€40

Being Catholic,
Being American

The Mary and Tim Gray Series
for the Study of Catholic Higher Education

VOLUME I

Being Catholic, Being American:
The Notre Dame Story,
1842–1934

1999

VOLUME II

Being American, Being Catholic:
The Notre Dame Story,
1934–1952

forthcoming

Being Catholic, Being American

The Notre Dame Story, 1842–1934

Robert E. Burns

UNIVERSITY OF NOTRE DAME PRESS
Notre Dame, Indiana

All university-related photos are courtesy of the Notre Dame Archives.
Photos of political figures and the Indiana Klan are courtesy
of the Indiana State Library.

Library of Congress Cataloging-in-Publication Data
Burns, Robert, E., 1927–
  Being Catholic, being American : the Notre Dame Story, 1842–1934 /
Robert E. Burns.
    p.   cm.
  Includes bibliographical references and index.
  ISBN 0-268-02156-2 (hardcover : alk. paper)
  1. University of Notre Dame—History.   I. Title.
  LD4113.B87   1999
378.772'89—dc21

98-31553
CIP

The Mary and Tim Gray
Series for the Study of
Catholic Higher Education

By this gift
Mary and Tim Gray
support the appreciation and understanding of the
richness and tradition of Catholic higher education

CONTENTS

PART III

PREFACE

Over the last century and a half, the history of the University of Notre Dame has been a small but important part of the larger history of how and when the majority of Catholics in this country rose from minority status to full participation in mainstream American life. Traditional anti-popery in America was not driven from public consciousness by righteous inspiration or by concerted action. It simply expired from natural causes. After all, by the end of the twentieth century, practicing Catholics are the largest religious group in the country and nonpracticing Catholics are the second largest. American Catholics had become too numerous and too affluent to ignore or demean.

At the same time, during the course of the century, American Catholics and their Church underwent changes in attitude and practices that even the most fervent supporters and severest critics in 1900 could not have imagined. As time passed, especially after implementation of the reforms of the Second Vatican Council, American Catholics tended to become less martial, a bit more tolerant, and at the end of the century more ecumenical in attitudes to Protestants and other Americans. The older very strong official American Catholic fear of indifferentism, meaning the attitude that one religion was as good as another, just faded away.

This process of achieving general acceptance of Catholics in this country as authentic Americans was by no means an inevitable one. It was painfully slow, and there are some who will argue that it is still incomplete. Yet, however long delayed and opposed along the way, by the last quarter of the century the vast majority of American Catholics are solidly in the mainstream of American life and have lost their minority status.

During the course of the century, the University of Notre Dame was always a witness, sometimes a contributor, and usually a mirror of the travails and triumphs of the American Catholic minority. It is with this mirror relationship of the university to the rise of the American Catholic minority and in lesser ways to the larger American society that this study is concerned.

Within the chronological period of this book, 1842 to 1934, there were two critical turning points in the institutional history of the university. Those two turning points were the death of Father Edward Sorin, C.S.C., founder of Notre Dame and the selection as president of the university of Father John F. O'Hara, C.S.C., who later became cardinal archbishop of Philadelphia.

The period between Sorin and O'Hara was scarred by war and depression, and by political corruption at all levels of government on a grand scale. It was a time when anti-Catholicism—driven by a revived, nationally organized Ku Klux Klan—intensified throughout the country but especially in Indiana. It was a time when a general acceptance of Catholics in this country as authentic Americans was very much in doubt. These were also the years when the leaders of Notre Dame strove mightily to find the new resources required to transform their successful Catholic boarding school with small colleges attached into a modern university.

Those new resources were found partly in gifts from generous alumni, and by soliciting grants from foundations and organizing national fund drives. However, most of the resources for new construction and general development were internally generated from the extraordinarily successful Notre Dame football enterprise. It was a money machine that for almost a decade utterly astounded the men charged with managing it.

While Notre Dame's winning football program made money for the university and was an incalculable public relations asset, it also caused moments of acute embarrassment. Perhaps even more important were those relatively few occasions when men who knew better made morally suspect decisions on behalf of the football program for the sake of a perceived higher cause. At the same time, however, during these years Notre Dame's football glory certainly raised American Catholic self-esteem at a time when it needed raising and functioned as a powerful riposte to Klan-inspired anti-Catholic bigotry.

My interest in the twentieth-century Notre Dame story is easily explained. I spent thirty-eight years of my life at the university as a teacher, working scholar, proposal writer, and academic administrator. In those roles one quickly realized that Notre Dame was a special place, or put another way, that Notre Dame was informed by an institutional culture that appeared to be unique.

This institutional culture contained many elements that were beneficent and a few that were not. Some faculty wits, during my early years at Notre Dame, affected to explain the unique quality of life and work at the university by burlesquing St. Thomas Aquinas' famous five rational proofs for the existence of God. For them, the existence and progress of Notre Dame was a sixth rational proof that St. Thomas failed to anticipate.

Other more thoughtful faculty hypothesized that whatever was good or bad in current rules and regulations governing the institution was rooted in some actual historical experience. According to them, nothing ever happened administratively at Notre Dame without having had a specific cause. For example, existing university policies restricting faculty behavior or activities had not come out of the blue. When established, such policies had been intended to prevent recurrence of an event or activity embarrassing to the university. Tracking down and identifying forgotten specific policy-establishing precedents led me into the complicated story of Notre Dame and its relationships with American Catholics and the larger society during the early twentieth century.

No book is ever completed without help from many people. Among those most generous with ideas and insights are two long-time friends and colleagues, J. Philip Gleason and Rev. Marvin R. O'Connell. They educated me greatly with their published works as well as with years of conversation, always listening patiently and sympathetically as I developed and redeveloped my story.

Other friends and colleagues, Thomas J. Stritch, Bruno Schlesinger, and Frederick J. Crosson, drew on their long memories of Notre Dame lore to provide perspectives on people and events that I might have missed. Among my friends in the Congregation of Holy Cross, Rev. Thomas E. Blantz, C.S.C., and Rev. Robert J. Austgen, C.S.C., recalled incidents in community history that provided leads into controversial events and insights to help capture the personalities of many of my subjects.

Finally, I must reiterate what other researchers have written about the resources and staff of the Notre Dame Archives. The collections in these archives are treasure troves of information about the university, the development of Catholic higher education, and American Catholic affairs generally. Excellent finding aids abound and most of them are accessible through the internet. Within the rules of access which in most cases are liberal, the staff is helpful and cooperative to a degree unencountered by me in any other archive facility. Special thanks must be given to University Archivist Wendy Clauson Schlereth, Associate Archivist Peter Lysy, Associate Archivist Charles Lamb, and to Sharon Sumpter, whose lives I burdened with endless queries and requests.

All of these people as well as others not mentioned helped me in so many ways, suggesting books and articles and directing me to unpublished and archive materials. However, they share no responsibility for the interpretation put upon the materials examined or for errors of fact or style. Those are mine alone.

PART I

— 1 —

Catholic, French, and Irish American

The University of Notre Dame was founded in 1842 in northern Indiana by the recently established Congregation of Holy Cross as a Catholic institution. The mid-nineteenth-century European Catholic world from which this American Catholic educational enterprise drew inspiration and obtained most of its initial intellectual and material resources was in turmoil. One long period of European Catholic Church history had come to a close and another was aborning. The collapse of the ancien régimes of Europe in the aftermath of the French Revolution and years of Napoleonic domination had ended three hundred years of support and protection of the Church and Church interests by Catholic monarchs.

Most of the powerful old local Church hierarchies were gone. Also gone were the traditionally mingled roles of religious officer and civic functionary so common in the ancien régimes. No longer were priests and bishops in effect officers in both Church and state. By the third quarter of the nineteenth century, state and church in Europe were either totally separate or moving apart. Whatever authority in society priests and bishops enjoyed in the changing European Catholic world derived solely from their status as men of religion. Without the assurance of protection and support from friendly heads of state and appointed ministers, European churchmen faced a future wherein old assumptions and past practices no longer spoke to present realities. Increasingly, many priests and bishops looked, *ultra montana*, across the mountains to Rome for the protection and support now denied by secularized states.

At midcentury, Rome was eager to oblige. Convinced that dangers and threats to the survival of the Catholic Church were genuine and numerous, the Roman response to the turmoil of the times was ecclesiastical centralization. From the Roman perspective, conformity was essential for Catholic unity, and Catholic unity was the only practical guarantee of security and institutional survival. The degree of conformity needed to achieve the extent of Catholic unity required was obtainable only through close papal supervision and regulation of local churches, liturgy, popular piety, uses of church property, appointment of bishops, clerical education, and most important of all, Catholic theology. This new and heightened sense of the centrality of the pope in the Catholic Church or ultramontanism, as it came to be called, was to be the dominant characteristic of Catholic affairs throughout the world for the next hundred years.

Although this new ultramontane mode was firmly set down during the long pontificate of Pius IX (1846–78), a somewhat earlier but well-established literary tradition as well as contemporary events went into the making of it.[1] However, it was the wonders of nineteenth-century transportation and communications technology that made implementation of an ultramontane program possible. The availability of railways and steamships that could bring people to Rome in increasing numbers and the establishment of effective postal services were essential prerequisites for effective Roman supervision and regulation of local churches and religious practices.

Accompanying and generally paralleling closer Roman supervision of local churches throughout the Catholic world during this period was a closer supervision of priests by bishops. Moreover, as time passed, bishops had more clergy to supervise. Almost everywhere in the Catholic world the number of priests and other religious men and women increased. Generally, this increase was qualitative as well as quantitative. Seminary preparation was better in the sense that it was more intense, but it also became narrower, more professional, and more isolated from contemporary intellectual interests. Nevertheless, clergy during the third quarter of the nineteenth century tended to be better trained, more professional, and more single-minded in their vocational commitments than had been the rule during the previous fifty years.[2]

To the waves of Hegelianism and infidelity sweeping out of European universities that seemed to be capturing the minds of the educated classes, the midcentury Church had nothing to offer. The revival of medieval Scholastic philosophy, especially the works of the thirteenth-century savant and saint Thomas Aquinas, under way in Italian Jesuit seminaries since the reconstitution of the order in 1815, had proceeded slowly and uncritically until the founding of *la Civilta cattolica* in 1850.[3] The Thomist aspect of this revival of Scholastic philosophy did not pass out of the seminaries into the European intellectual mainstream until sometime after the issuance of Leo XIII's *Aeterni Patris* (1878). It would take another forty years before the philosophy of St. Thomas Aquinas, or Thomism, achieved the practical status of an official Catholic ideology and of a required subject in European and American Catholic universities.

Similarly, to the great social challenges of an industrializing economy, the Church of Pius IX had little to say, secure in the hopeful notion that in time such things would either improve on their own or pass away. The spread of socialism among French and German workers continued no matter what Church leaders said or did. Nationalism, however, was a different matter entirely. Nationalism was a powerful all-embracing mass movement and nothing about it suggested a quick passing. Encounters between the Church and Italian nationalism were devastating. Those occurring in Prussia were not much better. Accommodations had to be made with nationalist-minded Catholics in Ireland and in America.

In the face of such challenges, a defensive posture was not enough. No matter how well directed by Rome or closely supervised by local bishops, most Catholic clergy were simply not in touch with the new intellectual developments and social movements of the time.[4] Consequently, no new suitable pastoral methods were devised for dealing with the messages and challenges of nineteenth-century liberalism, nationalism, and socialism. Of course, a minority of clergy and a few bishops were very much in touch with the new age. However, their efforts to move the institutional Church away from its defensive stance were generally unappreciated by a majority of their brethren in religion. Such so-called liberal, reformist, accommodationist priests and bishops frequently found themselves in trouble with their hierarchical superiors.

By and large the majority of clergy and bishops, as directed by Pius IX and his officials, put their faith in pastoral methods devised many years ago at the Council of Trent. To be sure, the leadership of the Church was able to develop and implement those methods more effectively through a more dedicated parish clergy and from religious orders revived and renewed after the disasters of the French Revolution. On the one hand, during these years everywhere in the Catholic world devotional practices changed. As directed by the clergy, devotions practiced by the Catholic laity became more personal, more distinctively Italian in general tone, and perhaps more sentimental. During the 1850s devotions to the Eucharistic presence, to the Sacred Heart, the Precious Blood, and especially the Blessed Virgin all became very popular. More people were enrolled in confraternities and sodalities. The practice of going to confession and

Communion on the first Fridays of nine consecutive months, and the distinctively Italian custom of placing Christmas cribs—plaster animals, shepherds, and angels—in churches at Christmastime spread throughout the Catholic world.[5] Taken together, all of these devotional practices had the effect of getting more people into more churches more often.

On the other hand, Catholic theology, being in a defensive mood, tended to give clearer answers to hard questions than informed believers had any right to expect.[6] For many believers, practical Catholicism could become a matter of rules and regulations, with moral theology becoming nothing more than a list of offenses that grew longer every year. There was a temptation in all of this, which some could not resist, to pose moral questions in terms of "how far can you go?"[7] When Pius IX died in 1878, there may have been in Rome and perhaps elsewhere in the Church a sense of partial failure, a lingering fear that the Church was losing ground and had not really come to terms with the intellectual, scientific, political, and social issues of the day.

At the same time, however, there can be no doubt that Pius IX had made a very big difference in the life of the Church. Indeed, the Papal States had been lost, sacrificed to the new omnipotent gods of Italian nationalism. Yet, the Catholic Church without the Papal States was far stronger organizationally and was experiencing a deeper, more active religious life than at any time in the last hundred years.[8]

— ii —

The origins of the University of Notre Dame were rooted in the Catholic religious revival movements of Restoration France. The years of the Revolution and of the Empire had severely tested the traditional religious faith and morals of all classes of Catholic people throughout the country. In France after 1815, insofar as Catholic religious life was concerned, virtually everything had to be begun anew. The challenge of rechristianizing the country was an enormous one that only extraordinarily religious-minded men and women could meet. In France, the morrow of Waterloo turned out to be a time of frenetic religious activities: establishing many new religious foundations, hastily reinforcing a depleted clergy, teaching catechism in rural communities, conducting missions in urban areas, raising the intellectual level of collegiate and seminary programs, and expanding foreign missionary works. Few periods of modern French religious history witnessed such an outburst of spiritual, intellectual, and organizational energies.

One of the participants in this flowering of early-nineteenth-century French religious activity was a small association of priests and brothers known later as the Congregation of Holy Cross (C.S.C.). This congregation of religious men was founded by Father Basil Antoine Marie Moreau in the Diocese of Le Mans in 1837 by the union of two independent existing religious societies: the Brothers of St. Joseph founded by Canon Jacques François Dujarié in 1820 and the Auxiliary Priests of Le Mans brought together by Moreau in 1833.[9] The mission of Dujarié's Brothers of St. Joseph in the France of Louis Philippe had been to provide primary education for children in rural areas, while that of the Auxiliary Priests was to preach, offer retreats for residents of rural parishes, and otherwise assist in the rechristianization of post-Revolution France.

The name Moreau chose for his new congregation was not selected because of any special devotion to the Holy Cross of the Crucifixion. The name derived from a suburb of Le Mans, Sainte-Croix, wherein lay a gift of property which Moreau had received in 1832 from an old priest-friend for pious and charitable works. This property was named in official documents and on old maps of Le Mans as Notre-Dame. Through the years, the parish of Sainte-Croix had been built up around a very old church of that same name. Though that church was destroyed in the Revolution, the name Notre-Dame for several centuries had been closely associated with Sainte-Croix.[10]

Born in the village of Laigne-en-Belin, a few miles south of Le Mans in 1799, Moreau was the ninth of his parents' living children. Moreau's father was a small-scale wine merchant and farmer. Other relatives were laborers and tradesmen. The Moreau family was solidly rural middle class. Both parents appear to have been actively religious persons at a time when it was not easy to be so.[11]

In 1816, the young Moreau was accepted into the major seminary at Le Mans, where he pursued his studies so successfully that the bishop allowed ordination in 1821, even though the candidate was almost two years under the canonical age.[12] Selected by the bishop to be a trainer of future priests, Moreau studied for two years at the Seminary of St. Sulpice in Paris. Then, in 1823, at the age of twenty-four this son of an illiterate rural wine merchant returned to the seminary in Le Mans to teach philosophy.

While at St. Sulpice, Moreau had turned away from the so-called clear-idea analytical modes of the Cartesian philosophical tradition and also from the Gallican theology taught in his seminary curriculum wherein French bishops in council were held to be authoritative in all matters affecting the French Church. Moreau had been converted by his masters at St. Sulpice to accept faith as the firmest basis for conviction and to embrace the ideals of papal infallibility and the primacy of the spiritual power of the Catholic Church in the world.[13] Between these two theological traditions were deep philosophical and practical differences. Much more than authority relationships were at issue here. Liturgical forms, devotional exercises, and even clerical dress were involved.

Upon returning to Le Mans in 1823 to teach philosophy, Moreau found himself in frequent philosophical disagreement with Jean-Baptiste Bouvier, superior of the seminary and a former teacher whose disposition and theological writings were distinctly Gallican,[14] so distinctly Gallican that in the last years of his life Bouvier had to accept papal correction of some of his books. Moreover, a full-scale purge of Gallican sentiments from all of his works was undertaken after Bouvier's death in 1854.

Two years at St. Sulpice had the effect of separating Moreau, the former student, from Bouvier, his old teacher. This separation begun in philosophy grew larger over the years and became increasingly personal, especially after 1834 when Bouvier, also a man of relatively humble social origins, a carpenter's son, became bishop of Le Mans. For example, in 1850, Moreau put aside the special winged rabat of the French clergy and adopted the Roman collar for himself and for all of the priests and brothers in his religious community.[15] Bishop Bouvier wore a rabat until the day he died.

As an ultramontane, Moreau became very uncomfortable with the authority claims of the Gallicans and frequently appealed to Rome for protection against what he perceived to be local episcopal tyranny. For his part, Bouvier's harshest language against Moreau was reserved for those instances when the superior at Sainte-Croix tried to overturn episcopal decisions in Le Mans by appealing to friendly influentials in the Roman Curia.[16] As a matter of fact, Moreau wrote so often to Rome protesting actions or inactions of Bishop Bouvier that friends there in 1847 urged him to desist for a while.[17]

When Moreau thought about how to proceed in the enormous task of repairing the great damage done to religion and to the Church by the French Revolution, he tried to be realistic in estimating the extent and complexity of the problems facing him and practical in his approaches to solving them. He was especially distressed by the climate of unbelief then prevailing in the country's universities that seemed to be undermining the faith and morals of the educated classes. Consequently, Moreau believed that his Auxiliary Priests had to be equipped to do more than preach and offer retreats. He saw the need for supplementing his missionaries with learned priests qualified to teach in preparatory schools, seminaries, and colleges.[18] It is clear that from the earliest days of the

Congregation of Holy Cross, a special dedication to education, preaching, and missionary activities informed the thinking and actions of
Moreau and his early companions.

What Dujarié and Moreau hoped the union of Brothers and Auxiliary
Priests would bring forth is not clear. Because the times were so unsettled
after the Revolution of 1830 and because Bishop Bouvier was alternately
and unpredictably supportive and hostile toward his former pupil's religious projects, Moreau found himself driven more by circumstances than
by intellectual principles. Though Moreau was perhaps more a man of
action than an intellectual, he was nonetheless interested in intellectual
matters. Ideas fascinated and moved him; he was at once a creator and
borrower of them.

At no time during his long and sometimes controversial life did
Moreau ever really cease being a professor of philosophy, that is, a professor of philosophy profoundly shaped and informed by French rural
lower-middle-class values. For Moreau, few tasks gave greater personal
satisfaction than those of composing and drafting regulations and constitutions for associations of religious men and women. He loved to make
up rules that would cover all possible situations. He never doubted that
such rules could be written and that they would work. Moreau believed
without reservation that perfect rules could obtain a perfect society if
imperfect men would only obey them. Obedience to authority and compliance with rules were behaviors that had been learned and internal-
ized in his father's house, were highly valued by his friends and neighbors
in Laigne-en-Belin, and later were also strongly reinforced by religious
training and philosophical study. Moreau expected such behavior from
his associates and frequent failure to get it occasioned some of the greatest disappointments of his life.

When Moreau thought about the nature and mission of his new religious congregation, one idea much discussed among his companions in
the Le Mans area was that of a union of three societies in one. This
notion of three in one was commonplace at the time and found numerous symbolic representations and applications at every level of Christian literature and art. The idea was by no means unique to the Le Mans
area and can be found in the rules and constitutions of many religious
foundations established in early-nineteenth-century France.[19] In the
Le Mans area, however, Dujarié had been particularly moved by it. Frequently during the mid-1820s, he had spoken and written about founding
a group of priests who would form an association with the Brothers of
St. Joseph and an organized community of sisters. Dujarié expected that
from the group of priests would emerge a superior to provide the general

government for all three societies.[20] He approached ecclesiastical authorities with this plan on several occasions, but nothing happened.

For his new congregation, Moreau adopted Dujarié's conception of a union of three societies in one as his ideal. Moreau proposed adding a third branch of religious women to his union of brothers and priests. To that end, he founded the Marianite Sisters of Holy Cross in Le Mans in 1841. Moreover, in thinking about the nature of his proposed union of three societies into one, Moreau went beyond Dujarié. For Moreau, the priests, brothers, and sisters were to be as one, while maintaining the particular characteristics of each. What Moreau had in mind was what he described as a mutual harmony, rooted in one general authority, with all branches sharing one common inspiration.

When thinking about the possible internal dynamics of his new congregation, Moreau made very clear what he believed the authority relationship between the priests and brothers ought to be. None of the brothers would be subordinate to any of the priests. No priest would have a right to give orders to any brother. No brother would be expected to obey all priests indiscriminately. Only those priests elected to an office or an employment to which special authority had been added could give orders to the brothers.[21]

About proper authority relationships between the sisters and the other branches, Moreau said little because there was very little that could be said. Bishop Bouvier showed himself to be extremely reluctant to sanction new foundations of religious women in his diocese.[22]

Bouvier was especially opposed to formalizing Moreau's Marianite group. Because Moreau could not imagine that any aspect of his religious foundations would be outside of the influence of a religious life, he had recruited three pious peasant girls and an equally pious daughter of a local physician to form a small religious community that would perform housekeeping and cooking functions in the priests' facilities.[23] While Bishop Bouvier recognized the need for domestic services in those facilities, he saw no necessity for organizing laundresses, cooks, and seamstresses into a religious congregation and would have nothing to do with them.[24]

Moreau's new religious congregation was unique in the Catholic Church of that time because it united priests and brothers in a single association that afforded equal constitutional rights in congregation governance to both groups. As the congregation expanded, it developed that at local and later at provincial levels in most things both societies remained distinct, each one having its own government and administration. Unity was maintained by a common general administration under a priest as superior general and a general council composed of an equal number of priests and brothers. Within this organizational structure, all priests and all professed brothers, irrespective of occupation, enjoyed full participation in the governance of the congregation. As the activities of the congregation multiplied, local houses and individual works had their own superiors and local councils. If both priests and brothers lived in such houses or participated in such works, priests and brothers enjoyed equal representation on the local councils.

This unusual combination of priests and brothers in a single congregation tested the patience and energy of all those religious chosen to manage it. From the beginning, this union was disturbed by arguments over finances, disputes over representation on congregation councils, and charges of unfair treatment.[25] As time passed, it became clear that the religious family which Moreau's union of fathers and brothers had created was not to be an entirely harmonious one.

The first education project undertaken by Moreau at Sainte-Croix was an elementary boarding school opened by the brothers in 1836 and then transferred to the Notre-Dame property in 1837. In opening this school and in effecting the transfer—across one street and from one house to another—Moreau found himself embroiled with several levels of French bureaucracy. Delays and requests for additional information were endless. Hostility toward religious education projects by public officials was a simple fact of French political life after 1830, and Moreau coped with that reality any way he could. In the end, Moreau succeeded in obtaining final permissions, inspections, and licenses only by seeking out and obtaining interventions by high-placed friends who could influence such decisions.[26]

This venture into elementary education was followed in 1838 by the establishment of a Latin school on the same property. The prospective opening of a new secondary school in Le Mans encountered not only the usual and predictable bureaucratic harassment from local educational authorities, but the project also met strong opposition from Bishop Bouvier. The bishop appears to have responded to pressure from the principal of another Catholic secondary school in Le Mans known as the Oratorical College.[27] Bouvier urged Moreau to abandon this project and ended his conversation with the zealous priest by threatening never again to set foot in Sainte-Croix if he persevered in opening a Latin school.[28] Moreau was embarrassed but not intimidated. The Latin school was a matter of supreme importance to him and to his new congregation. As he tried to explain to the bishop, establishment of this school was a first but vitally necessary step in a plan for recruiting and training priests for his congregation. Only a Latin school, a secondary school, could provide access to the class of young men from which potential vocations for his congregation would most likely come. Moreau made very clear to Bishop Bouvier that he would not remain at the head of any religious work where opportunities for expansion were denied. He offered to resign.

On this matter, the bishop had said enough and chose to say no more. To be sure, Moreau was visited later by two emissaries from Bishop Bouvier, but the priest would not step back from the line that he had drawn. Tempers cooled, and the school opened quietly without further incident.[29] Moreau got his Latin school but at the price of very chilly future relations with his bishop—a condition that was to become chronic in the years ahead for the leadership of Sainte-Croix. As a matter of fact, relations with Bishop Bouvier became so strained that Moreau was unable to obtain even a formal Roman decree of praise for his congregation until 1855, six months after Bouvier's death. When definitive approval of the Congregation of Holy Cross was finally obtained from Rome in 1857, the Marianite Sisters of Holy Cross were excluded. Moreau was instructed to govern them as a separate and autonomous congregation.[30]

Moreau and his followers in Sainte-Croix did much more in the late 1830s than dispute with their bishop. The congregation had specific, practical religious objectives, and its members pursued them vigorously. Throughout 1837–38, Moreau and other priests from Sainte-Croix undertook the preaching of missions in and near Le Mans. By all accounts, the efforts of these energetic priests brought large numbers to church and to confession. Conversions were effected among all classes.[31] Preaching the gospel in country parishes and providing Christian teaching for youth were the principal works of the new congregation until 1840. In that year came the first of several opportunities for missionary service in foreign parts.

As early as 1839 three bishops from foreign lands had knocked on Moreau's door at Sainte-Croix asking for priests and brothers for their respective dioceses. The bishop-elect of Vincennes, Indiana, the bishop of Montreal, and the bishop of Algiers within a space of a few months all applied to Moreau for help. The needs of Bishop DuPuch of Algiers seemed most urgent. He was desperately short of clergy and churches to minister to the growing French colonial population in that country. Moreau agreed to help, and in May 1840 two priests and four brothers went off to teach in a preparatory seminary and take charge of an orphanage for French children outside of Algiers. All things followed the flag in this colonial venture, and bureaucratic harassment and official hostility to religious schools was almost as intense in Algiers as it had been in Le Mans.

Very soon the health of the missionaries was undermined by over-work, the hot Algerian summer, and the unsanitary conditions in the country. All of Moreau's missionaries were stricken with fever and dysentery. Thoughts about dying in Africa were never absent from their minds.[32] The bishop was too impoverished to help. Local resources were inadequate. Most important, the French government simply did not regard the presence of Christian missionaries in Algeria as important and made no effort to provide financial or administrative support. It became obvious to Moreau that under existing circumstances this present missionary experiment could not be prolonged. He recalled all Sainte-Croix priests and brothers from Algeria in June 1842.

The mission to Algeria had been a failure, and Moreau did not try to delude himself about how complete that failure had been. He did not dwell upon it or lose any of his optimism about the future for Sainte-Croix, because new requests for religious men had arrived from America. The possibility of doing God's work in an environment where French bureaucracy and regulations did not prevail and where anticlerical politicians and officials did not harass must have pleased everyone at Sainte-Croix. The prospect of going to America made memories of the failures in Algeria fade.

Celestin Guynemer de la Hailandière, recently appointed as the second bishop of Vincennes, first wrote to Moreau in July 1839 and later, in August of the same year, visited Le Mans seeking teaching brothers for religious work in his diocese. That diocese was enormous in area, covering the entire state of Indiana. Within a population of over nine hundred thousand, Catholics were a small minority and were scattered in isolated communities from Lake Michigan to the Ohio River. Churches were few, priests were in short supply, Catholic schools were virtually nonexistent, and the largely Protestant population was frequently unfriendly and prejudiced. What de la Hailandière found and saw at Sainte-Croix pleased him very much. Very quickly the bishop saw in the growing community at Sainte-Croix an answer to his prayers. He pressed upon Moreau the captivating idea of establishing in Vincennes a motherhouse modeled on Sainte-Croix.

By early summer 1840, for Moreau and others close to him in Le Mans the idea of establishing a colony from Sainte-Croix in America and from that small foundation eventually dispatching preaching and teaching missions intended to bring all of the people of North America into communion with the Catholic Church had become so overpowering that some sort of start, no matter how small, had to be made. Moreau decided to try to mount a maximum effort out of available Sainte-Croix financial and human resources for Vincennes. He turned to friends of Sainte-Croix in Le Mans for money, linen, clothing, sacred vessels, and sanctuary lamps. Since virtually nothing for religious work was available in Vincennes, everything had to be brought.

In the selection of personnel for this mission, Moreau tried to be as generous as possible. He decided to send six brothers and a priest as their superior. For this important post of superior, upon whom the future of the new colony would surely depend, Moreau chose a priest regarded in the community as one of the best and brightest. Though only twenty-six years old, Father Edward Frederick Sorin de la Gaulterie was Moreau's choice to lead the mission for America. Sorin had been born on February 6, 1814, in the Manoir de la Roche, at Ahuillé, in La Mayenne into a family belonging to the modest country nobility. The Sorin family was large—he was the seventh of nine children—but comfortable. At about the age of fourteen Sorin had decided to become a priest. His family approved, and he transferred to the Petite Seminary at Precigné. After completing the Latin course in Precigné, Sorin entered the Grand Seminary in Le Mans.

While in the seminary, Sorin's imagination was stirred by stories about French missionary activities in distant lands, especially in China. As a matter of fact, this interest in China missionary work never left him. Priests who knew Sorin in later years recalled his enduring fascination with accounts of the trials and triumphs of China missionaries.[33] Sorin made no secret of his interest in the China mission, and Moreau as one of his philosophy teachers must have known about it. However, at that time and for several years thereafter the prospect of obtaining an assignment to China from the diocese of Le Mans was remote. Yet, opportunities for service in other missionary areas not so distant or as exotic as China presented themselves to the young men studying at Le Mans.

For example, in 1836 Simon Bruté de Rémur, first bishop of Vincennes, visited the seminary at Le Mans while on a begging expedition for money and for personnel to work in his sprawling diocese. Already passed fifty-seven years of age when he visited Le Mans, Bishop Bruté had spent more than a quarter of a century in different American religious works. The bishop was not only a man of extraordinary presence, but when he spoke about religious work in America he spoke from experience and with conviction. The man's undoubted apostolic zeal and straightforward accounts of preaching and ministering to Indians and to white families living in isolated and frontier conditions deeply moved all of those who heard him. Sorin remembered the experience of hearing Bruté and credited the bishop with making him think about the possibilty of going to

Indiana. About going to America or to China or anywhere else, Sorin could dream but not act. When Bruté visited Le Mans in 1836, Sorin was still two years away from ordination. At long last, that much anticipated event occurred on May 27, 1838. Sorin was a priest, but for the moment he was not to be a missionary. His bishop assigned him to serve as an assistant pastor in the parish church at Parce.

For Sorin, fifteen months in that role was enough. He craved greater challenges and more personal sacrifice than Parce or any other country parish could provide.[34] Although nothing at Sainte-Croix in 1839 indicated that Moreau's tiny congregation would engage in foreign missionary work, Sorin persuaded himself that somehow his heart's desire would be fulfilled by joining the Auxiliary Priests. Sorin knew Moreau from his seminary days and adopted wholeheartedly the religious ideals articulated and projects mounted by his former teacher. Sorin was one of the four priests who pronounced their vows with Moreau before Bishop Bouvier on August 15, 1840. Sorin and the others swore to live chaste lives in poverty and promised to live in obedience to Moreau as their superior.[35]

Clearly, Moreau had recognized that Sorin was a most worthy priest, but also that he was one of those rarest of men who simply could not be intimidated by any task or any person. Indeed, Moreau had perceived correctly the qualities which leadership of an enterprise of such enormous potential required, and Sorin seemed to possess most of them. Simply stated, Sorin was capable of anything.

By all accounts, Sorin was a man gifted with boundless energy who was ever sustained by an unfailing optimism. He was blessed with a keen intuitive sense of the need of virtually any moment; he had no difficulty whatsoever in viewing a problem and deciding what ought to be the most practical way of dealing with it. At the same time, Sorin was always receptive to inspiration from great ideals. In most things, he was spontaneous, quick to decide and to react, and above all else supremely self-confident in all of his undertakings. In a long and busy life, there may have been some moments when Sorin would have admitted not being right; but in his own mind, as God's instrument he could never be wrong.[36]

Sorin's extraordinary self-confidence was far greater than what one would normally expect to find in a person of his class. More than the easy certitude of the lesser rural French nobility was involved here. Sorin's self-confidence seems to have been rooted in an almost childlike belief that he, Edward Sorin, had a special relationship with God. For example, shortly after being chosen to lead the Indiana colony, Sorin wrote to Bishop de la Hailendière describing his enthusiasm for the great venture to America, and then with touching frankness and candor explained how certain he was that "God loves me in a very special manner."[37] Men thus constituted and driven frequently become superb leaders, but they also tend to perform very poorly as subordinates. In the summer of 1841, neither Moreau nor Bishop de la Hailendière appear to have given that possibility serious thought. Sorin was the best available man for the mission, and Sorin was very anxious to go.[38]

In any case, once Sorin became leader of the mission to Indiana, and notwithstanding his limited knowledge of the English language, in his own mind he had become an American. Sorin tried to explain his new mentality to Bishop de la Hailendière by observing that in his present state of mind, the road to America stood out as clearly to himself as did the road to heaven. Henceforth, Sorin exclaimed in a letter to de la Hailendière, "I live only for my brethren in America. America is my fatherland; it is the center of all my affections and the object of all my thoughts."[39] Even before leaving Sainte-Croix for Le Havre, Sorin in effect had prepared himself mentally to be pleased with whatever he might find in his new country. Departure day from Sainte-Croix and Le Mans was set for August 5, 1841. For Sorin, it could not arrive soon enough.

— iii —

When Sorin and his party left Le Mans for the Diocese of Vincennes in distant Indiana in 1841, the idea of establishing a university in the United States formed no part of their purpose or thinking. As a matter of fact, not one member of the Sorin party could speak a word of English, not one had ever attended a university, only one was an experienced elementary school teacher, two were teenagers lately out of school themselves, two were craftsmen, and one was an illiterate farm laborer. Nonetheless, the mission of this band as perceived by Sorin, the leader, was grand indeed. They ventured across the Atlantic to bring the Catholic religion to the unchurched and heretic population of the Indiana frontier. Their mission was to assist in the Catholicizing of America.

Once in Vincennes, where the group remained about a year, several of the brothers quickly learned enough English to open two elementary schools in the area. During their brief time in Vincennes new recruits, including several immigrants from Ireland, joined the brothers, raising the number there to about eighteen. Disputes between Sorin and Bishop de la Hailendière over money and autonomy had begun on arrival day in Vincennes and were chronic thereafter.

As a matter of fact, only a week after arriving in Vincennes and meeting the bishop for the first time, Sorin wrote to Moreau explaining that the man could not be trusted. After a single week of living and hearing gossip in Vincennes, Sorin advised Moreau that Bishop de la Hailandière had acquired the reputation here of "being a slick politician and of never getting caught; he has a thousand and one tricks for getting himself out of embarrassing situations."[40] Time did not improve Sorin's first impression of de la Hailandière. Over the course of his five-year relationship with the bishop, Sorin made many written and spoken judgments about him. When the bishop resigned his post in 1847, Sorin rendered his final one, describing de la Hailandière as in many ways an excellent man, pious as an angel, but at the same time he was to a fault, "suspicious, defiant, and stubborn."[41] Sorin did not like Bishop de la Hailandière and could not work under his governance.

In order to insure an adequate living from teaching for their small community and to be able to acquire property in their own name and, most of all, to put as much distance as possible between themselves and the bishop, Sorin seized an opportunity to move his group to the northern extremity of the diocese, near South Bend. Sorin agreed to open a school at an unmanned old Indian mission station on land owned by the bishop in St. Joseph County, and the bishop promised to transfer the land to the congregation if the school succeeded.

Located on two small lakes north of South Bend, near the St. Joseph River, and only forty miles from St. Joseph, Michigan, for both Sorin and the Brothers of St. Joseph, the identification of this northern region of the Diocese of Vincennes with St. Joseph, their patron saint, was a providential sign. How could this group of religious men turn away from such a place? They could not and did not. Sorin moved his group north in two phases. The first group of Sorin and seven of the brothers left Vincennes on November 16, 1842, traveling north in an old stagecoach and ox cart, and reached the old mission station by the lakes eleven days later. The second group of ten brothers traveling in midwinter in a large four-horse-drawn wagon, accompanied by eight head of cattle, took about three weeks to make the journey, arriving at the lakes on February 27, 1843.

Sorin's first sight of the lakes was a memorable one. He described that moment in a letter to Moreau heavily laden with highly emotional religious imagery. The frozen lakes with their mantles of new white snow struck Sorin as a symbol of the stainless purity of Our Lady. Henceforth, this land and these lakes would be the spiritual and actual home of Holy Cross in America. Appropriately remembering and honoring the motherhouse in Le Mans, the mission station by the lakes and all that came after would be forever known as Notre Dame du Lac.

In the first group traveling with Sorin from Vincennes, only two had been among the original companions from Le Mans. Five of this first group had joined the society in Vincennes, and four of them were re-cent immigrants from Ireland. To be sure, the roots of Notre Dame were French, but half of the party arriving first at the site of the future Uni-versity of Notre Dame had been born in Ireland.

Even though four Irishmen had made the long cold weather journey from Vincennes to the lakes with Sorin and shared all of the difficulties of a new foundation with their leader, it is clear that in the early years of Notre Dame, Sorin was not pleased with the way Irishmen adjusted to life in a religious community. In the 1840s, Sorin shared the prejudices of his nationality and class about the Irish. While Irishmen exhibited many of the virtues essential for the religious life, according to Sorin, they were a people possessed with one terrible flaw that had the effect of negating all of those virtues. That flaw was instability, that is, they were the most changeable of all races.[42] Dissatisfaction, a penchant for complaint, and a disposition to blame others for their own failings along with an excessive affection for hard liquor were all behaviors that followed from this unfor-tunate racial flaw.

In dealing with Irishmen generally during the early years of his mis-sion, Sorin adopted a stance toward them that was similar to one fre-quently encountered among high-placed ecclesiastics in Rome: listen sympathetically to complaints, counsel patience, and then discount much of what had been alleged in complaints because opposition and indig-nation were only matters of course with them.[43] Over the next forty years Sorin had to deal with a great many priests and students of Irish birth or descent. As a matter of fact, he was overwhelmed by them. Though he moderated his views about Irishmen somewhat and evinced genuine sympathy for the goals of Irish nationalism, he was always inclined to attribute instances of perceived religious disobedience by priests and brothers or mischievous or bizarre behavior by students of Irish descent to the Gaelic temper.[44]

The tiny boarding and day school which Sorin began with two stu-dents in the winter of 1842–43 consisted of a few log buildings and a teaching staff that included only one person who had completed sec-ondary school. Amazingly, through the good offices of a local member of the state legislature, in 1844 this primitive but zealously managed school was chartered by the State of Indiana as a university. How unlike France was this part of America. No long negotiations with a ministry of educa-tion had been required. No nosey inspectors arrived to harass a religious school. Overwhelmed by the ease with which virtually all future state li-censing requirements had been satisfied, Sorin quickly realized that as far as state and local governments were concerned, he was free to do whatever he wanted at his now chartered university.

From this fortuitous beginning, the school grew slowly and precariously. It grew because Sorin was psychologically and temperamentally prepared to do almost anything to ensure survival. Sorin willingly committed his own inherited patrimony to the common cause and encouraged other members of his society to do the same. Funds were solicited and obtained from the Societies for the Propagation of the Faith in Lyons and Paris. Timely gifts were obtained from relatives of members of the congregation. Begging trips were made throughout the east and northeastern parts of the United States and into other areas where Catholics were concentrated.

In addition, by means that will not bear close examination, Sorin simply forced Moreau to divert monies from Holy Cross religious works in France and elsewhere to Notre Dame. On more occasions than Moreau was disposed to excuse, Sorin would sign promissory notes on his own authority to fund needed building projects and then simply send them off to Moreau to pay. Also, without much regard for either the intellectual or physical resources in hand, Sorin was always ready to direct some member of his society to teach any student any subject at any time.

Ever anxious to expand, Sorin managed the purchase in 1855 of 185 acres of land west of the lakes. The next year, he transferred fifty acres of that land to a group of Holy Cross sisters who had been working at Notre Dame and elsewhere in the area since 1843. He also provided the sisters with $5,000 from a recent large benefaction to begin construction of permanent living quarters for them and a girls' school and college to be known henceforth as St. Mary's. Thus began a long and complex relationship between two separate but cooperating institutions with many mutual interests and occasional conflicting ones.

In 1856, twelve years after receiving the state charter, five years after railroad connections had been established between South Bend and Chicago, and a year after the foundation of St. Mary's, Sorin had in place at Notre Dame for boarding male students a preparatory or secondary school and a college taught by priests, religious brothers, and a few laymen, an elementary boarding school for little boys taught by brothers but soon to be taken over by Holy Cross sisters, and a manual labor or trade school also taught by the brothers. Moreover by 1858 student enrollment in all departments exceeded 200, which was the number of paid tuitions required to keep all parts of the enterprise solvent and growing.

The heart of Father Sorin's university was the six-year preparatory/ college course of studies which students entered at the ages of twelve or thirteen and usually completed before turning nineteen. Initially, that course tried to replicate in the environment of northern Indiana the curriculum of a French boarding school with all of its strict supervision of virtually every waking moment of a student's academic and social life. That style and level of discipline proved unworkable and was dropped by Sorin after two years and replaced by a modified version of a curriculum offered by the Jesuits at St. Louis University.[45] Begining in 1848 students were permitted to follow either a classical course of studies or a commercial one and so began a long and tortuous series of curriculum adaptations whereby this six-year preparatory/college course of studies evolved into a four-year preparatory school and a four-year college.

Between 1854 and 1857, the first two years of the preparatory/college courses of study were reorganized into what was called the Junior Department and the last four years became the Senior Department. In 1858 that nomenclature was dropped in favor of a preparatory course of studies and a collegiate course of studies. It would appear that Sorin and other members of the Congregation of Holy Cross charged with managing the university during these years struggled valiantly to maintain the six-year sequence intact while at the same time modifying it to meet the changing needs of their students.

In the 1850s bookkeeping and penmanship offerings were added to the preparatory course, and then in 1863 a two-year commercial sequence became part of the preparatory course. Commercial and business offerings did not appear as a college-level program until 1913 when a four-year collegiate commercial course of studies was made available. Other important curriculum innovations occurred during and after the Civil War. In 1865 a scientific course was installed at the college level and the existing collegiate course was renamed classical in order to distinguish it from the new alternative scientific course of studies as a pathway to a baccalaureate degree.

Occasional law lectures had been offered as early as 1858, and by 1869 those occasional lectures had become a two-year law course. Similarly, lectures in surveying led to the establishment of a two-year sequence in civil engineering by 1873. Other engineering subjects were added during the 1890s, so that by 1900 the two-year sequence in civil engineering had grown into a four-year course, and degrees were also being offered in mechanical, electrical, and architectural engineering.

All of these curriculum additions and adaptations, particularly those occurring after the war, imposed an unbearable strain on the concept of a six-year preparatory/college course of study. In 1873 that concept was abandoned. A third year was added to the preparatory course and the four collegiate years henceforth were denominated respectively as freshman, sophomore, junior, and senior. Organizational and name changes continued when, in 1882, the four-year college courses and the three-year preparatory ones were regrouped into separate collegiate and preparatory departments. Finally, in 1903, a fourth year was added to the preparatory department. Notre Dame began the twentieth century as an institution with a small trade school, a stable elementary school staffed by Holy Cross sisters, a thriving four-year preparatory school, and a collection of four-year collegiate programs offering courses of study in classics, science, business and commerce, engineering, pharmacy, and law.

Although the first two baccalaureate degrees were awarded in 1849, Sorin's university had been largely a school, and thus it remained until well after the founder's death in 1893. To be sure, student enrollment in all departments of the institution reached 800 by 1900, but many who came during the nineteenth century received neither certificates, diplomas, nor degrees. Such persons came for a year or so, and for a variety of personal and financial reasons left the institution before completing the courses required for diplomas or degrees. In any case, between 1849 and 1880 the number of degrees awarded to Notre Dame collegians averaged only ten a year; between 1881 and 1900 that yearly average rose to thirty-two. Collegians did not regularly outnumber the combined total of preparatory, trade school, and elementary pupils in the general student body until after 1910.

— iv —

The fact that Notre Dame was the only Catholic boarding school between Cleveland and Chicago was only one reason why the institution was able to attain economically sustainable enrollment levels. The most important reason for the institution's successful ascent to the happy condition of relative economic viability was the enormous increase in the American Catholic population between 1840 and 1860. A major part of that increase of course was made up of immigrants from Ireland. The rising tide of Irish immigrants in the 1830s became a torrent of working-class and peasant refugees after 1846. However, there were enough economic success stories occurring among the families swept out of Ireland into the eastern and midwestern United States, first by the tide and then by the torrent, to provide tuition-paying boarding students attractable to the various departments of Notre Dame.

This torrent of peasants and workers from Ireland utterly changed the character and status of the Catholic Church in America. It became a church of the immigrant poor and was increasingly viewed as a largely foreign and working-class institution by the general population of the country. Leadership positions in the American Catholic hierarchy and in religious orders were taken over by clergymen of Irish birth or descent to such an extent by the 1880s, if not sooner, that the Church in America was widely perceived here, in Europe, and by religious authorities in Rome as functioning and behaving like an Irish national church.

One of the characteristics of an Irish national church in midcentury was an ambivalent, nearly condescending, religious attitude toward non-Catholics. That ambivalence was rooted in a long historical experience of Protestant persecution in Ireland and in a strong tradition of *nulla salus extra ecclesiam* in Irish Catholicism. As Paul Cullen, rector of the Irish College in Rome and later archbishop of Dublin, explained to a correspondent in 1841, "We should always entertain the most expansive sentiments of charity towards Protestants, but at the same time we should let them know that there is but one true church and that they are strayed sheep from the fold. . . . Otherwise we might lull them into a false sense of security in their errors and by doing so we would really violate charity."[46]

Priests trained in Ireland, especially after Cullen became an archbishop there in 1849, and lay persons influenced by them in both Ireland and America tended to be quite comfortable with the principle of one true Church and no salvation for anyone outside of it. To be sure, this principle was not widely trumpeted by clerical and lay leaders of the Catholic minority in America during the late nineteenth century, but whether spoken of in public or not, it was always present in Irish American Catholicism of those years. Being always present, it affected relations with the country's Protestant and unchurched majority.

One consequence for all Americans of this sudden and rapid increase of foreign-born Catholics with a strong tradition of salvation exclusivity was the appearance during the 1850s of anti-Catholic and anti-foreign political movements. Some ugly incidents occurred in the eastern cities and elsewhere. Repressive local and state legislation against Catholics was threatened and in some instances enacted and enforced. While such movements did not last, anti-Catholic prejudice remained endemic in American society for a very long time.

American Catholic bishops and priests reacted to the bigotry of the 1850s and to later manifestations of anti-Catholic prejudice in two ways. One party of Church leaders fully accepted American values and public culture. This party generally advocated a liberal accommodationist stance toward American Protestants and unbelievers, confident that in time if a few minor adjustments were made to some traditional Catholic practices, America's lightly churched and unchurched majority would embrace the true faith. They were not fearful of mixing and competing with Protestants in the larger society and enthusiastically supported social movements such as Temperance, which had a large Protestant following. The leaders of this party had persuaded themselves that American institutions, especially our country's unique near-absolute separation of church and state, were providentially inspired and were replicable models exportable to the rest of the world.

Another party of Church leaders, while accepting American institutions and constitutional practices, especially church-state relations, as appropriate for this country, were not disposed to try and recommend American arrangements as models for the rest of the world. Moreover, this party was suspicious of American values and public culture and advocated a more conservative and segregationist stance toward other American religious groups. They saw no virtue and much danger in mixing with Protestants in society or in making adjustments in Catholic practices to accommodate majority opinion in this country. Simply stated, the one true Church was in place and thriving in America. Protestants and other non-Catholics could embrace Holy Mother Church or go to hell in their own way. While disagreeing principally about how to relate to the other Christian and non-Christian groups in the United States, both parties agreed that piety, manliness, and patriotism were highly valued ideals for Catholics in this country.

Clerics of Irish birth and descent were prominent in the leadership of both parties: James Cardinal Gibbons, Archbishop John Ireland, Bishop John J. Keane, and Monsignor Denis J. O'Connell, later bishop of Richmond, for the liberal accommodationist party, and Archbishop Michael A. Corrigan and Bishop Bernard J. McQuaid, for the conservatives. Differences between the leaders of the two parties became deep, personal, and very public. In the end, Rome sided first with the liberals, switched to the conservatives, and then tried to end party conflict by only elevating to episcopal rank clerics who were unattached to either of the two parties and who were possessed with unblemished records of absolute loyalty to Rome. By the 1890s, both the liberal and conservative parties could find friends and allies at Notre Dame. As elsewhere in the American Catholic Church those party differences at Notre Dame were frequently and sometimes sharply contested.

— v —

While adversity had been no stranger to Notre Dame during its early years, overall the institution had grown and prospered. Yet, like so many other organizations in American life during the 1860s, Notre Dame was tried and severely tested by the Civil War. Though most of the students attending the university in the years before the war had been drawn from the northern states, some young men from the South had been attracted there as well. Because Notre Dame students tended generally to follow the politics of their parents and of their locales, the great issues dividing the country at that time intruded into campus life.

Aware that a building adjacent to the campus had been used for years as a safe house in the anti-slavery underground railway and himself staunchly northern in sympathies and allegiance, Sorin believed that public discussion by faculty and students of such powerfully divisive issues as abolitionism and secession would divide the university community and lead only to bitterness and recrimination. For Sorin, preserving the internal peace and insuring the prosperity of Notre Dame simply outweighed all other considerations, no matter how exhalted or compelling others may have regarded them. To preserve that peace and to insure that prosperity, Sorin tried to ban all on-campus public discussion of the great moral and political issues presently driving the country into civil war, and he failed.

As early as 1858 a group of senior collegians formed a military company, the Continental Cadets, complete with buff and blue uniforms, to learn the military arts, turn out for parades, and publicly display their patriotism.[47] Not to be outdone by the seniors in patriotic zeal, a group of younger students also from the northern states formed a military company of their own, the Washington Cadets.[48] As war excitement intensified after Lincoln's inauguration, incidents occurring between campus unionists and secessionists were reported in the local press. Sorin admitted that incidents had occurred but denied that politics had been involved. Nonetheless, he declared that political contention had no place at Notre Dame and, if unsuppressed, would utterly destroy the spirit of study. Those who wanted to take up arms should go away and do so.[49]

Many Notre Dame students and several lay faculty did go away and took up arms to preserve the Union. A much smaller number of Notre Dame students returned to their homes in the South to fight for that cause. Moreover, seven Holy Cross priests volunteered for service as chaplains in Union regiments, participating in some of the bloodiest battles of the war.

The most celebrated of the Civil War chaplains was Father William E. Corby, C.S.C., who joined General Thomas F. Meagher's New York Irish Brigade and served with that regiment in the battles of Fair Oaks, Antietam, Fredericksburg, Chancellorsville, and Gettysburg. At a critical stage in the battle of Gettysburg, this priest from Notre Dame performed an act that seized the imagination of his countrymen. Corby climbed to the top of a large rock, put on a purple stole, raised his arm, and offered general absolution to all of the Union troops, Catholic and non-Catholic alike, about to engage the main Confederate force. Thirty minutes after this absolution, 506 of the several thousand soldiers in sight of Corby who had received it lay on the battlefield, dead or wounded.[50]

Holy Cross sisters did their part for the Union cause in the Civil War as well. No less than eighty sisters from St. Mary's served as nurses in eight Union army hospitals. Working often in primitive conditions caring for both wounded soldiers and for many afflicted with deadly contagious diseases, the sisters commanded respect from all of the soldiers fortunate enough to come under their care. Not to be outdone by the priests in anything, the sisters produced their share of heroines as well. Attached to an army hospital in Mound City, Sister Josephine bravely confronted an enraged group of Union soldiers and prevented them from lynching a wounded Confederate officer believed responsible for cruel treatment of their dying captain.[51]

At the same time, battles of a lesser sort were being waged by Sorin with local and national politicians to secure draft-exempt status for the Holy Cross brothers needed to keep the university running. Exemptions for the brothers were obtained first by employing influential friends to bring the matter to the attention of the secretary of war and to President Lincoln. That first exemption was lost after the elections of 1864, when Sorin had promised a prominent local politician more than he could deliver.

Convinced by the experience of the Holy Cross Congregation in France that religion and politics should not be mixed, Sorin had maintained a policy of strict neutrality in local, state, and national politics. As a matter of fact, members of the congregation had been directed not even to go to the polls. However, in the elections of 1864, the local Republican member of Congress, Schuyler Colfax, had pressed Sorin to show some gratitude for Sorin's appointment as Notre Dame postmaster and for the brothers' draft-exempt status by voting Republican in the forthcoming election.

Sorin agreed to oblige the congressman. Through an intermediary Sorin urged the brothers to go to the polls and vote Republican all the way. But most of the brothers were of Irish descent and like the rest of their ethnic group disposed to vote for Irish names, if they voted at all. Since most of the candidates with Irish names were Democrats, the brothers went to the polls and despite the indirectly expressed wishes of their

superior voted for their own kind. Sorin was embarrassed by the result. Though reelected anyway, Congressman Colfax was furious, and about a month after the brothers' unexpected display of political independence, their draft-exempt status was withdrawn.

Once again influential friends, including General William T. Sherman's wife, who was a Catholic, were asked to intervene. At the time, Sherman's young son was enrolled in the Minim department at Notre Dame, and a young daughter was a boarding student at St. Mary's. After Sherman captured Savannah in late December 1864, the brothers' draft-exempt status was reinstated.

Unlike the conditions faced by troops in the field or in hospitals, life at the university proceeded generally in an untroubled fashion. Throughout the entire war, enrollment remained comfortably above the financially viable level of 200, actually rising to 236 by 1863. Apart from a nationwide inflation of paper money, the demands of a wartime econony had virtually no effect upon Notre Dame. Sorin coped with the inflation of paper money in a straightforward way. When paid in gold, tuition and board cost $160. Parents electing to pay those bills with paper money were charged $320.[52]

By war's end there was not a vacant bed anywhere in the school, and the need for additional student living space to cope with expected postwar enrollment increases was apparent to all. Additions to the main college building were one way to meet that need. A new free-standing building was another. At the appropriate time, Sorin would decide, and then the brothers would pick up their tools and provide. During the postwar years at Notre Dame, that was the way of their world.

— vi —

Having successfully avoided enrollment problems and other forms of adversity during the difficult wartime years, Sorin faced the future with great confidence. That confidence was severely tested on April 23, 1879, when a devastating fire destroyed all of the principal university buildings. Away from the university when this catastrophe struck, Sorin returned to view the smoldering ruins of his life's work. Without a moment's hesitation, he decided to rebuild and to begin at once. Within a week of the fire the brothers had set themselves to clearing away the debris of the old building and preparing the ground for a new one.

Though only $45,000 of an estimated $200,000 loss was covered by insurance,[53] plans to obtain and select a design for a new, larger, and improved college building and raise the money to pay for it were prepared and implemented. Designs were received from thirty architectural firms, and the one submitted by Willoughby J. Edbrooke of Chicago was approved by Sorin. Funds for the project came in part from insurance payments, cash and credit from the Congregation of Holy Cross, gifts from the South Bend area, and from special fund-raising campaigns and benefit programs organized in Chicago, elsewhere in the Midwest, and in the East.

Ground was broken for the Edbrooke design on May 17. In addition to all of the brothers put to work on the project, more than 300 local workmen were hired. Of that number, fifty-six were bricklayers required to set the 4,350,000 bricks needed to complete the building. Most of the stone foundation was in place by June 21, and a week later, walls for two stories were up. By the Fourth of July, the third story had been completed. This hectic construction marathon went on throughout the hot Indiana summer. By September 1879 the building was sufficiently finished and improved with gas illumination, steam heat, hot and cold running water in the lavatories, that it was ready to receive the 324 collegians, preparatory students, and minims enrolled for the fall semester. Even Sorin must have been astonished by what the Notre Dame community had accomplished during that extraordinary summer.

To be sure, the energy and enterprise demonstrated in 1879 was not sustainable. Nonetheless, improvements in the physical plant continued over the next few years, and indeed, some progress was made acquiring books to replace library holdings destroyed in the fire. In any case, by 1885 enrollment in all departments passed 900, with preparatory and elementary students predominating. The university was secure, financially viable, and the great fire a fast-fading memory.

Sorin's leadership during the first half-century of university history had been at once authoritarian and fortuitous. As a crisis manager at Notre Dame and as some might say with regard to his troublemaking role in Holy Cross affairs generally and in diverting resources away from religious works elsewhere, Sorin had no peer.

However, not even a man as dominating as Sorin could deter the aging process. At the Third Plenary Council in Baltimore in 1884 Sorin was seventy-two and recognized by all as one of the grand old men of the American Church. That status pleased him very much. Indeed, since coming to America in 1841 Sorin had risen very high in the Catholic world. That rise had not been without cost, and most of it had been paid by Holy Cross religious works in France. A combination of clerical politics in which Sorin played a significant role, financial scandal, and unmanageable debts forced Father Basil Moreau, C.S.C., founder and life-time superior general of the Congregation of Holy Cross, out of office and into retirement in 1866. Two years later, with the Congregation of Holy Cross on the verge of dissolution because of internal strife and enormous debts, a live or die meeting was held in Rome to determine the future of the society. Out of that meeting came personnel changes, internal reforms, sales of property to pay some debts and ordinary foreclosure procedures to discharge others, and election of Father Sorin as the third superior general of the Congregation of Holy Cross.

As superior general, Sorin immediately took charge as both friends and enemies in the congregation expected that he would. He abandoned Le Mans, eliminated some Holy Cross religious work in France and elsewhere, and moved the generalate of the order to Notre Dame, where it remained with only a few interruptions until 1941. Though Sorin had given up the presidency of Notre Dame when chosen as provincial in 1865, he never gave up administrative direction of the institution and appointed or dismissed Holy Cross priests to that presidency as he saw fit.

Sorin's immediate successor as president was Patrick Dillon who served four years (1865–69), being replaced by the heroic Union Army chaplain, the ever loyal and always cooperative William Corby (1869–72). Corby stepped aside for Sorin's nephew, the gentle but frail Auguste Lemonnier, who died after serving only two years in office (1872–74). After Lemonnier's death, Sorin left the office vacant for three months and then against his better judgment appointed the ill-fated Patrick J. Colovin to be fifth president of the university (1875–77). Two years of Colovin was enough for Sorin. Corby was brought back again for five years as both president and provincial (1877–82).

Compelled by Rome to give up one of his offices, Corby was succeeded as president by a young French-speaking Canadian favorite of Sorin with an Irish name, Thomas E. Walsh (1882–93). Walsh served eleven years before dying in office in 1893. A few months before his own death, Sorin selected Andrew J. Morrissey (1893–1905) to head the university and lead it into the next century. From the time Sorin gave up the presidency in 1865 until his death in 1893, final authority over all personnel and financial decisions was his to exercise whenever he chose to do so.

During the years of Sorin's generalate, priests and brothers at Notre Dame frequently would appeal to him to overturn particular decisions of local superiors which they believed had affected them adversely. For example, when some brothers became convinced that Colovin, as president, abetted by a number of priest-faculty members, intended to force them out of their teaching positions in the college, they appealed to Sorin for protection.[54] In the end, for this reason as well as others combined under the general accusation of "contempt of authority," Sorin dismissed Colovin from the presidency, compelled him to leave Notre Dame, and eventually drove him out of the country and out of the congregation.[55] For his part, Colovin accused one of the brothers of having too much business with the superior general and attributed his own difficulties with him to clashes over the authority of the Provincial Council.[56]

While Sorin was authoritarian, and often arbitrary, in relations with those persons under his governance, in other matters he was pragmatic and flexible. As a matter of fact, when some French members of the congregation derisively described Sorin's pragmatism as American, he accepted that description as a compliment. Simply stated, Sorin adjusted to the world as it was very easily.

— vii —

Sorin and his early companions had founded a school which from the very beginning had been both solidly Catholic and predominantly residential in character. This predominantly residential character of Notre Dame was no accident. The place could hardly have grown and prospered in any other way. Notre Dame simply could not operate on tuition income alone; in order to survive the institution needed the revenues from room and board. As a matter of fact, Notre Dame was a pioneer and innovator among American Catholic colleges and schools in the development of academic residential facilities and ambiance.

In order to accommodate and retain more of the older students attracted to Notre Dame by the newer nontraditional programs being offered in the collegiate departments and in the law school, in 1886 some individual rooms in the main college building were provided to a few students judged sufficiently mature to be able to study without regular supervision. Abandoning the very powerful tradition of open dormitories and supervised open study halls was not a decision easily made or one that commanded unanimity among the leaders of Notre Dame. Conservatives within the Congregation of Holy Cross—and on this issue Father Thomas E. Walsh, C.S.C., president of the university, was a conservative—feared that any acknowledgment of possible imperfections in the open dormitory system would lead to anarchy.[57]

However, improving the retention rate of students attending the school seemed dependent on the greater availability of individual rooms. The availability of such accommodations was one trend observable in contemporary American boarding schools that a few influentials in the Congregation of Holy Cross believed Notre Dame would have to follow. As one Notre Dame faculty member argued, compelling students to use crowded study halls and open dormitories where they slept like patients in a hospital ward was intensely disliked by American Catholic students. Young men wanted independence and an essential part of that independence was to have one's own room. Catholic colleges which failed to provide individual rooms would either lose enrollment or become preparatory schools catering to junior students. No other circumstances operative in contemporary American Catholic colleges had a more retarding effect on academic development and intellectual progress than open dormitories and supervised study halls.[58] Whatever the state of affairs in schools and colleges in the larger society, at Notre Dame the availability of individual rooms was so popular among students and the competition for them was so intense that additional private rooms had to be provided.

For this so-called audacious experiment to become a privilege regularly extended to juniors and seniors in all college departments who had maintained high scholastic standing and exemplary conduct, a new building was required. However, in the 1880s no other Catholic college in the United States had a student residence with individual rooms, and opposition to building such a facility at Notre Dame was very strong. As president, Father Walsh refused even to consider such a project. At the same time, the leading advocate for a new residence hall with individual rooms was Walsh's vice president at that time, Father John A. Zahm, C.S.C. According to an account left by Zahm's brother, Albert, Father Zahm managed to overcome Walsh's objections by going to Sorin and persuading him that this project was essential for the future development of Notre Dame.

According to Albert Zahm, Sorin sent Walsh off to Europe to attend the International Scientific Congress in March 1888 and during his absence W. J. Edbrooke was commissioned to design a new student residence hall with sixty individual rooms and space for law lectures, a room for holding mock court, a law library, and a chapel. Edbrooke's design, originally styled as Collegiate Hall, was later renamed, appropriately, Sorin Hall. Sorin pressed for construction to begin as soon as possible.

The cornerstone dedication with Sorin and Zahm officiating took place on May 27, 1888, two days before Walsh returned from Europe.[59] Whether Walsh knew about Zahm's intrigue with Sorin at the time that it occurred is unknown, but he clearly learned about it later. Consequently, after suffering a few more bad experiences coming out of the special

Zahm/Sorin relationship and when the state of community politics finally allowed the president some freedom of action, Walsh replaced Zahm as vice president.

However obtained, the commitment to individual rooms for Notre Dame students was irreversible. Sorin Hall, the first student residential facility with individual rooms ever established on an American Catholic college campus, opened and received its first students in early January 1889. Though Walsh initially had opposed the idea of building such a residence hall and could not have been pleased by the means employed to launch the project, he wanted it to succeed. With that end in mind, Walsh appointed his director of studies and protégé, Andrew J. Morrissey, as rector of the new residence hall.

Though conservative and no admirer of Zahm, Morrissey was hardworking and charming. As rector of this splendid new facility, he found himself in a situation where failure was virtually impossible. Sorin Hall was the most desirable living situation at the school and only the best and brightest students were able to obtain rooms there. The discipline, order, and cleanliness maintained in the new facility pleased everyone. A way had been found to attract and retain older students at Notre Dame.[60] In a few years two new wings providing seventy-five more rooms were added.

A turning point in the development of the residential character of Notre Dame had been reached. Henceforth, collegians would be housed whenever possible in individual rooms and would be responsible for organizing their own study time. Henceforth, most—but not all—of the preparatory students and those collegians afflicted with poor study habits or otherwise needing closer supervision were assigned to the open dormitories and study halls of the main college building.

In general, the residential situation at Notre Dame provided opportunities for young men to grow spiritually through regular participation in religious exercises and intellectually through individual study and regular recitation. At the same time, many Notre Dame collegians were able to enjoy some of that privacy and independence that adolescents craved and only distance from home and parents could provide. Yet, that degree of privacy and independence was encountered in a well-protected environment where no one would be seriously hurt by the experience. So important did the special quality of residential life become to the institutional character and mission of the school that the kind of residentiality perceived to be experienced here was one of the principal reasons so many Catholic parents wanted to send their sons to Notre Dame. By 1912 Notre Dame proudly advertised itself as the largest and most successful Catholic boarding school in the world, an institution founded and built by the Congregation of Holy Cross by themselves alone without benefit of support from the government or from millionaires.

— viii —

Sorin was a man of many accomplishments, but above all else he was an extremely lucky ecclesiastical politician. Viewing the intensifying conflict between the liberal and conservative parties in the American Catholic hierarchy from a safe distance, Sorin was too old and too wise to take an active part in it. He professed admiration for both sides and allowed representatives of both camps to hold influential positions in the university administration.

With the liberals, Sorin believed passionately in a brilliant future for the Catholic Church in America. While it is unlikely that he ever shared completely the grand vision of Archbishop John Ireland and Monsignor Denis O'Connell about the practices of the American Church and of American political democracy being exportable models for the rest of the world, there were moments when he came close to doing so. However, there were also many moments when conservative criticism of some aspects of the liberal program must have appealed to this grand old man of the American Church. As the superior of a religious order, Sorin had no truck whatsoever with Archbishop Ireland's distrust of religious orders, especially of their autonomy from episcopal control. Moreover, as the founder and head of a developing Catholic educational enterprise, Sorin could not have been supportive of Archbishop Ireland's schemes to find publicly funded alternatives to privately funded parochial schools. With the conservatives, Sorin believed absolutely in the necessity of a religious education delivered to Catholic students in the secure philosophical and moral environment of a Catholic school.

The leading liberal accommodationist cleric on campus was Father John A. Zahm. He was a protégé of Sorin, a self-taught scientist, a science teacher, a popular writer on scientific and religious subjects, and for a time vice president and director of studies for the university. He was a personal friend of Archbishop Ireland and imagined himself as one of a special band of Catholic clerics called to assist in the reform and modernizing of the Church.

Zahm was convinced that scientific truth and revealed religion could never be in conflict. The truth of science and the truth of faith were derived from the source of all truth, namely, the mind of God. In lectures and in articles Zahm insisted that the conclusions of modern science properly understood were not contrary to the dogmas of the Church. After publication of his controversial book *Evolution and Dogma* in 1896, Zahm became one of the leading Catholic apologists for evolution. For Zahm, science was an important intellectual component in any religion-based education. For that reason as well as others, Zahm promoted science and engineering courses of study at Notre Dame. Beyond that, he also believed that collegiate work of all sorts ought to be expanded, even at the expense of limiting or reducing the size of the preparatory school departments. He was not fearful about borrowing money for new facilities that would promote his personal vision of what he believed the course of the university over the next decade ought to be. Impatient with those who disagreed with him about the future of Notre Dame or about the agenda of the liberal bishops, Zahm lacked the political instincts and skills required to achieve his goals at the university or in the Church at large.

Zahm's most formidable opponent and leading campus religious conservative was Father Andrew J. Morrissey, C.S.C. Known by friends and foes alike as the "Kilkenny Chieftain" from the Irish county of his birth, Morrissey possessed all of the political instincts and skills that Zahm lacked and virtually none of his intellectual and scientific interests. Morrissey had been a teacher of elementary Greek and Latin who had captured Sorin's eye and had risen through the university administrative hierarchy, alternating over a number of years with Zahm in the office of vice president and director of studies. Knowing something of the history of Holy Cross difficulties in France, terrified by the prospect of incurring institutional debt, ever watchful over salaries paid to lay faculty, and never convinced that advanced study and graduate degrees were necessary for college teachers,[61] Morrissey was thoroughly satisfied with Notre Dame as it was—that is, as a large preparatory school with small colleges attached. Moreover, he had no patience with what he perceived as dreamy schemes to please American Protestants or reform the Catholic Church according to some new American model.

At Notre Dame the differences between the liberal and conservative Catholic parties, between Zahm and Morrissey, were as much personal as they were ideological. Neither of these men liked the other very much. In July 1893, three months before Sorin died, Morrissey had enough support among the factions within the congregation to win Sorin's approval of his appointment as president of the university. In the context of congregation politics, the aged Sorin's approval of Morrissey was a clear victory for the Kilkenny Chieftain over the dour and sometimes arrogant Zahm. After Sorin died and a new superior general, Father Gilbert Français, C.S.C., had been chosen, Morrissey helped facilitate the exile of Zahm from campus in 1896 by releasing him from his duties at Notre Dame so that he had to accept an appointment as procurator general of the Congregation of Holy Cross, resident in Rome.

Zahm accepted this appointment with no small reluctance, but as it turned out his twenty months exile in Rome was a happy and exciting time for him. He liked the company of important people and got on very well in Vatican high society. He came face to face with the great men in the American Church visiting the city and got to know most of them personally. Zahm was at once an observer and a participant in the intellectual controversies and ecclesiastical power politics which were under way in Rome at the turn of the century and would do so much to shape the direction of the American Church for the next sixty years.

Zahm's position and growing reputation in Rome led to increased contact and socialization with the new superior general whenever official business brought him to Rome. Français was much impressed by Zahm's intellect and by the contacts which the procurator had developed in the Eternal City. Consequently, when death removed Corby from the post of provincial of the American Province of the Congregation of Holy Cross resident at Notre Dame, Français appointed Zahm in early 1898 to serve out the remaining seven months of Corby's term. Then, in August 1899, Français managed the election of Zahm to a full term.

Zahm returned to Notre Dame immediately and began to implement reforms that in time would begin the transformation of Notre Dame into a modern university. It became immediately evident that Zahm as provincial could not depend on the full cooperation of brethren in the university administration. Morrissey was as hostile to Zahm and his ideas as ever. Moreover, there were reasons aplenty to encourage the president to ignore or not take seriously the educational ideas of his provincial.

For his part, during most of 1899 Zahm was deeply distracted and in a state of high anxiety. His controversial book *Evolution and Dogma*, wherein he had accepted evolutionary processes as a viable creation mechanism while rejecting the Darwinian notion of natural selection, had been referred to the Sacred Congregation of the Index. Zahm's book was formally condemned by that body on September 10, 1898, nine months after he had been appointed provincial and just weeks after he had won election in his own right to a full term of eight years. Taking Français's advice, Zahm submitted completely and unreservedly to the decree and to all of its injunctions and voluntarily withdrew the book from sale. In the future, he would attempt no more reconciliations of science and religion. At the same time, both Français and Zahm systematically and diligently called upon all of their Roman friends high and low with influence in official Vatican circles and managed to get publication of the decree suspended. That process took about a year to complete.

However, at Notre Dame word of Zahm's difficulties began to leak out in May and early June 1899 and rumors about the possibility of his being deposed from office circulated widely.[62] Though such rumors in the end turned out to be groundless, a letter reporting Cardinal Miecislaus Ledochowski's question to the new procurator general about why members of Holy Cross placed Father Zahm in such a high office was passed around.[63] It was a fact that Zahm began the highly politicized process of educational reform at Notre Dame with very high vulnerability. To be sure, he was the provincial and endowed with all the powers vested in that authoritarian office, but at the time that Français made the appointment every superior in the province with influence was against it.[64] Also, every superior in the province knew that Zahm was only provincial for the time being.

Transformation of Notre Dame into a modern university would require time and intellectual and financial resources greater than those at hand. Zahm's strategy for finding and deploying them suggests that he was indeed a man of his own time and place. In at least one very important respect, Zahm and Morrissey were in agreement. They were both extremely wary, with some good reason as will be shown, of hiring laymen with advanced degrees to teach at Notre Dame. Both Zahm and Morrissey recently had very bad experiences with such a lay faculty member, experiences that led to the most serious public relations crisis in university history up to that time. Smarting from this unpleasant episode, Zahm and Morrissey remembered the wisdom of Sorin's instruction to the congregation, delivered in a formal circular letter as long ago as 1870, to reduce the number of lay faculty employed at the university and to hire no more.

On this subject Sorin had been very clear. He urged that as teachers in the university "strangers [should] be gradually dispensed with; otherwise you will never derive much profit from all of your pains and labors . . . let it be clearly understood that no strangers should be employed where one of ours will do as well."[65] Sorin's distinction between "our men," meaning members of Holy Cross, and "strangers," meaning lay faculty, did not die with him in 1893. It survived formally at least until 1919 in the listing of faculty in the general catalogue of the university. Holy Cross priests as a group were listed first, followed by Holy Cross brothers and other religious; third and last came the names of the lay faculty.

As a man of his time and place, Zahm was not disposed to look beyond the Congregation of Holy Cross and Notre Dame for the men and money necessary to begin modernization of the university. In Zahm's view, candidates for advanced training in needed academic specialties could be selected from the congregation and sent off for study at an appropriate graduate school. Monies to pay for such training as well as to build new academic facilities could be borrowed and then repaid out of operating revenues. To implement such an internally financed self-improvement strategy, only the will to begin appeared to be wanting. Clearly, Zahm had the will to initiate educational reforms at Notre Dame, but unpleasant decisions avoided early on suggest that he lacked the hardheaded realism and common sense required to see them through to completion.

Though advised to do so, Zahm did not turn out Morrissey and his friends from their places in the university administration until July 1905. So for six years, conflict, both personal and substantive, between the provincial and the president, exacerbated by a public relations disaster damaging to both Morrissey and Zahm, formed the context for academic changes at Notre Dame and for the way members of the congregation were trained. The idea of sending Holy Cross priests to study at secular universities was never seriously considered. Even for Zahm, that prospect was far too advanced. A true believer in the liberal agenda of Archbishop Ireland and his allies in the American hierarchy, Zahm was an enthusiastic supporter of the recently established Catholic University of America as a center for Catholic graduate studies and that was where the men of Holy Cross would be trained. As a matter of fact, Notre Dame was the first large Catholic institution to ally with the Catholic University of America in any common educational effort.

With those ends in mind, Zahm simply ignored the opposition of the Morrissey party and acquired property in Washington, D.C., in 1899 for a permanent house of studies for Holy Cross priests pursuing graduate studies there. The provincial installed a protégé, Father James A. Burns, C.S.C., a former chemist soon to earn a doctorate in education, as superior there in 1900.

Meanwhile, at Notre Dame building projects proceeded with great rapidity. Over $300,000 was spent on improvements to the physical plant. Provincial funds were committed for a new college in Portland, Oregon, and to repair fire damage to Holy Cross facilities in Texas. Property was mortgaged to pay for Zahm's projects and debts mounted. Opponents protested Zahm's disregard of traditional decision-making procedures and his perceived contempt for other points of view. The provincial's reputation as a highly opinionated spendthrift grew.

Finally, in July 1905, when new assignments were given out, Zahm decided to deal with his critics directly. Perhaps influenced also by Morrissey's very rough handling of a lay professor, Charles Veneziani, whose subsequent public protests visited upon the university damaging negative publicity and embarrassing scrutiny by higher religious authorities, Zahm required Morrissey to resign as president, and Father James French, C.S.C., to step down as vice president. At the same time, Morrissey's director of studies, Father Martin J. Regan, C.S.C., moved from that office to the post of prefect of discipline. According to a deeply disappointed friend of Morrissey, Regan as prefect of discipline would "give correct and sincere information about Notre Dame to the new administration."[66]

What shocked Morrissey supporters most was not that changes had been made, because after the Veneziani fiasco, it was clear that some were needed. In the end, Zahm acted as Zahm had always acted. The shock was not so much in the changes themselves as in "the want of manner with which they had been brought about: so sudden, so radical, so heartless!"[67] Zahm replaced his old adversary in the presidency with a protégé, the energetic Father John W. Cavanaugh, C.S.C., best known for his oratory and appealing public persona.

For Zahm, the elevation of two of his protégés, Burns and Cavanaugh, and the dismissal of Morrissey was the beginning of the end to his power at Notre Dame. Morrissey had no intention of accepting this defeat as anything but a temporary setback. Given a leave of absence for a year, he accompanied the superior general on an inspection tour of Holy Cross houses and works throughout the American Province. While on this tour, Morrissey tirelessly advised friends at Notre Dame and elsewhere in the province about what to say to the superior general on the subjects of morale in the congregation and on the general state of affairs in the province.

Morrissey urged his friends at Notre Dame to speak their minds, to make very clear to the superior general as often as possible that their positions were well supported in the congregation. Zahm's supporters (he did not have many friends) were younger, louder, but fewer.[68] The special problem facing the conservatives in their guerrilla war against Zahm was an extremely delicate one. They had to persuade Français that he had erred in promoting Zahm but do so in an inoffensive and noncritical way. Morrissey was up to the task and accomplished it in a year's time. When Zahm's term as provincial ended in August 1906, he was not renewed.

Frightened by Zahm's strategy of financing expansion through borrowing, aware that Zahm's liberal friends in the hierarchy had fallen out of favor in Rome, observing that conservatives were routing liberals in the Church everywhere, and fearful that present divisions within the community at Notre Dame would become permanent, Français turned back to the Kilkenny Chieftain. Français approved the selection of Morrissey to succeed Zahm as provincial. Clearly, Zahm was deeply wounded by this rejection. He went into a voluntary exile. With the approval of the new provincial, Zahm remained away from the university for the rest of his life, pursuing a successful writing career and traveling with celebrities until he died in Munich in 1921.

In the long term, Zahm's most enduring contribution to the development of the university was the elevation of Cavanaugh and Burns to positions of influence. Even more than Zahm, Cavanaugh and Burns were the architects of the modern university. Together, they gave a direction to future development and profoundly influenced university affairs for the next thirty-five years.

Perhaps tamed a bit by his recent experiences and ever under the watchful eyes of the superior general, Morrissey continued as provincial almost to the day he died in 1918. However, conflict between the provincial and the president of the sort that had divided the Notre Dame community since 1898 ended when Zahm left the campus in 1906. As provincial, Morrissey stayed out of the operational affairs and got on well with Cavanaugh as president of the university and with Burns as superior of the House of Studies in Washington. Burns remained in Washington as superior and supervised the graduate education of a whole generation of Holy Cross priests until he succeeded Cavanaugh as president in 1919.

—   ix   —

By the first decade of the twentieth century, Notre Dame had become a very important part of an enormous and seemingly ever-expanding American Catholic educational and eleemosynary enterprise. Formally committed to the creation and development of this enterprise by the predominantly Irish American episcopal leadership of the Catholic Church in this country at the Third Plenary Council in Baltimore in 1884, American Catholics proceeded over the next seventy-five years to build, staff, finance, and patronize an alternative all-inclusive system of religious, educational, medical, and charitable institutions. What they managed to create and maintain during this period was extraordinary, made even more so by the fact that it was done by themselves virtually without assistance from government funding. In doing what they did the way they did it, American Catholics were unique in the world. No other group in the twentieth century has matched their effort.

To be sure, the ideal proclaimed at Baltimore in 1884 of a Catholic school for every Catholic child was never realized. There never were financial and human resources sufficient for that. It was probably true that development of this American Catholic educational enterprise was driven more by a desire to self-segregate American Catholics from the social institutions of the larger society in order to protect and preserve religious faith than to achieve educational and intellectual excellence. It was also certainly true that while there was much to praise in the history of the American Catholic educational enterprise between 1884 and 1962, there were some things to regret and fault. Mistakes and missteps were inevitable. Intergroup relations suffered. No set of issues was more divisive in early-twentieth-century America than the school question.

During those same years American Catholic leaders knew very well that by whatever standard chosen, Catholic schools, colleges, and universities had less to offer than publicly supported institutions or long-established and well-endowed private ones. Yet in American Catholic circles, Catholic schools, colleges, and universities were generally perceived to be morally and philosophically safer. For that perceived safety, large numbers of American Catholics were willing to send their children to such institutions and to pay for the opportunity of doing so.

How much American Catholics willingly paid through tuition and fees and other forms of financial contributions to the creation and maintenance of morally and philosophically secure schools and colleges can never be known. Over the course of the twentieth century the amounts given were enormous and the demands and solicitations for more were endless. As a matter of fact, fund raising and responding to financial solicitations became a leading characteristic of America Catholic culture. So characteristic in fact that even the most severe critics and opponents of a large Catholic presence in the United States agreed that giving money to their church was what American Catholics appeared to do best.

Paying and contributing so much so often to the American Catholic educational enterprise became a habit for American Catholics. However, until after midcentury that habit of giving did not generally extend to Catholic universities and colleges. As John William Cavanaugh, Morrissey's successor as president of Notre Dame, observed in early 1906 to a staff member of the General Education Board, later to become the Rockefeller Foundation, contributions to the Notre Dame endowment for the previous year had been minuscule. Why American Catholics gave so little to their universities and colleges was one of the great puzzles of life for Cavanaugh.[69] "Our people, so generous to most religious enterprises," Cavanaugh remarked, "have not yet begun to encourage in a practical way schools of higher education." It was that condition, he concluded, that "accounts for the slow development of some of our Catholic colleges."[70]

In time, all of this would change. By the end of the century, given the enormous increase in the size and wealth of the American Catholic community, their giving to Catholic universities and colleges had far surpassed John Cavanaugh's most optimistic expectations. All in all, during the last half of the century the American Catholic habit of giving to religious and educational causes was transformed into a powerful group tradition of generosity unsurpassed anywhere.

By the end of the twentieth century, American Catholics were not per capita the richest of Americans. However, of the large groups in our country, American Catholics had become the most affluent and the most generous. It was out of this tradition of group generosity that the University of Notre Dame and other Catholic colleges and universities found the support and resources with which to grow and prosper.

2

The President
and the Professor

D uring the first two decades of the twentieth century a new sense of discipline was on the rise everywhere in the Catholic Church. The papacy had
strengthened the foundations of orthodoxy by reasserting the authority
of St. Thomas Aquinas in philosophy and theology. Under the rubric of
Americanism condemned in 1899, the idea that the Catholic Church in
America ought to develop its own style was rejected. After the accession
of Pius X in 1903, modernism or the notion that the Church had to adapt
itself to changing times and to the work of scholarly critics of the Bible
and of other sources of religious authority was condemned.

All of these measures had a chilling effect on intellectual activity
within the Church. Independent inquiries into philosophical and theological subjects in Catholic institutions capable of conducting them became suspect and were discouraged. If answers were needed for questions
raised in those areas, Rome would provide them. It was a very difficult
time for dissenters and protesters of any sort. In this climate, obedience
and loyalty were the virtues most highly valued and rewarded.

Where needed, this Roman model of orthodoxy, obedience, and loyalty was adopted and implemented throughout the Church. The progress
of this model through the various levels of authority in the American
Church had little impact on Notre Dame. Threats to orthodoxy were
nonexistent. Problems of obedience were more frequent than superiors
and university officials wanted to admit and would continue to be so.
Loyalty to the university, meaning no public criticism of persons or policies, was taken for granted. At least it was up to 1900.

In that year, the customary canons of institutional loyalty were grossly violated in the most public way and produced the greatest public relations crisis in the history of Notre Dame up to that time. The cause of this most unwanted and embarrassing situation was the appearance in early 1900 of a privately printed pamphlet written by Charles Veneziani, a dismissed Notre Dame lay faculty member. In this pamphlet, extensively titled *A Plea For The Higher Education Of Young Catholic Men Of America With An Exposure Of The Frauds Of The University Of Notre Dame, IND, Preceded By A Circular Letter To The Archbishops, Bishops, And Prominent Clergy Of The United States,* Veneziani attacked Morrissey and the university for a variety of alleged fraudulent educational and financial activities, a range of serious and petty misrepresentations, and some very mean-spirited behavior toward himself. As indicated in the title, in early 1900 the author distributed copies of this pamphlet to all of the archbishops and bishops in the country and also to the members of the all clerical Board of Trustees of the university.

Veneziani followed up with a second pamphlet in 1902, entitled *Frauds Of The University of Notre Dame, Notre Dame, Indiana, Or How The Catholic University Of Notre Dame With Her Fraudulent Doctor's Degrees, Courses, Etc., Prostitutes The Prestige Which A Religious Order Enjoys In The Eyes Of Catholics To Obtain Their Money Under False Pretenses.* He returned to some of the same subjects again along with an account of his efforts to obtain redress of grievances and satisfaction from various levels of ecclesiastical authority. This account appeared as an undated compilation of papers put into a newspaper format, probably printed in 1912, titled with the Jesuit motto, *A.M.D.G.* (*ad majorem Dei gloriam* or "to the greater glory of God"). Being so public, this Veneziani affair was something that could not be ignored at the time. Over the years, Veneziani's business touched a great many very important Catholic Church officials and lasted in one forum or another until 1924.

Born in Italy, fluent in Italian, French, German, English, and a zealous Catholic, Veneziani came to Notre Dame in September 1896. Though carrying a spotty employment record during his time in the United States—only one full-year and the rest part-time appointments—Veneziani came to the university extremely well credentialed, perhaps the most highly credentialed faculty member, clerical or lay, ever employed by the institution up to that time. Veneziani had received an A.M. and a Ph.D. in mathematics from Heidelberg.

As president of the university, Morrissey personally handled all of the negotiations and signed all of the correspondence about the appointment of Veneziani. According to Veneziani, he had been hired to teach

French and had been promised appointment to a chair in mathematics as soon as one opened up. He also claimed later to have been told that in view of his qualifications, his contracted salary of $600 was more than was usually paid to first-time appointees.[1] Ever conscious of his highly credentialed status and always expecting proper deference to it, being the highest paid first-time appointee was important to him.

However, soon after arriving at the university, Veneziani discovered that his salary was not the highest paid to a first-time appointee and that there were no chairs in mathematics or for that matter in any other discipline for him or anyone else to get. At the same time, Veneziani discovered also that he had been listed in the local newspaper as holder of a chair in romance language in a nonexistent Department of Romance Languages.

As one might suspect, Morrissey's version of Veneziani's arrival and three-year teaching career at Notre Dame is very different and, as events will show, was self-serving. Before Veneziani's first year at Notre Dame was over, the president claimed to have realized that hiring him had been a serious mistake. According to Morrissey, from the moment Veneziani had set foot on campus he had received special treatment and kept demanding more. The man had been paid a rent subsidy in addition to his salary. Though married, he was allowed to take his meals in the university refectory. Moreover, Veneziani's young son was admitted to the university elementary school with all fees, including board, waived.[2]

In Morrissey's view, Veneziani was a much better seeker of favors and special treatment than a teacher, being "utterly unfit to have charge of students, and his work here was not worth half the amount he received for it."[3] The president described Veneziani's attempts to teach mathematics as disastrous; the students could not understand his presentations and generally regarded him as a mere pretender. Morrissey professed great pity for the man in his apparent helpless state, insisting that he had been retained after the first year only because of a misguided sense of charity.[4]

Moreover, several times during Veneziani's first two years at Notre Dame, Morrissey had met with him to discuss his situation and prospects, urging that he try and find a post elsewhere.[5] Though belied by later events, Morrissey insisted that, after two years at Notre Dame, Veneziani seemed incapable of helping himself. He had become a man who saw persecution everywhere and was driven mentally to construct huge mountains out of tiny molehills. According to Morrissey, the root cause of Veneziani's problems was mental instability.[6]

Veneziani recalled those same meetings with Morrissey, but his account of them is vastly different. According to Veneziani, at no time during any of the meetings with Morrissey did the president deny that a promise of a chair in mathematics had been made to him. The professor did say that at one meeting Morrissey told him, because the branches of mathematics taught at the university were so elementary, a scholar of his knowledge and ability could not be of much use at Notre Dame. The president urged the professor to look for a position at another institution where his scholarship could be better utilized. At the same time, Morrissey assured Veneziani that he could remain at Notre Dame until a better post elsewhere could be found.[7] On still another occasion, Veneziani stated, Morrissey had told him that present university policy was "to get rid of the laymen Professors as soon as they can be replaced by members of the Congregation of Holy Cross."[8] Again, Morrissey advised Veneziani to look for another job.

Why, then, did not Veneziani heed the president's advice and leave Notre Dame? A simple answer is that a man with a family and not possessed with independent means could not leave one job until he had found another. A more complex answer reflecting the reality of Veneziani's situation was that no teaching positions equal to or better than his place at Notre Dame were available at that time or were ever likely to be. Veneziani assumed correctly that a teaching post at another Catholic college would be no gain. Salaries elsewhere in Catholic higher education would not be better.

Moreover, escaping to a state university was not a viable option for lay professors in Catholic colleges. Once in the Catholic system, one was trapped there forever. At this time and for many years thereafter, lay professors with work experience in Catholic colleges were not welcome in state universities. Veneziani claimed that throughout its entire fifty-six year history, not one Notre Dame lay professor had ever managed to get a position at a state university.[9] Veneziani wanted very much to keep his job at Notre Dame because he did not think a better one could be found.

— ii —

Clearly, for Veneziani, who had been to Heidelberg, and for Morrissey, who had spent his entire learning life at Notre Dame, the notion of an academic chair had completely different meanings. As Veneziani understood the concept, an academic chair was a special appointment, most likely specifically endowed, given only to the most distinguished persons on the faculty. Indeed, an academic chair was not for everyone. For Morrissey, an academic chair was just a more elegant way of describing an academic appointment. Styling Veneziani as holder of the chair in romance languages made better-appearing news copy than simply stating that he had been hired to teach French. The deliberate lying and immorality which Veneziani imputed to the president in this instance and railed against so stridently in his pamphlets was utter fantasy. Morrissey was so astonished by Veneziani's outrage over a press release and by what the man wrote later about this matter that he attributed it to mental instability.

What drove Veneziani in early 1900 to write and circulate his first pamphlet attacking Notre Dame was a series of encounters with Morrissey in the fall of 1898 and in the early winter of 1899. Actually, trouble began in the late spring of 1897, when Veneziani asked Morrissey how much his salary increase for the next year would be. Believing that a salary increase for the second year had been promised when hired, Veneziani was shocked when Morrissey replied that there would be no salary increases for lay faculty during 1897–98 because the university had to support the missions in India.[10] Appalled by what the president had said, Veneziani appears to have discussed it with other lay faculty and learned that his treatment on the matter of a promised salary increase was not exceptional. The policy of the university, Veneziani claimed, was to pay first-time appointees as little as possible, promise much in the future, and then find reasons for reneging on what had been promised.[11] When that happened and it happened often, the faculty member had to forget about past promises and take what was offered or leave.

Fully aware by the end of 1898 that neither promised salary increases nor an academic chair would be given to him and humiliated by having an extra course in German for which extra pay had been promised taken from him and assigned to a Holy Cross brother lately employed as a college porter,[12] Veneziani decided to try and obtain what he believed was justice from the Board of Trustees of the university. In January 1899 he sent letters to all three clerical members of the board stating his claim to a salary increase and to a chair in mathematics. He supported his claims with copies of passages from Morrissey's letters sent to him in 1896.[13]

Within two days, Veneziani received a response from the board that was succinct and to the point. The board referred the matter to the president, who, in their judgment, had exclusive authority to act in such matters.[14] When Veneziani called upon the president shortly thereafter, Morrissey told him that his services would not be required after June 15, 1899. By appealing actions of the president to the board, Veneziani, as a lay professor, had crossed a line and lost his job for doing so.

When Veneziani asked Morrissey why he had been discharged, the president responded by saying that if Mr. Studebaker could discharge workmen in his shop at a moment's notice without giving reasons, so could he.[15] Insofar as Morrissey was concerned, the short sad story of Charles Veneziani at Notre Dame was now over. In truth, Morrissey had ended only one chapter of that story, but Veneziani was busily preparing others.

In March 1899 Veneziani addressed the board once again requesting that his claims respecting an academic chair and a promised salary increase be referred to Bishop Scanlan of Salt Lake City for review and adjudication.[16] The board neither acknowledged receipt of the letter nor responded to it. Thus matters rested until May 17, when Morrissey sent Veneziani a formal notification that his employment at the university would end on June 15. At this point Veneziani did two things. First, he began working on a pamphlet intended to expose Morrissey and all of the alleged petty hypocrisies and frauds witnessed and experienced by him during his three years at Notre Dame. Second, Veneziani answered Morrissey's dismissal notification on June 1 with a very angry insulting letter that invited a harsh response.

In this letter of June 1 Veneziani accused Morrissey of being a liar for his many misrepresentations about academic status and salary prospects and of acting like a thief for withholding payment for that extra German course well begun but reassigned to a Holy Cross brother. Even Veneziani admitted later that perhaps the letter itself was "rather too strong," even though the facts in it were all true.[17] The letter so infuriated Morrissey that he acted hastily and foolishly, in effect confirming Veneziani's allegation that the university had robbed him of monies justly due.

Outraged by Veneziani's strongly put allegations and believing the university a victim of attempted extortion, Morrissey instructed the assistant treasurer, a Holy Cross brother, to withhold the balance of Veneziani's contracted salary ($140) until the man had signed a statement that all university financial obligations to him had been discharged. Veneziani heatedly refused to sign such a statement, and the assistant treasurer would not release the check until he did.[18] Veneziani left university employment with approximately one quarter of his contracted salary unpaid.

Morrissey's attempt to obtain a signed acknowledgment that the university had discharged all of its financial obligations to Veneziani had misfired. The president had grossly underestimated the former professor's willingness to endure financial hardship for the sake of standing on what he believed was an important principle, namely, that men should be paid for what they do. Morrissey also realized that even a partial nonpayment of a contracted salary could have serious public relations if not legal consequences for the university. With those unhappy prospects in mind, the president twice tried to pay Veneziani the unpaid balance of his contracted salary, including sending a courier to the man's house with a check in hand for $140. Moreover, no signed acknowledgment that all university financial obligations to him had been satisfied was sought.[19]

According to Morrissey, when Veneziani observed that the check brought by the courier included only the unpaid balance of the contracted salary and nothing for the extra German course begun but then taken away, the man virtually exploded. He began "gesticulating and muttering incoherent menaces, precisely as might an escaped inmate of an asylum."[20] Veneziani crumpled the check, tore it into pieces, and threw it on the floor. While Mrs. Veneziani intervened to calm her husband, the courier hastily retrieved the check fragments and returned them to the president. After this incident, Morrissey sought out his former employee no more but made very clear that Veneziani could collect his $140 any time he wanted by writing or sending for it. Once again, Morrissey believed that the Veneziani matter had been closed, and once again he was wrong.

Disgusted by his experiences with Morrissey, Veneziani turned to the provincial and to the Board of Trustees for what he hoped would be a measure of justice. During the summer and continuing into October, Veneziani sent several letters to Zahm as provincial and to the board urging that his case be reviewed by Bishop Scanlan of Salt Lake City or by Archbishop Riordan of San Francisco. Veneziani claimed to have sent no less that twenty registered letters to the provincial and to the board during this period. None of these registered letters were answered by Zahm or by any of the trustees. The only response received was an oral one from Morrissey that "the Community brooks no interference from outsiders."[21]

For Veneziani, Zahm's silence in this matter of a request for justice through outside arbitration was proof positive that he was of no mind to see justice done because lay professors at Notre Dame possessed no rights that he, as provincial, was bound to respect.[22] In Veneziani's mind, by that silence Zahm had become an abettor and supporter of Morrissey's lies and injustices. If in this instance the provincial was as much a villain as the president, nothing further could be accomplished toward obtaining justice by dealing with either of them. With all patience and forbearance utterly exhausted, Veneziani drafted an open letter attacking Father Zahm. To his pamphlet *A Plea For The Higher Education Of Young Catholic Men Of America With An Exposure Of The Frauds Of The University Of Notre Dame*, attacking Morrissey and the university, Veneziani appended his attack letter against Zahm. In early 1900, Veneziani distributed the letter and pamphlet to all of the bishops and archbishops in the country.

Along with the copy of the pamphlet sent to Archbishop William Henry Elder of Cincinnati, the prelate with territorial jurisdiction over Notre Dame, Veneziani sent also a request that the archbishop review his case and render a judgment about the justice of it. Archbishop Elder read the pamphlet and must have been disturbed by what he found there. Immediately, he solicited from Zahm, as provincial, an explanation of what had gone on between Morrissey and Veneziani and why the man had not been paid the monies due him.

Certainly no admirer of Morrissey, Zahm did not want to be placed between the archbishop and the president or otherwise involve himself in this matter. He decided to be a conduit and nothing more. The provincial passed on to Morrissey the archbishop's request for information and asked him to prepare a full written explanation of how the present situation with Veneziani had developed. Unsure of how much support would be forthcoming from Zahm, Morrissey set to his task at once. He researched university payroll records and wrote a lengthy, self-serving, and largely untrue account and interpretation of Veneziani's career at Notre Dame.

The version of events that Morrissey prepared for the eyes of the provincial and of the archbishop alone was very strong medicine indeed. Veneziani was an utter rascal with no redeeming qualities whatsoever. Morrissey described Veneziani as an incompetent teacher and, his Heidelberg degrees notwithstanding, as an academic charlatan who was also probably mentally unbalanced. The man was an unsuccessful blackmailer of the university who, frustrated by failure, now vengefully attempted to blacken the reputation of Notre Dame in a thoroughly libelous pamphlet.[23]

In his account sent to the archbishop, Morrissey made no mention of Veneziani's allegations about promises of a salary increase or of a chair in mathematics for the professor and professed, out of charity, no intention of proceeding with a libel action against his dismissed employee. Morrissey insisted that the pamphlet should not and would not be taken seriously by honest men because it was nothing more than a collection of "puerile inanities" and "vituperative and vindictive ravings."[24] The president sent his account of events to Zahm on March 22, 1900, along with a check for $140 to settle the matter of unpaid salary. Zahm dispatched Morrissey's version of the Veneziani story and the check to the archbishop forthwith. Elder sought counsel from trusted persons in Cincinnati and then responded to Veneziani on April 17, 1900.[25]

Archbishop Elder acknowledged receipt of a long document from Morrissey and that he had discussed the case with people in Cincinnati. According to advice received and what he understood about the laws of equity, Elder had not been persuaded that Veneziani's case would have much standing in a civil court. Moreover, he did not believe that all of the claims put forward in Veneziani's pamphlet were reasonable. In any case, such a publication was not a proper means for obtaining justice. Veneziani had appealed to popular opinion, whereas justice and law were provided only in authorized courts. Finally, the archbishop believed that Morrissey's proposed settlement, payment of the $140 owed to the former professor, was correct. Elder hoped that Veneziani would accept it, be satisfied, dispute no more, and go away.[26]

Then, Archbishop Elder did an incredible thing. With his letter of April 17, 1900, to Veneziani, the archbishop enclosed and sent off to him the original copy of Morrissey's lengthy account and interpretation of his relations with the former professor. When Veneziani received and read what Morrissey had written for the eyes of the archbishop alone, he was at once outraged and euphoric, outraged over what Morrissey had said about him and euphoric over the possibility of exposing and damning the president with his own words. Henceforth, Veneziani always referred to Elder as the "saintly Metropolitan of Cincinnati."[27]

By sending Morrissey's document to Veneziani, Elder changed the whole nature of Veneziani's dispute with Morrissey and the university. The principal issues were no longer simply those of money. To be sure, that issue remained operative, but other embittering ones were added to complicate, protract, and prevent an acceptable settlement. The professor's grievances against Morrissey and Zahm now included defamation, and he sought repair of severely damaged personal honor and some form of retraction of the lies spoken against him. All of this would require a formal investigation by appropriate ecclesiastical authorities of the charges contained in the Morrissey document. With so much emotion and ego invested by both sides and given the powerful clerical abhorrence of public scandal, any sort of mutually satisfying compromise was unlikely. Indeed, Archbishop Elder had let a genie out of its bottle. Veneziani was absolutely determined that no one would be able to put it back inside again.

— iii —

After receiving Morrissey's document from Archbishop Elder, Veneziani made an important decision. He collected materials for the basis of an appeal of his case to the apostolic delegate, Archbishop Sebastian Martinelli, for review and possible intervention. What Veneziani wanted as a final outcome was a more equitable settlement of the university's unpaid financial obligations to him and a formal investigation by appropriate ecclesiastical authorities into the charges contained in the Morrissey document. Confident that the Morrissey document would force such an inquiry, he sent off a packet of materials to the apostolic delegate in August 1900.[28]

Whatever Veneziani's expectations about the prospects, the appeal turned out to be time and effort wasted. Archbishop Martinelli responded to Veneziani's letter and materials briefly but unambiguously on September 16, 1900. The apostolic delegate saw no basis for going further with Veneziani's business than Archbishop Elder had taken it. Martinelli minced no words, stating that "you will acquiesce in the decision of the Archbishop of Cincinnati and cease further prosecution of the matter."[29]

Archbishop Martinelli spoke and wrote Italian and English fluently so there should have been no mistaking the meaning of his message. However, after overanalyzing all ten lines of the apostolic delegate's letter, Veneziani concluded that Martinelli had made a terrible but understandable blunder. The apostolic delegate had assumed that Archbishop Elder had investigated the charges contained in the Morrissey document, which he had not. Since Martinelli's judgment in this matter and instruction to him had been based on a mistaken assumption, Veneziani could treat both the judgment and instruction as inoperative and non-binding.[30]

After explaining away Martinelli's instruction to cease further prosecution of his case, Veneziani began working on his second pamphlet viciously titled *Frauds Of The University Of Notre Dame . . .Or How The Catholic University Of Notre Dame With Her Fraudulent Doctor's Degrees, Courses, Etc., Prostitutes The Prestige Which A Religious Order Enjoys In The Eyes Of Catholics To Obtain Their Money Under False Pretenses.* In addition to the subject matter mentioned in the title, this pamphlet contained a withering attack on one of Zahm's science-popularizing books, *Catholic Science and Catholic Scientists.* Veneziani began circulating this pamphlet in 1902.

What inspired Veneziani's second pamphlet and sent his indignation soaring almost out of control was a discovery that a Spanish-language version of the general catalogue of the university printed in 1899 contained falsehoods and misrepresentations too shameful to be printed in the English-language version. According to Veneziani, in order to attract students to Notre Dame from recently acquired Puerto Rico and from Cuba, Mexico, and Central and South America, university officials deliberately lied in this new Spanish-language general catalogue about opportunities to obtain doctor's degrees in the fields of philosophy, literature, science, and law by attending Notre Dame.

A doctorate in philosophy would be awarded after completion of three years of postgraduate work under professors with higher degrees not yet hired in courses never taught or even listed in the English-language version of the general catalogue. Doctorates in literature, science, and law would be awarded to those Notre Dame students who, after graduation, had managed to do remarkable work in any one of those areas.[31] Clearly, that was not the way things had been done at Heidelberg, as Veneziani was always ready to point out, or how he believed things were being done at Harvard, Chicago, or Johns Hopkins in 1900.

What Veneziani wrote about the Spanish-language version of the general catalogue was generally true. However, the opportunities for obtaining doctorates from Notre Dame described in that version of the general catalogue were far less sinister than Veneziani would have us believe. First of all, the Spanish-language version was much more the work of the provincial than of the president, though the latter clearly went along with the project. Zahm spoke Spanish and had more contacts in Latin America and experience with Spanish-speaking culture than Morrissey. Zahm assumed that academic titles were so highly valued in upper-class Latin American societies that opportunities to obtain such a title might persuade parents to send their sons to Notre Dame. Zahm's purpose in preparing this Spanish-language catalogue was to attract Catholic students from Spanish-speaking areas to Notre Dame. If deception there was, it was unintentional.

As a matter of fact, not much deception was actually involved. Only one of those doctoral opportunities, philosophy, was intended to be an earned degree program. To be sure, all of the courses required for an earned doctorate in philosophy were not in place in 1899. However, a formal commitment to Thomism as the official Catholic philosophy had been made twenty years earlier and providing teachers of it was a high priority for American Catholic higher education.

In 1899 the prospects were very good that the newly acquired Notre Dame House of Studies in Washington, D.C., to be directed by Father James A. Burns would provide enough Holy Cross priests with doctorates in Thomistic philosophy from the Catholic University of America in a few years to launch such a doctoral program at Notre Dame. The other doctoral opportunities—in literature, science, and law—would be, in effect, honorary degrees given to Notre Dame graduates who had distinguished themselves in those fields, much like the unearned doctorate in philosophy that Zahm had received from the Vatican in 1895. Indeed, rewarding distinguished alumni with honorary degrees was commonplace in American higher education at that time and has continued to be so ever after.

Veneziani's attack on Zahm's book was a bit of mean-spirited vindictive work of his own. *Catholic Science and Catholic Scientists* was a popular work, not a scholarly one, and had no bearing whatsoever on Veneziani's case. Because Zahm, as provincial, was in Veneziani's mind an abettor of Morrissey's lies and injustices, the man could not have been possessed by the passion for truth that scholarship demanded. If Zahm had difficulty recognizing truth in the particulars of Veneziani's case, what was the likelihood that he could recognize it in the history of science? Veneziani believed that Zahm could not and had not. According to Veneziani, Zahm's main argument that the Church had generally supported science and scientists was historically fallacious, and the abundance of basic factual errors in the book was inexcusable. Unfairly, Veneziani read Zahm's book as if it was a representative piece of American Catholic scholarship and implied that American Catholics really ought to be able to do better than that.[32]

— iv —

This sort of public relations attack was a new experience for the university. Morrissey and other officials did not know how to cope with it. Because the overall Notre Dame student retention rate was so low in 1900 any public relations situations that would discourage students from coming to the university threatened the future prosperity and perhaps even the existence of the institution. What Veneziani was doing was a very serious matter for Notre Dame.

So far the audience targeted by Veneziani had been strictly clerical, and there may have been some comfort in that. The general public, especially people in areas where Notre Dame recruited students, had not been specifically addressed or reached in any meaningful way and showed little interest in Veneziani or his charges. Though the former professor, in his pamphlets, had actually invited Morrissey and the university to prosecute him if what he had written against them was untrue, undertaking a libel action would only attract more attention to the whole business. The decision of Zahm and Morrissey not to prosecute was a prudent one.

The only public response to Veneziani's charges mounted by the university was an indirect one. Morrissey hired persons better known than Veneziani, a popular priest/writer, John Talbot Smith, and some Chicago journalists, to write short introductory pieces for the general catalogue of the university praising the religious atmosphere and academic excellence of the place. The main hope for repairing the damage done by Archbishop Elder and for defending the university's reputation from further attacks by Veneziani resided in the presumed ability of the apostolic delegate to contain and silence him. Archbishop Martinelli's decision and instruction to the former professor appeared to be a good beginning.

However, Veneziani was a man richly endowed with the virtue of persistence, a passion for overanalysis, and a person not easily intimidated. After receiving and explaining away the Martinelli instruction, Veneziani looked for justice in the civil courts. He filed a defamation action against Morrissey in the St. Joseph County Circuit Court. Apparently, the judge there ruled against assuming jurisdiction, whereupon Veneziani appealed that decision into the Indiana Supreme Court on May 8, 1903.[33] No satisfactory result was obtainable from that court either.

Disappointed but not discouraged, Veneziani found cause for hope in the fact Archbishop Martinelli was replaced as apostolic delegate by Archbishop Diomede Falconio in 1902. Perhaps, the new delegate would be more diligent and correct the mistakes that his predecessor had made when reviewing Veneziani's case. Amazingly, Providence seemed to have provided an opportunity for Veneziani to pursue the new apostolic delegate in person. Archbishop Falconio had scheduled a visit to attend a function at Notre Dame at the end of October 1904. Veneziani determined to attend that function, meet the apostolic delegate, and engage the archbishop in a conversation about his cause.

When Veneziani met Archbishop Falconio at a reception in the Main College Building, he was surprised to discover that the delegate was familiar with the details of his case.[34] After Falconio learned who Veneziani was, he immediately asked the former professor in Italian, what possible harm could have been done to him by the Morrissey document which had been read only by a few people pledged to secrecy?[35] Veneziani explained in Italian that any professor seeking a post at another university was bound to provide references from his last employment. If Morrissey responded to a reference inquiry as he had to Archbishop Elder or if he did not respond at all, Veneziani's prospects for finding employment elsewhere were hopeless.[36]

According to Veneziani, the delegate listened intently, repeated the substance of what he had said, and concluded their conversation by admitting that "You are right, those charges are really harmful to you."[37] At this meeting or sometime thereafter, Falconio advised Veneziani that if there were wrongs in the Morrissey document that needed to be righted, he should address Father Gilbert Français, superior general of the Congregation of Holy Cross.[38]

However, because Morrissey had been turned out of the presidency of Notre Dame by Zahm in 1905, Veneziani saw some possible advantage in meeting with the new president, John W. Cavanaugh, before addressing the superior general. Veneziani met with Cavanaugh in the fall of 1905. The men were polite to one another, and in general their meeting went well. The former professor asked the president to read the Morrissey document, and then, according to conscience, do what he believed was appropriate. The president and the former professor read the Morrissey document together without comment. Cavanaugh asked Veneziani if any money was due him, and he said that there was.[39]

After thinking about what he had read in the document and also about the delicate state of community politics at that time, Cavanaugh looked for a way out and found one. After several minutes of reflection, Cavanaugh told Veneziani that the duties of the office of president of Notre Dame were so onerous that "he could not undertake to look after any obligation that he had not personally contracted."[40] The meeting ended. Veneziani had received sympathy from Cavanaugh but no promise of action. At this point, given the turmoil in congregation politics at Notre Dame, it was clear that Archbishop Falconio's advice had been correct. The proper man to see about this business was the superior general.

Scheduling a meeting with Father Français was not easily done. As a matter of fact, it took almost three years. Only by stating that Archbishop Falconio had recommended such a meeting was Veneziani able to arrange it. By the time the former professor was able to meet with the superior general, in September 1908, the internal political situation at the university had changed greatly. Morrissey had replaced Zahm as provincial and the latter had chosen to exile himself from Notre Dame. With a more subdued Morrissey installed as provincial and reporting directly to the superior general but largely removed from university affairs, Français was ready to put an end to the Veneziani business.

Unscathed by previous encounters with the former professor, the superior general had no impudent remarks or insults to forgive. However, Français was seriously constrained by a powerful fraternal obligation to protect Morrissey from the consequences of what he had written about Veneziani to Archbishop Elder. Français dropped Morrissey's principle of defending the university against extortion and was ready to pay whatever the professor said was owed, but that was all. There would be no admission of wrong or satisfaction of any sort given to Veneziani that Morrissey would be reprimanded. The superior general could not allow that to happen to his new provincial. In this instance, ranks did not have to be closed because they really had never been open.

At this meeting, Français was polite to Veneziani, and the former professor put the superior general somewhat at ease by conversing with him in French. Discussion about the monies due Veneziani went well while those about a formal investigation of the charges in the Morrissey document did not. The superior general admitted that more than the unpaid balance ($140) of his contracted salary was due. Veneziani insisted that he wanted only what was justly owed for services performed. He accepted a figure of $298 as appropriate for the services he had performed. However, since these funds had been withheld for almost ten years, Veneziani expected that at least 4 percent interest ought to be paid. Français agreed, and the final sum accepted by both parties was $417.20.[41]

Alas, reaching agreement on the sum was the easiest part of the negotiation. Disputes about the specific wording of the release that Veneziani would have to sign in order to be paid went on for about two weeks between the former professor and the brother/treasurer with the university lawyer mediating. Finally, Veneziani was allowed to put whatever he wanted into the release to bring the matter to closure. The former professor received his money and signed a release acknowledging that all of his financial claims against the university "valid in justice and conscience" had been satisfied. He passed the signed release to the treasurer and neglected to keep a copy.[42]

As was immediately apparent, settling only the financial aspects of Veneziani's case would not end it. During the negotiations over the financial settlement, Veneziani had pressed the superior general to initiate a formal investigation of the charges in the Morrissey document to determine their truth or falsehood. Français absolutely refused even to consider such an action, justifying his refusal with a freedom of speech argument. Questionable statements in the Morrissey document were only personal opinions, and after all, Morrissey like any other citizen was entitled to hold and express personal opinions in a private letter.[43] In the brief discussion over an investigation of the Morrissey document, Zahm's name was not mentioned by either party, even though the document had passed through his hands on its way to Archbishop Elder.

By the end of 1908 Veneziani had been paid the money owed with interest. However, he had received no satisfaction or even the prospect of satisfaction for damaged personal honor. That issue turned out to be even more important to the professor than had been his unpaid salary. Because Français would not move an inch away from absolute opposition to any investigation of the Morrissey document, Veneziani spent much of the next few years searching for ways to persuade Français to reconsider that position.

First, Veneziani tried a direct approach. He wrote to the superior general on January 14, 1910, and formally demanded an investigation of the charges in the Morrissey document. The former professor supported that demand with a packet of papers containing what he believed were new and unanswerable arguments for such an investigation as well as supporting documents. Français responded at once. He returned all of the papers and documents to Veneziani unopened, saying that "in conscience" he could not help the professor a second time in his fight with Notre Dame. By this time, for the superior general, Morrissey had become a victim of the former professor's insatiable lust for revenge. Moreover, since Français believed the case to be completely settled by the signed release, he stated unequivocally that he would never discuss this subject again with Veneziani, either orally or in writing.[44]

Having been stopped from pressing further for a formal investigation of the charges in the Morrissey document, Veneziani decided to appeal to the highest authority in the Catholic Church. He drafted in elegant Italian a petition to Pius X asking the pope to communicate His Holiness' desire to the apostolic delegate in Washington, D.C., that if the facts of Veneziani's case respecting the Morrissey document as he had stated them were true, the superior general of the Congregation of Holy Cross resident at Notre Dame should undertake a thorough investigation of the contents of the said document.[45]

To give credibility to his petition, Veneziani sent it on July 20, 1910, to Archbishop Falconio in Washington, D.C., a man from whom the former professor incorrectly expected sympathy, for transmittal to the Vatican.[46] Falconio responded on July 24, 1910, returning the petition to the sender, stating that since the apostolic delegation had given its final decision on the professor's case, he could not forward the petition to the Holy Father. The archbishop noted, however, that Veneziani could send his petition directly to His Holiness if he wished. That was precisely what the former professor did, sending the petition off to Rome in late July 1910.

Veneziani waited patiently for six months for a response from Rome, and when nothing came, he wrote to Falconio asking whether or not a communication from the Vatican about his business had arrived at the delegation. Falconio's secretary answered Veneziani immediately. He stated that no correspondence concerning the former professor or his case had been received by the archbishop, adding that Veneziani should cease troubling himself about "those vain imaginings and give all of your thoughts to the execution of the various duties which fall to your share."[47]

Veneziani was pleased by the archbishop's concern for his well-being but did not heed his advice.

After not hearing from Rome and having been closed off by Français and Falconio, most men would have given up, but Veneziani was not like most men. He was so obsessed by a need to have personal honor satisfied through a formal investigation of the Morrissey document that nothing else in life seemed to matter. His professional prospects had been ruined, even his family had been lost to him, but still the man went on. Believing that in the end, somehow persistence would bring the justice he craved, Veneziani bided his time until Providence would provide a new opportunity for proceeding. He did not have much time to bide.

Archbishop John Bonzano replaced Falconio as apostolic delegate in 1911, and Veneziani sent his first packet of materials to the new delegate in June 1912. The former professor went over what was by now very old ground. In his letter to the archbishop, Veneziani argued in detail why he was entitled to a formal investigation of the charges in the Morrissey document. He asked that Bonzano send a copy of the letter containing the arguments for an investigation to the superior general, along with an order to proceed with such an investigation.[48]

Bonzano is perhaps best remembered as the principal investigator of corruption charges filed against Cardinal William O'Connell, archbishop of Boston, by some bishops of that archdiocese and for a famous photograph widely distributed during the American presidential election of 1928 showing Alfred E. Smith kneeling before Bonzano kissing his archiepiscopal ring. Though Bonzano believed the archbishop of Boston was guilty as charged but did not press for action against him,[49] he was not a man of faint heart when dealing with an ordinary layman. He intended to waste no time on a man such as Veneziani. Bonzano answered the former professor's request quickly and succinctly by returning Veneziani's materials, saying that the former professor could send them to superior general if he wished, the apostolic delegate would not.

Regarding the case itself, the archbishop stated that once and for all it had been definitely settled by his predecessor, now Cardinal Martinelli. Moreover, Veneziani had been told repeatedly by his immediate predecessor, now Cardinal Falconio that the case was closed. Bonzano refused to take up the matter again in any way whatsoever. In the future, all correspondence from Veneziani to the delegation concerning his case would be ignored.

At this point, even Veneziani must have realized that all avenues ecclesiastical and civil had been closed. The former professor simply could not find anyone in religious authority willing to receive correspondence from him about his business. The provincial had supported the president. The archbishop with jurisdiction had supported the president and the provincial. One apostolic delegate had supported the archbishop, and two other delegates had supported him. Neither the pope nor anyone in the Vatican had acknowledged receipt or responded to his petition. No one at any level had lifted a finger to determine the truth or falsehood of the charges against Veneziani contained in the Morrissey document. The hope for this layman to prevail in a dispute with high-placed clerics was forlorn indeed. It would appear that, at long last, Veneziani's search for what he believed was justice for an ordinary layman from Catholic religious authorities was over. At least it was over for the time being.

— v —

Sometime during the middle of the decade, Veneziani left South Bend to find non-academic work in Indianapolis. He was not in this largely Protestant city very long before he had an encounter with the local Catholic bishop, Joseph Chartrand, that was a new experience for that prelate. According to Veneziani, the bishop had recommended a pamphlet written by a Catholic priest and published by the Knights of Columbus as a guide to good Catholic reading for the people of his diocese. The heart of the pamphlet was a list of books entitled "Catholic Words by Catholic Authors" that could be found in the Indianapolis public library. Apparently, the author of the list had collected Catholic-sounding titles but had not examined or read very many of the works on it.

Veneziani was a diligent reader and upon examining the list of "Catholic Words by Catholic Authors" discovered that many of the authors on the list that Bishop Chartrand had recommended were not Catholic at all. Many of the books on the list had been written by Unitarians, Baptists, Methodists, and even a few rabidly anti-Catholic authors. In a letter to the bishop Veneziani pointed out the error of recommending this list as guide to good Catholic reading. Whether Bishop Chartrand was displeased by being caught in an embarrassing error or simply annoyed by the fact that Veneziani was the one who had detected it can never be known. Though Chartrand never acknowledged receipt or responded to Veneziani's letter, he certainly acted upon it. All copies of the pamphlet in stock were destroyed, and Catholics in possession of copies distributed by the Knights of Columbus were asked to destroy them as well.[50]

However, keeping Bishop Chartrand up to standard was only a casual interest for Veneziani, his major preoccupation was still getting a formal investigation of the Morrissey document. Why he returned to that subject again in early 1918 is unclear. While there was no hope of changing the mind of Archbishop Bonzano, who was still the serving apostolic delegate, Veneziani persuaded himself that the superior general might be manipulated in such a way so that the apostolic delegate would have to intervene.

Veneziani wrote to Français on January 2, 1918, enclosing affidavits drafted by himself which he wanted signed by the superior general, Zahm, and Morrissey stating that they believed that the charges against the former professor in the Morrissey document were true. Veneziani wanted Français to forward these signed affidavits to the apostolic delegate. If these principals in the Veneziani case would swear on their priestly character that they believed the charges against the man were true, then the former professor promised never to bother them again.[51] However, convinced that none of these priests would sign such an affidavit, Veneziani expected to be able to interpret their refusal to the apostolic delegate as proof positive that Morrissey and Zahm had known that the charges were false when they passed the Morrissey document on to Archbishop Elder in 1900.

Whether that sort of argument would have moved Bonzano from his position of opposition to further discussion of the case is highly unlikely. In any case, Veneziani never had an opportunity to find out. When the former professor's latest letter reached the superior general, he was in the middle of a serious crisis over community governance with a faction of priests at Notre Dame. That faction had appealed one of the superior general's decisions on the composition of local councils to Rome. Français was appalled by that action and was bent upon restoring that faction of priests to proper discipline and punishing their leaders. At that moment, he had time for little else.

Whether Veneziani knew about Français's political problems at Notre Dame at this time and decided to try to exploit them for his own cause is unknown. If he did, the tactic did not work. Another letter about a very old matter believed settled from a man the superior general wanted most to forget could only be counterproductive. Français had no time or energy to waste on this man or on his cause. The superior general would have nothing to do with Veneziani or his affidavits and told the man in a one-paragraph letter that the case was closed and would never be reopened. Veneziani's affidavit scheme had collapsed after the first mailing.[52]

Defeated once again in 1918, amazingly Veneziani refused to abandon his cause. Even though Morrissey had died in 1918 and Zahm passed away in 1921, Veneziani planned for 1924 what was to be his final effort to repair

his personal honor so damaged a quarter century ago. The former professor intended to visit Rome in June 1924 and make a personal appeal to the
pope for justice so long delayed. Essential for this personal appeal to the
pope was a written argument properly documented. Veneziani believed
that he could prepare a persuasive argument, but he lacked an important
document, a copy of the release signed by him at the time of the final
financial settlement. Veneziani had neglected to retain one in 1908 and
subsequent requests to the superior general for a copy had been ignored.[53]

Since Archbishop Bonzano had been replaced by Archbishop Pietro
Fumasoni-Biondi as apostolic delegate in 1922, Veneziani applied to the
new delegate on April 8, 1924, for assistance in getting a copy of the release signed at Notre Dame in 1908 from the superior general.[54] At this
point, Veneziani's presence in the Notre Dame historical record abruptly
ends. Whether Fumasoni-Biondi helped Veneziani obtain a copy of the
release from Français, how the man intended to use it, whether he actually traveled to Rome and proceeded with an appeal, or even how long
he lived are all unknown. It would appear that insofar as the leadership of
the university and of the Congregation of Holy Cross was concerned, in
the spring of 1924 the Veneziani case was closed finally and definitively.

— vi —

The Veneziani case was unusual for at least three reasons. First, the case
was unusual in that a Catholic layman in this country would even bother
to try to obtain remedies for grievances against two prominent, highly
placed priests by applying through several levels of religious authorities.

Second, the case was unusual certainly for the length of time it went on
and for the tenacity with which Veneziani pursued it after a financial settlement had been reached in 1908.

Third, it was unusual in that all of the religious authorities involved
were unanimous in their opposition to dealing with Veneziani even
though the charges against him in the Morrissey document had never
been examined. The possibility that Morrissey may have lied about
Veneziani's performance at Notre Dame and other things in a letter never
intended to be public was either not faced by the various religious authorities solicited or not faced in ways that were sufficient to bring about
a judgment for the layman.

In addition to being unusual, the Veneziani case was important for
Notre Dame and also, though less directly so, for Catholic higher education as a whole. The entire Veneziani affair, protracted as it was and bitter

as it became, was important for the development of Notre Dame because it reinforced the old Sorin admonition about the dangers of hiring lay professors. Sorin had been concerned primarily with the financial burden that the presence of lay faculty would impose on the university and on the religious community. However, the Veneziani affair had shown that there were more dangers than just rising salary budgets by having too many lay faculty around. Lay faculty, particularly highly credentialed ones such as Veneziani, could turn out to be powerfully disruptive forces within the university community. Who knows, some of them, especially those with higher degrees, might even presume to tell the priests how the place ought to be run?

After 1900 a very strong attitude against hiring and retaining lay faculty developed among university leaders and appears to have been shared by much of the religious community. From that point of view, the presence of too many lay faculty could change the character of Notre Dame from what Sorin and the Holy Cross Congregation had started into something different and unrecognizable. Certainly, recent events had shown that one Veneziani was too much for the president and prefect of studies to handle. One dreaded to speculate what might happen to Notre Dame if two or three or four Venezianis were hired. Far better to send Holy Cross priests off to Father Burns' House of Studies at the Catholic University of America to receive graduate training in needed academic specialties than to take on the added costs and ancillary dangers of filling up the faculty with lay professors. This traditional attitude against hiring lay professors was intensified in 1900 by the Veneziani experience and hardened into a university policy that remained operative and unchallenged until after 1920.

Between 1900 and 1915, student enrollment at Notre Dame rose by a half whereas overall faculty size increased only a quarter. However, during those same years the percentage of laymen on the faculty decreased from 40 percent in 1900 to 35 percent in 1915. That trend continued through the very difficult war years. By 1920, with student enrollment exceeding 1,200 and the number of overall faculty reaching 165, only 60 or 36 percent of that number were laymen.

So it happened that during the first twenty years of this century, Holy Cross priest-professors dominated instructional activity at the university. The best credentialed teachers were usually Holy Cross priests. Students generally perceived them as being the best the university had to offer. Holy Cross priests were the men who taught those few highly regarded classes that bright students wanted to take before graduating. Altogether, the period 1900–1920 was perhaps the golden age of Holy Cross priest-professors. Ironically, it was the indefatigable enemy of Notre Dame, Charles Veneziani, who in an entirely accidental way helped make that time a golden one for them.

The Veneziani affair was important for the development of Notre Dame in another respect as well. Morrissey had roughly handled Veneziani while at Notre Dame. As president of the university, Morrissey had probably lied about the former professor in a private communication to Archbishop Elder. That Morrissey had a capacity for ruthless action when aroused surprised no one at the university. Many, especially Zahm, could testify to it. Unfortunately for everyone involved in this matter, Veneziani quickly displayed an extraordinary talent for arousing Morrissey. When confronted by the professor's demands and refusal to take no for an answer, Morrissey simply could not stop being himself. The result was ruinous for Veneziani and painfully embarrassing for everyone else. Having said all of that, Morrissey's treatment of Veneziani was inexcusable, especially so because he was a priest.

Morrissey's culpability as the creator of this embarrassing, interminable situation for the university was only one side of the Veneziani affair. From the perspective of most members of the university community, both clerical and lay, by publishing and circulating pamphlets attacking Notre Dame, Veneziani had gone far beyond what redress of grievances required. They do not even seem to have recognized that by circulating his pamphlets Veneziani, in effect, was trying to do to Notre Dame what Morrissey had done to him, destroy a professional reputation.

In the opinion of persons of this mindset by attacking Our Blessed Lady's university as he did, Veneziani had committed a form of public sacrilege that was unforgivable. Beyond that, by attempting to damage the reputation of Notre Dame he threatened the prosperity and perhaps even the very existence of the place. By the grace of God, they thought, those threats to the viability of the institution never materialized. However, the memory of the sacrilege remained.

While the former professor could not be forgiven for what he had tried to do to the reputation of the university, he could be forgotten and was. With the passing of time, the memory of Veneziani's great public sacrilege became completely disconnected from him. Henceforth, severe public criticism of Notre Dame, especially by lay faculty members, in print or in speeches, was generally regarded by successive generations of university officials—and by most of the faculty—as an act of disloyalty, never to be forgotten and seldom forgiven.

Finally, the Veneziani case, in a less direct way, was important for Catholic higher education because of the issues raised by it. In his pamphlets as in his life, Veneziani sharply underscored the issue of the place of lay men and women in Catholic universities and colleges and the roles they could or should play. That issue was present everywhere in Catholic higher education, and sooner or later, every Catholic university and college would have to confront and resolve it. From a historical perspective, however, the most important issue for Catholic higher education raised in Veneziani's pamphlets was the everlasting one of why, given their numbers and wealth, American Catholics were so underrepresented as participants in their country's scientific, intellectual, and cultural life.

Veneziani asked that question and found answers for it in his own experience. He attributed the conspicuous absence of American Catholics from scientific and intellectual activities to the condition of their universities and colleges. When compared with the great endowed private universities of the land—Harvard, Yale, Princeton, Johns Hopkins, Chicago, Northwestern, and Brown—Veneziani argued, American Catholic universities and colleges were of a very low standard.[55]

The reasons for that low standard were clear enough. According to Veneziani, among those reasons were a lack of financial endowment, an inability to pay salaries high enough to attract trained and credentialed lay professors, and most important of all the fact that most Catholic universities and colleges were controlled by religious orders. Control of American Catholic higher education by religious orders, Veneziani insisted, was a problem because those religious orders were accountable only to themselves for what they did or did not do.[56] Being accountable only to themselves and paying lay faculty as little as possible, Veneziani asserted, these religious orders "enrich themselves and are grievously sinning against the natural law of justice and charity so strongly upheld by Pope Leo XIII in his encyclical on the labor question."[57] According to Veneziani, what American Catholics needed were endowed Catholic universities and colleges not controlled by religious orders, staffed by competent lay professors, and equipped with functioning boards of trustees with bishops as chairmen.[58]

However, none of these happy prospects would ever be fulfilled, Veneziani regretted, until American Catholics realized the importance of higher education and financially supported their universities and colleges as generously as Protestants and nonreligious Americans supported theirs.[59] If American Catholics wanted their children to be taught by thoroughly trained and cultivated teachers in Catholic universities and colleges, they would have to provide those institutions with the financial means necessary to do so. Only then would American Catholics contribute scientific, intellectual, and cultural leaders to their country commensurate with their numbers in the general population.[60]

Veneziani's treatment of the question of American Catholic scientific and intellectual underperformance was brief, insightful, but largely ignored. What he had to say on that question was buried in the pages of two pamphlets written in attack against Notre Dame and would have been missed by persons reading them for what their very long titles promised. While Veneziani's linking of quality higher education with endowment size was prescient, his strictures about the management of American Catholic higher education by religious orders were highly experiential and exaggerated. However, his comments on the accountability of religious orders to themselves alone were hardly controversial.

In the case of the Congregation of Holy Cross, Archbishop Elder had implicitly confirmed their virtual independence from him, and the apostolic delegate, Archbishop Falconio, did so explicitly. If asked about the accountability of religious orders operating in their dioceses, many other American prelates would have agreed with Veneziani. Similarly, his observations about the apparent disinterest of American Catholics in higher education were common complaints of Catholic university and college presidents and some prelates in the years before World War I and were repeated many times by Catholic journalists over the next half-century.

While Veneziani, if remembered at all, will not be recalled as the first, second, or third man who asked why American Catholics had produced so few scientific and intellectual leaders, the man's observations on that subject are more than just historically interesting. Though Veneziani appears to have had no influence on American Catholic thinking about the quality of their expanding system of higher education, he certainly made those in charge of Notre Dame think about it. Finding ways to improve the quality of the education delivered at Notre Dame and paying for it had been one of several points of contention between Morrissey and Zahm. Similarly, improving the quality of education, with himself personifying quality, was one of many points of contention between Veneziani and Morrissey. Right in the center of the quality of education issue at Notre Dame stood the smiling, portly, determined figure of Andrew J. Morrissey.

While Morrissey was not opposed to improving the quality of education at the university, he was content with Notre Dame the way it was. He wanted the university to do the best possible instructional job it could with the resources at hand. It must be said, however, that Morrissey tended to view Notre Dame as a family business, the principal and most successful business of the Congregation of Holy Cross. Insuring financial survival of that family business was for Morrissey a constant preoccupation, because he knew what debt had done to Holy Cross works in France and elsewhere. He would say or do almost anything to protect the reputation and financial viability of Notre Dame. That was why he opposed Zahm's spending schemes for facilities expansion and for acquisition of the property in Washington, D.C., for a House of Studies at the Catholic University of America. That was why he argued heatedly with Veneziani about paying a $4.00 a month partial house rent subsidy and why he probably lied to Archbishop Elder about Veneziani. More to the point, Morrissey doubted whether Notre Dame would ever be able to compete in any way with the renown of well-endowed private universities of the country and was unimpressed by arguments contending that they should try.

Zahm had wanted to try. He assumed that the unsalaried instructional services provided by Holy Cross priests would compensate to some extent for the university's lack of endowment. Zahm also believed strongly that Holy Cross priests trained in graduate programs offered at the Catholic University of America would be able to provide the scientific and intellectual resources needed to expand offerings and raise the quality of education at Notre Dame. For his part, Veneziani had seen the quality of education issue simply as a matter of hiring well-credentialed Catholic laymen, like himself, and paying them decent salaries. They would bring to Catholic higher education levels of knowledge and cultural awareness presently wanting.

Over the next few years, experience would prove the schemes of both Zahm and Veneziani to be impractical. The Congregation of Holy Cross was a small society. Until the turn of the century, the entire American Province numbered less than fifty priests.[61] The supply of priests in the congregation willing and able to obtain higher degrees could not meet the demand for them. Moreover, many of those priests who returned to the university after earning a doctorate would soon find themselves out of the classroom and in an administrative post. Veneziani's scheme fared no better. The supply of Catholic laymen with higher degrees was too small and uncertain to meet the needs of those few Catholic institutions willing to pay for them. For this reason, when Catholic lay persons had to be hired, those engaged tended to be men well recommended as good teachers but without higher degrees.

Even more important than the general problems of finding qualified teachers from among priests of the congregation or from among credentialed Catholic laymen were the special difficulties of filling particular academic or professional specialties from those two sources of teaching personnel. As time passed and as the university expanded its offerings and activities, more and more of these specialties would be needed. If

Holy Cross priests or qualified Catholic laymen could not be found to staff them, then the best men available regardless of religious affiliation would have to be sought out.

Whether or not hiring academics or professionals from other religious traditions or, for that matter, from no religious tradition at all would change significantly the Catholic character of Notre Dame was something that Holy Cross priests and the small number of long-serving lay faculty could argue about among themselves. However, the realities of institutional growth, trying to improve quality, and expanding offerings put Notre Dame on an evolutionary track from which it could not escape. Sorin's Catholic school would become in almost every way a modern American university without ceasing to have a strong Catholic orientation.

The modernization of Notre Dame was a very long process that consisted largely of a series of institutional responses to changing practical circumstances and to unanticipated opportunities. The next generation of university leaders continued to pay attention to the religious practices and moral values of the university community. Yet, after 1905 they recognized and accepted the fact that their principal function was to raise the enormous sums of money required to pay for modernization.

Over the next seventy-five years, Notre Dame presidents would have to learn how to develop relationships with wealthy individuals, solicit the great foundations, persuade large corporations to contribute to fund drives, and deal with national and local government officials and agencies. Above all else, the priests in charge of Notre Dame would have to understand and be sensitive to the importance of positive public relations. The university had a reputation to protect. That was its greatest asset. Advice on how best to do that in a given set of circumstances should be sought from friends who were professionals and from employees who were experienced and had mastered the arts of this sometimes arcane business. After receiving such professional advice, the president was on his own and would have to say or do what he thought was in the best interests of Notre Dame.

None of this would be easy, always pleasant, accomplished with complete truthfulness, or entirely successful, but it had to be done if the university was to grow and prosper in the world as it was. The Holy Cross priest who as president of Notre Dame would be in charge of coming to terms with the modern world for the next fourteen years was the temperamental but unforgettable John William Cavanaugh, C.S.C.

— 3 —

MAKING A PLACE
IN THE WORLD AS IT IS

F ather John William Cavanaugh's fourteen-year presidency (1905–1919) was critical in the development of the university from a school-centered institution into a college-centered one. His views about the mission of the university and about the nature and form of the Catholic education to be offered at Notre Dame were more developed and advanced than had been those of his predecessor. Cavanaugh believed that the future of the university would be shaped by the colleges and that the colleges would attract and hold students if their curricula provided courses of study that were modern, scientific, and practical as well as traditional and literary.

The priest who directed the affairs of the university during one of the most critical stages of its development had been born in Leetonia, Ohio, in 1870. Both of Cavanaugh's parents had immigrated from Ireland. They met and married in America, settled in Ohio, and prospered as farmers. Young John was educated in Leetonia parochial schools, decided early to become a priest, and came to Notre Dame and the Congregation of Holy Cross in 1886, at the age of sixteen. Cavanaugh was ordained in 1893 and spent the next five years at Notre Dame assisting Father Daniel E. Hudson, C.S.C., editor of the *Ave Maria* magazine. Hudson was a conservative in Holy Cross affairs and a strong supporter of Morrissey. However, in 1898, Father Zahm, newly appointed provincial, selected Cavanaugh to be superior of the Holy Cross Seminary and then in 1905 elevated him to succeed Morrissey as president of the university. Cavanaugh's rise had been rapid and facilitated by the fact that he had remained on good terms with both the Morrissey and Zahm factions at Notre Dame. Neither side opposed his advance, and the superior general was fond of him.

The young priest who had fared so well during a period of extremely turbulent Holy Cross politics was a tall, well-proportioned man blessed with a gracious smile and a marvelous speaking and preaching voice. Upon first meeting John Cavanaugh, almost everyone liked him. To most people, Cavanaugh was an interesting person. He always had something to say and usually said it well. As president of the university, Cavanaugh frequently encountered celebrities in all sorts of settings and thoroughly enjoyed being in their company. However, he was rarely ever intimidated by the rich and powerful and was never fearful of speaking his mind in front of them.

By nature, Cavanaugh was a man of pleasant and cheerful disposition. To close friends and people he admired, Cavanaugh's loyalty was absolute. He wanted to like and trust most people and generally did so until crossed or deceived. When that happened, it was best to avoid him. Extreme temper could and did drive him to say things regretted later, to make unreasonable demands, or to issue impossible orders. Happily those moments were infrequent but unforgettable for those unfortunate enough to have experienced them.[1] In a word, Cavanaugh was a passionate man. He was passionate about Church and country, about his beloved Notre Dame, and extremely so about the impoverished and troubled birthplace of his parents. Cavanaugh loved God and Notre Dame, lived and breathed American patriotism, and accepted totally the ideals and values of Irish nationalism.

The special place of Irish nationalism in the emotional life of the university during the years of the Cavanaugh presidency cannot be overestimated. Administrators, faculty, students, and alumni were all deeply touched by it, and none more so than the local leadership of the Congregation of Holy Cross and the decision makers of the university. Morrissey, the old Kilkenny Chieftain, who was provincial during these years, was Ireland-born. Cavanaugh as president of the university and Burns as superior of the Holy Cross House of Studies in Washington were both of Irish descent. All three were extremely self-conscious Irish Americans, strongly committed to the cause of Irish nationalism, and intensely anti-English.

Cavanaugh's tenure as president coincided with the revival of the Home Rule movement and the growth of revolutionary nationalism in Ireland. Because Cavanaugh was so outspoken for the Irish cause so often, the university was popularly and accurately identified as stridently Irish nationalist and anti-English. Cavanaugh had acquired his nationalism naturally in his father's house—his father, Patrick, had been born in Tyrone and his mother was from Armagh. As Cavanaugh himself would say many times, as a boy he had learned Robert Emmet's speeches by heart and then would deliver them to rows of cabbages on the family farm in Leetonia, Ohio. When the Great War began in 1914 and Home Rule was suspended for the duration, Cavanaugh and other like-thinking Notre Dame faculty and students were outraged. Publicly and privately during 1914 and 1915, Cavanaugh hailed every disaster to British arms with acclaim.[2] After the Easter Rising in Dublin in 1916, Cavanaugh's anti-English rhetoric simply went out of control. As a featured speaker at the Friendly Sons of St. Patrick Convention in New York on March 17, 1918, Cavanaugh addressed an audience that included the vice president of the United States, Cabinet members, three U.S. senators, and a sprinkling of congressmen, generals, and admirals. It was a speech which those present and hearing it would never forget.

Cavanaugh began with a direct assertion that he, John William Cavanaugh, hated England because of her treatment of Ireland.[3] It was a fact, sad but true, that England had made Ireland a ravaged Belgium for the last seven hundred years. Elsewhere in this speech, Cavanaugh raised the question whether he or any other man had to love England in order to be a good American? According to Cavanaugh, Senator New of Indiana was visibly angered by this question, but Secretary of the Navy Josephus Daniels congratulated him for asking it.[4] As he summarized the message of his speech that evening for a friend later, it was "briefly and piously, to hell with England."[5]

The intensity of Cavanaugh's commitment to Irish nationalism and the frequency of his public statements in support of it contrasted sharply with what he said and wrote about education. Apart from occasional denunciations of John Dewey and his followers, which was usual among Catholic educators of that time, Cavanaugh said and wrote very little about the place and role of education in America that was striking or worth remembering. He identified with no existing school of educational philosophy and expounded no particular theory of learning. His favorite and much-used educational dictum that students learned as much or more from social intercourse with each other than from teachers and books was about as profound as he ever got on the matter of education in America.

About the nature and purposes of Catholic education and the necessity for it, Cavanaugh could be and often was eloquent. However, even on this subject the substance of Cavanaugh's message was conventional and commonplace in Catholic circles. The president of the university of Notre Dame offered no new rationales for why American Catholics should avoid public schools and tax-supported colleges and universities. He said what others had said but always said it so well.

Cavanaugh and others in leadership positions at Notre Dame agreed with the bishops that Catholic education was absolutely necessary for the survival and growth of the faith in America and that Catholic institutions would have to find the resources to deliver it. Cavanaugh along with other Catholic educators believed that a Catholic education had to be different and was special. It was a whole much greater than the sum of its parts. Catholic education was much more than an aggregation of buildings, books, and teachers. An authentic Catholic education should provide the best kind of instruction in the arts and sciences while insuring that moral training and virtuous example would produce students who were superior in the way they conducted their lives.

First of all, in practice a Catholic education at Notre Dame was protective. Faculty and students were protected from the dangerous antitheistic doctrines of the late nineteenth century by the Index Librorum Prohibitorum and by the several canons regulating access to proscribed literature. Skepticism, materialism, irreligion, and all doctrines believed to be false and condemned as such by Roman authorities had no place in Notre Dame courses of study. Simply stated, in the form of Catholic education delivered at Notre Dame error had no rights to be heard, argued, or propagated. Because truth alone should imbue minds of young people during their student years, it was the duty of all who were teachers to banish error from the thinking of their students and close all openings to false convictions. In a Catholic university such as Notre Dame, teachers had no right to teach whatever they pleased. University leaders agreed completely with the official Catholic position sanctioned by the American hierarchy that freedom to teach must have limitations; otherwise the office of teacher could be with impunity turned into an instrument of corruption. Academic freedom was not a concept highly valued at Notre Dame or at other American Catholic educational institutions during the first half of the twentieth century.[6]

Second, the Catholic education taught and studied at Notre Dame was supposed to be infused by Christian doctrine. That infusion could not be left to mechanisms of structured courses alone. Ideally, Christian doctrine would be presented to students by persons who professed the Catholic faith and practiced it in their own lives.

Third and most important, an authentic Catholic education should also be a moralizing experience. Indeed, residential hall staff at Notre Dame were expected to watch over the morals of their youthful charges, and the young men studying there should turn out to be better persons for having been watched.

Indeed, Notre Dame students were watched on campus and whenever they ventured into the city. Among residence hall rectors, conventional wisdom held that male teenagers removed from parental influences, as most of them were at Notre Dame, courted "a dangerous liberty" and could not recognize the presence of temptations until after serious moral damage had been done.[7] With the objective of safeguarding morals in mind, the prefect of discipline and his assistants strove to provide Notre Dame students with forms of recreation, mainly athletic, that would engage their interest in on-campus activities and events and keep them out of the city of South Bend.

From the perspective of the authorities at Notre Dame, South Bend was no better or worse than other cities of a similar size. However, it was in cities where resided the most serious threats to Catholic morality. According to priests with residential hall experience, the greatest danger for Catholic boys and young men in any city were its public dance halls. South Bend had its share, of which The Tokio was the most notorious. In the judgment of the prefect of discipline and of virtually all of the priests on campus, the young women frequenting such places were little more than tarts. Notre Dame students of all ages and classes were strictly forbidden to go to The Tokio or to other dance halls. Students were even forbidden to take jobs there as musicians. The dance halls were believed to be lascivious places and in campus chapels and confessionals were preached against and counseled against regularly. Students were admonished to avoid frequenting places where they would be ashamed to bring their sisters.[8]

Casual pick ups leading to sexual encounters were of course the principal danger to be guarded against. No less threatening and perhaps even more embarrassing to the institution was the possibility that older students might be seduced or trapped into undesirable marriages below their stations by designing local girls. The prospect of presenting an unknown and most likely unwanted daughter-in-law to distant parents who had placed their sons in the presumed morally secure environment of Notre Dame was not a pleasant one. The public dance halls were off limits, and students seen entering or leaving them were subject to immediate dismissal.

— ii —

When Cavanaugh was appointed president in 1905, the student body of the university was evenly divided between collegians and students in the preparatory, elementary, and manual labor departments. By 1912 overall student enrollment passed 1,500, with about a thousand students being registered in collegiate programs and 500 pupils attending classes in the preparatory school. Students in the college were taught by a faculty of sixty-six while the staff of the preparatory department numbered twenty-seven. About a hundred elementary pupils, known as Minims, were taught by the Sisters of the Holy Cross.

Of the college faculty in 1912, half were priests or brothers and half were laymen. Out of the sixteen faculty members listed in the general catalogue as holding doctorates, fourteen were priests and two were laymen. Of the sixteen holders of doctorates, seven were in science departments and nine taught humanities or social science subjects. Science courses were shared between priests and laymen. Engineering courses were taught exclusively by laymen. Humanities and social science subjects were taught mostly by priests with laymen largely handling skill-development courses such as foreign-language instruction, journalism, instrumental and vocal music instruction, speech, and drawing.

With regard to university governance at this time, every decision-making position and most of the lesser administrative posts at the university were held by Holy Cross priests. Any other arrangement was unthinkable. Notre Dame was very much and in every way a Holy Cross institution. At that time it was a fact that the men with the best reputations for intellectual rigor and good teaching as well as the person of most renown at Notre Dame for scientific research were all Holy Cross priests.

Father Julius A. Nieuwland, C.S.C., botanist and chemist, graduated from Notre Dame in 1899, was ordained in 1903, received his doctorate in chemistry from the Catholic University of America in 1904, and returned to Notre Dame as a faculty member in that same year. As a graduate student Nieuwland developed a lifelong interest in acetylene chemistry. From that interest came the discovery of reactions and processes leading to the development of a form of synthetic rubber. At the same time, while in graduate school, he made and published his findings on reactions that others would use at the end of World War I to develop the deadly arsenic-based poison gas known as the "dew of death," Lewisite.

Despite this extraordinary promise as a research chemist, when Nieuwland returned to Notre Dame, university needs required that he teach classes in botany. Accepting such an assignment with good humor, Nieuwland immediately proceeded to learn as much as he could about local flora and fauna. So extensive were his notes and studies of the northern Indiana environment that Nieuwland established and became the editor of a bimonthly botanical magazine, the *American Midland Naturalist*. Nieuwland remained a working and publishing botanist until 1918, when he was allowed to return to his first love, chemistry. But not for long. Once again university needs took him out of full-time research and teaching. He served as dean of the College of Science, 1920–23.

Relieved at last from administrative duties and regular undergraduate teaching, Nieuwland returned to his laboratory where he could be found every day and most of the evening hours working with highly toxic chemicals. He regularly published the results of his work and quickly won recognition as a leading authority in acetylene chemistry and pioneer developer of synthetic rubber. With that recognition came medals and awards, from the International Acetylene Association in 1932, from the American Chemical Society in 1934 for his work studying dangerous chemicals, and from other scientific associations in 1935 and 1936. After a lifetime exposure to highly toxic chemicals and as befitted a man so totally dedicated to scientific research, he died suddenly at the age of fifty-eight in 1936 while visiting a chemistry laboratory at the Catholic University of America.

Though Nieuwland cannot be remembered as a great teacher of undergraduates (few ever took his courses), he was an inspired chemist and, during the decade before his death, mentor to a generation of graduate students. During his lifetime, Father Nieuwland was the university's premier man of science and most published and respected scholar.

While Nieuwland's work as a botanist or as a chemist had little impact on many undergraduates or on prewar undergraduate education generally, there were, at that time, other Holy Cross priests and a few lay professors who did. However, they did so largely by the force of personality and character rather than by the subject matter presented in their courses. Course options were limited and, by later standards, not particularly interesting. Great teachers were remembered, great courses were not.

To be sure, course catalogues are notoriously deceptive, but they do tell us something about the range and depth of subject matter to which Notre Dame collegians were exposed. Required philosophy courses were largely perfunctory and taught out of Scholastic philosophy study manuals. Required religion courses were nonexistent. Such courses did not become part of the curriculum until 1920–21. Literature courses were limited in number and breadth of subject matter. Rhetoric, both written and spoken, was an important offering. Literary history and criticism courses were few, and by later Notre Dame standards unattractive. The general catalogue listed one course entitled Poetry and the Poets: Texts, Theory, and Critical Study. There were two offerings in fiction. A course in the novel and a course in the short story were described in the general catalogue as being courses where those respective genres were "technically, historically, and critically considered." Students interested in drama had

four options. A historical survey of ancient dramatists with some attention to medieval liturgical, morality, and miracle plays was one possibility.
The Elizabethan dramatists and Shakespeare each had a course. Modern
drama from Sheridan to the present was offered three hours a week for six
weeks. There were no offerings in American literature as such in the general catalogue.

Courses available in history were what one would expect. There was
one offering in ancient history, a two-course survey of medieval and
modern European history from the Christian era to the present. The history of the British Isles from the Roman invasions to the present was
covered in one semester. All of American history was taught in a one-
semester course. American Church history was given equal treatment in a
one-semester course. Other history offerings clearly reflected the ethnic
backgrounds and ethnic-oriented political and international interests of
the faculty and student body. Irish history and modern Irish literature
had a one-semester course apiece. Poland was not forgotten. As a matter
of fact, the general catalogue listed three courses in Polish history and one
in Polish emigration. The foreign language department listed comple-
menting courses in the Gaelic language and in Polish language and
literature.

During Cavanaugh's long tenure as president, some old things were
abandoned at the university while many new ones were begun. Among
those things abandoned was the Manual Labor School. By 1912 this program had become increasingly anachronistic at Notre Dame. The brothers were no longer able to staff it, and student enrollment had declined to
a mere handful. Perhaps even more important in accounting for the
demise of the Manual Labor School than diminished enrollment was
the fact that the locus of the program known at that time as St. Joseph's
Hall was coveted for other uses. More dormitory space was needed to
house the increasing numbers of collegians coming to the university and
a renovated St. Joseph's Hall could provide it.

In any case, the Manual Labor School was closed in 1916 and renovation of its former home began in the next year. Several extremely important educational consequences followed from the decision to invest
$25,000 in a major reconstruction of St. Joseph's Hall. Two new wings
were added to the existing structure, a cafeteria-restaurant was laid out
for the ground floor, and three enterprising recent immigrants from
Greece were given a three-year contract to establish and run this new
food-service facility. This new dormitory was renamed Badin Hall.

Traditionally, food services at Notre Dame had been provided from
college kitchens staffed by Holy Cross sisters. Over the years, complaints

about the variety and quality of food offered to students had been regular occurrences. Establishment of the new cafeteria on campus would give students choices about what, how much, where, and when they could eat. This was a first step in a lengthy process whereby campus food services were taken out of the hands of Holy Cross sisters and turned over to professional caterers. It was also a key element in Cavanaugh's scheme to pay for the reconstruction of St. Joseph's into Badin Hall.

Cavanaugh began the reconstruction of what became Badin Hall with only $10,000 in ready money received in gifts from two donors. The remaining $15,000 of project costs would have to be borrowed from the Congregation of Holy Cross. Cavanaugh had no misgivings about asking Morrissey for such a sum because dormitory fees from the new facility and income from the cafeteria contract would enable that borrowing to be repaid in less than two years.[9] Cavanaugh was very proud of this scheme. It was, in his view, a very low-cost and much-needed redevelopment of a hitherto underutilized university resource that was long overdue. Having done it once, the president was quickly persuaded by his director of studies to try to do it again.

Father Matthew A. Schumacher, C.S.C., Cavanaugh's energetic and creative director of studies, for several years had been urging the president to consider opening a summer school at Notre Dame. Schumacher had received a doctorate in Thomistic philosophy from the Catholic University of America in 1904 and had served as director of studies since 1907. He had been very active in the recently established Catholic Educational Association and was a leader in the accreditation movement presently affecting and causing some problems for Catholic schools and colleges. Schumacher knew that most of the priests, brothers, sisters, and lay persons teaching in Catholic schools had educational needs made more urgent by state certification requirements and the progress of the accreditation movement. He had persuaded himself and tried to persuade Cavanaugh that a Notre Dame summer school could be a place where those educational needs and professional requirements could be satisfied.

Cavanaugh liked Schumacher personally and trusted his judgment in most matters absolutely. Of all of the university administrators reporting to Cavanaugh, Schumacher was the one whose authority was usually upheld and whose recommendations were most often approved.[10] Despite all of Schumacher's urging, Cavanaugh had steadfastly refused to approve the establishment of a summer school at Notre Dame out of concern for the Holy Cross sisters who worked in the college kitchens. The president would not even consider burdening those sisters with food preparation work during the hot Indiana summers.[11]

However, the opening of the new cafeteria staffed entirely by lay people in the fall of 1917 made possible a summer school in 1918. Once the problem of the sisters working in the kitchens during the hot months of July and August had been resolved, the project could proceed even though a successful summer program would require some of the regular priest faculty to give up part of their summer vacations in order to teach in it. For Cavanaugh, persuading Holy Cross priests to teach in a summer program was much less formidable than asking the sisters to prepare meals for a hundred or more students during July and August.

In a memorandum to Morrissey justifying the summer school, Cavanaugh argued that a summer program organized and run in a Catholic environment and focused on the specific educational and state certification needs of Catholic schools was something that Notre Dame ought to do for Catholic education in America. Such a program would be a service, a good work, that the university owed to American Catholic education.

At the same time, Cavanaugh argued, opening a summer school would meet at least three very important immediate university needs without incurring undue financial risk or creating foreseeable difficulties. The first of these university needs was obvious. Under present circumstances, the enormous Notre Dame plant was idle and produced no revenue for one quarter of the year. A summer school would virtually end such inefficiency and provide some income during the hitherto financially barren summer months. Second, payment of a living wage to lay faculty to date had been difficult because of the enforced idleness of the long summer vacation. Cavanaugh was certain that lay faculty would gladly take up the new employment opportunities provided by a summer school in order to "piece out their salaries." Higher annual salaries would enable the university to attract and retain good men. Third, the teaching priests, brothers, sisters, and lay persons coming to the Notre Dame summer school in the future most likely would be inclined to recommend the university to their college-bound male students as a place to pursue their higher education.

Of possible difficulties or disadvantages to the Notre Dame community, Cavanaugh foresaw none. Historically for the Notre Dame community, the university had been a quiet and private place during July and August. Cavanaugh simply refused to believe that this privacy would be seriously disturbed by the advent of summer school students. After all, certain portions of the campus could be designated as areas set aside for the use and recreation of the sisters attending summer programs.[12] The newly renovated residential wings of Badin Hall could be reserved for the sisters. Once the urinals in the lavatories had been discreetly covered with white sheets, the accommodations in Badin Hall would be at once proper and comfortable for religious women. With food service available and close-by, all details seemed accounted for. There was no reason for not proceeding with a summer school project forthwith. Morrissey agreed.

Summer school instructors were selected from those regular Notre Dame faculty prepared to offer courses believed to be attractive to sisters and other Catholic school teachers. Lay teachers were paid a modest stipend for their services; Holy Cross priests were not. Nonetheless, most of the instructors in this first Notre Dame summer session were Holy Cross priests. Summer school student recruitment began in earnest at the end of March 1918. Printed cards were sent to all of the American bishops advising them of the establishment of a summer session at Notre Dame, listing the courses offered, and mentioning the availability of Badin Hall as a special residence facility for sisters. Similar cards were sent to all mothers superior in the United States, and notices were sent to local superiors of religious women and men in Indiana, Ohio, Michigan, Illinois, and Kentucky. In addition, advertisements were placed in Catholic periodicals and magazines.

Summer school recruitment succeeded grandly. Registration exceeded two hundred, twice the most optimistic projections. Students seemed generally pleased with the course offerings. They were delighted with campus accommodations and recreational opportunities. Being away from their religious communities, most of the sisters enjoyed the inevitable relaxation of discipline and the absence of menial housekeeping assignments. Despite the reading and writing demands of the courses, a vacationlike atmosphere prevailed among the sisters. There were not a few tears and many hand squeezings when the session ended. Most important of all, virtually all of the university departments participating in the summer school earned a profit. It was clear after the books were closed on the first summer session at Notre Dame that a summer school would be a continuing part of university operations for the foreseeable future.

Cavanaugh was personally delighted with the results. He wrote to a friend, "Every body is well pleased, and in a few years I expect Notre Dame to be one of the three or four most popular Summer Schools in America." Indeed, even to casual visitors the campus was remarkably picturesque "dotted with sisters of the various orders" dressed in distinctive religious habits. Most significant of all was the appearance of laywomen as students at Notre Dame. The summer school was the first opening for them. Cavanaugh noted the impact of a significant lay female presence on campus when he observed to a correspondent, "it seems strange to have secular women parading to class-rooms and loafing about the grounds."

The experience of this first summer session forced Cavanaugh and other administrators to think seriously about developing some sort of organization and program of postgraduate education at the university. The basic educational purpose of starting a summer program at Notre Dame had been to provide opportunities for religious teachers to finish their baccalaureate degrees and otherwise satisfy certification requirements increasingly being imposed on Catholic schools by state educational agencies. Inevitably, the summer school became the focus of postgraduate education at the university.[13]

As early as 1905, a faculty committee on graduate study had been formed, but no set program of graduate studies had ever been developed and no identifiable graduate courses had ever been offered before 1919. Nonetheless, between 1906 and 1919 fourteen master's degrees and six doctorates had been conferred. No records of what the recipients had to do in order to earn them has survived. One can guess that most of the recipients received their degrees for good behavior. No less than four of the six doctorates conferred were awarded to working members of the Notre Dame lay faculty.[14]

Though nothing serious was done about graduate work at Notre Dame during the Cavanaugh presidency, requests for courses carrying graduate credit during the summer session of 1918 were numerous.[15] It was clear to those in charge of the university in the fall of that year that future successful summer sessions would have to offer graduate courses. Religious and lay teachers in Catholic schools had educational needs that could be met most effectively by summer graduate programs offered by a Catholic university. Cavanaugh and others in the Main Building recognized that Notre Dame could play a major role in meeting those needs. However, the problem of what to do about postgraduate education at Notre Dame and what portion of university resources ought to be devoted to it was to be left to Cavanaugh's successors. Surprisingly, all of these educational developments and important future educational policy decisions had followed from a relatively straightforward economic decision to open a public cafeteria on the ground floor of Badin Hall in the fall of 1917. Indeed, from tiny acorns do mighty oaks grow.

—   iii   —

Another extremely important new venture beginning in Cavanaugh's time was Notre Dame's entry into the exciting and risky world of intercollegiate athletics as a major football power in the Midwest. Intercollegiate athletics began in the United States with eight-oared barge races between Harvard and Yale in 1852. During the next two decades colleges competed with one another in baseball and track. The first intercollegiate football game was not played until 1869. It took about ten years to standardize football rules and equipment and to organize regular schedules. During the 1880s paid professional coaches, elaborate equipment, and paid admission tickets all became essential parts of intercollegiate football activity. By 1890 intercollegiate football had become an important business activity for those colleges participating in it and a very popular spectator sport.[16]

Organized team sports first appeared at Notre Dame in the early 1860s when students formed a cricket club.[17] Athletic competition with an outside team occurred in 1885 when a senior baseball team played the South Bend Green Stockings. From this beginning, baseball became the most popular intermural and intercollegiate athletic activity at Notre Dame for the next twenty years. Also in the 1860s, informal student-organized football games began at the university.[18] The first intercollegiate football game at Notre Dame was played against the University of Michigan on November 23, 1887.[19] The first intercollegiate football game played away from the university and the only football game played that year occurred at Northwestern in 1889. No intercollegiate football games were played in 1890 or 1891. However, beginning in 1892, when only two games were played and one of them was against South Bend High School, regularly scheduled games with regional colleges, clubs, and high schools became the norm.

The university did not hire a paid coach until 1894. Coaches employed between 1894 and 1913 were part-time employees, mostly young former players from state universities. As such, few of them remained at Notre Dame for more than one or two years. Scheduling games with worthy and challenging opponents at convenient times within the midwest region was a continuing problem during the 1890s. Consequently, when a loosely organized alliance of midwestern universities and colleges fielding football teams known as the Western Conference was formed in 1896 to standardize rules and facilitate scheduling, Notre Dame applied for admission to it. At that time, the university's application was denied on the grounds that its caliber of play was below the standards of the other conference members.

That argument was difficult to refute. Between 1887 and 1896, Notre Dame had played thirty-two games against universities, colleges, clubs, and high schools, winning twenty-two, losing eight, and tieing two. However, during those same years, the university's record against major opponents was dismal. Between 1887 and 1896, Notre Dame played the

Universities of Michigan, Purdue, Chicago, and Northwestern eight times, winning only two games and losing six.

Over the next decade Notre Dame coaches came and went, but the record against major opponents got worse. Between 1897 and 1905, when Cavanaugh became president, Notre Dame had played seventy-six games overall, winning fifty-two, losing sixteen, and tieing six. Against major opponents such as Michigan, Chicago, Indiana, Purdue, Illinois, Northwestern, Wisconsin, and Kansas during those years, Notre Dame played twenty games, winning only two, while losing sixteen and tieing two. In 1905 it was even more difficult to argue that the quality of Notre Dame football had improved sufficiently over the past decade to merit admission of the university to the Western Conference. Nevertheless, when Michigan dropped out of the Western Conference in 1905, Notre Dame re-applied, and once again was rejected.

In any case, during 1906 intercollegiate football in the United States underwent a major reform and reorganization. New regional conferences were established and the National Collegiate Athletic Association (NCAA) was founded. These new organizations legislated a series of reforms to try to make football less injurious to players, insure amateurism, regulate recruitment procedures, and set reasonable academic standards for players. The impact of this organizational and reformist activity upon the Western Conference was immediate and radical.[20]

Under the leadership of Amos Alonzo Stagg of Chicago and Fielding Yost of Michigan, the loosely organized Western Conference was transformed into the "Big Nine," a smaller conference composed of teams from the major public and private universities of the Midwest. The possibility that Notre Dame would ever find a place in this smaller, new but very prestigious conference so long as Stagg and Yost were influential in it was extremely remote. Those two coaches had no respect whatsoever for the caliber of Notre Dame football and by extension very little for the university as an institution of higher education. After all, between 1887 and 1908 Notre Dame had played Michigan eight times and Chicago three times without winning or tieing a single game. Chicago had dropped Notre Dame from its schedule in 1900. Michigan was to do the same after 1909 under circumstances that would be long remembered.

Notre Dame had scheduled a series of games with Michigan in 1908, 1909, and 1910. Michigan won a closely contested game against Notre Dame, 12 to 6, in 1908. The following year, for the first time in history, Notre Dame defeated Michigan, 11 to 3. Immediately, the glory of this much-savored victory was diminished by bitter controversy. Athletic authorities at Michigan accused Notre Dame of using two players in that game who were ineligible by conference standards. The specific point at issue was whether or not an Oregon educational institution attended by these two linemen before coming to Notre Dame was a preparatory school or a college.[21] Notre Dame officials denied the charge, insisting that the Oregon institution had been a preparatory school. Also, spokesmen for the university countered the charge of conference rules violations by raising questions about the eligibility of some Michigan players.

In the end, Michigan authorities canceled the Notre Dame game scheduled for 1910. Moreover, they did so at the last minute, informing university officials by telegram just before the team boarded the train at Niles for Ann Arbor. Father Thomas V. Crumley, C.S.C., vice president of Notre Dame and the administrator directly responsible for the football program, scorned the course of compromise and the role of peacemaker by attributing the exclusion of Notre Dame from conference membership, Yost's charges of rules violations, and the manner of canceling the Notre Dame-Michigan game in 1910 to religious bigotry.[22]

In effect, Notre Dame football teams had been ostracized by the major football powers in the Midwest. Games with the university's natural opponents, the public universities in Indiana and in neighboring states became virtually impossible to schedule. Notre Dame played Purdue in 1906 but was unable to schedule another football game with them until 1918. With Indiana, the time between games lasted from 1908 to 1919. After the controversial victory over Michigan in 1909, Notre Dame did not play Michigan again until 1942. It was a fact that for over half a century neither the administrative nor athletic department leaderships of either institution exhibited much interest in renewing this historic football series, that is, the series that had actually initiated Notre Dame football. Moreover, the series was not renewed until the reasons it had been ended were long forgotten.

Denied games with their midwestern neighbors, Notre Dame had to look farther east and west for opponents who would attract ticket-buying customers. Pittsburgh was added to the schedule in 1909 and then again in 1911 and 1912. However, large or long-established eastern colleges and universities with football programs were not excited by the prospect of a game with a Catholic university from northern Indiana and none were scheduled.

During 1911 and 1912 half of the university's football opponents were small or developing Catholic colleges without much experience and virtually no success in intercollegiate football competition. A tie with Pittsburgh in 1911 and a narrow victory over them in 1912 were the only games worth paying to see during those two years. Enormous one-sided defeats of Loyola, 80 to 0, in 1911, Marquette, 69 to 0, in 1912, and an incredible mismatch with humble little St. Viator, 116 to 0, also in 1912, proved nothing about Notre Dame's football prowess except an inability to schedule competitive opponents.

Something had to be done to achieve football respectability and end such disgraceful overmatching and exploitation of small Catholic colleges. At the end of 1912 something was done. Notre Dame hired Jesse C. Harper as their first full-time professional coach. Harper was experienced, having come to Notre Dame from a similar position at Wabash College. He was very well connected in intercollegiate athletic circles, having played baseball for A. A. Stagg at Chicago. Also, Harper was a Protestant. He was one of those needed specialists whose religious affiliation did not matter.

Harper went to work at once trying to improve the schedule. Actually, the task turned out to be easier than most had expected. First, he wrote letters to friends in the West and successfully obtained contracts for games with South Dakota and Texas for the fall season. Next, he followed the scheduling pattern set by the baseball team during their spring seasons in 1912 and 1913. The baseball team had made eastern tours during those years and had established contacts and played games with Penn State and Army, defeating the former but losing to the latter. Harper wrote to both of those institutions seeking games with them also for 1913.

The inquiry to the United States Military Academy was no shot in the dark. Two other schools had just dropped the Army team from their football schedules because of alleged violations of eligibility rules. Harper knew that Army needed opponents to complete its schedule for 1913.[23] As a matter of fact, Harper's letter offering to bring Notre Dame to West Point could not have come at a better moment. Army accepted a game with Notre Dame, as did Penn State.

In just a few months Harper had raised the competitive level of Notre Dame football beyond all expectations. Only one Catholic institution and two small regional colleges remained on the schedule. Three new Notre Dame opponents were state universities. Army, the United States Military Academy, was one of the most widely reported and closely followed football teams in the country. The public relations value of football victories over Penn State and Texas would be great, over Army it would be incalculable.

Next, Harper turned to the team that he had inherited. That team had enjoyed an undefeated season against very weak opponents during 1912. Most of the better and experienced players were returning. Among them were Raymond J. Eichenlaub, a bruising fullback, Charles E. Dorais, a steady quarterback with an accurate throwing arm, and Knute K. Rockne, a speedy twenty-five-year-old left end with pass-catching ability. Generally, successful football coaches in 1912 assumed that footballs were made for kicking and carrying, not for throwing. To be sure, rules changes made in 1906 legitimized forward passing as an offensive tactic, but it had not become a widely used weapon of choice. In 1912 football games were contests of strength, weight, and endurance between linemen and running backs. Harper's new schedule required a new approach to the game if the public relations opportunities open to the university were to be realized.

Harper was open-minded about football tactics and strategies and was one of the few active coaches aware of the game-breaking potential of accurate forward passing. Moreover, in Dorais and Rockne, Harper believed he had a talented combination of passer and receiver that could introduce elements of surprise, deception, and speed into a style of football play that sorely needed them. During the summer of 1913 both Dorais and Rockne took jobs at the Cedar Point Amusement Park near Cleveland and found ample time to practice and perfect their passing and receiving skills. When the season began in early October, Harper with Dorais, Rockne, Eichenlaub, and the rest of the team were the future. The future was ready.

The first three games of the season were one-sided victories reminiscent of the previous year. The game against Army, played on November 1, 1913, was another matter. For all of Harper's vision, the practiced skills of Dorais and Rockne, and Eichenlaub's strength and courage, the simple fact of being outweighed by almost fifteen pounds a man was felt as a reality. By halftime Notre Dame had managed a lead of only a single point. In the second half, the combination of Dorais' passing and Eichenlaub's powerful running was too much for the larger but slower Cadet line to contain. On that memorable day, Dorais completed fourteen out of seventeen passes for 220 yards. Notre Dame defeated Army 35 to 13.

Coverage in both the eastern and national press was extraordinary. Harper and Notre Dame were credited with having originated a new style of play which pundits predicted would change the tempo and the nature of the game forever. A sense of being present at a critical moment in the history of American sports informed the prose of the reporters covering the game for the *New York Times*. The university had achieved an enormous public relations triumph. Everyone in the country would know about the football heroics of the team from Notre Dame. Most important of all, American Catholic pride in this single athletic victory was unbounded. In an afternoon the university had acquired intense emotional commitments from a whole generation of Catholic working-class supporters and defenders that would endure for years.

After the Army game, even though Notre Dame defeated Texas and Penn State handily and had finished the season undefeated, the rest of the schedule was anticlimactic. The team's spectacular performance against Army had utterly changed the university's football fortunes. Well-known teams became eager to play Notre Dame. Harper arranged a game with Yale for 1914 which Notre Dame proceeded to lose in a most decisive fashion. Nebraska was added for 1915 and became a regular opponent for many years thereafter. Wisconsin broke the conference blacklisting of Notre Dame and arranged a game for 1917. Purdue and Indiana came back on the schedule in 1918 and 1919.

After the loss to Notre Dame in 1913, Army wanted a rematch, which they got the following year and won, 20 to 7. A third game in 1917 which Notre Dame barely won, 7 to 2, initiated a series of games played every year beginning in 1919 that lasted through 1947. The Army-Notre Dame series became one of the greatest and most closely followed intercollegiate football rivalries in the history of American sports. By 1920 this game had become such a renowned sports event that no major eastern sports writer would dare miss it.[24] Because popular interest in this game had become so intense and the demand for tickets so great, in 1923 the site of the game was moved from the sparse bleachers on the plains of West Point to the great baseball stadiums of New York City. First, in 1923, the game was moved to Ebbets Field, the home of the Brooklyn Dodgers, where mounted police were required to manage the crowd pressing to get in.[25] Later, the game would be played in even larger facilities at the Polo Grounds and in Yankee Stadium. Within a decade of the memorable victory over Army in 1913, Notre Dame had risen to an exalted status in intercollegiate football. Not only could Notre Dame teams fill almost any stadium anywhere in the country during the 1920s, but there seemed to be something special, perhaps even inspired, about the way they played the game. Notre Dame provided the football heroes that ticket-buying spectators most wanted to see.

Jesse Harper remained at Notre Dame for five years, resigning in 1918 when the unexpected death of a wealthy relative required him to take charge of a cattle ranch in western Kansas. During those five years at Notre Dame, Harper-coached teams won thirty-three games, lost five, and tied one. Harper did much more for Notre Dame football than win 85 percent of the games played. He developed a schedule that insured continuing regional and national interest in the fortunes of Notre Dame football. In doing that, Harper created a football enterprise which in time the university could barely control. This Notre Dame football enterprise became an important component of the university's corporate culture and principal sources of institutional distinction and popular identity. Once begun and established the Notre Dame football enterprise could not be stopped or even much diminished, only continued.

During Harper's years at the university, the profits of the Notre Dame football enterprise were measured more in the coin of public relations than in real money. Between 1913 and 1918 football revenues rarely and barely covered costs. For example, when Notre Dame played Army in 1913, the financial guarantee for that game was only $1,000.[26] Moreover, when Harper was hired in 1913 he was the highest paid person employed by the university and continued to be so during his time as head football coach. At that time and later as well there were some at Notre Dame who worried about the financial costs of a winning football program when cash-flow problems were endemic at the university, when faculty salaries were low, and new facilities so much needed.

Persons of such a mind would admit that Harper had done wonders for university public relations but were prepared to argue that a new library building might do more. As president, Cavanaugh had listened to such arguments sympathetically and had been persuaded that the university needed a new library. He was prepared to borrow money in order to build one. Yet, he did not regard money spent on football as being in any way diverted from educational services.

As a matter of fact, Cavanaugh insisted that salaries paid to football coaches were "questions not of faculty expenses but of athletics."[27] Generally, football coaches have brought in "considerably more than we pay out for them. Good athletic men are inevitably high priced."[28] Having said that, there is no suggestion in Cavanaugh's correspondence that he imagined for a moment a future time when football revenues would increase to levels where they could be used to support academic programs or build new facilities. Indeed, Cavanaugh knew that by Notre Dame standards in 1913 or in 1918, Harper's salary was excessive. However, so long as Cavanaugh was president, he believed that Harper's salary was money well spent for which commensurate value had been received.

Harper had done more to insure the continuity and success of the Notre Dame football enterprise than merely improve the schedule. He recruited a successor coach who would build upon his foundations and then create the most celebrated and successful intercollegiate football program in the country.

Knute K. Rockne had graduated from Notre Dame with a degree in pharmacy in June 1914. After thinking about the possibility of attending medical school in St. Louis, Rockne decided to get married and then pursue a career in coaching. Harper facilitated appointments for him at

Notre Dame, beginning in September 1914 as an assistant football coach, head track coach, and as a chemistry teacher in the preparatory school. Harper and Rockne worked well together, and very quickly the new assistant football coach emerged as the person in the athletic department reputed as best able to broker disputes with the university administration and to solve academic and disciplinary problems for athletes. Though a Protestant, Rockne was comfortable in the American Catholic environment of Notre Dame, got on well with most of the Holy Cross priests, and was liked by influential alumni who were especially devoted to Notre Dame football. When Harper resigned, Rockne's appointment as head football coach and athletic director in 1918 was by no means automatic, but it came as no surprise. With Rockne as head football coach, the golden age of Notre Dame football was about to begin.

—　iv　—

An important university development begun during the Cavanaugh presidency that focused more directly on educational needs and services was the construction of a new large free-standing library building. In considering and undertaking such a project at a Catholic institution, Cavanaugh and Morrissey were pioneers. No other Catholic college or university in the country possessed such a facility. The case for a new library building at the university was easily made. As a matter of fact, such a case had been made as early as 1887 and preliminary plans for a new building actually had been prepared in 1900.

The present library located in the Main Building was simply taxed beyond its capacity. Some books and magazines had to be stored on the floor because of a shortage of shelving space. Catalogued books were not available as located. Service was slow and poor. Stress on the girders of the Main Building from the overweighting of library holdings threatened the structural integrity and safety of the building. Beyond those conditions was the undeniable fact that during the previous twenty years a well-stocked and properly serviced library had become the most important single element in higher education. Notre Dame desperately needed a new library facility if it was to survive and prosper as an institution of higher learning. However, nothing serious about providing the students and faculty with a modern library occurred until Father Paul J. Foik, C.S.C., became librarian in 1912.

Foik was a highly energetic priest of Canadian origins who had entered the Congregation of Holy Cross in 1905. Ordained in 1909, he was sent off to the Holy Cross House of Studies in Washington, D.C., to pursue doctoral studies in history at the Catholic University of America. While residing in the House of Studies, Foik attracted the attention of the local superior, Father James A. Burns, who put him in charge of the small seminary library there.[29] After Foik completed his doctoral work, Burns recommended him to Morrissey as a strong candidate for the post of university librarian vacated by the death of James F. Edwards in early 1911. Morrissey acted upon Burns' recommendation and kept the post unfilled until Foik was able to return to the university in 1912.

When Foik arrived to take charge of the library, he was supremely self-confident and absolutely determined to provide the university with a library and library services worthy of its educational mission. Though deficient in technical knowledge of library services and procedures, Foik brought to the challenges of his new post an unfailing persistence, very little patience, and a fondness for intrigue. In short, Foik had more energy for the job than knowledge of it. However, he had other assets. He was a charming but highly adept, perhaps even unscrupulous, clerical politician who was very comfortable in the changing political environment at Notre Dame during the last half of Cavanaugh's long presidency. Foik was perfectly suited to initiate and undertake what others in the congregation desired, had discussed, but were too cautious to try to obtain.[30]

Foik began his campaign for a new library immediately after being appointed librarian. In truth, only three very important persons—Français as superior general, Morrissey as provincial, and Cavanaugh as president—had to be persuaded to seize the moment and try to put up a building that would be the pride of the university.[31] As provincial, Morrissey's support was absolutely essential. Given the urgency of the need for a new facility and the lack of any sort of fund-raising experience or apparatus, funds for building a new library would have to be advanced by the American Province of the Congregation of Holy Cross and then hopefully be repaid by the university over a period of years out of operating revenues.

It took Foik almost two years of constant agitation to get the necessary approvals and appointment of a library building committee with himself as chairman. The most difficult and time-consuming aspect of the local approval process was overcoming the provincial's innate parsimony and conservatism. In the end, Morrissey's support was obtained, but not easily. He had to be convinced that Notre Dame ought to have "the finest library in the whole state of Indiana and the finest Catholic library in the whole United States."[32]

This library building project turned out to be the most costly and most complicated ever undertaken in university history up to that time. It also turned out to be an important modernizing experience for the leadership of the university and of Holy Cross. Among the many things that Morrissey, Cavanaugh, and others had to learn was that over the previous thirty years construction technology and general contractor business practices had changed greatly. Unlike the great reconstruction of the Main Building after the terrible fire of 1879, where the skilled and unskilled labor provided by Holy Cross brothers contributed significantly to the timely completion and cost-effectiveness of that building, by 1914 the available manpower resources of the congregation were insufficiently skilled and professionalized for deployment on the library project. For Notre Dame the era of self-sufficiency was long past. Money was more important than free labor. Cavanaugh and Morrissey had difficulty accepting that reality.

As a matter of fact, Morrissey never fully accepted it at all. The provincial insisted that Brother Irenaeus, styled as the congregation's master mechanic, be given complete charge and responsibility for all electrical, plumbing, and heating installations in the new building. In effect, the university through Brother Irenaeus became an unpaid electrical and heating subcontractor for this project. However, Brother Irenaeus was a subcontractor who was not under the direct supervision or financial discipline of either the architect or the general contractor. While the long-term consequences of this arrangement were to be disastrous, the immediate short-term effect was to reduce initial cost estimates down to a range of between $180,000 and $250,000. Morrissey always plumped for the lowest possible figure while Foik invariably argued for a more costly building that would be beautiful and functional and would serve the students and faculty for the next seventy-five years.

Foik had begun his campaign for a new library in 1913. He pursued his objective with a degree of indefatigability that was astonishing. During 1913 and 1914, Foik had contacted prominent American librarians and leaders of state and national library associations. He corresponded or met with the librarians of the University of Michigan, Harvard, Yale, the director of public libraries for the city of Chicago, and W. Dawson Johnston of the Carnegie Foundation for the Advancement of Teaching.[33]

At the same time, Foik lobbied influentials in the Congregation of Holy Cross ceaselessly, insisting that the intellectual reputation of Notre Dame as an American Catholic university would turn on what was done about the library. He envisaged a graduate program in library science being established in the new building and perhaps even a learned journal similar to the one published by the Catholic University of America.[34] By 1915, Foik had become a man of a single idea. Building the library and doing it right was never out of his mind or off his lips.

Next, Foik identified Edward L. Tilton of New York as one of the country's leading library architects and managed his selection by the library building committee in the spring of 1915. Actually, Tilton was one of five architects who submitted drawings to the committee that spring. Tilton had come highly recommended. He was a graduate of the Ecole des Beaux Arts in Paris, had written monographs and articles on classical Greek architecture, and most important, had designed more than sixty libraries in the United States and Canada. Tilton submitted plans for a building done in the Renaissance style. It was to be built of stone, the first of its kind at Notre Dame, and had a planned capacity of 618,000 volumes. Since the present collection approached 100,000 volumes, this new facility promised to meet the needs of the university for many years to come.

Some of the details of the Tilton design were striking. The delivery hall and main staircases were to be finished in marble and patterned after similar ones in the Louvre. Two large reading rooms would accommodate three hundred readers at the same time, and sixty cubicles in the stacks would be available for serious scholarship and private study. There was room also, 6,500 square feet, for museum purposes, the Catholic Archives of America, and art collections. Lecture rooms would be available in the basement area, and the school of journalism might even be located there. Executives of the American Library Association, the president of the Illinois Library Association, and the editor of *Public Libraries* had all praised the design and modernity of the proposed new facility.[35]

Though excavation work did not begin until November 1915 and a general contractor, Bedford Stone Company, was not selected until the end of the year, Foik had accomplished a great deal during the spring of 1915. However, during that summer a major crisis in internal Holy Cross politics arose suddenly which threatened to put aside all plans and decisions made up to that time on the library project and delay indefinitely the start of actual construction. To be sure, Foik was extremely knowledgeable about and skilled in the sometimes Byzantine ways of Holy Cross politics; all of that knowledge and all of those political skills had to be quickly deployed in order to save the project from major modification and possible failure.

According to Foik, by June 1915 the library building committee had clearly indicated its preference for the Tilton design. Thereupon, he insisted, "sinister influences" were brought to bear on the committee by a member of it, and the whole selection process had to be repeated in order to prove which of the submitted designs was the best. Only after what Foik described as a "stern fight" was the matter resolved and the architectural contract actually awarded to Tilton.[36]

The sinister influences to which Foik referred emanated from Father Michael A. Quinlan, C.S.C., a professor of philosophy and a member of the committee. Father Quinlan had a brother-in-law—William Kelley of Pittsburgh—with some experience in the construction business who became seriously interested in the Notre Dame project only after the committee had decided unanimously in June to award the architectural contract to Tilton.[37]

William Kelley had worked for many years as a supervisor of building construction for the Jarvis Hunt Company in Pittsburgh. By all accounts, in the capacity of supervisor William Kelley had shown himself to be an able man. However, he had neither been trained nor had any work experience as an architect. Being ambitious and knowing that his wife's brother, Father Quinlan, was a member of the library building committee, William Kelley decided to form his own architectural firm with the assistance of his brother, Joseph, and two Chicago architects. With this new company Kelley intended to pursue the Notre Dame contract as vigorously as possible even though the committee had already decided unanimously to select Tilton as architect.[38]

In July, William Kelley submitted two sets of elevations and floor plans with his name on them to Foik.[39] One set of plans was patterned after the Widener Library in Cambridge, Massachusetts and the other was modeled on the Morgan Library in New York.[40] Foik was of no mind to cooperate with Kelley, but he agreed to meet with him in August. After the meeting, Foik's distrust of Kelley hardened. It was clear that Kelley's technical knowledge of architectural design and procedures was limited. He could not answer simple questions relating to reading room and stack capacities. Moreover, when pressed to provide the address and location of standing buildings that he had designed and built, Kelley could not do so. Foik was disgusted by Kelley's ineffective efforts to present someone else's work as his own and showed it clearly. After this meeting Foik received no more communications from William Kelley. All future negotiations were to be left in the capable hands of Father Quinlan.[41]

Quinlan's strategy was simple. He tried to circumvent Foik and the committee by dealing directly with Cavanaugh. According to Foik, Quinlan tried to convince Cavanaugh that the whole question of architect selection had become a personal one between himself and the chairman of the library building committee and that Kelley's designs had not been given a fair evaluation.[42] Next, Quinlan began soliciting support from prominent persons in the library world for the Kelley designs. In the end, Quinlan failed to persuade the president to reject the committee's recommendation for Tilton. Cavanaugh simply asked the committee to review the Kelley designs, even though the time for formal submission had passed. With Father Quinlan absent, the committee obliged the president, reviewed Kelley's plans, and then unanimously rejected them.[43] The immediate effect of Quinlan's failed coup was to establish Tilton as the university architect. While this was a status that would not last, it enabled the New York architect to get another commission in 1916 to design a new chemistry building and begin construction of it in 1917.

Foik had won this battle and was inclined to be a magnanimous victor. He wrote to Miss M. E. Aherne of the Chicago public libraries, whose support for the Kelley designs Quinlan had solicited, and asked her not to think ill of this Notre Dame priest for trying to do a service for his brother-in-law. Nepotism of the sort attempted by Father Quinlan was not particularly widespread at Notre Dame at that time, but it occurred with sufficient frequency to be a problem. If nepotism of this kind was regarded as sinful by a majority of the Holy Cross priests of Foik's generation, it was understood to be only venially so and easily forgiven. However, Tilton was well aware of the political necessity of placating Holy Cross influentials at the university and worried about it. He hesitated before hiring Joseph Schumacher as clerk of works for the library project because Schumacher's only qualification for the post was the fact that his brother was Father Matthew Schumacher, then director of studies at the university.

Even Foik himself was not above doing favors for friends. He pressed the president to approve the appointment of Edward Flynn as a resident evening caretaker of the new library. Flynn was a long-serving university employee, an active member of the local chapter of the Knights of Columbus, and much distraught by the recent death of his wife. Cavanaugh approved Foik's recommendation and Flynn was given living accommodations in the new building. As Foik observed to a friend, Flynn was an old man who had not much longer to live. We all ought to take care of our own, he added; Flynn's presence in the library as an evening caretaker was more desirable "than perhaps some Polock or Huniak from the city."[44]

When excavation of the site and actual construction began in November 1915, the biggest problem with the project turned out to be neither nepotism nor Holy Cross patronage. It was Brother Irenaeus' installation of electrical, plumbing, and heating equipment. While his knowledge of and skill in installing modern equipment in a project of this size was inadequate, his capacity for disputing with contractors was endless. Moreover, by temperament, Brother Irenaeus was incapable of seeking or receiving technical assistance from anyone. Virtually everything that Irenaeus and his crew installed failed to work properly.

The Devoe telephone system wired by Irenaeus and his crew was use-less. Downspouts installed according to Irenaeus' layout rather than by the one provided by the architect flooded the library basement during heavy rain storms.[45] Drinking fountains were in place two years before corrections in piping allowed water to flow through them.[46] Most serious of all was Irenaeus' faulty installation of the heating and ventilation system. During the winter of 1917–18, the new building was barely habit-able. According to Foik, "the thermometer was stuck at fifty." Only after threatening to resign his post as librarian was Foik able to get sufficient heat into the building to keep it comfortable.[47]

Foik lost all patience with Irenaeus, the "Enfant Terrible" of the pro-ject.[48] Foik worked very hard to persuade Morrissey and Cavanaugh to relieve Irenaeus of all responsibility for work on the project and re-place him with a qualified heating and ventilating engineer.[49] That was not done, and Irenaeus remained in charge of heating and ventilation throughout the entire period of construction. The damage he wrought was not corrected until three years after the library had been dedi-cated and opened for use. At long last and after much expense, in 1920 a Chicago heating and ventilation company replaced some valves in the university heating system, properly installed others, and managed to get the system balanced so that some buildings would not be super heated and others, such as the new library, left frigid. Notwithstanding all of the difficulties with Irenaeus and with local contractors and no matter how chastening the construction experience had been for all concerned, the library was completed in time to be formally dedicated and become the centerpiece of the university's festive and spectacular diamond jubilee ceremonies in June 1917.

From Tilton's perspective, Brother Irenaeus had been only one reason why a smooth-running building operation had been so difficult to estab-lish. Both Cavanaugh and Morrissey shared responsibility with Irenaeus for the delays, failures, and disputes that marred the progress of the li-brary and other construction projects at the university at that time. Re-tention of Irenaeus in a position where he could continue to mismanage the installation of critical elements in the library had been Cavanaugh's fault. According to Tilton, Cavanaugh had been warned about Irenaeus' faulty wiring of the telephones while the work was in progress, but no corrective action was taken.[50]

As a matter of fact, Tilton evinced no small pleasure in lecturing the president about the many unnecessary difficulties following from the Notre Dame method of insisting that parts of the building opera-tion should be handled by a member of the university. Coordination and quality control became impossible and rectification of poor work was costly.[51] Cavanaugh was annoyed by Tilton's manner and quickly developed a strong personal dislike of the man. As that dislike intensified, the president was more inclined to blame Tilton for the failures and problems in the building operations than Irenaeus.

As Tilton saw the situation at Notre Dame, on the one hand, Cavanaugh had allowed problems to develop on the library project by failing to act when Irenaeus' incompetence had been brought to his attention. On the other hand, Morrissey himself had caused serious problems during the construction of the new chemistry hall by acting on his own in matters properly left to the architect.

Morrissey personally had taken over the direction of the chemistry hall project. While Tilton remained as architect, the provincial had insisted on a strict utilitarian design that consisted of little more than four walls and a roof. Consequently, details were extremely important to Father Maguire and the rest of the chemistry professors. Requests for small changes from Maguire and his colleagues were endless and delaying. Morrissey selected the local contractors and negotiated all contracts, which in Tilton's view he did neither wisely nor well. In order to save $5,000, Morrissey allowed the contractor to reduce the thickness of the walls and change the system of floor construction.[52]

Even more damaging to the project was the contract negotiated for bricks. With the objective of avoiding payment of an architect's fee on brick, Morrissey sought out the cheapest local supplier and signed a contract without any specification or guarantees of product quality. What Morrissey got for his efforts were improperly fired bricks that began deteriorating within days of being laid. Tilton reported the delivery of inferior material, but no notice was taken of his warning and no tests of the bricks were made.[53] In Tilton's judgment, local suppliers had taken advantage of Morrissey's naiveté and had sold the university "a material falsely represented as brick." The architect urged authorities at Notre Dame to take legal action to recover damages from all dishonest suppliers. Because Tilton claimed total ignorance of the terms of the brick contract and had charged no fee on it, he denied any responsibility for what had happened.[54]

Cavanaugh explained project failures and delays in a different way. He blamed Tilton for the painfully disappointing experience of the chemistry hall project. According to the president, Tilton was the project architect and was therefore responsible for seeing the project through to a successful completion. After all, the principal reason for hiring an architect was to insure competent settlement of all technical questions for the client. In the matter of the chemistry hall project, the president insisted that this most important professional function had not been done with general satisfaction. Cavanaugh did not state directly but strongly implied that Tilton had received his last architectural commission from Notre Dame.[55]

For his part, Tilton refused the role of scapegoat. He complained to Foik many times that prompt delivery and quality performance of professional services in the administrative environment of Notre Dame was almost impossible. There was an unusual lack of cooperation among university administrators and supervisors. Middle management was either nonexistent or incompetent. Affairs at the university, Tilton contended, "seemed to be without a centralizing grasp." To be sure, things were not left entirely to chance. Directions from the top were issued often enough to supervisors responsible for particular functions, but rarely and haphazardly were such directions carried out.[56] The whole system of contract negotiation and procurement without adequate safeguards had to change or university money would be wasted. The way things were, Tilton insisted, neither he nor any other architect could "protect the University against themselves."[57]

Foik accepted Tilton's complaints as well-founded and tried to raise his extremely frustrated friend's spirits. He agreed that Morrissey had allowed himself to be duped by unscrupulous contractors. Foik came very close to admitting that Cavanaugh had been unfair to the architect. He did say, however, that the president had complicated matters by many prolonged absences from the university at critical moments when quick decisions were needed. Those frequent presidential absences had annoyed Foik greatly, but he accepted them as necessary to preserve Cavanaugh's rumored precarious state of health. Cavanaugh would simply go away and not tell anyone at the university where he had gone. The president was "some where in the United States," Foik complained to Tilton on one occasion, "Should the whole University burn down tomorrow, he would have to get his information from the newspapers."[58]

In December 1918, Foik tried to assure Tilton that his association with Notre Dame might possibly be continued. Morrissey and Cavanaugh would not be in office forever. "The time may not be very distant," he wrote to his friend, "when we may not have these men to deal with, but others." This bit of information, he said, was "a secret between yourself and myself."[59] The librarian turned out to be correct about the tenure of Morrissey and Cavanaugh but wrong about the prospect of Tilton doing more work at Notre Dame. Over the next decade, several new buildings would be erected, but other architects would design and build them in an administrative environment that had become much more conducive to the performance of quality professional services.

— v —

Cavanaugh's last years were not an easy time for him or for Notre Dame. Physically and mentally, he was a man who always required adequate rest in order to function efficiently. In the best of circumstances, he did not handle excessive work loads well. During the war years, his work load became so excessive that he could barely cope with it. Part of this was due to the illness of the provincial. Morrissey was frequently ill during 1917 and 1918, suffering several serious attacks of pneumonia, and was unable to perform the duties of provincial most of the time. Those responsibilities, which were extraordinarily heavy and politically complex, during these years passed to Cavanaugh.[60] Matthew J. Walsh, vice president since 1911, volunteered along with seven other popular and experienced Holy Cross priests to serve in the war as chaplains. Walsh's counsel and energy were sorely missed.

There simply was not time enough for Cavanaugh to tend to all of the matters referred to him and just about anything that happened at the university or in the Holy Cross Congregation was referred to him. For Cavanaugh, not only had decision-making responsibilities multiplied, during these years they had become extraordinarily complex politically. Internal Holy Cross politics had reached a crisis. A majority of the priests at Notre Dame and elsewhere in the American Province of the congregation were in sharp disagreement with the superior general, Gilbert Français, over possible changes in congregation rules.

By 1918 cooperation between priests and brothers in congregation governance, never entirely amicable, had become especially strained. The union of clerical and lay religious in a single association affording equal rights in governance established by Moreau so many years ago was not working well. Clearly, since Sorin's time the instructional presence of the brothers at Notre Dame had diminished. Moreover, events since the closing of the Manual Labor School suggested that it would be diminished further. Understandably, the brothers were uncertain about what their future roles at Notre Dame and in congregation educational works would be.[61] As a matter of fact, in 1910 a group of brothers petitioned Rome for a formal separation from the priests. That appeal had been denied, but the superior general had tried to allay anxiety and give new purpose and direction to their work by decreeing that henceforth the brothers would concentrate their teaching efforts in high schools.[62] The problem with this solution, of course, was that the high school movement in many parts of the country was only recently established and that Catholic high schools were few and far between.

At the end of 1918, a group of priests at Notre Dame petitioned the superior general to support changes in the constitutions of the congregation. These changes were intended to change current practices whereby priests and brothers enjoyed equal voting rights in the selection of superiors and in other matters determined in formal meetings known as Provincial Chapters. The priest petitioners wanted to limit voting for superiors in priests' houses to priests only and in brothers' houses to brothers only. The petitioners believed that the traditional practice of allowing brothers to vote in Provincial Chapters on matters concerning the priests should be ended.[63]

In addition, the petitioners sought to democratize the selection of delegates to the Provincial Chapter. Traditionally, this chapter was composed entirely of superiors, all approved by the superior general and in practice easily managed by him. The petitioners urged that at least two-thirds of the delegates to the chapter should be elected by the priests of the province.[64]

Father Français rejected the priests' petition, stating that the constitutions of the congregation presently were being revised to conform to the new code of canon law promulgated in May 1918. For this reason, all other proposed changes would have to be deferred until the General Chapter of the congregation in 1920. In his reply, the superior general denounced the priests responsible for preparing the petition, describing their meetings as unauthorized and their proposals as extreme and an "entire overthrow of our past."[65]

The petitioners were not intimidated. They feared that if their reform proposal was referred to a General Chapter chosen by existing procedures, it would fail absolutely. Instead, the petitioners, now being called "Bolsheviki" by opponents, decided to appeal over the authority of the superior general to the Sacred Congregation of Religious in Rome.[66] Though history and prudence warned that in the end such appeals would be fruitless and serve neither the interests of the petitioners nor the superior general and his friends, it was sent off to Rome in March 1919.[67]

Out of 129 priests in the American Province, 71 signed the petition. At Notre Dame, no less than 27 out of 32 priests signed. None of the 21 priests and brothers constituting the Provincial Chapter signed, and most significantly, not one of the eight priests living and studying under the direction of Father Burns in the Washington House of Studies signed the petition.[68] Challenging the superior general's authority before a branch of the Roman Curia was a serious matter. However, a majority of the priests in the American Province decided that regardless of the outcome, it was worth doing.

As local superior at Notre Dame, Cavanaugh was in a very difficult position. He stood with Français and Morrissey against the petitioners, but one very important university administrator and several popular teachers did not. Cavanaugh's director of studies, Matthew Schumacher, was a leader of the petitioners. The combination of mounting problems at the university and increasingly bitter intra-congregation conflict stretched Cavanaugh to his limits. As he complained to a woman friend in the fall of 1917, "Every moment in my day is mortgaged in advance. If time is money as the ancient wisdom said, then I have been living in debtor's prison all my life."[69] Not even choice seats for the World Series in New York could liberate him from his office in the Main Building.

In 1917 and 1918, Cavanaugh's list of worries, obligations, and problems was very long. In addition to the frustrations and disappointments of Holy Cross politics, he was deeply distressed by events occurring in Ireland and much disturbed by Americans who spoke out against our participation in the Great War. During these years, Cavanaugh's hatred of the English government and English policy in Ireland intensified. From his point of view, English policy in Ireland was irrational and evil. After the United States entered the Great War in the spring of 1917, Cavanaugh's fierce anti-English rhetoric diminished not one whit. After all, if English policy in Ireland had not been moderated by America's declaration of war on Germany, why should Cavanaugh soften his verbal assaults on that policy and on the authors of it. For the president of the University of Notre Dame, simultaneously despising England, our ally, and hating Germany, our enemy, was not illogic. It was the highest form of American patriotism.

In personal correspondence Cavanaugh described himself as a "red hot American through and through."[70] Moreover, as the official spokesman for the university and all constituencies contained therein on public policy issues, Cavanaugh's speeches proclaimed Notre Dame to be the most patriotic and pro-war place in the country. Immediately after war had been declared, insofar as possible, Notre Dame went onto a war footing. All students enlisting and called up any time during a term would receive full credits for that term.[71] The spring semester in 1917 was even shortened to enable students to travel home before railroad rates were increased.

At Notre Dame, dissidents, slackers, and copperheads had better beware. They would get neither aid nor encouragement from the president of Our Lady's university. Cavanaugh could not abide "the wise, cold, philosophers who fear enthusiasm and advise prudence." He quarreled with such people whenever and wherever encountered.[72] In speeches delivered to students at campus war rallies when in this red hot condition, Cavanaugh became a patriotic cheerleader. Invariably, he urged the men and boys of Notre Dame to thank God they were Americans. Sometimes, however, when seized by the patriotic fervor of the moment, Cavanaugh could descend to levels of banality that no one could take seriously or raise oversimplification to an unintended comedic art form.

On one occasion, Cavanaugh assured friends and students that by divine arrangement the Germans essentially were cowards and that once a proper rod was put to their hides, they would scamper off to the tall timbers. In a widely reported campus speech, he referred to a handful of students and faculty reputed to be against the war as "concrete copperheads" who embarrassed everyone at Notre Dame with utterances which, if not frankly disloyal, were lacking in the spirit of patriotism. Stupid pride of opinion, he continued, and a silly desire to appear independent in judgment had combined to reveal the shallowness of second-, third-, and fourth-rate minds.

For those unfortunates afflicted with such shallowness, Cavanaugh added, perhaps a condign punishment would be appropriate. Any American who was not heart and soul with his country in this war, he concluded, ought to be segregated and obliged to associate with their own kind. A cruel and unusual punishment in the extreme, to be sure, but disparaging this great cause was a serious matter. According to a reporter for the *South Bend News Times,* students attending this rally hung on every word and cheered their reverend president's patriotic harangue.

Cavanaugh's frequent public denunciations of English policy in Ireland as well as his extreme American patriotic rhetoric was for him possibly one way of coping with a very difficult situation at the university. The war years, but especially 1918, brought very hard times to Notre Dame. In addition to the priests commissioned as chaplains, about a half dozen of the younger lay faculty had gone off to the army. From enlistments and other causes, overall enrollment at the university between October 1916 and October 1918 declined by one-third. With virtually no endowment and burdened by substantial debt from the new library building, this sharp decline in paid tuitions and loss of room and board revenues created serious financial problems for the university.

To be sure, part of that revenue loss was made up from the presence of a Student Army Training Corps (SATC) on campus for a few months before war's end in November 1918. However, the soldier students created more trouble the short time they were on campus than their government-subsidized tuition payments were worth. Of the seven hundred soldier students assigned to Notre Dame not many were Catholics, and virtually none of them were amenable to the sort of disciplined behavior expected from Notre Dame students. They would not conform, and their training officers were of no mind to try and make them do so. Simply stated, the soldier students drank too much too often. University prohibitions against frequenting the Tokio and other public dance halls were derided and ignored. Moreover, they pursued local women with a vigor and determination that the prefect of discipline and hall rectors had not thought possible. Clearly, the soldier students daily were setting horrible examples of lascivious behavior which the young boys in the preparatory school did not need.

Cavanaugh was himself personally disturbed and annoyed by the noise and endless carousing. His bedroom was directly under one of the soldier student dormitory areas. He complained bitterly to the officer in charge of the training unit and presented him with a list of grievances. Nothing was done, and Cavanaugh's sleepless nights continued until the soldier students departed in December 1918. When that happy event came to pass, Cavanaugh observed to a Chicago nun how much he hoped that "God love[d] those poor fellows, because nobody else did, not even themselves apparently."[73] All things considered, the experience of having soldier students at Notre Dame seemed to have been all bad. Memories of their raucous and uninhibited behavior lingered well into 1919 and helped produce an uncooperative reaction to a proposal sent to the university from the Bureau of Venereal Diseases of the Indiana State Board of Health.

As part of both national and state campaigns against venereal diseases in 1919, the Indiana State Board of Health offered to supply a film for viewing at Notre Dame produced by the United States Public Health Service about such diseases entitled "Fit to Win." The State Board of Health also offered to provide a speaker who would introduce the film and then answer viewer questions after the showing.

Cavanaugh thanked the State Board of Health for their offer but rejected it. He then proceeded to explain how such matters were normally handled at Notre Dame. Indeed, the president was aware of the national and state campaigns against venereal diseases and stated that a "proper kind of lecture" on that subject was given once a year at the university. Since that lecture already had been delivered, there was no reason to do it again.[74] Furthermore, Cavanaugh added, "we reach the question of immorality effectively through sermons and the confessional."[75] At Notre Dame, there really was no need for much more than that.

Cavanaugh simply had no interest whatsoever in facilitating a public discussion at Notre Dame about venereal diseases. He saw no relevance between venereal diseases as a social problem and the prevailing lifestyle of Notre Dame students. Now that the soldier students were gone, so also was any reason for a campus anti-venereal diseases program. The old college spirit had come back with a rush, he wrote, and seeing the old boys return and take up the old ways, the old loves, and even their old tricks was a delight.[76] In any case, Cavanaugh had things much more important to worry about than a Public Health Service film on venereal diseases.

So serious were university financial problems between September 1917 and September 1919 that Cavanaugh and other university officials were ready to try almost anything to raise money for debt retirement and operating costs. Consequently in 1917 Cavanaugh, joined by Burns, who had come up from Washington, visited the General Education Board, forerunner of the Rockefeller Foundation in New York, seeking funds. The visit was friendly and cordial, but at that time the board had no general purpose funds available. Thrown back on his own meager resources and pressed by his ever-resourceful director of studies, Matthew A. Schumacher, to do something, to try anything that might attract students and raise revenues, Cavanaugh authorized the starting of a medical school. That was a project that lasted only two years. In addition, Cavanaugh approved an agricultural school, a school of education, as well as a summer school. He even considered opening a correspondence school department but was shamed out of that idea by the registrar, Father William A. Moloney, C.S.C., who described correspondence schools as "the patent medicine factories of education."[77]

Indeed, between 1916 and 1918, especially in the fall of 1918, times were very hard at Notre Dame. If financial problems and unruly soldier students on campus were not enough, the terrible nationwide epidemic of Spanish influenza reached the South Bend area in mid-October and lasted until early November. Public gatherings were banned for three weeks, schools were closed, and fatality lists were published daily in the *South Bend Tribune.*[78]

At Notre Dame before the epidemic abated, over two hundred students were afflicted, classes were canceled for several days, and at least nine students died. This epidemic was so serious at Notre Dame that Cavanaugh described its impact on the campus in a private letter written ten months later as "the death of all human joy."[79] However, in a public statement issued on October 15, 1918, in order to lessen student and parental panic published in the *South Bend Tribune* and in campus publications, the president denied the presence of influenza at Notre Dame, admitting only that some students suffered from colds.[80] A week later, Cavanaugh issued another statement wherein he admitted that sixty-four students were sick and that two had died in St. Joseph's Hospital, asserting nonetheless that conditions on campus were not a cause for alarm. He tried to minimize the danger by suggesting that the contagion on campus was not the virulent form of Spanish influenza presently ravaging the rest of the country but a more common and less fatal type of pneumonia. Cavanaugh praised the local physicians for their devoted service and implied that the two fatalities reported were young boys already weak and run-down when they arrived on campus in September.[81] Saying something was perhaps better than saying nothing in a near crisis situation, when one could do nothing.

Yet, at that darkest of moments, the wonder-working Providence upon whom Cavanaugh had called so often in recent months for intervention on behalf of the Irish cause or on behalf of American military arms at the front seems to have come to his rescue. The war ended. The influenza epidemic passed. Most important, Cavanaugh was delighted to learn that his time as president of the university would soon be over. The new codification of canon law required that terms of religious superiors be limited to six years. The rumor that both Morrissey and Cavanaugh would soon be out of power reported by Foik to Tilton in December 1918 was true. Morrissey and Cavanaugh at Notre Dame and Burns in Washington had all served much longer than six years in their respective offices and all would have to resign. Cavanaugh announced his intended resignation on April 11, 1919, to be effective when the Provincial Chapter chose a successor in July.

At the time of Cavanaugh's announcement, Matthew J. Walsh, thirty-seven years old, lately returned from the war, and serving vice president, seemed to be the candidate most likely to succeed. Cavanaugh described Walsh as the most popular but suspected that the superior general preferred Burns, who was much older, at age fifty-two, and much more experienced as a religious superior.[82] At the Washington House of Studies, Burns had earned the reputation as a superior who was strongly directive but fair. In the judgment of the superior general, Burns as local religious superior and president of the university would be strong enough to end the political turmoil that had unsettled congregation affairs over the last several years.[83]

Français was not content to wait and see what measures the new president would take to bring the priests at Notre Dame back to more acceptable standards of obedience and performance. He intended to make the new man's task a bit easier by instituting major personnel changes effective in July. Matthew Schumacher, Cavanaugh's director of studies and the most notorious Bolshevik of them all, had become particularly obnoxious to Français after a verbal encounter which the superior general regarded as unforgivably impertinent.[84] Schumacher was transferred away from Notre Dame and appointed president of St. Edward's College

in Texas. In addition, four of the leading petitioners, priests with doctorates, were banished from Notre Dame and assigned to teach in secondary
schools.[85] In the case of Schumacher, Cavanaugh tried to intervene and
save him to direct the recently established school of education, but
Français would not be deterred.[86] The need to restore the priests at Notre
Dame to what the superior general believed was a proper state of obedience was far greater than the inconvenience of finding someone to direct
the school of education. Examples needed to be made. Schumacher went
off to Texas.

In July the unreformed Provincial Chapter composed entirely of superiors and under the guidance of the superior general ratified his personnel decisions and installed a new cadre of leadership at the university.
Charles L. O'Donnell, thirty-five years old, a published poet, and also
lately home from the war, succeeded Morrissey as provincial. James A.
Burns was chosen as president and local religious superior. Walsh agreed
to continue as vice president.

Even though Burns was the oldest, best trained, and most academically
qualified priest ever to become president of the university, neither that
training nor those academic qualifications accounted for his selection. He
came to the presidency because the superior general believed he would be
a strong and effective religious superior. In a sense, the selection of Burns
was a counter-revolutionary tactic. As local religious superior, he did not
disappoint the superior general. Very quickly the priests at Notre Dame
were made aware that a new superior had taken charge. Burns introduced
a custom familiar to alumni of the Washington House of Studies but unknown at Notre Dame. He appointed Brother Maurilius to act as an exci-
tator, knocking on the bedroom doors of the priests in the early morning making certain they were awake, up, and ready to begin work at an
appropriate hour.[87] Generally, Burns tried to set high standards of obedience and performance for himself, and he expected others to do the same.

Understanding the nature of the administrative and organizational
changes presently reshaping the structure of American higher education,
Burns applied some of them to the Notre Dame situation. In the process,
he changed completely the direction and principal educational mission
of the university. Moreover, he did all of this in three years' time. Placed
in office as local religious superior to help put down one revolution, as
president he initiated another one far more radical in outcome than
Français or any of the priests and brothers voting in the Provincial Chapter could have imagined.

— 4 —

THE BURNS AND
O'HARA REVOLUTIONS

J ames Aloysius Burns was one of the most creative Catholic educators of his generation. A son of Irish immigrant
parents, Burns had been born in Michigan City, Indiana, in
1867. He came first to Notre Dame in 1882 at the age of fifteen to enroll
in the Manual Labor School as an apprentice printer. The following year
he transferred to the college, graduating in 1888. Burns entered the Holy
Cross Novitiate in that same year. He studied theology at Notre Dame and
elsewhere, finally receiving ordination in 1893.

Burns began teaching chemistry at the university in 1893. Attracted to
Father Zahm, Burns soon became one of that controversial priest's most
devoted followers. Zahm obtained permission for him to study chemistry
during a summer session at Cornell University in 1895. Back at Notre
Dame, Burns favored Zahm in that priest's celebrated conflict with Morrissey. Distraught when Zahm was exiled to Rome in 1896, Burns' spirits
soared and expectations rose when his patron returned to Notre Dame
in 1898 as provincial.

In 1900 Zahm appointed Burns superior of the recently established
Holy Cross House of Studies in Washington, where he remained until
being selected for the presidency of Notre Dame in 1919. While in Washington, Burns used his time wisely. He began graduate studies in education at the Catholic University of America, completing all of his
doctoral work in 1906. While a graduate student, he found time to play a
major role in founding the Catholic Education Association in 1904. A pioneer historian of Catholic education in America, Burns published three
books and many articles on different aspects of American Catholic history and educational policy between 1908 and 1917.

Burns was not intimidated by the magnitude of the problems facing him and the university in the summer of 1919. With the tunnel vision of a zealot, he set out to resolve and reform as much as he could as quickly as possible. He did not believe that difficulties were made easier by protracted discussion and careful consideration of all sides of every question. Burns explained his plans and expected that they would be carried out. While he held the office of president, they were.

As president of the university, Burns preferred formality in personal and professional relations. He rarely ever addressed friends, acquaintances, or persons reporting to him by their Christian names. In Burns' usage, religious men and women were always to be addressed as Father, Brother, and Sister. Lay faculty were always styled as Professor or, if appropriate, as Doctor. As an educational administrator and religious superior, Burns was not an easy man to work under. While he did have some favorites and treated them generously, most remember him as a direct man, excessively so, who usually preferred candor over dissimulation, kept confidences well, and shared information on a need to know basis. Others recall Burns as cagey by nature and a bit too willing to shift responsibility for mistakes to others.

Consequently, when persons under Burns' governance did not perform as expected, he would tell them so in a manner not quickly forgotten. This combination of demanding high standards of performance and near compulsive candor probably accounts for his enduring reputation as a difficult person. One elderly member of the Holy Cross Congregation at Notre Dame during the 1960s, remembering Burns and reflecting on his personality and roles in university and congregation affairs, described him as the meanest man he had ever known.[1]

However formal and perhaps even insensitive Burns may have appeared in some of his personal relations, he was the oldest and demonstrably the best-prepared Holy Cross priest ever to assume the presidency of the university. He was also probably the luckiest man ever to hold that office. The financial crises of Cavanaugh's last years ended with the war. Students returned to the university in the fall of 1919 in record numbers, and no one was turned away. As Burns reported to the National Association of State Universities in 1921, Notre Dame did not "favor adoption of specially rigid standards of admission" or "any measures for the purpose of excluding students either from the institution as a whole or from the professional schools."[2] Such a policy might become necessary in the future, he added, when we knew how many students we could care for, but at the moment we have "accepted all students who came to us."[3]

Young men, many former veterans of the war, flooded into the collegiate departments in the fall of 1919, raising enrollments there to over a thousand, that is, amounting to almost 65 percent of all of the students attending Notre Dame. Residence halls were filled to capacity. Nearly two hundred and fifty collegians had to find lodgings in South Bend. Two years later, collegiate enrollment passed fifteen hundred and nearly six hundred students were living in town. Indeed, Burns faced what was for him a happy problem, but a problem nonetheless and one whose solution could not be deferred and would profoundly affect the future development of the university. Being the man he was, Burns knew what to do and without much deliberation or discussion proceeded to do it.

Burns decided to find space for this sudden influx of postwar college students by limiting the enrollment of preparatory pupils. Moreover, if the growing number of collegians seeking admission to the university held up, Burns was ready and willing to begin phasing out the entire preparatory school department. Burns made these decisions after a close examination of admission applications during the summer of 1920.[4]

While the preparatory school was a long-established and profitable operation, it consumed more than a third of the teaching time of the staff, occupied space and facilities much needed by the college, and impacted negatively upon overall faculty quality.[5] Simply stated, in Burns' judgment, the presence of large numbers of small boys at the university added nothing to the intellectual quality of life or academic excellence of the institution.

To be sure, Burns made this decision on his own without much input from other university officials, but it was not a decision suddenly or lightly made. For many years Burns had argued in print and in private correspondence for formal separation of Catholic colleges from their feeder preparatory schools. As early as 1899, Burns had observed that in the United States there was not a single Catholic college wherein a majority of enrolled students were not preparatory pupils. Moreover, for the past twenty years the Catholic Education Association had been advocating the establishment of diocesan high schools in areas with large Catholic populations. Burns strongly supported the diocesan high school project, in large part because it could be a mechanism for moving Catholic secondary students off Catholic college campuses.[6]

As Burns saw the developing world of American higher education at that time, the simple fact of Catholic colleges sharing facilities, faculty, and resources with secondary schools located on their campuses had prevented them from achieving levels of academic performance comparable to other private and public colleges.[7] He eliminated the freshman and sophomore years of the preparatory department in the fall of 1920 and closed the entire school after graduating the last senior class in the spring of 1922.

Surprisingly, Burns made no moves against the Minim department during his tenure as president. These elementary students, numbering about one hundred, were completely separate from the collegians. Taught by the Sisters of Holy Cross, installed in their own residential and class-room facility, St. Edward's Hall, and directed for almost half a century by the formidable Brother Cajetan, C.S.C., the Minim department survived until the end of the spring term in 1929. Brother Cajetan had died in 1927 and within a year of that long-serving director's demise a decision was made to end the Minim program at Notre Dame. In the fall of 1929, two hundred collegians moved into a newly renovated St. Edward's Hall. For the first time in its eighty-seven-year history the University of Notre Dame was entirely and completely an institution of higher education.

Having irrevocably committed Notre Dame to an institutional future that would involve only Catholic higher education, Burns moved quickly to maximize the effectiveness of that commitment by improving organizational efficiency. On paper, for many years the university had been divided into colleges and departments. In fact, however, they were colleges and departments without deans or chairmen. It was a highly centralized, relatively inexpensive, inefficient, and almost totally nonresponsive system. A single academic administrator, the director of studies, personally administered all academic operations. He hired all faculty members, arranged all teaching schedules, and set the curriculum. Adopting virtually without amendment a reorganization plan prepared by the now exiled former director of studies, Matthew Schumacher, Burns proceeded in the summer of 1919 to divide the university into four distinct colleges—Arts and Letters, Science, Engineering, and Law. The College of Commerce was added as another distinct unit in 1921. A dean was appointed to each of the colleges and heads of departments within each of the colleges were named.

Another part of the Schumacher reorganization plan that Burns adopted was the establishment of a University Council, a body modeled on the Academic Senate of the Catholic University of America. This council would be composed of administrative officers, the deans, and one person elected by the faculty of each college. This council was intended to be a place where academic policies could be initiated, discussed, and formulated before presentation to the president for final approval and before implementation by the new deans and department chairmen. By early February 1920 this new University Council, or Academic Council as it later became known, was in place and functioning.[8]

Neither the appointment of deans and department chairmen nor the deliberations of the University Council precipitated an immediate academic or any other sort of revolution at the university. So many years of centralized power had left the faculty, whether cleric or lay, totally unprepared for undirected academic policy initiatives or action. Generally, during these years deans and department chairmen did whatever the director of studies told them to do and the new University Coucil approved whatever the president or director of studies presented to them.[9] All of these administrative changes, nonetheless, were significant because they created an institutional basis for a gradual development of an effective policy-making structure for the university. Whatever the future practical influence of individual directors of studies over academic affairs at Notre Dame might be, the formal authority of that office had been much diminished.

Henceforth, instead of only one academic officer being responsible under the president for the formulation of academic policy for the entire university, for recruitment and evaluation of faculty, and for setting college curricula, several deans and department chairmen, each presumably an expert in a particular area, shared some of these responsibilities with the director of studies. Burns and his friends assumed that the effect of such sharing would be beneficial for the entire university community and was absolutely necessary if Notre Dame was to make any sort of mark in American higher education.

In truth, however, substantial changes in the way decisions were made or who made them were minimal. In 1921 Burns candidly responded to a survey on the role of faculty in governance in American colleges and universities conducted by the American Association of University Professors (AAUP) by admitting that in matters such as the selection of the president or of other academic officers and in the making of the budget, "The faculty has no voice."[10] Thus it was to remain at Notre Dame for over half a century.

By 1920, 35 percent of the Notre Dame faculty who had no voice in important matters of university governance were laymen. On the issue of hiring lay professors, the Veneziani affair notwithstanding, Burns totally abandoned the policies of his predecessors. He did so out of necessity and because of his knowledge of what was happening in American higher education.

Bright students, or for that matter even average students, no longer studied the classics. That trend was clear enough at Notre Dame. Two-thirds of the college students at the university in 1920 were taking courses in business, law, science, and engineering. After many years of experience as director of the Holy Cross House of Studies in Washington, D.C., Burns knew that few Holy Cross priests were prepared to teach courses in those fields. If Notre Dame was to grow and prosper, it needed to provide the kind of specialized courses that would attract students. In the end, the combined realities of a small religious community and ever-increasing student enrollments in professional courses forced the hiring of more lay faculty.

Burns did more than just hire lay faculty, his administrative reorganization actually brought laymen into positions of influence at Notre Dame for the first time. Two of the first five deans and fourteen of the first twenty-two department chairmen were laymen, as were five members of the first University Council.[11] Other lay faculty not in policy-influencing positions now had easier access to someone who was, and of course possibilities for expression quickly became abundantly available for those desiring it in the new mechanism of departmental meetings.

However, it must also be said that while laymen might be needed at the university as teachers, scholars, scientists, and even as administrators, neither Burns nor anyone else at Notre Dame in 1920 thought for a moment that perhaps someday laymen might actually run the place. Indeed, the university could not survive and grow without lay faculty, but no one doubted that Notre Dame present or future would be a far different place if the Congregation of Holy Cross was not firmly in charge.

— ii —

Burns' only reservations about introducing more laymen into the Notre Dame faculty were financial ones. He worried about the inability of the university to pay the salaries required to attract highly qualified teachers and scholars to Notre Dame.[12] Nevertheless, Burns was determined to recruit as many qualified laymen as his resources would allow. All things considered, Burns did rather well.

Between 1919 and 1922 the size of the lay faculty increased from 34 out of about 100 to 62 out of about 165. This expansion was qualitative as well as quantitative. As an acute and knowledgeable observer of American higher education and as a former chemist, Burns was absolutely convinced that excellence in American colleges and universities was achievable only through strong science programs. He also understood that doing successful science meant doing research. If the president had his way, Notre Dame would offer strong science programs and its science faculty would have the time and resources to do research.

For example, in the department of chemistry, Burns opened a splendid new research laboratory and hired Henry B. Froning, lately director of a research project at Nizer Laboratories to manage it.[13] He also hired a young man with a master of science degree from the Massachusetts Institute of Technology to teach industrial chemistry.[14] About Froning, Burns wrote to a friend in 1921, "we have a man who devotes most of his time to research. . . . My ambition is to have this kind of work going on in every department. But money is necessary for this and we have to proceed slowly and patiently."[15] Nothing would please me more, he continued, than to have a biologist here "who shall devote a considerable part of his life to research, but I am unable to provide for this at the present time." Unfortunately, biology teachers at Notre Dame were so overburdened with instructional duties that they had no time for research.[16]

Burns amplified futher his views of the value and importance of research activities in American colleges and universities in a response to an inquiry from the Division of Educational Relations of the National Research Council. There were "very few college or university teachers in the country," wrote Burns, "who cannot devote a little time to research or advanced study if they have the will to do so." He complimented the National Research Council for "most excellently serving the best interests of higher education by emphasizing the need of research."[17]

Finding the kind of men that Burns wanted and could afford to bring to Notre Dame was a difficult and protracted enterprise. He negotiated with Henry B. Froning for six months. Froning came to Notre Dame in 1920 and remained for the next twenty years, building a career as a distinguished teacher, researcher, and administrator, experiencing during that time moments of both high satisfaction and deep disappointment.

Even though Burns considered science and perhaps engineering to be the most important elements in the future academic progress of Notre Dame, he could not ignore the staffing needs of the commerce program and of the College of Arts and Letters. In 1919 Father John F. O'Hara, C.S.C., director of the commerce program and destined to become the first dean of the College of Commerce a year hence, desperately needed an assistant.[18] O'Hara's work load had become enormous.

The commerce program and the College of Commerce after it had been established had absorbed the bulk of the enormous postwar collegiate enrollment increase. It was a particularly attractive program for that generation. The commerce program promised good to excellent employment prospects after graduation and was not difficult to enter or to finish. It required no special language or mathematics prerequisites for admission, not much exposure to those subjects or to library work of any sort to complete.[19] Enrollment in the commerce program had increased from six students in 1913 when business courses were moved out of the preparatory department into the College of Arts and Letters to over three hundred in 1919. It rose further to 421 in 1921, when it became the college with the largest enrollment in the university, a position which it has rarely relinquished ever since.

While serving as dean and as one of six men teaching courses in this college, O'Hara was also prefect of religion for the entire university, as well as functioning as a tireless personal religious counselor for hundreds of students. Burns was well aware of O'Hara's work load and understood that there was not much more that O'Hara could be expected to do. This much overworked priest needed help at once even though teachers of business subjects were in short supply and very expensive.

Help finally arrived in the person of James E. McCarthy in September 1921. McCarthy was a recent graduate of Columbia University who had worked for two years as an overseas representative of the United States Transport Company in Buenos Aires. O'Hara had met McCarthy while visiting Argentina during the summer of 1920. He was greatly impressed by McCarthy as much as a potential candidate for recruitment into the congregation as for a teaching post in the commerce program. On O'Hara's strong recommendation, Burns hired McCarthy, a handsome and ingratiating man with no advanced degrees and only a few years of business experience, to teach students the principles and practices of foreign commerce. Once at Notre Dame, McCarthy was there to stay. Very conservative and outspoken on Catholic matters, McCarthy became a close and lifelong friend of O'Hara and succeeded him as dean of the College of Commerce. Opting for marriage and a career as a teacher and academic administrator over a religious vocation, McCarthy became a mainstay of the College of Commerce and a pillar of local and state Republican party politics.

Though liberal arts and humanities programs were never popular with Notre Dame students whenever utilitarian alternatives were available, Arts and Letters staffing needs remained high because of the many service courses provided for students in other colleges and programs. In 1921 the College of Arts and Letters enrolled less than a quarter of the student body but employed half of the faculty. Nonetheless, the enrollment increases in the fall of 1919 and thereafter had created a need for additional teachers of Spanish, history, and English. Burns wrote to friends at the Catholic University of America for assistance in identifying candidates.[20]

As an education theorist of some standing, Burns had written extensively over the years and spoken often about the special place of humanities subjects, especially philosophy, literature, and what he called a Catholic instinct or Catholic insight into cultural activities, in Catholic colleges and universities.[21] Though Notre Dame had clearly developed and was continuing to develop in a different direction, Burns' articles and papers on this subject argued that Catholic colleges and universities, because of their religious commitment, had both a unique competence and special mission to explain and interpret modern culture to a generation of confused and misdirected men and women. It was a most important mission and one that was eminently practical for Catholic colleges and universities to undertake, being nowhere near as costly as science or engineering programs.[22]

However, there were special problems in 1920 for teachers of humanities and social science subjects at Notre Dame as well as at other Catholic colleges and universities. The largest of these special problems was the Index of Prohibited Books. Many of the most important books regularly used in literature, economics, sociology, and history courses offered by most American colleges and universities at that time were on the Index.[23] The simple meaning of that fact was that without special permission from appropriate religious authorities Catholic professors and students were forbidden to read any and all of such banned material.

In the past, local bishops had been empowered to provide Catholic professors and students with limited permission to access prohibited books, but in the reactionary postwar climate of Rome, diocesan authority for granting such permission had been withdrawn. As Burns reported to a friend, this situation had created a major educational crisis at the university. With over sixteen hundred students registered in all sorts of courses, it was inevitable that "prohibited books would have to be dealt with and used sometimes." One could not teach economics without referring to John Stuart Mill, and John Stuart Mill was on the Index.[24] There were also many books advocating socialism *ex professo* that had to be read if for no other reason than to refute them.

Burns believed that the present policy relating to prohibited books was educationally destructive and an embarrassment to the university. Because Bishop Herman J. Alerding would do nothing about this matter at all, Burns decided to try to deal with Rome himself, indirectly, through a trusted personal intermediary, Father George H. Sauvage, C.S.C.

Sauvage was procurator for the Congregation of Holy Cross living in Rome. He was an energetic, experienced man of affairs, having spent most of the late war as a French army chaplain. Sauvage knew his way around the Roman Curia and enjoyed performing the kind of task that Burns had laid upon him. Burns explained to Sauvage the nature of his problem and then asked his friend to speak with contacts in the Holy Office and try to obtain for him as president and religious superior at

Notre Dame "a faculty of permitting to professors and students the use of such books whenever I would deem it expedient to do so." If possible, Burns wanted "the faculty to cover both books simply prohibited and books prohibited by censure." He did not ask for any faculty relating to "libri ex professe obscaoni" (obscene books).[25]

Sauvage had been well chosen for the job. Within ten weeks Sauvage was able to send Burns formal faculties for books on the Index. The president was much pleased by Sauvage's industry. He rewarded the procurator with a box of fine Havana cigars and thanked his friend for relieving him "from a very serious embarrassment."[26] Yet the faculties issued by the Holy Office and sent to Notre Dame were so limited as to have been hardly worth the effort expended to obtain them.

The permission given to Burns was personal and would last only as long as Burns was president and superior. It also had three limiting conditions. First, permission was granted to professors and students to read only those books which were proper for their education and whose reading was practically necessary. Second, the danger of "imbibing the poison contained in such books must be guarded against as carefully as possible." Third, professors and students must be advised that the permission obtained from the president to read such books was valid only while they were actually studying at the university.[27]

Indeed, being at once a modern university and Catholic was difficult in 1920 and because of the Index would continue to be so for the next forty-four years. Burns admitted as much to Sauvage, stating that without the faculties obtained by his friend, limited as they were, his difficulties on this issue were "from a view point of conscience, unendurable."[28] Though at the time Burns could not imagine that some sort of relief would ever be forthcoming, it was.

Because the permission given to Burns was personal, it would have to be sought again when Burns left office. Burns' successor, Matthew J. Walsh, had to ask Sauvage to go back to the Holy Office in the fall of 1922 and try to get the faculties renewed. This time Sauvage managed to work a minor miracle. He obtained the same limited permissions, but they were granted not to Walsh personally. The renewed faculties were granted to whomever was president of the University of Notre Dame and local religious superior without limits of time. Once granted, they would not have to be renewed.

Sauvage understood immediately what an extraordinary privilege he had obtained and urged Walsh to preserve very carefully the official document authorizing the new faculties and, above all else, not to misplace it. For his part, Walsh fully appreciated what Sauvage had managed and secured this now treasured document in the university safe. Never again would a president of Notre Dame have to go back to the Holy Office on this matter.

Anxiety and frustration over the problem of prohibited books notwithstanding, Burns understood clearly that the heart of a modern university was creation and dissemination of knowledge through research and publication. As a university president, Burns wanted to believe that a research and publication thrust was as important in humanities disciplines as in science and social science fields. While research and publication in the humanities was important, he did not consider it to be as essential or vital as in chemistry or economics.

What Burns believed was needed for humanities at Notre Dame as well as in Catholic colleges and universities generally were great teachers, that is, intellectually alert communicators of Catholic insights into the great cultural and moral issues of the day.[29] Such insights could come only from persons who were good Catholics, generally at peace with the Church as it was, tolerant of institutional eccentricities, and at the end of the day, mindful of hierarchical authority. If such great teachers were also of a scholarly disposition, did research and published the results of it, so much the better. In this matter as in so many others, Burns was lucky. Father Charles L. O'Donnell, C.S.C., lately back from wartime chaplain service knew of such a person and recommended George N. Shuster to the president.

Shuster was twenty-six years old in 1920. Born in Wisconsin, educated in Catholic schools, Shuster had graduated from Notre Dame in 1915. Like other bright students studying the liberal arts at Notre Dame at that time, Shuster had aspired to a career in journalism and creative writing. Indeed, after graduation Shuster had occasion to experience some of the uncertainties and hardships of Chicago journalistic life. However, in 1917 the war took the young man away from the Midwest, first to France and then to Germany, where he served as a sergeant in the Army of Occupation. Discharged in 1919, returning to Chicago and unable to find a job to his liking, Shuster was pleased to receive an invitation at the end of 1919 to come to Notre Dame and teach English beginning in the fall of 1920.

O'Donnell had known Shuster as a student. As a matter of fact, while a student Shuster had assisted O'Donnell in the preparation of a locally published eleven-page pamphlet, *Catholic Literature, a Reading List.* Moreover, as a published poet of some distinction himself and possessed by a profound and passionate interest in the late-nineteenth-century English Catholic poet Francis Thompson,[30] O'Donnell had a sharp eye for writing talent. Something that Shuster had published came to O'Donnell's attention, and knowing that the young man had a genuine appreciation for the author of "The Hound of Heaven," O'Donnell, now provincial of the Indiana Province of the Congregation of Holy Cross, asked Burns to make young Shuster an offer. Unaware that important people at the university had very high hopes for him, Shuster accepted the invitation, believing that a year at Notre Dame would be restful and agreeable. He left Chicago fully expecting that his time at Notre Dame would be brief.[31]

Once at Notre Dame Shuster had an opportunity to meet Burns and immediately the young man became one of Burns' favorites. For his part, Shuster was much taken by the intellectual power, knowledge, and candor of the president. Burns knew about Shuster from conversations with O'Donnell and also had been much impressed by the fact that during the year the young man had researched and written some scholarly articles offering a different interpretation of "The Hound of Heaven." Since scholarship of any sort in the College of Arts and Letters at that time was rare, recalled Shuster, the completion of these papers was perceived by Shuster's colleagues in the English department, and especially by Father Burns, as something of an event.[32] In time, Burns shared his vision of what Notre Dame could become with Shuster and urged the young man to help him realize it.[33] The president raised Shuster's salary for the next year by 57 percent, and although Shuster was only twenty-seven and had only one year of teaching experience and no advanced degrees of any sort, Burns appointed him head of the department of letters (English).[34]

Because of Burns' hiring, between 1919 and 1922 the budget for lay faculty salaries rose from $38,000 to $95,000.[35] Burns found the funds to handle the increases in the lay faculty budget wherever he could. He refused to renew the cafeteria and restaurant contract with Mr. Tsiolis and the Balbanes brothers upon expiration in September 1920. Instead, Burns awarded this contract to O. A. Clark of the Kable restaurant chain for six years at a higher annual rent and on the condition that Clark invest $18,000 of his own money to improve food preparation facilities in Badin Hall.[36]

Also in some instances Burns simply and unceremoniously denied contract renewal to lay faculty whom he believed could be replaced with better-qualified men.[37] He reallocated monies and deferred projects so regularly that even his vice president and other associates were chagrined by his apparent neglect of the university's physical plant.[38] Most of the funds for new faculty, however, came from the tuition income generated by the 50 percent increase in collegiate enrollment occurring between 1919 and 1922.

While managing this expansion of lay faculty to meet the needs of an increased enrollment, Burns tried to be as sensitive to their morale requirements as he was to their financial ones. In the first year of his administration Burns changed the order of faculty listing in the general catalogue of the university. No longer were priests listed first. Length of service at the university determined the placement of names. To the public at least, Sorin's "strangers" were now indistinguishable from other members of what was coming to be known as the Notre Dame family.[39]

— iii —

The academic unit most needing attention during the Burns' presidency was the law school. Admitting, training, and graduating students since 1869, the Notre Dame law school had enjoyed a checkered academic history. The lowest point of that history occurred during the very difficult year of 1917 when the American Association of Law Schools (AALS) rejected its most recent application for membership.[40] Since the spring of 1919 the law school had been housed in a renovated old science building renamed the Hoynes College of Law after the long-serving director of the law program and for many years its sole full-time teacher William Hoynes.

In charge of the law program since 1882, Hoynes was a genial, slightly pompous but very popular bachelor don residing in Sorin Hall, remembered best and affectionately as a campus character given to polysyllabic expression and grandiloquent gesturing.[41] One of the last acts of the expiring Cavanaugh administration was to proclaim Hoynes "Dean Emeritus" and remove him from his post as director of the law program. For that action Cavanaugh had every right to expect from Burns nothing less than eternal gratitude.

In the fall of 1919, the Notre Dame law school consisted of about 190 students, a faculty of four full-time and two part-time teachers, and a newly hired full-time priest-librarian to manage a law materials collection of about seven thousand volumes. The mode of instruction was a combination of lectures and case law analyses. Three of the faculty either were or had been city or circuit court judges and four of the faculty were practicing lawyers. Both admission and general academic standards were minimal. For students admitted out of high school, the program would take four years to complete. Students with one or more years of college work could finish in three years. Among Notre Dame students, the law program was perceived as a singularly undemanding refuge for dropouts from other university courses of study. The law program was described by the student weekly magazine in 1920 as a haven for "all of an athletic or oratorical turn of mind."[42]

As a first step toward improving academic standards for the law program, Burns chose Judge Francis J. Vurpillat, a member of the law faculty to be dean of the Notre Dame law school when he appointed deans to the other colleges in the fall of 1919. Next, as a second step, Burns imposed a prerequisite of a full year of college work, sophomore standing, for admission to the law school, with an expressed promise of a requirement of junior standing as soon as it was safe to do so.[43] Also introduced in 1920 was a one-year graduate program leading to a master of law degree and a six-year program combining regular undergraduate bachelor work with law courses leading to the awarding of two degrees. While the prerequisite of sophomore standing and other reforms had a positive effect on the development of the law school, the selection of Vurpillat as dean did not. He turned out to be the least effective of the president's deanship choices.

Vurpillat had graduated from Notre Dame in 1891, practiced law for many years in South Bend, and had served as a city judge. He joined the faculty of the law school in 1917. In 1918 Vurpillat had prepared a memorandum for Cavanaugh explaining why the application of the law program had been rejected by the AALS and detailing what he believed were the principal weaknesses and problems in the law program. The apparent good sense and clarity of that memorandum had been the basis for Burns' selection of Vurpillat as dean. However, once installed as dean, Vurpillat acted as if the post was an honorific one, a recognition of his personal worth rather than as an academic office with some authority and many responsibilities.

As a matter of fact, Vurpillat had convinced himself that an easy solution for some of the many problems presently afflicting the law school was to increase the prestige and dignity of the dean. A few months after becoming dean, Vurpillat began a campaign to have the university award him both a master of arts and a master of law degree. He insisted that this very small recognition given to an alumnus of thirty years' standing and to one who had given several years of service and sacrifice to the law school was appropriate and overdue.[44] Moreover, awarding the dean higher degrees, Vurpillat argued, would add some prestige to a law school that needed it, dress up the law school catalogue a bit, and it would make sense for the dean as the administrator of a new master of law program to be a master himself. Without any acceptance of this argument by university authorities or public announcement of conferral of a master of law degree by any institution anywhere, Vurpillat simply listed himself in the law school catalogue in 1920 as holding a master of law degree.[45]

For Burns and other university administrators, the dean of the law school had gone too far. His requests for a higher degree based on teaching and service were denied, and the catalogue listing wherein he had claimed to possess one was corrected in 1921. Meanwhile, other difficulties had arisen in the law school. Both teachers and students began missing classes. When Burns directed Vurpillat in the winter of 1922 to find out the extent of such transgressions and the reasons for them, the dean expressed surprise that keeping track of teacher and student absences was part of his duties.[46]

Advised that providing such an accounting was indeed the responsibility of a dean, Vurpillat supplied Burns with the information and explanations requested. He then proceeded to annoy the president and exasperate some of the law faculty and many of the law students by confounding his decanal responsibilities with an exaggerated notion of judicial discretion. Henceforth, Vurpillat tried to protect and govern his academic jurisdiction in the manner of an angry judge arbitrarily ruling disrespectful counsel and uncooperative witnesses in contempt. Consequently, for the remaining eighteen months of Vurpillat's time at Notre Dame the law school would be in a state of near constant turmoil.

In effect, by installing Vurpillat as dean and insisting that he perform as a dean should, the president had created an enormous leadership and morale problem in the law school. However, because of the press of so many other important and absolutely unavoidable issues Burns had neither the time nor opportunity to resolve the law school problem the only way it could be resolved. That very unpleasant task had to be left to his successor.

— iv —

One of the paradoxes of the Burns presidency was the circumstance that while he changed so much so quickly about Notre Dame, he touched college curricula hardly at all and was under virtually no pressure to do so. Apart from beginning a process which would limit the variety of bachelor degrees offered by the university and reducing the number of hours required to earn one, curricula changes during Burns' time were minimal. However, Burns could not avoid addressing the special problems of teaching and studying in Catholic higher education at that time, namely, philosophy offerings and required religion courses.

The special problem of philosophy offerings was by no means unique to Notre Dame. It was a common problem for all of American Catholic higher education. In 1879 Pope Leo XIII had mandated the study of

St. Thomas Aquinas as the official philosophy of the Catholic Church, but the progress of the neoscholastic revival had been uneven. This was particularly so at Notre Dame, because there was no easy way for persons to be trained as teachers of Thomistic philosophy. Father Stanislaus Fitte, C.S.C., one of Morrissey's conservative friends, offered Scholastic disputation as part of a course in formal logic in 1897. Also before the turn of the century, a course relating epistemological theories of early modern and modern philosophers from Descartes to Spencer to Thomistic epistemolgy was offered along with one that compared fundamental concepts of natural science with Thomistic positions. The first course explicitly described as Scholastic philosophy did not enter the general catalogue of the university until 1912.

Most of the students enrolled in programs in the College of Arts and Letters at the turn of the century studied Catholic philosophy for three years, while students in law, business, science, and engineering programs did so for only one. Most of the courses offered to complete these requirements had some Thomistic elements in them, but they met only once a week and were not perceived by students as very difficult or even serious. George Shuster remembered these courses as being taught out of study manuals without much understanding or interest by either teachers or students.[47]

However, Pius X's suppression of efforts by some European Catholic intellectuals to reconcile traditional Catholic dogmas with late-nineteenth-century thought in his condemnation of Modernism in 1907 was to change all of that. Subsequent papal decrees reaffirming Thomism as the official intellectual guarantor of orthodoxy had the long-term effect of making Thomistic philosophy the centerpiece of Catholic higher education. As such, for at least three generations of educated Catholics in America, Thomism was to be an exclusive way of knowing that inspired a distinctive manner of intellectual discourse and a range of perspectives on public policy issues readily recognizable by other Americans as Catholic.

The first trained and self-proclaimed Thomist at Notre Dame was the indefatigable and irrepressible Matthew Schumacher, who came to Notre Dame in 1904 aglow with his recent doctorate in philosophy from the Catholic University of America. Though required to teach German, English, and history between 1904 and 1906, he returned to philosophy after Cavanaugh appointed him director of studies in 1907. Immediately, he styled his field in the general catalogue of the university as that of "special philosophy." The description changed to that of "Scholastic philosophy" in 1912, when he offered the first course at Notre Dame explicitly so described. Schumacher continued to describe his field in the same manner until he left Notre Dame in 1919. He was the only person, cleric or lay, teaching philosophy during those years to do so.

Given the time demands of the office of director of studies and the very difficult problems confronting the university during the war years, the number of Notre Dame students actually encountering Thomistic philosophy presented by someone with genuine expertise such as Schumacher must have been very small. Consequently, the Thomist revival did not really get underway at Notre Dame until 1918, when a brilliant teacher, Father Charles Miltner, C.S.C., returned from graduate study with a doctorate from Laval University.

In 1919 Burns was a true believer in the centrality of neoscholasticism in the intellectual and theological life of the Church. As the superior of the Holy Cross House of Studies at the Catholic University of America, Burns had followed events connected with the suppression of Modernism. Like most priests of his generation with serious intellectual and educational interests, Burns fully accepted the pope's condemnation of the Modernists. He also accepted without question subsequent papal decrees imposing an oath on aspirants to the priesthood against the prescribed doctrines of the Modernists as well as regulations requiring acceptance of Thomism as the basis of the "sacred sciences" and of capital theses of St. Thomas as being non-debatable propositions.[48]

Many European and American Catholic thinkers embraced Thomism out of genuine intellectual conviction, and enduring and sophisticated works were certainly written out of that tradition. Indeed, careful definition and redefinition of terminology and subtle distinction making produced a method of analysis and an understanding of political and theological complexity that was insightful and persuasive. However, because the purpose of the Thomistic endeavor was to recover timeless truths from a medieval system of thought that would relate to contemporary moral and philosophical uncertainties, the whole Thomistic enterprise appeared to have an anti-historical cast to it.[49] After all, truth was truth and would remain the same notwithstanding the passage of time or changing circumstances.

For most American Catholic intellectuals and teachers neoscholasticism came to them by fiat. Acceptance of Thomist doctrines and principles was a function of authority and mastery of its methodology was a serious and difficult intellectual exercise. However, this exercise was supposed to have a mind-improving quality to it that purportedly stimulated clear thinking in those persons engaging it. Thomism was thought, by some true believers, to do for educated minds in the 1920s what study and recitation of Latin and Greek grammar had done for the educated

minds of generations past. Other enthusiasts, including one very prominent archbishop, believed that because of the clear thinking stimulated by
Thomistic methodology, mastery of it would make a person a better
lawyer, physicist, chemist, teacher, or physician.[50]

In American Catholic classrooms, Thomism largely became a required
curriculum to be studied and learned. That curriculum provided official
answers to a series of speculative questions about the rational foundations of Catholic beliefs and practices, assured believers that faith was
indeed compatible with the findings of modern science and scholarship,
and that great issues like the existence of God could be proved with certainty by rational argument. A few persons properly schooled and trained
could provide such rational proofs, many could not do it at all, but everyone attending Catholic colleges and universities between 1920 and 1960
was expected to try.[51]

No system of philosophy could be offered on such a scale without
losing substance in the process. As Philip Gleason has so persuasively
argued, Thomism assumed the role of an ideology in American Catholic
culture.[52] It provided the basis for an American Catholic intellectual outlook, a worldview, and, more narrowly considered, a Catholic viewpoint
on everything and a Catholic way of doing just about anything.[53] Most
important, the Thomistic methods of analysis and explication of theological and philosophical issues became a mode of argument easily trans-
ferable to other fields of intellectual activity. By the middle of the 1920s
the Thomistic mode of redefining terms and drawing distinctions had
become a uniquely and widely used American Catholic form of arguing
public policy issues.

The probative force of Thomistic theological and philosophical argumentation resided in its systematic employment of Aristotelian logic. In
such disputations, verifiable facts were generally not available, and conclusions logically derived decided the issue. However, in public policy
discussions verifiable facts were available, and logic, no matter how
perfectly cast, unsupported by verifiable facts was unpersuasive to most
of the larger society. As a matter of fact, Thomistic argumentation won
virtually no support outside of Catholic circles.[54] When employed in
public controversies, the Thomistic method was generally recognized as
a uniquely Catholic form of argument, frequently misunderstood, sometimes dismissed as a quaint medieval anachronism, and occasionally condemned as a devious technique for making bad causes appear good.

Within Catholic circles the commitment to Thomistic methodology
as an exclusive way of knowing was by no means universal or equally intense. There were extremists such as Father George Bull, S.J., chairman of

the philosophy department at Fordham University, who insisted that Thomistic methodology was not just the *best* way of unlocking the great treasury of truth and wisdom discoverable in the Catholic tradition, it was the *only* way.[55] For Bull and others of a similar mindset, answers to all questions that really mattered were already in the possession of the Catholic Church, embedded in its traditions as principles waiting to be discovered and explained.[56] Thomistic methodology, assisted by contemplation rather than by fact-accumulation research, was the proper route to the discovery and articulation of such vital principles.[57] From Bull's point of view, mastery of principles was much more important for achieving understanding than accumulation and rearrangement of facts. Other Catholic intellectuals and educators, including fellow Jesuits, disagreed with Bull's extremist views on Thomism and Thomistic methodology but recognized Thomism in every practical way as the official ideology of the Church.

When compared with Bull on the matter of Thomistic methodology, Burns, Miltner, and others at Notre Dame were moderates. Nonetheless, like most other American Catholic educators of that time, Burns fully accepted for Thomism the august and privileged position in Catholic theological and intellectual life that papal authority had given it. Moreover, as the new president of Notre Dame, Burns adopted as a first priority the introduction of Thomistic principles and methods into all collegiate curricula at the university. As a first step, Burns established a department of philosophy at Notre Dame for the first time in 1920 and appointed Miltner to head it.

Once installed, Miltner made the point in a report to the president that "Catholic philosophy should be in reality as well as in theory the main subject in the curriculum of the University."[58] Moreover, the three members of the philosophy department, Miltner added, had "formulated a full four-year program leading to a Bachelor in Philosophy, but for lack of sufficient professors it is impossible to put this program into effect."[59] At the moment, Burns and Miltner did what they could. They founded the St. Thomas Aquinas Philosophical Society, a club open only to philosophy majors wherein special lecturers appeared and student papers were presented and discussed. The shortage of professors was remedied as soon as resources would allow. For new positions, no department in the College of Arts and Letters would have a higher priority. After all, it was Thomistic philosophy that made Catholic higher education authentically Catholic. It followed then that required courses in Thomistic philosophy would be taught to masses of students in all of the undergraduate colleges of the university for the next fifty years.

Throughout American higher education as well as at Notre Dame, required courses have always been the bedrock upon which academic empires were built. The imperialist tendencies of the Notre Dame philosophy department appeared early and have remained generally unchallenged ever since. The best and brightest members of the Holy Cross Congregation were sent off to study Thomistic philosophy and the best-credentialed, most published, and highest paid lay professors in the College of Arts and Letters were hired to teach it. Within the context of Notre Dame academic politics over the next half century Thomism became a protected special interest and its locus, the philosophy department, an ever-expanding monopolizer of available human and financial resources.

What is extraordinary about this preferred status for philosophy in the Notre Dame curriculum was the fact that this status outlived the confessional reasons that had established it. Even when, fifty years later, Thomism was quietly abandoned as the official ideology of the Catholic Church after the Second Vatican Council and when divisions among and between Thomists had become sharp and deep enough to diminish the authenticity of any one version, a two-course philosophy requirement remained for all Notre Dame undergraduates.

During the many years of preferred status for Thomistic philosophy in the curriculum, too much had been invested in faculty, too many professors receiving relatively high pay held permanent contracts to risk the possible staff reductions that elimination of a university-wide philosophy requirement might necessitate. Neither academic politics nor current perceptions of financial reality would allow further reduction of the philosophy requirement, no matter what had happened to Thomism as an official ideology. Students had to be found for some quality professors who, for many good reasons, could not and should not be let go. To be sure, in time, some professors who were uncomfortable in what was to become a changed and much more eclectic philosophical environment at Notre Dame, and perhaps personally wounded by the diminished status of a tradition to which they had given much of their working life, left or retired. Others turned to the field of history of philosophy or even to creative literature as a principal academic activity. In the end, the philosophy department adjusted internally to the demise of Thomism as the official Catholic way of knowing by recruiting new people trained in other traditions. Because the two-course philosophy requirement for all Notre Dame students continued, the philosophy department more or less maintained its size, overall academic quality improved immeasurably, and its budget continued to grow and grow.

No longer, however, was the justification for the privileged status of philosophy in the curriculum one of providing much-needed mental exercises in clear thinking or of mastering an official Catholic way of knowing. Students should experience two required courses in philosophy in order to encounter intellectually in a formal and systematic way teleological and epistemological problems that Catholics ought to be interested in. In facilitating these intellectual encounters over issues such as the existence of God, the nature of knowledge and belief, or immortality, and depending on the skill of the facilitator, one philosopher or philosophical system was almost as good as any other. Neither Fathers Burns nor Miltner, to say nothing of Bull, would have approved. These three men never said or wrote that it would be better to have no philosophy requirement at all if the philosophy taught and studied was not Thomist, but they probably would have if asked.

— v —

In American Catholic higher education, required courses in religion were not the norm until well after the turn of the century. As a matter of fact, probably the first person to offer religion courses to undergraduates as formal academic subjects was Father John Montgomery Cooper of the Catholic University of America in 1909.[60] Required religion courses did not come to Notre Dame on a regular basis in either the college or the preparatory department until 1920, and an academic department of religion was not established until 1923.

The sparsity of such offerings in American Catholic colleges and universities does not mean that the place of formal courses in religion in Catholic higher education curricula had not been discussed often and passionately at meetings of the Catholic Education Association, because it had. Catholic educators were uncertain about what the objectives of such courses ought to be, how objectives once defined were to be achieved, and what Protestants and other American educators might think or say about the American Catholic higher educational enterprise for trying to teach religion as an academic subject. For all of these reasons movement had been slow.

All of the speakers presenting papers at meetings of the Catholic Education Association during the early 1920s accepted the commonplace Catholic notion that any education which ignored religion and morality was a radically defective education. To be sure, historically Catholic schools and colleges had justified their existence by emphasizing the religious and moral dimensions of their programs. However, expecting that religion and morality would be absorbed by students from the general atmosphere of Catholic schools or from peer pressure to participate in liturgical events did not appear to have worked. Most Catholic schools and colleges either had not taken up religious and moral education as a serious academic enterprise or had not yet learned how to do it effectively.

During the early 1920s there was great concern among much of the membership of the Catholic Education Association that Catholic schools and colleges were not successfully fulfilling their self-proclaimed educational mission. Generally, American Catholics were not Bible readers, and for most of them religious instruction of any sort ended at the ages of twelve or thirteen upon reception of the sacrament of confirmation.[61] Certainly, the behavior of elements of the American Catholic community as reported in the press and in criminal court proceedings testified to the failure of Catholic schools to effect either much moral improvement or transmit knowledge of religious truth. American Catholics were vastly overrepresented in prisons and in other institutions for social delinquents. Even spokesmen for an organization such as the Knights of Columbus had recently embarrassed themselves and their Church by displaying in a public controversy an appalling ignorance of Catholic doctrine.[62]

Part of the explanation offered for why Catholic religious instruction had only minimal impact upon the students receiving it was ineffective teaching. Most teachers of religion in Catholic schools wanted their students to like religion and therefore refrained from challenging them intellectually in religion classes. The rector of St. Thomas College complained that far too many teachers of religion preferred to entertain students rather than make intellectual demands upon them. Students were not held accountable for factual content and were rarely asked to generalize on the basis of learned facts. He insisted that the intellectual rigor of courses in religion should be comparable to what was demanded in other courses—a lesson in religion requiring as much reasoning as one in mathematics, as much imagination as in literature, and as much careful analysis as in science.[63]

Much more was at issue on the matter of teaching religion as a formal academic subject in Catholic schools and colleges than an alleged lack of rigor. Leaders of the Catholic religious instruction movement were much annoyed by Protestant criticism of their efforts. Catholics heard Protestant critics saying that their whole approach to religious instruction was misdirected and in the long term possibly even bad for the country. The substance of this criticism was that religion courses in Catholic schools and colleges overemphasized supernatural virtues, such as prayer, a sense of sin, the need for penitence, the necessity of grace, and ignored the natural virtues of honesty, truthfulness, loyalty to friends, and charity for the sick and needy.[64]

One Catholic authority on the purposes of teaching religion, Father Joseph V. McClancy, responded to such criticisms in 1922 by asserting the much stated Catholic principle that in all things service of God surpassed in dignity the service of man. Supernatural virtues always outstripped in value the merely natural virtues.[65] However, once having asserted that important Catholic principle as a justification of Catholic instructional priorities and practices, McClancy all but admitted that Protestant criticisms were close to the truth and ought to be taken seriously. At no time, McClancy declared, had the Catholic Church ever officially committed herself to the neglect of the natural virtues. After all, Christ had practiced those virtues fully and so should we. Time simply had to be found in an already crowded curriculum to deal with them.[66]

There was a similar ambiguity frequently voiced about the nature and complexity of specific theological knowledge communicated in high school and collegiate religious education programs. McClancy described as a misconception the notion that informing youth about the beliefs of their religion was or ought to be a major objective of formal courses in religion. He admitted that development of intellect entered prominently into religious education. It had to. For him as for most teachers of that generation, development of intellect through selected reading and recitation was the only way to teach anything. However, the principal objective of all religion courses, the fundamental purpose of the whole Catholic religious instruction enterprise was formation of character, development of the will through acquiring habits of right service of God.[67]

In the end, the practical point of religious instruction was to get students to frequent the sacraments of confession and Holy Communion.[68] To be sure, nothing approaching a full or perfect knowledge of Catholic doctrine had ever been a prerequisite for fulfilling the traditional Catholic religious obligation of annual confession and Communion. However, advocates of more frequent Communion assumed that greater knowledge of Catholic doctrine and liturgical practices would encourage young people to confess and receive more often. Formal courses in religion offered by Catholic high schools and colleges would provide that knowledge.

The important decree issued by Pius X in 1905, *Sacra Tridentina Syndodus*, recommending greater frequency of Communion for all Catholics had pointed the way. Even more than those observant Catholics who customarily received Communion at least once a month, those receiving on a daily or weekly basis had to be more constantly in a state of grace and have right intentions about taking the sacrament so often. According to *Sacra Tridentina Syndodus* frequent communicants ought to be free of deliberate venial sin, appropriately confessed, and properly penitent.[69] Fulfillment of these conditions took time, demanded personal effort, and required cooperation from individual priests. Formal high school and collegiate courses in religion followed by frequent confession and Communion was after all "right service of God," but also it could be a method of moral training.[70] Furthermore, frequent communicants, it was assumed, more often than not in a state of grace and generally free of deliberate venial sin would exemplify most probably in their personal lives the natural virtues that Protestant critics had berated Catholics for neglecting in their religious instruction programs.

All was well that ended well. Some day, perhaps, Protestants and other Americans would understand that genuine American Catholic character, "ornamented, impregnated, supernaturalized by our holy religion,"[71] was rooted in Christian morality and supportive of good government and of the happiness of all Americans. Then again, perhaps they would not.

—   vi   —

As a frequent participant in the meetings and deliberations of the Catholic Education Association and a regular reader of its *Bulletin,* Burns was well aware of the movement to introduce religion courses into Catholic collegiate curricula. He accepted the arguments justifying such courses as requirements for all Catholic students and once installed as president was ready and willing to begin such a program at the university. However, the inspiration for introducing required courses in religion in all study programs at Notre Dame in 1921 and for establishing a department of religion at the university in 1924 was not really derived from movements in Catholic higher education. Instead, this inspiration came from within the university, from the industry and insistence of Father John F. O'Hara, C.S.C., the energetic teacher of commerce subjects and the serving prefect of religion.

Simply stated, Father John F. O'Hara was one of the most extraordinary men ever to be associated with Notre Dame, as his later career as auxiliary bishop of the Military Ordinariate, bishop of Buffalo, and cardinal archbishop of Philadelphia testifies.[72] O'Hara was blessed with a very high level of intelligence, an enormous capacity for work, an unshakable optimism about any project undertaken, and a most retentive memory. Though not trained in science or in any other academic discipline for that matter, he highly valued scientific research and greatly respected scientists. O'Hara was interested in history, especially Latin American history and was fascinated by economics. He accepted all contemporary Catholic assumptions about the place of Scholastic philosophy in Catholic higher education and its presumed value in developing clear thinking. O'Hara had no patience and considerable antipathy for sociology and other social sciences. He absolutely abominated the name and the concept of social studies. Unless literature provided some sort of moral inspiration, he saw little value and much danger in it. O'Hara had no use whatsoever for contemporary American literature and regarded such a writer as Hemingway as a purveyor of pornography. He was a perfervid anticommunist and valued loyalty to Church, country, and Notre Dame as a standard by which students and faculty should be measured. O'Hara was absolutely devoted to Father Burns and to the task of developing Notre Dame into a major university.

To most people who knew O'Hara with any degree of intimacy, he appeared supremely self-confident and ever optimistic. Difficulties did not intimidate him, and problems were to be solved. Blessed with an extraordinary memory and a quick if not always reflective mind, O'Hara preferred immediate answers and action to deliberation and delay. His manner of delivering rapid responses to all sorts of questions never failed to impress. When in that mode, any response, even a wisecrack, was better than no response at all. Not everyone would be or could be satisfied, but no one went away unanswered.

For others who did not know O'Hara well that self-confidence and rapid response technique projected arrogance. On most matters and in most situations he was a decisive man, but when pressed by time and circumstances that otherwise admirable quality sometimes became uncomfortably arbitrary. Father John O'Hara could be the best of friends and the worst of enemies.

All accounts of O'Hara agree on three things. First, in the many jobs he had in a long and illustrious career he never displayed a single iota of vainglory or pretension. Second, no priest on the Notre Dame campus ever served more time in the confessional than Father John O'Hara. He was most satisfied in the role of confessor and happiest in the job of prefect of religion at Notre Dame, an office that he enriched and transformed by completely disassociating it from enforcement of disciplinary regulations. To all students O'Hara tried to be a friend and counselor, never a cop. His friendliness to students was limitless; most of them knew that and responded to his pastoral programs accordingly. Third, he had a lifelong love affair with statistics. O'Hara collected statistics on all sorts of subjects throughout his entire life. Once collected, he manipulated them this way and that way. He drew inferences and made judgments, saw meaning in such numbers when others did not. He was very proprietary about the data he collected and was extremely loathe to share any of it with other investigators.

For all of his ability and energy, O'Hara was no intellectual. He had no patience whatsoever for the criticizing and evaluative social roles of intellectuals. If anyone had mistakenly described O'Hara as an intellectual, he would have been the first one to deny that such an appellation fitted him.

Ever since becoming prefect of religion in October 1917, O'Hara had been a tireless advocate of the practice of frequent confession and Holy Communion. O'Hara believed strongly that students who deported themselves in ways that would enable them to receive Communion daily would be living authentic Christian lives and be so constantly in a state of grace that all other problems of life and work would be solved or significantly minimized. O'Hara saw himself in his role as prefect of religion and as an advocate of frequent Communion as obliged to banish from the lives of students as much as possible anything that might obstruct the pursuit of that sort of sacramental life.[73] For O'Hara, the principal deterrents to daily Communion were improper books, contemporary American novels, and the girls who frequented South Bend's public dance halls.[74] In the words of O'Hara's biographer and longtime personal acquaintance, Father O'Hara's notion of an ideal Notre Dame man was one "who found clean living and happiness in his work because he lived so that he could receive Holy Communion every day."[75]

In order to help fashion such ideal Notre Dame men, O'Hara needed a media more efficient than personal counseling and preaching. During the fall of 1921, he found one. It was the *Religious Bulletin.* Within a year of its first appearance the *Religious Bulletin* became a one-page daily newspaper packed with special messages, statistics about Communions received, requests for prayers for the sick or the dead, exhortations to turn away from improper books, and observations on what was called the evils of naturalistic philosophies. The *Religious Bulletin* quickly became a running dialogue between a talented religious journalist and the student body. It also became a thorough-going Notre Dame institution for the next fifty years. Under O'Hara's editorship the language of the *Religious Bulletin* was seldom pious and never elegant. On one never to be forgotten occasion, O'Hara referred to the young women who frequented South Bend public dance halls as "pigs"[76] and on another he described some contemporary American novels as "best smellers."[77]

Appropriate perhaps for a sometime dean of an undergraduate school of business, O'Hara insisted that the content and style of the *Religious*

Bulletin was no more and no less than an application of modern principles of advertising to the spiritual life.[78] Day after day he hammered at student foibles and suggested ways of expanding and improving one's personal spiritual life. His overall objective in writing and distributing the *Religious Bulletin* was to increase the number of frequent communicants among the student body, and in reaching that objective he appears to have succeeded grandly.

O'Hara kept careful records of the number of students receiving daily Communion in various university chapels. He prepared graphs from those records and correlated peaks and valleys on the graphs with campus events. All Catholic students living on campus were required to receive Communion on every First Friday. O'Hara's graphs show that large numbers of campus residents complied with that requirement. The graphs also reveal that the number of daily communicants increased significantly during examination periods, on holy days, and whenever a student died from illness or accidental causes. Numbers decreased sharply during periods of very cold and snowy weather and after football games, Knights of Columbus dances, and St. Patrick's Day celebrations. Overall during the decade of the 1920s, the number of daily communicants at the university increased steadily, rising from a daily average of 507 in December 1920 to 1,324 in December 1928. Whatever critics might say about O'Hara's pastoral methods, there was no doubt that students responded to them and came to the altar rail in ever increasing numbers.[79]

Much of what O'Hara wrote in the *Religious Bulletin,* as he himself claimed, was caricature rather than portrait, "for a portrait is too true to be comfortable, while the exaggerations of a caricature carry home a point without leaving too much of a sting."[80] In other words, O'Hara purposely exaggerated language and situations for effect. His statements in the *Religious Bulletin* about life and work at Notre Dame should not have been taken literally, though they frequently were when read off campus by critics of his pastoral policies and of his controversial advocacy of frequent Communion, especially Communion received outside of Mass.

The idealized community of young Catholic gentlemen, daily communicants and ever in a state of grace, praying, excelling in sport, studying, and avoiding all occasions of sin in literature, film, popular music, and life describable from O'Hara's statements in the *Religious Bulletin* never existed anywhere. Father John O'Hara knew that. However, he absolutely refused to believe that steps toward creating such a community of young Catholic gentlemen at Notre Dame were either misdirected or wasted efforts. During O'Hara's tenure as prefect of religion undeniably the practice of frequent Communion became a widespread devotional experience for a large part of the Notre Dame student body. At the same time, under

O'Hara's editorship the *Religious Bulletin* was undeniably a primary vehicle for the dissemination of anti-intellectual prejudices and attitudes among that same student body.

In order to discover whether or not his pastoral program was in fact making a difference in the lives of Notre Dame students, O'Hara prepared in 1921 the first of several questionnaires probing into the extent and quality of student religious practices. The data collected by this questionnaire as well as later ones were collated and analyzed by O'Hara with the results being published and circulated in 1921 and thereafter as the *Religious Survey*.[81]

All items on the questionnaire were to be answered anonymously, and in 1921 those items included questions about the effect of daily Communion on one's personal reverence for the Blessed Sacrament and whether or not frequent Communion had helped respondents become better Catholics and better students, as well as questions seeking information about study habits, general behavior, and recreational preferences. To be sure, not all students responded to this first questionnaire, and some rude and uncomplimentary observations were scrawled on returned incompleted forms. The rate of return of completed questionnaires for 1921 was about 33 percent, more than enough for O'Hara to proceed with collation and analysis. O'Hara presented the results of his analysis along with selected student comments on each question in a special report to the president and then later to the general public in a small pamphlet of twenty-eight pages entitled *Religious Survey*.[82] The first printing of this pamphlet was a mere one thousand copies. Within four months three other printings totaling 19,000 copies were required.[83]

The *Religious Survey* attracted wide attention in the Catholic press in 1921 and became an annual offering with yearly printing runs exceeding 15,000 copies. The last *Religious Survey* of this type appeared in 1938. During the 1920s copies of the *Religious Survey* were bound up with the official general catalogue of the university and distributed to prospective freshmen students by the admissions office. Despite the inevitable controversy surrounding the preparation, publication, interpretation, and use of the *Religious Survey*, it was perceived by university officials as an effective recruiting device.

In the data collected and analyzed in 1921, O'Hara found abundant evidence that the practice of frequent Communion had improved the spiritual and personal lives of the vast majority of respondents to his questionnaire. According to O'Hara, students who were or had become frequent communicants believed themselves to be more devout Catholics, better persons, and brighter students because of that practice.

The *Religious Survey* also provided O'Hara with information about circumstances and situations affecting student morale and spiritual growth that needed correction. For example, he concluded from the survey that the Sunday High Mass in Sacred Heart was unpopular because the music was unappealing, student knowledge of the Mass was so meager, and liturgical expectations were so low.[84]

Also, responses to items on the questionnaire appeared to have confirmed the existence of a situation in the College of Arts and Letters that O'Hara did not like, had long suspected, but could not prove. Responses revealed what O'Hara described as a "woeful neglect" of Catholic authors and Catholic reading in English courses. More than half of the respondents had never read a Catholic book of any sort while in college. Of those students responding to a question asking the name of their favorite Catholic author, the most preferred writer was Father Francis James Finn, S.J., author of the very popular children's book *Tom Playfair* and twenty-six others in the same genre. Cardinal Newman, required reading in several English courses, was the second choice, followed in a distant third place by Monsignor Robert Hugh Benson, an English Catholic convert best known for melodramatic historical novels about the English Reformation.

O'Hara believed absolutely that one's faith could be lost through reading. He turned out to be much better at banning books than reading and recommending Catholic authors for others to study and enjoy. The only serious Catholic intellectual ever publicly recommended as essential Catholic reading by O'Hara was Newman.[85] He was unable to identify any other.

However, identifying serious Catholic intellectual writing was not his chosen line of work. Others at Notre Dame ought to be more knowledgeable about such matters. He suggested to Burns that perhaps a talk with George Shuster, the new head of the English department, might resolve the neglect of serious Catholic reading which his questionnaire had disclosed.[86]

Apparently such a talk occurred. While cause and effect should not be assumed, because Shuster was already moving in this direction, the head of the English department first offered a course in the fall of 1921, "The Catholic Spirit in Modern English Literature." Shuster's course examined English Catholic literary revival writers from Newman to Chesterton, along with non-Catholic writers from the same period such as Ruskin, Pater, and the Rossettis, who were fascinated by the unity and aesthetics of medieval Catholic culture. Rebelling against the sordid monotony of industrial civilization and realizing that life was not all utility, Shuster argued, this latter group were Catholic in spirit if not in formal commitment. Shuster's course was immediately successful and became the basis of a book published by the Macmillan Company in 1922. For his part, O'Hara was pleased by Shuster's quick response to the neglect of Catholic authors by the English department but was deeply suspicious of Shuster's notion that Protestant, agnostic, and socialist-minded writers could be Catholic in spirit.

Other bits of information collected from the questionnaires persuaded O'Hara that greater freedom in relations with students at St. Mary's College was overdue. The high percentage of respondents to the questionnaire (37 percent) admitting to regular correspondence with non-Catholic girls was surprising. Better communication and more organized social activities with St. Mary's students might have the effect of reducing that correspondence and thereby perhaps avoid the dangers of immoral relationships or the many inevitable difficulties of mixed marriages.[87]

O'Hara also culled from his data miscellaneous remarks and complaints about the impact of disciplinary policies on student life and dutifully passed them on to the president for thought and action. One student complained that young men at the university were being governed by kindergarten principles. Another complained that the enforcement of disciplinary regulations at Notre Dame was more appropriate for an army camp or penitentiary than a college. One student, according to O'Hara, even described Notre Dame as a reform school for rich boys. Still another bitterly condemned those rectors who presumed to intercept, open, and read student mail. However, one student made precisely the point that O'Hara most wanted Father Burns to grasp in the summer of 1921.

Notre Dame is a fine old school, an unnamed student was quoted as writing on his questionnaire, but the whole student body would agree, he added, "that the enforcement of regulations is at present in the wrong hands."[88] In July 1922, the serving prefect of discipline was replaced. O'Hara's influence in the affairs of the university already great was growing.

The principal reason for establishing required religion courses at Notre Dame was O'Hara's concern for the spiritual welfare of off-campus students. With so many students living off campus, O'Hara complained, the spirit of the world will infiltrate into the student body. That infiltration, he added, "is one of the things our cloister is intended to combat."[89] Any sort of monitoring of Mass attendance of off-campus students was impossible. Requirements about receiving Communion on First Fridays were unenforceable. All that the prefect of religion could do was to require all Notre Dame students to take regular courses in Christian doctrine. In that way, off-campus students would be involved in some sort of spiritual program wherein perhaps the worst aspects of the worldly spirit might be countered.[90] Burns agreed.

In the fall of 1920 Burns approved introduction of a required sequence of religion courses into the curricula of all colleges. These courses were to meet only one hour a week for six semesters. Moral issues relating to the natural virtues, sin, and the Commandments were to be addressed first during the sophomore year, while dogma and worship were to be taken up later. These courses were designed and prepared by the prefect of religion and staffed by interested priests drawn from the College of Arts and Letters. The experience of this first year indicated that one hour a week was insufficient to cover the subject matter desired. Beginning in the fall of 1921, all required religion courses in the program were increased from one to two meetings a week and remained so for the next twenty years.

Required religion courses developed by the prefect of religion and taught by interested priests drawn more or less at large from the university community simply did not obtain an immediate academic authenticity with students or from faculty. The promise that such courses amounted to more than a walk through the Baltimore Catechism with time out for liturgical experiences had to be demonstrated. O'Hara was well aware of this problem and, true to character, was ready with a solution for it.

In order to obtain academic authenticity and uniformity in the subject matters treated and to provide proper supervision of religion teachers, O'Hara urged the president to authorize establishment of a new academic department of religion within the College of Arts and Letters. This new academic unit should be authentic in every way, that is, staffed by a regular faculty and supervised by a department head who was responsible to the director of studies for his personnel and programs. Once again, the president agreed. The department of religion was in place with O'Hara as head by the opening of the fall term in 1923. The special status of this new department was exemplified by placing it first, ahead of all others in the departmental listings for the College of Arts and Letters printed in the general catalogue of the university.

This union of the office of prefect of religion with the post of head of the department of religion in a person as energetic and as committed to a specific pastoral policy as O'Hara created a new situation at Notre Dame. O'Hara quickly emerged as an informal academic censor and as a moral arbiter of all things at the university. No one since Sorin had ever exercised such moral authority over the affairs of the university as did O'Hara during the 1920s and 1930s. For the next twenty years whenever O'Hara spoke, everyone listened, and increasingly responded to this dynamic prefect of religion and formidable head of the department of religion with a very polite "Yes, Father" or "Right away, Father."

As head of the department of religion, O'Hara was ready "to assist the department of English by suggesting courses of Catholic reading."[91] As prefect of religion, he placed the university humor magazine, the *Juggler,* under close observation. That magazine had been criticized in the Catholic press for printing off-color humor. O'Hara had several talks with the editors of the *Juggler* about the danger of scandal from unseemly jokes. He faulted them for not grasping the principle that suggestive jokes were out of place in a magazine published at a school dedicated to the Blessed Virgin.[92] He demanded and got an apology and a change in editorial procedure so that future scandal would be avoided. In addition, O'Hara recommended publicly that all copies of the offending issue should be destroyed and that all persons touched by this affair should participate in a Communion of reparation.[93]

As pastoral leader of the university community, O'Hara persuaded the president to include chapels in all plans for new student residence hall construction. According to O'Hara, chapels in residence halls were absolutely essential for the success of his pastoral programs. Students, especially freshmen, needed a good talker for a rector, he added, because they often have to be kidded out of their foolishness; but they also need a meeting place of dignity which chapels in residence halls would provide.[94] Again the president agreed. The revenue loss from rooms eliminated to create chapel space was a modest price to pay for the spiritual advantages of having chapels in residence halls.[95]

For Burns, introduction of regular courses in religion, creation of an academic department of religion, and agreeing to include chapels in all future residence halls completed the internal aspects of his modernization program for the university. However, modernization also required extensive changes in the way the university handled external relations and how it related to important outside public constituencies, that is, publics upon whom the institution was becoming increasingly dependent.

This external aspect of modernization in the long run would turn out to be more radical than anything Burns had done internally. As in most of his other undertakings while president, Burns' attempts to rationalize and improve relations with outside publics succeeded. However, he did so at heavy personal, emotional, and physical cost. The man almost worked himself to death.

The first of these outside publics requiring Burns' time and energy was Irish America, that very powerful and unforgiving custodian of the university's other ideology, Irish nationalism.

— 5 —

IDEOLOGIES AND MONEY

Among the outside publics to whom the university had become increasingly beholden was Irish America. The identification of Notre Dame with Irish America and with the cause of Irish freedom was long established and widely recognized. Even Sorin, whose early misgivings about the sensitivities and perceived behavior problems of Irishmen and Irish Americans have been recounted, recognized that both Notre Dame and the Holy Cross Congregation in the United States in effect had become Irish American institutions. On October 10, 1885, Sorin publicly embraced the cause of Irish nationalism.

In his capacity as superior general of the Congregation of Holy Cross, Sorin made a contribution of $100 to the Parliamentary Fund being raised in Chicago by local Irish nationalist groups organized through the *Chicago Citizen*. When making this contribution, Sorin announced in a letter published in the *Chicago Citizen* that it was offered on behalf of himself and on behalf of the members of his religious community, faculty, and students of the University of Notre Dame, most of whom were of Irish birth or descent.

There is no doubt that Sorin's embrace of Irish nationalism in 1885 was genuine and that this contribution and his statement accompanying it were very popular at Notre Dame and in Irish American communities throughout the country. For Sorin as well as for others at Notre Dame in 1885, in its righteousness the cause of Ireland was the cause of God. As such, over the next thirty years Irish nationalism became the most enduring and dominant element in the emotional life of the university community.

The specific element of Irish nationalism most evident at the university and perhaps best exemplified in the public speeches and private correspondence of Father Cavanaugh was a powerful disposition to be anti-English. Faculty and students were disposed to believe the worst about English society, institutions, and customs. English leaders were regarded as self-interested and untrustworthy, while English policies were assumed to be wrong and exploitative. Roughly and sacrilegiously put, the British Empire was God's only mistake.

When Burns became president of the university in July 1919, because of the war in Ireland and the atrocities daily reported, interest in the Irish cause was great. Emotions about the course of the struggle were intense, and the new president was deeply touched by them. Two large and flourishing chapters of the Friends of Irish Freedom were in place at Notre Dame, one for residential students and the other for off-campus students. In September 1919 Burns learned that Eamon DeValera was going to visit Indiana and be in the South Bend area in mid-October. Burns invited DeValera through Harry Boland in New York to come to Notre Dame to speak while he was in South Bend. Though the Irish Revolution was far from over and British forces appeared determined to put down the rebels at whatever cost, Burns addressed DeValera as the president of the Irish Republic and assured him of a very warm reception at Notre Dame. Faculty and students here, Burns insisted, were anxious to greet and pay their respects to the hero of the Easter Rising.[1]

The great man and his entourage of Harry Boland and Rev. James Grattan Mythen, an Episcopal priest from Norfolk, Virginia, arrived in South Bend on October 15, 1919, to a tumultuous welcome that included a reception committee of a hundred, an automobile cavalcade through the city, parades and bands, greetings from city and county officials, a speech to an audience of more than two thousand packed into a local high school, and a dinner and evening of entertainment at the Oliver Hotel. The next day DeValera went first to St. Mary's College, where he spoke at 11:30, then moved on to Notre Dame for lunch and another speech, leaving the campus for Detroit by way of Niles, Michigan, at 2:00 P.M.

Though DeValera was on campus for only about two hours, they were a memorable two hours. When his automobile cavalcade passed along Notre Dame Avenue toward the main campus, the great bell in Sacred Heart Church, which was rung only on special occasions, boomed out its welcome. The students were wildly enthusiastic. After lunch with university dignitaries, DeValera placed a wreath before Father Corby's statue. At the statue of this former president of the university and chaplain hero of the Battle of Gettysburg, DeValera drew a parallel between Corby giving general absolution to the troops before that battle with the absolution given to the Irish rebels before the Easter Rising in 1916.[2]

Next, he went to another part of the campus and planted a tree to commemorate his visit.[3] From there, DeValera went to Washington Hall, where the Irish leader addressed an audience of more than twelve hundred students, faculty, and guests. He spoke generally about the state of things in his country and then proceeded to make the same point that he had made over and over again ever since coming to America. He urged the United States government officially to recognize "the republic established in Ireland by the will of the people."[4] When DeValera concluded, he received what the *Scholastic* weekly described as one of the greatest ovations in the history of the university. It was a grand moment, and according to DeValera in a letter sent to the university later, the happiest day since he had arrived in America.[5]

The student turnout and rousing welcome for DeValera in the fall of 1919 was only one indicator of campus commitment to the Irish cause. Another indicator was administrative and faculty reactions to the tragic events occurring in Ireland at that time. Burns and others here were appalled by the Black and Tan outrages. In letters and in conversations with colleagues the new president questioned whether the very worst of German atrocities equaled what the Black and Tans were doing on a daily basis in Ireland. The government-directed terror in Ireland, Burns wrote, seemed to him to be the opening stages of a renewed Cromwellian-type massacre in the twentieth century. Burns was particularly heartsick over the devilish doings in his ancestral county, Tipperary, and could not understand why after so many years English leaders had not learned the simple truth that Ireland could not be suppressed.[6] Campus commitment to Ireland's cause amounted to more than student rallies and presidential statements. The university mounted two new academic projects intended as much to counter British censorship and propaganda as they were to generate tuition revenues. While courses in Irish history had been offered during the regular academic year for many years, the university offered an ambitious Celtic Studies program to interested students in the summer of 1919. No special degree or certificate was to be awarded upon completion of the program. This program was open to anyone, including those students not seeking college credits. Celtic Studies had been planned with the expectation that members of Irish American organizations such as the Ancient Order of Hibernians and the Ladies Auxiliary would come to Notre Dame in the summer and fill up these courses.

The objective of this program was to give students a correct and thorough knowledge of the language, history, and life of the Irish people from the earliest times to the present day. Burns strongly supported this project because he believed that the subject matter would soon find a place in

American public and parochial school curricula. He hoped that teachers would be especially attracted by the opportunity to study Irish history, literature, and language in the pleasant surroundings of the Notre Dame summer school.[7]

A grandiose schedule of offerings was planned. Three levels of Gaelic language instruction were intended. No less than four history courses, including the Social History of Ireland, Irish Political Movements of the Nineteenth Century, and Irish Influences upon Western Civilization, were advertised along with special courses in Irish Music and Gaelic Literature.[8] Staffing such an array of offerings proved to be impossible and student interest in Celtic Studies courses did not fulfill expectations. Two teachers were engaged and some Gaelic language and general Irish history courses were offered.[9] Not many Hibernians or their Ladies made the trip to South Bend to confront the intricacies of Gaelic grammar.

Celtic Studies courses were offered again during the summer of 1920, and Burns tried not to be disappointed by the lack of student interest in them. As he wrote in a letter to the national president of the Ancient Order of Hibernians at the end of the summer session of 1920, the Gaelic work done here should be viewed only as a modest beginning. He hoped that it would be possible to continue and expand what had been begun. The future of Celtic subjects in the summer school would turn on the number and quality of students attracted to them. Burns believed that a major intellectual movement would be required to arouse Americans to the value of the language, literature, and history of Ireland. "Educated Americans," Burns concluded, "who are not of Irish descent will appreciate nonetheless Ireland's contributions to the world's culture as soon as the evidence is brought home to them."[10]

No such intellectual movement among American Catholics occurred, even though incentives of a sort were offered. The Ancient Order of Hibernians and their Ladies Auxiliary provided handsome medals adorned with harps and shamrocks to be awarded for distinguished work in Celtic subjects in the Notre Dame summer school. However, very few students were sufficiently inspired or motivated to take the courses necessary to qualify for them. The summer school program in Celtic Studies did not survive Burns' term as president. The Celtic Studies summer program was offered for the last time in 1922.

Related to, but separate from, the Celtic Studies summer program was the heroic effort of Father Paul L. Foik, C.S.C., university librarian, to establish at Notre Dame an Irish National Library Foundation. Foik was a Canadian-born Holy Cross priest of very strong Irish nationalist opinions. As university librarian with a new and largely unfilled building in his charge, sometime in 1918 he conceived the idea of organizing an Irish National Library and providing space for it in his new facility.[11]

According to Foik, the establishment of an Irish National Library was a means to an end. That end was placing all of the resources of Irish achievement and learning obtainable in America and elsewhere within reach of all Irish people and their friends. The success of the Irish movement for self-determination would mean a renaissance of Irish culture and learning. Already, Foik believed, intellectual activity and moral strength had begun to alter minds and souls of all true Irishmen in the home island as well as in the adopted land of America. Foik had special Irish National Library Foundation stationery printed, wrote a fund-raising letter, and initiated through the mail a fund-raising campaign among clergy and other prospects in the United States and in Ireland.

Foik urged all true Irishmen everywhere to advance the cause of Irish liberty, help promote a new Irish cultural renaissance, counter English censorship of the press, and combat English propaganda by subscribing to the Irish National Library Foundation at Notre Dame. In his appeal Foik solicited gifts of money and books and promised to provide space in the new Notre Dame Library building for Irish books, periodicals, and manuscripts, as well as custodial and bibliographic services. Fund raising for the Irish National Library Foundation began in March 1919, and by 1923 Foik had raised only $1,500 for the purchase of Irish books.[12] It would appear that the project never progressed farther than Foik's original appeal. In the end, internal Holy Cross politics, abetted by an encounter with O'Hara over allowing a book on the Index to circulate, took Foik out of his post as librarian in 1924 and forced him into exile with Schumacher at St. Edward's College in Texas.[13] Though never formally dissolved, not much was heard about the Irish National Library Foundation after Foik left the university.

Although the Irish National Library Foundation turned out to be a dream unfulfilled, Foik's efforts to obtain funds for it had an absolutely unforeseen outcome. Foik sent out his first fund-raising appeal to Catholic clergy and other friends of the Irish cause in the United States and Ireland on March 15, 1919. One of those appeals, sent to a priest in County Roscommon, was intercepted, that is, taken out of the British Post Office by Security Forces. Extracts were made from Foik's covering letter and then dispatched to the Bureau of Investigation of the Department of Justice in Washington, D.C., on March 22, 1919. On May 21, W. E. Allen, acting chief of the Bureau of Investigation, sent a photostat of the extracts from Foik's covering letter to the bureau's resident agent in Fort Wayne, Indiana, with the observation that Foik appeared to be engaged in

Sinn Fein activities and that the agent in Fort Wayne, George W. Green, should take appropriate action.[14]

By some extraordinary error, Acting Chief Allen's letter to Agent George W. Green in Fort Wayne was misdirected to a man at Notre Dame with the same name, who then delivered it to the president. Given Burns' views on the Irish question, one can imagine what happened next. The incredible incompetence of Justice Department officials in this instance mirrored what most of the faculty and students at Notre Dame believed was President Wilson's very foolish national policy toward Ireland. Many at Notre Dame must have been amused. Certainly, Foik did not suffer from the experience. A copy of the extract along with a copy of Allen's letter to Green typed on University of Notre Dame stationery were passed on to Foik and then filed with other Irish National Library materials.[15]

Altogether, the end of fighting in Ireland in 1921, the establishment of the Irish Free State in 1922, and the Civil War that followed had the effect of diminishing the influence of Irish affairs on the life of the university. The long struggle against England was over. To most of the faculty and students here, the conflict between Irishmen in the Civil War was incomprehensible and embarrassing. Indeed, fighting for the sake of fighting seemed to be a national avocation. In any case, during the mid-1920s few at Notre Dame maintained an informed interest in contemporary Irish politics.

All of the university presidents for the next thirty years had distinctive Irish names and possessed distant relatives living in Ireland, but for them as for most faculty and students, the great cause was done. The Irish question was a memory and Irish nationalism had become historically interesting. To be sure, Irish writers and politicians visited the campus frequently during the 1930s, but they came here as curiosities, not as brothers. The easy identification with the Irish cause and the familiarity with Irish culture that had come so naturally to Fathers Cavanaugh and Burns and to so many other Holy Cross priests of their generation diminished and then all but disappeared. It disappeared also from most Notre Dame students. By 1930 not many of the young men proudly bearing Irish surnames were certain whether Munster was a county or a province.

However, one important aspect of Irish nationalism at Notre Dame lingered, quiescent usually but at times stridently active. Irish independence did virtually nothing to end or even soften the very long-standing anti-English disposition of most Notre Dame faculty and students. It would surface again with great intensity during the deeply divisive isolationist-interventionist controversy in the country and at the university during 1940 and 1941.

— ii —

Another of the outside publics with whom the university would have to deal in the new postwar world was the narrowly based, highly selective community of financial contributors, philanthropic foundations, and fund raisers. This was a community that university leaders knew little about and over the years had not tried very hard to reach. Finding endowment money for Catholic higher education in the years before World War I was very difficult. In 1919 the university possessed virtually no endowment. Outside of campus buildings and land, the only other permanent assets were some unproductive real estate in Chicago worth $75,000, funded scholarships and prizes in the amount of $17,000, and an endowed professorship in journalism worth $5,000. The only other source of cash income was tuition and fees.[16]

In a real sense, when university leaders publicly prided themselves on the fact that Notre Dame had grown and prospered without aid from the government or millionaires, they were making a virtue out of necessity. In the United States, government subsidies for Catholic education were simply not available, and the number of wealthy Catholics willing to make large gifts to Catholic higher education was small.

Middle- and working-class Catholics were extraordinarily generous toward highly visible projects that touched their lives directly. They supported parochial and diocesan church and school building projects with an enthusiasm that astonished Protestant observers. However, that enthusiasm did not usually extend to Catholic higher education. It did not extend to Catholic universities and colleges because for many middle-class and virtually all working-class Catholics, postsecondary education of any sort was an unrealistic expectation. Even if middle- and working-class Catholics had been disposed to give to Catholic higher education, which they were not, there were no mechanisms in place to encourage them to do so.

Even the alumni of Catholic universities and colleges had not been organized into fund-raising appeal groups. For example, when Burns became president of Notre Dame in 1919, the university was able to identify more than 1,200 living twentieth-century graduates. Of that number, only 10 percent had paid their annual dues to the Alumni Association in 1918.[17] The first organized fund drive of any sort had been launched among alumni in the fall of 1915 to raise $125,000 for a dormitory to be known as Old Students' Hall. Progress had been disappointing. In four years' time less than $50,000 had been collected.

To be sure, inexperience and inadequate organization were certainly some of the reasons for this failure, but there were others. One Chicago alumnus, James R. Hayden, suggested to Cavanaugh in 1916 that Notre Dame alumni had never been taught to give to their alma mater. The university, he continued, had "bred in her students and friends a spirit of *taking* rather than a spirit of *giving* . . . like an over indulgent parent you have served too well and demanded too little from their gratitude."[18] Whatever the reasons, Notre Dame alumni had not been pressed for contributions and few had given anything.

American philanthropic foundations had played no role whatever in the development of Notre Dame or of any other Catholic university or college. Applications from Catholic schools for assistance were unwelcome, and leaders of Catholic higher education knew it. For their part, those leaders acting through the Catholic Education Association had publicly censured the work of the foundations for exercising alleged dechristianizing influences upon higher education in this country.[19]

In view of that censure, the visit of Cavanaugh and Burns to the General Education Board and the Carnegie Foundation in the spring of 1917 was a bold move but also a desperate one. Burns reported to Morrissey how frankly Cavanaugh had explained the university's financial problems, the politeness of foundation staff to them, but the utter absence of any encouragement about future grant possibilities.[20]

That visit with Cavanaugh to the foundation offices in New York in 1917 made a lasting impression upon Burns. For him, the foundations became places to be revisited, resources to be developed. Through all of the exchanges and meetings following from Burns' administrative and academic reforms, the pressing need for money was never out of his mind and very often on his lips. While Burns was not the first president of Notre Dame to realize the importance of an endowment for the university, he was the first to take the steps necessary to obtain one.

Burns contacted the General Education Board in the fall of 1919 and began a correspondence with its president, Wallace Buttrick. The president of the General Education Board had not encountered many Catholic priests in his professional life and had never met one as knowledgeable and competent as Burns. Buttrick was much impressed by Burns' candor about the present state of the university and by his determination to improve academic quality there. Very quickly, Burns and Buttrick became personal friends who greatly respected and trusted one another. Though Burns was probably unaware of the importance of his friendship with Buttrick, by establishing it he had secured for himself and Notre Dame an advocate for the university within the foundation. After Buttrick's visit to Notre Dame in the late fall of 1919, Burns regularly received advice from Buttrick about how to improve the university's prospects for grant application success.

That advice included establishment of a Board of Trustees composed of laymen to oversee any endowment funds received from future grants or collected in fund-raising campaigns.[21] Burns recognized at once how important the creation and establishment of such a body would be for the university. Indeed, no written statements were ever received from Buttrick unofficially or from the General Education Board that laymen had to be involved in the management of future grant funds. Nonetheless, Burns understood that the existence of such a board at Notre Dame was a necessary condition for getting grants from foundations such as the General Education Board.[22] None of the great American philanthropic foundations of that time would give funds to a Catholic university managed by priests and brothers to use as they saw fit. When Burns argued the case for a lay Board of Trustees, the Provincial Council of the Congregation of Holy Cross accepted his conclusion that without such a lay board to manage grant funds there would be no grant funds forthcoming, ever.[23]

Burns moved quickly to establish a board of lay trustees. He asked William P. Breen, an alumnus and a former president of the American Bar Association to draft a set of bylaws for such a board. Breen's bylaws provided for a board of fifteen members. Three were to be *ex officio* members: the provincial, president, and treasurer of the university. Six members were to be chosen from alumni, and six were to be members at large. For the original board, Burns appointed the twelve laymen. Thereafter, vacancies among alumni members would be filled by men elected by the Alumni Association. Vacancies among at-large members would be chosen by the board itself.[24]

According to Breen's bylaws, Notre Dame's lay trustees were much less empowered than would be their counterparts in a private corporation. Board members at Notre Dame had no authority over institutional property or educational operations.[25] The board had complete control over all endowment funds, but that was all. A three-member finance committee elected by the board was authorized to make investment recommendations to the full board. All such recommendations had to be unanimous to go forward from the finance committee to the board. Majority approval by the board was required to implement finance committee investment recommendations.[26]

In time, however, as the board acquired more experience, advice would be sought from them on all sorts of issues affecting the financial operations of the university. When given, such advice was strictly advisory and in no way binding on the Notre Dame administrators receiving it.[27] Burns obtained easy approval of the new board from the Provincial Council because real authority in university affairs remained safely and securely vested in the Congregation of Holy Cross. By creating and establishing this board, the president had given up very little to gain a lot.

Burns proceeded slowly and carefully during the last half of 1920 to select board members. Among the first of the alumni members chosen was William P. Breen, the author of the bylaws. Breen accepted the appointment and in due course was elected by other board members to be the first president of the body. Other important alumni members were Joseph M. Byrne '79, a Newark stockbroker; Warren A. Cartier '87, a Michigan industrialist and financier; and Clement C. Mitchell '02, a Chicago banker. The most prominent and active at-large members chosen by Burns were Edward N. Hurley, a Chicago industrialist and chairman of the U.S. Shipping Board and Solon O. Richardson of Toledo, president of the Libby Glass Company.

The original board members appointed by Burns met for the first time on January 25, 1921, and attended largely to organizational matters. After hearing a speech from the president about grant prospects with the General Education Board, members proceeded to elect officers and then schedule their first business meeting for mid-November 1921. However, before the November meeting was held, Breen resigned from the presidency of the board because of poor health but retained his seat on it. Consequently, when the board met in November, it did so without a president. Burns set the stage for what turned out to be the most brilliant personnel coup of his entire presidency. He managed the election of Albert R. Erskine, president of the Studebaker Corporation, as president of the Board of Trustees and as chairman of the three-person finance committee.[28]

Erskine was an extraordinary self-made man. Born in Alabama in 1871, he was a moderately observant Protestant who had left school at the age of fifteen to become an office boy. A gifted salesman, Erskine did not remain an office boy very long. He joined the Studebaker Corporation in 1911 and rose through the corporate hierarchy, in 1915 becoming the first company president who was not a member of the Studebaker family. Extremely well connected with the leaders of corporate America and very knowledgeable about corporate managerial practices, he brought an enormous store of practical business experience and financial expertise to the university's new Board of Trustees.

For his part, Erskine was delighted to serve. He accepted Burns' invitation and attended the first business meeting on November 16, 1921. In the morning of that day, the board formally admitted Erskine to membership. Then, in the afternoon, the other members proceeded to elect him president of the board and chairman of the finance committee. Erskine described the event to his friend, Charles M. Schwab, president of the Bethlehem Steel Corporation, as being "railroaded through as president."[29] However done, Erskine, a man who had never finished high school, was flattered by the confidence that so many university-trained people had placed in him. He expressed to Schwab his great respect for Burns and the university for "the great educational work they are doing."[30]

With the board established in mid-1920 and with Erskine heading it in late 1921, Burns had in place a required mechanism to qualify for a General Education Board grant. The president was extremely optimistic in early 1920 that a grant would be forthcoming. He was optimistic because in December 1919 the General Education Board announced that John D. Rockefeller had made an extraordinary gift to them of over fifty million dollars for the specific purposes of assisting private colleges and universities to raise faculty salaries.[31]

On the basis of his contacts and correspondence with the General Education Board, Burns believed that an application from Notre Dame would be favorably received and made his plans accordingly. Since grants of this type were usually contingent upon matching sums being raised from other sources, Burns began discussions with other university officials about organizing a fund drive. Initially, the president had hoped to be able to announce a grant award and the start of a major fund drive at the June commencement.[32]

Though Burns' optimism about the prospects of a grant were well founded, the June announcement date was unrealistic. Before making a grant, the General Education Board was obligated under the terms of the Rockefeller gift to examine all institutional applicants thoroughly. Part of that examination was a formal site visit by foundation staff, and Burns tried very hard to get one as soon as possible. One of his tactics was to ask William Lowe Bryan, president of Indiana University, to write to Buttrick requesting the immediate dispatch of a visitation team to Notre Dame. Bryan obliged on January 21, 1920. He justified the urgency of the Notre Dame case on the grounds of the very important and unique mission of the university.

According to Bryan, Notre Dame was able to reach "a class of men, especially the Slavonic races, who will not go to any other than Catholic universities." Future leaders of our Slavonic groups, Bryan continued, will come from these institutions and will lead their ethnic brothers in this country either toward anarchy or toward a well-ordered civilization. Great benevolent foundations, Bryan concluded, can do much to insure the latter result. Nothing is more important at this present moment of bolshevism abroad and socialist threats at home than "to strengthen the hands of Catholic universities in this great and necessary work."[33]

Buttrick responded to Bryan's letter promptly and assured him that "two of our experts will visit the institution at the earliest practicable date."[34] However, Notre Dame's turn for such a visit was delayed until mid-January 1921. In the meantime, the chief financial officer of the General Education Board, Trevor Arnett, sent a number of inquiries to Burns intended to clarify the relations between the university and the superiors of the Congregation of Holy Cross.[35]

Burns prepared a lengthy explanation for Arnett's inquiries and in effect told him what he believed would best serve the interests of Notre Dame. He minimized the influence of the superior general and provincial in university affairs. Burns limited the role and jurisdiction of those two superiors to "purely religious matters."[36] The president emphasized the point that those two superiors had no authority over university property. The purpose of making that point was to assure Arnett that no part of any grant funds awarded to the university could be diverted or appropriated by the superiors of the congregation for other Holy Cross religious works. However, Burns' silence on at least one very important aspect of the authority exercised by those superiors in university business affairs was less than honest. He neglected to mention the fact that in 1920 expenditures of more than three hundred dollars of university funds required the permission of both the provincial and superior general.[37]

Arnett was satisfied with Burns' explanation of the relationship between Holy Cross superiors and the university. At least, he did not press further on this point. Burns had verbal assurances of a sort as early as the end of May 1920 that a grant would be forthcoming, but he had no idea how much or when the grant would be approved.[38] Arnett did not arrive for the required site visit until mid-January 1921; once that formality had been satisfied, the university's application was complete and the award process could proceed.

Arnett's report on his visit to Notre Dame was very positive. He had been much impressed by the president's realistic attitude toward the problems of the university and toward the important education services that Notre Dame could provide to the nation. Arnett had been fully persuaded that any grant the General Education Board might choose to make "would be carefully guarded by the Lay Board of Trustees, and would be rendering a real service toward education." Before leaving Notre Dame, Arnett told Burns that a grant request "would be given sympathetic and prompt attention."[39] One could easily argue that Notre Dame received this grant because Father Burns was its president.

On February 21, 1921, the General Education Board voted to award Notre Dame $250,000 for building a lay faculty salary endowment under the following six conditions. First, the university would have to raise $750,000 from other sources. This sum would be combined with the General Education Board grant to create a lay faculty salary endowment of $1,000,000. Second, pledges for the university's share of the proposed endowment ($750,000) had to be subscribed by June 30, 1922. Third, pledges obtained by that date were to be redeemable and the cash actually collected by June 30, 1925. Fourth, no legacies could be counted toward the university's share. Fifth, none of the income from the new endowment could be used for religious instruction. Six, the contribution from the General Education Board would be paid only when the university was debt free.[40] In addition, the General Education Board also authorized a special grant of $12,500 "to relieve immediate necessities of the University with respect to teachers' salaries,"[41] that is, to raise the salaries of valued faculty who were underpaid or who, like George Shuster, had a job offer elsewhere.[42]

Of these conditions, the only troublesome one was the requirement that the university be debt free in order to receive payment of the grant. When the grant had been approved, the university had debts of $73,500. This deficit, as had been the case with smaller ones incurred between 1916 and 1918 from construction of the new library, would be covered by funds provided by the Congregation of Holy Cross.[43] The problem for Burns and for the university was to maintain a debt-free condition until the grant payment was made.

This debt-free requirement for receiving the grant prevented Burns from borrowing funds to construct much-needed revenue-producing residence halls and not revenue-producing but equally needed teaching facilities. Consequently, at various times between 1920 and 1923 up to one-third of the student body lived off campus, enriching South Bend landlords and restauranteurs.[44] Similarly, classrooms were crowded, and class scheduling had to be extraordinarily creative in order to accommodate the flood of postwar students coming to the university. These circumstances were annoying and inconvenient but well worth enduring for the sake of the grant.

As a matter of fact, just about anything was worth enduring or doing for the sake of the grant. Burns believed absolutely that the life of the university was at stake. He wrote a deeply moving personal letter of thanks to Buttrick for all of his help and courtesies during the grant solicitation process. Burns stated his belief that the decision to approve the Notre Dame application had been strictly an educational one, fully in compliance with the rules and principles of all such General Education Board actions. It was a fact, however, that the grant to Notre Dame "was the largest appropriation that the Board has made to a Catholic institution."[45] Moreover, it would be amiss for me, Burns continued, not to thank you for "the warm-hearted desire you evinced from the very beginning to co-operate with us in the development of Notre Dame when we should make it possible for you to do so."[46]

In addition, there was a personal satisfaction in this grant award deci-sion that transcended the very generous financial benefits it brought to the university. This grant was proof positive that the General Education Board "does not discriminate between educational institutions on reli-gious grounds. . . . I have long believed that the time has come when Catholics and Protestants in America must stand closer together in order to preserve our common heritage of Christian civilization."[47]

Apparently, upon receipt this letter overwhelmed Buttrick emotion-ally. He referred it at once to John D. Rockefeller, the great benefactor of the General Education Board, to read. After a few days, Rockefeller returned what he described as "a beautiful letter" and observed that "making this appropriation was a wise thing to do."[48]

When Burns formally announced the grant award and the proposed fund drive to the university community on March 5, 1921, the president was very clear about the importance of the task before them. "The high-est interests of the University are too vitally involved in the matter," he wrote, "to allow the possibility of failure."[49] All true friends of the univer-sity, Burns concluded, "will appreciate the greatness of the opportunity which has come and will see that the necessary money will not be lack-ing."[50] Nothing in this world would be more important to Burns and to other university leaders over the next four years than the fund drive, and every other university interest, priority, and activity would have to defer to it. As the president had said, the possibility of failure could not be al-lowed and was not.

— iii —

Burns' determination to say or do whatever was necessary to insure the success of the fund drive was implemented forthwith. While courting the General Education Board in early 1920, Burns had not forgotten about the Carnegie Foundation. In January 1920 Burns went to New York to renew contacts with Carnegie Foundation staff that had been established when he and Cavanaugh had visited them in 1917. President Prichett was unavailable because of illness, so Burns had to settle for conversations with lesser officials. Burns submitted a formal request for a contribution to the proposed fund drive and then began mobilizing support for the Notre Dame application from friends of the university assumed to have influence with Carnegie officials. As Burns saw the present state of things at the Foundation insofar as Notre Dame was concerned, the prospects for a grant were very good, but nothing should be left to chance or to the vagaries of ordinary grant processing procedures.[51]

Burns enlisted the support of two newly appointed members of the Notre Dame Lay Board of Trustees, Samuel T. Murdock of Indianapolis and James D. Callery of Pittsburgh, who were known to some of the officials at the Foundation.[52] Burns went even further in that direction. He selected Morgan J. O'Brien, a justice of the Supreme Court of New York and friend of some Carnegie Foundation trustees, to be Commencement speaker in 1920 and an honorary degree recipient.[53] How effective Burns' influence-garnering efforts were is impossible to know. He certainly believed they were worth undertaking. The positive judgment by the General Education Board on the university's worthiness was probably far more decisive with Carnegie Foundation decision makers than these personal interventions on behalf of the university, however earnestly or perfunctorily performed.

In any case, the result of Burns' essay into influence mongering was a happy one. The Carnegie Foundation awarded Notre Dame a grant of $75,000 in late May 1921, and this grant became the first contribution to the fund drive. It was a very good beginning, perhaps too good and too easy. Burns had 10 percent of the required fund-raising match in hand before the drive had even started. Getting the rest would be much more difficult.

In the spring of 1921, the economy of the country was still languishing in the grip of the postwar depression. Consumer confidence was low. Housing was in short supply. Widespread labor troubles fueled exaggerated fears within the affluent classes of the spread of socialism among American workers as well as other forms of social and economic radicalism. For many reasons, public anxiety levels were high. Short-term thinking and present-mindedness prevailed. It was not the best of times for Notre Dame or any institution to begin a major fund drive.

Several other Catholic colleges and universities were already actively engaged in fund raising. Holy Cross, St. Louis, Duquesne, and Canisius all had campaigns underway.[54] Father John A. O'Brien, the popular convert maker, pastor of St. John's Church in Champaign, Illinois, and Catholic chaplain at the University of Illinois had mounted a formidable fund drive in Chicago for his controversial Catholic Center at that university. Even St. Edward's, a Congregation of Holy Cross college in Texas, lately devastated by a tornado, under its ever-entrepreneurial president, Father Matthew A. Schumacher, had planned a million-dollar appeal. Notwithstanding all of this competition for Catholic money, Burns went ahead and officially began the Notre Dame fund drive with a formal dinner for seventy-five South Bend dignitaries and special friends of the university at the Oliver Hotel on May 23, 1921.

Before this group of South Bend businessmen Burns was at his best. He communicated a sense of both deep crisis and great opportunity. Burns explained that much more was involved in this fund drive than simply raising a matching sum to qualify for the General Education Board grant. His objective was to raise two million dollars for the university in two years. The first million dollars, including the grants from the General Education Board and Carnegie Foundation, had to be pledged by June 30, 1922, and would be invested as a permanent endowment for lay faculty salaries. The second million dollars in pledges should be obtained by June 30, 1923, and would provide funds for constructing much-needed residence halls, engineering and commerce buildings, and additions to the gymnasium and athletic field.[55]

Burns' plan was an ambitious one but absolutely essential for the survival and progress of Notre Dame. As Burns saw the present state of the university, a moment of great crisis was at hand. Notre Dame would either have to increase capacity or limit enrollment. Every available room was reserved for next year. More than five hundred students would have to find rooms off campus. To increase capacity sufficiently to accommodate all of those Catholic young men wanting to come to Notre Dame, the university must erect new buildings and hire more lay professors. A successful fund drive in the order of magnitude proposed was the only way to pay for that expansion.[56]

The special roles of the South Bend and Chicago business communities in raising the needed two million dollars was critical. Burns estimated that at least $500,000 would have to be pledged and collected locally and another $500,000 raised in Chicago for the drive to succeed.[57] Not only would this fund drive affect the development of Notre Dame for the next fifty years, but the drive would bring the university and city of South Bend into a new cooperative and mutually beneficial relationship. A greater Notre Dame would mean a better-known and more prosperous South Bend. Most of the businessmen attending the dinner in the Oliver Hotel that night believed that Burns was right, and at least one of them, Albert R. Erskine, president of the Studebaker Corporation, was determined to do everything he could to make it happen.

Burns had begun well at the Oliver Hotel dinner with candor and inspiration. He turned next to organization, tactics, and strategies. The organization created for the drive was simple. It consisted of Burns, Vice President Walsh, Father John McGinn, C.S.C., a sociology professor given leave to work on the drive full time, and many interested alumni scattered across the country. Authority lines were also simple. Burns was in charge absolutely. He made all important decisions and initially tried to deal directly with everyone actively involved in the drive.

As the campaign developed, rough divisions of labor occurred. Burns handled the South Bend area and Indiana generally. Walsh opened an office in the Congress Hotel in Chicago, appropriately named on office stationery "The $500,000 Campaign for Notre Dame," and worked that region. McGinn was more or less responsible for everywhere else. Within a few months, it became apparent that after South Bend and Chicago, the most promising areas were New England, New York, Pennsylvania, and Ohio.[58] Consequently, McGinn spent most of his time traveling in those regions, calling on prospects, and meeting with local alumni groups.

With the drive officially under way, insofar as possible, Burns' first concern was to eliminate or otherwise undercut other fund-raising projects competing with Notre Dame at that time for Catholic dollars. Burns could do nothing about current fund-raising campaigns mounted by Jesuit institutions, but he was able to persuade his provincial to direct Father Schumacher to delay the start of his campaign to rebuild St. Edward's in Texas until after the Notre Dame fund drive was over.[59]

Another worthy Catholic charitable effort delayed in the South Bend area because of the Notre Dame fund drive was the project to restore the library of the University of Louvain, which had been destroyed by the Germans in the late war. Though approached by Judge Victor Dowling of New York, acting on behalf of the executive committee of the project, and Archbishop Patrick J. Hayes, who strongly supported it, Burns denied Whitney Johnson permission to come to Notre Dame and solicit one dollar from each student for the restoration.

Unmoved by the archbishop's involvement, Burns explained to Dowling that the university was in the midst of an endowment and building fund-raising campaign and that students here were targeted for contributions to it. Restoration of the library at Louvain was a most important and stirring endeavor, Burns wrote, "but under our special circumstances it seems to me that the principle of charity beginning at home has application."[60] Johnson could come to Notre Dame after September 1923 but not before.

Once again Burns had been candid and, from his perspective, brutally realistic. Some resources were simply not shareable. No matter how noble in purpose or by whom endorsed, no cause or project could be allowed to compete for resources that properly and rightly belonged in the Notre

Dame fund drive. That was the way Burns saw the situation and that was the way things would be.

About Father John A. O'Brien's campaign to raise funds in Chicago for his Catholic Center in Champaign, Illinois, Burns had several good reasons to be uneasy. As envisaged by O'Brien, the Catholic Center at the university would include residential, dining, classroom, and meeting room facilities. The purpose of the center was to take advantage of an opportunity lately offered by the University of Illinois to provide university credit for religion courses taught by properly credentialed persons in off-campus facilities. O'Brien saw this possibility as a marvelous opportunity to minister to the religious needs of six hundred Catholic students attending the university and to reach potential Catholic converts among the unchurched and lightly churched in the general student population.

The Catholic Center idea was controversial because O'Brien had represented it in fund-raising literature as a viable alternative to an authentic Catholic education provided in Catholic colleges and universities. O'Brien was and would be continuously attacked publicly in a series of articles appearing in the Jesuit periodical *America* for undermining Catholic education with his Catholic Center project. Though protected by his bishop, Edmund M. Dunne of Peoria, O'Brien incurred the hostility of Michael J. Curley, archbishop of Baltimore, for the same reasons. Curley formally complained to Rome about O'Brien's alleged damaging activities to Catholic education. Escalating controversy about O'Brien and his project made fund raising in some Catholic areas very difficult. O'Brien tried to counter those difficulties by obtaining endorsements from prominent Catholic educators about the importance of providing religious education to Catholic students already attending state universities. He sought such an endorsement from Burns early in 1922.

Burns was probably not intimidated by the rising controversy surrounding O'Brien. He actually wrote an endorsement of the Catholic Center project along lines suggested by O'Brien but decided against sending it to him. Apparently, Walsh advised against sending an endorsement because O'Brien had opened up a fund-raising office in the Hotel Sherman in Chicago, a few blocks away from Walsh's office in the Congress Hotel. Walsh feared that O'Brien's "Million Dollar Campaign for the Catholic Center at the University of Illinois" would compete with his "$500,000 Campaign for Notre Dame."

Burns explained to O'Brien on February 14, 1922, that because of the great importance of the Notre Dame fund drive in Chicago, it would be unwise for him to join any appeal for O'Brien's Catholic Center in that city. If O'Brien could delay his appeal in Chicago and in other Illinois cities until next year, then at that time Burns would be pleased to send him a letter of endorsement.[61] For whatever reason, O'Brien called off his appeal in Chicago in late March 1922.[62] In due course, as promised, Burns sent a letter endorsing the Catholic Center project and, as requested, urged O'Brien to do the project in a manner "worthy of the name and position of the Catholic Church in the great State of Illinois."[63]

Despite the continuing criticism of the Jesuits and of Archbishop Curley, O'Brien persevered and in 1929 completed and dedicated a magnificent new chapel, residential and educational center in Champaign. To be sure, the manner whereby O'Brien raised and borrowed the funds required will not bear close scrutiny and got him into serious trouble with his new bishop. Yet, the completed chapel and other facilities were grand enough to compare favorably with what Protestant groups in Champaign had been able to build.

For Burns, Walsh, and others working in the fund drive, eliminating competition for Catholic dollars was important, but in the end the success of the drive would turn on their ability to get pledges and then collect the cash or marketable securities promised. In raising money the university was blessed with a champion. The hero of the entire fund drive was Albert R. Erskine of the Studebaker Corporation, who had lately been elected president of Notre Dame's new Board of Lay Trustees.

Not a university man himself, Erskine obtained enormous personal satisfaction from working for Notre Dame and from publicly identifying himself as a leader of the Notre Dame fund drive. For Erskine, helping Notre Dame raise money was much more than a worthy charitable work or form of useful community service. Raising funds for a salary endowment and new buildings at a private university was a socially desirable activity that all true believers in the efficacy and virtues of American capitalism, all responsible industrial leaders and persons of means ought to undertake.

It was a fact that Erskine wanted very much to be and to be perceived as a responsible industrial leader. He had worked very hard to insure labor peace at Studebaker. Under Erskine's direction, the Studebaker Corporation had purchased land in the south and southwestern parts of South Bend and had organized a $1.5-million housing company to build 500 workers' houses in the city. He was very proud that workers' wages at Studebaker had risen 150 percent since 1913 and 30 percent since the end of the war.[64] Studebaker workers were paid enough, Erskine was fond of saying, "to provide the comforts of life and permit savings."[65]

Erskine poured all of his considerable energy into the Notre Dame fund drive. He shamelessly pressed and pressured friends, associates,

Studebaker dealers and suppliers, and South Bend businessmen to contribute to it. What he sought from others, he willingly gave from his
own resources. Erskine personally contributed $10,000 and arranged for
$50,000 to be given in the name of the Studebaker Corporation. Lesser
Studebaker officials contributed amounts ranging from $1,000 upwards.[66]

Studebaker dealers from Boston to Baton Rouge contributed similar
amounts as well, usually sending their checks to the university through
Erskine to insure that their boss would know that they had done the right
thing. That same pattern was followed with Studebaker suppliers. The
owner of the Kelsey Wheel Company in Detroit sent $1,000 to the fund
drive by way of Erskine.[67]

Erskine's solicitation of the South Bend business and professional
community was total. Anyone who sold or wanted to sell services and
goods to the Studebaker Corporation contributed. Under any circumstances, Erskine was a difficult person to refuse. In South Bend few people
in the business community dared even consider saying no to this extremely influential man's solicitation for the Notre Dame fund drive. By
early October 1921, six months into the drive, pledges and contributions
collected in South Bend reached $200,000.[68]

For Burns and Walsh, a major strategic priority of the drive was
to identify potential large givers and then find ways of approaching them
either directly or indirectly through mutual friends. Erskine was extremely helpful in doing this. Successful solicitation of persons of that
sort, most of whom were not Catholics, would turn on their respective
attitudes toward Notre Dame and their perceptions of the university's
educational mission. To insure that no one at Notre Dame would offend
or embarrass potential donors through public statements or publications,
Burns simply ordered the lay faculty to avoid such behavior and threatened them with dismissal if they did not. He added a new clause to the
annual contracts offered to lay faculty for 1921–22 prohibiting them from
jeopardizing "the confidence and good will of patrons and friends of the
University."[69]

— iv —

To reach potential non-Catholic large givers, Burns and Walsh realized
that an approach different from the ones employed to solicit funds from
Catholic contributors had to be developed. Potential non-Catholic contributors would not be moved very far by arguments extolling the virtues
of studying and living in the philosophically and morally secure Catholic

environment of Notre Dame. If that sort of appeal would not work, perhaps one based more on strident opposition to bolshevism and socialism, and preservation of the present social and economic order would do better.

The standard appeal letter for non-Catholics was developed before the campaign began but was not made public until published in a special endowment campaign number of the *Scholastic* on June 11, 1921. This standard appeal letter presented three arguments why "all those who are interested in the preservation of the present social and economic order" ought to contribute to the Notre Dame fund drive.[70]

First, the type of economic thinking taught to Notre Dame students was very conservative. Students at Notre Dame were taught that property rights had to be respected, that capital had inviolable rights as well as labor, and that moral and spiritual principles were appropriate considerations in the settlement of practical economic questions. Above all else, this standard letter continued, "we are working to uphold the rights of property holders."[71]

Second, according to Burns and Walsh, thinking men generally regarded the Catholic Church as a great bulwark against the spread of socialism. That was true in the past, but in more recent days the ability of the Catholic Church to play that role was much diminished. Catholic workingmen no longer looked to the clergy and bishops for guidance in social and economic matters. Priests and bishops were unable to deter Catholic workingmen from consorting with or even joining socialist parties except by supplying them with lay leaders raised up from among themselves through the instrumentality of higher education. Burns and Walsh hoped that this extraordinary image of Notre Dame graduates acting out roles as new apostles of social and economic conservatism would inspire affluent Protestants and Jews to think favorably of Notre Dame and other Catholic colleges and universities and contribute generously to the Notre Dame fund drive.

Third, enlarging upon the theme developed by William Lowe Bryan for Burns in a supportive letter sent to Buttrick in January 1920, Burns and Walsh insisted that Notre Dame and other Catholic colleges and universities had special opportunities to reach elements of the country's population that other institutions of higher education could not. Many young men of Magyar and Slavic ancestry wanted to come to Notre Dame and would probably go nowhere else. If such young men were not given opportunities to become leaders in constructive activities, as they would if Notre Dame had room for them, in many cases they would find easy paths to leadership along destructive lines. The entire nation would benefit, the letter concluded, if Notre Dame were "enabled to care for all such applicants, afford them intellectual opportunity and train them to become efficient leaders of our Catholic people along lines of sound social and economic progress."[72]

In this appeal letter, Burns and Walsh added a new dimension to the conventional Catholic educational idea of receiving instruction in a philosophically and morally secure environment. According to what Burns and Walsh wrote in this letter, the concept of being taught in a philosophically and morally secure environment now included the indoctrination of future leaders of our country's ethnic groups in economic principles likely to reinforce and preserve the present social and economic order. Indeed, this was a cause that should benefit the entire country and one that affluent non-Catholics ought to support out of enlightened self-interest.

With what Burns and Walsh believed was an effective appeal letter in hand to send to industrial leaders with some possible interest in the university, they were anxious to use it. One inviting first target was the celebrated Judge Elbert H. Gary of the nearby United States Steel Corporation. There was, however, a small problem of deciding how to approach one of the greatest men in corporate America. No one in the inner circle at Notre Dame, not even Erskine, was personally acquainted with him. The only connection between U.S. Steel and Notre Dame was their common northern Indiana locations. If there was no existing connection between Judge Gary and Notre Dame, the obvious strategy was to establish one.

To that end, Burns made a personal call upon Judge Gary on December 20, 1920, in his corporate offices in New York. He explained his plans for the forthcoming fund drive, emphasizing the point that Notre Dame was the closest engineering school to the sprawling U.S. Steel works in Gary, Indiana. Burns also talked at some length about Notre Dame being a place where the sons of the company's Slavonic and Magyar employees could be educated in sound social and economic principles. Burns' notes of this meeting record the judge as saying that "he would personally favor such a contribution."[73]

When Burns returned to the university, he sent Gary a letter thanking him for the courtesies shown to him during his recent visit and then asked the judge for a memorandum confirming his interest in contributing to the fund drive once the campaign had formally opened.[74] No such memorandum appears to have been written or sent. After the drive had been officially launched and nothing had been heard from Judge Gary, Burns decided to send off a gentle reminder of what he hoped had been a genuine commitment. On August 3, 1921, Burns wrote to Gary requesting a copy of a speech that the judge had given at Syracuse University in June.

In the highly competitive and sometimes unreal world of fund raising where the best of ends frequently justifies the most obsequious of means, Burns' letter to Gary is a classically embarrassing example. For fund raisers, the line between excessive flattery and near apotheosis of potential donors is always a shadowy one. In this instance, Burns crossed it. In his letter to Judge Gary, Burns began by saying that there was so much to admire about the Syracuse speech that he wanted a copy to study and keep. It was a most timely speech, wrote Burns, that ought to be widely circulated among college and university students. What Burns admired most in it was the judge's "straight forward, forceful, exposition of fundamental principles, such as, equality of opportunity . . . [being] the keynote to national and individual success and attainment." Moreover, Burns continued, "The solution of our worst industrial ills . . . is conditioned upon a general acceptance of that principle which as you show lies at the base of our entire governmental structure."[75]

There was so much wisdom in Judge Gary's speech, Burns suggested, that internalization of all of it required serious study. For example, the moral aspects of the principle of equality of opportunity involved the idea of justice and equity. The entire country, Burns wrote, must return "to this bedrock of virtue before we can have permanent industrial peace."[76] He concluded with the observation that Dr. Bolger, head of Notre Dame's economics department, was fond of emphasizing those points in his courses.

What Father Bolger may have thought about Burns putting such a conservative cast on his opinions is unknown. Most likely, Bolger was unaware of how Burns had used his name to approach U.S. Steel for a contribution to the fund drive. In any case, Burns' effort to reach Judge Gary failed. Burns had intended to send off to the judge a variation of the standard appeal letter upon receipt of a copy of the speech. However, nothing appears to have happened. There is no evidence that Judge Gary responded to Burns' letter of August 3, 1921, that a copy of the speech was received, that a copy of the standard appeal letter was sent, or that Gary or U.S. Steel made a contribution. This was one scheme that did not work.

Other potential large givers suggested by Notre Dame alumni were the oil magnates Harry F. Sinclair and Edward L. Doheny. Father McGinn put both of these men on his prospects list, aware that Doheny was a Catholic and Sinclair was not. The strategy employed to reach these men was a variation of the one employed in trying to influence the Carnegie Foundation, that is, approach them through personal or business acquaintances who were men of wealth themselves and friendly to Notre Dame. This strategy seemed to be a sound one, but as events would soon show was fraught with risks for the naive and uninformed.

McGinn attempted to arrange a meeting with Sinclair in New York City with a letter of introduction from Patrick Molloy, a Notre Dame alumnus working in the oil business in Tulsa. Whenever McGinn tried to set an appointment, Sinclair was unavailable. McGinn learned from H. F. Standford, general counsel for the Sinclair Oil Corporation and also a Notre Dame alumnus, that Molloy had become *persona non grata* with Sinclair because of a break between himself and some of the Tulsa oil people. McGinn advised Burns to drop Molloy as an intervenor and use Standford instead.[77]

Standford was full of ideas about how to proceed with Sinclair. To succeed with this man, one had to move in the right way, which was to appeal to Sinclair's extraordinary vanity without appearing to do so. He had much to be vain about. Sinclair had been a millionaire since 1910. He owned a regal estate in Long Island, lived in an elegant town house in New York City, owned part of the St. Louis Browns baseball team as well as a string of race horses that included the celebrated Kentucky Zev, Kentucky Derby winner in 1923. Sinclair lived as a great American oil prince. He found great personal satisfaction in having the best, being the biggest, and doing the most as his chosen name of Mammoth Oil for one of his companies and the famous corporate logo of a dinosaur testify.

Standford advised McGinn to have Father Burns write the standard anti-bolshevik, anti-socialist, ethnic leaders letter with a few special paragraphs added. The letter should be addressed and sent to Standford, not to Sinclair.[78] Even though the drive was still in the planning stage, the General Education Board grant had not yet been awarded, and no contributions of any size had been pledged or received from anyone, this letter to Standford should state that substantial donations already had been received.[79]

Standford suggested to McGinn that these special paragraphs should contain confidential information that one of the largest corporations in the country had donated $35,000 to the Notre Dame fund drive, another corporation had given $30,000, and that $25,000 had been sent from a person in Tulsa. No names should be mentioned, but stating that donations had been received was extremely important.[80]

The next step was for Standford to give this letter to Mrs. Sinclair and get her approval. She would tell her husband that he was about to be asked to make a substantial contribution to the Notre Dame fund drive. If Sinclair received that news favorably, Standford would present the letter addressed to himself to Sinclair. McGinn had no problems with the fundamental immorality of this utterly Machiavellian scheme and asked Burns to write to him for additional information if his explanation had not been clear.[81]

Burns was pleased to have the information about Molloy's present relationship with Sinclair. His reaction to the Standford scheme can only be guessed. He made no comments whatsoever to McGinn about the immorality of it.[82] However, in a letter to a Catholic prospect in Racine written shortly after receiving the elaborate details of the Standford scheme from McGinn, Burns mentioned that an influential non-Catholic who could not be identified at the moment had promised a donation of $35,000 to the drive. Experience had shown, Burns continued, that non-Catholics can be interested as easily in Notre Dame as Catholics. Non-Catholics appreciate "keenly the value of the social work Notre Dame is doing especially in training up leaders for our Catholic people of foreign origin."[83]

Quite apart from the morality of Standford's scheme, it was far too complicated to implement. There was just too much deception to keep track of. Whether Burns ever wrote such a letter to Standford is unknown. If such a letter was written and sent to Standford, there is no evidence that he passed it on to the Sinclairs. In the end, neither of the Sinclairs contributed to the Notre Dame fund drive. They were preoccupied with other matters. During the year and a half of the first phase of the Notre Dame fund drive, Sinclair and Standford, as chief counsel of the Sinclair Oil Corporation, were engaged in obtaining oil leases in the United States Naval Reserve No. 3 about fifty miles north of Casper, Wyoming, at a place called Teapot Dome. Sinclair obtained these leases from Secretary of the Interior Albert B. Fall without the inconvenience of a competitive bidding process.

A self-made oil man of great wealth, a good Catholic with strong Irish nationalist opinions but much less enamored of celebrity status than Sinclair, Edward L. Doheny appeared to be an excellent prospective contributor to the fund drive. Doheny had been a pioneer of the oil business in the Los Angeles area who had expanded his operations into Mexico. He organized the Mexico Petroleum Company and managed to obtain leases to 250,000 acres near Tampico.

Doheny was close to the Díaz regime, and one of his companies provided about half of all of the asphalt used to pave the streets of Mexico City. When Díaz was overthrown in 1911 and the country was convulsed by its long revolution, Doheny's fortunes along with other American companies operating there rose and fell as the revolution wound its confusing course. A consistent problem for Doheny during the turbulent decade 1911 to 1921 was finding ways of getting his oil out of Mexico into world markets. That problem was resolvable in large part with assistance from the United Sates Shipping Board.

A Notre Dame alumnus associated with a Washington, D.C., law firm, Tim Ainsberry, recommended Doheny as a prospect to McGinn and suggested a way of reaching him. Ainsberry, who knew Doheny personally, proposed Admiral William Benson as an intervenor.[84] Benson was an extremely devout Catholic, a convert of many years' standing. He was deeply interested in Catholic lay organizations and served as first president of the National Conference of Catholic Men, 1921–1925. Benson had enjoyed a long and distinguished naval career, reaching the post of chief of naval operations in 1915. After retirement from active service in 1919, President Wilson appointed Benson chairman of the United States Shipping Board, 1920–21. Thereafter, Benson served as a member of that board until his retirement from public service in 1928. Most important, Notre Dame had awarded Benson the Laetare Medal in 1917, a medal given annually to an outstanding Catholic lay person.

Ainsberry advised McGinn that any favor asked of Doheny by a member of the United States Shipping Board would receive the most immediate and serious consideration. McGinn learned also that Doheny was a man easily moved by causes that interested him, for example Irish nationalism, but without an aroused interest nothing would be heard from him. Clearly, Benson was the man to arouse Doheny's interest in the cause of Notre Dame.[85]

Ainsberry advised McGinn to prepare and send to Benson an appropriate letter emphasizing the special role of a Notre Dame education in the broader mission of the Catholic Church in the world. The next step would be for McGinn to call upon Benson in the company of Father John W. Cavanaugh.[86] If anyone could bring Benson into this Doheny project enthusiastically, it would be Cavanaugh.

McGinn prepared a letter for Benson along the lines suggested by Ainsberry. It was a letter meant to touch all of Benson's emotional vulnerabilities that McGinn had been able to identify. McGinn began by stating that our cause is the cause of the Church and that means the cause of men and women throughout the world. "We are laboring for the spread of Christ's Kingdom and the salvation of souls."

We want to provide opportunities for young men "to get the best possible education without running the risk of losing their faith by exposing themselves to the unbelief and . . . [loose] philosophy that prevails in practically all secular institutions."[87] Friends of the university who are able to assist us by laying this situation before men of wealth will be doing an invaluable service to their Church and country.[88]

Next followed the standard anti-bolshevik, anti-socialist argument, supported in this instance with the observation that the university presently had enrolled ninety students "of the Slavonic and Magyar races." McGinn concluded by making a point that would often be made during the next year and a half. All persons seriously "concerned about the conservation and preservation of the 'Right' and the 'Just' in their present social and economic order . . . [should] help Notre Dame in her work for society and progress."[89]

Indeed, McGinn had done his best. It is difficult to think of anything he left out. The letter was sent to Benson in early September 1920, but in the end, the entire Doheny project turned out to be a dry hole. Whether Benson ever actually communicated with Doheny on behalf of the Notre Dame fund drive, or in any way even considered compromising his position as a member of the United States Shipping Board by doing so, is unknown. Doheny gave nothing to the drive. It would appear that while McGinn was drafting his letter to Benson and awaiting a response, Doheny approached a much more important, if not more worthy, beneficiary than Notre Dame and paid him.

Like Sinclair, Doheny had extremely delicate business matters to attend to at that time. On November 30, 1921, Doheny's son delivered a now famous "little black bag" containing $100,000 in cash to Albert B. Fall, secretary of the interior. Though Doheny later described this donation as a loan, that is, a loan without collateral or interest requirements, bribe would more accurately describe the transaction. For this donation/loan/bribe, Doheny received a lucrative contract for his Pan-American Petroleum and Transportation Company to build a fuel tank complex at Pearl Harbor as well as leases to drill for oil in the Naval Oil Reserve in Elk Hills, California. This contract and the way it was obtained would have serious consequences for all involved in the awarding of it.

— v —

After doing so poorly with oil, Burns and McGinn went back to steel. Another potential large giver from that industry even more hotly pursued than Judge Gary, Sinclair, or Doheny was Charles M. Schwab of the Bethlehem Steel Corporation. Schwab was a personal friend of Erskine and had grown into one of the giants of steel making and of corporate America generally as a protégé of the legendary Andrew Carnegie. Schwab was as much a true believer in the virtues of corporate philanthropy as his great mentor but harbored no special feelings toward or sense of obligation for Catholic institutions.

At Notre Dame, Schwab was believed to be a Catholic. In fact, Schwab was a nonobservant Catholic who had married a nonobservant Protestant woman. Neither of the Schwabs turned out to be much amenable to specifically Catholic religious appeals. However, unaware of Schwab's ambivalence toward Catholic causes and issues, Burns approached Schwab and his wife as if they were regulars at Mass and frequent communicants. Mrs. Schwab received presents of specially blessed devotional aids. Burns awarded Schwab an honorary degree in June 1921 and had hired his brother to teach in the Notre Dame Law School. Erskine pressed Schwab to be generous and in effect to become a contributing member of the Notre Dame family.

All of these appeals produced no result. Mrs. Schwab evidenced no appreciation of or gratitude for the holy medals and beads, and Schwab said no to both Burns and Erskine. As Schwab explained to Erskine, he was a trustee of Cornell, Pennsylvania State University, and Lehigh, "to all of whom I have contributed this year, taxing all resources." He would have "to leave Notre Dame to my friends in Chicago."[90]

Schwab's refusal was disappointing, but his reference to the important role of Chicago in the fund drive was well made. Because time was short to reach the goal of $250,000 to be raised in the Chicago area by June 30, 1922, Burns and Walsh decided to hire a local fund-raising agency, M. F. Kern and Associates, to organize and manage the drive in Cook County. According to the terms of the agreement with the Kern organization, their involvement in the drive was to begin on February 20, 1922, and run for three months.

Specifically, the Kern organization would provide one experienced fund raiser for two weeks and then two experienced people for ten weeks. For the services of these people during the three-month contract period, the university agreed to pay Kern $6,600 plus all travel expenses.[91] Walsh would keep the office in the Congress Hotel open, and all Notre Dame fund drive workers and volunteers in the Chicago area would operate under the direction of Kern representatives. It became clear at once that the Kern people knew their business and would earn their fees. Pledges from the Chicago area increased significantly, and the prospect of raising the overall General Education Board matching requirement on time seemed achievable.

Having an achievable goal did not make reaching it easy. Among the first of the many Chicago corporations approached was the Armour

Company. Burns sent Armour the standard anti-bolshevik, anti-socialist, future ethnic leader letter, but prefaced with a paragraph pointing out that Notre Dame had been a customer of Armour for many years, spending as much as $1,200 a month for meat products. A contribution to the Notre Dame fund drive by Armour would be at once a way of satisfying an old customer who could easily take his business elsewhere and an action consequential for the future social and political peace of the country.[92]

J. Ogden Armour responded with a personal pledge of $1,000 but offered nothing in the name of the company, pleading business losses of over $30 million during the past year. Other prominent Chicago industrial families did the same. William Wrigley gave only $1,000 in his own name, while Marshall Field pledged $5,000. Field insisted that company policy limited corporate giving to only a few local charities, such as the Red Cross, Salvation Army, and YMCA.[93] For Samuel Insull of Commonwealth Edison and spokesman for the Morgan interests in Chicago, the situation was a bit more complicated.

Insull was a very wealthy industrialist who lived in a princely fashion on a 4,000-acre estate in Libertyville, Illinois. Neither a Catholic nor a university man, Insull had met Father Cavanaugh some years previously and liked him very much. Insull was pleased and flattered by the attention of university people, artists, classical musicians, and opera stars. He enjoyed classical music and opera immensely as his later large gift toward the construction of the Chicago Civic Opera House testifies. At the same time, Insull was also much attracted to Notre Dame football. As a matter of fact, he frequently allowed university officials the use of his private railway car for games played at distant sites. By both Cavanaugh and Burns, Insull was regarded as a friend of the university and a potential large contributor. Insull appeared to be eminently qualified for possible appointment to the new Board of Lay Trustees, especially qualified because Burns believed that the man was Jewish and would thereby give the board a unique ecumenical dimension.

Burns assigned Walsh the task of researching and making a case for appointing Insull to the board, and what Walsh discovered quickly put an end to Insull's candidacy. According to Walsh's informants, Insull was not Jewish. He was English and strongly pro-British on the Irish question. So pro-British on that issue was Insull, Walsh reported, that he had broken off several long-standing personal friendships because of it.[94]

Walsh advised against putting Insull on the board, observing that "his relations to the Irish question would certainly start comment."[95] That sort of comment the university did not need in the midst of a major fund drive in Chicago. Because affluent Irish American Catholics in the Chicago area were so important for the success of the drive, there was much more to lose from such a public embrace of the man and of his pro-English stance than could ever be gained from the level of contribution he was prepared to give. Irish nationalism was a very serious matter in Chicago, and Irish American Catholics in that city would be most unforgiving of persons and institutions believed to have demeaned it for money.

Burns accepted his vice president's advice, and Insull was not asked to become a member of the board. In the long term, Walsh's advice respecting Insull proved to be very sound. Insull only contributed a total of $3,000 to the drive between 1922 and 1925. That sum was much less than amounts received from some Studebaker Corporation executives in South Bend and even less than contributions from executives in companies doing business with Studebaker Corporation.

However, university officials never stopped hoping for more. Insull was still a very rich philanthropically minded man, and he continued to be friendly toward the university. Though Insull had been inappropriate for the Board of Lay Trustees in 1921, much had changed by 1925. With the ultimate triumph of Irish nationalism in Anglo-Irish relations the emotional power of that most enduring cause in Irish America greatly diminished. In this new emotional climate, perhaps Insull's past pro-English positions could be forgotten and some other honor or accolade calculated to inspire warm and generous feelings toward the university could be given to him. In 1925 Insull was put on the Advisory Board of the College of Commerce, and in 1926 he was given an honorary degree. Insull's affection for Notre Dame may have been intensified thereby, but he chose not to demonstrate it with additional contributions.

To be sure, offenses against Irish nationalism in 1921 were of the nature of mortal sins and were not easily forgiven. Walsh's concern over possible negative reactions by Irish American Catholics to Notre Dame by honoring Insull had to be taken seriously. It made no sense at all to provide potential donors with a reason for not contributing. The managers of the drive had to be sensitive to ideological issues and avoid offending potential donors because of them. However, the primary task of Burns, Walsh, and especially the Kern organization was to convince American Catholics that contributing to the Notre Dame fund drive was the most worthy Catholic charitable action that one could undertake at that time. Because of the tremendous competition for Catholic charitable dollars, that argument was not easily made or readily believed.

The most successful fund raisers are born not made. The ability to charm any personality type however eccentric, speak with conviction for any cause, endure frequent rejection with equanimity are skills and traits much more God-given than learned. Asking persons that one does not know for money is difficult for most, embarrassing for many, and absolutely humiliating for a few. Father McGinn was one of those few. In time, he grew to detest the assignment that Burns had given him. McGinn could cope with outright refusals but not with the procrastinations and polite untruths from people that he knew were deceiving him. He tried to explain to Burns the depth of his frustration over a series of unrewarding calls made to prospects in New York City in March 1922. Some men were visited eight times and no subscription was obtained. However, each time McGinn went away from that much-visited prospect with a promise that he would contribute and with a request to call again.[96]

Though the men working Chicago for the fund drive were more experienced and tougher minded than McGinn, they also encountered much of the same. Several important prospects missed scheduled appointments in May, one volunteer complained, because they had been taken out of the city by the Kentucky Derby.[97] As in New York City, many Chicago prospects were reluctant to give an unequivocal no to Notre Dame fund drive representatives, especially if that representative was a priest. At the same time, however, some of the prospects reluctant to say no to priests were also unwilling to pledge more than minimal amounts.

One such example was Joseph Downey, a prominent Chicago Irish American contractor and builder. According to the conventional wisdom of that time and place, Downey was an old-time Chicago contractor who had done much work for the city over the years and was reputed to be very wealthy.[98] Consequently, as a major potential large donor, Downey was given special attention.

Early in the fund drive, Burns made a personal visit to the Downey home in St. Gertrude's parish. James T. Foley, a Notre Dame alumnus and volunteer fund drive worker called upon Downey in his LaSalle Street office and visited with him at home no less than fifteen times. Finally, after all of that special attention, Downey gave Foley a check as his contribution to the drive. However, the amount of the check was so small that Foley was almost too embarrassed to send it to Burns.[99]

Downey justified the small donation on the grounds that everyone was after him for money, especially Father John A. O'Brien for a contribution to his proposed Catholic Center at the University of Illinois. Since Downey had shown himself reluctant to say no to priests asking for money in face-to-face situations, Foley advised Father Walsh either to visit Downey personally in his office or to send some other priests to do so. Obviously, Downey was good for more than he had given, Foley insisted, and most likely more could be obtained if some priests did the asking.[100]

Whether Walsh or any other Notre Dame priest pursued the Downey matter further or regarded additional investments of time in him as a waste is unknown. Generally, during March and April 1922 Notre Dame officials were preoccupied with trying to reverse a slowdown of pledge and cash collections during those months. By the end of May anxiety levels in the Main Building rose significantly. With only a month remaining before the General Education Board deadline of June 30, pledges had reached a grand total of only $600,000. To meet the deadline and qualify for the full amount promised in the grant, the university would have to collect in pledges or cash $150,000 in thirty days' time.[101]

Burns was prepared to do or say almost anything in order to obtain the necessary pledges in time. All of those prospects who had promised to give something later but had not, received urgent appeal letters, telegrams, telephone calls, or visits. Most thus contacted responded with pledges. Many of the old alumni and long-standing non-alumni friends of the university rose to the challenge of the moment. An Irish American industrialist from Rockaway, New Jersey, provided a timely $25,000. A non-Catholic president of a Chicago insurance company contributed $10,000. Edward N. Hurley responded with $15,000. An alumnus building contractor from Washington, D.C., sent bonds issued by his own corporation worth $10,000. Other loyal alumni, such as Clement Mitchell of Chicago and Angus MacDonald, Joseph Byrne, and Robert Sweeney of New York City, all of whom had given once, pledged more.[102]

The graduating class of 1922 pledged $12,000, and most important of all, the Alumni Association agreed to transfer to the fund drive $60,000 collected since 1915 for the construction of a large new student residence facility to be known as "Old Students' Hall." The transfer of these funds effected only two weeks before the end of the drive was critical for the successful and timely completion of it. To get this money, Burns promised the Alumni Association that the first new residence hall built at the university would be called "Old Students' Hall" and would conform in every way to the architectural plans prepared for it. Burns had made this promise in good faith, but it was a promise that neither he nor his successor would be able to keep.[103]

Burns announced the successful completion of the General Education Board phase of the fund drive at graduation exercises on June 12, 1922. A few days later, he traveled to New York City to report in person the details of his accomplishment. In all, 1,387 pledges amounting to $824,765 had been collected. The expenses of the fund drive were reported as being $50,000. Of the amount pledged, $252,000 had come from South Bend, $197,000 had been subscribed in Chicago, the Knights of Columbus of Indiana had promised $50,000, and current students pledged $27,000. The rest had come from alumni and friends in the New York City area, New England, Indiana, and elsewhere in the Midwest.[104] Since a little more than $260,000 had been collected in cash or in marketable securities by June 30, 1922, in accord with the grant agreement to provide one dollar for every three dollars collected, the General Education Board authorized payment of $86,907.[105]

In contrast to the generally modest contributions obtained from the great men of corporate America or from well-known affluent Catholics, the generosity of devoted old guard alumni at this critical moment in the history of the university was stretched beyond all reasonable expectations. They gave what they could afford, often more than they could afford, but always regretting that they could not do more. Except for Erskine and those men coerced by him into making contributions and a few others, the successful completion of the General Education Board phase of this fund drive was indeed for that time a major philanthropic achievement of Catholic America, accomplished in large part by an extremely devoted band of Notre Dame alumni.

— vi —

Shortly after completing the first phase of the fund drive and then getting through graduation exercises, Burns had to make a major decision about his future roles in university and congregation affairs. His three-year term as local religious superior and president of the university was about to expire. Under the terms of canon law Burns was eligible to serve for another three years in those offices but no longer. On June 30, 1922, the Provincial Chapter met to consider reelecting Burns for a second term and to dispose of other congregation business.

Just back from his New York meeting on June 26 with Trevor Arnett of the General Education Board, Burns went to the chapter meeting on June 30 with only about one day's rest. Physically exhausted by the wear and tear of long-distance train travel and by the stresses and anxieties of the last six months, Burns seems to have become aware that a man of his age could not continue to manage the second phase of the fund drive, travel far and wide calling on prospects, and also run the university on a daily basis as president. As he explained to a friend, Burns found the combination of those two very difficult tasks, running the university and meeting a large-scale fund-raising deadline, "about all I could stand and I am thoroughly played out. I hope to get some rest now."[106]

Burns believed that he could handle one of those jobs but not both. Moreover, the next three years promised to be even more physically demanding and anxiety-laden than the last. Most likely there would not be the incentive of a large matching grant to encourage donations to a building and facilities improvement drive. In any case, only the pledge collection aspect of the General Education Board phase of the drive had been completed. By June 30, 1922, only one-third of the total amount pledged had been collected in cash and only one-third of the grant money promised had been paid. Under the terms of the grant, the university had three years to collect the rest.

Burns seems to have decided sometime during the spring of 1922 that collecting pledges from the first phase of the drive and successfully managing the building and facilities improvement phase of it would be more important for the university and for the congregation in the long term than serving another three years as president. Moreover, within the congregation there was a highly qualified alternative to Burns for the presidency—Walsh had served ten years as vice president—but there was no one with comparable fund-raising experience and contacts with foundations to replace Burns as the leader of the drive.

Although there is no available evidence that Burns revealed his intentions to anyone, most likely he shared his thoughts about the drive and the presidency with the serving provincial, Father Charles L. O'Donnell, and with Walsh. However politically prepared or surprised, the Provincial Chapter assembled as scheduled at Notre Dame on June 30, 1922. Before deliberations about Burns' reelection could begin, Burns formally requested to be relieved as local superior and president of the university. The minutes of this meeting are brief and state only that Burns "gave many good reasons for his request."[107] In effect, the chapter accepted Burns' resignation and did so without much contention. After an adjournment of several hours, the chapter reassembled and elected Matthew J. Walsh as local superior and president of the university by a wide margin.[108] Walsh chose Thomas P. Irving, C.S.C., to be his vice president, the first of three Holy Cross priests to serve under Walsh in that office.

This change in leadership was a great surprise to most people interested in Notre Dame affairs. Certainly, Burns had given no hints of his intentions during his meeting with Arnett in New York on June 26, 1922. Yet, four days later Burns was out of office, titled "president emeritus" by the provincial, assigned office space in the Main Building, and charged to complete the second phase of the fund drive. To outsiders, this sudden and totally unexpected removal of a man who had taken the university so far in such a short time was mystifying. There simply had to be some un-stated reasons for it.

At the time of the resignation as well as later, there were some campus observers of Holy Cross politics prepared to believe that Burns had been forced out of office. Persons of such a mind would point out that Burns had been a rigorous and sometimes severe religious superior. As local superior, he appears to have resolved the obedience problems that had annoyed the superior general so much in 1919, but in so doing probably aroused resentment among some of the priests and brothers under his direction.

For example, Burns was a strong believer in the vow of poverty and on occasion ruthlessly confiscated dollars, however so few, that may have come into the hands of his priests as earnings or gifts.[109] At the same time, the educational priorities established by Burns, the range and number of reforms pressed, as well as the manner of their implementation could not have commanded full support in either the Congregation of Holy Cross or in the larger university community. There were priests and laymen at the university who were convinced that Burns' academic goals for the in-stitution were impossible. There were others, no doubt, who believed that their president's academic goals were undesirable.

However, even if there was a party of discontented priests and broth-ers who wanted to be rid of Burns, there was no way to do it as long as the provincial and superior general supported him. To do so would mean turning the entire political culture of the Holy Cross Congregation upside down. In any case, there is no evidence whatsoever that the su-perior general or provincial in 1922 or any of their successors lost con-fidence in Burns or doubted his judgment.

If either the perception or reality of resentment or hostility from within the congregation had been involved in Burns' decision of July 1922, it vanished quickly. In fact, in July 1927 Burns was appointed pro-vincial of the Indiana Province of the Congregation of Holy Cross and by virtue of that office he also served as chairman of the Board of Trustees of the university and held those posts for the canonical limit of six years. His influence in university and congregation affairs was to continue until his death in 1940.

— vii —

After several weeks of relaxation and golfing in the late summer of 1922, Burns was sufficiently refreshed to begin again the serious pursuit of Catholic dollars. He started the new campaign with high hopes. As a matter of fact, between 1922 and 1924 Burns managed to spend $100,000 for campaign expenses.[110] With the indefatigable but always pessimistic McGinn as an assistant and two laymen for staff, Burns started the building and facilities improvement phase of the fund drive with a canvasing tour through the eastern states in the fall of 1922.

For this tour Burns' new prospect list was not much different from the old one. Consequently, Burns and McGinn revisited many Catholic gentlemen of means who had already contributed to the first phase of the drive. As one might expect, these gentlemen were not anxious to meet again so soon with Burns and McGinn and hear about the special needs of Notre Dame and the all-important mission of Catholic higher education in America.

Pittsburgh turned out to be especially difficult territory to work. There was the very large matter of competition from Duquesne University and from a Catholic women's college. However, neither of those institutions were able to raise more than 50 percent of their respective publicly advertised goals and had to abandon their campaigns. One of Burns' staff described the situation in Pittsburgh as rooted in a "peculiar attitude here toward Catholic higher education."[111] Giving to Catholic universities and colleges in that area was not regarded as a high priority Catholic charity. Men who should have known better, complained the staff member, did not.

It became very clear that giving to Catholic universities and colleges was not a high priority charitable cause in many other areas either. Without the incentive of a foundation matching grant, raising a million dollars for new buildings in three, four, or even five years would be very difficult. The wisest course seemed to be that of persuading some foundation to provide such an incentive. However, for Burns and his group realistic options were few. There was, of course, the great Rockefeller well from which Burns had already drunk.

On January 15, 1923, Burns wrote to Buttrick at the General Education Board to test the depth of water in that well. He requested consideration of a grant to Notre Dame to help finance the construction of a new engineering building and to insure "the successful prosecution of our building campaign in general."[112] Buttrick passed Burns' letter to Arnett, who took a month to respond. Arnett politely informed Burns that at present it was not the policy of the General Education Board "to make contributions to colleges and universities toward the cost of building."[113] Whatever the leadership at Notre Dame decided to do about new buildings and facilities improvement, they would have to do on their own.

Burns toured the West Coast during the fall of 1923 and then traveled about the Midwest in early 1924. The results of the California tour were embarrassing. Only $11,000 was pledged for the entire state. The Midwest tour was better. Cleveland achieved its goal, as did Kansas City with the help of the local bishop. New York City responded well, but in general the campaign for the second million dollars never came close to the publicly announced goal.[114] There were enough affluent Notre Dame alumni who could afford one substantial gift to the fund drive but not many who could afford to give twice.

By early May 1923 pledges and cash from the second phase totaled $200,000.[115] A year later, pledges and cash had increased to $344,000.[116] That was about as close to the final goal as the drive ever got. In the end, virtually none of the money pledged and collected was ever actually spent on building projects. As Erskine explained to the Notre Dame alumni in April 1924, no funds raised for new buildings or facilities improvement could be spent on construction projects until all of the General Education Board pledges had been collected and the matching grant was paid in full.[117]

By the end of April 1925, two months before the closure date for pledge redemption and final grant payment, almost $200,000 in uncollected pledges from the General Education Board phase of the drive were outstanding. Even though Erskine urged Notre Dame officials to pursue delinquents with sharp pointed sticks,[118] it was easier and less embarrassing to close the books on the General Education Board grant by raiding the building and facilities improvement collections. That was done. The matching grant was paid in full during the summer of 1925. With most of the funds raised for new buildings now gone, Burns and Walsh faced reality and recognized the impossibility of ever raising a second million dollars. In effect, they closed out the new buildings and facilities improvement campaign.

While there was no public admission that the second phase of the fund drive had failed or that it had been formally ended, university leaders simply decided for the time being against investing more time and money in fund-raising campaigns. The charitable resources available to the university had been worked over and out. No new pledges would be sought, the lay professionals would be let go, but efforts to collect pledges already made would continue. Implementation of this new policy began in August 1925, when the provincial reassigned Burns to his old post as director of the Holy Cross House of Studies in Washington, D.C.[119]

This decision to end the new buildings and facilities improvement phase of the fund drive was a very easy one to make because the drive had become almost superfluous. Since 1922, the gains from fund-raising activities had been hardly worth the time and energy expended to get them. In any case, several new buildings funded out of internal resources had been built or were under construction. Between 1922 and 1925, two temporary student residences had been put up, a permanent student residence hall was started, and extensions had been added to Science Hall and to the gymnasium.

The cost of these five projects was $550,000 and the money for them had been found. Notre Dame had been surprisingly and suddenly blessed with what seemed to be a new and ever-expanding financial resource to pay for new buildings and facilities improvement. That new resource was football revenues. No one could be sure how much it would grow or how long it would last, but large sums of money were in hand for one-time projects.

Enjoying extraordinary football success between 1922 and 1925, Knute Rockne created a football enterprise at Notre Dame that dazzled the American sports world. It would do much more for the university than generate profits to pay for new buildings. Football success at Notre Dame during the 1920s gave the country great sports heroes at a time when ordinary Americans craved them and made the name of the university a household word. Rockne's football enterprise established a new public image of Notre Dame and profoundly affected the development of the university for the rest of the century.

After all of the time and effort invested in the Notre Dame fund drive, by 1925 the income from the newly established faculty salary endowment was only $46,000. In contrast, profits from Notre Dame athletic programs—virtually all from football—for 1925 was $191,000.[120] For Notre Dame officials of that time, football profits must have seemed like a Providential gift. Providential or not, football success was a more certain and more lucrative way of acquiring funds for expansion of university facilities than asking rich people for them. This was a fortuitous condition, alas, that would not last forever. So the most ought to be made of this new but troublesome and sometimes embarrassing source of revenue as long as it lasted.

— 6 —

THE DEVELOPMENT OF THE
NOTRE DAME FOOTBALL
ENTERPRISE, 1918–1922

An important outside public to whom the university had to pay increasing regard in the early 1920s was the sports media establishment and the hundreds of thousands of American sports fans and ticket buyers served by them. In the years following the end of the war, the popularity of intercollegiate football increased enormously. During the 1920s large football stadia were built across the length and breadth of the country. For those colleges and universities able to field winning teams, intercollegiate football became a very big and ruthless business.

Notre Dame was marvelously situated both geographically and athletically to participate in the popularity explosion of intercollegiate football. Jesse Harper had improved the schedule, recruited talented players, and won important games widely reported in the regional and national media. Harper's successor hired by Father Cavanaugh in 1918, Knute K. Rockne, was much more than an extremely able man fortuitously placed in an opportunity-laden job at the right moment. Rockne was a genius at self-promotion who promoted the university while promoting himself. He also turned out to be one of the greatest and most successful coaches in the history of intercollegiate football.

No single coach in the immediate postwar years was more responsible for the extraordinary popularity of intercollegiate football than Rockne. He understood the value of making the game more interesting and easier to watch and did so by introducing an easily identified uniform for his team and assigned numbers to individual players. Moreover, his open style of football, emphasizing speed and deception, was far better suited for public consumption than the traditional closed style of play.

In the closed style of football, ball action was limited and generally obscured by the players themselves, who massed together and smashed into their opponents, gaining or losing a few yards at a time. Success came to the heaviest, strongest, and most durable players. Rockne's open style of play abandoned most of this. In the early and middle years of his career Rockne's players tended to be a bit smaller but much faster than the norm. His reliance on speed and deception rather than weight and strength confused defenders but allowed spectators to see who was carrying the ball, the direction of attack, and—if all worked as planned—running and passing plays that covered more yardage per play than usually occurred in the closed game.[1]

The university unit overseeing Notre Dame football fortunes during the 1920s was the Faculty Board in Control of Athletics. Established in 1898, the board was reformed and in effect reestablished in 1924. Prior to 1924, the board was entirely the creature of the president. It consisted of whomever and however many the president chose to put on it. Normally, before 1924, the board was composed of six or seven faculty members, of whom two or three were usually Holy Cross priests. One of the priest members, generally the same one, assumed the informal role of chairman. During the early 1920s, Father Burns' chairman of choice was Father William A. Carey, C.S.C., a professor of Greek.

Another board member, usually a layman recommended by the president, served as secretary. Cavanaugh had preferred Professor William Farrell of the department of history and politics for this post. Burns facilitated Farrell's resignation as secretary but allowed him to remain on the board. In 1920, at a very critical moment, Burns replaced Farrell with George Shuster, a special favorite of the president and lately appointed head of the department of English. The principal duty of the secretary of the board was to keep an official record of board actions, sometimes including with that record abbreviated accounts, rather than formal minutes, explaining in part why the board acted as it did.

The reforms of 1924 provided that the board should consist of at least five faculty members, all appointed by the president. In addition to the faculty members, three alumni members chosen by their association were to act as advisors to the board. After 1924 terms of members were not fixed. However, an indication of the vastly increased importance of the football enterprise in the financial and social life of the university was the fact that the president normally appointed his vice president to serve as chairman of the board. The secretary of the newly reformed board was elected by the appointed faculty members, and the treasurer, being the treasurer of the university, held his place on the board *ex officio.*

In theory, both before and after 1924, the board had full control over all aspects of the Notre Dame athletics, establishing policy, setting standards, and approving financial expenditures. Before 1924, there were no special mechanisms to oversee compliance with board decisions. After 1924, compliance was monitored through three standing committees: schedules, finances, and eligibility.

However, reality was a bit different. The board met only when summoned by its chairman. Furthermore, all of the board's authority, before and after 1924, was circumscribed by presidential prerogatives. The president reserved the right to set aside any decision of the board, disapprove any policy or expenditure of money proposed by them.[2] In practice, the old board, as well as the reformed one, usually recommended or approved only what they knew the president wanted. In most cases, the president wanted what the coaches wanted.

On those rare occasions when the president's views on a particular matter were unclear or misunderstood and the board went ahead and decided a matter that turned out to be contrary to his wishes, correction was usually uncontested and quickly done. The board would cheerfully and sometimes ingeniously find a way to rescind today what they had approved unanimously a week ago.

Examples of the board doing what either the president or the coaches wanted are not hard to find. Burns became infuriated over what he believed was a libelous attack upon the university, the football team, and the coaching staff that appeared in late October 1920 in *The Torch*, a student newspaper published at Valparaiso University. The occasion for the article was Notre Dame's one-sided football victory over the Valparaiso team, 28 to 3, on October 23 before a better than average crowd of 8,000 at Cartier Field.

A disappointed Valparaiso fan wrote a disparaging account of the game, attributing the final result to extremely unsportsmanlike conduct by the Notre Dame team, coaches, and fans. The author, identifying himself only as "a Valpo Nutt," sent his account of the event to *The Torch*, and the student editors without any consultation with the Valparaiso administration published it as it came in.[3]

The writer was very good at what he had chosen to do. He described the Notre Dame players as a lot of "muckers," who had deliberately tried to injure key members of the Valparaiso team to get them out of the game. In the parlance of the time, "mucker" was an anti-Irish epithet of English origin meaning dirty, violence-prone people with disgusting habits.

Rockne was not accused of being a "mucker," his well-known Norse ancestry prevented that, only of behaving like one. The writer charged
Rockne with having actually struck an official. Notre Dame fans were represented as being totally out of control. All in all, the author suggested,
that Cartier Field at Notre Dame was a very dangerous place to be on a
Saturday afternoon.[4]

The fact that this unfounded attack on the athletic program of Our
Lady's university and the insulting ethnic slur accompanying it appeared
in a student newspaper published at a Lutheran school obligated Burns to
respond. Being president of the best-known Catholic university in the
country and only one generation removed from the green fields of Tipperary, he could not do otherwise. According to Rockne, Burns stormed
into his office in the Main Building with a copy of the offending article in
hand shortly after it appeared, demanding that all games with Valparaiso
in all sports be canceled at once.[5] Other evidence suggests that Rockne's
description of Burns' anger was an accurate one.

The matter was brought before the Faculty Board in Control of Athletics by Carey, presumably speaking for the president, as early as November 4—that is, only two weeks after the game had been played—in a special meeting called to deal with it and nothing else. Carey explained what
had happened and concluded his presentation with the observation that
"competition with Valparaiso in the future should be considered undesirable." The rest of the board concurred absolutely, but formal action was
put off until an expression of opinion from the Student Academic Committee could be obtained.[6]

Whether that expression of opinion ever came about, or what it was if
obtained, is unknown. The board addressed the matter of future football
relations with Valparaiso in an entirely different context on November 27.
Questions were raised about the championship quality of games with
Valparaiso and how games with teams of their caliber of play would affect
our team's chances for regional or national championship recognition.
The very sparse record of this meeting reveals only that the problem was
discussed and not that any action was taken.[7]

Certainly, Rockne's unceasing efforts to improve the schedule have to
be considered as a factor in this controversy. Rockne claimed that he had
scheduled this game with Valparaiso in the first place only because Coach
George Keogan was a personal friend. Because of the great and growing
demand by major football powers all over the country for opportunities
to play against Notre Dame, Rockne's totally supportive position in this
Valparaiso matter has to be suspect.

Outrage over an egregious institutional and ethnic insult was real.
Members of the Notre Dame community were particularly sensitive to

a thoroughly opprobrious anti-Irish epithet such as "mucker." Rockne must have felt some of that resentment as well, but not too much. His very hard line against Valparaiso was inspired much more by the timely schedule improvement opportunities which the incident provided and that he needed.

Whatever the emotions and motives driving this controversy, Rockne advised Coach Keogan by letter on December 18 that football relations between Notre Dame and Valparaiso were over and the reasons why. Within a week, Daniel Russell Hogdon, president of Valparaiso, wrote an apologetic letter to Burns expressing sincere regret that friction had developed between their respective institutions. He explained that *The Torch* was not an official university publication and that the offending article had been written by an outsider from Chicago and would not have been published if the student newspaper had been properly regulated and supervised, which he promised would be the case in the future.

However, Hogdon mentioned also that Valparaiso fans attending the game complained about partisan officiating and allowing "violation of certain courtesies and rules connected with football, especially that of permitting the coach to go onto the field during a game."[8] He complained also that Rockne did not notify Coach Keogan that future scheduled football games would be canceled until after the Notre Dame coach had filled Valparaiso's date with another team. In Hogdon's opinion, that sort of action "hardly complied with the spirit of true sportsmanship."[9]

Hogdon believed that a heart to heart talk among the principals involved could resolve this situation amicably. He was completely mistaken. To that end, however, he invited Rockne, Carey, and any other interested parties to come to Valparaiso and dine with him.

In this response, perhaps President Hogdon had protested a bit too much. It was a fact, as Rockne had pointed out to Keogan, that no one at Valparaiso had officially noticed, said, or did anything about the offending article in *The Torch* for seven weeks. No apologies were forthcoming from Valparaiso until after Rockne had informed Keogan of Burns' anger over the incident and of his determination to end athletic relations with them. Hogdon's dinner invitation was not accepted.

Clearly, greater forces were at work here than the president of Valparaiso could imagine. Nothing could be done about the football schedule for next year. Valparaiso was out and would stay out. Rockne had already increased the schedule from the nine games played in 1920 to eleven games for 1921 with no open dates between September 24 and November 24. As a matter of fact, Rockne had agreed to play three games in only seven days—one against Army at West Point on Saturday, November 5; another against Rutgers in the Polo Grounds in New York City on election day, Tuesday, November 8; and then still another against Haskell at Notre Dame on Saturday, November 12. Rutgers was a brand new opponent, and that game was the first appearance of a Notre Dame team in a New York City stadium. There was just not time enough or room enough in the expanding world of Notre Dame football for poor little Valparaiso.

President Hogdon did know how stretched Rockne was to meet all of his football game-date commitments, so when the dinner invitation failed, he made one more effort to set matters aright. Father William McGowan, a Catholic pastor in the city of Valparaiso, traveled to Notre Dame in late January to plead in person before the faculty board for adding a football game with Valparaiso to next year's schedule.

McGowen took himself and his mission very seriously, did his best, but had no way of knowing how utterly hopeless his mission was. McGowan described the *The Torch* as unofficial, an enterprise of doubtful repute in the university community, and for the moment out of control. He praised President Hogdon's character and spoke at length about how much the students and people generally in Valparaiso respected Notre Dame.[10] With that assertion, Father McGowan had said too much and stayed too long.

Shuster's minutes of this meeting reflected the very low interest of the board in this matter and their impatience with the style and length of McGowan's presentation. Shuster noted in the minute book how extraordinary was the goodwill allegedly exhibited by "the student body and citizenry of Valpo" toward "the school that had allowed only 3 pts. via a field goal." When McGowan finally finished and had withdrawn from the room, Shuster noted the board's intention "to weigh this matter in the scales of justice and to reconsider its virtual decision to hang out a not-at-home sign when Valpo called."[11]

Indeed, McGowan's mission had accomplished something. To be sure, there was no room for Valparaiso on either the football or baseball schedules, but basketball was open. In a spirit of reconciliation, Rockne allowed Coach Keogan to pick his dates for the 1921–22 season. Understandably, the authorities at Valparaiso declined to do so. Revenge, or at least vindication, of a sort was obtained by Valparaiso on February 23, 1921, when in a previously scheduled game, their basketball team defeated Notre Dame's squad, 32 to 26. That was to be the last intercollegiate game in any sport between Notre Dame and Valparaiso for a very long time.

The final Notre Dame insult to Valparaiso's battered and bruised athletic self-esteem occurred two years hence when Rockne hired away their football coach, his friend George Keogan, to coach baseball at Notre Dame. No wonder the hiatus in athletics as well as in other relations between these two neighboring schools was so enduring.

As the president had used the Faculty Board in Control of Athletics in the Valparaiso matter to respond to what he believed was an unwarranted attack on the university and on Irish Americans generally, Rockne used it as a mechanism for canceling scheduled games and replacing them with more renowned opponents likely to attract larger crowds. Managing the board to improve the schedule was not difficult. The president and board members admired Rockne's enormous football successes in 1919 and in 1920 and generally did not question his recommendations about such technical matters as scheduling. In practice, Rockne did what he thought was right and best for his program in such matters. Generally, though not in every instance, during Burns' presidency the board agreed with him.

— ii —

Ever since becoming head coach at Notre Dame, Rockne had been extremely anxious to bring his team to New York City. After the undefeated season of 1919 the prospects were very good that such an opportunity would arise. When Notre Dame continued to defeat all opponents in 1920, an offer to play Georgia Tech in a postseason game in the Polo Grounds crossed Rockne's desk in early November of that year. Put together by the managers of the Polo Grounds, the offer was vague about financial guarantees, but Rockne and others close to the football program were excited by it. In fact, the board went so far as to approve the principle of a postseason game before serious negotiations about financial guarantees were completed.[12]

However, when negotiations proceeded, the Polo Grounds managers turned out to be very hard bargainers. They knew how much Rockne wanted a game in New York and believed they could get the Notre Dame team into their facility on the cheap. Rockne understood numbers and immediately recognized that the financial guarantees offered were inadequate. He advised the board that guarantees were too low and that the lion's share of the anticipated gate receipts would go to the Polo Grounds management. The board behaved as Rockne knew they would and formally withdrew their approval of the game on November 27, 1920.

Chastened by losing an attractive postseason game for their facility in 1920, the management of the Polo Grounds became more reasonable. They quickly and successfully negotiated an acceptable contract with Rockne to play Rutgers in their stadium on election day, November 8, 1921. The principal loser in these negotiations so far was Georgia Tech. Authorities from that institution approached Rockne at the end of November 1920 about the possibility of a game with them in Atlanta on October 22, 1921. According to spokesmen for Georgia Tech, Rockne agreed to a $9,000 guarantee by telephone on December 1 and then confirmed the game date and guarantee by telegram shortly thereafter.[13]

Thus matters stood until Rockne recalled a commitment with Nebraska for a game on the same day as the one lately scheduled with Georgia Tech. The Nebraska series had been underway since 1915 and was very important to Notre Dame. Rockne was of no mind to do anything to jeopardize it. Embarrassed but without any room to maneuver in the very crowded schedule for 1921, Rockne told the people at Georgia Tech that the game would have to be canceled because it had not been approved by the Notre Dame Faculty Board in Control of Athletics.[14]

Upon hearing of Rockne's cancellation of the game, the people at Georgia Tech were shocked. They could not believe that Notre Dame would break a confirmed agreement in such a cavalier fashion. Two representatives from Georgia Tech traveled to Notre Dame in mid-January 1921 to try and persuade the board to reconsider the cancellation. Neither of these gentlemen were aware of the Nebraska complication. They were allowed to meet with the board and mentioned first the fact that unrecoverable monies already had been spent on game publicity. Next, one representative insisted that no suitable replacement opponent could be found for October 22, 1921. The other talked about the mutual benefits accruing to both schools if an intersectional series could be initiated. He cautioned the board about killing golden geese that laid golden eggs. This point was well made and well taken.[15]

According to Shuster's notes of the meeting, the board expressed a willingness to reconsider the matter seriously, and then, the secretary noted, "with long faces, more enigmatic than that of the presiding bust of Socrates dominating the meeting room, we withdrew and went our separate ways."[16] Four days later, the board met again in order to try and decide how some good could be salvaged from Rockne's inexplicable embarrassment of the university.[17] While nothing could be done about the Nebraska situation in 1921, there was always next year. Carey had prepared a carefully worded apology to Georgia Tech for the cancellation. The board approved Carey's letter as an appropriate response, and then voted to leave the entire business of future relations with Georgia Tech in that persuasive priest's capable hands.[18]

The shock and disappointment of Rockne's game cancellation in 1921 did not last. Carey was determined that this particular golden goose would survive. A game with Georgia Tech was scheduled for 1922 to be played in Atlanta. That game initiated a home and away series between the two schools that lasted through 1929.

No less than the university president who had appointed them, board members were fully committed to defending the interests and reputation of Our Lady's university against critics, detractors, and nay-sayers. Board members were prepared to do or say whatever the protection of those interests and that reputation required. They were also generally disposed to accommodate the coaches with supportive rulings and interpretations and usually were willing to rescue them from embarrassments of their own making.

To be sure, the board was the creature of the president and not of the coaches. The reality of their situation required that members defer to the president's wishes on all matters under their purview or leave the board. With the coaches, there were lines that most board members would not cross. There was moral ground that they would not abandon easily. One of those lines was the one separating amateurs from professionals.

The problem of varsity intercollegiate football athletes being paid for participating in professional and semiprofessional games under assumed names on Sundays or of receiving money for teaching or demonstrating football skills to aspiring players was acute and ubiquitous in the American sports world during the early 1920s. Notre Dame certainly had more than a fair share of such malefactors. Usually, players thus discovered and brought to the attention of the board were suspended from varsity competition in all intercollegiate sports. However, the risk-reward ratio of detection and punishment was too low to function as much of a deterrent between 1919 and 1922. The practice continued at Notre Dame, and Rockne was either unable or unenthusiastic about doing much to stop it.

The most blatant offenders at Notre Dame were varsity players who had completed their third year of eligibility. The temptation to play in professional games and be paid for what they did well and enjoyed doing after their final intercollegiate season had ended was very great. If detected, however, operational rules required banishment from all participation in intercollegiate basketball, baseball, and track. Some varsity players and a few local advocates for them argued that such a policy was hypocritical and unfair. Receiving money for playing football was professionalism in football only, they insisted, and therefore should not be regarded as a loss of amateur status in other intercollegiate sports.

Father Carey brought this issue before the board on November 27, 1920, argued the case against hypocrisy and for fairness. He moved that varsity football players whose eligibility had expired and had thereafter participated in professional football games should be allowed to compete in other intercollegiate sports during their final semester at Notre Dame.

Whether Carey spoke for himself alone, the president, the coaches, or for some specific players detected and facing suspension, or for all of the above is unknown. The rest of the board was neither moved by Carey's argument nor disposed to change the operative policy. Carey's motion was disapproved. In addition, according to Shuster's notes of the meeting, the board insisted upon placing in the official record a strong statement that any player whose eligibility in a sport had expired and who then had participated in a professional game should be suspended from all inter-collegiate sports for the rest of his time at Notre Dame.

Formal toleration of professionalism in intercollegiate athletics was a piece of moral ground that a majority of the board would not abandon on their own. If pushed by the president, some probably would have complied, others would have resigned. On this issue at this time, the president was of no mind to push anyone. Living with this problem and with the hypocrisy and alleged unfairness associated with it would cause less in public relations damage to the university than legitimizing inter-collegiate athletic rules violations. In this instance, the majority of the board was politically correct. Father Carey was not. The president supported the board.

The locus of football activities at Notre Dame during these years was the office of the Notre Dame Athletic Association in the Main Building. As director of athletics, Rockne administered this department with the help of a small secretarial staff and his assistant coaches. Rockne was responsible for everything that went on there. His office made schedules, purchased equipment, authorized all travel arrangements, supervised the preparation and sale of tickets, handled sports public relations, and prepared an annual operating budget. As part of his duties as director of athletics, he was also charged with preparing and administering a separate financial account wherein all Athletic Association receipts, expenditures, assets, and liabilities were properly listed and presented according to the accounting practices of those days. This account was very carefully protected from prying eyes inside the university as well as without.

Rockne was the boss of the entire athletic enterprise, and every vice president to whom he reported for thirteen years knew that and acted accordingly. He was a very special person and quickly became the one and only absolutely indispensable person at Notre Dame. He was one man the university could not afford to lose, and the only faculty or staff member at the university during the 1920s to receive an employment contract running more than one year. Rockne had been given annual contracts for a yearly salary of $3,500 in 1918 and 1919. After the undefeated season of 1919, he was given another annual contract for 1920, but his salary was raised to $5,000, plus a bonus of an additional $1,000 if he won all of his games in that year.[19] Rockne won all of his games in 1920 and collected his bonus, but in 1921 he lost only one game and did not.

Perhaps disappointed by the loss of his bonus payment in 1921, Rockne seriously considered the offer of a higher salary to move to Northwestern. He did not share his salary concerns with Father Burns at all and only did so indirectly and unspecificly with other university officials. Instead, Rockne communicated the details of the Northwestern offer and his salary concerns to two very influential alumni, Byron V. Kanaley and Angus McDonald, and wisely allowed them to deal with Burns.

Kanaley was a Chicago mortgage and bond broker who had graduated from Notre Dame in 1904 and had been a four-year baseball monogram winner. McDonald was a New York stockbroker and later president of the Southern Pacific Railroad Company, a member of the class of 1900, a monogram winner in both football and baseball, and a team captain in both of those sports. Both Kanaley and McDonald were devoted to Notre Dame, great boosters of the football program, and strong admirers of Rockne. They were absolutely determined not to let Rockne slip away from Notre Dame if they could prevent it.

Apparently, Rockne had either written to or visited with these men in late November. McDonald traveled to Chicago in early December and met with Kanaley at the Blackstone Hotel. They spent two days together discussing the Notre Dame football program and how to proceed with Burns and with Rockne in order to prevent the coach from defecting to Northwestern.[20] They decided that both of them would write to Burns separately urging the same policy, that is, offer Rockne a higher salary and a longer contract.

Kanaley wrote to Burns on December 7, 1921, advising him of his meeting with McDonald at the Blackstone and expressed their mutual fear that Rockne might leave Notre Dame. Kanaley assured Burns that the Northwestern alumni were very serious about getting Rockne as a recent story in the *Chicago Tribune* testified. He urged Burns to consider what an invaluable asset Rockne was to the university. The public relations value of a winning football program was incalculable. Money could not buy the advertising obtained by the football team for the university during last season. Moreover, Rockne was important not only for his winning teams, but also because the manly qualities of his teams reflected "such tremendous credit on our school."[21]

Kanaley suggested that Rockne's extraordinary football successes and the increased paid attendance at home and away justified a new contract for the head coach. Kanaley believed the best way to keep Rockne at Notre Dame would be to offer him a five-year contract with a substantial salary increase, and then eliminate payment of a bonus for winning every game. The bonus system, he insisted, was inappropriate for collegiate coaches and not right for Notre Dame. Aware that Burns was almost totally preoccupied with the final phase of the fund drive, Kanaley concluded by noting that among Notre Dame men in the Chicago area the possibility that Rockne might leave the university was much discussed and much deplored.[22] The point intended was clear enough but entirely unnecessary. Once Burns learned from Kanaley and McDonald that Rockne was unhappy with his contract, the president took immediate corrective action.

Burns had a long discussion with Rockne on the day after Christmas that went very well. The discussion went well because both parties were in substantial agreement about the outcome before it began. Kanaley had informed Rockne about his meeting with McDonald at the Blackstone Hotel and of the fact that he had written to Burns on behalf of all Chicago Notre Dame men urging the president to keep Rockne as head coach.[23] For his part, Burns knew that Rockne knew about the meeting at the Blackstone Hotel and that Kanaley had written to him about the football situation at the university.[24] The amiability of Burns and Rockne was appropriate for the holiday season, and the two came to terms easily. The president offered Rockne a five-year contract and raised his salary by 40 percent to $7,000 a year. The coach accepted the new contract at once and promised Burns that he would "stay at Notre Dame permanently as long as he was in the coaching business."[25]

Burns had no illusions about what had happened and why. He understood clearly that Rockne's role at the university was special and different from any other faculty member. No professor had ever or in the foreseeable future would ever be treated so deferentially and so extravagantly. The president had agreed with Kanaley, McDonald, and other likeminded alumni that such deference and extravagance were reasonable prices to pay for the financial and public relations gains of football glory.

What neither Burns, Kanaley, nor McDonald realized at the end of 1921 was that Rockne's price for football glory would have to be paid over and over again. The coach's promise to the president about remaining at Notre Dame as long as he was in the coaching business was made to Burns only and not to Burns' successor. Contract crises, threats of defection to another football program, continuing demands for salary increases, and for off-season opportunities to make more money occurred regularly at the end of every football season between 1922 and 1930. Even a ten-year contract virtually extorted from the university in 1924 turned out to be insufficient by 1928. Rockne's demands never stopped because the growth of paid attendance at Notre Dame football games during his years as head coach never stopped. The simple fact of scheduling a football game with Notre Dame was enough for a host team to justify expansion of existing seating capacity in the host's playing field or stadium.

This spectacular growth of Notre Dame football during the Rockne years is statistically traceable. In 1919 Rockne's first undefeated team played a nine-game schedule with a combined paid attendance of 56,500. The championship team of 1924 played ten games, including an appearance at the Rose Bowl; combined attendance was 318,000. By 1929 Rockne's fourth undefeated team played nine games before more than 550,000 spectators; the game at Soldier Field, Chicago, against the University of Southern California alone attracted 112,000 people. Rockne's record-breaking paid attendance statistics for 1929 would remain unsurpassed until 1947 and unequaled again until 1969 and 1978.

The enormous popular interest in Notre Dame football and the huge crowds attending games translated into increasing revenues and profits for the Notre Dame Athletic Association. For the 1919–20 season net gain (revenues minus expenditures) on football for the Notre Dame Athletic Association was $3,508. Football profits were only a few dollars more than Rockne's salary. Yet, during 1920–21 net gain on football was $14,951 or more than twice Rockne's salary and bonus.[26] That pattern did not last, however. Over the next several years, net gains from football increased enormously. Rockne wanted more of those gains for his program and for himself.

In addition, Rockne earned more than $15,000 in some years from his summer coaching clinics, although his budgeted salary for serving as director of athletics and head football coach never exceeded $12,500.[27] However, during the 1920s a combined income from the university derived from salary and summer coaching clinic stipends of $27,500 was a lot of money. By way of comparison, the highest paid faculty member, dean of the Law School, during that period earned $6,000 and no other professor earned more than $5,000.[28]

While total football expenditures rose from a modest $20,100 in 1919 to $427,000 in 1929,[29] revenues and net gains raced far ahead of that. Over the next few years, the number of games played in a season varied between nine and ten. Ticket prices were regularly increased, and revenues from radio broadcasts significantly added to net gains. Most important, paid attendance at football games doubled, tripled, and quadrupled. The result being that net gains from football rose steadily after 1922 reaching in 1929–30 a spectacular $529,400.[30]

The extent of football profitability was not fully appreciated by university leaders until after 1922 and scarcely believed then. No one thought it would last. The problem of deciding whether football profits ought to be worked into the university operating budget or reserved to finance high-priority university or Holy Cross Congregation projects was left to Burns' successors. Lay faculty always wanted and needed salary increases.

Rockne wanted a new football stadium. The university required additional residence halls and a modern dining facility. In Washington, D.C., the Holy Cross House of Studies needed an immediate and extensive renovation. Deciding what to do and when to do it would not be easy.

—   iii   —

Rockne's career as head coach of the Notre Dame football team in the fall of 1918 began unspectacularly. Because of wartime conditions and the influenza epidemic, the schedule had been shortened to six games, all in the Midwest. Many of the players were members of the Student Army Training Corps program at Notre Dame, rejected draftees, or freshmen.[31] Eligibility rules regarding freshmen and just about everything else in intercollegiate football were suspended or simply ignored during the seasons of 1917 and 1918. The team fielded in 1918 won three games, lost one, and tied two, easily defeating two overmatched small colleges and performing well against only one major opponent. Some excellent players were on this team, and the few bright moments in an otherwise lackluster season were the performance of one of them, the future national football hero *par excellence* and media darling, George Gipp.

Gipp had come to Notre Dame in 1916 from Laurium, Michigan, a copper-mining region in the Upper Peninsula, as a twenty-one-year-old freshman. Gipp's presence at Notre Dame at that time was an extraordinarily fortuitous event. There was absolutely no reason for him to be there except that he had nothing better or more interesting to do. He had been raised in a large and observant Protestant family wherein higher education was not a legitimate expectation. Not very serious about religion himself, or about anything else at that time, Gipp had been directed toward Notre Dame by a priest from nearby Calumet, who had a passion for baseball, Father Joseph Paquet. Recognizing talent when he saw it, Father Paquet had urged Gipp to go to Notre Dame, play baseball there, and perhaps follow other successful Notre Dame players into the game as a professional.[32] Father Paquet's advice was reinforced by Wilbur "Dolly" Gray, another young man from Laurium, who had spent four years at Notre Dame (1910–1914) on a baseball scholarship. Gray had spent two years thereafter playing semiprofessional baseball in Indianapolis before returning to Laurium in 1916.

Gipp was endowed with extraordinary athletic ability. For his time, he was big, strong, and fast. Despite great natural gifts of speed, coordination, strength, and endurance, however, Gipp sorely lacked the mental and physical discipline required to compete and excel. Moreover, Gipp had never been properly coached in any sport. He had not played baseball or football while in high school, usually being ineligible because of poor grades. As a matter of fact, there is no evidence that he ever graduated from high school.

Apart from much demonstrated skills at card sharking and pool hustling, some success in YMCA basketball, and impressive statistics as an amateur baseball player in the Michigan Trolley League, his life in Laurium had no direction whatsoever. In spite of Gipp's terrible high school academic and deportment records, through Father Paquet contact was made with athletic officials at Notre Dame, a scholarship was offered, and Gipp arrived at the university in the fall of 1916, registering as a freshman in the Arts and Letters course of studies.

Rockne's discovery of Gipp in the fall of 1916 while watching students pass time kicking footballs is a much-told tale. The coach persuaded Gipp to report for freshman football practice, which he did and performed spectacularly at his first practice. The first time Gipp ever touched the ball in an offensive scrimmage, he ran through the entire freshman defense and scored a touchdown. Thus began one of the most astounding collegiate football careers in American sports history.

Altogether Gipp played five seasons of football at Notre Dame between September 1916 and December 1920, that is, one three-game season of freshman football in 1916 and then twenty-six varsity games spread over four seasons, 1917 through 1920. He was a wonderful athlete and an absolutely superb football player in all aspects of the sport. In his first freshman game, Gipp drop-kicked a record sixty-two-yard game-winning field goal when both Coach Harper and his quarterback had directed him to punt. In twenty-six varsity games, Gipp rushed for more than a hundred yards ten times. In a celebrated 1920 game against Army at West Point, before a crowd of only ten thousand but widely reported in the regional and national press, Gipp personally accounted for an incredible 480 offensive yards running, passing, and returning kicks. During that same season Gipp amassed an amazing total of 1,883 offensive yards. He averaged a stunning 185 all-purpose yards in every game played during 1920. Moreover, his rushing average of 8.1 yards per carry during that same season has yet to be equaled by a Notre Dame player.[33] Gipp was a coach's wildest fantasy made real.

Having said that, it must also be said that at no time after the fall semester of 1916 was Gipp ever really a bona fide Notre Dame student. Ordinary rules and regulations governing academic progress and student life were rarely applied to him. Generally indifferent to any sort of authority and recklessly indiscreet, Gipp was pampered and protected by coaches, university administrators, and influentials in the South Bend community. Indeed, Gipp was officially registered every semester he played for Notre Dame, but that was about as far as he ever progressed toward completing a course of studies. Between September 1916 when Gipp first came to Notre Dame and December 1920 when he died, the young man spent nine semesters at the university. Of those nine semesters, he received grades for academic work during only four of them. During the other five semesters of residence at Notre Dame—fall 1917, spring and fall of 1918, spring 1919, and fall 1920—Gipp received not a single grade, passing or failing, in any courses at all. He was a registered student and played varsity football during that time but took no courses for which the university has any record.

Gipp was a classic example of an extraordinarily gifted collegiate athlete out of control. In everything he did while at Notre Dame, he was exceptional. No one in the entire history of the institution has ever surpassed his athletic performance, and no Notre Dame athlete has come close to matching his disregard for and successful avoidance of academics. The best that Rockne could say about Gipp's career at the university was that he had "fewer than the usual faults of star athletes."[34]

Gipp and many other athletes attending Notre Dame during 1917 and 1918 who had played freshman football were able to spend four years on the varsity because playing time during the war years was simply not counted in the total three-year collegiate eligibility. In any case, external supervision of collegiate eligibility requirements was virtually nonexistent during these years, and each college or university was more or less responsible for policing its own programs. Given the enormous public interest in intercollegiate football and the fact that so many men were off to war, the popular assumption was that rules violations were widespread, everyone was doing it, and that coaches simply could not produce winning programs and comply with eligibility rules.

In such an environment excesses were inevitable. Even though Notre Dame officials generally acted against rules violations when brought to their attention, during the early Rockne years by no means were all violations "brought to their attention." In the case of a celebrity athlete like George Gipp, university officials merely averted their eyes from possible violations of their own eligibilty requirements as well as disciplinary regulations.

Perhaps as potentially embarrassing to the university during these years were the flagrant perversions, if not violations, of eligibility rules by former Notre Dame players after leaving the school. Leonard "Pete"

Bahan played one year as a freshman at Notre Dame in 1916 and three years as varsity quarterback, 1917 through 1919, serving as team captain in 1918 and 1919. Because his playing time in 1917 and 1918 was not counted against his collegiate eligibility, he would have played again for Notre Dame in 1920 except for the fact that his dean suspended him for academic delinquency on September 21.[35] Bahan promptly enrolled at the University of Detroit and played there during 1920.[36]

The next year Bahan received a frantic cry for help from Edward "Slip" Madigan, a former teammate and two-year monogram winner. Madigan had played guard and center for Notre Dame 1916 through 1919 with a year out for military service. In 1921 Madigan was a young new coach attempting to install at St. Mary's College near Oakland, California, a hasty imitation of the Notre Dame football program. At St. Mary's the "Fighting Irish" had become the "Galloping Gaels."

Madigan invited Bahan to play out his final year of eligibility, actually his fifth year of varsity play, as the starting quarterback. Bahan obliged his former teammate by enrolling at St. Mary's, serving as team captain, and winning selection by the Bay area press as "All West Coast Quarterback." Heartley "Hunk" Anderson, a teammate of both Bahan and Madigan and later a coach at Notre Dame and with the Chicago Bears, observed that unlike other tramp athletes of that time, Bahan had actually enrolled at the colleges for which he played.[37]

Of course Notre Dame officials really bore no responsibility for the behavior of Bahan and Madigan, occurring as it did in circumstances over which they had no control, except perhaps as it reflected the athletic culture tolerated at the university. However, there were many in the country ready to believe the worst about the Notre Dame athletic program as well as about programs at other Catholic schools. After all, the Bahan-Madigan relationship had begun at Notre Dame, and however innocent or culpable, three Catholic schools had been involved in this sorry affair. One such person ready to believe the worst about Notre Dame and its football program was Walter Albert Jessup, president of the University of Iowa, 1916–1934, and thereafter president of the Carnegie Foundation for the Advancement of Teaching. President Jessup was an Indiana native, a very good Methodist, a Mason, a strong Republican, who was also extremely cynical about the integrity of the Notre Dame athletic program.

Mrs. Raymond Wright of Des Moines attended the Notre Dame-Iowa football game on October 8, 1921, in Iowa City, which Iowa managed to win 10 to 7. After the game Mrs. Wright attended a social gathering hosted by President Jessup wherein she heard him say that from an advertising standpoint a win over Notre Dame meant more to the University of Iowa than defeating any other team on its schedule. However, from the perspective of the quality of football played, winning or losing to Notre Dame meant absolutely nothing one way or another. It meant nothing, according to President Jessup, because Notre Dame players were not required to pass their examinations or have any certain number of credits to be eligible to play and that fellows could stay on and play five or six years. Moreover, continued Jessup, if one asked why a player had not passed his examinations and finished, the reply would be that he is a "football player." Jessup believed that possibly Iowa had some better football players on their squad; but in order to play on the first team Iowa players had to earn many more credits than was required at Notre Dame.[38]

Good Catholic lady that she was, Mrs. Wright was shocked by President Jessup's matter-of-fact condemnation of the Notre Dame athletic program and unmistakable, though unstated assumption, that a Catholic school ran a dishonest program in order to win. She wrote to Burns forthwith, four days after the game, asking him to explain the university's eligibility requirements and to send her "the truth of the matter so I may pass it on to President Jessup."[39]

What neither Mrs. Wright nor President Jessup could have appreciated at that moment was the cruel irony of his strictures on the Notre Dame athletic program. In 1929, eight years after this incident but still during Jessup's presidency, the University of Iowa was suspended by the Big Ten for illegal subsidization of athletes.

Burns answered Mrs. Wright's letter promptly on October 18, 1921. Generally, Burns' response to Mrs. Wright focused on the present and future whereas Jessup's accusations had been about the past. Burns said nothing about the eligibility waivers for athletes who had played during the war years of 1917 and 1918. Rather he said that all of the players participating in the recent game with Iowa as well as all others engaged in varsity sports at Notre Dame conformed "strictly to the regulations of the Western Intercollegiate Conference." In compliance with those regulations freshmen were not allowed to play in varsity games, postgraduates were barred from varsity sports, and consequently, students were not allowed to play a varsity sport longer than three years. Furthermore, no student was allowed to compete in varsity sports who fell "below the academic standard required for passing examinations."[40]

To reinforce that point, Burns mentioned that last year two starting varsity players had been dropped from the squad "because they had fallen below this standard." He concluded by stating categorically that the statements quoted in Mrs. Wright's letter about eligibility standards at Notre Dame were altogether untrue.[41]

Presumably, Mrs. Wright communicated Father Burns' message to President Jessup, but that message would have done little to raise Jessup's estimation of the integrity of athletics at Catholic schools. The best that can be said for Burns' response was that he meant well and said nothing that would injure anyone. Clearly by the fall of 1921, the president knew as much of the truth about rules violations in the Notre Dame football program as did President Jessup. However, for the sake of the good reputation of the university and for the progress of the fund-raising campaign with which he was at that time preoccupied, he chose not to tell it. In Burns' letter to Mrs. Wright, he denied what every sports writer in the country knew to be true. Some Notre Dame football players, especially those of star quality, spent more than three years as varsity players. The speedy halfback Alfred "Dutch" Bergman earned four monograms for varsity play in 1910, 1911, 1913, and 1914. Raymond J. Eichenlaub battered opposition defenses as a fullback for four years, receiving a monogram for each of the seasons, 1911–1914. Maurice "Clipper" Smith was a starting guard for both Harper and Rockne, 1917–1920, and collected four varsity monograms.

The great George Gipp, whose escapades Burns could not have forgotten in a year's time, had earned four monograms for varsity play, 1917–1920. Finally, Heartley Anderson at guard and Edward Anderson at end played four years for Rockne, 1918–1921, and each of the Andersons won four varsity monograms. As a matter of fact, both Andersons, completing their fourth year on the varsity, participated in the game against Iowa on October 8, 1921, that had precipitated President Jessup's accusatory remarks.

While completion of the college program and graduation of Notre Dame football players with their class was by no means as frequent in the early Rockne years as it was to become later, the graduation record of the four-year varsity players was dismal even by the standards of that time. Bergman did not graduate at all. Eichenlaub received a two-year short course certificate in architecture a year after his playing days were over. Smith and the two Andersons all graduated, but a year after their class. George Gipp could never have graduated. Of the unusual three-year varsity men mentioned above, neither the peripatetic Pete Bahan nor the enterprising Slip Madigan ever graduated.

On the central question of academic eligibility the issue is not as clear-cut as playing more than three years, but here Jessup was close to that mark as well. In his letter to Mrs. Wright, Burns had been vague about academic eligibility standards for athletes, mentioning "the standard required for passing examinations" but not explaining it. He was vague because in 1921 the standard itself was vague and only recently established.

Until the fall of 1919, there was no published official university statement defining academic good standing or delinquency for Notre Dame collegians. Academic good standing did not turn on passing a specific number of courses, maintaining a particular average, or even of carrying a certain number of courses. It was a matter of personal academic progress toward completion of a prescribed course of studies sufficient to satisfy the director of studies. Similarly, operative academic eligibility statements regulating the Notre Dame Athletic Association at this time were wondrously unspecific, declaring only that for athletes "delinquency in studies is determined by the Prefect of Studies."[42]

With the establishment in the fall of 1919 of viable colleges, academic departments, and of credit-hour requirements for completion of major study sequences and graduation, the entire academic landscape and many of the record-keeping practices at the university were changed and improved. In 1919, an official statement defining academic delinquency, not academic failure, was added to the general catalogue of the university under the rubric of "Conditions and Failures." However, that rubric notwithstanding, university officials were extremely hesitant about precisely defining academic failure. Any such definition would involve to some degree a surrender of administrative discretion in matters of student academic discipline. Within the body of the official statement published in the general catalogue, no definition of failure appeared. Avoidance of that word in the statement was deliberate. After all, parents did not send their sons to the university and pay Notre Dame prices to experience failure. Delinquency was correctable, failure was not.

Under the new rule of 1919, the passing grade in all courses was specified as 70. Failure to attain a passing grade in a course rendered a student "conditioned," that is, obligated to remove the condition in the next term by achieving a grade of 70 on a special examination or repeating the course. In addition, under this rule, students would suffer a grade penalty of 2 percent for each unexcused class absence, with the penalty rising to 5 percent for such absences occurring on days before or after vacations. Few failing grades appeared on the student transcripts of those years. The more common practice before Burns' reforms was to enter no grade at all for an absolutely unsatisfactory performance. The course had not been passed and no credit for it was recorded.

On a close technical reading of the rule of 1919 as presented in the general catalogue, the only way a student could irredeemably fail a course was to drop one without the permission of the director of studies. Jessup's point that Notre Dame football players during the season of 1921 were not required to pass their examinations or accumulate a certain number of credits in order to remain eligible was true, but it was also true for every other student in academic good standing at Notre Dame as well.

After a few years of use, the ambiguities and flaws of this system were obvious. The concept of academic probation—exclusion from all extra-curricular activities—was introduced at Notre Dame for the first time and added to academic regulations in 1923. Probation was defined simply as faculty censure for low scholarship and left at that. How students got on or off probation was to be determined by the college faculty imposing the censure. Then, in the following year, 1924, the entire system of academic discipline at Notre Dame was elaborated and reformed. Being "conditioned" was defined as obtaining a grade in a course of between 60 and 69. Grades of 59 or below were failures, that is, at least by implication, though the word "failure" was not used in the official statement printed in the general catalogue.

Any student whose work fell below the passing grade of 70 in more than one third of the courses for which he was registered "*might*" be placed on probation at the discretion of his college. Although this amount of specification certainly modernized and improved the academic discipline system at Notre Dame, accurate information about the number of students failing courses was difficult to obtain. For example, one report on academic delinquencies for 1921 issued in January 1922 put the failure rate in all courses offered at 14 percent. Another report on failures for the fall of 1922 prepared in March 1923 placed that rate at 10.9 percent.[43] Administrators really did not have reliable information about what was happening, and in large part the traditional reluctance to take a hard and fast line against academic deficiency continued.

For athletes in 1924, the constitution and bylaws of the Faculty Board in Control of Athletics were reformed as well. In effect, the eligibility regulations of the Western Conference became formal Athletic Association policy at Notre Dame. After 1924, the rules operative at Notre Dame required that athletes be full-time bona fide students, in residence for at least one year before participating in an intercollegiate sport. Students could not participate in varsity intercollegiate sports for more than three years and could not ever have accepted pay for playing or teaching a sport.[44]

To remain eligible for intercollegiate competition, student athletes had to carry the regular number of hours prescribed by the college or department in which he was enrolled. In addition, all student athletes must have passed all of the courses required since being admitted to the university.

The meaning of this eligibility requirement was interpreted in the light of the new university rule regarding academic probation, only given a positive instead of negative twist. Instead of describing the condition of probation as achieving grades below 70 in one-third of the courses taken, academic good standing and eligibility for athletes in the new Constitution and Regulations of the Faculty Board in Control of Athletics was interpreted to mean achieving passing grades in two-thirds of all courses taken.[45]

In the eyes of critics of the university's athletic programs, particularly Fielding Yost and Alonzo Stagg of the Big Nine, this two-thirds requirement for academic good standing and collegiate eligibility was below Western Conference standards. For them, the two-thirds requirement was a ploy whereby Notre Dame claimed to comply with Western Conference standards while interpreting them less rigorously than did regular conference members. This accusation formed the substance of one of the reasons Notre Dame was denied admission to the Intercollegiate Association of Amateur Athletics of America in 1929.[46]

Because present regulations of the university archives interpret rights of privacy as broadly as possible, access to Notre Dame student grade reports are highly restricted. Student academic records are closed for 100 years from the date a given record was created or fifty years from the death of the student who created it. Disciplinary records are closed forever, except to the student who created the record or to blood relatives of such students, if the student is deceased. For this reason, no analysis of student athlete academic standing during the Harper and early Rockne years is possible.

Even if student athlete grade reports were open for examination and analysis, definitive answers about the integrity of the Notre Dame football program during the early Rockne years might not be forthcoming. Normally, students received a grade at the end of each quarter, that is, two grades in a single semester course and four grades in courses running through the entire academic year. By modern standards, record-keeping practices at that time were primitive and haphazard and all record entries were by hand.

Certainly, the reform of the constitution and bylaws of the Faculty Board in Control of Athletics in 1924 was undertaken to address some real problems as well as to satisfy critics. One of those problems was that of Notre Dame athletes playing in professional and semiprofessional games under assumed names. Without analyzing student athlete grades, one cannot know how the director of studies before 1919 exercised his discretion in determining academic good standing and intercollegiate eligibility or how the college faculties acting through their new deans decided such matters thereafter.

While judgments about the academic honesty of the football program as a whole between 1913 and 1923 must be suspended, no such caveats apply in the cases of some of the university's celebrity athletes, especially George Gipp, who died in 1920 and whose academic file is open. Official university academic records support absolutely the testimony of contemporary newspapers and memoirs from that time that this greatest of all American postwar football heroes was not by any standard beyond the simple fact of registration a bona fide student during four of his five playing seasons at Notre Dame.

George Gipp lived and acted without much regard for accepted social norms and seemed unconcerned with the moral ideals of piety, manliness, and patriotism as they were preached by Cavanaugh and later articulated by O'Hara in the *Religious Bulletin*. To be sure, Gipp enjoyed the company of men as good Notre Dame students were expected to do, but he always maintained a serious active interest in women.

Unlike the performance of later star athletes who achieved notoriety and status in sheer numbers of conquests, Gipp was content to pursue one woman at a time most of the time. If recollections of friends can be believed, Gipp's pursuit could be as overpowering as his broken field running. During one stretch in early 1920, one friend recalled Gipp's infatuation with a petite brunette, Iris Tripeer from Indianapolis, as being so intense that he made five consecutive daily round trips by train from South Bend to Indianapolis just to spend a few hours with her.[47] However, neither that pace of pursuit nor the relationship itself could last. Partly because her attorney father had little use for twenty-five-year-old football players and partly because of Gipp's addiction to gambling and affection for night life and pool-hall culture, she turned elsewhere and married another before the football season of 1920 began.[48]

— iv —

What can be said with certainty about George Gipp as a student at the University of Notre Dame? In 1916, Gipp registered as a student in the Arts and Letters course of studies. He stayed in that program during fall of that year and through the end of the spring semester in 1917. A friend, recalling Gipp's behavior during this year, stated that he attended most of his classes, sat quietly in the back of the classroom, never volunteered or was called upon for recitations, and showed little interest in the subject matter.[49] Gipp's academic record indicates that his friend's assessment of his academic interests and performance was an accurate one.

During 1916–17, Gipp carried a course load of four collegiate courses and one German course taught by the Preparatory Department. He passed German and political science for the year. In biology and history failing quarterly grades were recorded, but those courses were passed by obtaining acceptable scores on "condition" examinations. English was passed only after the grade for the final quarter was changed from 66 to 70. By the end of his freshman year, Gipp had satisfied local eligibility requirements for participating in intercollegiate varsity football in the fall of 1917.

However, the declaration of war in April and enactment of a draft law shortly thereafter complicated everyone's plans. None of the coaches expected to see Gipp in the fall. He spent the summer of 1917 playing baseball for a local team near Calumet, Michigan, while waiting to see where he stood in the draft.[50] In September he found out. The Laurium Draft Board announced that Gipp would be drafted and sent along with other inductees to an army camp near Battle Creek, Michigan.

When the train left Calumet to make connections for Battle Creek, Gipp missed it. He simply did not appear with the other draftees and was not formerly inducted into the army. Gipp disappeared for about a month and no action by the draft board appears to have been taken against him. One account places him in Kenosha, Wisconsin, playing semiprofessional baseball until September. The same account states that Rockne, acting as Harper's assistant, traveled to Kenosha and persuaded Gipp to return to Notre Dame, which he did on October 14, the day after the second football game of the season and about a month into the fall term.[51]

Still formally enrolled in the Arts and Letters course of studies but returning to campus so late, there is no evidence that Gipp bothered to attend class at all. Nonetheless, he played in the next four games, suffering a broken ankle in the game against Morningside College in Iowa on November 10. After spending eleven days in an Iowa hospital, he returned to South Bend, dropped out of school before Thanksgiving, and went back to Laurium. Since Gipp was only on campus for about five weeks during the fall semester of 1917 and had been injured, his academic record for that entire year, whatever it may have been, was simply erased.

The football injury apparently resolved Gipp's status with the Laurium Draft Board. He reported for a physical examination on January 31, 1918, and was given a six months' deferment.[52] Upon returning to Notre Dame in the fall of 1918, Gipp enrolled in the Student Army Training Corps and managed to avoid active service until war's end. At that point, mid-

November 1918, Gipp dropped out of the SATC program and in effect was not actively enrolled in any academic program for half of that football season.

The six-game season played during the fall of 1918 had been shortened by wartime conditions and by the influenza epidemic. Only one game that year was played at home. Five games—one home and four away— were played during a twenty-six-day period between November 2 and November 28. The final game, a tie with Nebraska, was played at Lincoln. Celebrating both the end of the war and of a mediocre football season, Gipp, Heartley Anderson, and Frederic Larson did not return to Notre Dame and academic work with the rest of the team after the Nebraska game. They had been enrolled in the SATC, and since that program was ordered demobilized in December, for them there was no academic work to return to.

These three Notre Damers remained in Lincoln on their own, playing poker and shooting pool with local gamblers before proceeding to the Calumet area for Christmas vacation.[53] In his first year as head coach, Rockne had not distinguished himself as a disciplinarian. He either could not or gave up trying to control the behavior of his players while on official university athletic trips.

By the end of Rockne's first season as head coach in late 1918, Gipp had proved himself to be the most valuable player on the team. With the war over and many experienced players returning after military service, the prospects for fielding a formidable team in 1919 were very good. Rockne was determined to make the most of the athletic and public relations possibilities achievable by the Notre Dame football program in the year ahead. From his perspective, that meant keeping Gipp content in his personal life, in school, and eligible.

With those ends in mind, Gipp was allowed to remain formally registered as a student although he was not enrolled in any course of studies during the spring of 1919. After a few weeks, Gipp became bored with campus life and spent most of his time at Hull and Calnon's (Hullie and Mike's), a South Bend restaurant, pool hall, poker parlor, and bookmaking establishment. By the end of the spring semester, Gipp had made absolutely no academic progress whatsoever. His official record for the entire academic year 1918–19, which lists only his enrollment in the SATC and carries no grade reports at all, includes the notation, "did not take any examinations."[54]

To be eligible for varsity play during the football season of 1919, Gipp had to be enrolled in some course of studies. At some point during the spring of 1919, he decided to follow several other athletes into Dean

Vurpillat's law department, the least demanding collegiate course of studies in the university. After three years of residence at Notre Dame and having earned no grades, passing or failing, for two of those years, once again Gipp was a beginning student, but in the rules-compliance environment of Notre Dame at that time, he was eligible to play varsity football during 1919.

With his affairs at Notre Dame thus arranged, Gipp departed for the Upper Peninsula before the 1919 spring semester ended and spent most of the summer playing baseball for a local Laurium team, remaining with them until their season ended on September 21. Gipp departed for South Bend forthwith, spent one day in Chicago gambling,[55] and arrived at Notre Dame on September 24,[56] eight days after fall practice had begun. Gipp immediately began practicing with the team for the opening game against Kalamazoo on October 4. Because all past academic problems had been so easily and painlessly resolved, neither Gipp nor Rockne worried about even the possibility of present ones. Though formally enrolled in six law department classes during the fall semester, Gipp did not much bother himself about attending many of them. Out of the twelve grades given to ordinary law students during the two marking periods of the first semester, Gipp received only three. Nine marking period entries are blank. His official transcript records no academic credit whatever for any course taken during the football season of 1919.

— v —

Rockne enjoyed his first undefeated season as head coach in 1919. During that season the team played a nine-game schedule, four games at home and five away, between October 4 and November 27 before a total paid attendance of only 56,500. The largest single turnout was slightly more than 10,000 people for the game against Nebraska played at Lincoln. Two of the away games during the season of 1919 involved relatively short trips to Indianapolis and West Lafayette, Indiana. However, the other three away games took the team to Nebraska, West Point, and Iowa and involved significant amounts of travel time. Because all of the games during this season were played without any open dates, on eight consecutive Saturdays and Thanksgiving Day, for Gipp and his teammates there was time enough only for football.

No one in authority at Notre Dame evidenced much distress over how the time demands of practice sessions or team travel affected academics because in 1919 football enthusiasm had become too great to contain or regulate. Simply stated, football frenzy had seized the entire Notre Dame–South Bend community. By the end of the third game, Gipp was an immensely popular local hero in South Bend and well on his way to becoming the most acclaimed collegiate football player in the country.

After defeating Indiana, 16 to 3, in a game played in Indianapolis on November 1, mobs of students and local supporters marched lockstep through South Bend hotel lobbies and department stores, performed snake dances through the city center, and obstructed traffic for several hours.[57] A week later, the win over Army, 12 to 9, in a game widely reported in the eastern press wherein Gipp's passing was described as the best in the nation, produced an even wilder celebration in South Bend. Virtually the entire student body marched through South Bend carrying banners proclaiming Notre Dame as the Champion of the West and asserting Notre Dame Always Wins.[58] Paul Foik described the occasion for Cavanaugh, who was in Washington, D.C., as one where the students went to town and paraded through the principal thoroughfares with a band at their head. "After three hours of ceaseless yelling," Foik continued, "they returned to Notre Dame, where a huge bon-fire made of packing boxes and old barrels sent flames high into the heavens."[59]

Ironically, Gipp was not in South Bend to show himself to his admirers and accept congratulations for his West Point triumph. According to Heartley Anderson's account of the events of November 8, the Notre Dame players raised $2,100 in cash and checks to bet on themselves against the Army team. No bookmakers were involved. The winner-take-all bet was covered by cash and checks collected from Army players and their friends. The money wagered by both teams was left for safekeeping in the shop of a West Point shoemaker located near the playing field. At game's end Anderson, still dressed in his football uniform, raced to the shop to collect the team's winnings. Gipp's share of this action was $400, so being a bit richer at the end of the day he was of no mind to leave the bright lights of New York City and return to South Bend.[60]

Gipp disappeared from the team in New York City, remained in places and parts unknown doing whatever he fancied for the following week. After missing all of his classes and all of the practices scheduled to prepare for the next game against Michigan State, Gipp turned up on campus on Saturday, November 15, in time to suit up for the game.[61]

It is difficult to believe that Rockne did not know what had happened or that Gipp was the only malefactor. The coach was so angry with the entire first team that he started only one member of it against Michigan State. However, punishment of Gipp and his mates lasted only a single quarter. The regulars played the rest of the game and managed to win it,

13 to 0. While in the game, Gipp did very well. He ran for forty-five yards, threw one touchdown pass, and completed four others, totaling seventy-three passing yards for the day. Once again, the Notre Dame student body demonstrated wildly in South Bend throughout the early evening. This time, Gipp showed himself to his admirers and watched students snake dance along Main Street from the lobby of the Oliver Hotel.

At Purdue on the following Saturday, November 23, Gipp, his favorite pass receiver Bernie Kirk, Bergman, and the others overwhelmed the Boilermaker team, 33 to 13. Gipp rushed for fifty-one yards and completed eleven out of fifteen passes for 217 yards. Both Bergman and Kirk scored touchdowns. However, this most convincing victory had a sorry sequel.

After the game, Gipp, Bahan, Bergman, Kirk, Madigan, and several other Notre Dame players disappeared from the playing field and made their way over to Rockford, Illinois, to play for a professional team there under assumed names against another professional team employing Purdue players. The affair had been arranged by the ever-enterprising Madigan, and each participating Notre Dame player was paid $150 for his services. The result of this game was the same as on the previous day. The Notre Dame–led team easily defeated the players on loan from Purdue.[62]

In this professional pickup game both Bergman and Madigan were injured. Bergman recovered sufficiently in a week's time from a strained knee and sprained ankle to be able to play in the final game of the season against Morningside College in Iowa. Madigan received a severe blow to an eye that took him out of the Morningside game. That injury suffered on the sandlots of Rockford effectively ended his playing days anywhere but enabled him to turn his considerable entrepreneurial skills to coaching. Gipp came through the pickup game in Rockford intact and then went on to lead the team to a hard-fought victory over Morningside, 14 to 6. In frigid late November weather, Gipp completed six out of eleven passes for sixty-six yards, including one to Kirk for the game-winning touchdown. Sports writers from coast to coast applauded Gipp's brilliant football performances during the late season and proclaimed him to be the premier passer in the country.

Even though Rockne attempted to capitalize on the enormous publicity of an undefeated season and tried to arrange a postseason game on the West Coast against Oregon, he was unsuccessful. The Notre Dame community had enough football heroics for one year. At last, the season of 1919 was over, and Rockne must have thanked God that it was. The season ended appropriately on December 14 with a team banquet in the Oliver Hotel hosted by Rockne and assistant coach Charles Dorais with the featured speaker being George Hull,[63] a perfervid Notre Dame football booster and one of the proprietors of the well-patronized restaurant, pool hall, and betting parlor known as "Hullie and Mike's." After the monograms for the season had been distributed, the players elected George Gipp as their team captain for 1920.

Glory had come with a price, and Rockne had paid dearly for it in anxiety. Gipp and most of the first team had been impossible to manage. It was an undeniable fact that during this season there were many occasions when Rockne had lost control of his charges. Many of the players on the team in 1919 were war veterans, older in years and very much older in life experiences than most Notre Dame students of that time. As a matter of fact, Rockne was himself only seven years older than Gipp. As a group, they were extremely talented athletes who were generally undisciplined in their personal lives, unmindful of rules, and enjoyed their newly acquired celebrity status immensely.

Also as a group, the team of 1919 was probably the most unrepresentative, opportunistic, antiheroic collection of players ever to put on Notre Dame football uniforms. They were indeed the stuff from which legends could arise. They were the first of the best, and there would never be another Notre Dame team quite like them.

After the difficulties and uncertainties of the war years, the unbridled enthusiasm inspired by Gipp and the team at the university and in the town during the season of 1919 was an invigorating experience for university leaders, and they liked it. They also liked the national and regional press coverage that football glory had provided for the university. Most important of all, Catholic America had taken the Notre Dame football team to its heart. Here was achievement and excellence, albeit in athletics, but an achievement and excellence nonetheless in which Catholic Americans of all ranks and stations could and did take enormous pride. Academic and behavior problems with Gipp and his teammates, if such there were, could be examined and corrected once this extraordinary football season was over.

Over the Christmas holidays, Gipp entered a series of local billiards and pool tournaments emerging on January 10, 1920, as the champion pool player in South Bend.[64] When Gipp was not playing pool, he did what he enjoyed most, frequenting area night spots, and participating in all-night poker parties in the Oliver Hotel or at Hullie and Mike's.[65] Classes began in mid-January. Gipp enrolled in only three and rarely attended any of them. Because Burns' newly appointed deans were just lately installed and very uncertain about their respective responsibilities and authorities, Gipp's absences and general academic delinquency was not reported by Dean Vurpillat to the president until March 29, 1920.[66] However, events had occurred and had been brought to Burns' attention in early March that compelled the president to expel Gipp from the university.

Baseball practice had begun on March 2, and Gipp reported to Dorais, the baseball coach, for a uniform. A few days after practice began, baseball scouts from both the Chicago White Sox and the Chicago Cubs came to Notre Dame to observe Gipp in action. In batting practice, Gipp's performance was dazzling. At the end of the day, scouts from both teams presented Gipp with identical contracts offering a salary of $4,000. He gave both contracts to Heartley Anderson to store in his locker for safekeeping and went out celebrating in South Bend.[67] Before the night was over, Gipp wound up in the Tokio public dance hall. His presence in that forbidden place was reported to Father Burns, and as disciplinary rules required, the president expelled Gipp from the university effective March 8.[68]

Gipp reacted to this disciplinary suspension as any twenty-five-year-old celebrity athlete in possession of two major league baseball contracts would. He simply did not seem to care that his sports career at the university appeared to be over. Of course, the adulation of Notre Dame students and the South Bend community would be missed. However, if he could not play football at Notre Dame in the fall of 1920, perhaps he could play it somewhere else, and the hero worship would continue. In any case, the baseball contracts had secured his immediate future. At long last, the petty hypocrisies and annoying inconveniences of university academic and disciplinary rules, however laxly enforced, need be endured no longer. Gipp moved all of his belongings out of Sorin Hall and took up permanent residence in the Oliver Hotel, where he could live as he pleased.

Not much is known for certain of Gipp's activities during March and April of 1920. He remained in South Bend and at the Oliver, and precisely who paid his hotel bills at this time is unknown. There are several candidates: Gipp could have paid them himself, boosters and friends in town might have done so, and of course, Rockne could have found a way to take care of this matter.

One account of this period has Gipp working as a house pool player at Hullie and Mike's.[69] Whatever he was doing or whoever was paying his bills, Gipp much enjoyed the free and uninhibited life-style of the Oliver Hotel. Apparently, he believed himself to be unwelcome at the university and therefore generally stayed away. Friends saw him in town rather than he bothering to visit them at the university. However, on one occasion in

April, Gipp showed up on campus as an umpire in an exhibition baseball game between Notre Dame and a team from Mishawaka.[70] That was
about all.

News of Gipp's expulsion from Notre Dame spread quickly throughout the small world of intercollegiate athletics. He received scholarship
offers to play out his final year of eligibility from one team that he had
played against—General Douglas MacArthur's West Point—and from at
least three that he had not—Glenn "Pop" Warner's University of Pittsburgh, Fielding Yost's University of Michigan, and the Jesuit University of
Detroit.[71] One thing about this time, however, is certain. Gipp did not
participate in spring football practice when it began on March 9.

Rockne could not have been happy with either the general condition
of the team or of its prospects in the forthcoming season. Since Gipp, the
elected team captain, had been expelled, the first order of business was
for monogram members of last year's team to choose a new team captain.
Frank Coughlin, the starting left tackle during the previous season, was
elected.

In addition to Gipp, several other familiar faces were absent when
practice began. The huge center from 1919, George Trafton, had been
expelled in January for playing in some professional games in Chicago
during the Christmas holidays. In 1920, he would be starting for the
Chicago Bears. Bernie Kirk, Gipp's favorite pass receiver, was in academic
difficulty and otherwise generally unhappy with the highly regulated student life situation at Notre Dame. He did not suit up for spring practice,
seriously considered an offer from the University of Detroit, and eventually enrolled at the University of Michigan to play out his final year of
eligibility for the intercollegiate football reformist zealot Fielding Yost.
Bahan had missed so many classes since January that his availability in the
fall was much in doubt. Indeed, several other starters from the previous
year were listening to offers from other schools.

To be sure, Rockne's problems were many that spring, but the loss of
Gipp was the most serious. Without Gipp, there was no chance for an undefeated season or for a salary bonus of $1,000 if he won all of his games
in 1920.[72] So serious in fact was the prospect of Gipp leaving Notre Dame
and playing for some other team that leading members of the South Bend
business and professional community decided to intervene.

Eighty-six prominent business and professional men from South Bend
presented a very respectful and carefully worded petition to Burns, probably in late April, urging the president and his associates to allow Gipp to
return to the university as a regular student. The petitioners included two
members of the Studebaker family, manufacturers, bankers, merchants,

lawyers, physicians, and elected officials. They professed a deep interest in the welfare of the university and contended ever-so-respectfully that reinstatement of Gipp would do no harm and much good.[73]

The petitioners noted that many of the signers knew Gipp personally and believed him to be possessed of many fine qualities in addition to his demonstrated athletic abilities. They also praised Gipp for the great notoriety and national recognition that his football triumphs had brought to South Bend. The petitioners understood that Gipp had violated some of the "fundamental and necessary laws of discipline" at the university. However, the signers hastened to add that they understood that the violations were of a kind, meaning visiting the Tokio public dance hall, "that would not reflect seriously upon the character of the young man; that they were infractions of your disciplinary code and not of morals or social conventions."[74]

There was, of course, the matter of Gipp's enormously successful avoidance of academics since the fall of 1916. The petitioners opined hopefully that if Gipp were reinstated, he would "accept as he should have accepted previously, the necessary discipline of the institution and that in the classroom, as well as upon the football field, he will, in the future, do creditable work." The petitioners concluded by assuring Burns that while their interest in this matter was personal, it was "in a larger sense a very deep interest in Notre Dame, and in everything that concerns her standing and prestige."[75]

The authors of this extraordinary document certainly knew the disposition, character, and psychology of the priest to whom it was addressed very well. So well in fact that one is tempted to hypothesize that the inspiration and even perhaps some of the language in it originated with some members of the Congregation of Holy Cross. The phrasing of the petition was so delicate and so calculated to touch the heart of such a long-serving priest and local religious superior as Burns and the timing of it was so perfect that no outsider could have written it alone. As written, the petition was one that Burns would never be able to deny.

To be sure, the petition did not begin the penitential formula, "Bless me Father for I have sinned," and then end with an Act of Contrition. Yet, the impact of the petition upon Father Burns when he read it must have been as if he had put on his stole and was waiting in the confessional box to ask the next penitent when he had last been to Confession. The petitioners, an entirely ecumenical lot, in effect had privately confessed George Gipp's sins to Father Burns and asked for absolution. If genuinely penitent, absolution could not be refused. Indeed, no fitting penance could be imposed on the sinner, and there were reasonable doubts whether in this instance the sinner was or ever would be properly penitent. Cast as it was, however, the petition employed a practiced Catholic stratagem for influencing authority, that is, never make it easy for an authority to say no.

However, there were other much less esoteric, very practical reasons why Burns would react positively to this petition. The perfect timing of it could not have been accidental. Someone with inside knowledge must have advised those outside to do what they did at the time they did it. In the spring of 1920, the need for goodwill and maintaining good relations with the South Bend business and professional community had never been greater. Ever since December 1919, when John D. Rockefeller had given $50 million to the General Education Board (GEB) to assist private colleges and universities with endowment grants for raising faculty salaries, Burns had been in serious and protracted negotiations with them about the possibility of a lay faculty salary endowment grant.

By mid-April 1920, Burns was very optimistic about getting a grant of $250,000 from the GEB to improve lay faculty salaries at Notre Dame. One of the conditions for obtaining such a grant was the university's ability to raise three dollars from other sources for every dollar given by the GEB. Organizing a fund-raising campaign to obtain pledges of $750,000 in a year and collecting those pledges in three years' time would be a new and very difficult undertaking for university leaders. As noted earlier, Burns had hoped to be able to announce the grant award and the start of the fund-raising campaign at Commencement ceremonies in June 1920. However, formal announcement of the grant and the start of the fund-raising campaign was delayed until February 25, 1921.

Whether the campaign began in the fall of 1920 as Burns had originally intended or as it did in February 1921, a prime target in that campaign would be the business and professional community of South Bend. When Burns received the petition on behalf of Gipp from eighty-six prominent South Bend business leaders, he was of no mind to disappoint or alienate any of them in any way. For the next several years nothing was more important than the fund drive. Every other university activity would have to be subordinated to it and was.

Because so much was expected from the South Bend business community and in the end so much was in fact obtained, a matter as trivial as Gipp's visit to the Tokio public dance hall had to be put into a proper perspective and quickly resolved. Burns did not dally long over the petition. Gipp was reinstated on April 29, 1920, and the good news was communicated to the sports world by the *South Bend Tribune* on May 7, 1920.[76]

Gipp was himself supremely indifferent and not at all grateful for the decisive intervention by South Bend businessmen on his behalf. Reinstatement did not mean very much to him. He kept his room in the Oliver Hotel and did not bother about returning to his classes. However, on May 10, Gipp made his first appearance as a varsity baseball player. His varsity career in this sport lasted only a week. He appeared in two games, quit the team on May 21, and then left the university shortly thereafter (without taking any final examinations) to accept an offer to play football for the Jesuit-run University of Detroit during the season of 1920.[77]

When Gipp left Notre Dame, his academic record was in a shambles. It was irreparable. There was absolutely no honest way that Gipp could be declared eligible for any intercollegiate sport anywhere. Because of class absences before the suspension as well as during it, Gipp's transcript recorded only two quarterly grades out of six for the entire spring semester and carried credit in only one course for the entire year. He went to Detroit firmly convinced that his football career at Notre Dame was over.

The offer from Detroit was one that Gipp could not refuse. Cash payments may have been part of it, but there is no hard evidence one way or the other.[78] The most appealing part of the offer was the end of all nonsense about courses, grades, and academic eligibility requirements. According to Dorais' recollection of a conversation with Gipp about the University of Detroit's offer, Gipp was much annoyed by his continuing eligibility problems at Notre Dame. He wanted to go to a school where he would be able to participate in all sports without worrying about academic standing.[79]

At Notre Dame, for one reason or another, he always had been ineligible after the football season was over. He wanted to play basketball and baseball but generally had been unable to do so at Notre Dame. As Dorais remembered Gipp's conversation, Coach Bingo Brown had assured Gipp, Bahan, and Kirk that eligibility would be no problem for any of them if they came to Detroit. They would be able to participate in all varsity sports for the year they would be there. In addition, Coach Brown assured them all that the University of Detroit would impose no restrictions on where or how they lived. They could come and go as they pleased.[80]

Coach Brown's assurances were good enough for Gipp. The offer had the additional virtue of being convenient. Gipp had already accepted an offer to play baseball for the Buick Motor Car Company team in the Factory League located in Flint. At that time the quality of play in the Factory League was comparable to Triple-A competition, and the Buick team in Flint was where the Chicago Cubs seasoned some of their best major league prospects. Since Gipp had a contract with the Chicago Cubs, the move to Flint was no surprise. After all Flint was near Detroit. He left Notre Dame, South Bend, and the Oliver Hotel sometime in late May or early June, not expecting to return.

During that summer the *Flint Journal* published stories that Gipp had received an offer to play for the Canton Bulldogs, a professional football team, and also that he would leave the Flint area and return to Notre Dame when the baseball season ended after September 25.[81] Instead, Gipp honored his commitment to Coach Brown and began practicing with the Detroit team. Somehow Rockne learned where Gipp was. The coach was in a state of near panic because along with Gipp, Bahan, and Kirk three other regulars from last year's undefeated team—John Mohardt, Frederic Larson, and Edward Degree—had failed to appear. Rockne dispatched Dorais—a graduate of the same law program in which Gipp had been enrolled—to Detroit to bring Gipp back to Notre Dame or else.

Rockne made very clear to his assistant that both of their jobs were in jeopardy if Gipp did not return. If Gipp came back, he was optimistic that the others would return as well, and they would have a team worth fielding.[82] No less important was the undeniable fact that many important people in the university and in South Bend had invested time and energy, broken rules, and ignored aberrant behavior in order to have George Gipp play his final year of intercollegiate football at Notre Dame. Explaining why Gipp was playing elsewhere would be neither easy nor pleasant.

Actually, Dorais' mission to Detroit succeeded grandly. Gipp was as indifferent about the University of Detroit and the Jesuit fathers as he had ever been about Notre Dame. However, he was certainly not indifferent about the coaching future of his friend, Dorais. The combination of Dorais' employment predicament and a reminder that playing for Notre Dame would insure selection as an All-American disposed Gipp to forget about Coach Brown and the University of Detroit. What convinced him to return to South Bend, however, was Dorais' assurance that the Faculty Board in Control of Athletics at Notre Dame had met last week and had ruled that Gipp would be eligible to participate in all varsity sports at the university in the forthcoming academic year.[83]

According to Dorais, if Gipp returned to Notre Dame, he would not have to worry about grades during his final year at the university. He would be able to enjoy the same arrangement about grades, eligibility, and life-style while playing for Notre Dame that had been offered to him at Detroit.[84] Dorais' assurances were utter fabrications, outright lies. There is no record of the board meeting between June 9 and September 21, 1920.[85] Dorais simply told Gipp what he believed would persuade the star halfback to return to South Bend. In the end, however, Dorais' lies turned out to be a self-fulfilling prophecy.

Apparently, Gipp believed Dorais, left Flint on September 5, traveled to Laurium, where he remained for a few weeks before proceeding to South Bend. Bahan remained at Detroit. Kirk went on to the University of Michigan. Mohardt, Smith, and Degree returned to Notre Dame on September 17. Finally, Gipp arrived on campus on September 26. Rockne had his team back, and Dorais could rest easy about having a coaching job for another year. At long last, the coaches and players could get serious and concentrate on winning football games.

Not quite yet. On September 21, while Gipp was en route from Laurium to South Bend, the Faculty Board in Control of Athletics met informally and, on the basis of final grade reports for spring semester of 1920 provided by the brand new director of studies, Father Joseph Burke, C.S.C., unanimously had declared Gipp and Bahan ineligible for varsity play during the forthcoming football season.[86] Since Gipp had earned credit in only one course during the entire year, neither the director of studies nor the board members, acting on their own authority, could have done otherwise. Somehow the action of this informal meeting of the board, a meeting for which no official minutes were taken, was reported in the *South Bend Tribune* on Wednesday, September 22, 1920. At once, things began to happen.

The simple truth of the case was that for extremely persuasive and compelling reasons Burns had decided last May that Gipp would play football for Notre Dame during the present season. At this moment, the specifics or lack thereof of Gipp's academic record did not matter. Too much had been said, explained, or promised explicitly or implicitly to too many important people for anything coming out of Father Burke's office at this eleventh hour to change that. Burns probably met with Father Carey sometime in the evening of Wednesday, September 22, or the next day to work out a scenario for resolving Gipp's eligibility problem as quickly as possible. Most certainly, discussions were also held, probably by Carey, with the coaches on Friday or over the weekend about how best to proceed.

Since an action of the board, informal but widely reported, had declared Gipp ineligible because of academic delinquency, only the board could restore what it had taken away. Because time was so important in this matter, probably on Friday, Carey scheduled a special meeting of the board for Monday, September 27, 1920, and notified the members accordingly. Because restoring Gipp's eligibility was so newsworthy and would be so widely reported, credible reasons explaining why the board had reversed itself so quickly had to be developed. This was one of those public relations situations that occur so frequently in the lives of large, complex organizations where telling the simple truth will not do. Indeed, Carey must have been a very busy man over the weekend of September 25–26.

Clearly, during that weekend, Burns' anxiety level had risen greatly. He wanted the Monday meeting of the board to go well. For the sake of relations with the South Bend business community and with football enthusiasts everywhere, Burns wanted Gipp's eligibility restored. At the same time, because negotiations with the General Education Board over an endowment grant were in a critical stage, the president wanted Gipp's restoration accomplished with minimum public relations damage to the university's academic reputation. Maintaining credibility was essential if that was to happen.

The board summoned to meet on September 27 consisted of six members: Fathers William A. Carey; Thomas E. Burke, secretary of the university; James Galligan, prefect of discipline, and Professors John Tiernan of the law department, William Benitz from mechanical engineering, William L. Farrell of the department of history and politics. Carey served as chairman, while Farrell performed secretarial duties. All of these men had served the university primarily as full-time administrators or as teachers but not as publishing scholars.

In order to strengthen the academic credibility of the board, Burns decided to add two men with scholarly records to it at once. He chose George Shuster, head of the English department, and Father William Cunningham of the philosophy department. Both of these men had serious scholarly interests, had published articles, and were working on books. Over the weekend, Burns contacted Shuster and Cunningham and directed them to present themselves at the board meeting on September 27 and join in its deliberations.[87] No doubt, the president made very clear to these two new board members the political complexities of the Gipp situation and what would be the best outcome of the forthcoming meeting for university interests as a whole.

The strategy developed over the weekend for the Monday meeting was simple and straightforward. The only way the board could reverse itself in the Gipp matter and maintain even the appearance of autonomy and credibility to the general public was to argue that the academic information on which the denial of eligibility had been based was inaccurate. If that information was inaccurate, then the denial of eligibility was wrong and should be suspended until an accurate report of Gipp's academic record for the spring semester of 1920 could be prepared and acted upon.

The strategy adopted for the Monday meeting amounted to representing the academic information on Gipp supplied to the board by the Director of Studies' Office as being incomplete and in part erroneous. Incomplete it was. Father Joseph Burke's predecessors would have to be paraded before the board and perhaps even the world as incompetent record keepers whose mistakes had created this problem in the first place. Who better to do the parading of such mistakes before the board than George Gipp himself? In truth, that could be done by no one else. At that time, certainly no layman could ever publicly reproach Father Burke's predecessors, who were Holy Cross priests, for any reason and remain an employee of the university. Similarly, no Holy Cross priest would even think about publicly criticizing his brothers in religion.

In this matter, given all of the political implications, there was only one way to go. To be sure, that way was unprecedented and could be very embarrassing to the Burns' administration however it turned out, but the president decided to go on with it anyway. Through Carey, Burns recommended that the board allow Gipp to appear before them and make his case in person about possible mistakes in Father Burke's records. In this instance as in so many others, the board willingly, if not enthusiastically, obliged their president.[88]

The meeting on September 27 proceeded as scheduled with Benitz, Tiernan, Farrell, and Fathers Carey, Thomas E. Burke, and Galligan all present. Carey took charge, and introduced Shuster and Father Cunningham as new board members recommended by the president. Next, Carey took up the business at hand, namely, the eligibility of George Gipp for varsity intercollegiate football. Carey informed the board that the president had recommended that Gipp with Assistant Coach Walter Halas attending should be "accorded the privilege of appearing before the Board and presenting his case in person."[89]

Gipp and Halas entered the room and greeted the board. Carey asked Gipp to proceed with his statement, which he did. After completing the statement, Gipp and Halas left the room. Farrell's minutes of this meeting are sparse indeed and do not report what Gipp said, how long he spoke, or whether or not Halas offered any comments or opinions. Farrell recorded only that "After hearing the statement of Gipp, the Board was convinced that there were errors in the records of the Director of Studies and it was decided that no further action be taken in this matter until the Director of Studies makes a formal report on his scholastic record."[90]

To be sure, the number of missing entries on Gipp's record was so extraordinary for any student with eight semesters of residence at Notre Dame that the possibility of misfiling and lost grade reports had to be considered. The board was willing to go that far. Father Thomas E. Burke moved that the director of studies be directed to submit such a report to the board. Farrell made no mention in his minutes of any other statement or motion by any of the board members. After Burke's motion, there being no further business, the meeting adjourned without specifying when they should meet next.[91]

Indeed, the meeting was over, but the business went on. Presumably, Carey discussed the meeting with Burns minutes after it had ended, and neither of them could have been satisfied with the outcome. Nothing of media interest had happened. What could be released to the press? A basis for resolving Gipp's eligibility problem had been laid, that was all. The problem itself had not been resolved one way or the other. More needed to be done, and before the day was out Burns and Carey had decided what to do and to do it quickly.

Gipp's record was so incomplete that nothing could be done with it. A more complete record that in good conscience the board could approve had to be provided. Gipp would have to make up and pass the examinations missed in May. According to a memoir written many years after the event by a contemporary of Gipp, an oral examination before a group of law professors was arranged for the athlete on the afternoon of September 28. If this source is credible, the oral examination lasted two hours and Gipp passed it handily.[92]

Rockne's recollection of this incident published in 1930 was different. Rockne placed the oral examination in the spring and related it to Gipp's reinstatement after the Tokio dance hall incident. He also stated that the oral examination was conducted personally by Father Burns and not by members of the law faculty.[93] Three of the most authoritative studies of Rockne and Gipp regard Rockne's version of the oral examination as pure fiction, an example of Rockne's much-demonstrated truth stretching.[94]

What did happen? After the board meeting on September 27 and Carey's discussion with Burns, Carey contacted all of the board members and scheduled another meeting for the late afternoon of September 28. At the same time, if indeed an oral examination actually took place, Tiernan probably made all arrangements with Dean Vurpillat.

What is known for certain is that the board met again on September 28 and took up the matter of Gipp's eligibility. However, the composition of the board that met on Tuesday was a bit different from the one that had sat on Monday. Father Galligan, prefect of discipline, did not attend. Farrell was present but had resigned as secretary. Shuster was elected to replace him in that role. Assistant Coach Halas was back as an observer.

The question of Gipp's eligibility was moved by Carey. Tiernan spoke next and in very carefully chosen words made a case for restoring Gipp's eligibility. He said nothing at all about an oral examination that found its way into Shuster's minutes. However, he assured the board members that Gipp had satisfied the requirements of the law department for the spring semester of 1920. Good lawyer that he was, Tiernan said only as much as needed to be said.

Among the board members hearing Tiernan's statement, not one was audacious or humorous enough to ask Tiernan how such a wondrous academic miracle had been wrought in the short space of twenty-four hours. No one asked such a question, because no one wanted to. All present believed on their own or had been convinced that the best interests of Our Lady's university would be served if George Gipp played football for Notre Dame that year. If Tiernan's lawyer's lies were a means to that end, so be it. Sins of that sort were venial and easily forgiven.

According to Shuster's minutes, "Professor Tiernan testified that the said Mr. Gipp had followed and successfully passed the subjects required for the [law] course [of studies] in the final semester of last year." Following Tiernan's statement, the question of Gipp's eligibility was put and carried unanimously in the affirmative. Again, there being no other business at hand, the meeting adjourned.[95]

A statement announcing the board's action was released to the *South Bend Tribune* and appeared in the newspaper on September 29, 1920. The newspaper account of the events of the past two days closely followed what Farrell and Shuster had put into their minutes: "Gipp, who returned to school last week, was granted a hearing before the board and on a presentation of a statement of satisfactory work in his June examinations from the law department his disqualification was removed."[96]

The deed was done. Gipp was eligible. Given the way authority was concentrated in the hands of the president at Notre Dame and the references to presidential recommendations in Farrell's minutes, and possibly even Farrell's resignation as secretary of the board, there is little doubt that the means of resolving Gipp's eligibility problem had been orchestrated from a convenient distance by Burns. There was a certain irony in the fact that the greatest and most successful academic reformer in the history of the university also probably managed what turned out to be the most celebrated case of academic fraud and eligibility-rules violations in university history as well.

Indeed, other interpretations of the events of September 27 and 28 are possible. However, to believe that an indifferent student such as Gipp, not known for taking class notes or participating in recitations, and who had missed at least six weeks of classes during his spring suspension could have done what Tiernan said he had done requires a leap of faith that few are able to make. Moreover, Gipp's transcript carries no record of an oral examination or any indication of corrections or additions to it. Gipp was declared eligible by the board, but his academic record was left as it was. As a matter of fact, Gipp's transcript ends with the spring semester of 1920. There are no extant university records of Gipp's enrollment in classes or of receiving any grades whatsoever during the football season of 1920.

After the board's actions of September 27 and 28, Dorais' lies to Gipp in Detroit about eligibility requirements and academic demands had become a self-fulfilling prophecy. Once eligibility had been restored, especially the way it had been restored, there was nothing that university officials or the coaching staff could do to, with, or about Gipp. He returned to his rooms at the Oliver Hotel, did not bother about classes, attended football practices whenever so inclined, and at times virtually functioned as a co-coach.[97] Rockne did not appreciate Gipp's special status but endured it for the sake of the overall good fortune of the football enterprise. And how that enterprise prospered during the season of 1920.

The price of football glory in the coin of academic integrity had been high, but the product purchased was genuine. Rockne enjoyed his second undefeated season, and on the football field Gipp did everything expected of him, everything that one could ask. By season's end, Gipp was recognized as the premier left halfback in the country and had won a place on Walter Camp's coveted list of All-Americans.

— vi —

Rockne's undefeated team played a nine-game schedule in 1920. The four games with Kalamazoo, Western State Normal, Purdue, and Michigan State were all relatively easy shutouts played against teams with weak programs. The games against Valparaiso and Northwestern were won handily by twenty-five points. Only the games against Nebraska, Army, and Indiana were genuine contests.

For Notre Dame teams, games played against Nebraska and Army were always hard fought and difficult. On October 16, against Nebraska in Lincoln, Notre Dame had to come from behind to win 16 to 7. Gipp played well in a largely defensive struggle, rushing for seventy yards, scoring one touchdown, and completing six passes. Two weeks later, on October 30 against Army at West Point, Notre Dame overcame a halftime deficit of two points to win going away, 27 to 17. In this game, attended by the most celebrated sports reporters in the East, Gipp's performance was spectacular. He rushed twenty times for 150 yards, completed five passes for 123 yards, and returned punts and kickoffs for another 207 yards, amassing an incredible total of 480 all-purpose yards in a single game against one of the strongest teams in the country. Newspaper coverage of Gipp's football achievements in this game with Army made him the most famous intercollegiate football player in the nation.

The game against Indiana in Indianapolis on November 13 was not supposed to be difficult but was. After the Army game, many of the Notre Dame players believed what New York sports writers had written about them. When preparing for the Indiana game, the team suffered from an acute case of overconfidence. The Indiana team had no such problem. They had been preparing for this game for months, running Notre Dame formations in practice every day since the season started.[98] The game turned out to be an extremely physical one. Late in the first quarter Gipp suffered the most serious football injury of his career, a shoulder separation and fractured collarbone. Leaving the game to be examined and heavily taped, Gipp was unable to return until the final ten minutes of the last quarter. By that time, the Indiana team had managed a ten-point lead and seemed well on its way to the upset victory of the year.

Inspired by Gipp's return late in the game, the Notre Dame team began one of the greatest comebacks in the school's football history. Notre Dame marched to the Indiana goal line, where after two running plays Gipp scored the first Notre Dame touchdown of the day. The game-winning touchdown occurred only minutes later. After Heartley Anderson recovered an Indiana fumble, Gipp's passing brought Notre Dame to the Indiana one yard line. Joe Brandy rushed for the final score of the day with Notre Dame winning 13 to 10.

The Indiana game had been a bruising one for all Notre Dame players. Several were injured, but none more seriously than Gipp. His shoulder was so painful that further football play for the rest of the season was doubtful. The team left Indianapolis by train for South Bend on Sunday, November 14. Gipp traveled with the team but did not leave the train in South Bend. He went on to Chicago, where he gave a demonstration of dropkicking to high school students at Loyola Academy. It was a bone-chilling Chicago day, with temperatures dropping into the twenties. After the demonstration, Gipp developed all of the symptoms of a severe cold and decided to remain in Chicago for a few days to rest and see a doctor.

After being treated by Dr. C. H. Johnson, an ear, nose, and throat specialist,[99] Gipp went back to South Bend on Wednesday, November 17. Instead of returning to his rooms at the Oliver Hotel, Gipp went to his old room at Sorin Hall where he could rest his shoulder, recover from his now worsening cold, and where an old priest friend, now rector of Sorin Hall, Father Patrick Haggerty, C.S.C., would look after him.[100]

By Thursday, Rockne had decided that Gipp was not healthy enough to play against Northwestern on Saturday, November 20. The coach did not include him in the starting lineup released to the press. However, by Friday Gipp felt well enough to travel. He made the trip to Chicago and checked into the Auditorium Hotel with the rest of the other twenty-nine members of the traveling squad.

With or without Gipp in the game, Notre Dame was heavily favored to win it. Alumni groups in the Chicago area rallied around the Blue and Gold and selected November 20 as George Gipp Day. The Notre Dame allotment of four thousand tickets was sold out by November 18.[101] On a very chilly game day, thirty special railway cars carried hundreds of Notre Dame supporters from the Loop to Evanston, and even though temporary bleachers had been erected, the game was sold out. The paid attendance in Evanston of over 20,000 was the largest crowd up to that time ever to attend a Notre Dame football game.

Gipp appeared on the field during the pregame warm-up, but did not start. He remained relatively inactive, standing on the sidelines on that cold Chicago day for over two hours, possibly experiencing hypothermia.[102] Even without Gipp in the game, Notre Dame had taken complete conrol of it early, holding a lead of 21 to 7 by the end of the third quarter. Throughout the game, Notre Dame supporters had chanted "We want Gipp," urging Rockne to play the star halfback they had come to see. With about ten minutes left to play and holding a comfortable two touchdown lead in the game, Rockne decided to give the crowd what they wanted. Rockne went ahead and put Gipp into the game.

Gipp's weakened condition was obvious. He tried one running play and fumbled. However, if Gipp could no longer run with authority, he was still able to pass. He completed five out of six passes for 129 yards and two touchdowns. As a poignant period to a brilliant football career, a feverish and exhausted Gipp tried to return a punt. He staggered after fielding the ball and clearly was unable to function.[103] According to one account of the game, at that moment occurred one of the most extraordinary incidents in the history of American sport. Two Northwestern players refused to hard tackle Gipp in his weakened condition and gently eased him to the ground.[104] Thus ended George Gipp's last football game. The crowd had seen their hero throw two touchdown passes, and at the end of the day, Notre Dame had defeated Northwestern, 33 to 7.

After the game, Gipp suffered chills, his throat was extremely sore, and he ran a high temperature. Upon returning to South Bend with the team, Gipp went straight to Sorin Hall and the friendly ministrations of Father

Haggerty to rest and recover. His condition worsened on Monday, November 22. Nonetheless, Gipp forced himself to attend a football banquet organized and hosted by South Bend businessmen that night. However, after about an hour at the banquet, his throat became so painful that he left the festivities early and returned to Sorin Hall. He did not improve there. With the help of Haggerty and Rockne, Gipp was admitted to St. Joseph's Hospital in the early morning of November 23.[105]

Rockne and the team were scheduled to travel to Lansing on the next day, Wednesday, November 24, to play their final game of the season against Michigan State on Thanksgiving Day, November 25. Rockne and hospital authorities issued no statements about Gipp's condition or hospitalization until after the team had departed for Lansing. On November 23, the *South Bend Tribune* reported the general physical condition of the team as being good. Gipp was described as hurt but likely "to play against the Aggies should the going get too rough for his mates."[106] On November 24, the hospital reported Gipp's diagnosis as tonsillitis, described his condition as serious, but indicated his prognosis was good and that he would probably be able to leave the hospital in a few days.[107] In Lansing, even without Gipp, the team routed Michigan State 25 to 0, giving Rockne his second undefeated season. In South Bend, Gipp's condition stabilized for a day or so but did not improve.

Over the long Thanksgiving Day weekend, Gipp took a turn for the worse. On November 29, the hospital announced that his tonsillitis had developed into pneumonia. The patient's relatives were notified of his condition, and Gipp's mother came down from Laurium, arriving in South Bend on November 29. George Gipp's brother, Matthew, arrived from Kalamazoo a week later. Ever the optimist, Rockne was reported in the press on November 29 as expecting that Gipp would be out of danger in a few days. That was not to be. Within hours of the publication of Rockne's optimistic expectation, the two local attending physicians, Doctors James E. McMeel and T. A. Olney, reported their patient's condition as being grave.[108]

Specialists were called in from Chicago. At the suggestion of Rockne, McMeel summoned Dr. S. R. Slaymakers, an eminent ear, nose, and throat specialist to enter the case as a consultant. Slaymakers arrived in South Bend on December 1, where he remained for one day. While Slaymakers reviewed the case with McMeel and Olney at the hospital, Dr. C. H. Johnson, the specialist who had treated Gipp in Chicago before the Northwestern game, arrived and announced that he had been summoned by some of Gipp's friends. Both Slaymakers and Johnson examined Gipp and neither appears to have recommended any changes in treatment. Both Slaymakers and Johnson returned to Chicago on December 2.[109]

On December 3, Gipp rallied and some of his strength returned. He was able to hold normal conversations with his mother, Rockne, and Father Haggerty, who had remained in the hospital and near his friend since bringing him there on November 23. That very small rally lasted about one day. On December 5, Gipp's condition worsened severely. McMeel and Olney expressed no hope of recovery and feared that he would not last the night.[110]

Gipp was still alive on December 6, but barely. Desperate to do anything that might help her stricken son, Mrs. Gipp directed Matthew Gipp to ask Dr. McMeel if Dr. Johnson could be brought back into the case. Matthew Gipp approached McMeel about summoning Johnson to come to South Bend, and McMeel did not object. Johnson agreed to come and arrived at the hospital on December 7.[111] Though Johnson left his Chicago practice for eight days in order to minister to his most famous patient, he was no more successful in arresting the progress of Gipp's illness than had been McMeel, Olney, or Slaymakers. Without antibiotics, there simply was not much that medical treatment of that time could do about pneumonia and streptococcal hemolytic septeropymia. For another week Gipp lingered, passing in and out of consciousness until lapsing into a final coma in the late afternoon of December 14. Gipp died in the early morning hours of December 15.

— vii —

Letters and telegrams praising Gipp's athletic triumphs poured into Notre Dame from all over the country. They came from governors, congressmen, alumni, sports personalities, and players. Rockne released a statement to the press declaring Gipp to be the greatest halfback ever to wear a Notre Dame uniform. He mentioned his own profound sense of personal loss upon the tragic passing of one of the country's greatest sports heroes and then described the outstanding feature of Gipp's character as being a deep affection for his mother.[112] Rockne's observation at this moment about Gipp's maternal affection must have struck Burns and others at Notre Dame, however unintended, as supremely ironic.

Distraught by the untimely death of their famous son, Mr. and Mrs. Gipp blamed university officials and the coaching staff for the terrible adversity visited upon them. They had convinced themselves totally that in life their son had been ruthlessly exploited by the university and were determined to prevent any more of it after his death. Mr. and Mrs. Gipp absolutely forbade the erection of any sort of memorial or plaque intended to perpetuate the memory of their son at Notre Dame. Students and friends had organized a benefit to help pay for George's funeral expenses, but the Gipps would not take a penny of it.[113] Mrs. Gipp insisted that her son's body be transported at once to Laurium and that funeral services be held there in her church. She also made very clear to Burns and to the coaches that no priests or coaches from Notre Dame would be welcome at the funeral.[114] At the heart of the Gipp family's hostility toward university officials was the fact that George Gipp had been formally received into the Catholic Church about nine hours before he died. Though in a semidelirious state, Gipp was baptized and given the last rites by Father Haggerty.[115]

According to Father Matthew J. Walsh, who investigated the matter, Gipp had identified himself as a Baptist when he had first come to Notre Dame in 1916. Several times during his years at the university, Walsh said, Gipp had discussed with some priests, especially with his friend Father Haggerty, the possibility of someday becoming a Catholic. When stricken by his fatal illness, he much appreciated the frequent visits of priests to his bedside and the near permanent presence of Haggerty. When Gipp's condition worsened, continued Walsh, he spoke of his intention to become a Catholic to several priests "without the matter having been suggested to him."[116] Burns mentioned in a letter to Cavanaugh as early as December 6 that Gipp "wants to be baptized before he dies, if he is to die."[117]

Walsh insisted that the desire to become a Catholic was repeated many times during the two or three days prior to his death. When offered the opportunity of doing so, Walsh stated, "he put the matter aside on the ground that he did not wish to offend his mother who was very devoted to her own religious belief" and wanted her son to die in the faith in which he had been reared. On the last day of his life, according to Walsh, Gipp told Haggerty that when he was "going out" he wanted the priest "to fix him up." In accord with that request, Walsh concluded, Father Haggerty baptized Gipp 4:00 P.M. the day he died (*sub conditionen*) because he "was in some what a delirious condition."[118]

On December 15, Mrs. Gipp allowed her son's body to be taken from the hospital to the McGann Funeral Parlor on North Michigan Street. Early in the morning of December 17, Mrs. Gipp's objections notwithstanding, a requiem Mass for Gipp was celebrated in Sacred Heart Church on campus. Classes were canceled for the day so students could attend the Mass and visit the funeral parlor to pay their last respects. At about 10:30 A.M. a long procession took the casket from the funeral parlor to the railroad station, where a large crowd had gathered to bid a final farewell to their dead hero.[119] At noon, Gipp's casket was put on a Chicago-bound train and began its long journey to Laurium, arriving there for a late afternoon funeral on December 18.[120]

Virtually all of the businesses in Laurium and Calumet were closed out of respect and most of the local dignitaries attended the funeral.[121] From Notre Dame, Heartley Anderson and Frederic Larson, who lived near Calumet, made the long trip north with the casket as did a few other players and some ordinary students. Mrs. Gipp's wishes were respected. No university officials, Holy Cross priests, or members of the coaching staff attended the funeral.[122] Frank Coughlin, who had replaced Gipp as team captain after the Tokio dance hall incident, delivered the eulogy. Coughlin described Gipp as one of a kind, a great athlete, a man among men, brilliant and unassuming, and filled with love for the old school. "He will forever be remembered," concluded Coughlin, "as a friend, a student, an athlete, and a gentleman, for to know him was to love him."[123]

Coughlin's eulogy was formal and appropriate for the time and place. It did what eulogies are supposed to do. Gipp was to be remembered positively and graciously by a fellow athlete for those friends and teammates who had known him longest and would miss him most. However formal the eulogy, Coughlin was absolutely correct in noting that Gipp was one of a kind. There would never be another like him at the university. No other Notre Dame player would ever again enjoy the celebrity status of a George Gipp, and never again would local and regional athlete eligibility rules be so regularly and so shamelessly violated as they had been on his behalf.

Moreover, no other player or group of players would ever again be publicly perceived as being so directly responsible for Notre Dame football success as had been Gipp. Henceforth, that responsibility and all of the celebrity status accompanying it would be reserved for the head coach. In time, a very short time, Rockne would become a media darling in his own right, a national football idol, and as much of a public relations and management problem for the university as Gipp had ever been for him.

— viii —

During Gipp's final days verbal exchanges between the dying athlete's family and university officials were frequent and heated. Father Burns had been particularly offended by remarks of Matthew Gipp about Notre Dame and by what he perceived to be an undisguised anti-Catholic attitude. Unable or unwilling to attribute Matthew Gipp's offensive remarks to grief over the untimely death of his brother, Burns could neither understand nor forgive the family's hostility toward the university and the Holy Cross Congregation. In return, Burns developed a profound dislike of the Gipps and ended all communication with them. The principal victim of this dislike was Dr. C. H. Johnson.

Dr. Johnson, a Chicago nose and throat specialist, had been invited into the Gipp case as a medical consultant by Matthew Gipp. He had spent eight days in South Bend attending to Gipp in concert with the local primary care physicians. After Gipp died, Johnson presented a bill for $750 to the Gipp family. He received no response whatever from the senior Gipps and an "insolent letter" from Matthew Gipp directing him to collect whatever he could from the university.[124] Next, in late December, Johnson sent a similar bill to the Athletic Association which Rockne neither acknowledged nor paid. Finally, on March 3, 1921, the doctor wrote to Burns explaining his version of what happened and asked for prompt settlement of this account.[125]

Burns responded at once but not in the manner expected by Johnson. The Athletic Association had already paid out $1,200 for hospital costs and physician's fees,[126] and Burns was not willing to pay any more. Burns advised Johnson that Rockne denied any responsibility for bringing him into the case. Moreover, Rockne had told Burns that Matthew Gipp had engaged Dr. Johnson, and Matthew Gipp should be responsible for the bill. Clearly much more than a bill of $750 was at issue here. Burns was of no mind to assist any of the Gipps in any way. If Dr. Johnson wanted his money, then he would have to find some way of getting it from them.

Throughout the spring of 1921 Johnson continued to press Burns for a settlement, insisting always that Rockne had assured him at the time he entered the case that the Athletic Association would pay for his services. Burns' response was always the same. The university had not been responsible for employing the doctor in the Gipp case and therefore had no obligation to pay him.

Discouraged by Burns' refusal to reconsider or compromise, Johnson tried another tactic. In late April, Johnson's nephew met with Rockne at the university and discussed the situation at length and probably threatened legal action. According to the nephew, at the end of that discussion, Rockne recommended that Johnson write another letter to Burns politely requesting that the president reconsider.[127]

Indeed, the doctor took Rockne's advice and wrote another letter to the president. However, by this time, June 1921, Burns had heard enough about this subject from Dr. Johnson. As far as Burns was concerned the matter was closed. He was not going to change his mind and decided not to answer any more of the doctor's letters.[128]

Frustrated and angered by Burns' adamant refusal, Johnson dropped the matter for almost a year. Then, in late March 1922, the doctor revived his cause against the university by engaging the law firm of Lowenthal and Mums to pursue the matter for him.[129] At that time, Mr. Lowenthal wrote to Burns informing him that his law firm had been retained to represent Dr. Johnson in a possible legal action against the university. He also advised Burns that several witnesses were prepared to come forward and testify under oath to overhearing Rockne ask Dr. Johnson to come to South Bend and attend to George Gipp. Because of this new circumstance, Lowenthal continued, "the University or Coach Rockne is responsible for Dr. Johnson's bill of $750." He requested a reply from the president by return mail and received one.[130]

Burns was not intimidated by Lowenthal's revelation about new witnesses or by his threat of legal action. The president simply reiterated his long-standing position that the University of Notre Dame had no responsibility for the employment of Dr. Johnson in the Gipp case and left the next step to Johnson and his lawyers.[131]

Lowenthal and Johnson realized that nothing could be done with Burns without going to court, but the amount recoverable was not worth the time and trouble of pursuing that remedy. If the threat of legal action could not move Burns and actually going to court was impractical, some other way of resolving the matter would have to be found and was.

Most likely, Johnson received advice from persons at Notre Dame about the best way to resolve his problem. Canon law requirements would take Burns out of the presidency three years hence, no later than July 1925, and at that time Johnson could reopen the matter with his successor, who might be more disposed to put an end to this embarrassing business. However Johnson did not have to wait that long. Burns chose not to be reappointed for a second three-year term as president in July 1922 and was succeeded in the presidency by Father Matthew J. Walsh, the serving vice president under both Cavanaugh and Burns.

The doctor wasted little time in approaching the new president. Johnson traveled to Notre Dame in mid-October and met with Walsh. He thought that meeting went well and came away believing that Walsh favored a settlement.[132] Yet nothing happened. So Johnson went back to Notre Dame in November, bringing legal counsel with him. Johnson and his lawyer met with a group of university officials that included Walsh, Rockne, and the university counsel. Out of this November meeting came a basis for settlement which was not fully and finally implemented until January 10, 1923.[133]

Walsh continued to assert that the university had no obligation to pay Johnson anything and steadfastly maintained that Burns' decision not to pay had been correct. Nonetheless, he offered the doctor a compromise settlement of $350. The settlement offer involved no acceptance of liability by the university. In effect, Rockne had forced Walsh into making it. Walsh admitted that when Rockne made a statement at their last meeting in front of witnesses that possibly "he had committed himself in some way [to engage Johnson] but had no definite recollection of doing so,"[134] denial of a financial obligation to Dr. Johnson had become impossible. The doctor accepted the compromise with thanks.[135] At long last for university leaders, the spectacular but corrupting era of George Gipp had finally come to an end.

In this controversy with Dr. Johnson as in others later, Walsh wanted to do right by the historical record. Walsh collected all of the Johnson correspondence and carefully filed it with the rest of the Burns presidential correspondence. At least one part of the George Gipp story, the final part, would be preserved as it actually had happened. In the years ahead, much of that story would be forgotten, some of it would be suppressed, and of course the heart of it would be compressed and transformed by Rockne and his media friends into one of the greatest and most enduring American sports myths of the twentieth century, the "Win one for the Gipper" story.

—   ix   —

Rockne's first published account of the "Win one for the Gipper" story appeared in *Collier's* magazine in November 1930. This article had been ghostwritten by John B. Kennedy, an associate editor of that magazine. It became the basis for Kennedy's completely ghostwritten *Autobiography of Knute Rockne,* published shortly after the coach's death in 1931.[136]

According to the magazine account, as George Gipp neared death there was a moment when he and Rockne were either alone or out of anyone else's range of hearing in his hospital room. At that moment, Rockne wrote, Gipp said to him, "Some time Rock, when the team is up against it, when things are wrong and the breaks are beating the boys—tell them to go in there with all they've got and win just one for the Gipper. I don't know where I'll be then, Rock. But I'll know about it, and I'll be happy."[137]

There were no witnesses to this alleged deathbed conversation related by Rockne. No mention was made of it by Rockne to anyone at the time. As a matter of fact, no mention was made of this alleged Gipp statement to anyone until Rockne used it in 1928 to inspire a mediocre Notre Dame team to defeat Army. Given the absence of direct corraborative evidence at the time or later, the probability that George Gipp said anything like what Rockne attributed to him in St. Joseph's Hospital in 1920 is low, and the probability that Rockne made it up in 1928 is high.

In December 1920, neither Rockne nor anyone except immediate family had easy access to Gipp's room when his condition deteriorated. So many students and local people wanted to visit their hero that visiting hours and the number of visitors allowed into Gipp's room had to be strictly limited. From December 5, when the doctors gave up any hope of recovery, until the moment of death in the early hours of December 15, Gipp was constantly attended by physicians, hospital staff, Mrs. Gipp, Matthew Gipp, and the ever-present Father Haggerty. Moreover, Rockne could not have visited the hospital at all between December 4 and December 7 because he was in Chicago attending a coaches' conference.[138] Most important, given the hostility of the Gipps toward university officials and the coaches, Rockne's visits to the hospital after returning from Chicago could not have been frequent, prolonged, or tension free. In any case, Gipp slipped in and out of consciousness during his last days and was unable to communicate lucidly with anyone. Overall, opportunities for a private moment between Rockne and Gipp when their famous alleged conversation could have taken place without others hearing it were rare, probably nonexistent, during the last week of Gipp's life.

If opportunities for a conversation as reported by Rockne were minimal, one has to ask whether an expression such as "Win one for the Gipper" was one that Gipp would have used? Was such an expression or the sentiments behind it characteristic of him? When he was healthy, the answer to these questions would probably be no. When stricken by a terminal illness and aware of it, the answer must be who can know? In 1979 Michael R. Steele interviewed two elderly former teammates of Gipp who, he hoped, might know. Paul Castner and Chet Grant were contemporaries of Gipp and past eighty years of age when Steele interviewed them. Grant had known Gipp longer and was a bit less admiring of Rockne than Castner.

Castner believed that Gipp was capable of saying what Rockne had attributed to him.[139] Grant admitted to doubting the truth of Rockne's account at one time, but in 1979 he thought that the story as told by Rockne was credible.[140] Both Castner and Grant agreed that Gipp had never referred to himself as "the Gipper." Grant took that point another step further by stating that he had "never heard Gipp referred to as Gipper before."[141] In this instance, however, Grant's memory had failed. A reporter for the *South Bend Tribune* used the word "Gipper" in a story published on December 17, 1920, about the progress of the Gipp cortege from the McGann Funeral Parlor to the Union Station.

In the end the recollections of these two octogenarian Rockne players decide nothing. They both believed that some sort of conversation about the team may have occurred between Rockne and Gipp in December 1920, but whatever it was, Rockne improved upon it in 1928. Castner and Grant did not know what actually had happened, if anything, in Gipp's hospital room in 1920. After two generations of sports writers and after-dinner speakers, as well as a popular Hollywood film and even a president of the United States had sanctified this great American sports legend, they were of no mind to challenge or even cast serious doubt upon it. Nonetheless, it is extremely unlikely that before dying George Gipp ever said to Rockne, "Win one for the Gipper."

Over the years, Rockne's famous exhortation to "Win one for the Gipper" has become a widely understood and much used American cultural expression for overachievement, success after extraordinary individual effort, and triumph of the underdogs. Having entered the spoken language of ordinary people and being understood by them, most Americans use the expression "Win one for the Gipper" without need for explanation in a variety of contexts. This expression is a distinctive Notre Dame contribution to our country's store of popular cultural values.

— 7 —

THE PREFECT
AND THE PROFESSOR

Matthew Walsh came to the presidency of the university extremely well recommended. All groups within the clerical community had great expectations for him. He was a close friend and protégé of Cavanaugh. Burns liked and trusted him. He was popular with both older and younger members of the congregation. The provincial superior and superior general believed that as president Walsh would continue modernization and academic improvement of the university while preserving the character of the old Notre Dame.

Except for congratulating the presidential choice of the Chapter, lay faculty normally did not publicly express themselves about Holy Cross politics, the presidential selection process, or about the priest chosen by it. One possible source of misgivings over the Walsh appointment might have been the athletic department. Even though there is no evidence one way or the other how Rockne or the other coaches regarded Walsh, they certainly must have been distressed by Burns' resignation. They would certainly miss him. No president could have been more accommodating to the special needs and problems of the athletic department than had been Burns.

Walsh's early career path was similar to that of his predecessor. Both had spent their early adolescent years at Notre Dame and had been virtually brought up there. Born in Chicago in 1882, the seventh of ten children, Walsh attended parochial schools in that city. In 1897, at the age of fifteen, with strong support from his mother, Walsh decided to become a priest. The provincial accepted the young man's application and installed him in the Preparatory Department of the university so he could finish secondary school.

Walsh entered the college in 1899 and graduated in 1903. After spending the next year in a novitiate, he went off to the Holy Cross House of Studies in Washington, D.C., to study theology. While doing his theology, Walsh found time to pursue graduate studies in history at the Catholic University of America, receiving his doctorate in 1907. He attended summer school at Columbia University in that same year and then enrolled in some economics courses in Johns Hopkins University in September. However, Walsh only stayed there for one semester. He was recalled to Notre Dame to begin teaching in January 1908 because a popular teacher of history had resigned to take a position in the U.S. Consular Service.

Ordained in Washington shortly before Christmas 1907, Walsh returned to the university to teach American history and serve as rector of Corby Hall. Only four years after ordination and being only twenty-nine years old, Cavanaugh selected him to serve as his vice president. Walsh remained in that post for six years, learning from Cavanaugh, marveling at how that man ran the university virtually single-handed, sometimes serving as acting president during his mentor's increasingly frequent absences, and trying to talk Schumacher out of attempting another new academic venture.

Knowing little of the world except James Burns' House of Studies in Washington, D.C., and John Canvanaugh's Notre Dame and wanting to know more, Walsh, along with several other Holy Cross priests, volunteered for military service as chaplains when the United States entered the World War in April 1917. He was commissioned and served with great distinction in combat with the Third Division in an infantry regiment. Later, Walsh was appointed senior American Army chaplain for the Paris District. There was not much occurring at the Front or behind the lines that this priest from Notre Dame did not personally witness or hear about from friends. In less than two years, Walsh had seen more of the world than most Holy Cross priests could even imagine after a lifetime of hearing student confessions.

Like so many others who had served in the Great War, Walsh had been changed by the experience of it. He brought back from the war a clear conviction that no one was indispensable. He also brought back a clear idea of what, good and bad, ordinary men were capable of. This is not to say that wartime experiences had turned Walsh into a pessimist or a cynic. However, during his presidency and later, arguments derived from idealism or from concerns about the human condition simply did not much affect him. In his relations with lay faculty, students, and even with some Holy

Cross priests, he faithfully believed and observed the principle that no one was indispensable. At the same time, Walsh tolerated levels of performance from each of those constituencies that would have appalled Burns.

People who knew Walsh well liked him, but for most, getting to know him well was difficult. One who did was Father Charles L. O'Donnell, a fellow chaplain veteran of the war and his successor as president. O'Donnell, who was inclined to give his friend a bit more credit than was deserved, asserted on more than one occasion that by carefully controlling operating costs and erecting revenue producing facilities on campus Walsh had saved the congregation from possible bankruptcy.[1] Others in the congregation saw Walsh as timid, hesitant, and unable to relate well to some lay faculty, particularly to some important ones who had been particularly close to Burns. He demanded deference from them and usually got it, but virtually none were ever brought into his inner circle, and none except Rockne were allowed to think that they were indispensable. Shuster had little respect for him as an academic leader, and Rockne positively disliked him.

Part of Walsh's problems with important lay faculty such as Shuster and Rockne were rooted in personality differences, in the widespread faculty anxiety over annual contract renewals, and in Walsh's administrative style. Walsh kept confidences well, too well for some, and was a true believer in the need-to-know principle. He did not believe in lengthy explanations and himself did not give away much information. Outbursts of candor that Burns had used so often and so effectively to charm foundation officials and terrify underachievers were not Walsh's style. One Holy Cross priest recalled observing Walsh in old age break off a personal recollection of an old controversy in midsentence when younger priests came within earshot.[2]

— ii —

When Walsh assumed the presidency of Notre Dame in July 1922, he found himself confronted by a most serious and ugly external problem. That problem was a strident anti-Catholicism propagated throughout the country but especially in Indiana by a newly revived Ku Klux Klan. Klan-inspired anti-Catholicism was an unpleasant fact of life of Hoosier politics throughout the 1920s. For most of the decade, in Indiana it was almost respectable to be anti-Catholic. As will be shown later in more detail, the Notre Dame community was touched directly by instances of Klan verbal abuse and actually threatened with physical attack. Elements of the Notre

Dame community reacted to such displays of Klan bigotry with embarrassing aggressive actions of their own.

Whatever Walsh and other university leaders proposed or did to improve facilities at Notre Dame, especially revenue-producing ones, during this troubling decade occurred within national and local contexts of intensifying anti-Catholicism. These very tense and difficult circumstances made university leaders a bit wary and cautious at times. However, no matter what was being said about or happening to Catholics in the larger society, the university had needs that could not be ignored or deferred. As was his way, Walsh slowly but deliberately found the resources to deal with them.

The root cause of the university's internal problems was the rapid expansion of student enrollment during the last two years of Burns' administration. During Walsh's six-year tenure as president that trend continued. Between 1922 and 1928 student enrollment increased 66 percent whereas over the same period, faculty size grew by only 21 percent.

Walsh's two preoccupations during those years were the initiation and completion of a building program that would enable the university to cope with and manage the growing student population and the containment of lay faculty salary costs. Walsh had no doubt that such priorities for resource allocation were needed. The financial problems and opportunities created by the enrollment increases were obvious. When Burns left office, more than 1,100 out of 1,600 students were living in off-campus housing. Only 135 students had paid for food service at the university dining halls in 1921–22.[3] The new president was determined to reroute the flow of student dollars from South Bend landlords and restauranteurs to the university.

To that end, no less than two temporary residence facilities—Freshman Hall and Sophomore Hall—and three permanent residence halls—Howard, Morrissey, and Lyons—with a total capacity for 900 students were constructed at a cost of $896,000 in five years' time.[4] After the plans for Freshman Hall had been completed, Father O'Hara, then prefect of religion, urged Walsh to add a chapel to the proposed building even though such remodeling would reduce the student capacity of the hall from 194 to 174. Walsh accepted O'Hara's recommendation, as he usually did, and thereafter all new residence halls were designed to include chapels.[5]

To complement the new housing arrangements as well as to meet a need of very long standing, Walsh also obtained authorization for construction of a large multipurpose central dining facility with a capacity for feeding over 3,000 students and faculty at a cost of $860,000. At the same time, a basketball arena extension budgeted at $149,000 was added to an existing gymnasium, new laundry and dry cleaning equipment costing $50,000 was installed in an existing facility, and one new academic facility—an extension to Science Hall providing seventeen new classrooms and seven laboratories—valued at $77,000 was completed.

The dollars spent reveal much about Walsh's priorities and also about the direction in which the ruling councils of the Congregation of Holy Cross wanted the university to move. The future religious and residential character and financial solvency of the university was affirmed. Completion of these projects involved no assumption of long-term debt. All of these projects except the extension of Science Hall were actual or potential revenue producers and all were financed in part out of football revenues.

By the time Walsh became president, residence halls were regarded by Notre Dame officials as an essential part of university life, as much for their impact on student religious and moral formation as for needed revenue. Notre Dame residence halls have been described variously over the years as miniature parishes, cloisters providing the quiet atmosphere for the mandatory three-hour evening study period, constituencies for student politicians, training centers for the university's extensive intramural athletic programs, and reformatories for rich Catholic adolescents. Students have remembered their residence-hall experiences in various ways. The personality and zeal of individual rectors would determine just what they remembered of it.

Rectors themselves tended to be more positive about the value of residence-hall living. One very popular and extremely successful rector, the close friend of the late George Gipp, Father Patrick Haggerty, wrote in 1925 that a residence hall was much more than a building where students studied and slept. It was a proper setting for character formation and a place where the indefinable but always recognizable spirit of Notre Dame could be promoted and nurtured.[6] In 1922, because of the lack of facilities, less than half of the students enrolled in the university were able to have a residence-hall experience of any sort. It must be admitted, however, that at that time a great many of the students living off-campus were content to do without one.

According to a report from the director of off-campus student housing sent to Walsh in 1922, about half of his charges had moved into the city because there was no space for them on campus. The other half moved there because they wanted to escape university rules. Most of this latter group disliked being continuously watched and objected to being checked for morning prayers and being required to obtain permission in order to go into the city.[7]

From the director's point of view, far too many students lived in housing unapproved by the university. Off-campus students were the principal violators of university rules against drinking and frequenting public dance halls. The director was especially fearful for those young men who had taken rooms in the local YMCA and would be subjected to the Protestant religious influences of that institution. He wanted a rule promulgated prohibiting students from living in the YMCA or in any clubs within five blocks of the business district. Though virtually everyone in the Notre Dame administration shared the director's concern about the spiritual danger to Catholic students living in the YMCA, he did not get the prohibition he wanted because the Notre Dame basketball team played its home game schedule there and had no place else to go. Finally, with so many students scattered about South Bend, there was no way to compel them to be in their rooms studying after 4:00 P.M.[8]

The director's concern for the religious and moral wellbeing of off-campus students was reinforced by data from the Registrar's office and by financial considerations. Ninety percent of the students suspended for excessive absences lived off campus, and the course failure rate of that group was much higher than that of students living in residence halls.[9] In the end, of course, the whole question of what kind and how many new residence halls ought to be built and when to do it turned on money.

The most pressing needs, however, were met first by closing the freshman and sophomore years of the Preparatory Department, which provided space for about two hundred new collegians. Next, a temporary wooden dormitory, known as Freshman Hall, to accommodate 200 students and costing only $39,600, was completed before the end of 1922. A second temporary wooden building named Sophomore Hall, a bit more commodious than Freshman Hall and costing $69,000, was finished in time to receive another 200 students in 1923. These two obvious temporary structures were quickly and quaintly named by students as the "Cardboard Palaces." Permanent architecturally attractive brick residence halls were much more expensive than unsightly, hastily built wooden dormitories. Nonetheless, many at Notre Dame urged the president to move ahead as soon as possible.

There was also the matter of Burns' unfulfilled promise to the alumni when the funds collected for "Old Students' Hall" had been raided to complete the fund drive. Legal complications had been raised by the architect who had designed "Old Students' Hall" when his plans were put aside. To avoid contract litigation, the name of the first new permanent brick residence facility was changed from "Old Students' Hall" to Howard Hall. Though the name "Old Students' Hall" was never used for a student residence, Burns' promise was in large part redeemed in 1931 when the university added Alumni Hall to its inventory of student residences.[10]

On the important subject of how much the university should spend on new permanent residence halls, the financial considerations underlying decision-making were succinctly put to Walsh by a Chicago financial advisor. Because any debt incurred in new construction would be very short-term and easily retired with football revenues and room rents, it was immaterial whether university officials decided to build one, two, or three new permanent residence halls. By putting up only one hall now and delaying the others until the cash for building them was in hand, immediate rental income would be lost, an income that "is now literally scattered along the streets of South Bend."[11] Walsh was not persuaded that haste was better. He opted for the cash-in-hand strategy, putting up Howard Hall in 1925, Morrissey Hall in 1926, and Lyons Hall in 1927 at a total cost of $787,300.[12]

After the funding for Howard Hall had been settled and ground broken, the next construction priority was expansion of the gymnasium to include a new basketball arena with a seating capacity of 5,000. Rockne got this new basketball arena because Walsh and O'Donnell knew that football revenues would pay for it. Times had changed since 1919 when Father Burns had been denied permission to spend $650 to improve Cartier Field.

The centerpiece of Walsh's building program was a central dining hall. When Walsh assumed office in 1922, students had a choice between two campus food services. Students could pay $375 a year and take all of their meals in the Brownson Hall Refectory or buy meals on a pay-as-you-go basis in a cafeteria located on the first floor of Badin Hall. In 1920, Father Burns had leased cafeteria space to Olin Clark of the Kable Restaurant group in South Bend.

Clark had been so successful in providing quality food service at reasonable prices in his cafeteria that 90 percent of the students chose to eat there rather than pay board and take their meals in the university dining hall. The reason for reforming food service and constructing a new dining facility was not to improve the food service but to direct student food-service dollars away from Clark's Cafeteria to the university.

Burns had given Clark a six-year contract with extraordinarily generous terms. The rents charged Clark were equivalent to what the space leased to him would have earned if used for student rooms. Because Clark had captured 90 percent of student food-service business, there is no doubt that he was making a very large profit from this contract.

As Walsh explained to an alumnus in 1924, "too much liberty was given to the proprietors of the cafeteria . . . [with the result] that practically the only dependable source of revenue has been taken away."[13] Clark's contract expired in July 1926, and as soon as that happened, Walsh intended "to erect a mess hall or convert one of the large dining rooms into a cafeteria and employ some experts as managers."[14]

After becoming president, Walsh took some immediate steps to correct a situation that had become financially ridiculous. He asked the Provincial Council as early as April 30, 1923, for permission to plan a central dining facility, but no action was taken. Then, in September 1924, Walsh required all freshmen living on campus to pay board and eat all of their meals in the university dining hall. At the same time, the president required that all other students make a choice between the cafeteria and the university dining hall and stay with that choice for an entire semester.[15] The effect of these two actions was dramatic and revealing. During 1924–25, with only 900 students paying board, dining-hall profits rose to $157,000.[16]

Thereby, Walsh had a fair idea of how profitable the Clark operation was and what the potential profit to Notre Dame might be if all students took their meals in a university-owned food-service operation. Whatever the cost of a new dining hall managed by professional food-service personnel for the university, it was worth paying, because the profit potential from this hitherto underdeveloped internal resource was so great.

Thus matters stood, more or less, until Commencement exercises in June 1924, when the university awarded an honorary degree to the distinguished Boston architect, Ralph Adams Cram. A passionate devotee of the Gothic style, Cram's work profoundly influenced the course of Protestant and Catholic church architecture during the first forty years of the twentieth century. He had worked on the Cathedral of St. John the Divine in New York City and was the principal architect in the rebuilding of West Point. Cram had served as the supervising architect at Princeton University for twenty-two years and produced a consistency in Gothic style there that was rare in American universities. His masterpiece was the state capitol in Lincoln, Nebraska.

In addition to his stunning array of architectural credits, Cram had been a professor of architecture at the Massachusetts Institute of Technology, a much-published scholar, a founder of the Medieval Academy of America, prolific popular writer on cultural and social issues, and a recipient of honorary degrees from Yale, Princeton, and Williams, as well as from Notre Dame. This extraordinary man was worthy of any accolade the university could bestow.

During Cram's few days at Notre Dame in June 1924, he expressed a willingness to Walsh to assist the university in any new building projects. Walsh seized the moment and explained to Cram his thinking about a new central dining hall for the university, a facility that could seat 3,000 students at a single sitting. Cram responded to Walsh's explanation by agreeing to design such a building at no charge to the university.[17]

Delighted with the prospect of having a Cram-designed building at Notre Dame, Walsh approached the Provincial Council and explained how food-service profits from the new facility would easily and quickly pay for it. He obtained authorization from the Provincial Council to spend $500,000 on the project. Walsh did not get back to Cram until 1926,[18] the expiration year of the Clark contract, and was pleased to learn that the architect's enthusiasm for the project had not waned. Cram promised to design a "gracious gothic building in stone" that would be "the finest in America," and proceeded to do so.[19]

When completed, Cram's design was spectacular in concept and in cost. As the architect had promised, he had produced a design of exquisite beauty. The proposed facility would be built of stone, was Gothic in design, and would accommodate 3,000 students in a single sitting in one very large dining room. Project costs were estimated to be $1,000,000, making this project the most expensive in the history of the university, and exactly twice the budget approved by the Provincial Council.[20]

As Walsh and others suspected, the council refused to approve a budget increase of that magnitude. Changes would have to be made in Cram's design if the project was to go forward. Professor Francis Kervick of the architecture department was prepared to offer some that he believed Cram would accept. In his estimate of Cram's willingness to compromise, Kervick was absolutely correct.

Kervick suggested that the one enormous dining hall envisaged by Cram be split into two rooms, each one 220 feet by 62 feet, with a combined seating capacity of 2,200. These two dining rooms would be connected by a two-story structure which would house the kitchen and a cafeteria large enough to accommodate 300 persons in a single sitting. The north end of the building would contain a spacious lobby and wide entrance vestibules. Also part of the plan was a well-appointed dining room for 150 lay faculty on the second floor, as well as a more elegant, exclusive smaller dining room appropriate for fifteen or twenty patrons. The floors of the dining areas were to be made of terrazzo, the ceilings would be wood beamed, and the walls finished with a beautiful oak wainscoting.[21]

This revised plan not only incorporated all of the food-service experience, good and bad, acquired by the university over the last twenty years;

it contained all of the features required for a central dining hall facility at Notre Dame for the foreseeable future. All of the persons involved in the decision-making process realized that in beauty, grace, and functionality, there would be nothing like this proposed new facility anywhere on campus and nothing like it many other campuses either. Even though, when final cost estimates had been calculated, this new dining hall would probably be the most expensive construction project in university history, somehow a way to go forward with it had to be found and was.

First, Cram agreed to the changes suggested by Kervick. Second, Walsh was able to assure the Provincial Council that nothing beyond the original authorization would be asked of them. That assurance was based on hard negotiating with contractors and vendors to get construction costs for the completed building down to $545,000 and equipment costs to $100,000. The estimated total project costs of $645,000 still exceeded the Provincial Council's authorization by $145,000.

This shortfall, Walsh informed the Provincial, would be "cared for out of current receipts of the University [meaning football revenues] and will not necessitate any additional loan."[22] However, when the final cost of building and equipping the dining hall were calculated, overruns escalated project costs far beyond Walsh's estimate of $645,000. In the end, the final cost of the new facility was $860,685.[23]

Work began on the dining hall in 1926 and was not completed until November 1927. With Clark's contract expiring in July and students due to arrive in September, a serious food-service problem was averted by the magnanimity of Clark. He offered to continue providing food services to the university until the new facility with which he would have nothing to do had opened.[24]

When the facility opened in November 1927, it was an immediate success. As time passed, Walsh's expectation of what the dining hall would earn for the university was exceeded. Even though board rates were not increased between 1927 and 1933, annual dining hall profits regularly exceeded $300,000 during that period.[25] Indeed, a most dependable internal revenue source had been recaptured. On that issue, Walsh had been right, absolutely.

The only academic building project undertaken during the Walsh presidency was a large extension to the rear of Science Hall. Completed in the late summer of 1924, this project added seventeen classrooms and seven laboratories at a cost of $77,000 to a much-used facility built almost forty years previously.[26] This extension to Science Hall was the least expensive of Walsh's permanent building projects, costing a bit more than new laundry and dry cleaning equipment installed in an old facility but only half as much as his improvement and expansion of the gymnasium.

In spite of all of Walsh's building activity, his goal of having all Notre Dame students in on-campus residence halls was unattainable. As he explained to an alumnus in 1925, "growth has been so rapid that unless we place a limitation on enrollment, there is little hope of our catching up with the situation." In order to reach some sort of solution, he continued, "we have about decided to limit the attendance to 3,000 and as rapidly as possible build up Notre Dame to care for that number."[27]

Even that proposed upper limit of 3,000 seemed too high for some of Walsh's administrators. In 1925, a policy of limiting student enrollment at the university to 2,600 and the number of lay professors to twenty-seven was adopted.[28] The lay faculty figure was obtained by dividing the average lay professor's salary into the yield of the recently established lay faculty salary endowment. Both of these stated goals turned out to be higly unrealistic, because the tradition of admitting every Catholic young man who could afford to come to Notre Dame was so very powerful. There were so many "interest cases"—that is, exceptions allowed to this policy because of one sort of local influence or another—that the official limit of 2,600 students was unenforceable. As Walsh reported to the trustees in November 1927, the policy "was hard to adhere to," and present student enrollment stood at 2,862, with about 1,000 of them living off campus.[29] It followed then that lay faculty beyond the magic number of twenty-seven would have to be hired on one-year contracts to teach them.

Walsh's goal of bringing the students back to campus residence halls was not achieved until two more halls, Alumni and Dillon, were built in 1931 and the terrible economic conditions of the Great Depression had sharply reduced student enrollment. By the fall of 1933, when the university by accepting virtually every application had managed to register 2,545 students, only twenty lived off campus.[30] For the six years of Walsh's presidency, 1922–1928, a large and troublesome off-campus student population was a situation that everyone in the Notre Dame administration wanted to change but did not know how to do it.

— iii —

The zeal for the kind of reforms pressed by Burns and the great value placed on intellectual achievement by him diminished during the administration of his successor. Walsh had not much sensitivity and little interest in expanding the role and influence of the lay faculty in university affairs. Burns' Academic Council became virtually a moribund institution during much of Walsh's time as president. The Academic Council met infrequently, sometimes only once a year, and usually transacted whatever business the president or director of studies presented to it.

The idea that lay faculty at Notre Dame had a role to play in university affairs other than teaching their classes had no appeal for Walsh at all. To say that Walsh regarded lay faculty as a necessary evil as Sorin had done would be an exaggeration but not by much. His attitude toward lay faculty was perhaps analogous to that exhibited by commissioned officers toward enlisted men, a setting with which Walsh was totally familiar.

Enlisted men were absolutely essential for completion of a military mission, as were lay faculty for fulfillment of an academic one at Notre Dame. In the army, privates and corporals were always told what to do, not asked. The situation with lay faculty ought to be about the same. For their own sake, individual faculty compliance with institutional rules should be watched and the identities of persistent violators noted. Privates and corporals were notorious complainers. Nothing was ever right, nothing would ever be right. Lay faculty were much the same.

To be sure, in the army or at the university, complaints must be heard. After all, that is what army chaplains and academic deans were for. In the army or at the university, a sympathetic hearing of complaints did not mean that a particular complainant would be satisfied. The mission came first, whether military or academic. Exceptions were made and available resources were deployed according to that principle. This is what Walsh and others close to him believed.

Walsh was convinced that since 1919 a great deal of presidential time had been expended on faculty problems and faculty welfare. The purpose of the General Education Board fund drive had been creation of a lay faculty salary endowment. For the time being, enough had been done for them. In a sense, Walsh signaled this turn of mind when he abandoned Burns' cumbersome general catalogue listing of faculty by years of service at the university. He replaced it with a simple alphabetical listing of all faculty, mixing priests and laymen together. After concentrating so much effort and energy on the lay faculty salary endowment drive, it was time now to do other things.

Walsh's institutional priorities are easy to discern from his actions. In the postwar economic environment, the financial integrity of the university and of the Congregation of Holy Cross should not be unduly stretched for any reason. Facilities improvement and expansion were long overdue and much needed. Moreover, as one-time expenditures new buildings were fundable in large part out of rising football revenues. Lay faculty salary increases were not one-time expenditures. Moreover, the lay faculty salary endowment was very conservatively invested and could not provide for regular increases. Once given, lay faculty salary increases were permanent parts of the operating budget and resources to pay them outside of the lay faculty salary endowment would have to be found every year. Except for Rockne, who was a very special case indeed, Walsh held the line on lay faculty salary increases throughout his time as president.

With the football team playing before record-breaking crowds and with new buildings rising every year, Walsh failed utterly to convince the lay faculty that few funds were available for salary increases. Given Walsh's firm stand on this issue and the intensity of the collective lay faculty high-anxiety experience at annual contract-renewal time, the inevitable result was a serious and enduring lay faculty morale problem. Every lay faculty member knew someone whose contract had not been renewed and virtually all of them believed themselves underpaid and unappreciated.

Many envied Rockne's special status within the university and resented the adulation and media attention visited upon him outside of it. While lay faculty generally did not know how much the university paid Rockne, they could guess. From reading newspaper accounts of Rockne's many contract flirtations with other institutions, those who were interested could figure out that Rockne received from the university three or four times what the highest paid professors were given. To all of this, Walsh gave little heed. As long as the officers, that is, members of the congregation were content, he would not distress himself about the corporals and privates. No one was indispensable, and unlike the army, those who were seriously unhappy with the way things were at Notre Dame could always leave.

Among those who were seriously unhappy after Walsh's ascent to the presidency of the university in July 1922 was George Shuster. He quickly discovered that he was no longer a favored person as had been the case during the Burns' years. Several incidents occurring during 1923 made his changed status abundantly clear.

Given Walsh's urgent building priorities and attitude toward faculty salaries, Shuster should not have been surprised when he, along with most of the lay faculty, received minuscule or no salary increments for the academic year 1923–24.[31] Walsh's salary policy was so severe throughout the rest of his tenure as president that some of the lay faculty with families were ready to do almost anything to earn more money. For example, when James E. McCarthy, dean of the College of Commerce, learned that the director of studies had set aside $2,500 to hire a professor to teach advanced marketing courses to juniors and seniors in his college, he wrote to Walsh urging the president to allow him to teach the four new courses that an additional professor would teach and earn the $2,500 set aside for the new man. Walsh refused McCarthy's request.[32] That, after all, was the dean, other lay faculty with pressing family financial needs had to think about finding part-time jobs in the city.

The heart of any university is its library. At Notre Dame during the 1920s that heart was a very weak one. First of all, library holdings were limited, the facility was understaffed, and acquisitions were seriously underfunded. Moreover, persons with professional library training were very slow in finding employment at Notre Dame. Neither Father Paul Foik, the librarian in 1922–23, nor Paul I. Fenlon, a library assistant, had professional library training or experience. As a matter of fact, Fenlon's formal education had ended with an undergraduate bachelor of laws from the Notre Dame law program. His time was split between teaching freshman writing courses and working at the circulation desk in the library. In any case, Walsh was as parsimonious with the library as he had been with lay faculty salaries. The scope of that continuing parsimony was disclosed in 1929 by the embarrassing revelation that the university had spent more money in that year on football uniforms than on books for the library.[33]

Evidence abounds suggesting that the library was so inadequate that many students, especially those in the College of Commerce, rarely used it at all. Dean McCarthy reported the substance of a College of Commerce faculty meeting about library problems to the director of studies in January 1926. Faculty complained that commerce students never used and did not know how to use the library. They faulted the teachers of freshman English for not adequately introducing them to the library. At the same time, however, because there was not enough money to purchase technical commerce books, there was not much in the library for these students to read. McCarthy suggested the reestablishment of a commerce book section in a suitable room in the library that could be staffed by someone who could help students find books and assist them in completing their out of class assignments.[34]

One of the alleged reasons why there was so little for students to read in the library was because professors checked out new books on the subjects of their lectures and students could not get access to them. Father George McNamara, assistant librarian, complained to Walsh in late 1923 that many books on philosophy, sociology, history, and science were checked out for six months and then immediately renewed for a like period. McNamara wanted to establish a two-week borrowing period for faculty with opportunities to reserve as many books in the library as they desired. McNamara insisted that the university was not obligated "to supply the private libraries of the professors."[35] Until a few days ago, McNamara continued, "many of the choicest books on nearly all subjects were in the hands of the professors, and from indications, these books are going back in January to the cozy study of someone." McNamara concluded by observing that if professors had to have books, let them get "an order and buy the copies outright."[36]

The assistant librarian's undisguised hostility to faculty who abused book-borrowing privileges was shared by Walsh. The president approved forthwith McNamara's two-week faculty book-borrowing policy.[37] This particular instance of hostility toward the lay faculty on the matter of a virtually unlimited book-borrowing policy derived in part certainly from a growing administrative indifference during the Walsh years to lay faculty circumstances, needs, and morale. In view of all of the things that Walsh had to worry about in 1923 and 1924, that growing indifference may be understandable, but as will be seen, sometimes it got out of hand.

In addition to the problems of lack of holdings and untrained staff, the Notre Dame library was subjected periodically to the stresses and strains connected with being a Catholic university. The special problem of denying faculty and student access to works on the official Index of Prohibited Books or to other works judged obscene and/or spiritually dangerous by local religious authority made the librarian's job extremely difficult. Given the small library staff and the fact that such books had not been labeled or identified in any way or even listed for the convenience of library staff and student library employees, strict enforcement of rules about faculty and student access to such books was impossible.

Like most Catholic clergymen of his generation, Foik believed absolutely that reading bad books could lead to spiritual confusion and immoral behavior. For this reason, faculty and student access to such books had to be tightly controlled, but given the present state of library staffing this was not easily done. Advocacy of censorship was one thing; finding ways of implementing it was another. Given the circumstances, short of the librarian spending all of his time at the circulation desk personally examining every book checked out, there was simply no other practical way to proceed. Furthermore, Foik did not want censorship responsibilities and urged that determining who could read what and when should be lodged with the prefect of religion, Father John F. O'Hara.

With that end in view, Foik wrote an extraordinary letter to O'Hara on October 28, 1922, urging the prefect of religion to assume responsibility for regulating faculty and student access to officially prohibited or morally suspect books. More than frustration with an unworkable system seems to have been driving Foik in this instance. There is no evidence that O'Hara sought to expand the authority of his office to include the role of official local university book censor, though on at least one occasion, as will be seen, he had personally removed an assigned book from the reserve book shelf and destroyed it.[38]

It is clear that Foik invited O'Hara to assume this responsibility, and it is also clear that when Foik offered O'Hara that responsibility, the prefect of religion must have admitted to himself and perhaps to a few close friends his general ignorance of literary history and criticism, but, nonetheless, O'Hara accepted Foik's offer. It also appears that Foik was having political problems within the Holy Cross community over the matter of prohibited books. When incidents happened, he was the person to blame. With no one formally designated as official censor, any priest of a mind to act like one could and did.

The source of the problem of student access to prohibited or morally suspect books, Foik believed, was advice given by irresponsible instructors to read them. Two recently hired lay instructors in the English department, Hale Moore and James Coyle, were the principal offenders. Foik believed that the assignment of such books had been done in ignorance of what was permitted and what was not. Neither of these young laymen had taken the time or trouble to come to the library and try to find out if their assigned readings were acceptable. Heretofore, Foik complained, whenever a case of an improper reading assignment came to his attention, "I have absolutely prohibited the issuance of such a book in spite of the assignment of the said instructor."[39]

One case involving Hale Moore was familiar to O'Hara because he had been involved in it. A freshman student, Jeffrey Sachs, had asked Paul Fenlon to check out Alexandre Dumas's *The Count of Monte Cristo*. Because this book was on the Index, Fenlon advised the young man not to read it, even though the book had been assigned to a class of nuns in the summer session. On that occasion all proper permissions had been easily obtained. The young Mr. Sachs insisted that the book had been assigned and that his instructor had obtained permission for him to read it. This statement by the student was untrue. Fenlon allowed the book to circulate, Foik reported, so "he could have a case against the man who had assigned it to bring to O'Hara's attention."[40] Among other things, Fenlon's action was a revealing and trenchant comment on the state of department politics and on faculty morale among the five laymen teaching English at Notre Dame at that time.

Once apprised of what had happened, the prefect of religion retrieved *The Count of Monte Cristo* from Mr. Sachs' room and destroyed it. Indeed, while Foik complained about O'Hara destroying university property without communicating to the librarian what he had done and why, Foik did not dispute the prefect of religion's authority to do it.[41] O'Hara's action was public and very quickly became widely known throughout the College of Arts and Letters. The fact that the book had been destroyed and that everyone on the faculty very quickly knew who had destroyed it must have had a chilling effect on what teachers directed their students to read. Hale Moore's contract was not renewed, and he did not return to the university.

The other case involving James Coyle was similar, except that O'Hara was not involved. Coyle had assigned Laurence Sterne's eighteenth-century picaresque novel *Tristram Shandy* for his students to read. This book was also on the Index. In this instance the book was not allowed to circulate or to be read by students but was not destroyed. This incident was not reported to O'Hara until October 1922, some time after the matter had been resolved. Though the Coyle incident was not as serious as Moore's transgression and notwithstanding the facts that the young man was related to a prominent monsignor and came from a well-known Catholic family in Taunton, Massachusetts, he also was dismissed. However, the manner of effecting the dismissal was extraordinarily mean-spirited, and Shuster was charged to do it.

As head of the English department in August 1923, Shuster was obliged to write to Coyle, who was spending the summer vacation with his family in Massachusetts, and inform the young man that his services would not be required in September. The given reason for this abrupt and absolutely unexpected termination of employment was not the *Tristram Shandy* matter but that Father Burke, the director of studies, opposed his return to the university. That was all that Shuster was able to tell him.

Coyle immediately sent a telegram to Walsh, asking for confirmation or denial of what Shuster had written. He described the news of his dismissal as amazing and complained that he was now without any prospects for the fall, adding that he had thought his work at Notre Dame had been "loyal, constructive, and successful."[42] Walsh responded with a collect telegram briefly and succinctly, "Father Burke objects to your return."[43] In Walsh's view, that was all the young man needed to know. The matter was closed.

At least one other priest had been as aggressive in such matters as O'Hara but had done so for reasons that Foik believed were questionable. Understandably, Foik was upset by unauthorized destruction of books which were, after all, Holy Cross community property and wanted free-lance book censorship activity stopped. Foik complained to O'Hara about one incident where Frank Arthur Swinnerton's recently published novel, *The Coquette* (1921), described by the librarian as unfit "to be placed in the hands of our Catholic students" was removed from the library. According to Foik, without so much as a by your leave, a certain unnamed priest "destroyed the book, at least so it was reported to the library." Foik added, "I have since been informed that the book was not destroyed but still reposes on the shelf in his room."[44]

Simply stated, Foik wanted help managing a situation that had become for him unmanageable. He looked naturally to O'Hara for that help because O'Hara had demonstrated time after time that he could manage anything. Though Foik may have harbored some concerns about the intellectual and educational consequences of censorship, he did not express them forthrightly to anyone. About as far as he would go in that direction was to observe to O'Hara that it might be necessary to read some of the works of Karl Marx in order to refute him.[45] He noted also that the same probably held true for literature as well. What Foik wanted was to be rid of all censorship responsibilities by passing them to O'Hara.

Foik proposed a plan whereby all books prohibited by the Roman Index would be labeled and stored in a secure location. Such books could not be examined by faculty or students except for serious study and only then "with the permission of the Prefect of Religion, who ought to notify the library in writing whenever this permission is granted." In this way, Foik concluded, "I think we can protect the faith and morals [of] our students and yet permit on the shelves for study the books in question."[46] Foik's scheme was adopted and remained in place for the next twenty years, as long as O'Hara was prefect of religion. When O'Hara became vice president of the university in 1933 and then president in 1934, he had to give up the office of prefect of religion, but he continued to function as university book censor during lunch hours and in other spare moments.

When O'Hara undertook the role of unofficial university censor of library books and of magazines sold in various campus facilities, he was wise enough to know that his knowledge of literature, literary history, and literary criticism was minimal. To be sure, he knew what he liked and disliked and was disposed to find rampant immorality in most modern literature and anti-Catholic attitudes and assumptions in many contemporary news magazines. O'Hara knew also that his own likes and dislikes were an unacceptable basis for a censorship program in an American Catholic university setting. He needed a recognized Catholic literary authority whose tastes and learned opinions could provide such a basis. O'Hara found that Catholic literary authority in the late Father John Talbot Smith, Catholic novelist and essayist and founder of the Catholic

Writer's Guild and the Catholic Actor's Guild, who had died in 1923. Smith was also known and resented in some Catholic circles for his scathing criticism of clerical training and seminary education.

Father Smith had come to Notre Dame in 1906 and had delivered a series of lectures on the evils of modern literature. O'Hara prepared a series of vignettes for the *Religious Bulletin* as part of a Lenten program in 1924. These vignettes were based principally on notes taken from Smith's lectures, expanded by more recent comments of Smith on contemporary authors, and a few trenchant observations by O'Hara on contemporary books brought to his attention by faculty and students offended by them. O'Hara entitled this Lenten series of literary vignettes, "A Critical History of the Development of Modern Trash Literature."[47]

O'Hara began this Lenten series with an explanation of the moral consequences of reading obscene books. In this matter, O'Hara's moral theology was straightforward and unambiguous. Such books "were condemned by a general decree of the Congregation of the Index."[48] Similar to missing Mass on Sunday or having sex prior to or outside of marriage, reading an obscene book was a mortal sin which would condemn unconfessed and unabsolved sinners to eternal damnation.[49] From that fearsome beginning, the series commenced with Father Smith's excoriation of the Norwegian dramatist, Henrik Ibsen (1828–1900). According to Smith, Ibsen was the beginning of that "open sewer" type of anti-Christian and anti-natural literature so common in the twentieth century. Ibsen's questioning and denial of traditional Christian values and near veneration of emancipated women was, in Smith's view, a form of situational morality and grossly sinful.

As for George Bernard Shaw, styled by Smith as the founder of the Ibsen school in the English-speaking world, this red-headed Irishman was no better and because of his ethnicity a great deal worse. Being Irish, albeit Protestant Irish, he still should have known better. Then, there was the Victorian poet and essayist Algernon Swinburne, whom Shuster had described in his first book, *The Catholic Spirit in Modern English Literature* published in 1922, a book read by many Notre Dame students, as being Catholic in spirit. Smith simply dismissed Swinburne as morally and intellectually rotten. Apart from John Henry Newman, Francis Thompson, and the Polish nobel laureate novelist Henryk Senkiewicz, there was not much worth reading in late Victorian and Edwardian English literature. Certainly, Smith asserted there was nothing in that literature comparable to the aesthetic and moral quality of Newman's *Apologia*, Thompson's "The Hound of Heaven," and Senkiewicz's *Quo Vadis*.[50]

Insofar as Smith was concerned, there was not much good that could be said about late nineteenth-century French and American literatures either. Smith complained that Dumas's *The Three Musketeers* was the first attempt to pervert Catholic drama and to falsify history. Casting a cardinal as the principal villain in an utterly preposterous story was only one of many measures of the author's anti-Catholic attitudes.[51] Victor Hugo was an idolater and Zola was worse.[52] Even though American authors generally were much less talented than their English and French counterparts, they had managed to absorb many of the same bigoted anti-Catholic attitudes.

Emerson was sorry that he had not been born a Puritan and was theologically confused. Longfellow was unable to conceal his anti-Catholicism. Even Anne Nichols' contemporary Broadway play *Abie's Irish Rose* was objectionable because one of the characters in it was, in Smith's words, "a stupid" (meaning a bigoted and thoroughly unattractive) priest.[53]

O'Hara learned literary taste and judgment from Smith and never forgot what he had been taught. Smith's tastes and judgments remained with O'Hara for the rest of his life. O'Hara believed that most modern literature, especially modern American literature, was worthless and dangerous. While running the Lenten series, O'Hara decided to venture some opinions of his own. He regarded Hemingway as a pornographer and nothing more. He had a special loathing for Percy Marks' recently published *The Plastic Age* (1924). O'Hara had condemned this book once in the *Religious Bulletin* for lewd scenes and lack of an objective morality. Nonetheless, the book was still circulating among Notre Dame students. As a matter of fact, *The Plastic Age* was assigned reading in an unnamed English professor's course, probably in one of Shuster's courses. According to O'Hara, the offending professor had tried to defend himself and justify his use of the book on the grounds of wanting to expose and illustrate the mediocrity of contemporary American cultural life. O'Hara's advice to students encountering this book in class or elsewhere was clear and direct, "Burn the book if it comes near you."[54]

Handling the Moore and Coyle matters had been very unpleasant for Shuster. At this time in his life, there was a limit to the number of unpleasant tasks he would undertake for the sake of institutional loyalty and Catholic unity. The utterly callous way that Moore and Coyle had been dismissed and O'Hara's Lenten series were only two of several indications for Shuster that the social and intellectual climate at Notre Dame either had changed or never was what he had imagined it to be. The general intellectual and instructional environment of the university had turned increasingly uncongenial.

All in all, the pervasive religious atmosphere, particularly O'Hara's pastoral programs, had become increasingly anti-intellectual. Shuster knew that in the present academic climate, teachers of literature, especially teachers of contemporary English and American novels, could certainly expect oversight and probable harassment from the prefect of religion. Moreover, it was an undeniable fact that for understandable financial reasons, athletic success was more highly valued by the administration than intellectual aspiration.

The impact upon Shuster of the way things had gone at Notre Dame since Father Burns' departure was one of embarrassment and frustration. He was particularly embarrassed, perhaps even personally humiliated, by his inability to work for a doctorate while holding a full-time professorship at Notre Dame or to develop a regular doctoral program in his department.

Shuster wanted very much to obtain the status and prestige of a doctorate, and in his early years at Notre Dame he wanted to get one as easily and conveniently as possible. How Shuster attempted to do this and why he failed is a complicated story worth telling because it speaks directly to the state of academic values at Notre Dame in the early 1920s and who in the university community were the strongest believers in them.

Soon after his arrival at Notre Dame, sometime in 1920, Shuster began collecting and organizing materials for what became his favorite and most popular undergraduate English course, "The Catholic Spirit in Modern English Literature." The course consisted of a series of lectures on Victorian and Edwardian English and Irish Catholic writers and poets along with a few non-Catholic writers—Swinburne, Ruskin, and Pater—that Shuster liked and designated as being Catholic in spirit.

While organizing and teaching this course, Shuster also began writing a textbook under the same title as the course to be used in it. Believing that a significant market existed in Catholic schools and colleges, the Macmillan Company offered Shuster a contract in 1921 to publish it and actually did so in 1922. They did so after Shuster agreed to guarantee the purchase of a large number of these textbooks for use at Notre Dame.[55]

Although *The Catholic Spirit in Modern English Literature* was a textbook and not a scholarly work, it was, after all, a book, and books of any sort published by Notre Dame English professors at that time were rare events indeed. Moreover, for a young man with not much training in either literary criticism or literary history, this textbook was mature and well written. It would appear that Shuster considered using this textbook as a form of leverage with the Walsh administration to obtain a doctorate from the university while remaining a full-time employee.

In the early 1920s there were no formal operative doctoral programs in any academic department, and the administration was in the process of considering but had not yet decided whether or not to commit scarce teaching and financial resources to graduate education. Nonetheless, a few doctorates had been awarded over the years on an *ad hoc* basis to Notre Dame professors deemed worthy of receiving them. Whether these degrees were more honorary than earned or more earned than honorary is difficult to ascertain from the academic records of that time.

In any case, on May 1, 1923, Shuster applied to the Committee on Graduate Studies—three priests and two lay professors, all with earned doctorates—for permission "to register as a student for the degree of Doctor of Philosophy."[56] The committee denied Shuster's application for two reasons. First, as the serving head of the English department, the committee believed it would be inappropriate for Shuster to pursue a degree in the department which he was charged to supervise. Second, the committee was governed by a general rule established in 1918 that no postgraduate degrees from Notre Dame should be awarded to any professor currently employed by the university.[57] The committee was entirely consistent in its application of this general rule. Two weeks later, the committee denied similar applications from two Holy Cross priests.[58]

Shuster did not give up easily. He returned to the committee on July 31, 1923, apparently hoping to support his case by pleading the special needs and circumstances of the English department. Shuster appeared before the committee and described the many difficulties experienced by the English department in trying to offer doctoral work. The very few teachers with doctorates in the department were too overburdened with undergraduate and master's degree work to mount any sort of serious doctoral program. No progress at this level of scholarly work was possible without hiring additional teachers with doctorates or encouraging serving faculty to obtain them. The idea of adding new faculty with advanced degrees to the English department or developing some of their own did not appeal to the committee at that time at all.

The members advised Shuster that if the burden of advanced graduate work was too great, the English department should not undertake it. The secretary for the committee noted in the minutes of this meeting, "It was with this understanding that Professor Shuster left the Committee."[59] If Shuster had not been aware of his changed status at the university before this encounter with the Committee on Graduate Studies, he clearly knew it now.

Shuster's earlier disappointments over no salary increases and over pursuing doctoral work while working at Notre Dame combined with this humiliating rejection of a move into advanced graduate work by the English department was more than enough to start Shuster thinking about leaving Notre Dame. As he confided in late 1923 to the woman he would soon marry, that is, before O'Hara's embarrassing and humiliating Lenten series in 1924, Notre Dame was no longer a place where he wanted to be. As matters are now, Shuster wrote,

> I should really very much like to get away from Notre Dame. Even though I love the place and love the purpose to which it has been dedicated, I must admit that it seems impossible to expect of Notre Dame anything like what I had once hoped for from it. We have an administration now without any vision or sense of scholarship—much less poetry. It has deteriorated so far that the candid opinion of all lay faculty is very pessimistic. And of course I saw the future as it could have been under Father Burns—a new Louvain, with dreams steadily coming true. I have spent many a bitter hour beside the ashes of a dying dream. . . .[60]

Total disenchantment could hardly have been more elegantly put.

— iv —

When Shuster wrote to his future wife that elegant statement of disenchantment with the university, he had been experiencing for some time an increasingly powerful sense of a drift away from Notre Dame. That sense of drift became a real shove during Lent 1924. In any case, during the spring of 1924 Shuster made two very important decisions. First, he proposed marriage to one of his former summer school students and was accepted. Shuster's friend and dean of the College of Arts and Letters, Father J. Leonard Carrico, performed the ceremony. Second, he requested and obtained an indefinite leave of absence to go to New York and begin graduate studies in English at Columbia University. He did not resign from the university and at that point intended to return. The precipitating cause of his decision to leave was undoubtedly O'Hara's Lenten program on the evils of modern literature. Such blatant anti-intellectual

prescriptions had to be unacceptable to persons with serious literary interests and commitments to scholarship. The Lenten series was the precipitating cause of Shuster's departure in 1924, but that was not the way Shuster wanted to remember it in later life.

To be sure, leaving the university for the sake of a dispute over an ephemeral work such as Marks' *The Plastic Age* was not worthy of the event which the attempted censorship of it had precipitated. Someone greater and more heroic than Percy Marks had to have been involved. In his later memory of the event Shuster appears to have substituted D. H. Lawrence for Percy Marks.

In an interview given to William M. Halsey for his book *The Survival of American Innocence* in 1967, Shuster described his reasons for leaving Notre Dame in dramatic terms, he took a stand on the side of truth. According to Shuster's recollection, given thirty-three years after the event, he had assigned D. H. Lawrence's *The Rainbow* to a class of Notre Dame freshmen. Suspecting that such an assignment would be controversial, Shuster claimed to have taken all possible precautions that the book would be read only by students in his class. According to this interview, despite these precautions, O'Hara somehow noticed the book on the reserved shelf, seized it, and proceeded to tear it up. Shuster told Halsey that he left Notre Dame because of this incident.[61]

The D. H. Lawrence incident finds no corroboration anywhere and most likely never happened. No one else mentions it, nor did Shuster at the time. This is not to say that O'Hara would not have mutilated a D. H. Lawrence novel if a virtuous spirit had moved him and if he thought that Notre Dame students were reading it. However there is no evidence other than Shuster's much-belated recollection that O'Hara destroyed the book.

Whatever his reasons, Shuster left the university on a leave of absence went to New York with his new bride and enrolled as a doctoral student in English at Columbia University. Having already published one textbook of literary history and criticism and hard at work on his second, Shuster was warmly received at Columbia. In his own words and implicitly contrasted with his treatment by the Committee on Graduate Studies at Notre Dame, he claimed to have entered the Columbia graduate program "through the front door."[62] Graduate studies went well, he found part-time teaching jobs in the New York area, and he made contact with the *Commonweal*, a newly founded weekly intellectual and public affairs magazine with a Catholic orientation. Contact developed quickly into association. Shuster joined the staff in early 1925 and very soon became managing editor, a post that he held for the next thirteen years.

The combination of a happy marriage, the intellectual stimulation of graduate students and faculty at Columbia, the often grueling but always fascinating work at the *Commonweal,* and the cultural climate of New York City in the late 1920s had brought George Shuster truly to where he wanted to be. His career as a faculty member at Notre Dame was over. Old ties of friendship and affection were as yet unstrained. Shuster returned to Notre Dame for the last time to teach in the summer session of 1925 and while there, according to a short memoir written many years later, he had several long talks with Father Burns. In those talks, Shuster claimed to have tried to explain to his old priest-friend the reasons for his decision to leave the university in as tempered a way as possible. It is extremely unlikely that he was as candid about his hostility to O'Hara in 1925 as he was to Halsey about it in 1967.

Burns and Shuster also talked about the younger man's experiences in New York, at Columbia, and with the people at the *Commonweal.* Burns loved stories about celebrities and Shuster loved to tell them.[63] In turn, Shuster recalled that Burns told him about some of the things presently occurring at Notre Dame and about problems with the second fund drive. Most of the obvious donors had already been solicited for the first drive. Then, apparently, the two men exchanged views about an old question in Catholic circles that Shuster believed related to his not so happy experiences as chairman of the English department at Notre Dame.

That larger question was how to explain the failure of American Catholics to produce scientists, scholars, artists, intellectuals, and financial and corporate leaders, or otherwise influence the cultural and economic life of the country in any way remotely commensurate with their numbers in the general population. The fact that American Catholics were so underrepresented among the country's scientific, intellectual, and financial elite had been the subject of serious discussion among American Catholic leaders and spokesmen for a long time. Indeed, Veneziani, another disenchanted lay professor, had raised it in 1900. Some commentators on this subject had been exculpatory and defensive. Others were stridently critical of what American Catholics had failed to achieve. A few proclaimed that intellectual underachievement seemed almost to have been elevated to the level of a virtue by the great mass of American Catholics. For all such commentators, the persistence and intensity of this perceived aversion to scientific and intellectual pursuits was a measure of the enduring minority status of American Catholics and a major failure of their very large and costly educational enterprise.[64]

For example, the indefatigable, sometimes vulgar but always direct Patrick Scanlan, managing editor of the *Tablet* of Brooklyn, New York, complained bitterly in 1921 about the utter failure of American Catholics to achieve intellectual distinction. Though American Catholics constituted one-fifth of the general population, they furnished less than one-fiftieth of the higher intellectual life of the country. Scanlan identified the source of the problem in what he described as a lamentable attitude toward higher education.[65] In the view of this managing editor, American Catholic parents were too anxious to get their children employed and earning money. Too many American Catholic youth entered the work force after grammar school. American Catholic parents were unwilling to make the kinds of sacrifices required to obtain a higher education for their children. If these attitudes and practices continued, Scanlan added, "The results will simply be that our people will be the followers, the hewers of wood and drawers of water, and not the leaders of the future." Scanlan finished off his point in a very heavy New York accent representative of the *Tablet* in the early 1920s, "The Jews will be the lawyers and doctors, the Catholics will be the clerks and laborers."[66]

Inevitably in such discussions about the failure of American Catholics to participate in intellectual activity or about the more serious related problem that they did not seem to care very much about their absence from such activities, critics contrasted that failure and that attitude with the excellent intellectual, scientific, and cultural achievements of European Catholics. For example, Carlton J. H. Hayes, the eminent historian teaching and writing at Columbia University, told the graduating class at the College of New Rochelle in July 1922 that the three million Catholics of Ireland and even the two million Catholics of England had produced more scholars, scientists, artists, and critics than had twenty million American Catholics. Without a large and vigorous intellectual class, Hayes continued, American Catholics would "never influence profoundly the life and thought of America."[67]

The contrast between the quality and number of European Catholic intellectuals and the perceived aversion of American Catholics to scholarly and scientific activities was a very important part of contemporary thinking about the entire problem. During 1927 *American Mercury* ran articles based on analyses of the relation of religious affiliation to names selected for inclusion in *Who's Who in America,* and then in 1931 a similar analysis of names selected for listing in *American Men of Science* was published in the *Scientific Monthly.* According to these tabulations, Catholic representation in *Who's Who in America* and in *American Men of Science* was minuscule. In the case of the latter work, out of 303 eminent scientists listed, only three were Catholics, prompting the embarrassing conclusion that "The conspicuous dearth of scientists among the Catholics suggests that the tenets of that church are not consonant with scientific endeavor."[68] The contrast between the scholarly and scientific achievement of European and American Catholics was an effective, if not always persuasive, response to allegations that the traditions, principles, policies, and leadership of the Catholic Church discouraged scholarly and scientific inquiry. It seems extraordinary that something which appeared almost self-evident to secularist and Protestant observers of Catholic affairs was so generally ignored by Catholic commentators during the 1920s. Not until the problem of American Catholics and the intellectual life was revived in the late 1950s did Catholic investigators raise questions about the chilling effects of the suppression of modernism upon research and speculative thought, of the impact of the *Index Librorum Prohibitorum* and certain provisions of Canon Law on the scholarship undertaken by American Catholics, and the effect of the dead hand of the study-manual variety of scholastic philosophy upon seminary education.[69]

This contrast between the scholarly and scientific reputations of American and European Catholics also had a special message for administrators of Catholic colleges and universities. For administrators intent upon raising the levels of scholarly and scientific production in their institutions, the shortest and quickest way to salvation seemed to be over the gangway of a Cunard ocean liner. Europe had in sufficient numbers what the American Catholic Church had failed to produce at all. Recruitment of European Catholic scholars, particularly English Catholic scholars, for regular or visiting appointments to American Catholic colleges and universities seemed to be the most sensible way to go.

If the failure of American Catholics to pursue intellectual activity and achieve distinction in scholarship and science during the years between the two world wars was not attributable to doctrinal or spiritual aspects of Catholicism, then the cause of the problem had to be rooted somewhere in the special historical experience of American Catholics. To those persons speaking and writing about the problem in the 1920s and 1930s, it seemed clear enough that neither by nature nor tradition was Catholicism anti-intellectual. However, it appeared equally clear that most American Catholics and many of their leaders and spokesmen were.

From the three generations of Catholic writers investigating the problem a consensus about cause has emerged. The reasons for the very slow development of intellectual and scientific traditions among American Catholics were primarily social.[70] American Catholics were largely descended from European peasant and working-class stock, and during the interwar period most of them had not progressed beyond lower middle-class status. An important consequence of the relatively low social status of American Catholics was a concomitant inferior economic position. Related to these two fundamental conditions were difficulties involved in the process of assimilating millions of immigrants, prejudice, hostility, discrimination, and the development of a defensive and sometimes martial mentality among American Catholics themselves. All of those circumstances tended to segregate American Catholics from the larger society and hindered their participation in national life.[71]

To effect a link between his own personal experiences as a lay faculty member at Notre Dame with this larger problem of American Catholic scientific and scholarly underachievement, Shuster planned two journalistic broadsides which he wanted to fire in late August 1925. Shuster claimed to have discussed his intentions with Father Burns during the early summer, and in one place he implied that Burns was an active participant in the preparation of them.[72] That Shuster discussed his intentions with Burns is likely. That Burns was in any way a coauthor in this enterprise is not. Under no circumstances would Burns have participated in a public attack on Father O'Hara, a fellow Holy Cross priest and protégé, which is what Shuster intended to do and did in these broadsides. There simply was no room in Burns' small world of Holy Cross fraternalism for anything like that.

In any case, the first of Shuster's broadsides, a short signed article entitled "Have We Any Scholars?" appeared in the Jesuit publication *America* during the week of August 13, 1925. The editors of *America* published it with a note stating that they did not agree completely with the article, but they believed that it would generate useful discussion. For all that the article said, it was relatively short. Shuster presented his case against American Catholic intellectual apathy in two parts. In the first part, he offered a total and absolute indictment of American Catholic scholarly and scientific performance. Next followed a discussion of the causes of the condition indicted and some suggestions about corrective action.

This first broadside was loaded with canister shot and tore up everyone and everything within range. During the last seventy-five years, argued Shuster, American Catholics had not produced a single great literary man, no historian, scientist, or economist whose work had discovered a new and better social direction. American Catholics had exerted virtually no influence on the general culture of the country.[73] According to Shuster, the dismal record of American Catholic cultural achievement was directly related to the inability of American Catholic higher education institutions to produce scholars.

One of the reasons so few scholars had emerged from American Catholic colleges and universities was the lack of understanding and appreciation of what scholarship was and how scholars worked by most of the leaders of American Catholic higher education institutions. "Scholarship is not a bundle of things to be weighed and measured," argued Shuster, "it is a state of mind, a certain discipline of personality, an attitude struck up by the human faculties."[74]

Moreover, scholarship was "guaranteed by neither libraries nor degrees, but only by the creation of an atmosphere in which knowledge and learning can grow." Upon scholars, he added, "has depended almost every single one of our useful ideas in all branches of endeavor, every rugged impulse to produce new ways of thinking or new attitudes toward life, every genuine contact with tradition." He concluded the indictment part of his article by insisting that Catholic influence upon the civilizing currents operative in contemporary America was "necessarily dependent upon Catholic ability to produce scholars."[75] Until American Catholics could achieve distinction in scholarly, scientific, and cultural affairs, the influence of Catholic values and American Catholics upon the larger society of their country would be minimal and American Catholics would continue to be subordinates and followers of others in their own land.

In the second part of the article, Shuster attributed many of the problems of American Catholic intellectuals to the relatively recent origin of so many Catholic educational institutions, the lack of prestige and the overall poverty of those institutions, and the deplorable but undeniable absence of American Catholic financial support for Catholic colleges and universities.[76] Not much had changed since Veneziani made the same point a quarter century earlier. Those circumstances, Shuster admitted were not readily amenable to change. However, a very important circumstance contributing to American Catholic intellectual backwardness was correctable, the overly ambitious school and college founding programs had to stop. In Shuster's judgment, the leadership of American Catholic higher education seemed intent upon creating an oversupply of schools and colleges rather than multiplying the number of teachers, who were needed.[77]

The present "gap between too many students and too few teachers," Shuster complained, was "bridged over by the employment of lay professors."[78] On the status and role of lay professors in American Catholic colleges and universities, Shuster had some very strong words, reminiscent of what Veneziani had said in his pamphlets. Clerical administrators of American Catholic colleges, as well as the members of the religious orders that staffed and ran them, viewed lay professors as "necessary evils or cheap benefits" who were not expected to develop themselves or become masters of their subjects.[79] Their sole function was "to relieve the congestion by holding forth during a number of hours for the sake of a pay-cheque trimmed down to the smallest dimensions possible." After a while, Shuster concluded, "the lay professor ceases to kick and struggle, settling down then perforce to be a placid second rate and eminently serviceable cog."[80] After the decks and rigging had been cleared with the first broadside of canister, Shuster fired a second round of solid shot, more accurately aimed lower at the waterline.

The second article was published, unsigned, as an editorial entitled "Insulated Catholics" in *Commonweal*, August 19, 1925, the same week as the article in *America*. This article was also very short but perhaps more reflective of Shuster's experience at Notre Dame. As the article in *America* had complained about conditions within American Catholic higher education that inhibited the development of scholarship and a more general appreciation and acceptance of scholarly values, the *Commonweal* editorial focused on a perceived self-centered, highly individualistic social outlook of American Catholics, more specifically of American Catholic students attending Notre Dame. For Shuster's tastes, far too many American Catholic students, of which those attending Notre Dame were highly representative, cared only about themselves and their own prospects in this world or in the next one. Accordingly, most of these young men gave little or no thought to how Christian charity ought to inform their lives or what obligations as educated men they had toward their neighbors and fellow citizens. This generation of American Catholic students struck Shuster as being so insulated from the realities of life in twentieth-century America in what they studied and did while students, so preoccupied with achieving financial success in this world and personal salvation in the next one, that they had put out of mind important virtues of the very faith to which great attachment was so often and so loudly professed.

Such young men were on their way to becoming poor citizens and, to large extent, only marginal Christians. They had forgotten or had never been taught the virtue of being their brother's keeper. The great fear implied by Shuster in this editorial was that American Catholic colleges and universities were graduating many young men possessed with anti-intellectual attitudes about scholarship and culture and otherwise bereft of any detectable social conscience.

In the first part of the *Commonweal* editorial Shuster mildly criticized quantitative approaches to extending and expanding spirituality among college students. He could not believe that statistics told us very much about the untidy and unruly elements of human spiritual needs. Next, he mentioned O'Hara by name, the university, and the *Religious Survey*.[81] However, Shuster was not sufficiently brave or foolish or liberated to criticize directly Father O'Hara's pastoral program as anti-intellectual or as devoid of social concern. In 1925 American Catholic laymen simply did not do that sort of thing. Instead, Shuster resorted to the timeless convention of using the words of a high-ranking ecclesiastic to confute the arguments and otherwise turn aside the assertions of a cleric of lesser rank.

Shuster reported in the editorial the dissatisfaction of an unnamed distinguished Canadian archbishop with the style of religious training reflected in O'Hara's *Religious Survey*. The remarks of students relating to experiences with frequent communion struck the archbishop as being highly individualistic.[82] To that negative observation, along with another from the archbishop that the *Religious Survey* suggested that Notre Dame students were not being trained for leadership positions in their country, Shuster added a comment that respondents to the *Religious Survey* "apparently looked at life without giving any thought whatever to public-spirited service or to their neighbors."[83] Shuster hastened to conclude that the archbishop had intended no direct criticism of the University of Notre Dame. The want of social interest exemplified in the *Religious Survey*, the archbishop believed, was characteristic of Catholics generally.

According to Shuster, the causes of this general abdication of social concern by American Catholics as well as their general indifference to intellectual activities were rooted in their immigrant history. Both social concern and cultural interest had to be sacrificed for the overall economic struggle. The psychological consequences of that struggle for most American Catholics were profound and long-lasting.

Shuster drew upon Father Burns' experience in two endowment-raising campaigns and described the great difficulty encountered by leaders of Catholic higher education in trying to persuade "very good people to see the need for supporting colleges and other institutions that lie beyond parish work."[84] Money could be raised only by basing appeals on religion as such. The needs of Catholic higher educational institutions simply did not seem as important to donors as parish schools and local charities. Shuster reinforced this latter point by quoting from a speech of Archbishop Austin Dowling of St. Paul who complained about "prodigious parochial activity and supine indifference to the general needs of the Church."[85] Because of that condition, argued Archbishop Dowling, "Catholics where they are strongest, are isolated, out of touch with the community, exerting no influence commensurate with their numbers, their enterprises, or their splendid constructive thought."[86]

In the second part of the editorial, Shuster quoted from a resolution introduced by Father Burns at the last meeting of the Catholic Education Association urging graduates of Catholic schools to exhibit greater interest in the welfare of their fellow men and exhorting "Catholic teachers to explain the meaning of Christian brotherhood and to show the opportunities for its exercise in modern social organization."[87] In Catholic colleges and universities, Burns had concluded in his resolution, "this may well be regarded as a necessary element in the training of men."[88]

Shuster ended the editorial by building upon what Father Burns had urged teachers in Catholic colleges and universities to do. He saw no useful purpose in haranguing students about social duties and the obligations of citizenship. Instead, Shuster returned to what was by now for him an old theme. What was needed, he insisted, was "an awakening of the students' intellectual life—the culture of the mind for its own sake with which will come a sympathetic realization of those broad issues upon which the stability of our human world ultimately depends."[89]

In a coda to this piece, Shuster's disappointment and frustrations with the dormitory building and athletic priorities of the new administration at Notre Dame intruded. So long as the leaders of Catholic higher education refused to concede that their goals were not quantity, not buildings, "but quality—excellent quality achieved at no matter what cost," Shuster pleaded, "Catholic educators will talk in vain about 'Christian brotherhood.'"[90]

For Shuster leadership was a by-product of intellectual exercise and fidelity to moral obligations. Catholics had failed to develop such leadership because they had not led in education. With the football glories of the past few years and the *Religious Survey* of 1925 clearly in mind, Shuster ended this piece and his association with Notre Dame by insisting that the leadership of American Catholic higher education had superimposed upon a splendid system of elementary training little more than excellence in football. "There is the rub. At least part of the remedy suggests itself."[91]

The near simultaneous appearance of the *America* and *Commonweal* pieces produced uproar and outrage at Notre Dame. Burns later observed to Shuster, in a letter thanking him for a gift of a book, that the *Commonweal* piece in which Shuster had quoted him on the lack of social concern of American Catholic students had "stirred things up for a while."[92] He made no mention of the *America* article at all and gave no indication that he had read it. Burns had hoped to see the on-campus discussion of the *Commonweal* piece continue a bit longer, but, he concluded, "I guess it just exhausted itself."[93] Burns had thought about contributing something substantial to the controversy at Notre Dame that Shuster's articles had aroused, but the press of other work had prevented him from doing so.[94] This was not the language of one closely involved with the two controversial pieces, as Shuster intimated many years later.

— v —

Shuster's actions in publishing what he did were regarded by many in authority at Notre Dame as *lèse majesté,* as an offense against the dignity of the university.[95] Nothing comparable had occurred since Veneziani's pamphlets at the turn of the century. In 1925, at least one Notre Dame faculty undertook to respond to Shuster's charges. The Honorable Dudley G. Wooten was seventy years old, a convert to Catholicism, a former judge, congressman, Texas state representative, and an associate professor of law at Notre Dame. Though only a faculty member for one year, Wooten had powerful personal reasons for holding deep affection for the university and for Walsh. The university had quietly helped pay Mrs. Wooten's substantial medical bills.

Wooten had been deeply offended by Shuster's article and unsigned editorial. In the early fall of 1925, Wooten wrote a carefully crafted response to Shuster's two pieces and sent it off to Michael Williams of *Commonweal* for possible publication. Wooten's article, fifteen pages, consisted of two parts, an almost poetic highly conservative defense of timeless Catholic principles abstractly considered and a severe, highly personalized attack on Shuster and upon his assumed laicism and liberal religious principles.

According to Wooten, Shuster's attack on Catholic achievements in every field of endeavor and upon Notre Dame was "palpably unfounded in fact" and a "phenomenal arrogance" to conceive and execute in so few pages.[96] Shuster had asserted much about an alleged condition afflicting American Catholic culture but had proved nothing. Wooten doubted whether Shuster had the scholarly skills to prove anything. For his part, Wooten proceeded in lawyerlike fashion to refute or explain away every point that Shuster had made in his article and unsigned editorial. Finally, in what Wooten described as a "matricidal attack" by an "unfilial son," Shuster's most grievous sin was disloyalty to "the institution that gave him whatever culture he possesses."[97]

In the end, Wooten's reply to Shuster was not accepted by the editors of *Commonweal.* The article had been read by Williams and by the other editors, most assuredly including Shuster, and then rejected, "being impossible to publish in its present form."[98] Upon receiving the rejection notice, Wooten admonished Williams for not having the courage and fairness to permit a reply. Wooten concluded by declaring the futility of trying to argue "with one so insensitive to the ordinary rules of decent controversy."[99] Indeed, the matter of Wooten's response was closed, but the charge of Shuster's disloyalty would resonate at Notre Dame for years. Shuster had not demeaned Our Lady's university as much as Veneziani, but he had come very close.

For some at Notre Dame, especially O'Hara, Shuster's offense was unforgivable. As a matter of fact, when serving as archbishop of Philadelphia in 1957, thirty-two years after the events, O'Hara referred to the *America* article and the *Commonweal* editorial in a letter to Cardinal Spellman as Shuster's attack on Notre Dame.[100] For O'Hara the pain of the memory of those events in 1957 was almost as sharp as it had been in 1925.

A few others outside of the Notre Dame community criticized Shuster because they had become very tired of hearing him and others complain about American Catholic scientific and intellectual underachievement. There were enough Protestants, secularists, and Ku Klux Klan members ready and willing to do that. Catholics had become increasingly annoyed by hearing that message from one of their own.

One early test of Shuster's reception in New York Catholic leadership circles occurred at the First Annual Convention of the National Catholic Alumni Federation in New York City on November 6, 1925. This convention had been planned as a grand affair in the Commodore Hotel to celebrate the role of Catholic colleges and universities in retaining and preserving faith in an age of unbelief.[101]

The *Commonweal* had tried to influence the agenda and content of the presentations by addressing in an editorial, probably written by Shuster, some real problems that the Catholic educational system ought to confront. One of these problems was better public relations. The world had to be told what the American Catholic educational system was trying to do. Catholic leaders should mount a major effort to persuade the public that colleges and universities "where religion had a home" were principal sources "for that moral integrity of which the nation stands so much in need."[102]

However, before convincing the world of their value, Catholic educators had to convince themselves that what they were doing was different, worthwhile, and that as teachers and scholars they were appreciated by their co-religionists. The *Commonweal* editors, probably speaking out of Shuster's experience at Notre Dame, complained mildly that in the past the Catholic college man was lonely in a special way. Catholic college men had found themselves separated from those educated outside of the Church and had been forced to recognize the indifference of their own brethren to the cultural training that college and university experiences provided.[103]

When the convention began, the special problem of being Catholic and intellectual found no place on the agenda. Cardinal Patrick J. Hayes, the keynote speaker and guest of honor, had other points to make. Hayes commended the Catholic Alumni Federation for maintaining their faith during a time when unbelief was rampant. He likened Catholic college men and women to a special elite band of defenders of the faith.

According to Hayes, the Catholic Alumni Federation was a movement driven by the faith and members of it should be leaders ever ready to answer questions about their faith. In that way, Hayes continued, they would be able to demonstrate to the world the quality of their religious training in Catholic universities and exhibit the fruits of Catholic teachings.[104] If Catholic education was supposed to have had an intellectual dimension as well as a religious one, Archbishop Hayes neglected to mention it.

Indeed, while other speakers spoke about intellectual proficiency and activity as being useful and desirable—particularly Bishop Shahan of the Catholic University of America—what emerged from the convention was a definition of Catholic education as being primarily religious and moral and only secondarily intellectual and scholarly. Most public colleges and universities had greater intellectual and scholarly resources and better facilities than their Catholic counterparts, but that was no reason why Catholics should attend them. In this instance better was worse. Because of the state of unbelief in those institutions, Catholic men and women should shun them.

All of this was too much for Shuster, who was present at the proceedings. Apparently, he could not control his disappointment and frustration with the way matters were unfolding at the convention. With Rockne as the featured speaker at the evening banquet, later described as the hit of the night, Shuster could take no more. The combination of Cardinal Hayes in the morning and Coach Rockne at night was too much for him to endure passively, as it symbolized for Shuster precisely what was troubling Catholic education. He responded by creating an embarrassing scene at the banquet.

According to Hugh O'Donnell of the *New York Times* and a frequent correspondent of Walsh, the evening had gone extremely well until after Rockne's speech. Shuster stood up in his place at the table and made an impromptu speech of which no record has survived. Yet, one can guess what the thrust of it was. Whatever Shuster said that night was not well received. O'Donnell informed Walsh that Shuster's remarks turned out to be the only ugly feature of the convention. The speech offended everyone, especially the cardinal. O'Donnell concluded by observing, "I think he [Shuster] is fast ruining himself with Catholics in general."[105] Walsh asked for a copy of Shuster's remarks but none was available to send.

For George N. Shuster, a Rubicon had been crossed; henceforth, his career went in other directions and prospered. Though work at *Commonweal* was at once time-consuming and exciting, his second textbook *The Catholic Spirit in America* was completed and published in 1927. Three novels, four books on Germany, and articles followed with unbroken regularity over the next thirteen years. At the same time graduate studies in English proceeded apace, with a Ph.D. being awarded in 1940 and his dissertation, *The English Ode from Milton to Keats,* appearing as a book the same year.

During the 1930s Shuster emerged as a leading spokesman for the liberal Catholic point of view on domestic and foreign affairs. That point of view, strongly anti-Fascist and often strongly put, frequently encountered sharp criticism and heated rejection by many prominent American Catholic clergy and laymen. Shuster's uncompromising opposition to the Franco forces in the Spanish Civil War precipitated his departure from the *Commonweal* in 1937.[106] A two-year fellowship from the Social Sciences Research Council for study and travel in Europe allowed him to exit gracefully from the magazine with which he had been so long associated. Upon his return from Europe in 1939, the curious calculus of New York City ethnic/religious politics provided Shuster with a new career opportunity.

Through the good offices of Carlton J. H. Hayes and others the presidency of Hunter College, traditionally reserved for a Catholic, was offered to Shuster.[107] He accepted the post, which began in controversy because he lacked a doctorate at the time of the appointment.[108] That situation was remedied a year later when Columbia University granted him his degree. With the passage of time, controversy about his appointment diminished, and thus began an association that lasted twenty-one years, broken by a leave of absence in 1950 for almost two years when he served as deputy high commissioner of Germany. Though Shuster was deeply and at times passionately involved in the affairs of a thriving women's college in a politically charged municipal higher-education system for a long period, he never lost sight of, or interest in, the problem of the status of American Catholic intellectuals and the quality of their performance as scholars, scientists, and artists. He continued to address such issues in speeches and in print in a variety of contexts throughout his entire professional life.

No matter what job he held or how he was regarded by some members of the Notre Dame community, Shuster never lost interest in the university or in the people there. For example, in the fall of 1943, Shuster played a major role in organizing popular support for Dr. Francis E. McMahon, a philosophy professor at Notre Dame who had been fired in midsemester for refusing to accept university censorship of articles and outside speeches on foreign policy and public policy issues. While the McMahon incident was a very complicated one that developed over a period of two years and was profoundly affected by forces outside of Notre Dame, it turned out to be the greatest public relations disaster in the history of the university. Shuster did much to make it so.

He helped organize a celebrity committee of intellectuals, scholars, scientists, and artists headed by Albert Einstein who all urged the university to reinstate McMahon. The university stood fast with its decision and refused all such entreaties which were many. University leaders elected to say and do nothing, waiting for war news to displace this story from newspaper front pages.

Shuster's role in this affair struck many at the university as a repeat of his so-called anti-Notre Dame performances in 1925 and made him more of a *persona non grata* at the institution. However, all of this was to change with the passage of time and the selection of a new president of Notre Dame in 1952 who was young enough to have had no connection with the events of 1925 or 1943. When Shuster retired from Hunter College in 1961, he accepted an invitation from Father Theodore M. Hesburgh, C.S.C., sixteenth president of the University of Notre Dame, to return to his alma mater as a professor of English and presidential assistant. Later he became a member of the Board of Trustees and helped develop research programs in the social sciences and humanities that were to be encouraged and sponsored, in part, by a Ford Foundation grant. He also played a major role in the complicated events leading to the admission of undergraduate women to the university in 1972.

The prospect of returning to Notre Dame in 1961 in Shuster's mind must have been accompanied by a very powerful sense of *déjà vu*. By that time the very old controversy about the role of American Catholic intellectuals in American life that Shuster had addressed in 1925 was experiencing a widespread and emotional revival in the late 1950s. Father John Tracy Ellis had addressed the subject of American Catholics and the intellectual life in a paper delivered to the Catholic Commission on Intellectual and Cultural Affairs in 1955 which was published later in the same year. In 1957 Father Gustave Weigel, S.J., published his "American Catholic Intellectualism—A Theologian's Reflection" in the *Review of Politics*, a scholarly journal published at Notre Dame. In the same year, Father John J. Cavanaugh, C.S.C., president of the University of Notre Dame, 1946–1952, and later director of the Notre Dame Foundation, spoke forcefully to the John Carroll Society in Washington, D.C., about the absence of American Catholics from the front ranks of scholarly and scientific achievement by asking his widely reported and much quoted rhetorical question, where were the Catholic Salks, Oppenheimers, and Einsteins?[109] If these events were not enough to recall memories of that summer in 1925 when Shuster tried to turn the world of Catholic higher education upside down, there was another that surely would. Shuster's old adversary, John F. O'Hara, C.S.C., Cardinal Archbishop of Philadelphia, had died in August 1960, and contrary to His Eminence's personal wishes had been grandly entombed in Sacred Heart Church on the Notre Dame campus.

In 1961 the events of an active and fulfilling life for George N. Shuster had come full circle. He continued to play an influential and respected role in university affairs until his death in January 1977. As Shuster certainly wished, his intellectual life ended in the very place where it had begun sixty-five years earlier.

When Shuster and his new wife moved from South Bend to New York City in the summer of 1925, the State of Indiana was not a congenial environment for Catholics and Catholic institutions. During 1924 and 1925 anti-Catholicism propagated by the Ku Klux Klan intensified dangerously. Moreover, in May 1924 the university community found itself in a virtual state of siege when local Klansmen hosted a state convention of their organization in South Bend. To that event, hundreds of Notre Dame students responded accordingly. Later, in the fall of 1924, when Klan-supported candidates won the state elections handily and captured control of state government, Catholics and Catholic institutions throughout Indiana were at risk from local Klan organizations and possibly even from agencies of state government. How much Klan-inspired anti-Catholic legislation the state legislature would enact and the governor would enforce was uncertain, but the threat of doing so was real. It was a very troubled time.

All of this Shuster left behind when he went off to New York. All of this was what Walsh and other Notre Dame officials had to face and deal with, sometimes on a daily basis. All of this had come to pass because of the appearance in Indiana politics of an extraordinary entrepreneur/politician/Klansman, David C. Stephenson, who never held elective office, but successfully managed many of those who did.

PART II

— 8 —

THE KU KLUX KLAN
COMES TO INDIANA

During the 1920s the country as a whole and Indiana in particular experienced a powerful resurgence of anti-Catholic attitudes and behaviors. The anti-Catholic hostility of such a significant part of the larger society was an unpleasant fact of life and affected virtually all decisions and activities undertaken by Walsh during his eight-year presidency. Walsh's undeserved reputation among some of his fellow priests and many of the lay faculty for timidity was derived from a great concern over what other people might think or say about Notre Dame or about Catholics generally. Consequently, he was disposed to let statements and behaviors perceived as indignities or as examples of bigotry by others in the university community pass unrefuted. Whether this disposition was a measure of prudence or weakness is difficult to say. It is clear, however, that if such a disposition was prudent, it was not shared by a majority of the priests, lay faculty, or students at the university. When the time came, Walsh was pushed by his constituents into responding and into action.

Driving this resurgence of anti-Catholic prejudice was a resurrection in 1915 of the long moribund Ku Klux Klan, first in the south then in the Midwest and Far West. As the Klan spread out of the South, its focus changed. To be sure, the traditional anti-Black, White-supremacist focus of the original Klan remained a major characteristic of that organization wherever it might appear. However, as Klan organizers moved into the Midwest and Far West, they promoted the Klan more as a fraternal organization than as night-riding vigilantes. William J. Simmons, the first Grand Imperial Wizard of the resurrected Klan and the man responsible for introducing the old Scottish clan custom of cross burning into modern Klan rituals, idealized his organization as an "order for men of intelligence and character; the World's greatest secret, social, patriotic, fraternal, beneficiary order."[1]

So successful was Simmons in promoting the Klan as a fraternal organization that in 1922 he actually inducted the president of the United States into the Klan. In a special ceremony in the Green Room of the White House, Simmons and the other four members of his induction team swore President Warren G. Harding into the Klan.[2] Afterwards, the president showed his appreciation by giving the members of the team War Department automobile license tags that allowed them to run red lights and park illegally anywhere in the country.[3]

As a fraternal organization, the resurrected Klan presented itself in the Midwest and Far West as committed to preserving the American Constitution and traditional Protestant religious and social values. Those values were best preserved by rigorously enforcing the Volstead Act (Prohibition), strongly opposing sexual promiscuity, and fighting crime. With this sort of an agenda, it was clear that Catholics and Jews, foreign immigrants, social and economic radicals, criminals, and bootleggers were more threatening to the country than were Black people.

Simmons' successor as Grand Imperial Wizard, Hiram Wesley Evans, a Dallas dentist, stated in a speech delivered in October 1923 that biology and anthropology would forever inhibit the progress of the colored races in America. The enormous handicap of low mentality inherited from savage ancestors was too great for a new environment or education to overcome.[4] According to Evans, Blacks had not, and would never be able to function in American society at Anglo-Saxon levels.[5] However, Blacks were not and never could be the same sort of menace to Americanism as were Jews and Roman Catholics. A Black person was not hostile to Americanism. He or she was "simply racially incapable of understanding, sharing, or contributing to Americanism."[6]

According to Evans, Jews were unblendable. Jews are a people apart from all others. Were the great American melting pot to burn for a hundred years, Evans insisted, Gentiles would be changed but Jews would not. Evolution had no effect upon them. Jews are of physically wholesome stock. They are mentally alert. Jews are a family people, but their homes are not American. Their homes are Jewish, from which they will never emerge for a real intermingling with America. Most important, already one-fifth of the entire Jewish race lives in this country. We need no more.[7]

For Evans as well as for Simmons and other Klan leaders of that time, Catholics were the most serious threat of all to American ideals and institutions. No nation, Evans argued, could long endure that permitted a higher temporal allegiance to some other government. The Roman Catholic hierarchy regarded the presidency in Washington as subordinate to the priesthood in Rome. The existence of parochial schools was absolute proof of the divided allegiance and separatist instincts of American Catholics.[8] The foremost threat to Americanism in the twentieth century was "the tremendous influx of foreign immigration, tutored in alien dogmas and alien creeds . . . slowly pushing the native-born white American into the center of the country, there to be ultimately overwhelmed and smothered."[9]

A majority of the fourteen million immigrants entering the United States between 1900 and 1920 were in origin Irish, Italian, Polish, Hungarian, Czech, Slovak, and Croatian. The alien creeds in which these immigrants had been tutored, if tutored in anything at all, was Roman Catholicism. Rome was the inveterate enemy of everything American. Americans must be aware of the Roman menace, take heart, and protect themselves from it.

The Klan did not invent anti-Catholicism. It was very much a part of our eighteenth-century English religious and political heritage. Throughout the nineteenth century anti-Catholicism had been both endemic and respectable in American society. Protestant ministers inspired their congregations with it, and politicians captured votes by employing it. The Klan was able to exploit anti-Catholicism in the 1920s because most Americans were already familiar with it and because it attracted support for their organization.

As has been noted, for a variety of internal and external reasons, Catholic doctrines and practices in America during the early years of the twentieth century had become extremely conservative. Liberal voices within the American Church had been stilled. Formal official statements emanating from the hierarchy tended to be severe and without ecumenical sensitivity. Official American Catholicism was determined to be absolutely in accord with Rome in dogma and theology and did not appear to worry about what Protestants or unchurched Americans perceived the American Catholic Church to be.

Most Protestants and unchurched Americans misunderstood contemporary American Catholic doctrine and practices; and when individuals were moved to explain or criticize, they frequently caricatured what they had read or observed. American Catholics were widely understood by Klansmen and by those Americans of a similar mind-set to be a menace to the country because, owing allegiance to a foreign power, namely, the pope of Rome, they never could be loyal Americans. It could not be otherwise. By all accounts, the pope was an absolute and infallible religious authority distant from our country and probably ignorant of or in many cases formally opposed to some of our most cherished institutions and values. From that formidable intellectual position, a number of propositions caricaturing American Catholic doctrine and practices easily followed.

First, American Catholics were by definition intolerant of other religions and thereby a threat to the religious peace of the country. Official American Catholicism condemned what they called indifferentism, that is, the idea that one religion was as good as another. Catholicism's contention that error (meaning all American Protestant churches) had no right to exist or propagate strongly suggested that if American Catholics were ever to become a majority in this country, religious freedom as we have known it would end.

Second, American Catholic leaders revealed their future plans for America by demeaning Protestant doctrines and practices at every opportunity. They insulted Protestants everywhere by asserting that the Catholic Church had been established by Christ himself and, of all Christian denominations, was the only true Church. By insisting that whenever Catholic bishops spoke formally on matters of faith and morals, they did so with the authority of the Lord Jesus Christ himself, Catholics blasphemed outrageously. Moreover, by claiming that Catholic priests alone had the power to forgive and thus determine who would be saved or damned was too monstrously arrogant for Protestants to let pass unchallenged.

Third, American Catholics could never be loyal Americans because they were of no mind to protect and defend the Constitution of the United States. American Catholics favored a union of church and state such as existed in Spain. When their numbers allowed them to do so, they were determined to breach the wall of separation between church and state as specified in the American Bill of Rights.

Fourth, American Catholics could never be good citizens and function in a free society because they had freely and willfully given their minds away to their priests. How could men and women who accepted censorship of their speech, writing, and reading materials by Church authorities understand and support the principles of free speech and a free press? In this regard, authorities on the Catholic problem in America insisted that American Catholics were different from other Americans.

Fifth, American Catholics could never be good neighbors or honest business associates because they had given away their consciences as well. How could Protestants and other Americans relate to and associate with people who were in effect given licenses to lie, cheat, and dissemble by their priests? Such sins were venial, not as serious as missing Sunday Mass or engaging in premarital or extramarital sex, and easily absolved with a few prayers after a Saturday afternoon Confession, Sunday morning Communion, and a better than average contribution in the collection basket. Having done that, American Catholics were free to sin again.

Scholars, of course, knew better. The Catholic Church was not the same everywhere, even though for very different reasons Catholic bishops and anti-Catholic bigots were both fond of saying so. The Church was not a seamless web, the same in Madrid, Manila, or Minneapolis. Essential doctrine was the same the world over, but adjustments in practices always had been made to social, political, and cultural realities. The fact that church and state were together in Spain did not mean that a similar model was appropriate for the United States and would at some future time prevail here if demographic and political circumstances permitted.

The problem was, of course, that few people embroiled in the nasty world of American religious controversy paid much attention to the opinions of scholars, and no spokesmen for the hierarchy was willing to provide the kind of public assurance about the church and state issue that most Protestants would believe. For Protestants of that turn of mind, separation of church and state had the special meaning of separation of the Catholic church from the American state, not banishment of all Christian religious practices from American civic life or from all forms of public support. After looking at their own loose forms of organization, American Protestants might well regard the Catholic Church in the United States as a tightly organized, well-financed institution respectful of no other authority, secular or religious, and capable of anything.[10]

With so much misinformation and misunderstanding of American Catholic doctrines and practices abroad in the country and largely unchallenged, it was no wonder that Klansmen in many states developed a legislative agenda intended to limit the breadth and scope of Catholic activities in their areas. Klansmen offered bills which they believed voters and legislators would support. On the federal level the greatest concern was limiting immigration, while the bills brought up in state legislatures were directed against Catholic parochial schools.

The Klan, along with many other interest groups, strongly supported the Immigration Bill of 1924. When that bill became law and ended an era in the history of immigration in this country, the Klan took full credit for facilitating its enactment. At the same time, in several state legislatures bills were introduced, sometimes with formal Klan endorsement and sometimes not, to prevent Catholic nuns from teaching in public schools, to require Catholic and other private schools to adopt the same textbooks as were being used in public schools, and even to require all elementary students in a state to attend public schools.

Apart from enacting a new restrictive immigration law in 1924, Congress showed itself to be as unresponsive to reform legislation pressed by the Klan as it was to measures put forward by other special-interest groups. At the state level, only two state legislatures—Oregon and Indiana—actually enacted laws intended to arrest the development of parochial schools in their jurisdictions. The Oregon law was a serious matter.

This Oregon school law required that all children between the ages of eight and twelve must attend public schools. This measure had been inspired by the Oregon Scottish Rite Masons, who collected enough signatures to put it on the ballot in November 1922 as a public initiative. Strongly supported by the Klan, the initiative carried by a majority of 15,000 votes. Contested immediately by the Catholic hierarchy, who were joined by other religious groups and interested parties, the case made its way through the courts until it reached the Supreme Court, where it was overturned in June 1925. Nonetheless, the emotional and financial cost to the leadership of American hierarchy of fighting a three-year court battle was very great. For much of that, the Klan had been responsible.

Klansmen and their sympathizers in Indiana tried very hard in the legislative session of 1925 to deal with the Catholic problem in their state in an effective fashion. Among the anti-Catholic measures introduced during this session were bills banning the wearing of items of religious clothing in the public schools, specifying graduation from a public school in Indiana or in some other state as a requirement for a teaching license, and requiring that the same textbooks be used in all public and private elementary and secondary schools in the state.[11] In the end, none of these severe measures mustered enough votes to pass both houses of the Indiana legislature, but if they had, the newly elected Republican governor most certainly would have signed them. Few states became as intensely anti-Catholic during the 1920s as Indiana.[12] Historically, Hoosiers had always distrusted Catholics and regarded the Latin mass, the custom of Friday abstinence, the sacramental system, ceremonial vestments, Roman collars, and other practices as alien and un-American. In a state that was 90 percent white and Protestant, Catholics, being about 11 percent of the population, were the most visible minority.[13] Moreover, of those foreign immigrants who had settled in Indiana, mostly in the northern areas of Lake County and St. Joseph County, virtually all of them were Catholics.

Anti-Catholicism was an extremely popular cause in the Hoosier state during the 1920s. Virtually every successful seeker of public office from dog catcher through governor and U.S. senator verbally bashed the pope in the 1924 Indiana elections.[14] Despite the popularity of anti-Catholicism in the state and the large number of Klan-endorsed candidates winning primaries in that year, or perhaps because of it, the Indiana Klan organization could not cope with success. So many political and financial opportunities were presented to Klan leaders throughout the state in that national election year that by the end of May 1924, Indiana Klansmen had split into three unequal but bitterly feuding factions.

For that reason, when the Klan-dominated state legislative session of 1925 was over, all that the divided Klan factions had managed to enact in the Indiana legislature were two innocuous laws that intimidated no one and stopped nothing. One of these laws mandated that all schoolchildren in the state study the Constitution of the United States at an appropriate time in their curriculum, and another required that American flags be publicly displayed at all schools in the state.

— ii —

The new Klan began serious organizational and recruiting work in Indiana in Evansville in the spring of 1922. Within fourteen months the Klan claimed a membership of four hundred thousand.[15] Even allowing for the inflated numbers inevitably reported by recruiters, the growth of the Klan in Indiana was phenomenal. In little more than a year, enrolled Klansmen amounted to 13 percent of the entire state population and outnumbered Hoosier Catholics by about one hundred thousand people. By 1924, 30 percent of the state's white native-born male population had joined the Klan,[16] and local chapters, known as Klaverns, had been established in each of the state's ninety-two counties.[17]

In no other state would the Klan enroll more members, publish a more successful newspaper, address more citizens in rallies and meetings, and elect more national, state, and local politicians than in Indiana. For four long and embarrassing years the Klan dominated Hoosier social and political life. That the Klan in Indiana went so far so fast is attributable to the extraordinary leadership of a gifted, absolutely unprincipled, and very reckless young man, David Curtis Stephenson.

Born in Houston, Texas, in 1891, Stephenson grew up in Oklahoma, where he became an apprentice printer as a teenager. After working in several small Oklahoma towns in the printing trade and for a while dabbling in Socialist politics, he moved to Iowa. In 1917 Stephenson joined the Iowa National Guard and managed to get a commission as a second lieutenant. After serving two years in various installations in the United States, he was discharged at Camp Devens in Massachusetts in February 1919.

From Massachusetts, Stephenson made his way to Evansville, Indiana, where he found employment as a salesman before entering the coal business in 1920. Though lacking much of a formal education, having left school in the eighth grade, he was blessed with a marvelous speaking voice and acquired a fluent and polished speaking style. Stephenson learned early in life that he was a superb salesman and could sell almost anything, especially himself. He understood situations intuitively and always knew what to say to turn them to his own advantage.

At first, Stephenson used this extraordinary talent to make himself attractive to women and then, over the years, proceeded to develop a series of casual and longer-term relationships that were amazing for their variety and duration. In the corner boy parlance of the time, Stephenson was an accomplished cocksman, that is, totally addicted to sexual activity with any woman, any way, anywhere, and any time. Next, he applied his talent for selling to business and succeeded grandly. From selling large amounts of coal throughout Evansville, Stephenson turned his attention in mid-1920 to politics. He announced his intention to seek nomination to Congress from largely Republican Evansville as a Democrat. Despite a substantial following among war veterans, local Democratic political leaders were unimpressed. Stephenson's political career as a Democrat went no further, and he ceased to be one.[18]

After this failed essay into Evansville Democratic politics in 1920, Stephenson turned his attention to Indiana Republicans and to the Klan. In the national elections of that year, he urged his supporters among local war veterans to support Republican candidates. Precisely when he joined the Klan is unclear, but by mid-1921 he had risen to a leadership position in the Evansville organization. He became a local leader even though there is virtually no evidence that he was a true believer in Klan ideology, that is, in overt racism, anti-Semitism, anti-Catholicism, collapsing moral standards, and vigorous enforcement of the Volstead Act.[19] As a matter of fact, there is little evidence that Stephenson believed in much of anything except himself. To be sure, Stephenson was a man driven, but a man driven more by ambition than by prejudice and contemporary racist ideas.

Stephenson had joined the Klan in the first place in order to build a power base for his personal political ambitions. For him, the Klan was available. It was an organization of opportunity. Had the Rotary, Elks, Moose, or whatever presented him a like opportunity for organizing an enormously powerful political lobbying group, Stephenson would have joined one or all of them.[20] He saw at once the political potential of the Klan as a fraternal organization and proceeded to develop and exploit it.

As Stephenson told an Indianapolis reporter in 1924, his way of selling the Klan in Indiana was to praise Americanism and the Constitution. Preaching hatred might appeal to a minority of Hoosiers, but masses would be turned away. Stephenson spoke eloquently about pure Americanism and the need for reform of immigration laws, the public school system, and politics. He extolled the Protestant way of life and, though a heavy drinker himself, extolled the virtues of prohibition and temperance.[21]

Stephenson frequently warned his audiences about the spread of what he called foreign influences in the country but did not himself verbally abuse Catholics or openly denounce the pope. As matters stood in the Klan and in the state, he did not have to. Other Klan speakers, lecturers, and especially the editors of the *Fiery Cross* did it for him. Stephenson made no efforts whatsoever to regulate the hatreds and outrageous slanders delivered daily by Klan publicists and speakers throughout the state during 1923 and 1924.[22]

Very quickly, Stephenson became the top Klan organizer in the state, remitting over $400,000 in initiation fees to Klan national headquarters in Atlanta. By 1922 the national Klan leadership recognized Stephenson as a rising star in Klan affairs in the North and admitted him into their inner circle. As a matter of fact, Stephenson played a major role in effecting a palace revolution at the national convention in Atlanta in late November 1922, wherein William Simmons, founder and national leader of the resurrected Klan, was replaced by Hiram Wesley Evans. For services rendered during this coup, Stephenson returned to Indiana as the acknowledged head of the Klan in that state with recruiting and organizing rights in twenty other states as well.[23] Stephenson was on his way.

Immediately, Stephenson mounted a massive recruiting drive in Indiana and in his other northern jurisdictions with all of the zeal and confidence of an experienced sales manager. The first group targeted for recruitment were Protestant fundamentalist ministers and properly so. The principal Klan publication in Indiana, *Fiery Cross*, "a perfect paper for Protestant readers and all who would see America saved from the alienization process now under way,"[24] represented the Klan movement in Indiana as a Protestant crusade to save the Constitution and the country from undesirable ethnic and religious pollution. No wonder that the popular Protestant hymn "Onward Christian Soldiers" became the anthem of the entire Klan movement.

Stephenson obtained lists of Protestant ministers from all over the state and offered every one of them honorary membership in the Indiana Klan, that is, full membership without paying the $10 admission fee.[25] Of course, many ministers thus solicited were suspicious of the methods and objectives of the Indiana Klan and refused to have anything to do with it, but a substantial number listened to Stephenson and others and liked what they heard. Those Protestant ministers who gave pro-Klan sermons in their churches were rewarded with substantial donations.[26]

Other ministers who joined were given titles in the organization and put on the Klan payroll. There were at least two Protestant fundamentalist ministers in South Bend who, as an elected local chapter leader and as a local chapter secretary, received $75 a week from the state organization.[27] Klan-oriented Protestant ministers were critical elements in spreading the Klan and its anti-Catholic message across the length and breadth of the state. Even without that sort of support, Stephenson would probably have done well in Indiana but not as well so fast.

In addition to the help purchased or freely given from Protestant fundamentalist ministers and that provided by the rank and file, Stephenson also employed professional sales people such as former stocks and bonds salesmen and Florida real estate promoters.[28] Compensated by percentages of initiation fees and commissions from sales of Klan robes and other paraphernalia, Stephenson's recruitment and public relations organizations were efficient, extremely successful, and bound together by the very strong ties of self-interest and greed.

At least for Stephenson, those ties turned out to be substantial. By 1924 the Indiana Klan leader, not yet thirty-four years of age, had amassed a fortune of $3 million from his share of initiation fees and other commissions. He lived in a mansion in suburban Indianapolis, had the use of a $75,000 yacht on Lake Erie, a summer residence on Buckeye Lake in Ohio, and a private airplane complete with a personal pilot. That was what anti-Catholicism was worth to one very skillful practitioner of it in middle America during the 1902s.

Stephenson's self-confidence was boundless. His ambition was limitless. He compared himself at various times to Napoleon and to Mussolini. Some contemporaries believe that by 1923 he had his eye on the United States Senate seat then held by the ailing Senator Samuel M. Ralston, who was not expected to live to the end of his term. Once in the Senate, Stephenson hoped to be a serious contender for the Republican presidential nomination in 1928.[29] Others believed that he had no personal desire for public office, except perhaps to be a Republican national committeeman from Indiana or possibly national chairman of the Republican party.[30] Public adulation had little meaning for him. Power and money were what he wanted and what he got in a surprisingly short period of time. In any case, Ralston did not die until October 1925. When that long-delayed fortuitous event occurred, the extraordinary career of D. C. Stephenson was over.

Before the federal government in Washington could be captured, there was much still to be done in Indiana. Never lacking spectacular projects, Stephenson concocted a scheme in 1923 to purchase the financially troubled Valparaiso University. He intended to turn this small but much respected academic institution into a Klan college for the children of Klansmen.[31] The national Klan leadership in Atlanta had no interest whatsoever in such a project and summarily rejected Stephenson's requests for money to proceed.

More important than the rejection of Stephenson's Valparaiso project in Atlanta was the fact that the president and trustees of that institution were completely uninterested in being purchased by the Klan. The university issued a public denial that any such negotiations with the Klan had been considered. At the same time, the president and a group of distinguished alumni released a statement formally repudiating the Klan and declaring the university "open to the education of all without thought of race, religion, social standing, wealth, politics, or influence."[32]

The effect of this rebuff of the Valparaiso project was to reinforce Stephenson's growing conviction that the Indiana Klan should break all ties with the national leaders in Atlanta and go their own way. Disputes between Stephenson and Grand Wizard Evans and the national Klan leadership in Atlanta were inevitable. Between two such men as these, engaged in an organization with the perspectives of the Klan, loyal and peaceful cooperation for longer than a month would have been a minor miracle.

Within a year of Evans' successful coup against Simmons for control of the national Klan organization, Evans and Stephenson found much to argue about. Initially, their disagreements arose out of policy differences and over the handling of finances, but soon they became intensely personal. There was not much that one could say or do that the other would praise. Evans suspected that Stephenson was making too much money from the sale of Klan regalia and was appalled by the stories of his reckless womanizing. Stephenson dismissed Evans as an uncouth, uncultured violence prone incompetent. The heart of the matter was that Evans actually believed in the white supremicist, anti-Catholic, anti-Semitic, anti-immigrant Klan ideology, whereas Stephenson did not believe in anything.

Given such mutual hostility, they simply could not get on with one another for very long. The final break between them did not occur until mid-October 1923, when, after an internal investigation of sorts, Evans stripped Stephenson of his formal Klan titles and Indiana Klan offices and bestowed them upon William F. Bossert, an attorney from Liberty, Indiana. The action against Stephenson was kept confidential until early April 1924, two weeks after the Muncie Klan had announced its formal separation from both the Indiana Klan and the national organization.[33]

Because he was preoccupied with the Indiana primary elections in early May, Stephenson remained silent until after Klan-endorsed Republican candidates swept to easy victories in primary elections across the state. Having virtually taken over the Indiana Republican party in the those elections, Stephenson could well afford to announce to the world in a firm and strident manner his separation from Evans and the national Klan organization. He followed that announcement with the issuance of a constitution and bylaws for a new Indiana Klan, which a majority, but not all, of the Indiana Klansmen chose to support.

In the process of creating his new organization, Stephenson lost all authority and influence in neighboring states, particularly in Ohio. Now his power would be confined to Indiana alone, and even there he would be continually challenged by the Bossert faction and the Muncie group. However, because of coming national and state elections, all Klan factions in Indiana agreed to temporarily put aside deep personal animosities and ideological differences and cooperate for the sake of the greater good. If these elections were won, as all experts predicted, then repair of America could begin.

— iii —

Despite their difficulties with the national Klan organization in 1923, the Indiana Klan was very much alive and well during that year. To be sure, for Stephenson, the collapse of the Valparaiso project had been a disappointment but not one that much diminished the enormous public relations achievements of Indiana Klan leadership during 1923. The high point of public relations success was the great Klan convention held on July 4 in Melfalfa Park outside of Kokomo. This meeting, estimated by some to exceed two hundred thousand and by others to range somewhere between ten and fifty thousand people,[34] was the largest northern gathering in Klan history. Klansmen and their families came from every county in Indiana and from neighboring states by special trains, by interurban railway, and in thousands of automobiles. At the convention site on July 3, a night parade of Klansmen and their families, accompanied by thirty bands, stretched for miles.[35]

On July 4, convention ceremonies began at 9:30 A.M. with a prayer followed by a rendition of "The Star Spangled Banner" performed by a fifty-piece boys' band from Newcastle, Indiana. After a brief welcome by a local dignitary, the national Klan leader, Hiram Wesley Evans, delivered a long speech warning Klansmen to beware of foreign influences and ended by urging his audience to vote only for United States congressmen and senators who would work for the rehabilitation of the nation and preservation of our American heritage.[36]

The crowd was attentive to Evans but restless. Stephenson, the hero of the hour, had not yet made an appearance and did not until well after lunch. At 2:00 P.M., a small yellow airplane emblazoned with Klan symbols approached the meeting grounds from the south, circled the area, and then landed in a field adjacent to the speaker's platform. [37]

Stephenson, attired in an ordinary business suit instead of Klan robes,[38] mounted the platform and began speaking. He disappointed no one. His sense of audience mood was uncanny. He got it absolutely right. No appeals to prejudice disfigured this speech. Stephenson said virtually nothing about Negroes, Jews, or Catholics. As reported in the *Kokomo Dispatch,* he talked at length in what seemed to be a reasonable fashion about reclaiming the power which the Constitution had given to the people, lately usurped by unprincipled politicians, big money interests, and the judges and courts supporting them. Totally disregarding the founding fathers' affection for constitutional checks and balances and their distrust of unrestrained majority rule, Stephenson invoked their complete approval of his own message urging the sovereign people to be sovereign once again.[39] The people applauded. Stephenson had told his audience what they wanted to hear. There was a way for pure Americanism to triumph in America.

All in all, the day was a demonstration of strength by that part of middle America unable to accept the changes which they believed thirty years of massive immigration, postwar changing moral standards, unscrupulous politicians, and corrupt big business had thrust upon them. Stephenson had spoken, so carefully, so measuredly to the people assembled in Melfalfa Park because he had plans for them and for himself. Winning trust was the first step in a plan to make a real difference in Indiana politics in 1924 in order to be able to make a greater difference in national politics in 1928.

When the election year of 1924 began, the Klan was strongest in small towns but had also recruited thousands of supporters in the state's largest cities. Indianapolis was the acknowledged center of Klan activity throughout the Midwest. Muncie, Fort Wayne, and Evansville were all hotbeds of Klan sympathizers. Local newspapers, initially hostile to the Klan in 1921, shifted to neutral positions as the organization grew and spread throughout the state.

Major exceptions to this general Indiana journalistic temporizing with bigotry was the *Indianapolis Times, Fort Wayne Journal-Gazette, Richmond Palladium,* and *Vincennes Commercial.*[40] Perhaps the most strident anti-Klan newspaper in the state was the *South Bend Tribune.* Under Frederick A. Miller, the *South Bend Tribune* gave front-page coverage to every act of violence attributed to the Klan anywhere in the country.[41] Miller's editors and reporters invariably referred to Klansmen as Klucks, Kluckers, or Knights of the Knight Shirt. Coverage of local Klan activities was continuous and complete. Nothing large or small was omitted. It was no-quarter journalism all the way.

Partly because of the relatively large Catholic population in the South Bend-Mishawaka area, the presence of the University of Notre Dame, and the strong anti-Klan disposition of the *South Bend Tribune,* the St. Joseph County Klan chapter was one of the weakest and least successful in the entire state. In due course, Stephenson would attempt to turn that local weakness into a statewide advantage in the fall election. Yet, for the moment, South Bend, the second largest city in the state, would have to remain his biggest unsolved problem.

However, before attempting to improve Klan prospects in the uniquely hostile environment of St. Joseph County, strategies and tactics calculated to win the hearts and minds of citizens in the other ninety-one counties had to be developed, explained to local leaders, and then successfully implemented. The most important of these strategies was one intended to persuade Hoosiers to think better of the Indiana Klan and differentiate it in their minds from the violent vigilante image of what Stephenson called the "Southern Crowd."

To that end, Stephenson instructed all Indiana Klan chapters to engage publicly in some form of activity likely to be perceived by local people as beneficial to their community, such as aiding the public schools, ministerial associations, or charitable organizations. Reports about the range and scope of such beneficial local activities were supposed to be sent to Klan headquarters in Indianapolis every week.[42]

Another strategy to improve popular perceptions of the Klan in Indiana was to demonstrate a strong organizational commitment to law and order. Existing law-enforcement agencies simply could not cope with the criminality and immorality of the times. Bootleggers, gamblers, and bawdy houses operated almost everywhere with impunity. Clearly, something had to be done. Perhaps the Klan could find a way to move against crime and immorality that decent people would approve and support.

Not surprisingly, Stephenson found such a way. He found it in a long-forgotten nineteenth-century county law-enforcement institution known as the Horse Thief Detective Association. Created by the Indiana state legislature at the end of the Civil War to combat the rampant horse thievery of those years, the Horse Thief Act authorized county governments to organize volunteer county constabularies for the apprehension of horse thieves and other felons.[43]

Under provisions of this act, after obtaining permission of appropriate county officials, any group of men could band together and function as a bona fide county police force, that is, carry weapons, make arrests, and hold persons in custody.[44] Unused but unrepealed, this statute provided modern county commissioners with the legal authority to increase county police protection without paying for it. Stephenson recognized at once the extraordinary opportunities which this situation presented.

When raised and put in place, volunteer Horse Thief Detectives were nominally independent of local Klan chapters. However, overlap between the two organizations was substantial. All Horse Thief Detectives were made honorary Klansmen with initiation fees completely waived. Local Klan chapters frequently subsidized the organization and outfitting of such groups, and Klansmen were encouraged to report law violations to Horse Thief Detectives.[45] The close cooperative relationship between the Horse Thief Detectives and local Klan chapters in publicizing law violations and bringing criminals to justice, Stephenson believed, would be proof positive to most Hoosiers that in Indiana, the Klan was different and worthy of respect and support.

By the spring of 1924, 25,000 members of the Horse Thief Detective Association were regularly qualified unpaid volunteer constables. Perhaps 22,000 of those constables were Klansmen.[46] Horse Thief Detectives raided bootleggers and gambling establishments, sometimes in the company of regular peace officers and sometimes not. In Indianapolis, one series of raids on speakeasies and gambling houses resulted in 125 arrests. Klan leaders claimed that between June 1922 and October 1923 in Indiana, more than 3,000 cases of Volstead Act violations were brought to trial because of police work by the Horse Thief Detectives.[47]

— iv —

While denouncing crime, immorality, and supporting law and order in speeches delivered across the state, Stephenson paid special attention to the arcane and serious business of state politics. As early as the summer of 1922, after abandoning his efforts to win the Democratic nomination for Congress in Evansville, Stephenson began establishing Klan political organizations in selected Indiana counties. Described by Stephenson as his "military machine," these county organizations consisted of an active, if not always accurate, network of carefully chosen Klan informers and spies.

The mission of this military machine was to collect and dispatch to Klan headquarters in Indianapolis information about instances of local corruption as well as the names, addresses, places of employment, and activities of so-called undesirables, meaning political leftists, bootleggers, gamblers, bawdy house operators and inmates, Catholics, Jews, and Negroes.[48] Beyond collecting rumors and facts about corruption and the activities of undesirables, local Klan informers were ordered to secure and send to Klan headquarters the names, addresses, religious denominations, ethnic backgrounds, and political affiliations of every county officeholder, district court judge, school board member, policeman, and fireman.

Finally, Klan informers were urged to make regular reports to Indianapolis about the number, ethnic background, and religious faith of all persons arrested by the police in their respective areas. Included in this data should be information about where the children of local and county officials went to school.[49] It would appear that in each county in Indiana during 1924 there were sufficient instances of corruption as well as one or more of these undesirable groups to keep local Klan informers busy sending reports to Indianapolis.

From the data collected about local and county officeholders, Stephenson was able to give money to their churches, donate milk or American flags to their children's schools, and otherwise try to persuade them to think of the Klan as a generous civic-minded fraternal organization. At the same time, from the lists of so-called undesirables forwarded to Klan headquarters, Stephenson would be able to determine if any on those lists were candidates for public office. If any were, their electoral prospects could be damaged by local campaigns of innuendo and slander or, after the summer of 1922, by exposure and denunciation in the *Fiery Cross*.[50]

Though up and running only in Evansville, Indianapolis, and a few other places for the November elections in 1922, Stephenson's county machines contributed significantly to the electoral success of Klan-endorsed candidates in both major parties. Stephenson took credit for engineering the upset victory of former Democratic governor Samuel M. Ralston over the distinguished, long-serving progressive Republican senator Albert J. Beveridge. Beveridge had brought into the state a well-known anti-Klan speaker and had appeared with him in three Indiana cities.

For his part, Ralston had given a strong separation of church and state speech to a largely Catholic audience at a Catholic women's college in Terre Haute. The Klan published Ralston's speech under the title of "Where Courage Counts" and distributed it widely throughout the state. Ralston defeated Beveridge by more than thirty-three thousand votes.[51]

In other state races that year Klan-endorsed Republican candidates easily defeated their Democratic opponents. More particularly, candidates identified in Klan literature as Catholics and at least one who was Jewish were overwhelmed. One Republican candidate for clerk of the Indiana Supreme Court who happened to be a Catholic trailed the Republican state ticket by more than fifty-two thousand votes. Stephenson and his friends knew what they were doing and succeeded grandly.[52]

By early 1924, Stephenson had in place in each of the state's ninety-two counties a military machine organization of some sort. Not all of the county organizations were equally effective. For example, the organization in Indianapolis was large, well financed, and efficient, while the one in St. Joseph County was poorly led and unreliable. Despite the inevitable personality conflicts, serious internal feuds, and, of course, widespread corruption, Stephenson's county machines were ready to meet the supreme test in 1924 of a presidential election.

The strength of the Indiana Klan's statewide political organization was in its hierarchical command structure and communications system. Stephenson's use of telephones was extensive and, for the times, highly innovative. The most important and most valuable communication link in the Indiana Klan's statewide political effort, however, was its weekly newspaper, the *Fiery Cross*.

Located in Indianapolis, with an estimated circulation of 500,000 in Indiana and in neighboring states, Stephenson gained control of the *Fiery Cross* in early 1923 and held it until May 1924, when the editor, Milton Elrod, defected to the Bossert faction of the Indiana Klan.[53] While under Stephenson's control, the paper affected a courageous new persona. The *Fiery Cross* dared to print what others would not. From this paper issued a steady stream of sophisticated anti-Catholic propaganda intended to persuade Hoosiers to vote for the right sort of candidates in the elections of 1924.

The anti-Catholic propaganda line developed by Stephenson's editors and writers at the *Fiery Cross* was difficult for Catholic publicists to refute or deny, because it was derived in part from existing Catholic practices or easily verifiable facts. During 1923 and 1924, Indiana Klan writers made four points over and over again. First, the unwillingness of Catholic leaders as religious men to recognize Prohibition as the greatest moral issue of the day and defend it as such was inexplicable. Second, the Catholic Church had been and would forever continue to be hostile to the public schools, but encouraged its members to seek teaching positions in them. Third, the Catholic Church regarded all Protestant marriages as invalid. Fourth, given the number of Catholics living in Indiana, they were greatly overrepresented among elected public officials and far too prominent in public affairs generally.[54]

Indeed, most Catholic leaders were opposed to Prohibition, and Catholics were conspicuous as elected public officials and as political candidates. Official Catholic statements warning Catholic parents against sending their children to public schools abounded. Many Catholic men and women were employed as administrators and teachers in the public schools throughout the country. Out-of-Church marriages by Catholics had no standing in canon law. It was a fact sad but true that mixed marriages performed by Catholic priests in rectories unnecessarily demeaned non-Catholic partners in such marriages, as did the absolutely unenforceable requirement that all issue must be raised as Catholics. All of these situations were real enough, but being real did not mean that inferences drawn from them by Klan writers and speakers about Catholic attitudes and intentions were true.

Catholic teachers had not been directed by their bishops to seek employment in the public schools in order to destroy them. Ordinary Catholics may have been indifferent to Protestant values and institutions but not contemptuous. The present perceived overrepresentation of Catholics in Indiana public life was not a prelude to some sort of planned electoral coup to establish Catholic minority rule in the state.

Monsignor John F. Noll, editor and publisher of *Our Sunday Visitor*, the official Catholic diocesan weekly for northern Indiana, tried to put such charges and innuendos to rest. As early as May 27, 1923, *Our Sunday Visitor* had offered a reward of $1,000 to anyone who could prove the truth of any so-called Catholic atrocity as alleged by Klan speakers and publications. No such proofs were ever offered, and no rewards were paid. In October 1924 Noll prepared a special preelection number of *Our Sunday Visitor* wherein Klan misstatements of Catholic religious and political positions were detailed, and erroneous Klan assumptions about Catholic practices and intentions were denied.[55] Indiana Catholics were probably pleased by Noll's defense of their community; perhaps some were even inspired by it. Someone had to try to do something and Noll did the best that he could. However, the carefully crafted Klan image of a grave Catholic menace operative in Indiana was damaged hardly at all.

Not many Hoosier Protestants and unchurched voters paid much attention to whatever appeared in *Our Sunday Visitor*. Like most Catholic leaders and organizations in the state in 1924, Noll and *Our Sunday Visitor* were no match for Stephenson's "military machine" or the *Fiery Cross* in public relations warfare. In such encounters where slander and innuendo were primary weapons, truth was always an early casualty. While Noll and *Our Sunday Visitor* may have been too fastidious and insufficiently reckless to compete successfully with Klan speakers and publicists, some other Catholic advocates were not, and Noll had no reservations about encouraging them to do so.[56] Patrick H. O'Donnell and his Chicago-based anti-Klan organization, the American Unity League (AUL), were ready to do or say whatever they believed would damage or defeat the Klan.

The American Unity League was founded in Chicago on June 21, 1922 by Robert H. Shepherd, Grady K. Rutledge, and Joseph G. Keller. Dedicated to the eradication of the Klan in Chicago and in the country at large, the founders of AUL intended to recruit members from all minority groups and find places for Blacks and Jews within its leadership. As the organization grew, reality turned out to be very different. The AUL neither sought nor received much cooperation from other minorities.[57]

The organization's most influential supporters were two prominent Chicago Catholic priests and Monsignor John F. Noll of *Our Sunday Visitor* in Huntington, Indiana. During its brief but very active organizational life of two years, the AUL was in fact what most observers knew it to be, an Irish American Catholic advocacy group specializing in very rough public relations warfare.[58]

— v —

The driving force within the AUL was its chairman, Patrick H. O'Donnell, a dynamic Chicago criminal lawyer who made speeches all over Chicago and the Midwest denouncing the Klan. The unique weapon deployed by the AUL against the Klan was *Tolerance,* a weekly newspaper of sixteen pages, edited by Grady K. Rutledge. Convinced that rending the curtain of secrecy surrounding Klan membership would in time destroy the organization, O'Donnell set for himself and *Tolerance* the formidable task of obtaining by whatever means membership lists of local Klan chapters in Chicago and elsewhere. Once such lists were obtained, *Tolerance* published the names, addresses, and occupations of all persons on them.

The first issue of *Tolerance,* 2,700 copies, appeared on September 17, 1922, and identified 150 Chicagoans as Klan members. That issue was an instant success and sold out quickly. The next issue of over 17,000 copies appeared a week later and also found a ready market. By year's end, the circulation of *Tolerance* exceeded 150,000,[59] and O'Donnell had become a regional celebrity.

Acquiring authentic Klan membership lists was not easily done. Even though as many as seven paid investigators were employed by the AUL at one time, most of the information about Klan membership came from disenchanted or expelled former Klansmen.[60] Through a combination of diligence, good luck, bribery, intrigue, and an occasional burglary, the AUL managed to obtain names of actual or suspected Klansmen.

The greatest coup of this sort occurred in the early hours of Easter Sunday, April 1, 1923, when someone broke into the offices of the Indianapolis Klan on the third floor of Buschmann Hall at Eleventh Street and College Avenue and stole a list of 12,208 names of local Klansmen. *Tolerance* immediately published seventy-four names and addresses from this list with the promise of more to come in future numbers of the paper.

Given the questionable means of acquiring Klan membership records, verification of information thus obtained was virtually impossible and rarely attempted. Consequently, mistakes, sometimes very serious mistakes, were made. Outraged citizens incorrectly identified as Klansmen in *Tolerance* responded with a barrage of lawsuits. Within that barrage, clearly the heaviest was a lawsuit filed against *Tolerance* in Chicago by the celebrated William R. Wrigley, Jr., whose name, picture, and mistaken identification as a Klansman appeared in *Tolerance* on December 31, 1923. Though Wrigley was not a Klansman and the signed Klan application was clearly a forgery, Chicago Klan chapters allegedly used Wrigley's famous name to try to build up memberships.[61]

The original statement in *Tolerance* naming Wrigley as a Klansman had been published over protests from Rutledge, the editor, and from majority stockholders and directors of the publishing company.[62] O'Donnell, however, was convinced that a Klan application with Wrigley's signature on it that had been delivered to him by an informer was authentic. He insisted that Wrigley's name and picture be included among the list of discovered Klan members published in the New Year's Eve edition of *Tolerance*. O'Donnell was absolutely wrong about this matter, and Wrigley's immediate denial was followed quickly by a public admission of forgery by the informer.[63]

As events would soon show, this Wrigley affair precipitated the final collapse of *Tolerance* and of the AUL, a collapse that would take six months to complete. Rutledge, editor of *Tolerance* and secretary of the AUL, went to court and secured a temporary injunction restraining Shepherd and O'Donnell from interfering with publication of the paper.

Shepherd and O'Donnell responded on February 24 by petitioning the court to dissolve Rutledge's temporary injunction, which the judge proceeded to do. The judge ruled that Rutledge had not produced sufficient evidence to justify the injunction.[64] Ownership and control of *Tolerance* reverted forthwith to Shepherd and O'Donnell.

Two serious consequences for the AUL, *Tolerance,* and the anti-Klan cause generally followed from the dissolution of Rutledge's injunction. First, Rutledge had become so angry with Shepherd and O'Donnell and was so disappointed by the dissolution of the injunction that he broke off all business and social relations with his former colleagues. As a mat-ter of fact, Rutledge deserted the anti-Klan cause and defected to the other side. Noting that he was after all a Protestant, Rutledge began a long series of articles for *Dawn,* the principal Chicago Klan publication, purporting to expose the inner workings of the AUL and revealing the names and methods of *Tolerance* informers. Subsequently, Rutledge summarized his *Dawn* articles and published his version of the AUL-Klan conflict in Chicago in a short book, colorfully entitled *The Flag Draped Skeleton.*[65]

Second, the departure of Rutledge from the AUL and *Tolerance* left O'Donnell in full charge of the organization and of the paper. Now answerable to no one for what he personally said, published, or did, O'Donnell was of no mind to discourage subordinates and anti-Klan zealots in his circle from undertaking spectacular and often illegal actions against the Klan. To O'Donnell and to those in the anti-Klan movement who believed as he did, the Klan was so bigoted, so odious an organization, and so disgraced by past instances of terror and violence that any means employed to damage or defeat it was acceptable. Anti-Klan activity directed by the AUL and encouraged by *Tolerance* intensified in Chicago and spread elsewhere, especially to northern Indiana.

During the campaign for the Chicago aldermanic elections of April 1923, the extent of Klan electoral activity in some wards was heavy. Ordinary election excitement, combined with the fearful prospect that Klan-supported candidates might win, led to a series of violent anti-Klan incidents before and after the elections. A dynamite bomb exploded in the doorway of a butcher shop whose owner had been listed in *Tolerance* as a Klan member.[66] On April 5, a black powder bomb demolished the former publishing office of *Dawn.* The police suspected that this bombing had been the work of the AUL, and *Dawn* openly accused a staff member of *Tolerance* of committing the crime.[67] Other bomb attacks upon businesses advertising in *Dawn* followed.[68] The role of victim was new to the Klan, and local leaders proceeded to make the most of it.

While anti-Klan activity in Chicago encouraged by *Tolerance* and the O'Donnell faction of the AUL turned violent in the spring of 1923, O'Donnell, himself, was busy elsewhere. He established a number of distribution locations for *Tolerance* in Gary, Michigan City, South Bend, and, of course, Indianapolis, Indiana. Then, with encouragement from Monsignor John F. Noll of *Our Sunday Visitor,* O'Donnell attempted to introduce active AUL presences in those northern Indiana cities as well.

Klan activity had intensified in northern Indiana since the first of the year. Though denying formal ties with the Klan, groups of Klan sympathizers in cities and small towns across northern Indiana had been pressing county officials for permission to establish local Horse Thief Detective Associations.[69] O'Donnell and his friends were particularly distressed by the relative ease with which those permissions had been obtained in other parts of the state. AUL mounted a major campaign of disinformation and innuendo in *Tolerance* to discourage county officials from legitimizing such associations in their areas. This campaign began in South Bend in mid-March 1923.[70]

— vi —

The reasons why O'Donnell selected South Bend as a proper place to declare war upon the Klan in Indiana are readily discoverable. Though generally supportive of conservative causes and Republican politics, the *South Bend Tribune* was utterly opposed to the Klan and missed no opportunity to say so. Certainly, the presence of the University of Notre Dame nearby insured a reliable cadre of local anti-Klan support for whatever sort of campaign AUL might choose to wage. In addition, the city contained a large Catholic population of Polish (4,200) and Hungarian (3,200) ethnicities with a demonstrated and easily aroused hostility to the Klan. At the same time, local Klan membership was small for a city of the size of South Bend (70,000). Except for a few fundamentalist Protestant ministers, local Klan leadership included no one of significant social or economic standing in the community.[71]

Klan activities in the area during the early months of 1923 had been minimal and ineffective. Efforts to establish a local Horse Thief Detective Association had failed. To be sure, a typewritten threatening letter had been sent to the Polish-American pastor of St. Hedwig's Catholic Church,[72] and someone had unsuccessfully attempted to burn a fiery cross in Mishawaka during the evening of St. Patrick's Day.[73] South Bend was an area where the Klan was weak and opposition to it was very strong.

O'Donnell announced his intention to speak at an anti-Klan rally in South Bend on March 13, 1923. Accompanying that announcement was a public invitation to Father John W. Cavanaugh to preside. Much more amenable to private invitations respectfully delivered than to one extended publicly in a newspaper story, suspicious of O'Donnell's Chicago activities, and disturbed by the recklessness of his public relations tactics, Cavanaugh made himself unavailable that evening. Because he needed a prominent Catholic clerical presence for the South Bend meeting, O'Donnell replaced the absent Cavanaugh with Father William J. McNamee of St. Patrick's Church, Chicago, a strong supporter of the Shepherd-O'Donnell faction of the AUL.

O'Donnell and Father McNamee appeared in South Bend as scheduled on March 13 at Place Hall, a facility that had been used recently for closed Klan meetings. Addressing a sympathetic crowd of about six hundred,[74] O'Donnell began by denying the central premise of Klan propaganda, namely, that the Klan represented any form of Americanism at all. Next, he asserted the contrary. As an organization, O'Donnell insisted, the Klan was totally un-American. He did not stop there. Any organization that un-American was probably guilty of treason as well.[75]

O'Donnell vowed that Indiana would be the next battleground for the war between the AUL and the Klan. Winning this war would not be easy because the power of state government would not remain neutral. The present conflict in the state of Oklahoma between the Klan-dominated legislature and an unpopular anti-Klan governor was a sign of the times. In Indiana, O'Donnell concluded, more than sixty Klansmen were sitting members of the state legislature. McNamee spoke briefly after O'Donnell and urged Hoosiers to support the AUL against the Klan.[76]

Following O'Donnell's March appearance in South Bend, Klan activities increased in that city. A speaker was dispatched from Klan headquarters in Indianapolis to go to Place Hall in April and hold the first Klan-sponsored open public meeting in South Bend. As was usual in such situations, the speaker was identified as a Klan lecturer but unnamed. The announced subject was the now familiar Klan theme of 100 percent Americanism.

An audience of about five hundred, including a large contingent of Notre Dame students, gathered in Place Hall to hear the lecturer. Police were present and visible. Dressed in ordinary street clothes and well prepared, the speaker began by saying that he had not come to South Bend to pick a fight with anyone and that he hoped no one would try and pick a fight with him. Speaking mainly in clichés, he claimed that Catholic activities against the Klan in Chicago and in St. Joseph County, meaning those of the AUL and *Tolerance,* had an opposite effect. Persecution, he added, had helped publicize the ideals and patriotic goals of the Indiana Klan. Recruitment in this area had grown by leaps and bounds.[77]

At the end of the evening, the speaker was questioned sharply by several Notre Dame students. He responded calmly but made the same cliché-ridden points over and over again. Though strongly affirming the absolute separation of church and state as provided in the Constitution, the speaker insisted that the Bible should be on every public school teacher's desk and read to students during regular class time. Immigration was out of control, needed to be limited, and a residence requirement of thirty-one years for citizenship ought to be imposed. With regard to Catholics, they could never be 100 percent Americans because of their allegiance to a foreign potentate.[78]

Many Notre Dame students had attended the Place Hall rally in March to hear O'Donnell and went there again in April to see and hear the Klan speaker. Most of what they heard from both of these speakers was familiar. Most likely, very few of the students went away from Place Hall impressed or inspired. O'Donnell and the Klan speaker were just not what these young men were used to. O'Donnell's exaggerations, assertion of facts, and general lack of urbanity had been embarrassing. The Klan speaker must have seemed to them at that time more a curiosity than a threat.

Insofar as the *Scholastic* can be taken as representative of Notre Dame student and faculty opinion on Indiana Klan activities and on the responses of the AUL and *Tolerance* in early 1923, it would appear that the university community was firmly opposed to the Klan and everything it stood for but at the same time was also disturbed by the tactics of the AUL and *Tolerance.* In an unsigned article, the editors of the *Scholastic* argued that by recklessly publishing alleged but unverified Klan membership lists, *Tolerance* had damaged its own credibility more than it had exposed Klan hypocrisy and error.[79]

Perhaps remembering the form and content of their recently established required Thomistic philosophy courses, the editors of the *Scholastic* solemnly assured their readers that "Error can be met only with truth, and hypocrisy can be destroyed only with honesty." Faced with an utterly unscrupulous enemy, *Tolerance* had abandoned that principle and that was why they were in trouble. Unprincipled methods and crude language always connote insincerity, and the editors suspected that *Tolerance* was more interested in looking for dollars than for truth.[80]

To be sure, perceptions of the Indiana Klan as an amusing curiosity by members of the Notre Dame community would change quickly and radically over the next six months as Klan political activities intensified throughout the state. Certainly, the public admission by Lawrence Lyons, chairman of the Indiana Republican party, that he had joined the Indiana Klan in February only to resign from it at the end of March was a fair warning of how far and high anti-Catholic religious bigotry might reach in Indiana politics during the elections of 1924.[81] The danger to Catholics and Catholic institutions in the state of Indiana was about to become clear and present.

One group much aware of that danger was O'Donnell and his friends at *Tolerance*. Evidence of it seemed to them to be everywhere. Petitions requesting constabulary status for Horse Thief Detective Associations flooded into county commissioners offices all over northern Indiana. The *South Bend Tribune* described the many petitions presented to the commissioners in St. Joseph County as an epidemic. So many people petitioned for constabulary status and thus the right to carry firearms that the county commissioners issued a ruling limiting such appointments to a maximum of ten applicants from any one organization.[82] O'Donnell decided to try to put an end to this epidemic by imposing high public embarrassment costs on as many of the Horse Thief Detective Association petitioners as possible.

In this phase of his war against the Klan, O'Donnell's chosen weapon was simple, straightforward defamation. An early victim of this tactic was the unfortunate William Hale of Michigan City, Indiana. Hale had signed a petition presented to the LaPorte county commissioners seeking constabulary status for the Michigan City Horse Thief Detective Association. *Tolerance* published a forceful denunciation of the Michigan City association on March 18 as a Klan front and proceeded to describe Hale and other signers of the petition as complete scoundrels.[83]

Well known in Michigan City and a trustee of a large local Protestant church, Hale may or may not have had an attitude toward Catholics. He had signed the Horse Thief Association petition and that was enough for O'Donnell. *Tolerance* described Hale as a notorious adulterer. Hale responded immediately with a libel suit against *Tolerance* and the proprietor of the Michigan City soft drink parlor that circulated and sold the paper.[84] Hale's libel action against *Tolerance* was only one of many.

As a matter of fact, the increasing number of lawsuits filed against *Tolerance* was proof positive that a recently implemented Klan strategy to ruin O'Donnell, the AUL, and *Tolerance* was working. Klan officials petitioned the U.S. District Court in Chicago for an injunction to prevent *Tolerance* from publishing a list of the names of 12,000 Indiana Klansmen.[85] Klan lawyers argued that O'Donnell was part of a criminal conspiracy against their client and had obtained the lists of Klan members improperly, purchasing them from disaffected former Klansmen. The judge was persuaded that the lists had been improperly obtained and issued a temporary injunction restraining *Tolerance* from publishing them. O'Donnell, in effect, proceeded to violate the injunction by filing a legal action of his own in another court, thereby making the lists part of the public record. Thereupon, a local printing company published them.[86]

In this matter, O'Donnell had behaved precisely as Stephenson and other Klansmen had expected that he would behave. Klan leadership had set a trap into which O'Donnell had eagerly run. Indiana Klan leaders deliberately fed O'Donnell with false information about local celebrities being Klan members.[87] O'Donnell accepted as true whatever his sources gave him and published it. The Wrigley situation in Chicago was clearly a case of uncritical acceptance of false information and the Hale matter in Michigan City may have been so as well. With regard to the South Bend area, *Tolerance* seems to have identified as a Klan member anyone whom local informers reported was a Klan member. The list was long, sprinkled with the names of local celebrities, and for persons familiar with South Bend, very hard to believe.

Among the local celebrities and ordinary people erroneously identified by *Tolerance* as Klan members were several Notre Dame persons. One of the university barbers was reported to be a Klansman. So also were some lay faculty members, including the head of the chemistry department. Even the chairman of the Lay Board of Trustees was represented as a Klan sympathizer.[88] Because both Henry B. Froning, head of the chemistry department, and Albert R. Erskine, chairman of the Lay Board of Trustees and president of the Studebaker Corporation, were Protestants, O'Donnell had assumed that the information delivered to him about their Klan involvements and sympathies was reliable enough to publish.

The allusion to Erskine in *Tolerance* drew an immediate and firm response from Erskine's lawyers. Already overwhelmed by lawsuits, O'Donnell apologized and retracted. He promised Erskine that in the future "your name will never appear in *Tolerance* unless it is with your consent and approval." However, there were some other South Bend men that O'Donnell wanted to discuss with Erskine, "some of them in your plant." O'Donnell wanted Erskine and other important people from South Bend to visit him in Chicago because he was fearful of bringing records in his possession into the South Bend jurisdiction.[89] There is no evidence that Erskine or any other important persons from South Bend visited O'Donnell in Chicago or that O'Donnell ever went back to South Bend to investigate or denounce anyone. By the summer of 1923, O'Donnell had lost all credibility. He had been outwitted, outmaneuvered, and within a year was to be defeated totally.

The identification of Froning as a Klansman in *Tolerance* on May 6, 1923, created a situation within the university community that Father Walsh handled very poorly. The day after Froning's name appeared in *Tolerance* four lay faculty members in the chemistry department issued a public statement expressing their confidence that Froning was not a member of the Klan.[90] Froning expected that Walsh would do the same, that is, say something supportive, make some effort to clear his name and honor from this false and utterly preposterous accusation. However, perhaps preoccupied with graduation exercises and other end of term business, or unwilling to criticize publicly O'Donnell's anti-Klan activities because the man frequently corresponded with him, Walsh made no public statement whatsoever about Froning or about the *Tolerance* accusation.

Froning waited eleven weeks for some sort of action on his behalf by Walsh, and when none occurred, he met with the president in mid-July and expressed his deep disappointment. According to Froning, Walsh admitted that his silence had been intentional and had stated "what he would do depended on the attitude of the student body and the alumni."[91] Froning also noted that Walsh affected surprise that the chemist was so upset with him. The president conceded that he had not said anything supportive of Froning in this matter, but he had not said anything against him either. Following that observation, Froning told Walsh to his face that the president did not appear to have much concern for his well-being.[92] After that, there was nothing further to discuss.

Since the student body was on summer vacation and Froning had no way of knowing whether the alumni even had an attitude on this matter, he assumed correctly that Walsh was of no mind to do or say anything, so he took matters in his own hands. Froning refused to sign his annual contract and in effect resigned from the university on July 24, 1923. Walsh acknowledged receipt of the unsigned contract three days later and accepted Froning's resignation with regrets.[93]

Fortunately for the university, matters did not end there and a public relations disaster of the highest order was averted. Intervention occurred at once, most likely in the persons of Burns and Cavanaugh. Burns, himself a former chemist and the person who had hired Froning, probably talked to Froning and helped persuade the man to reconsider. Cavanaugh, close friend and confidant of Walsh as well as the person who had first brought him into the Notre Dame administration, was fully capable of changing Walsh's mind about almost anything.

Moreover, at the time of Froning's resignation, Cavanaugh was actively engaged in an all-out war to drive O'Donnell and his investigators out of South Bend and put *Tolerance* out of business.[94] How much Froning knew of Walsh's epistolary relationship with O'Donnell or of Cavanaugh's campaign against O'Donnell's slanderous activity of *Tolerance* is unknown, but Froning reconsidered his decision about leaving Notre Dame and stayed at the university until his retirement in 1940.

As has been noted, John W. Cavanaugh was a strong personality. Congenial and affable in most situations, he was a man afflicted with a terrible temper that career or life experience had done little to moderate. In most things, his patience was finite, and he was never one to suffer fools gladly or easily. Cavanaugh's mood changes could be instantaneous and spectacular. Nothing would move him from absolute composure to unbridled rage faster than encounters with behavior in others that he perceived to be hypocritical or dishonorable.

One often repeated but undocumented incident purporting to illustrate Cavanaugh's character and utter abhorrence of hypocrisy is contained in a widely read history of Notre Dame.[95] This incident involved a supposed confrontation between Cavanaugh and a group of local Protestant ministers at a public meeting in South Bend in the spring of 1923. According to this account, written twenty years after the incident described, the South Bend Chamber of Commerce had called a meeting of South Bend worthies to discuss and find ways and means of dealing with O'Donnell's slanderous and inaccurate identification and exposure of local Klansmen in *Tolerance*.

During the course of this meeting, Cavanaugh was supposed to have lost his famous temper and publicly excoriated the Protestant ministers there present for the rankest sort of hypocrisy and bigotry. As related in this account, several of the Protestant ministers had spoken out forcefully against *Tolerance* and urged banning the sale of it in the city. However, much to the chagrin of Cavanaugh, these same ministers had said nothing at all about the frequent libeling and slandering of Catholics in the *Fiery Cross*. How the ministers and others at the meeting reacted to Cavanaugh's severe tongue-lashing is not mentioned.

To be sure, this kind of direct, face to face denunciation of hypocrisy and bigotry was something that Cavanaugh could have done, perhaps should have done, but there is simply no documentary evidence that he did it in the place and manner described. O'Donnell's devilry in the South

Bend and Chicago areas and Klan and anti-Klan activities in the city and elsewhere were widely reported in the *South Bend Tribune,* but no mention of such a meeting or of a denunciation of Protestant clerical hypocrisy on this matter is mentioned in this newspaper during all of 1923. Similarly, no confirmation of this incident can be found in the Cavanaugh or Walsh correspondence or in university publications of this time. It is a good story, an anecdote perhaps illustrative of Cavanaugh's character, but not a documentable historical event.

About Cavanaugh's conviction that O'Donnell was an unscrupulous and dishonorable man corrupting a good cause by employment of nefarious means and that *Tolerance* was an embarrassment to Catholics everywhere, there is no doubt. About his determination to drive O'Donnell and his operatives out of South Bend and *Tolerance* out of business, there can be no doubt either. However, given the state of public opinion on the Klan and the reality of Catholic-Protestant relations at that time, the O'Donnell and *Tolerance* problems were better resolved through private action than by public denunciation.

This is to say that neither Walsh nor Cavanaugh were disposed to denounce O'Donnell or *Tolerance* publicly for exposing and attacking the Klan. O'Donnell was a scoundrel, but he was a Catholic scoundrel, and in 1923 that made a difference. To be sure, O'Donnell's methods were outrageous, embarrassing, and immoral. Both Walsh and Cavanaugh knew that, but to say so publicly to a largely Protestant country would be for both of these Irish American priests an action tantamount to religious and race betrayal.

At that time, one prominent Catholic simply did not publicly denounce another prominent Catholic engaged in a cause as important to the Catholic community as combatting Klan-inspired anti-Catholic bigotry. In any case, whatever Notre Dame presidents might say publicly about a subject of this nature would be at once highly newsworthy and amenable to distortion. Neither Walsh nor Cavanaugh were of a mind to provide reporters with quotes or headlines that would please the enemy. In these circumstances, if O'Donnell was a scoundrel, albeit a Catholic scoundrel, and *Tolerance* was a nuisance, both the man and the paper were Catholic responsibilities. Cavanaugh believed that and acted accordingly. He took appropriate measures to insure that South Bend would be rid of both of them.

Cavanaugh's campaign against O'Donnell was one of his finest hours. He communicated clearly and directly to O'Donnell that he must stop all AUL activity in South Bend and remove himself and his employees from the city at once. In addition, Cavanaugh contacted personal friends and

Notre Dame alumni in South Bend and in Chicago and urged them to cease all moral and financial support of the AUL and *Tolerance* and to distance themselves as much as possible from O'Donnell.

The former Notre Dame president's attack on O'Donnell, the AUL, and *Tolerance* was extremely effective. O'Donnell wrote to Walsh on May 26, 1923, stating that AUL "efforts to overthrow the Klan in South Bend [had] met with such furious opposition from Father Cavanaugh and others that we have considered that further efforts there would be unwise." Furthermore, "Father Cavanaugh's opposition [had] reached with such disastrous effect the Notre Dame alumni in Chicago . . . Our financial position and limited power are too precarious to hazard them any longer in South Bend." After having spent $1,000 of AUL money and kept two of his most experienced investigators in South Bend for over a month, O'Donnell complained, "we have, therefore, concluded to transfer our endeavors elsewhere."[96] O'Donnell would embarrass and disgrace Catholics and Catholic institutions in the South Bend area no more.

Cavanaugh's expulsion of the AUL from South Bend and his highly successful discouragement of Catholic financial support for that organization and for *Tolerance* was the beginning of the end for O'Donnell's anti-Klan movement. Because of the Wrigley affair and other incidents in Chicago and the infiltration of the New York chapter of AUL by a paid Klan spy, by the summer of 1924 the AUL was bankrupt, and *Tolerance* had ceased publication.[97] Cavanaugh was pleased by the collapse of AUL activity in South Bend, and, of course, so was Stephenson.

— vii —

The departure of O'Donnell and the AUL from South Bend had no appreciable effect upon Klan activities in St. Joseph County or elsewhere in northern Indiana one way or the other. However, the increased Klan presence in St. Joseph and neighboring counties following the April appearance of a Klan lecturer in South Bend continued and grew. Two hundred neophytes were initiated into the Klan in an open-air meeting held in the hills south of Mishawaka that was attended by 700 people.[98] Klansmen paraded through LaPorte on May 17, and on the next day about 5,000 Klansmen virtually took possession of Valparaiso.[99]

Ten days later, 500 Klansmen staged a parade in Walkerton, Indiana, and burned a large fiery cross on the main street.[100] A month later, 500 robed Klansmen marched through Plymouth, accompanied by brass bands and floats. A huge fiery cross made of telegraph poles was burned at the fairgrounds.[101] The extent and intensity of anti-Catholicism evidenced by these demonstrations in the environs of South Bend was truly astonishing. Local Catholics could have no illusions about what some of their Protestant neighbors thought of them or what those same neighbors might try to do to them. However, the most incredible and threatening expressions of anti-Catholic bigotry in the region were yet to occur, and when they did, it would be in Elkhart, fourteen miles east of South Bend.

According to the *South Bend Tribune*, Klan membership was larger and anti-Catholic attitudes were stronger in Elkhart than in South Bend. Many more otherwise respectable people, especially some prominent lawyers and Protestant ministers, were believed to be Klan members.[102] During the first week of June, local anti-Catholic feelings were greatly intensified by the ridiculous rumor that Pope Pius XI had made a secret visit to Elkhart to confer with Catholic leaders there about taking over the city.[103] More serious were the numerous warnings sent to individuals to mend their ways.

One such person thus singled out and threatened was Robert E. Proctor, a lawyer, former state senator, and a Catholic. Proctor had delivered anti-Klan speeches all over Elkhart and for that kind of activity was directed by anonymous letters to leave the city forthwith or face the consequences. What those consequences would be was revealed on the weekend of June 9–10.

Elkhart Klansmen planned a major demonstration in the city for June 9. Ed Jackson, the serving secretary of the state of Indiana, a Klansman, and a candidate for the Republican gubernatorial nomination, had promised to appear and did. The highlight of the day was a parade of Klansmen through the city. Proctor attended the parade as a spectator, and after refusing to remove his hat as the Klan color guard passed, Proctor was set upon by a group of Klansmen and sympathizers intent upon removing his hat and teaching him a lesson. Only timely intervention by the police prevented an assault and possible serious injury to Proctor. Though Proctor was able to walk away from this incident without injury, the message that ordinary citizens, especially Catholics, in Elkhart were expected by many in the community to bare their heads before white-robed men carrying the American flag was a frightening one to hear.[104]

Emboldened by Klan successes in Elkhart, South Bend Klansmen announced their intention to hold an outdoor public meeting and stage their first parade through the South Bend business center before the end of June. The timing was carefully chosen. On previous occasions when a Klan parade in South Bend had been rumored for a particular day, the downtown streets of the city on that day had been crowded with Notre Dame students anxious to see and harass the hooded marchers. For that reason and uncertain about adequate police protection, no Klan parades had actually taken place in South Bend. At the end of June, Notre Dame students would be on summer vacation and therefore pose no threat to the intended parade or outdoor meeting.[105]

The continuing problem of inadequate police protection for Klan-sponsored activities remained. The possibility of hostile action against a Klan parade by South Bend Polish American Catholic organizations had to be taken seriously. For that reason as well as others, Klan leadership in St. Joseph County decided to forgo a parade through the South Bend business district as part of their planned demonstration in the city. Instead, Klan activities in St. Joseph County would begin on Friday evening, June 22, with a parade through New Carlisle, a small town a few miles west of South Bend, featuring motorcycles carrying crosses composed of electric lights and followed by an open-air meeting.[106]

Next, an outdoor meeting would be held in South Bend on Monday, June 25, in a meadow off Portage Road on the northwest side of the city. This site would be difficult for opponents to access, and all approaches would be heavily guarded by Klansmen.[107] Indeed, the meeting was held as scheduled and about two hundred automobiles appeared at the site. However, the elements, not the Polish American Falcon organizations, intervened to break it up. Heavy rains made any sort of outdoor program impossible.[108]

The only newsworthy fact of this entire affair was the presence at the meeting of Gordon Ostot of South Bend. Ostot was the official solicitor of memberships of the St. Joseph County Klan organization and was also one of the most visible members of local Klan leadership. Ostot was employed as a state highway patrolman and always appeared at Klan functions dressed in his State Police uniform.[109] Since no one in the Indiana State Highway Commission or in other branches of Indiana state government publicly objected to when and where Ostot wore his uniform, the color of state government approval was given to Klan activities.

To South Bend Catholics and university officials, the regular and uncontested appearance of Ostot in his State Policeman's uniform at Klan functions communicated an unpleasant but very clear message. Some agencies of the Indiana state government had become passive, if not active, supporters of the current fashionable form of anti-Catholic bigotry. From the perspective of local Klan leadership, the color of state government approval that Ostot brought to Klan activities was a partial compensation for the perceived uncertain protection available from South

Bend police for Klan demonstrations and meetings. In this regard, South Bend was different from any other city or town in the state. Stephenson and his followers in Indianapolis and also the Bossert faction in Evansville and elsewhere agreed that all of this needed to be changed.

— viii —

Though driven out of South Bend, O'Donnell had not lost interest in either intelligence-gathering activities or in the general progress of the Klan in St. Joseph County or elsewhere in Indiana. Throughout the fall of 1923 he kept Father Walsh apprised of what his intelligence sources managed to collect. O'Donnell reported on the rift between Stephenson and Evans, the reasons why the Stephenson faction of the Indiana Klan had decided to separate from the national organization, and on what appeared to be an extraordinary increase of Klan membership in the Northeast. This information, O'Donnell added, was "food for serious thought and prayerful reflection."[110]

About the situation in South Bend and St. Joseph County, O'Donnell was very optimistic. According to his sources, there were fewer than eighty Klansmen in good standing and active in the city. O'Donnell believed that in the near future an organizer would probably be sent up from Indianapolis to try and improve Klan recruiting, but "at present in St. Joe county," he concluded, "they were dead, dead, dead."[111]

As might be expected, O'Donnell's sources of information about the vitality of the Klan in St. Joseph County were inaccurate. Indeed, he had been correctly informed about the divisions among Indiana Klan leaders, but, as events were soon to show, those divisions were not widely publicized and were to have no serious consequences until after the primary and general elections of 1924. Moreover, O'Donnell was taken entirely by surprise by the enormous increase in Klan political activity throughout the state, especially in northern Indiana, in late 1923 and during most of 1924. Ideological disagreements and personal animosities between Stephenson and the Bossert-Evans faction were simply not allowed to intrude upon or otherwise disrupt the smooth-running Klan political organizations that Stephenson had put in place across the state. Those matters could be settled or worked out, one way or another, later. For the moment, however, all factions within the Indiana Klan agreed that there were candidates to get nominated and elections to win.

At the same time, a few anti-Klan activists in Indianapolis and elsewhere in the state attempted to force incumbent officeholders as well as aspiring ones to take a public position either for or against the Klan. Generally, this effort was singularly unsuccessful. Most Indiana politicians were of no mind to risk alienating anyone by taking firm positions on anything. The Marion County chapter of the AUL made the task of position avoidance on the Klan issue easier by giving both political parties only seven days to declare whether as organizations they stood "for the American republic and the constitution or the invisible empire."[112] Spokesmen for both parties and virtually every individual who chose to answer pronounced for the American republic and the Constitution, but only a handful denounced the Klan by name.

Senator Samuel W. Ralston (D-Ind) was not one who did. He had defeated Beveridge in 1922 with strong Klan support and was currently a contender for selection as the Democratic vice-presidential candidate. Ralston proclaimed his belief in religious and racial toleration, denied that he was or ever had been a Klan member but would not repudiate the Klan as an organization.[113] Ralston had a great many emulators.

Closer to Notre Dame, in Elkhart County, the indefatigable and courageous Robert E. Proctor addressed an announced anti-Klan meeting in the Elkhart Armory that had been packed by 900 Klansmen.[114] A small fiery cross had been burned in front of Proctor's law office in the Monger Building during the evening of the meeting, and newsboys sold Klan publications at the Armory door. For Proctor, the audience was difficult, perhaps even dangerous, but according to the *South Bend Tribune,* he was up to all challenges encountered and never lost his composure. When Proctor made a point in his indictment of the Klan, there would be a moment or two of silence, followed inevitably by "a burst of jeering laughter from the Kluxers."[115]

In his speech, Proctor denied emphatically that Catholics owed any political or temporal allegiance to the pope or that Catholics took their politics from their bishops or priests. Also, he denied specifically that Catholics were plotting to take over the city by electing their own to public office. Such a contention was absolutely preposterous. The truth was that neither in the city of Elkhart nor in Elkhart County were there enough Catholic voters sufficiently organized or disciplined to elect members of their faith to any office. Moreover, during the past forty years, Proctor argued, no more than half a dozen Catholics had served in elective or appointive city offices, and in the entire recorded history of Elkhart County only one Catholic had ever been elected to office there. These facts notwithstanding, anti-Catholicism had been preached throughout the city and county more this past year than ever before.[116]

Proctor turned next to an aggressive examination of the record of the Klan in Elkhart. According to Proctor, the Klan had attempted to elect a slate of officeholders for the Elkhart Chamber of Commerce but had succeeded in returning only one Klansman as president of that body.[117] Next, he quoted passages from the Constitution of the United States and of the state of Indiana and then perhaps personalized his remarks a bit. Proctor asserted his opinion that Klansmen and ordinary citizens who attended meetings where boycotts of Catholic or Jewish merchants or professional men were promulgated became responsible for any crimes which followed from their actions.[118]

Proctor stated also that the Klan had made a similar attempt to capture the local hospital board but failed. Now, he contended, the Klan was trying to organize a junior Klan among high-school age youth. For Proctor, that was too much. "It is bad enough," he insisted, "to say the things you do about my people and my church without passing it on to the children," but with this junior Klan organization "you are going beyond the realm of all human decency."[119]

During the speech, Proctor was challenged frequently, several times by a reporter from the *Fiery Cross*, but according to the *South Bend Tribune*, managed to silence critics in a good-natured way. It is unlikely that Proctor changed many minds that evening, but he was able to complete his remarks and get out of the Armory without suffering personal injury.

The extent of Klan support in Elkhart during late 1923 and early 1924 as evidenced by the amount and intensity of popular participation in Klan activities there was by no means unusual for northern Indiana at that time. For example, Michigan City was even more Klan oriented than Elkhart. In preparation for a large Klan demonstration in Michigan City on January 11, 1924, complete with a horse parade and an elaborate open-air initiation ceremony, the newly elected Republican Board of Commissioners, at their normal weekly meeting on January 9, repealed an ordinance adopted the previous September by the former Board that prohibited all masked parades and masked gatherings in the city. The *South Bend Tribune* reported that the four Republican commissioners voting to repeal the ordinance either were Klansmen or had been elected on a ticket put up by the Klan.[120]

The successful capture of the Michigan City Republican party organization by the Klan was indicative of what was happening all over the state in early 1924. At this time, because the Indiana Republican party was in such a state of disarray, it was especially vulnerable to infiltration and domination by an organization such as the Klan. Since November 30, 1923, the serving Republican governor of the state, Warren T. McCray, had been under indictment for embezzlement and larceny of $155,000 of state funds. On February 25, 1924, a federal grand jury returned an additional indictment against McCray for mail fraud.[121]

In April, McCray was found guilty of the mail fraud charge, was fined $10,000 and sentenced to serve ten years in the federal penitentiary in Atlanta.[122] He was succeeded by the lieutenant governor, Emmett Branch, who would administer the state until the primary election and state convention in May and general election in November filled the leadership vacuum in the Indiana Republican party. Both Stephenson and Bossert were anxious to have their very good friend, Secretary of State Ed Jackson, properly politically positioned and financed to fill it.

Throughout February and March, Indiana Republican leaders tried to make the best of a bad situation. Not only was the governor and nominal head of the state party organization under indictment and on his way to a long term in a federal prison, but local party leaders were divided over several issues certain to be raised in the party platform committee at the state Republican convention scheduled for May 21, 1924, in Indianapolis. Old issues such as whether or not the controversial State Public Service Commission ought to be abolished and the state's primary election law ought to be repealed enjoyed no consensus among local party leaders and would be sharply contested in the meetings of platform committee at the convention.[123]

A new issue certain to be raised in the platform committee, but one that most Republican leaders hoped would go away, was that of the influence of the Klan in Indiana public affairs. Newspapers reported that "the most astute politicians do not know at this time [February 2, 1924] how the state convention will handle this problem."[124] Great pressure was being applied to Republican party leaders to prepare and approve a plank for the platform that would condemn the Klan. At the same time, an equal amount of pressure was being exerted on those same party leaders to say nothing at all about the Klan in the party platform. To be sure, the outcome of the Indiana primary elections on May 6, 1924, would go a long way toward settling this issue, but whatever candidates Indiana Republican voters chose on Primary Tuesday would have to be ratified by the state Republican party convention three weeks later.[125]

Stephenson and local Klan leaders across the state planned very carefully to insure that the primary elections would nominate as many pro-Klan Republicans for national, state, county, and local offices as possible and that the state Republican convention would refrain from any and all formal pronouncements against the Klan. Competent electioneering on behalf of Republican candidates sympathetic to Klan principles in normally low voter-participation elections was one proven way to win them. Some sort of incident staged at the proper time and demonstrating the dangerous reality of Catholic power in Indiana ought to persuade the state convention to lean toward the Klan and Klan-endorsed candidates. Preparations for effective electioneering and staging such an incident proceeded apace.

On April 2, 1924, the *South Bend Tribune* announced in front-page headlines that the Klan was making a serious bid for political power in Indiana. Picking up on stories in Indianapolis newspapers, the *South Bend Tribune* described Jackson as an "openly known . . . Klux candidate for Governor" and stated categorically that the hooded organization was determined to seize control of the "Hoosier G.O.P. organization if possible" in the forthcoming primary election. The paper reported estimated Klan membership in the state to be 600,000, and on the strength of those numbers rated the prospects for electoral victories in the primaries and capturing the Republican party organization as even-money betting propositions.[126]

This general newspaper story about Klan political objectives in Indiana was put out because of greatly increased political activities by local Klan chapters all over the state. Stephenson's military machine was in high gear. Local Klan chapters had prepared and were circulating slates of Klan-approved candidates for national, state, and local offices in every county in the state. Though official Klan spokesmen affected to be nonpartisan, far more Hoosier Republican candidates received Klan endorsements than did Democrats. Those same spokesmen insisted that because so much of professional politics was crooked and detrimental to American life and institutions, irrespective of political party, only honest, clean, high-minded, right-thinking men who were ready to place honor and duty above material gain had been endorsed.[127]

Stephenson reportedly sent out 600,000 letters urging the nomination of Ed Jackson for governor in the Republican primary. Stephenson stated in some of those letters that bootleggers, criminals, and shysters have resorted to every resource of treachery, falsehood, and double-dealing to defeat our program, "but God still reigns in heaven, we cannot fail." We are "not interested in Ed Jackson because he is a Republican, but because he is a Christian gentleman and a good citizen who loves his country and his God."[128]

In other letters sent out on behalf of Jackson, Stephenson reminded all members of his organization that "Our power to nominate a governor of Indiana has been challenged." He urged all Klansmen, Republicans and Democrats alike, to rally to Jackson.[129] At the same time, Bossert, for many years a Republican activist in his county, put aside temporarily his differences with Stephenson and also strongly supported Jackson.[130] For his part, throughout his campaign Jackson never mentioned the Klan issue and disregarded all questionnaires designed to get him on record about the Klan.[131]

The names of Klan-supported candidates in St. Joseph County were reported in the *South Bend Tribune* as early as April 6, 1924, and were repeated again with additional details and comment on May 2. Slates of Republican candidates for offices in St. Joseph County were broadcast throughout the city and county on Saturday, May 3, the last weekend before the primary election. These slates were typewritten on ruled paper, duplicated with carbon paper, mailed out in plain white envelopes, and carried no identification or indication that they were Klan-inspired. These slates urged "Votes for these 100 per cent Americans and for law enforcement."[132]

Republican leaders in St. Joseph County as well as in counties in other parts of the state were distressed by the prospect that Stephenson and other Klansmen were just a step or two from seizing control of their state political party organization. Efforts were made by local Republican leaders in many Indiana counties to put forward as candidates respectable men unaffiliated with the Klan.[133] In St. Joseph County, where the Klan was probably weaker than anywhere else in the state, local Republican leaders offered a slate that made very clear to the voters which candidates were Klan-endorsed and which were not. The *South Bend Tribune* assisted local Republican leaders by widely publicizing the names of non-Klan Republican candidates.[134]

In any case, because of the weakness of the Klan organization in St. Joseph County relative to other Indiana counties there was no possibility that Klansmen could win control of the St. Joseph County Republican organization, no matter how Klan candidates fared in the primary election. As a matter of fact, local Klan leaders did not even try. Only fifteen out of eighty-four candidates filing for election as Republican precinct committeemen were known to be connected with the local Klan organization. The declarations of candidacy for these fifteen men had been brought to the county clerk's office by men who were prominent in the local Horse Thief Detective Association.[135] Regular Republican leaders in St. Joseph County were safe.

The relative weakness of the Klan in St. Joseph County had been a matter of concern to both Stephenson and Bossert for some time. The cause of that weakness was the relatively large foreign-born Polish and Hungarian Catholic population in that county. In the two largest cities in the county, South Bend and Mishawaka, the Klan had very little working-class support, perhaps in part reflective of the $10 initiation fee. One student of the South Bend Klan concluded on the basis of an analysis of a sample of fifty-four known Klan members that Klansmen in that city were solidly middle- and lower-middle-class. Typically, an average South Bend Klansman held a white-collar job, was married, owned his own home, and regarded the city as his permanent residence.[136] Whatever the causes of Klan organizational weakness in St. Joseph County, weakness there was. During early 1924 Stephenson and others began viewing Klan weakness and the large number of working-class Catholics in that county as an opportunity to be exploited rather than as a problem to be resolved.

Convinced that his military machine would work and that Klan-endorsed candidates would win a great many Republican primary elections on May 6, Stephenson had at least two reasons to be uncertain about how state Republican leaders would react to that result. First, Stephenson had reason to be uncertain because many Republican leaders were so strongly opposed to the idea of holding state primary elections in Indiana at all. Second, few established state Republican leaders would be pleased by the prospect of their party organization and places being taken over by newcomers through the controversial mechanism of primary elections.

Opponents of the Indiana primary election law among Republicans had increased significantly during the preceding two years. Many Indiana Republicans hoped to put the State Convention on record as favoring an amendment to the state primary law that would eliminate the presidential preference entirely and limit gubernatorial nominations to party conventions only.[137] With anti-primary sentiments so strong among Republican leaders, the fact that Klan-endorsed candidates had won primary election victories might even work against, rather than for, them at the state Republican convention.

To forestall such a development, Stephenson and other Klan leaders, certainly Bossert and perhaps even Evans in Atlanta, began thinking seriously about staging an incident during the two-week interval in May between Primary Day in Indiana, May 6, and the opening of the state Republican Convention in Indianapolis on May 21. Such an incident might help persuade convention delegates to accept the anticipated primary election victories of Klan-endorsed candidates as politically correct and irrevocable. To succeed, such an incident should provide some convincing examples of Catholic aggression, and all indications pointed to St. Joseph County as the place to stage it.

Local Klansmen in St. Joseph County were contacted and agreed to host on Saturday, May 17, 1924, a tri-state meeting in South Bend for Klan members and their families from Indiana and neighboring Michigan and Illinois. The event was announced and planned as a typical large outdoor Klan function of that time, including speeches by both Evans and

Stephenson, a parade with marching bands through the South Bend business district, evening cross burnings, and a picnic. The meeting was well publicized in the *Fiery Cross* and by posters tacked up on telephone poles throughout the county. No one could be unaware that the Klan was planning to come to South Bend in force.

The timing of this Klan event was critical and was of Stephenson's choosing. It would occur after the Indiana primary elections, one day before Evans had scheduled a meeting of local Klan leaders in Indianapolis to denounce Stephenson for trying to take a majority of the Indiana Klan out of the national organization, three days before the opening of the state Republican convention also in Indianapolis, and while the University of Notre Dame was in session with all students residing on campus. Many extremely important matters, far beyond anything imagined by officials at Notre Dame or in South Bend at the time, would be profoundly affected by what happened in South Bend on May 17. Preparations proceeded apace.

South Bend Klansmen were very busy. The indefatigable Gordon Ostot was everywhere. Local Klansmen had never tried to organize an event of this magnitude. Nothing like this had ever happened in South Bend before. Indeed, the Klan had held several closed and a few open meetings. Some cross burnings had occurred. No public parades had ever been held in the city. Klan parades had been advertized in the past, but well-founded fears of disruption had always forced cancellation of them. For a public parade of any sort an official city permit was required and that would be very difficult to obtain. All previous requests for Klan parade permits had been denied.

While few Klan visitors from Michigan and Illinois were likely to appear, no one could be certain. Meeting headquarters in the city center had to be rented, open-air meeting grounds obtained, hotel and catering services arranged, and adequate police protection assured. All of these preparations took time and quickly became public knowledge. What people did not hear as rumor, they could read in the *South Bend Tribune*. Clearly, the Klan was coming, and a large number of both respectable and rough elements in the city were not pleased at all by the prospect. The city fathers worried, Notre Dame officials appointed committees and held meetings. Notre Dame students and Father Zubowicz's West Side Polish Falcon Club stockpiled bushel baskets of potatoes.

The month of May 1924 was a time that just about everyone in St. Joseph County wanted to forget as quickly as possible. Most members of the university community, if they were not already aware, had learned how important and defining were the characteristics of religion and "nationality," meaning ethnic origin, in contemporary American life. Confronting directly the sometimes painful reality of minority status in America as did middle-class Notre Dame students and South Bend Polish and Hungarian working-class ethnics during the Indiana primary elections, a violent response to a much publicized Klan meeting in the city was predictable. The presence in the city of a large number of easily identifiable persons who were known to despise the Catholic religion, had publicly demeaned ethnic backgrounds, impugned the citizens' patriotism, and made a point of disliking people for who they were was not likely to pass unnoticed or without incident. Stephenson counted on the very high probability that it would not, and he was right.

For the university, the events occurring in May were a turning point. In terms of university relations with city officials, with communities in the region, with state government and state institutions generally, everything would be changed for the worst. Not forever, of course, with most of these elements, but with state government and state institutions deep distrust bordering on hostility would persist for thirty years. Subsequent events occurring elsewhere in the country would recall and reinforce the harsh experience of being Catholic, foreign-born, or a child of foreign-born parents in America during the 1920s and 1930s. This series of defining moments for the university community began with the primary elections on May 6, 1924.

Notre Dame campus, 1848

Rev. William E. Corby, C.S.C., served as a chaplin in the Civil War and was twice president of the university, 1869–72 and 1877–82.

Rev. John Zahm, C.S.C.

Rev. Andrew
Morrissey, C.S.C.,
president 1893–1905

Rev. John W. Cavanaugh, C.S.C., president
1905–18

Rev. Julius A. Nieuwland,
C.S.C., served as dean of
the College of Science,
1920–23, and was later
renowned for his
scientific achievements.

Rev. Paul J. Foik, C.S.C., university librarian 1912–24

Rev. James Burns, C.S.C., president 1919–22

Rev. Matthew Walsh, C.S.C., president 1922–28

British author G.K. Chesterton was presented an honorary doctorate by President O'Donnell in 1930 and gave a course of lectures at the university.

Rev. John F. O'Hara, C.S.C., president 1934–1940

George N. Shuster

Governor Ed Jackson, Senators Arthur Robinson and James Watson attend a groundbreaking ceremony.

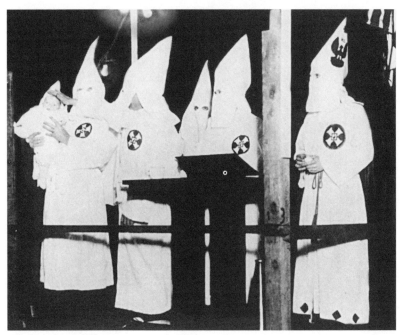

Christening at Klan ceremony in 1924

Indiana head
Klansman, D. C.
Stephenson in 1920s
newspaper photo

Klan drill team at Knox, Indiana

KKK visiting a Christian Church in Knox, Indiana

Senator James E. Watson

Above:
Madge Oberholtzer

Below:
D.C. Stephenson at the time of his trial

Headquarters of the South Bend Klan

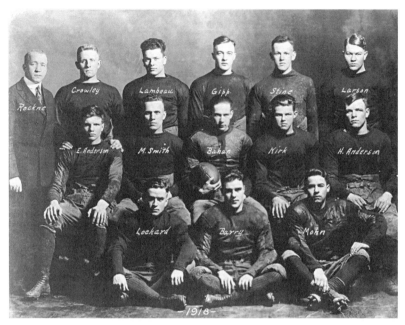
Rockne's team of 1918 included George Gipp as well as the two Andersons.

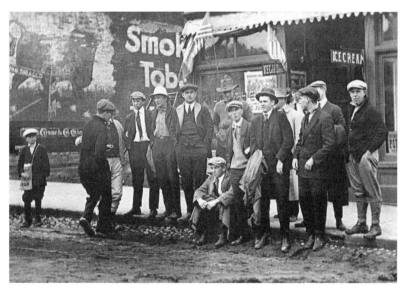
Hullie and Mike's cigar store and pool hall was a favorite haunt.

George Gipp

The Four Horsemen: Don Miller, right halfback; Elmer Layden, fullback; Jim Crowley, left halfback; Harry Stuhldreher, quarterback

A hugh crowd attended the Rockne funeral at Sacred Heart, April 3, 1931.

Notre Dame campus, 1938

— 9 —

CONFRONTATION IN
SOUTH BEND AND AFTER

O
n Primary Tuesday the weather was fair and warm.
Voter turnout in St. Joseph County as well as across
the state was heavy for a primary election. Early in
the day yellow tickets listing Klan-endorsed candidates were placed on
hundreds of door steps all over South Bend and Mishawaka. Incidents at
polling places were few. One dispute occurring in the fifth precinct of the
Fourth Ward in South Bend arose over the display of a campaign placard
belonging to Harry Taylor, the Klan-endorsed candidate for the Republican nomination for public prosecutor. Friends of the Republican incumbent, Frank E. Coughlin, objected, blows were struck, and police were
required to separate the combatants. One person was removed from the
area, but no charges were filed.[1]

At the end of the day, Klan-supported candidates did very well across
the state and surprisingly well in St. Joseph County. Ed Jackson won the
Republican gubernatorial nomination easily and so many other Klan-
endorsed candidates won Republican nominations for state, county, and
local offices that the Democratic choice for governor, Carleton H. McCulloch, declared publicly on May 11 that the Republican party in Indiana
had been taken over by the Klan and "has, as a political party, for the
present ceased to exist."[2] The main issue in the fall election, he continued,
would be whether or not the state would be run by a Klan or anti-Klan
government.

In St. Joseph County, five of the seven Klan-endorsed candidates for
county offices running in Republican primary elections won their respective offices, one lost by only 120 votes, and one lost decisively. The greatest
disappointment was the failure of the Rev. Albert N. Vermillion of Argos

to defeat the incumbent Republican congressman for the thirteenth district, Andrew J. Hickey of LaPorte. Klansmen had campaigned very hard for Vermillion but to no avail. Hickey carried every county in the district and captured 62 percent of the Republican primary votes cast.[3]

Notwithstanding the disappointing loss to Hickey, the success of Klan-endorsed candidates in St. Joseph County was extraordinary, especially Harry Taylor's upset victory over the popular incumbent Republican public prosecutor, Frank E. Coughlin. Longtime county Republican leaders expressed astonishment to reporters that Klan-endorsed candidates had done so well. They attributed their great success to the effectiveness of the local Klan organization, citing "hard and effective political work in getting out the vote and planning the campaign."[4]

While most Indiana Republican leaders were astounded at Klan success in the recent primary elections, some were appalled by what had happened, and at least one publicly disassociated himself from the result. Charles L. Kinney, a Goshen Republican and long-serving Republican county surveyor for Elkhart County refused renomination after winning the primary election. Kinney advised D. M. Hoover, Elkhart County Republican chairman, by letter to withdraw his name as the "nominee for county surveyor on the republican ticket."[5]

Kinney declared himself now as always a strong Republican and fully intending to vote for Coolidge for president in the fall election. However, Kinney could not support Jackson for governor and some Republican nominees for county offices because of their obligations to the Klan. Since he could not support the entire Republican county ticket, Kinney was not comfortable asking for the support of the Elkhart County Republican party in the forthcoming election.

Kinney also made the point in his letter that he was not a Catholic and had never been inside of a Catholic Church in his life. He believed that Elkhart County Republicans were "treading on dangerous ground when we undertake to curtail the political and religious liberty of anyone as is set forth in the constitution of the United States."[6] Kinney's action was widely publicized throughout northern Indiana by the *South Bend Tribune,* but it turned out to be a solitary act by one sensitive honorable man. Others may have felt the same as Kinney, but no one else followed his example.

In Indianapolis, Stephenson probably knew about Kinney's withdrawal but certainly did not trouble himself much about it. The primary election results had provided so much good news for Stephenson that he decided to go public with his decision to separate the Indiana Klan from the national organization. Again, timing was critical in achieving his objectives. He delayed going public with this matter until the primary elections had established the Klan as a major political force in Indiana and himself as the most powerful political boss in the state. He went public five days before the tri-state meeting in South Bend, six days before Evans' scheduled appearance at a Klan meeting in Indianapolis on May 18, and nine days before the opening of the state Republican convention in the same city.

Stephenson announced at a meeting in Indianapolis on May 12 that henceforth Indiana Klansmen intended to shape their own futures and take control of their own organization.[7] It was true that Stephenson invariably told audiences what he believed they wanted to hear. It was also true that when his own interests were at issue, Stephenson never worried about telling the truth. Moreover, as time passed he probably did not know what the truth in a particular set of circumstances actually was. With such caveats in mind, the reasons Stephenson offered to his audience and through the press to people across the state for disassociating the Indiana Klan from the national organization are of more than passing interest. In them, he also provided this audience and readers of the Indiana press with a glimpse of his own extraordinary future political ambitions.

If the Klan was to succeed as a national movement, it would have to change completely both its program and its public image. Stephenson could not believe that the present national leadership was up to that sort of a challenge. However, Indiana was ready and willing to show the way. The future business of the Indiana Klan would be politics, and it should be for the national organization as well. With respect to the national Klan leadership, Stephenson stated, "Indiana Klansmen have thrown off an outside control which was out of harmony with their purposes." Fear, intimidation, and blind animosity, Stephenson insisted, will have no part in the great new mission of the Indiana Klan. By exercising an influence for constructive citizenship, Indiana Klansmen would bring out what was best in the city, state, and nation.[8]

According to Stephenson, making an impact on national politics was clearly a part of the new mission of the Indiana Klan. Indiana, Stephenson added, "has 92 per cent of native born citizens with the best blood and traditions of America. It is in a pivotal position and will play an important part in shaping the future of our government." Then came the now famous and much quoted phrase, "we are going out to Klux Indiana as she has never been Kluxed before."[9]

Next, Stephenson praised Republican Ed Jackson as the candidate for governor best qualified to run the state for the next four years, describing him as the "highest type of Christian gentleman who ever served a public office in Indiana."[10] He picked up on the statement of the winner of the Democratic gubernatorial primary election, Carleton B. McCulloch, that the principal issue in the fall election would be the role of the Klan in state government. In effect, Stephenson agreed with McCulloch on that point. We must elect Jackson "who we nominated on May 6, because if we don't the challenge that this man, McCulloch, has thrown at our feet will be picked up and hurled in our faces."[11]

A large majority of the audience apparently believed what Stephenson told them. Some undoubtedly were moved by the prospect of the Indiana Klan leading the entire nation into a brave new world of constructive citizenship and political purity. In any case, an overwhelming majority of those attending the meeting approved his plan of disassociation and elected him leader of the now autonomous Indiana Klan.[12]

Throughout his entire speech, Stephenson was very careful not to say that the Indiana Klan intended to break all formal ties with the national Klan. According to Stephenson, Indiana Klansmen had "decided to take control of their organization, but will not secede from the national organization."[13] The onus of splitting the national organization would be passed to Evans and to Evans loyalists in Indiana, known hereafter as the Bossert faction.

At Stephenson's Indianapolis meeting on May 12, a few members of the Bossert faction were present, and one of them, Joseph Huffington, head of the Evansville Klan, announced to the press that Stephenson had been expelled from the Klan organizations, both local and national.[14] Huffington described Stephenson's efforts to disassociate a majority of the Indiana Klan as certain to fail and warned the state's Republican leaders that Stephenson was a political chameleon. That man had been a Democrat in Evansville, Huffington declared, but now he claims to be a Republican. Prophetically, Huffington added, Stephenson "will embarrass the republican party by butting in to it."[15]

Stephenson worried not at all about Huffington's statement. Events were moving too fast for him to find the time to respond to it. He had to be in South Bend by noon on May 17 to participate in the special tri-state meeting of Klansmen in that city. Stephenson had to be in South Bend early enough on Saturday, May 17, for an afternoon conference with local Klan leaders, then to attend a planned Klan parade through the city center in the early evening, finally to address a large picnic of Klansmen and their families at Island Park by the St. Joseph River. To travel to South Bend by car with his usual entourage and be there ready for the conference, parade, and speech on May 17, Stephenson would have to leave

Indianapolis on Friday, May 16. There would be time enough to deal with Evans, Bossert, and Huffington after the South Bend meeting.

— ii —

Just about everyone in South Bend knew that large numbers of Klansmen and their families would be in their city over the weekend of May 17–18, 1924. City and university officials expected that during the weekend trouble of some sort was likely to occur and made plans to deal with it. While Stephenson and his entourage were making the long four-hour journey from Indianapolis to South Bend, Father J. Hugh O'Donnell, C.S.C., prefect of discipline at the university, met with Laurence J. Lane, the chief of police in South Bend, to exchange information and coordinate security measures. Both O'Donnell and Lane agreed that avoidance of confrontation was the wisest strategy to adopt.

For his part, Lane assured O'Donnell that no Klan parade permit would be issued and that no Klan parade through South Bend would be allowed. He also assured O'Donnell that city and county law enforcement personnel would be up to whatever challenges the weekend might offer. In turn, O'Donnell assured Lane that university officials would do everything they could to keep Notre Dame students on campus while Klan meetings and gatherings in and about the city were in progress.[16] With so many students living off campus that assurance was nothing more than an expression of good intentions. In truth, both Lane and O'Donnell had promised more than either one of them could deliver.

O'Donnell reported to Walsh what Lane had said. Together, the president and prefect of discipline decided that the best way to keep Notre Dame students on campus over the forthcoming weekend was to issue a special bulletin stating the possibility of "riotous situations" occurring in the city and strongly urging all Notre Dame men to ignore demonstrations and provocations, remain on campus, and allow local authorities to take care of whatever situations might develop.[17] Walsh drafted such a bulletin during the evening of May 16 and released it to the student body and to the *South Bend Tribune* on May 17. However, trouble had already broken out near the interurban railroad station in the late afternoon of May 16. So, when released, the principal effect of the bulletin was only to advertise that a riotous situation existed in South Bend and that some Notre Dame students were much involved.

According to the recollection of Chester Grant, a student athlete who arrived from Chicago at the South Shore Railroad Station during the early evening of May 16, groups of people carrying bundles disembarked from the train with him. The people with bundles were immediately accosted by groups of young men who skirmished with them and tried to seize their bundles.[18] The persons with the bundles were Klansmen from Chicago and Michigan City coming to South Bend for the Klan meeting. The young men accosting them were Notre Dame students.

The encounters at the railroad station were not serious and did not spread to other parts of the city. A few Klansmen lost bundles containing Klan regalia, which were promptly and derisively displayed.[19] However, there were at this time no injuries or arrests. Nonetheless, these incidents were a fair warning to the local Klan organizers of what to expect on the next day, which they proceeded to disregard totally. During the course of the evening, local Klansmen erected a large fiery cross composed of red-tinted electric light bulbs outside of Klan headquarters in the old Knights of Pythias Building at the corner of Michigan and Wayne Streets.[20] This sort of provocation could not and would not go unchallenged.

Notwithstanding the release of Walsh's special bulletin to the Notre Dame student body on May 17, 1924, trouble began early that day in the South Bend business district, with several hundred Notre Dame students fully and enthusiastically involved. That morning the people of South Bend received their first glimpse of groups of white-robed, hooded, masked men in their city. Klan spokesmen would claim the presence of twenty-five thousand visiting members in South Bend on that day. Police estimates were more modest, stating that no more than two thousand Klansmen were ever assembled at one time anywhere in the city on May 17.[21] Whatever the number, by 9:00 A.M. Klansmen appeared in full regalia on street corners in the city center directing their brethren arriving by automobile, streetcar, bus, or interurban trains to the Klan meeting grounds at Island Park.[22]

Soon after the hooded men appeared on the downtown streets, automobiles crowded with young men, identified by reporters for the *South Bend Tribune* as Notre Dame students, traversed the main thoroughfares of the business district. At the same time, bands of young men showing intense hostility to the Klansmen showed up on foot and began surrounding the masked men wherever they could find them. Some of these bands were identified as being composed of Notre Dame students. Others were made up of West Side Polish and Hungarian ethnics. Within an hour, robes and masks had been torn from about a half a dozen Klansmen and several of them had been very roughly handled.[23]

During the course of the morning, the police were conspicuously absent. The bands of anti-Klan young men ranging through the city center grew into a crowd and showed signs of organization. Flying columns went from corner to corner, wherever a white-robed figure appeared.

Some of the most violent disturbances occurred at Washington Street and Jefferson Boulevard and at the intersection of Lincolnway and Jefferson Boulevard where two Klansmen had their robes torn off and were forced to flee to a nearby gasoline station for protection. So intimidating and effective were these flying columns that by 11:30 A.M., not a single Klansman could be seen in the business district.[24]

While the bands of Notre Dame students and West Side Polish and Hungarian ethnics were cleaning the city center of white-robed Klansmen, local Klan officials met with the mayor, police chief, and board of safety about a parade permit. Once again, a parade permit was denied. So evident were anti-Klan demonstrators in the downtown areas in the early afternoon that both the day and night shifts of the city police were kept on duty for the rest of the day.[25] In addition, Deputy Sheriff John Culley, reputedly a Klan sympathizer,[26] acting in the absence from the county of Sheriff Michael J. Hanley, called Governor Emmett T. Branch seeking a mobilization order for Company D, 152nd Infantry of the Indiana National Guard, to assist the Sheriff's department, if needed, in riot control. Governor Branch refused to mobilize the National Guard, insisting that local authorities were sufficient to handle the situation in South Bend.[27] Deputy Sheriff Culley responded to the governor's refusal by deputizing thirty members of the local Horse Thief Detective Association. He ordered the new special deputies to duty immediately, ready to intervene if and when the situation in South Bend worsened.[28]

By 1:00 P.M., a large crowd of anti-Klan demonstrators congregated in front of the local Klan headquarters on the corner of Michigan and Wayne Streets. The crowd assembled there turned menacing.[29] Individual Klansmen who appeared on the street or passed by in automobiles were harassed. Some automobiles carrying Klansmen had draped American flags over their hoods and fenders. Several of those vehicles were stopped, the flags were removed, and the occupants roughed up. Before the crowd turned completely riotous, four mounted policemen and a squad of foot patrolmen arrived on the scene and immediately seized control of the situation. Also present assisting the police was the ubiquitous Gordon Ostot, conspicuous in his State Policeman's uniform. The mounted policemen kept their tempers, impressed the crowd with their firm but good-natured professionalism, and managed to break it up into several small groups.[30]

However, despite the efforts of the police, several of the smaller groups successfully resisted dispersal and remained on the scene. One such group began hurling potatoes at Klan headquarters, breaking several windows on the second and third floors. Another group chose the red light bulbs in the fiery cross display as targets for their potatoes and exhibited an extraordinary accuracy in hitting them. So many bulbs were smashed that the cross had to be removed.[31]

Next, about a hundred students and others stormed up the stairs of Klan headquarters. They were met and stopped at the top of the stairs by the Reverend Jack H. Horton of the Calvary Baptist Church, Blaine and California avenues, with a loaded revolver in hand. Horton, a local Klan leader and the official spokesman for the St. Joseph County organization, stated later that he had threatened the invading students with a gun in order to protect a number of women who were eating lunch in a meeting room in Klan headquarters.[32]

About 2:00 P.M., four Notre Dame student leaders were invited into Klan headquarters to confer with Klan officials about how best to avoid serious trouble if the Klan parade went forward as planned. According to the account of this meeting published in the *South Bend Tribune,* the student leaders insisted that in the event of a parade the only way to avoid trouble was for the Klansmen participating in it to put aside their hoods and guns. If hoods were not worn and guns not displayed, the student spokesmen believed that the students and their allies would promise not to molest the paraders.[33] At this meeting, Klan leaders assured the student spokesmen that no weapons would be carried or displayed during the intended parade, if such a parade should occur. The matter of wearing hoods and masks was not so easily given up, but in the end it was. The student spokesmen announced the results of their meeting with Klan leaders to the crowd below from one of the windows. The mood of the students and their allies changed from one of hostility to triumph, and they began to disperse.[34]

Most of the crowd moved away from Klan headquarters to a large pool room at the corner of Washington Avenue and Michigan Street, where at 3:30 P.M. a meeting of about five hundred students and others was underway. Those present heard a student speaker plead for vigilance and restraint. The speaker announced that no permission for a Klan parade had been given. If a parade proceeded without official permission, the speaker urged the poolroom crowd to allow the Klansmen to parade unmolested and let the police handle the situation. However, if the police required assistance, all of those present should be ready to provide it, respond "2,000 strong." He asked the crowd to disperse for the time being and reassemble at the Jefferson Boulevard bridge over the St. Joseph River at 6:30 P.M. to prevent Klansmen from coming into the city center from the east and participating in an illegal parade.[35]

Meanwhile, after the meeting with student leaders at Klan headquarters on Michigan Street had ended, Horton traveled to Island Park to discuss the latest turn of events with Stephenson, who had arrived there with his entourage. After reviewing what had already happened since the previous evening, being fairly certain that no parade permit would be issued, and perhaps reading the weather forecast for the South Bend area, Stephenson decided to call off the planned early evening Klan parade and advised the chief of police accordingly.[36]

As Stephenson saw the present situation, no useful purpose would be served by proceeding with the parade and forcing a confrontation with the local police. The events of the day had already given him an enormous public relations advantage which could be easily thrown away by encounters with the police. The fact that peaceful Klansmen had been attacked by Catholic students and ethnic ruffians and then denied their constitutional right of peaceful demonstration was a clear warning to the Protestant voters of Indiana and neighboring states. Here was proof positive of the Catholic menace in action and of what could happen in an American city when Catholics were in control of civic institutions. Unwilling or unable to control the Notre Dame student body, university administrators and city officials had unwittingly handed Stephenson a public relations opportunity, which he began exploiting at once.

Rain began in the South Bend area around 4:00 P.M., became very heavy after 6:00 P.M., and continued until midnight, putting an end to all thoughts of a parade and to the scheduled program in Island Park. However, in the early evening of May 17, between rain showers, Stephenson met with reporters in Island Park and told them that the decision to cancel the parade had been made as early as 2:30, before there were any signs of rain. He had made the decision about the parade to avoid further trouble. Next, Stephenson severely criticized city and county authorities for not keeping the peace and preventing the disgraceful events of that day from happening in an American city. He promised that at some future date a Klan parade would be held in South Bend and that, if necessary, appeals would be made to the U.S. Army for protection.[37]

Despite the continuing rain, crowds of anti-Klan demonstrators remained in the city center, milling about, and waiting for something to happen. Many Klansmen began leaving the city in the early evening. Others arrived on a special train from Chicago, on four special interurban train loads from Michigan City, and still more in automobiles from other points. The new arrivals were met at the railway stations by hostile crowds who made very clear just how unwelcome Klansmen were in South Bend.[38]

Back at the Jefferson Boulevard bridge, in the early evening a very belligerent anti-Klan crowd filled the area. Among the city police observing the situation was the ever-present Gordon Ostot. In uniform and armed,

Ostot walked among the crowd at the bridge telling students and others there that the parade had been canceled. He was also overheard warning the students that fifty thousand members of the hooded organization from various states were gathered at a point near South Bend ready to intervene if needed.[39]

Trouble occurred on Jefferson Boulevard near the Yellow Taxi Company garage when an overzealous anti-Klan demonstrator stopped an electric streetcar by jerking down the trolley pole from the overhead wire. He was arrested at once and transported to the police station without interference from the crowd on the bridge. At the police station, he joined seven others arrested during the day. Of those eight, six were anti-Klan demonstrators, three had been arrested for assault and battery, two for using profane language, and one for interfering with a streetcar. Two Klansmen had been arrested for carrying weapons, one for threatening with a baseball bat, and one for brandishing a revolver.[40]

Surprisingly, none of the numerous clashes occurring during the day and evening in different parts of the city resulted in serious injuries. Neither local hospital reported a single emergency call. By midnight downtown streets were clear.[41] Much to the relief of the overworked city and county police departments and extremely anxious and fearful university administrators, a very long and potentially dangerous day was over.

For Notre Dame students as well as for most of the people in South Bend, Sunday was a day for reading about the events of May 17 in the *South Bend Tribune.* For university administrators and city officials, Sunday was an occasion to read the Sunday papers, but it was also a time for reflection and stocktaking. Fathers Walsh and O'Donnell were embarrassed by what had happened. They had been unable to control the student body and at the moment did not know what to do to prevent future recurrences. The students involved in the disturbances simply had not respected authority or behaved as Notre Dame men were supposed to behave. Perhaps most important of all, the president and prefect of discipline worried about what local and regional newspaper accounts of student lawlessness would do to the good name of the university.[42]

Not knowing how local reporters would handle this story, Walsh and O'Donnell had good reason to worry. Much that had happened in the city simply reinforced current negative stereotypes of Irish American behavior. Some Notre Dame students had roughly handled and in some cases actually assaulted Klansmen and persons believed to be Klan sympathizers. Several students had torn off Klan robes and hoods from persons wearing them, stole bundles of Klan regalia from others, and then returned to the campus with their purloined trophies to exhibit them.

Exhilarated, perhaps, by the experience of successful combat, students in possession of Klan robes and hoods wore them for photo opportunities and then marched around their residence halls thus attired.

Most scandalous of all, some students either captured a large home-made Klan banner in the city or manufactured it themselves on campus. Students took this banner, a white bed sheet with KKK painted on it, and ran it up the university flagpole. With that despised symbol of contemporary anti-Catholicism fluttering overhead, Notre Dame students paraded around the flagpole shocking clerical onlookers with language and gestures never tolerated and rarely ever displayed publicly at the university. This was one incident that neither the *South Bend Tribune*, nor the *Fiery Cross* reported.[43] Walsh and O'Donnell had to be grateful for that.

City officials had little cause for satisfaction either. They had been ill-prepared to contend with a potentially riotous situation that they knew was coming. City officials had reacted much too slowly as trouble developed. Not timely and coordinated police work but the fortuitous advent of heavy rains had saved the city from possible major property damage and some citizens from serious injury. Certainly, the mayor and chief of police were justifiably angered by the inability of university officials to keep their charges on campus. Most important of all, the mayor and chief of police were determined to assure the citizens of South Bend that henceforth elected and appointed officials would run the city, not the Klan and certainly not two thousand undisciplined, overprivileged adolescents from the University of Notre Dame. Next time, if there was a next time, things would be different.[44]

Local Klan leaders were indignant over the events of May 16 and 17.[45] Nothing had gone right. City officials had repeatedly denied their organization a parade permit. Police protection for their activities was so inadequate that visiting Klansmen were assaulted with impunity, and even their headquarters had been invaded. Peaceful adult citizens displaying patriotic symbols and Klan emblems had been harassed and driven from the city center by a mob of Catholic teenagers. No local Klan organization anywhere in the state had ever been so publicly and so thoroughly humiliated. With the St. Joseph County Klansmen, Notre Dame students had run up a very large bill. Settlement of this account began on Monday, May 19, and would not be paid in full until election day, November 4.

Monday began quiet enough. Notre Dame students returned to their classes. Local Klansmen went off to their jobs and businesses. Early Monday evening the first indication of possible trouble was the reinstallation and relighting of the electric fiery cross outside of Klan headquarters at Michigan and Wayne Streets. By 7:00 P.M. a meeting of some sort was in progress there and, as later events suggest, plans for a partial payback to Notre Dame students for their hooliganism of Friday and Saturday were being prepared and implemented.

Telephone calls were placed to Notre Dame dormitories reporting a Klan meeting in progress at their headquarters, the reappearance of the electric fiery cross, and that some students were being assaulted near Michigan and Wayne. The message quickly passed from residence hall to residence hall.[46] Quickly about 500 students dashed out to Michigan Street and gathered near the city center. Around 9:00 P.M. the students began marching toward the intersection of Michigan and Wayne and right into an ambush.[47] Boys who had been playing at men's games and enjoying it were about to be taught a lesson that neither they nor those in charge of them would forget for a very long time.

According to the report of the ensuing disturbances carried in the *South Bend Tribune,* most of the Klansmen attending the early evening meeting in Klan headquarters had dispersed to nearby strategic locations to await the arrival of the students. Similarly, local police were also on the scene in force, ready and waiting for the students. "With the police, they [Klansmen] surprised the anti-Klan forces as they neared the intersection of Wayne and Michigan streets. Bottles, stones, clubs, and any other objects were thrown about at random."[48]

Next, "The police charged the crowd, employing their clubs in an effort to disperse the throngs."[49] Members of both factions as well as non-participating bystanders were injured in the rioting that followed. Several injured persons were transported to nearby hospitals, where fortunately only minor injuries—cuts and bruises—were reported. The most serious reported injury was a South Bend police sergeant whose jaw had been broken after being struck with a heavy object. Only one person treated in the hospitals chose to give his name.[50]

News of the clashes between students and Klansmen and between students and police spread rapidly throughout the city and the Notre Dame campus. The situation downtown had become very serious. Crowds from all quarters began gathering. Police apprised university authorities about what was occurring and requested an immediate official presence from them on the scene to direct student rioters back to the campus. At the same time, police assistance was summoned from the neighboring community of Mishawaka. A detail of Mishawaka police led by Chief Corwin Hartwick arrived and joined with South Bend police arresting whoever could be apprehended. Members of both factions were among those apprehended and taken to the city jail, uncharged but detained until order was restored.[51]

Shortly after 10:00 P.M., Walsh and Hugh O'Donnell arrived and were first appalled and then severely frightened by what they saw. Students had been roughly handled by police. Some had been struck with night sticks. Some had been injured, no one knew or could easily find out how seriously. When Walsh and O'Donnell reached the city center, the police had driven the students away from the intersection of Wayne and Michigan streets. Some had retreated north on Michigan, but most had run west on Wayne to Main and then north on Main about two blocks as far as the Courthouse. It was a dangerously critical moment. Students were milling about, taking stock of themselves, and considering what to do next.[52]

Walsh and other Notre Dame officials had been unable to keep their students on campus during the weekend presence of the Klan in South Bend as they had promised the mayor and police chief they would try to do. Now after a full half hour of battering by the police, Walsh managed to persuade most of them to give up a very uneven fight, disperse, and return to the campus.

Walsh climbed atop a ledge on the Civil War Memorial outside of the Courthouse and addressed all of the students within earshot. He urged them to avoid and ignore provocations. In his judgment, any injury to a single Notre Dame student was too great a price to pay for what they had undertaken to do that night. He admonished them to respect the law by obeying it. No one, Walsh concluded, was more loyal or patriotic than Notre Dame students. They should demonstrate their loyalty by showing respect for South Bend and for constituted authorities by dispersing at once.[53] Much has been made of this speech by a later writer,[54] but given the noise and confusion in front of the Courthouse, how many students actually could hear what Walsh said can only be guessed. They saw him there and could easily imagine what he was trying to tell them. In any case, the students drifted away in small groups and by midnight were back in their campus residence halls.

What time Walsh and O'Donnell were able to get back to the campus is unknown, but whenever it was, the enormity of the security and public relations problems confronting the university had to be faced at once. The possibility of retaliation against university people, facilities, and property had to be considered, and appropriate protective measures devised. The inability of Notre Dame officials to keep students on campus or otherwise control off-campus student behavior was apparent to everyone. Some sort of scheme to correct that embarrassing and dangerous situation had to be developed and implemented. In the meantime, parents had to be reassured that their sons were safe at Notre Dame and would continue to be so. News releases putting the events of the last few days in the best possible light would have to be written. All of these things would have to be done in due course, but not all at once on Tuesday morning.

The most pressing immediate problem that had to be faced on Tuesday morning was the now tense and awkward state of relations between the university and city officials. On Tuesday morning, May 20, Mayor Eli F. Seebirt summoned Walsh and O'Donnell to a special meeting of prominent Catholics and other interested parties in the mayor's office to discuss ways and means of restoring and maintaining peace in the city. A similar meeting in the same place with the same agenda had been scheduled by the mayor with Klan leaders for the afternoon.[55]

Both meetings were held, but no statements indicating who attended or what was discussed were released. The mayor admitted only that such meetings had taken place. For the morning meeting, it is clear that along with the mayor, police chief, and perhaps one or two other city officials, Walsh and O'Donnell represented Notre Dame, and several other Catholic clergy and Catholic businessmen were there to speak for the Catholic community at large.[56]

On the basis of a few details leaked to the *South Bend Tribune* and suggested by a personal letter written by Walsh to the provincial superior several months later, it would appear that the meeting did not go well at all. The actions of Notre Dame students over the weekend past were condemned by everyone there. Some of the Catholic leaders at the meeting regarded the students as the principal aggressors and were disposed to blame them for most of the trouble. In their view, not only had the students caused most of the disturbances, but as students they would escape completely all consequences of their irresponsible behavior by going home when the present term ended. Local Catholics living permanently in St. Joseph County would be here to reap whatever whirlwinds these undisciplined but transient adolescents had sown. At the mayor's meeting, there was no disposition by anyone to criticize police actions on either Saturday or Monday. Those present agreed that future disturbances should "be prevented if it is humanly possible" to do so but dealt with quickly and firmly if not.[57]

There were no leaks to the press about any specific thoughts, observations, or comments by the Notre Dame representatives at the meeting. Walsh had been at the riot scene Monday night and had seen some results of student battering by the police. Apparently, he decided that the mayor's meeting was not the place to argue that point and said very little about much of anything while there. Walsh knew that Notre Dame students were by no means blameless, but believed strongly that West Side Polish and Hungarian ethnics had been as much involved in the rioting as were Notre Dame students.

Placing full blame for what had happened in the city on Notre Dame students alone as, representatives of the Catholic community attending the mayor's meeting seemed anxious to do, struck Walsh as unfair and unwise. Unwise, because if the Klan came back to South Bend in force at a later date as its leaders were threatening, disturbances would occur whether Notre Dame students were around to participate in them or not. Father Zubowicz's Polish Falcons were a formidable lot, indeed.[58] Unfortunately for future relations between the university and the city, Walsh came away from this meeting with a deep distrust and personal dislike of the chief of police. In the future, these two men would have little to say to one another and cooperation on matters of mutual concern would be minimal.[59]

Though Walsh believed Chief Lane had handled the situation in South Bend poorly, he was sensitive to the chief's problems because he faced similar ones on campus. The matter of campus security had to be addressed at once and was. Volunteer night patrols of lay faculty and priests were put in place during the rest of May and most of June. What would have happened if the volunteers had actually encountered intruders was unclear. Fortunately, this hastily organized system never had to be tested. Though no Klan avengers, hooded or otherwise, visited the campus during the spring and summer of 1924, there had been serious talk among local Klansmen about doing so. One local Klan leader testified to the Indiana attorney general in February 1928 that at one of the South Bend Klan meetings, one hot-headed Klansman volunteered to dynamite one or more buildings at Notre Dame if explosives could be obtained.[60]

As important as the security patrols was the need for developing and implementing an effective scheme for controlling student behavior when in South Bend. The scheme adopted was inspired by a widely used tactic to curb alcohol abuse. If taking temperance pledges effectively reduced adolescent and young adult drinking, why not solicit similar pledges from students to abstain from aggressive and riotous behavior against Klansmen in South Bend? Extremely naive perhaps, but lacking a better idea, it was what Walsh and his advisors decided to do.

Upon returning to campus from the mayor's meeting in town on May 20, Walsh conferred with Rockne about speaking to the student body on the importance of gentlemanly and law-abiding conduct. Then, in the afternoon, both the coach and the president addressed the students assembled in Washington Hall about the virtues of obeying local laws, avoiding confrontations with local police, playing by the rules, respecting themselves, their religion, and the university by exemplary behavior under provocation. Following these speeches, a pledge to abstain from clashes with the Klan in the city was administered to the students.[61] Most present complied and raised their hands.

Even if the pledge were observed most of the time by the students who took it, a significant part of the university's in-town student behavior problems would remain unaddressed. In 1924 over a thousand students lived off campus in largely unsupervised situations. As registered Notre Dame students, the university recognized a responsibility for them but was generally unable to exercise any control over what they did while in town or when and where they did it. Off-campus students for the most part were on their own for meals and time management, and went in and out of the city center at will. The possibilities for mischief from this group were infinite.

The only way to reach that group as well as other students who had not attended the Washington Hall meeting or taken the pledge was through the *Religious Bulletin*. O'Hara acted on this matter promptly, first, with a conciliatory religious appeal and, later, with a stern condemnation. On May 24, 1924, O'Hara announced in the *Religious Bulletin* a special Holy Communion on the following day for the welfare and prosperity of Notre Dame. He observed, first, that the students had evidenced great eagerness to fight for Notre Dame and in that eagerness had rushed into a trap prepared for them. Be just as eager, he added, to pray for our alma mater as to fight for her.[62]

"Be in a state of grace," O'Hara counseled. "While your first concern was for Notre Dame, your first duty of charity should be toward yourself." Hatred stalks the streets, he continued, and lies in wait for you day and night. We must be prepared. "Look to the golden lady on the Dome," he concluded, "and ask her not to forget us in our trials. She has brought us through many a crisis."[63]

Two days later, O'Hara excoriated those students who had broken university rules by going into the city and had taken the law into their own hands. Simply stated, those students were no better than the bigots they had attacked. Particularly, the seniors involved in the disturbances should have known better. Those seniors disgraced the university and the Catholic Church by what they did last week, wrote O'Hara; they might just as well go out and join the Klan. As Klansmen, they would do less harm to the university from without than they had done as students from within.[64] In this instance, O'Hara made his points about gentlemanly

behavior as well as such points could have been made in the circumstances of that time. Everyone in the university community, especially the
off-campus students, knew where the prefect of religion stood and what
he had said about the late disturbances. Whether the students would heed
his counsel and act accordingly, if and when another crisis with the Klan
should arise, time alone would tell.

To be sure, the events of May 16–19 in South Bend had neither created
university administrative perceptions nor the realities of the university's
off-campus student problems, but that weekend in May certainly raised
anxiety levels about them in the Main Building. Walsh and his advisors
pressed ahead with plans to construct three new dormitories and then
require as many Notre Dame students as possible to reside on campus.
There were other good reasons for building dormitories at this time, but
projects appearing desirable before that unforgettable turbulent May
weekend became urgent after it.

Leaks to the press about the mayor's May 20 meeting with local Klan
leaders were fewer and less informative than those from the morning
meeting with Catholics. Klan leaders were described in the *South Bend
Tribune* as being indignant over affronts to their organization and attacks
upon their membership. Most important, they wanted assurances "that
rioting will be prevented in the future."[65] Such assurances from city officials were necessary because the Klan intended to come back to South
Bend and finish in October what they had been prevented from doing
in May.

Some time shortly before the election on November 4, 1924, Klansmen from Indiana and elsewhere planned to revisit South Bend, obtain a
parade permit, and then exercise their constitutional rights by marching
peacefully through the city center. After all, South Bend was part of
America, not DeValera's Dublin, and in America there was supposed to be
justice for all. The events of May 16–19 had settled nothing and ended
nothing. The battle for South Bend was not over; it had only begun.

—   iii   —

Stephenson had returned to Indianapolis late Saturday night, May 17, in
order to be ready to respond to whatever might happen after Evans held
his Klan meeting and berated him for taking the Indiana Klan out of the
national organization. Stephenson had good reasons to be apprehensive
about what Evans and Bossert might do. Before traveling to South Bend
on May 16, he had attended a Republican organizational meeting in New

Castle, Bossert's home district. The two men met face to face, exchanged heated words, and actually threw punches at one another.[66] An angry Bossert and many of his equally angry friends would be in Indianapolis on May 18 for Evans' speech, so Stephenson had to be ready for anything.

The Sunday Klan meeting in Indianapolis turned out to be anti-climactic. The Evans-Bossert faction simply could not bring the Indiana Klan together. There was confusion about the meeting site and disputes about credentials. Though about nine hundred Klansmen showed up for the meeting, many were turned away from the hall. In his speech, Evans avoided the principal issue dividing the Indiana Klan, namely, whether Hoosier Klansmen should be directed by Atlanta and governed by their goals and methods or by regional and local organizations with more specific political objectives. At the end of the day, the Evans-Bossert faction simply issued a statement that Indiana Klansmen were of one mind and would remain loyal to the present national leadership.[67] In Indianapolis, Evans had done little to diminish Stephenson's dominating role in Indiana Klan affairs. That would have to be done very soon, but somewhere other than in Indianapolis.

Evans and his Indiana supporters decided that Stephenson should be tried by a special Klan tribunal for "certain charges" and "a major offense." Evansville was chosen to be the site of the trial, and Huffington was assigned responsibility for preparing the indictments against Stephenson, collecting evidence, and securing a correct verdict. A tribunal was appointed forthwith and dutifully indicted Stephenson on six counts: violating the Klan oath of allegiance, disrespect of virtuous womanhood, conspiring against the interests and prosperity of the order, lascivious acts unworthy of a Klansman, and violation of the constitution and bylaws of the Klan.[68] Formal charges against Stephenson were filed on May 31. On June 3 he was informed of the process begun against him and advised that his trial would begin on June 23.

For his part, Stephenson responded to Evans' Indianapolis speech with a press release stating that about half of all of the Indiana counties, especially those in the northern part of the state, had withheld representatives from Evans' meeting.[69] Believing himself to be supreme in Indianapolis and virtually invincible in Indiana, Stephenson refused to be intimidated by Evans or Bossert. After Evans' disappointing performance in Indianapolis, he went after both of his enemies with no holds barred. Nothing was too outrageous to say or write about them.

In papers distributed among local Klan organizations, Stephenson accused the Imperial Wizard of dishonesty, deception, and irremediable boorish behavior.[70] Bossert was accused of having sold out to the Roman

Catholics and to the political enemies of Ed Jackson, of maintaining law offices in a Jewish-owned building, and of living in an anti-Klan hotel when staying in Indianapolis. Finally, Stephenson's lawyers filed two lawsuits against several officers in the national Klan organization. One suit filed against Bossert for slander asked for $100,000 in damages. The other, a libel suit against Evans, Bossert, and Robert Lyon, treasurer of the national Klan organization in Indiana, also asked for $100,000.[71]

Apparently at this moment, Stephenson was supremely self-confident and not at all worried about whatever Bossert and Huffington were up to in Evansville. His eyes were on the biggest prizes of all. The Republican State Convention was to open in Indianapolis on May 21, and shortly thereafter, on June 10, the Republican National Convention in Cleveland was scheduled to begin. He intended to be actively present at both.

As Stephenson saw the world on Sunday evening May 18, his future place in it promised to be a very important one. If all went well at the Republican State Convention, within a week he could be the most powerful political boss in the Indiana Republican party. Within a month, after the National Republican Party Convention, who could guess where good fortune would leave him?

When the state convention opened in Indianapolis on Wednesday, Senator James E. Watson was elected temporary chairman and then delivered a keynote address to the delegates on Republican principles. As both delegates and observers, Klan supporters and sympathizers were everywhere. So was Stephenson. He was all over the convention hall, sometimes holding court, other times asking questions or giving orders. Reporters came away from the convention with a clear impression that he was in charge.[72]

Charles Maurice, writing for the *South Bend Tribune* from the convention site, described Stephenson as "the central figure in pre-convention arrangements and on the floor of the convention itself."[73] An obscure Evansville citizen only three years ago, Maurice wrote, Stephenson was as picturesque as a great fictional character. With unlimited funds at his command, he reminded observers of "the Count of Monte Cristo." Credited as the organizer of the Indiana Klan, Maurice continued, national Klan leaders now insist that Stephenson is no longer in good standing as a Klansman, is presently under suspension while awaiting trial and probable banishment from the national organization. According to Maurice, Stephenson had demonstrated both in the convention and in the reorganized Republican state committee that he had lieutenants everywhere ready to obey each and every command. Those lieutenants, Maurice stated, were all Klansmen.[74]

Whether Stephenson actually controlled events or merely assisted Senator Watson and his supporters in running the convention is unclear. Stephenson was present at all of the conferences and meetings where decisions had been made, and was the person delegates turned to when confused, upset, or in need of a favor. Most impressive to reporters covering the convention was the coup engineered by Stephenson to take over the Republican state committee and through it the Indiana Republican party.

Senator Watson was king of the convention. However, he had neither supported nor voted for Jackson in the recent primary election. In his keynote address on May 21, Watson admitted publically that indeed he had not voted for Jackson but urged all Republicans to come together, vote for Jackson in November, and help win the fight for Republican principles in the country. At that point in the speech, Jackson appeared at the podium and stood by Watson's side. The two men joined hands and received an enormous ovation from the delegates.[75]

Stephenson certainly must have savored this moment, because it had been entirely of his own making. The fruits of this Watson-Jackson public embrace were not long in coming. On the next day, May 22, an Evans-Bossert slate of candidates for openings on the Republican state committee was presented to the convention for approval but was rejected totally. Next, a Stephenson-Watson-Jackson slate of candidates for the same posts on the state committee was submitted to the convention and approved immediately. Thus was the Republican state committee captured and reorganized.[76]

What astonished experienced observers such as Charles Maurice was the precision with which the Stephenson-Watson-Jackson coup had been managed. There simply had been nothing like this Republican State Convention in the recent history of Indiana politics.[77] It was also very clear to reporters covering the event that Evans and Bossert were very angry over the way business had been managed. Something would have to be done very soon to separate Stephenson from his powerful political friends.

So dominant was Klan influence during this convention that one local newspaper described it as just another Klan rally, a warm-up for a larger statewide Klan rally and barbecue scheduled for the State Fairgrounds just north of Indianapolis on May 24.[78] Before the convention ended, all of the Klan-supported Republican candidates elected in the May primaries were approved by the convention as official candidates. With the exception of Arthur Gilliom, Republican candidate for attorney general who was anti-Klan, the entire top of the Republican state ticket were all Klan-endorsed candidates.

When the Republican State Convention completed its business on May 24, thousands of Indiana Klansmen and their families descended upon the State Fairgrounds for a rally and barbecue that was to be an Evans-Bossert reprise to the Stephenson-dominated convention. Bossert spoke at the rally. Stephenson did not attend. That same evening, more than six thousand five hundred Klansmen, accompanied by bands, floats, and a drum and bugle corps, paraded south on Capitol Avenue through the center of Indianapolis to celebrate the nomination of Ed Jackson.[79]

Parade units took almost an hour and a half to pass a given point. Supportive crowds estimated at seventy-five thousand assembled to watch the spectacle of white-robed, hooded, but unmasked men and women demonstrating the strength of their organization in the shadow of the state capitol.[80] Although no political banners or placards were displayed, the timing of this Klan rally and parade for the final day of the Republican State Convention was deliberate. An unmistakably clear political message was there for everyone to hear. Earlier in the day, Bossert and other Klan speakers at the Fairgrounds had urged Klansmen to support Jackson for governor and elect as many of their own men as possible to local, county, and state offices in the November elections.[81]

For Evans and Bossert, the Republican State Convention had been a humiliating and disappointing experience. Stephenson had toyed with them almost at will, nothing had gone their way, and they were extremely resentful over what had happened. On May 22, just after convention approval of the Stephenson-Watson-Jackson slate for the state committee, Bossert issued a news release stating that Senator Watson "could not be on both sides of the Klan political controversy."[82] Watson could not ally himself with Stephenson and then expect support and cooperation from the regular Klan organization in Indiana.

Watson's response was predictable. As was his normal political posture, he tried to avoid controversial issues altogether. Since he was not a Klansman, the senator failed to see how a controversy in that organization could interest or involve him. Furthermore, Watson denied that he had made a slate with either Bossert or Stephenson. He denied assisting either of those men in slate making of any sort. In any case, the present Republican ticket had been set, Watson supported it, and "invited the citizens of Indiana regardless of race, creed, or color to join in electing it."[83] That was not what Bossert wanted to hear, and apparently he decided that perhaps the senator needed to be taught a lesson.

For Stephenson, the Republican State Convention in Indianapolis had been a triumph. Just about everything had turned out right. Generally perceived by state Republican politicians and by reporters as Ed Jackson's most trusted political advisor and as one of Jim Watson's closest friends, Stephenson made the most of his new celebrity status in Indiana Republican circles. He took full credit for the Jackson primary election victory and assured anyone who would listen that his candidate would win handily in November.

Having managed the Republican State Convention so effectively, Stephenson was ready to try his hand at the Republican National Convention in Cleveland, June 10–12. Rumors flew around Indianapolis suggesting that he might be able to manage a surprise or two for Indiana Republicans in what otherwise promised to be a very unexciting convention. Stephenson made arrangements to go to the Republican National Convention in grand style. He traveled with his usual entourage to Toledo, where they boarded his yacht, *Reomar II,* and then sailed to Cleveland for the big event. While attending the convention, through a combination of quiet negotiation and ostentatious displays of hospitality, Stephenson hoped to advance the national political ambitions of his new ally, Senator Watson.

The nomination of President Calvin Coolidge in Cleveland was a foregone conclusion. Selection of a vice presidential running mate for Coolidge was believed to be open and undecided. Speculation in the press about Coolidge's range of choices invariably mentioned Senator James E. Watson of Indiana. Watson certainly coveted the nomination, and Stephenson was prepared to spend or do whatever was required to persuade the president and his advisors, particularly William M. Butler, chairman of the Republican National Committee, to think seriously about Watson. As Stephenson analyzed the situation at the Republican National Convention, the less said about past and present Klan support of Watson the better.

In any case, obscuring present associations with Indiana Klansmen and past support from that organization was by now habitual with Watson. Toward the end of his keynote address at the Republican State Convention in Indianapolis, Watson cleverly talked around his relationships with Klansmen and their organizations in Indiana. He denied personal membership in the Klan but saw nothing objectionable about a man belonging to it, if that was his wish. At the same time, Watson stated that he was not a Catholic either and had no objection to anyone belonging to that church. For himself, he was a Methodist and as such was not opposed to any creed or order.[84]

Meanwhile, harried by the scandalous revelation of the Teapot Dome investigation, the president's political strategists, particularly Butler, were determined that this convention would be as orderly and noncontroversial as they could make it. The most effective way to obtain that result was for the president to say as little as possible about anything important. Certainly, the activities of the Klan in but especially out of the South were important to millions of Americans as readers of the regional and national press could testify. As a rule, local Klan organizations tended to support the party in power, Republicans in the East, Midwest, and West, and Democrats in the South. It seemed clear that any formal Republican party position for or against the Klan was bound to offend some important voting bloc somewhere.

Justifiably, Republicans were fearful that because of the many scandals connected with the Harding administration, 1924 might be a Democratic year. Coolidge and Butler were of no mind to risk alienating voters in any state that they had a chance of winning. They agreed that the most prudent course for the party at the Cleveland convention was to make no mention whatsoever of the Klan in their party platform.[85] Stephenson understood and accepted this Republican rationale for avoiding the issue and maintained a low profile while working on behalf of Watson in the hotels and on his yacht.

Evans arrived in Cleveland early and moved into the Statler Hotel with an entourage of about sixty Klansmen. In that entourage were Bossert and Milton Elrod, editor of the *Fiery Cross*. Both of these men had developed a deep and abiding loathing of Senator Watson. Both of these men, especially Bossert, despised the man as the worst sort of self-serving politician responsible for the sorry state in which the country now found itself. Bossert and Elrod decided to teach Watson a lesson that he would not soon forget. How involved Evans was in this scheme is unclear. Thus staffed, supported, and well aware that in Indiana, at least, there were lost constituencies to be recovered, Evans proceeded to play a much more conspicuously public role at the Republican National Convention than did Stephenson.[86] For all of his very busy work that week Evans made the cover of *Time* magazine.

The scheme to cut Watson down to a very small size in the vice-presidential race began at once. On June 9, the day before the formal opening of the Republican National Convention, Elrod released a statement from Klan headquarters in the Statler Hotel naming the vice-presidential candidate most preferred by the Klan. It was Senator James E. Watson of Indiana.

Elrod was perfectly clear, "All of our boys throughout the nation will understand only one thing," he declared, "and that is Senator James E. Watson for Vice President—flat. We will deny any responsibility for the defeat of the Republican Party at the polls in November if Watson is not selected for Vice President, on the ground that he is the best available candidate to carry the Middle Western States which are necessary for the election of Coolidge."[87]

Watson, shocked beyond belief by Elrod's statement, immediately and vociferously denied that he was or ever had been a member of the Klan. "If they have issued a statement naming me," he continued, "they have done it for the express purpose of ruining me. Such a statement was made without my knowledge or consent and is wholly without authority from me or anyone having the right to represent me."[88] Stephenson agreed completely with Watson's interpretation of this incident but could not believe that Elrod had acted without the approval of Bossert and Evans.[89]

Watson did not know who was ultimately responsible for Elrod's statement and probably did not care; he was more concerned about damage control. A closed conference of Indiana delegates was called to discuss the general situation, but no action was taken. Watson took heart and refused to release those Indiana delegates already pledged to him.[90] Next, Watson moved very quickly to obtain some sort of retraction from Klan officials. Sometime either in the evening of June 9 or in the early hours of June 10, Watson met with Bossert and Evans to make peace and try to salvage whatever remained of his vice-presidential aspirations. Watson managed a lasting peace with Evans but only a temporary truce with Bossert.

The *Louisville Courier Journal* reported on June 10 that Bossert had forced Watson into a "gentlemen's agreement" with the national Klan organization in Indiana about cooperation in the forthcoming election.[91] On the same day Bossert was reported in the *New York Times* as dismissing the entire Watson incident with the observation that the senator did not appreciate the value of the "endorsement."[92] Evans did much better. He provided a retraction and an explanation why such an endorsement had not and should not have been given.

Evans denied that the Klan had demanded the nomination of any man to any national office. That was not the way the Klan worked. The Klan was not now and never would be owned or beholden to any political party for anything. Evans stated unequivocally that he was the only person authorized to speak for the Klan on such matters, and he had not even been interviewed on the subject of the vice-presidential nomination.[93] The statement concerning Senator Watson lately appearing in the press and attributed to me, Evans insisted, was utterly "without foundation of fact."[94] There simply was no danger, Evans concluded, that either the Democratic or Republican parties would nominate for "the President or Vice President any man who is not worthy in life and character to hold the position."[95]

Watson was certainly pleased with Evans' retraction and explanation, but it had no effect whatsoever upon his vice-presidential prospects. The leadership of the Republican party had never been seriously interested in Watson and became positively antipathetic after the release of the Elrod statement. Though Watson was not invited to any of the closed meetings where party leaders interviewed vice-presidential candidates, he refused to abandon all hope.[96] Anything was possible at a national convention.

Because Frank O. Lowden, former governor of Illinois, declined the vice-presidential nomination when offered to him, Watson decided to stay the course. He allowed his name to go forward, explaining to a *New York Times* reporter, as a protest candidate against William M. Butler's heavy-handed management of the convention.[97] In the end, the convention, heavy-handedly managed or not, chose Charles G. Dawes, a former general and a Chicago banker as Coolidge's running mate. Watson stayed in the balloting and managed to collect seventy-nine votes before the convention made Dawes' selection unanimous.[98]

Whereas Bossert and Elrod had been angered and were much more exercised over Senator Watson's close relationship with Stephenson than was Evans, all three of these Klan leaders became increasingly concerned about the possibility of an anti-Klan plank appearing in the Republican party platform. R. B. Creager, national committeeman from Texas and a member of the Committee on Platform and Resolutions, headed a small group of delegates who demanded a formal party declaration against the Klan.[99] Indeed, such an anti-Klan plank was presented to the Committee on Platform and Resolutions on June 10, and a seven-hour animated discussion followed.

Butler and other Republican party leaders, including a majority of the Committee on Platform and Resolutions, were opposed to taking an open stand against the Klan. Some committee members saw no useful purpose in irritating the Klan by any sort of declaration. Others favored a simple declaration affirming religious freedom as guaranteed by the Constitution.[100] What the committee finally presented, and the convention promptly approved, was a plan that made no direct mention of the Klan but declared the "unyielding devotion" of the Republican party to the Constitution and to the guarantees of civil, political, and religious liberty therein contained.[101]

Neither Stephenson nor the Evans-Bossert-Elrod group attending the convention could complain about that. They all left Cleveland reasonably satisfied with what had been done there. Stephenson returned to Indianapolis to manage Jackson's gubernatorial campaign and to learn the results of the Klan inquiry into his separatist activities underway in

Evansville. The Klan tribunal collecting and hearing evidence against Stephenson reached a decision on June 23. Not surprisingly, Stephenson was found guilty as charged on all counts and sentenced to banishment from the organization and to ostracism by every member in it.[102]

To make certain that the banishment and ostracism would be widely publicized, the tribunal authorized publication of all materials collected to make the case against Stephenson. Letters, copies of depositions, testimony, and formal Klan decrees were made into a booklet of about fifty pages and distributed throughout Indiana and elsewhere in the hope of permanently damaging Stephenson and putting an end to his separatist movement.[103]

For his part, Stephenson simply dismissed the verdict of the tribunal as well as the report issued by it as just another shameful plot of Evans, Bossert, and the Atlanta crowd. Indiana Klansmen would have to make up their own minds about which leader to follow. As Stephenson took charge of the Jackson campaign, he had no doubt about who that leader would be. For the moment at least, Stephenson was correct, it would be him.

Though Stephenson dismissed the whole Evansville trial as a meaningless exercise, others did not. The seriousness of the sentence of banishment and ostracism was made clear to Stephenson very soon. At 3:30 a.m. on June 27, 1924, three days after the Evansville Klan tribunal had judged and sentenced Stephenson, his yacht *Reomar II* was rocked by an explosion and totally destroyed by fire. Stephenson himself was not on board at the time, but a bodyguard was knocked unconscious and narrowly escaped death. Six months later a Muncie, Indiana, Klansman confessed to setting the fire, only to retract his confession two days later. No other arrests were ever made, and the case has never been solved.[104]

There was absolutely no evidence linking Evans, Bossert, or other Klansmen to this almost certain act of arson. They were all in New York attending the Democratic National Convention when the crime occurred. If Evans had ordered it as a warning to Stephenson, the warning was received and heeded. During the next several months Stephenson exhibited a near paranoid fear for his own life. More bodyguards were added to his entourage, and Stephenson never left his home or office unarmed or unaccompanied. He knew from experience that bad things seemed to happen to people who had crossed Evans. Henceforth, Stephenson kept a low profile in Klan affairs, stayed away from large and well-publicized Klan activities but remained visible and active in state politics.[105] During this very frightening period for Stephenson, the press cooperated, always referring to him as a former Klan leader or simply as Ed Jackson's political advisor.

Evans, Bossert, Elrod, and others traveled to New York for the Democratic National Convention opening in Madison Square Garden on
June 24. With Evans' Klan entourage being daily reinforced by new arrivals from the South, he installed his party in the McAlpin and Great
Northern hotels. Unlike the situation with the Republicans in Cleveland,
in the Democratic National Convention in New York the Klan issue could
not be contained, controlled, compromised, or resolved. For this failure,
the Democratic party would pay dearly in November.

Evans and his entourage had come to New York confident that the
Klan was too powerful to be challenged or condemned by name as an un-
American organization in the Democratic party platform. Upon arriving
at the convention, Evans and others were surprised to learn that the Klan
issue had emerged as the dominating one in the entire convention. Next,
they were shocked to discover that the number of actual Klansmen and
dependable supporters among delegates was far below what they had
expected. Moreover, it was also clear that no one in the convention was
willing to defend the Klan or its white, Protestant, American principles
in public.

As a matter of fact, only about three hundred forty delegates could
be reckoned as Klansmen or sympathizers.[106] The practical political effect
of those numbers was that Klan sympathizers could block the nomination of candidates such as the conservative Senator Oscar W. Underwood
of Alabama, who was stridently anti-Klan, or Governor Alfred E. Smith
of New York, strongly anti-Klan, against Prohibition, and himself a
Catholic. At the same time, those numbers were too small to make viable
the candidacy of the Klan favorite, Senator Samuel M. Ralston of Indiana,
perhaps best remembered for fearlessly lecturing nuns and the young
ladies in their charge in a Catholic women's college in southern Indiana
on the virtues of separation of church and state.

Klan strength in the convention was too weak even when joined
with many others to win the nomination for William G. McAdoo, former
President Wilson's son-in-law. McAdoo was certainly not a Klan sympathizer. Yet for political reasons, he had emerged as the candidate most
circumspect and hesitant about denouncing them. Klan sympathizers in
the convention were able to stop candidates obnoxious to them but were
unable to advance the prospects of anyone perceived to be even neutral
toward them. Klan sympathizers were absolutely intransigent. So were
their Catholic and urban-oriented opponents. The result was absolute
impasse, and the longest and most chaotic Democratic National Convention in modern history.

Unlike the Republican Convention where the issue of a formal condemnation of the Klan had been contained within the Committee on

Platform and Resolutions, the Democrats waged a bitter and widely reported floor battle over it. Virtually all of the delegates who spoke against naming the Klan in the platform said nothing positive about the organization or its principles. For them, the Klan was bad, but a great many good people mistakenly had joined it. The end of Ku Kluxism, pleaded the venerable William Jennings Bryan, will come about sooner by recognizing "their honesty and teaching them that they are wrong." Condemning the Klan by name in the platform, Bryan continued, would bring discord into the party and perhaps even divide the Christian Church in this country. Both applause and catcalls followed Bryan's plea for compassion and forgiveness. One who did not utter a catcall but probably wanted to do so was William Allen White. Later, he characterized Bryan's performance at the convention as nothing but "an apology for expediency."[107] When the convention finally acted on this matter the Klan escaped formal condemnation by name in the platform by only one vote.

This narrowest of victories in the fight over the Democratic party platform was certainly no encouragement for Klan supporters and sympathizers at the convention. In particular, Evans and Bossert had no reason to be pleased by it. Even though the supporters of a McAdoo presidential nomination as well as those of Ambassador John W. Davis had opposed a strong anti-Klan plank in the party platform, both of those men had used their good offices to try and work out some sort of compromise between delegates demanding condemnation of the Klan by name and those urging no declaration at all.[108] Even Senator Ralston, the Klan's preferred choice, denied he was a Klan sympathizer.

Nonetheless, the Klan issue so deeply divided the delegates at the Democratic National Convention that neither front-runner, McAdoo or Smith, could win the nomination. It took no less than nine more anxiety-laden, frustrating days and 103 ballots for the Democrats to nominate Ambassador John W. Davis for president and William Jennings Bryan's brother, Charles Bryan, for vice president. The delegates returned to their home districts exhausted, angry, embarrassed, and generally apathetic about the national ticket. Thus disillusioned, they began the post–Labor Day election campaign willing to try to win but in their hearts expecting to lose.

— iv —

Back at Notre Dame, faculty and students read about and followed the not so great events occurring at the national conventions in Cleveland and New York but do not appear to have been much moved by them. The nomination of Coolidge for a term of his own was certainly no surprise. The nomination of Davis must have disappointed most people at Notre Dame and surprised many. Smith was clearly the candidate of choice among priests, lay faculty, and students. However, the national election was a distant event and all members of the Notre Dame community were preoccupied with other concerns.

For priests, rumors about new assignments at Notre Dame or elsewhere were widespread. Among faculty, anxiety about annual contract renewals was particularly high that year. For students, completion of end-of-semester work, getting through graduation ceremonies, and planning for summer employment or a vacation somewhere well populated with girls were priority activities. Even though the post-student-riot public relations warfare with Klan newspapers and other anti-Catholic periodicals had begun at once, the burden of that activity fell first upon Walsh and Hugh O'Donnell, who did not do it very well, and then later upon O'Hara, who did it very well indeed.

First, there was hate mail in the form of letters and postcards addressed to Walsh. Virtually all of this material was unsigned. Much of it was semi-literate. One local citizen, addressing Walsh as Mr., warned him to keep his hoodlums on campus and out of South Bend. Next time, "there will be hot lead for you."[109] Another local resident, identifying himself as "A Klansman Now and Always," sounded a theme that would become familiar from repetition. He berated Walsh for harboring students who had disgraced the flag, adding that "not even a Negro has done what the Roman Catholics have."[110]

Still another local resident communicated a blunt but simple message to university officials in a blunt and simple fashion, "Keep those ruff neck anarchists attending your school out of South Bend."[111] Finally, an Indianapolis reader of the *Fiery Cross* sent Walsh a copy dated May 30, 1924 with a warning handwritten across the top of the front page, "You Dirty UnAmerican Degenerate Skunks will pay for your Mob Action at South Bend."[112]

Of more immediate importance to Walsh and other university officials than the hate mail received was a serious effort by Klansmen in Lansing, Michigan, to have a scheduled baseball game with Notre Dame on June 6, 1924, canceled and then, if possible, to persuade the president of Michigan Agricultural and Mechanical College to terminate all future formal and informal athletic relations with this Catholic university. No doubt inspired by Stephenson in Indianapolis,[113] Lansing Klansmen actually petitioned the president of Michigan A & M to take such drastic punitive action on the grounds that the generally outrageous and specifically disloyal behavior of Notre Dame students during the late civic disturbances in South Bend warranted it.[114] The desecration and trampling of the American flag by Catholic students there should not be forgotten and never could be forgiven. Something serious needed to be done to bring the Catholics at Notre Dame to their senses.

Neither Walsh nor anyone else at the university made any public comment about the Klan petition, which in the end produced no result at all. This was entirely a matter for officials at Michigan A & M to decide. The baseball game in question was played as scheduled on June 6 with Notre Dame winning a close contest, 4 to 3. Another game between the two schools scheduled for June 14 was also played with Notre Dame winning that one more convincingly, 8 to 2. Future athletic relations between Notre Dame and Michigan A & M were in no way interrupted or impaired by Klan-inspired anti-Notre Dame and anti-Catholic propaganda. Games were scheduled, played, won, and lost as before.

While the Indianapolis Klan leaders failed to obtain cancellation of the Notre Dame baseball games with Michigan A & M, they were absolutely determined to see that their charges of scandalously unpatriotic and disloyal behavior by Notre Dame students would get the widest possible circulation and high credibility. H. M. Trausch, a staff member of the *Fiery Cross* in Indianapolis, hastily prepared a small booklet entitled *The Truth about the Notre Dame Riot on Saturday, May 17, 1924,* which the Fiery Cross Publishing Company released in June.

Trausch's crudely written account of the events of that day gave the whole incident a new political and anti-Protestant twist. According to Trausch, the precipitating cause of the riot was the extraordinary success of Klan-sponsored candidates in the Indiana Republican primary elections on May 7. That political success, Trausch wrote, "has goaded the alien element to desperation." Moreover all Americans should know and never forget that Catholic hatred on that day "was directed not all toward the Klan, but that Protestantism was that against which the hatred was being spent."[115]

This point about Protestantism, America's religion, being threatened by Catholic conspirators and Protestants being attacked by Catholic hooligans was repeated many times over in Klan papers as well as by other anti-Catholic publications throughout the summer and fall. As a matter of fact, in October, during a moment of historical reflection, the *Fiery Cross* described the South Bend disturbances as the worst anti-Protestant riot in American history.[116]

What Trausch had started in Indianapolis with his booklet for distribution in Indiana and in neighboring states was taken up and disseminated

nationally in the pages of a stridently anti-Catholic and pro-Klan publication published in Washington, D.C., by James S. Vance, a drugstore
tycoon.[117] Popular with fraternal associations, Vance's publication, the
Fellowship Forum, was taken by many of them on a subscription basis.
The circulation of the *Fellowship Forum* was probably not large, but it was
widespread across the country.

The anti-Protestant twist that Trausch gave to the South Bend disturbances was embellished in the *Fellowship Forum* with details not hitherto
reported elsewhere. According to the story there, the entire affair in South
Bend had been carefully planned and orchestrated. Roman Catholic
students from Notre Dame showed their contempt for American ideals
and values and their disloyalty by trampling on the flag. Cursing mobs
of papist students harassed American women with insulting remarks and
obscene gestures. Masonic pins were snatched from the lapels of innocent
Protestant bystanders. A masonic button was even torn from the collar
of a South Bend motorcycle officer. The South Bend chief of police, a
Catholic himself, was disgusted with the performance of his men. He attributed their inability or unwillingness to maintain order to the fact that
so many of them were Catholics.[118]

If Trausch in his booklet and the writers for the *Fellowship Forum*
reported the truth, then the men writing the accounts of May 17 to 19 for
the *South Bend Tribune* had to have been blind or invincibly biased. They
were afflicted by neither of those conditions. The men reporting this
story for the *South Bend Tribune* had been on the scene and described
what they saw. Trausch and the writers for the *Fellowship Forum* reported
what they wanted their readers to believe.

After Trausch and the *Fellowship Forum*, the story got better with the
telling. An editorial published under a KKK symbol in the *Youngstown
Citizen,* a weekly paper styling itself as the only Republican paper in
Youngstown, stretched the anti-Protestant, un-American interpretation
of the South Bend disturbances about as far as it could go. At the same
time, the editors made a special point of emphasizing that the South Bend
Klansmen were American citizens who had been victimized and denied
constitutional rights.

A tough steel town with a large foreign-born and Catholic population,
Youngstown was a hotbed of Klan activity in that part of the state. In such
an environment, the editors of the *Youngstown Citizen* were surely not
speaking for themselves alone when they attacked the "gang of Papal pi-
rates" from Notre Dame. The editors saw the events occurring in South
Bend on May 17 as part of an American tragedy that had to be reversed.
Anyone should be able to demonstrate for a worthy cause. Americanism

was certainly a worthy cause. Anyone should be able to parade and light fiery crosses if they desired, yes anyone, even white, Protestant, English-speaking, native-born Americans.[119]

Innocent Klansmen, along with their wives and children, had been assaulted by groups of students from the Roman Catholic University of Notre Dame. Those assaults had occurred in broad daylight on the public streets of an American city against peaceable people participating in fraternal festivities. Moreover, these innocent victims of unprovoked assault had been exercising every American citizen's privilege of free assemblage. During these assaults knives had been freely used, and at least one young Klansman had been badly cut before being rescued by police.[120]

Although the national press services burlesqued the situation in South Bend and had sent out only meager and biased accounts of what was happening there, protecting the right of peaceable assembly for all citizens was a serious matter. The Klansmen of South Bend must be able to enjoy the right of peaceable assembly "even if it takes every Klansman in Indiana and Ohio to secure it." If this right guaranteed by the Constitution cannot be exercised without the risk of attack by papist students, the editors concluded, then the existence of the Klan is justified and horse whipping is a permissible administration of justice.[121]

Walsh was certainly not a man easily intimidated, especially when angered. Clearly, this sort of material angered him. Walsh saved some cards and letters, destroyed many, and answered none. Nevertheless, warnings and threats of this sort distressed him. Unaware of the confusion and personal hostilities presently dividing Klan leadership in Indiana, Walsh suspected that the probability of Klan members coming back to South Bend in force sometime before the national election was high. What troubled him most about that probability was the fact that he did not know who in local or state authority could be trusted to assist the university, if assistance was needed. Patience and discreet silence seemed to be the only sensible course open to him at this juncture.

For Walsh and others at Notre Dame the summer was a quiet respite before an exciting and anxiety-laden fall. The fall began soon enough after Labor Day, as expected with the intensification of national and local electioneering, followed in mid-September by the return of the students to campus in record numbers, and then in early October by the opening of one of the most glorious and celebrated football seasons in Notre Dame history. What was unexpected in the fall was the announced visits to South Bend of two notorious anti-Catholic lecturers, Mrs. Helen Jackson, a professional ex-nun from Toledo, and L. J. King, a self-styled ex-priest. Both Mrs. Jackson and King frequently spoke under

Klan sponsorship to Protestant church groups about their Catholic experiences.[122]

Walsh first heard about the intended visits of Mrs. Jackson and L. J. King to South Bend from a most surprising source. In a letter dated September 16, 1924, Pat Emmons, a Stephenson partisan in Indiana Klan affairs and a leader of the St. Joseph County organization, advised Walsh that Mrs. Jackson and King were coming to South Bend but denied that the Klan was sponsoring their appearance. "Meetings of this nature," Emmons wrote, "conflict with the purposes and ideals of our institution, for ours is one which prevails only by brotherly love for every race, color, creed, and lineage."[123] Walsh was positively mystified by this letter. He had no idea why it had been sent, made no effort to try and find out why, but acted upon the information in it forthwith.

Precisely what Walsh tried to do about the proposed South Bend speaking engagements of Mrs. Jackson and King is unclear. Not a strong believer in unlimited freedom of speech in any and all circumstances, Walsh could do nothing on his own to prevent Mrs. Jackson and King from speaking in South Bend. He had no reason to hope for assistance from city officials in this matter, so most likely he looked to Frederick Miller of the *South Bend Tribune* for help. If Mrs. Jackson and King could not be kept out of South Bend, reports of their activities while in the city could be kept out of the *South Bend Tribune*. All that is known for certain is that Walsh informed his Provincial that "We tried our best to keep . . . [Mrs. Jackson and King] out without stirring up any publicity but failed."[124] What Walsh meant was that he had failed to keep King out of South Bend. There is no record that Mrs. Jackson ever spoke in the city at this time, and it is a fact that the *South Bend Tribune* made no mention whatsoever of King's appearances in the city, September 19–22, 1924.

King arrived in South Bend as announced on Friday, September 19, 1924. He was scheduled to speak at evening meetings on Friday and Saturday, with another talk scheduled in between on Saturday afternoon.[125] Heavy rains kept down attendance at both evening meetings. The Saturday afternoon session was completely overshadowed by the appearance in the city of John W. Davis, the Democrat presidential candidate. Davis' speech was delivered at the same hour of King's Saturday afternoon meeting; so very few came out to hear the ex-priest.[126] Because of the bad weather, Davis' appearance, and the lack of publicity in the *South Bend Tribune*, for most people in South Bend, King's presence in the city had been a non-event.

On Monday, September 22, King intended to leave South Bend for a speaking engagement elsewhere. However, while preparing for his departure, King was visited by South Bend police and detained. Local Klan officials had filed a complaint against King with the police, alleging that he had stolen two hundred dollars from the funds collected at his several South Bend appearances.[127] Notwithstanding Emmons' letter to Walsh denying Klan sponsorship of King's lectures, local Klan officials insisted that the money taken by King belonged to them and should be returned. According to what Walsh had been told, the matter was resolved in the office of Edwin Hunter, the local Klan attorney, by King returning some of the money.[128] Hunter must have brokered a mutually satisfying compromise of some sort about a proper sharing of the proceeds. King did not go off to his speaking engagement angry or disgruntled, because he returned to South Bend directly, where he remained for a few days with friends, but made no additional public appearances or speeches.[129]

For Walsh and others in the Notre Dame community, this bizarre King affair seemed to be another example of how utterly deceitful and treacherous local Klan leaders were. These men seemed absolutely incapable of truthful communication to anyone about anything. However, more appears to have been involved in this episode than Klan deceit and treachery for its own sake. The King affair was an indication of just how divided and disorganized the Indiana Klan had become since Stephenson had been tried by the Evansville tribunal and formally banished. It was also an indication of growing concern by local and state Republican leaders over the possible impact of the Klan issue on local and state election outcomes.

Most likely King's appearance in South Bend had been arranged by the Evans-Bossert faction. Emmons, for the moment faithful to Stephenson, was under pressure from local Republican leaders to refrain from embarrassing and confrontational activities in St. Joseph County.[130] Walsh learned from what he described as a reliable source that the St. Joseph County Republican party chairman, E. M. Morris, had written a letter to the local Klan organization advising them to be cautious about engaging in any new public demonstrations.[131] It would appear that Emmons wrote that mystifying disclaimer to Walsh on September 16 in part to try and disassociate local Klansmen from King's explicit anti-Catholic message and in part to lessen Republican anxieties about negative effects following from Klan support of local Republican candidates.

When the campaigning season began after Labor Day, the people running the Jackson political operation in the state seemed to have changed their minds about keeping the Klan quiet. Walsh learned from what he described as a "very reliable source" that a scheme to bring back large numbers of Klansmen to South Bend for a mid-October meeting and hold a parade there in full Klan regalia had been "instigated by the backers of Ed Jackson." According to Walsh's unnamed "very reliable source," the Jackson managers believed that "a life sized riot in South Bend would go a long way towards bolstering up Jackson's candidacy and gaining sympathy for the Kluxers."[132] How serious Jackson's managers and backers were about this scheme is unknown. In any case, what might have appeared as a good idea in September was clearly a very bad one in October.

Virtually all observers of the Indiana political scene in late September and October reported the same finding. The Klan issue had turned the world of Hoosier politics upside down. Both of the old parties were to some degree split over it. No one could be sure what Hoosier voters would do, but most agreed that except among Indiana Catholics, who were mostly Democrats, straight ticket voting would not be widespread. The largest contingent of Indiana voters most likely to be alienated from normal party affiliations were Jews and Negroes. Both of these groups usually voted Republican; few were expected to do so in November.[133]

Factions in both parties were realigning. Even families were divided over the prospect of a Klan-dominated state government.[134] There was a general feeling among politicians in both parties that forcing the Klan issue into the primary and general elections had been a mistake, especially so for the Republicans. As one long-serving Republican leader in Marshall County observed to a reporter from the *South Bend Tribune,* by allowing Jackson to win the primary election and then by approving him in the state convention, Republican leaders left themselves without any escape from an issue that currently overshadowed all others in the state.[135]

Though Coolidge and Dawes were not believed to be in any danger in Indiana, Jackson was another matter. His close identification with the Klan was a cause of embarrassment to many old-line Republican politicians, longtime supporters, and financial contributors. One such very important person was Joseph Kealing, Republican national committeeman. Because of the importance of the Klan issue in Indiana and because of the divisions among Republicans, especially among rich Republicans, over it, Kealing urged his wealthy Republican friends to maintain a hands-off policy toward the state ticket. This policy was ingeniously Machiavellian, because by ignoring the controversial state ticket, Kealing hoped to be able to attract both pro-Klan and anti-Klan supporters to Coolidge and Dawes.[136] Moreover, if Coolidge won and Jackson lost, Kealing and all other Indiana Republicans who agreed with him had an excellent chance of recapturing control of the party lost to Jackson and Stephenson in the May primary elections.

Other less Machiavellian Indiana Republican leaders were also angered by the Klan takeover of their party. A Republican congressional candidate in the Fourth District, William Hill, wrote a letter to Clyde Walb, Republican state chairman, on October 18, 1924, and gave a copy to the press on the same day in which he condemned Klan conduct of the Republican congressional campaign in his district. Hill complained that the Republican county chairman for Dearborn County, E. W. Caldwell, had refused to arrange speaking dates for him, and he cited specific instances where the Dearborn County Republican organization had failed to publicize his meetings. Hill had no doubts at all as to why. He was an outspoken anti-Klan Republican who believed very strongly that the Klan question was a national issue that should not be avoided by Republican congressional candidates.[137] In his campaign, he had not avoided it. Hill advised Walb that no matter what, he intended to maintain his anti-Klan stance. He appealed to the Republican state chairman to find out and then report back to him which Republican county organizations in the Fourth District were prepared to arrange meetings for him in their respective counties and which were not.[138] At that moment State Chairman Walb's plate of problems was getting very full.

Throughout the state, hundreds of solid Republican businessmen, bankers, manufacturers, and men prominent and active in county organizations had become so fearful of Klan domination of state affairs if Jackson was elected that they turned away from the state ticket and gave their money and time exclusively to the Coolidge-Dawes campaign.[139] One could do that very easily because the Coolidge campaign was run entirely separate from the state ticket. As a matter of fact, the national and state campaign organizations were separated physically as well as philosophically and financially. Indiana Coolidge headquarters was located on one end of the third floor of the Hotel Severin in Indianapolis, while Indiana State Republican headquarters was installed at the other. Signs posted outside of the elevators directed visitors to one or the other.[140]

In mid-October, in his capacity as Republican state chairman, Walb appeared to be much disturbed by the attitude of Kealing and others toward the state ticket. Campaign contributions were not coming in from many prominent longtime Republican supporters, and Walb had been obliged to shut down several campaign bureaus in Indianapolis and elsewhere.[141] He sent out eighty thousand letters to Republican activists throughout the state criticizing "certain Republicans" for failing to support Ed Jackson and the state ticket.[142] One reporter claimed that Walb had signed and sent out such letters under protest. He had been pressured by Jackson's managers and had agreed to send out the letters because he viewed them more as an alibi or explanation for poor fund-raising than as a serious appeal for last minute contributions to the Jackson campaign.[143]

According to Walb's letter, some of these unnamed "certain Republicans" were strong for Coolidge and Dawes but had remained "perfectly quiescent" about the state and local tickets. Moreover, too many of the speakers appearing in the state for Coolidge and Dawes avoided "anything more than a passing reference to the state ticket." Why such persons believed that ignoring state and local candidates would help Coolidge and Dawes carry Indiana was a conclusion that Walb affected neither to understand or accept. With or without such people, Walb insisted, success was certain on election day "for all our tickets."[144]

— v —

During late September the *Fiery Cross,* now controlled by the Evans-Bossert faction, published stories and notices about the return of Klansmen to South Bend for a pre-election meeting and parade. As set out in the *Fiery Cross,* the event, scheduled for Saturday, October 18, 1924, promised to be historic. The outrages and humiliations of last May would be properly avenged. The Catholic toughs of Notre Dame would be revealed to the world as nothing more than bullies and cowards. According to the *Fiery Cross,* to accomplish these ends more than two hundred thousand Klansmen were expected to attend the South Bend meeting. Special trains would be chartered to bring Klansmen directly from Indianapolis and Kokomo. Thousands of Oklahoma Klansmen, exultant over their successful impeachment of their stridently anti-Klan governor, Jack Walton, were expected to come to South Bend in special trains.[145]

Neither city officials nor university administrators had any way of knowing whether the stories in the *Fiery Cross* about this intended meeting and parade were credible or just more examples of Klan hyperbole. The possibility of two hundred thousand Klansmen descending upon South Bend on October 18 was a frightening prospect that might turn out to be true. City officials had to take this prospect seriously and plan and prepare accordingly. If the *Fiery Cross* can be believed, local Klan officials actually met with the mayor and chief of police in early October and received assurances that there would be no repetition of the May riots.[146] Police protection would be provided for visitors and citizens alike, but the issue of granting a parade permit for October 18 was left undecided. The Board of Public Safety and Chief Lane also communicated with Walsh about the university's intentions and plans if the Klan returned to South Bend on October 18, but Walsh was singularly uncooperative and told them nothing.[147]

Walsh told them nothing because he did not trust them and could neither forget nor forgive what he believed was a deliberate police attack on the students outside of Klan headquarters on May 19. He advised his provincial superior, Charles L. O'Donnell, who was traveling in New York City and Washington, D.C., that by October 11 the Board of Public Safety and chief of police had not yet made up their collective minds about issuing a parade permit to the local Klan. Several board members as well as Chief Lane had asked Walsh about what he intended to do if the Klan actually paraded in South Bend. He absolutely refused to give any information to the board or to the chief until they had decided officially whether or not the Klan would be allowed to parade.[148]

Walsh explained to O'Donnell that the board and the chief "would like very much to have me say that the boys will not go into South Bend on that night, but I have them in a box and intend to keep close mouthed until they make a definite decision." Walsh described his conversations with Chief Lane as "nauseating." The chief's obsequious professions of loyalty to his alma mater were beyond both belief and description. Walsh wanted to have nothing to do with him.[149]

Regardless of what decisions the Board of Public Safety might make about a Klan parade permit, Walsh assured O'Donnell, "We have no intention of looking for trouble and have our plans for a demonstration of our own." If Klansmen actually came back to South Bend and paraded, trouble there would be, but probably not from Notre Dame students. A "head on collision with Father Zubowicz's Falcons could not be avoided."[151] These angry men were ready, anxious, and in no mood even to think about rights of free assembly, averting one's eyes, or turning the other cheek.

As provincial, O'Donnell had complete confidence in Walsh's ability to cope with the impending crisis. He offered to return to South Bend from New York, forgo attending the Notre Dame-Army football game at the Polo Grounds, and serve with his friend and fellow war veteran on whatever sort of reception committee Walsh had in mind for the Klan visitors on October 18.[152] Missing that football game was personal sacrifice of some significance, because over the past few years it had become one of the most popular fall sporting events in New York City. So popular in fact had that game become, O'Donnell had promised to deliver five tickets to the residence of John Cardinal Hayes, archbishop of New York, for the use of His Eminence or of members of his household. One way or another, either in South Bend or in New York City, October 18, 1924, promised to be a most important day in the history of the university.

As the intended great Klan meeting and parade in South Bend approached and the enormous logistical problems associated with staging such an event were not being addressed, the anxiety levels of Mayor See-birt, Chief Lane, and Walsh all dropped. Moreover, information received by Walsh from old-line Hoosier Republicans persuaded him that the great Klan event would not happen. "Taking in the whole situation," he wrote on October 11, 1924, to O'Donnell, "it appears to me that the political powers are likely to get busy at the last moment and induce the down-state leaders to call off the whole affair."[153]

Walsh's Republican friends were absolutely correct in the advice they had given him. Clyde Walb, Republican state chairman, forced cancellation of the South Bend Klan meeting, but it was not easily done. Walb had serious misgivings about the political effects of such a meeting for some time. In the end, Walb issued an ultimatum that he would close Republican state headquarters and leave all candidates on the state ticket to shift for themselves if the South Bend Klan meeting was not called off.[154] Much to the relief of South Bend city officials and university administrators, it was.

The *Fiery Cross* announced cancellation of the South Bend meeting but offered a much more colorful but distinctly less credible explanation for doing so. According to the *Fiery Cross*, the reasons for canceling the meeting were humanitarian. An unnamed Roman Catholic corporation was supposed to have made arrangements to import gunmen into South Bend from New York, Massachusetts, Missouri, Illinois, and New Jersey to disrupt the meeting and terrorize the participants.[155] In effect, the Klan called off the meeting for the noble purpose of saving lives and prevention of serious injury to Klansmen and other innocent Protestant Americans. Such was the sorry state to which the country had been reduced.

Indeed, October 18 turned out to be a quiet Saturday in St. Joseph County. An important piece of Notre Dame history would be made on that day but not in South Bend or out on the university campus. All eyes in the city and on campus were focused on New York, where Notre Dame and Army played their annual football game in the Polo Grounds before 60,000 people, the second largest football crowd in New York City history.

In that game an excellent Notre Dame team defeated a fine Army squad 13 to 7. Out of that decisive but hard-fought victory came Grantland Rice's stylization of the Notre Dame backfield as the legendary Four Horsemen of the Apocalypse. In time, that stylization properly promoted would persuade the country to forget the hooligan image of the university and Notre Dame student body so assiduously propagated by Klan papers and magazines after the May riots. Everybody loves a football hero. Notre Dame had four of them. That was special. Clearly there was one area where Catholics excelled and performed as genuine American heroes should.

All of this was yet to come and would take time, effort, and a great deal of luck to work out. Meanwhile, in Indiana there were state and local elections where anti-Catholicism had become a major issue. It was time for those whom William Jennings Bryan had described as mistaken good people to stand up and be counted. After cancellation of the South Bend Klan meeting and parade scheduled for October 18, the final days of the election campaign in Indiana, especially in the northern part of the state, were distinguished by the utter absence of public Klan electioneering activity of any sort. Apparently the word had gone out loud and clear to local Klan organizations that nothing should be done that would embarrass the Jackson campaign, and nothing was.

On election day, November 4, 1924, Coolidge and Dawes overwhelmed Davis and Bryan, capturing 54 percent of the popular vote. Coolidge and Dawes won the electoral votes of every state outside of the traditionally Democratic South except Oklahoma and Wisconsin. Davis even lost his native state of West Virginia. The election was a Republican landslide. Klan-supported favorites won handsomely in Colorado, Oklahoma, Kansas, Kentucky, Iowa, and probably in Illinois. Then there was Indiana, and of course, St. Joseph County.

Coolidge and Dawes swept Indiana, carrying the state by two hundred thousand votes. Jackson ran behind Coolidge and Dawes, but the widely known fact of Klan support for him, contrary to some Republican leadership fears, does not seem to have turned away many Hoosier voters. Jackson defeated McCullough handily by eighty-two thousand votes, and Klan-supported candidates generally did well across the state.

Harry E. Rowbottom, a Republican with Klan support, defeated William E. Wilson, the incumbent Democrat congressman from the First District who was a Catholic and anti-Klan. Rowbottom distinguished himself several years later by being indicted and convicted of selling federal postmaster appointments in Indiana. The anti-Klan Republican congressional candidate in the Fourth District, William Hill, who had complained publicly to the Republican state chairman about Klan opposition and harassment during his campaign, failed to unseat the Democrat incumbent, David Canfield. However, incumbent Republican Congressman Andrew J. Hickey of Laporte, who was strongly anti-Klan, easily defeated his Democratic challenger in the Thirteenth District.

In St. Joseph County voter turnout was very heavy. Anti-Klan sentiments were expected to be very high there among voters but were not. Local resentments over the May riots and understandable concerns over what trouble-making Notre Dame students might do next to disrupt community life translated into substantial majorities for local Republican candidates, whether they were Klan-endorsed or not. Coolidge and Dawes were not touched by such anxieties and carried the county handily. Though Jackson trailed the national ticket significantly, he managed to carry the county by 1,900 votes.

Most important for local affairs, Republican candidates won every county and local office up for election. Even the very popular incumbent Democrat sheriff, Michael C. Hanley, was defeated by Thomas S. Goodrich, a Klan-supported Republican, by five thousand votes. The election in St. Joseph County was as the *South Bend Tribune* described, "a clean sweep" for the Republicans.

In the state as a whole, the Republican victory was a triumph for the Indiana Klan, no matter how divided it might be. Klansmen had worked very hard in the May primary elections to win control of the state Republican party, and now in November they had captured the governorship, the Indiana House of Representatives, and had established themselves as a powerful influence in the Indiana State Senate. Both Stephenson and the Evans-Bossert group had reasons to rejoice. For the former, the prospects for power and money were enormous. For the latter, legislative remedies for the alien Catholic menace were now possible. The consequences of these radically altered political situations in state government for Indiana Catholics and in St. Joseph County for the University of Notre Dame were not to be long in coming. Neither was deliverance.

— 10 —

Against a Blue-Gray Sky

W hen the students returned to Notre Dame for the opening of the fall term in September 1924, the memory of those exciting days in May were still vivid. The confrontation with local police and Klansmen on May 19 could not be forgotten or forgiven. The prospect of a renewed encounter with the Klan and possibly with the police on October 18 excited some students, distressed others, and seriously worried Notre Dame officials.

It became very clear very soon that there was not much that anyone at the university could do about preventing a Klan parade in South Bend on October 18, and whatever happened on that day if the Klan came back to South Bend would happen. However, in September most members of the Notre Dame community were more concerned, some greatly angered, over the hooligan image of the student body and university so successfully propagated by Klan publicists. This image of overprivileged Irish Catholic teenagers assaulting innocent American Protestant patriots had not dissipated over the summer. If that image would not go away, perhaps something might be done to replace it in the media with one that was more attractive and honorable. O'Hara was convinced that the present extremely negative image of the university could be changed and that the means for doing so were at hand. That means was intercollegiate football success.

As a matter of fact, this strategy of countering the Klan-propagated hooligan image of the university through intensified publication of Notre Dame's football triumphs was inspired, if not actually suggested, by a tongue-in-cheek editorial about the activities of the Klan in Indiana published in the *New York Times* in 1923. This *Times* editorial was reprinted in the *Notre Dame Alumnus* in December 1923, months before the South Bend riots had occurred and long before the need for such a public relations campaign had even been considered.

Trying to be humorous about a situation that had little humor in it, the *Times* editors wrote: "There is in Indiana a militant Catholic organization . . . engaged in secret drills. They make long cross country raiding expeditions. . . . worst of all, they lately fought and defeated a detachment of the United States Army. Yet we have not heard of the Indiana Klansmen rising up to exterminate the Notre Dame football team."[1] Whatever the source, O'Hara's idea about publicizing Notre Dame's extraordinary football prowess turned out to be a most timely and effective public relations strategy.

To be sure, corruption was endemic in intercollegiate athletics during most of the 1920s, and using success in a corrupt intercollegiate athletic system as a strategy to change a negative institutional image was risky. However, the public tended to be extraordinarily forgiving of corrupt practices in intercollegiate athletics if their favorite teams won.

Under Coach Rockne during these years, the Notre Dame football program, like so many other intercollegiate football programs of that time, had been touched by recruiting violations and embarrassed by widely publicized instances of varsity players participating in professional games on Sundays and holidays. It is certainly not clear just how corrupt the Notre Dame program was relative to others or how much the president of the university and his top advisors knew about the extent of rules violations. Some did know, such as Father William Carey, an activist member of the Faculty Board in Control of Athletics who strove mightily during the 1920s to obtain strict rules compliance and maintain an honest program at the university.[2] Others in the administration were disposed to be more tolerant of violations, especially when pressured by influential alumni to be practical about such matters. Indeed, Rockne stretched and broke intercollegiate athletic rules, as did most other major coach of that time. However, because his teams won so often and so convincingly and because the athletic enterprise had become so profitable, Rockne generally ran the program as he saw fit. Rules violations whether petty or major notwithstanding, the Notre Dame football program had become by 1923 the university's most valuable and effective public relations asset.

Since becoming head football coach and athletic director in 1918, Rockne's teams had done extremely well, managing two undefeated seasons out of six, winning forty-eight games, tying three, and losing only four. Two of those defeats (1922 and 1923) were hard-fought one-touchdown losses to Nebraska in Lincoln before a rabidly anti-Catholic crowd overgenerous with epithets and insults.[3] Rockne's football team in 1924 promised to be one of his best ever.

Every starter on this team had earned at least one monogram, and several had won two. The starting backfield of Harry Stuhldreyer, Don Miller, Jim Crowley, and Elmer Layden had been recruited in 1921. Stuhl-dreyer and Miller had followed older brothers to Notre Dame. Crowley and Layden had been directed to the university by their high school coaches, who were former Rockne players, and by the prospect of substantial but illegal subsidies.[4] These four superb athletes had played together regularly as freshmen and on the varsity for two years. The team was ready now for a spectacular season, and the coaches knew it.

What made this team so psychologically prepared for a great season was, of course, the Klan-inspired anti-Catholicism lately experienced in Indiana. However, these players also had a fierce determination to defeat Nebraska so decisively in South Bend that Cornhusker supporters in the Lincoln area would think about changing their bigoted crowd behavior. Next time the Notre Dame team came to Lincoln to play football perhaps the fans there would think seriously about the wisdom of insulting and demeaning them.

O'Hara and other university officials appreciated the enormous public relations value of an undefeated football season and possible selection as national collegiate champion. There was not much that the *Fiery Cross, Fellowship Forum,* or other like-minded publications could say about that. By playing very hard, but always according to the rules, never complaining or making excuses, and winning, Notre Dame players would show the American public what Catholics and Catholic education was all about.

According to O'Hara, the football campaign of 1924 "was looked upon by the players as a sort of a spiritual crusade."[5] In truth, this football season was much more than a spiritual crusade. For O'Hara and millions of American Catholics throughout the country who believed and felt as he did, and especially for the 300,000 Catholics living in Indiana—11 percent of the population of the state—the performance of the Notre Dame football team in that year gave them all a supreme moment of restored pride and dignity. In the bigoted parlance of the times, the football fortunes of Notre Dame became the "Crossbacks" and the "mackerel snappers" revenge, albeit accomplished in a proper Catholic gentlemanly and sportsmanlike manner.

The football season began as Rockne preferred to begin most of his seasons with two home games against easy opponents. The October 4 opening game against Lombard played before only 8,000 people was a hopeless mismatch, with Notre Dame winning easily 40 to 0. In the second game, against Wabash College a week later, 10,000 people witnessed the same one-sided result. The crusading zeal of the Catholic Notre Dame squad displayed against the smaller, outclassed but Presbyterian-affiliated opponent was reflected in the *South Bend Tribune*'s headline, "Notre Dame defeats Wabash 34-0, Presbyterians Helpless before Attack."[6]

On the next Saturday, October 18, the day the Klan was supposed to return to South Bend, a very serious game was scheduled in New York City against a very powerful and undefeated Army team. The West Point squad was the most American, most patriotic, and most notoriously corrupt team in intercollegiate football. West Point authorities paid no heed to rules about three-year varsity play whatsoever. Because the mission of the institution was to train officers for the United States Army, the West Point administration simply did not believe that ordinary intercollegiate rules about recruiting athletes ought to apply to them. Army coaches regularly recruited outstanding players from other college and university football programs.

For example, the great running back, Elmer Oliphant, had played three years at Purdue, 1911–13, and attained All-American status before coming to West Point in 1914. Oliphant played brilliantly for Army for three more years, achieving All-American status there as well.[7] In a game with Army in 1923, Notre Dame players were reported to have taunted their opponents by asking whether the stripes on their uniforms indicated how many years of college football experience they had before enrolling at West Point.[8] In 1926, nine of the eleven starters on the Army team had played college football elsewhere, and for the season of 1927, Army coaches had deliberately and flagrantly recruited several former All-Americans for their team. One running back on that team had played college football for seven years and another had played for six years.[9]

The situation had become so bad by 1927 that the coaches at the United States Naval Academy who generally tried to observe intercollegiate football recruiting rules actually broke off football relations with West Point for a few years. As a matter of fact, West Point did not regularly comply with the three-year eligibility rule until ordered to do so by President Roosevelt in 1938.[10]

Because of consistent intercollegiate recruiting rules violations by West Point authorities during the 1920s, defeating an Army team was a major athletic achievement for any football program anywhere. Between 1920 and 1929 Notre Dame managed it seven times, losing only twice and tieing once. Indeed, the football game played against Army in the Polo Grounds on October 18, 1924, was very serious business. The entire American sports world awaited the outcome.

Stories about the extraordinary importance of this game filled New York City newspapers during the second week of October. Publicity about the game had become intense because Rockne and his friends among the New York City alumni had moved heaven and earth to make it so. In addition to the regular university publicists assigned to such an event,

Rockne authorized the hiring of a man from the *New York Times* for about a week's work at twice the average New York sportswriter's monthly salary. This local publicity man was to feed stories about Notre Dame and the team to as many New York City papers as possible.[11]

Consequently, during the week before the game feature stories about the two teams, the coaches, and players appeared in virtually all of the local papers. The messages delivered about the university and the team were all highly positive ones. Rockne was a coaching genius, a superb football tactician who would always do the unexpected. The players were all excellent athletes, well coached and conditioned, intelligent, highly disciplined, respectable young men proud of themselves, their university, and their religion. Gone entirely from these stories was any reference or allusion to the hooligan roughneck image so assiduously propagated in some quarters after the events of the previous May.

Rockne and influential New York alumni managed the New York City press so well and the pregame publicity was so successful that the game not only sold out but became a major celebrity event. Local, national, and even international dignitaries were in attendance. On the East Coast on October 18, the Army-Notre Dame game was the place to be. Sinclair Weeks, Secretary of War, had come up from Washington to attend the contest and host the celebrated Dr. Hugo Eckener, commander of the record-breaking German Zeppelin, ZK-3. Weeks and Eckener showed themselves to the crowd by walking twice around the playing field in the third period and then went around again together in the final period.[12] How much Dr. Eckener and Secretary Weeks appreciated or even understood American football is problematic, but if local newspaper accounts of the game can be believed what they saw along with what 60,000 other football fans saw was spectacular.

Although Notre Dame only defeated Army in this game 13 to 7, the defeat was far more decisive than the one-touchdown margin would suggest. According to the account of the game carried in the *New York Times,* though outweighed in both line and backfield, "Knute Rockne's Notre Dame football machine, 1924 model," devastated the Army team. "Not by brawn but by brains did the Notre Dame attack open great holes in the Cadets forward wall." Indeed, the West Pointers were a fine upstanding team, but at the Polo Grounds on October 18, they had the misfortune of encountering one of the best football aggregations in the country. West Point pluck, the *New York Times* account declared, was simply no match for Notre Dame football excellence.[13]

Although Notre Dame threw only twelve forward passes in the entire game, the *New York Times* report continued, its backfield men "ripped and tore" through an Army defense that was unprepared for this sort of a running attack. End runs, sometimes without interference, and off-tackle slants did the most damage. Yet, it was Rockne's affection for surprise and his absolute determination to do the unexpected that underlay this victory.

For example, Rockne startled the crowd and the opposition by fielding a team of substitutes and second stringers after the opening kickoff. To be sure, early in the first quarter after Army had made three consecutive first downs he replaced this substitute team with his all-star backfield and first team linemen.[14] But this game-opening diversion appeared to have unsettled Army's defenses because they were unable to contain the rushes of Don Miller, Jim Crowley, and Elmer Layden, led by the brilliant blocking of Harry Stuhldreyer. However, when the Notre Dame attack appeared to have stalled on the Army one yard line in the second period, Rockne once again resorted to the unexpected. He called upon Adam Walsh, first team center and at 187 pounds the largest man on the team, to move out of the line into the backfield, take the pass from center, and plunge into the end zone for the first touchdown.

Notre Dame scored again in the third period on Crowley's sixteen-yard end run. Visibly tiring in the fourth period, the Notre Dame line managed to limit Army's great running back, "Light Horse" Harry Wilson, a former All-American and three-year varsity player at Penn State, to only one long run of twenty-four yards. Notre Dame's defenses kept the Cadets scoreless until five minutes into the final period when, after a critical fifteen-yard penalty, a substitute Army quarterback ran fifteen yards for the West Pointer's only touchdown. The game ended ten minutes later with Notre Dame in possession of the ball on their own thirty-five yard line.[15] The *New York Times* reporter concluded his account of the game by observing that "Speed, deception, decisive punch, and to boot the coaching genius of Knute Rockne" combined to produce "a clean cut victory."[16]

Most other New York newspapers headlined the Notre Dame victory and provided detailed accounts of the game. The most famous of these accounts, probably the most celebrated piece of American sports journalism ever written, was composed by Grantland Rice for the *New York Herald-Tribune*. Rice had watched the first half of the game from the press box in the Polo Grounds, and it is not clear that he followed the action in the game up to that point very closely. Rice attributed the first Notre Dame touchdown not to Walsh, who had actually scored it, but to Layden on a ten-yard run, "as if he had been fired from the black mouth of a howitzer."[17]

However, that very important factual error notwithstanding, during halftime, while thinking about a lead for his story, Rice conversed with other writers and sports publicity men in the press box, including George A. Strickler, an extremely enterprising twenty-year-old Notre Dame sophomore student press assistant.[18] Strickler had recently seen the popular Rudolph Valentino movie *The Four Horsemen of the Apocalypse* and recalled the vivid film effect of the eerie figures of Death, Pestilence, Famine, and War charging through the clouds. When a reporter hyperbolized about the performance of the Notre Dame backfield during the first half of the game, Strickler remarked "that they were just like the Four Horsemen in the film." Rice heard Strickler's remark and turned it into his story lead.[19]

According to Murray Sperber, that lead became the "single most famous passage in modern American sports journalism." It changed the style of American sports writing and established Rice as the best known and highest paid sports writer of his day.[20] Rice began by adapting a well-known scene from the Valentino film to the events of the day: "Outlined against a blue, gray October sky, the Four Horsemen rode again. In dramatic lore, they are Famine, Pestilence, Destruction and Death. They are only aliases. Their real names are Stuhldreyer, Miller, Crowley, and Layden. They formed the crest of a cyclone before which another fighting Army team was swept over the precipice at the Polo Grounds this afternoon . . . ."[21]

To be sure, Rice took enormous liberties with "dramatic lore" by changing the Horseman of War into one of Destruction. He also created for popular imaginations and located somewhere in the Polo Grounds an image of a precipice over which the Army team had been swept and a track where Rockne's ethereal Four Horsemen came to earth and rode down everything in sight. He conjured up for his readers an image of Notre Dame running backs carrying the mixed blood of tigers and antelopes and ended with Army players frustrated and exhausted from tackling cyclones.

Rice got away with this sort of silliness because in the third paragraph of his story, he made a point that American Catholics throughout the country during the 1920s desperately wanted to hear from someone of the other persuasion, namely, that Catholics were very good at doing something. Rice, an important public man of the other persuasion had said just that, Notre Dame's Four Horsemen were the greatest running backs of all time, "the greatest backfield that ever churned up the turf of any gridiron in any football age." Brilliant backfields may come and go, Rice proclaimed, "but in Stuhldreyer, Miller, Crowley and Layden, covered by a fast charging line, Notre Dame can take its place in the front of the field." Being respected and respectable, being in the front of the field in something in 1924 was important to Notre Dame and to American Catholics everywhere.[22]

The night editor of the *Herald-Tribune* recognized the appeal of the Rice's lead and put it on the front page of the Sunday edition. It also appeared on the front page of the Sunday edition of the *South Bend Tribune* as well as in other papers taking Rice's story direct from the *Herald-Tribune.* Young George Strickler was delighted with the use Rice had made of his Four Horsemen idea and with the way the *Herald-Tribune* had featured it. So delighted was Strickler with what had happened that he got inspired once again and figured out a way to make some money out of his idea so flamboyantly fleshed out by Rice. From New York, Strickler telegraphed to South Bend to arrange for Harold C. Elmore, a staff photographer for the *South Bend News-Times* to take pictures of Stuhldreyer, Miller, Crowley, and Layden in full football regalia but mounted on horseback as soon as he and they returned to the Notre Dame campus.[23]

Once back at Notre Dame, Strickler collected the only horses available to him. What he got were hardly the sort of steeds favored by ethereal biblical avengers. Strickler's father was employed as a manager of the university farms, and he obligingly provided four farm work animals for his son's project. Young Strickler and Elmore mounted Stuhldreyer, Miller, Crowley, and Layden attired in football uniforms and helmets on these weary-looking animals and photographed them. None of the players could ride or were familiar with horses. Though nervous about what they were doing, they cooperated with Strickler and Elmore and completed the photographing session.[24]

Strickler intended to print these pictures in an 8 x 10 format and make them available for distribution and sale to wire services, newspapers, magazines, and individuals around the country. He sent the Four Horsemen pictures to the wire services and to selected newspapers and awaited a reaction. It was not long in coming. Strickler's idea succeeded grandly and changed the young man's life completely.

In the weeks ahead wire services widely distributed Strickler's photographs along with Rice's lead. A Four Horsemen phenomenon captured the imaginations of sports enthusiasts across the country, creating a brisk market for Strickler's photographs, and he sold several thousand of them for a dollar apiece. By the end of January 1925, Strickler had netted for himself the substantial sum of $3,000.[25] So much had come so fast for Strickler that after the Army game he simply had no further time for academics. He kept his part-time job with Rockne until the end of the football season but stopped going to classes after returning to South Bend from New York.

Strickler left the university in January 1925 without having passed a course or earned a single academic credit during the one semester he was there. Financially secure for the moment with the proceeds from the sale of Four Horsemen photographs and known locally as the originator of the Four Horsemen idea, Strickler took a job as a reporter with the *South Bend News-Times* and began what was to be a long and varied but highly successful career in sports journalism and public relations. Justly and appropriately, Strickler was the first beneficiary of the Four Horsemen phenomenon that he had inspired and Rice had launched. There would be others.

— ii —

Of the four players immortalized as the Four Horsemen, not one of them suspected at the time that Rice's story appeared that their lives would be permanently changed by it. However, by mid-January 1925 these four young men had become living legends and knew it. Rice had given each of them a new special identity that would last as long as young men played intercollegiate football.

What of Grantland Rice the author of it all? In the month immediately following the appearance of the Four Horsemen story, he turned his attention to other teams and players. Rice had no idea at the time the Four Horsemen story was published that he was making sports journalism history. As a matter of fact, the author of it all did not even bother to travel from New York to Princeton, a week after the Notre Dame-Army game, to watch what he had described as the greatest backfield of any football age perform against Princeton. At the *Herald-Tribune,* the job of covering the Notre Dame-Princeton game was given to W. B. Hanna. Rice stayed in New York to report Columbia's win over tiny Williams College.[26]

On October 25, 1924, Notre Dame defeated Princeton 12 to 0, but the team did not play well. The players had experienced an obvious letdown after the Army game. Crowley scored two touchdowns, but overall team performance was enough to win but not much more. While covering this game, W. B. Hanna saw no shadowy horsemen galloping across a blue-gray sky. He described the game as unexciting and criticized Rice's backfield immortals for excessive fumbling.[27] It would appear that, for the moment at least, Rice's Four Horsemen had come to earth as mere mortals and had played as such against Princeton. At the end of October, Rice did not seem to care.

Actually, the game at Princeton on October 25, 1924, was the last opportunity for Rice to see Notre Dame play during the current season. The rest of Notre Dame football games would be played at home on Cartier Field or in the Midwest. Whatever Rice might say or write about Notre Dame, Rockne, or the Four Horsemen for the rest of this season would have to be derived from the reporting of others. Before Rice would say or write anything more or new about Notre Dame football, his interest would have to be piqued. That process took about a month.

It began with the game against Georgia Tech at Cartier Field on November 1. Notre Dame overwhelmed the southern team, 34 to 3 before a crowd of 22,000. As was by now a familiar Rockne tactic, the coach started the game with reserves. After Georgia Tech scored first on a field goal, Rockne brought in his first-stringers. Of the Four Horsemen, Stuhldreyer did not play at all. The other three only played for about a quarter, but when on the field their performance was spectacular. Crowley scored one touchdown and Layden scored two. Kenneth S. Conn, who covered the game for the *South Bend Tribune,* summarized the quality of play by writing that Tech had been beaten by "Notre Dame's wonder team and fell gloriously."[28] After the running of Crowley and Layden, another highlight of the day was the halftime presentation to Rockne of a new Studebaker Big Six touring car. This luxury automobile was given by a group of Chicago alumni in appreciation of the fame and glory that the coach had brought to their alma mater.[29]

A week later and only four days after Klan election triumphs in Indiana and elsewhere in the country, the game against Wisconsin was played before a capacity crowd in Madison. None of the many Notre Dame supporters traveling there from Chicago were disappointed with the result. Notre Dame easily defeated Wisconsin, 38 to 3. Though Rockne again started his second-stringers, the speed, power, and conditioning of the Notre Dame players, whether reserves or regulars, was too much for the Wisconsin team to handle. Again the Four Horsemen played up to expectations. Crowley, a native of Green Bay, Wisconsin, scored two touchdowns, including a sixty-five-yard run through the entire Wisconsin team. Miller and Layden also scored touchdowns. If Rice had been in Madison to see his creation perform, he would have been proud of them.

Because influentials in the Big Ten had regularly denied applications from Notre Dame for admission to their conference, any victory over a Big Ten team delighted Notre Dame administrators and faculty. Under ordinary circumstances a victory as decisive and one-sided as this one over a Big Ten school would have been a cause for celebration. However, in early November, the circumstances were not ordinary.

No one seriously interested in Notre Dame football fortunes believed that Wisconsin was a formidable opponent. Wisconsin was expected to lose, the only dispute was by how much. Most Notre Dame supporters regarded the Wisconsin game as a warm-up for the very serious encounter with Nebraska at Cartier Field on November 15. The visits of the Notre Dame team to play the Cornhuskers in Lincoln in 1922 and 1923 had been very unpleasant experiences. Not only had Nebraska narrowly defeated Notre Dame in hard-fought contests in both of those games, but the Notre Dame players were insulted and demeaned by words and signs in the stadium and in the city because they were Catholic and of Irish ethnicity.[30] There was a lot to remember about those previous visits to Lincoln, nothing to forgive, and a great deal to pay back. For some of those people described by William Jennings Bryan at the 1924 Democratic National Convention as being good in most things but mistaken in their anti-Catholic attitudes and needing to be taught the errors of their ways, a lesson was about to begin.

The lesson taught was a humiliating one. Notre Dame routed the Cornhuskers, 34 to 6, before 22,500 people, the largest paid attendance at Cartier Field up to that time. This game also reached directly and immediately thousands of people who were miles from the bleacher seats of the Notre Dame playing field. It was broadcast by the *Chicago Tribune* radio station WGN and was the first radio broadcast of a Notre Dame home game. With an intensely partisan crowd behind them, the Notre Dame team did just about everything right while Nebraska could hardly do anything at all.

Reporting the game for the *South Bend Tribune,* Kenneth S. Conn observed that Nebraska had been so badly beaten and was so outclassed that even the lopsided score of 34 to 6 failed to show the superiority of the Notre Dame team. Other statistics did. Notre Dame rushed and passed for twenty-one first downs while Nebraska managed only two. Notre Dame completed seven out of ten forward passes; Nebraska completed only one out of seven.

With statistics such as that against a team as highly regarded as Nebraska, no small wonder that the *South Bend Tribune* crowed loudly and proudly about Rockne's team being the crowned kings of intercollegiate football. Against Nebraska, the Notre Dame team, especially the incomparable Four Horsemen, had passed an acid test which entitled them to the praise of the critics as "the best backfield in modern football history."[31] Indeed, continued Conn, the football capitol of the universe has been moved to South Bend for this season. Rockne's extraordinary players have the "undeniable right to wear the purple toga and wave the football sceptre with undisputed authority."[32]

What gave the Notre Dame that right, Conn's purple prose notwith-standing, was a near perfect performance on the gridiron against one of the best teams in the country. Again Rockne started reserves, and poor ball handling allowed Nebraska to score the first touchdown of the game after recovering a fumble inside the Notre Dame ten yard line. That was all that Nebraska was able to do for the rest of the game. Rockne sent in his regulars, and the Four Horsemen ran wild. Crowley, Layden, and Stuhldreyer scored a touchdown apiece, and Miller scored two. The most spectacular play of the day occurred late in the third quarter when Layden slipped and from a near sitting position threw a short pass to Crowley, who then ran sixty-five yards for a touchdown.

Though few penalties were assessed during the game, play was ex-tremely rough. At one point near the end of the final quarter when the game was irretrievably lost, several Nebraska players piled on Stuhldreyer after he had been taken down. A fight on the field was averted only by the timely intervention of game officials.[33] No unnecessary roughness penalty was called for this incident or for any others occurring during the game. When officials purposefully do not look for rules violations, they are not likely to find any. In the interests of neutrality in this very important game, the officials were generally inclined to look the other way and let the winners win without much interference from them. Indeed, at the end of the day the defeats and insults of 1922 and 1923 had been properly avenged at Cartier Field in 1924. Nebraska had been humiliated. Notre Dame's past-due accounts with the Cornhuskers had been settled, but now Nebraska had a very large new one to pay off against Notre Dame next year at Lincoln.

Rockne was immensely satisfied with the outcome of the game with Nebraska. This win, he wrote to a former player on November 17, 1924, was "the most pleasing thing that has happened to me in years." It was so pleasing, Rockne reminded his correspondent, because "Nebraska, as usual was the dirtiest team we played, and after the game, a few of their players even called *me* a few choice epithets."[34]

As for Rice, he was absolutely overwhelmed by the phenomenon he had visited upon the curious and unpredictable world of sports jour-nalism. Sports writers all over the country used the words and the concept of the Four Horsemen in all sorts of contexts and in an endless variety of ways. After the Nebraska game, Rice seems to have recognized at long last that his Four Horsemen creation was the greatest thing he had ever done and proceeded to exploit it shamelessly. One newspaper executive re-ported to a friend at Notre Dame in November that Rice had "gone crazy about the Notre Dame backfield and has personally given you about as much publicity as his newspaper will permit. Every day he mentions them." Rice not only stated in his column on several occasions that the Four Horsemen were the finest backfield ever to play intercollegiate football anywhere, but he was inspired to compose doggerel verse about the exploits of his heroes and then publish samples of it in his column.[35]

Claiming national intercollegiate championship status with two games still to be played was risky business. The game against Northwestern played before 34,000 people on November 29 in the recently expanded municipal stadium, Soldier Field, in Chicago was the largest crowd up to that time ever to attend a football game in that city. Though Notre Dame was heavily favored to win, the two teams turned out to be evenly matched with Rockne's squad obtaining a closely contested narrow victory, 13 to 6.

Kenneth S. Conn noted that "Northwestern had two horsemen of its own," Ralph Baker and Robert Wienecke, "to pit against the four horsemen of Notre Dame and all six rode up and down the gridiron of the Grant Park stadium."[36] Actually, Northwestern scored first in the opening quarter when Ralph Baker kicked two field goals. Notre Dame took the lead in the second period when, after completing a pass to Miller on the Northwestern five yard line, Stuhldreyer rushed for a touchdown and Crowley kicked the extra point. Layden scored the second Notre Dame touchdown by intercepting a pass and running thirty-five yards for the final six points.

In this game, the Four Horsemen were unable to run against Northwestern as they had against other teams. Generally, Crowley and Miller were contained all afternoon. Passing won the game for Rockne's team and averted what might well have been the biggest upset of the football season. Notre Dame supporters left Soldier Field satisfied with the win but much chastened by the difficulty of obtaining it. Among other things, the well conditioned and coached Northwestern players had managed to bring the celebrated Four Horsemen to earth and demonstrated to the sports world their essential football mortality. There would not be much written in South Bend newspapers about Notre Dame as the national intercollegiate football champion until the final game of the season had been won.

Formally, the season ended a week later on November 29 against Carnegie Tech before a crowd of 35,000 in Forbes Field, Pittsburgh. In the Carnegie Tech game, as had been the case against Northwestern, the issue was very much in doubt throughout the first half. Once again Rockne employed the strategy of starting the game with reserves, and things did not go well at all. The Tech men scored first after blocking a Notre Dame punt. Immediately, Rockne put his regular players into the game, but they were unable to run successfully against the Carnegie Tech defense. Rockne's men were unable to score until well into the second quarter, when Crowley completed a pass to Miller for a touchdown and kicked the extra point, giving his team a one-point lead. Notre Dame extended that lead to seven points by quickly scoring another touchdown but failed to kick the extra point.

Carnegie Tech responded fiercely with a long drive of their own resulting in a touchdown, a successful extra point, and a tie score at halftime. The Tech team sensed the possibility of a major upset and played with utter abandon throughout the second quarter. According to Charles J. Doyle, who covered the game for the *South Bend Tribune,* Carnegie Tech players "exchanged punches with the crack South Benders and when the gong sounded the end of the first half the adversaries were still fighting toe to toe."[37] No officials intervened, and no penalties were assessed.

During the halftime interval Rockne surely said something to his charges that changed them utterly. Whatever Rockne said or did in Forbes Field on that day posterity has failed to record. Yet whatever it was, it worked. The Notre Dame team absolutely overwhelmed the Carnegie Tech team in the second half. Crowley and Stuhldreyer were brilliant, with forward passes being their weapon of choice. Notre Dame required only seven plays in the third quarter to take the lead. Rockne's men were never behind thereafter. The Four Horsemen could not be contained, scoring another touchdown in the third period and two more in the final one. Not until the closing minutes of the game and against third- and fourth-stringers was Carnegie Tech able to mount an offense and score a touchdown.

By defeating Carnegie Tech, 40 to 19, Notre Dame had finished the season undefeated and untied. According to Charles J. Doyle, Rockne's team was "the greatest eleven in the U.S.A. in 1924."[38] The claim of this Catholic school to be national intercollegiate football champions was indisputable. It would be up to others to try and prove otherwise.

— iii —

As the Four Horsemen public relations phenomenon grew after the Army game and when the prospects for an undefeated season became stronger after the humiliation of Nebraska in mid-November, California alumni began lobbying university officials and Rockne to bring the team to the West Coast for a postseason appearance in the Rose Bowl. Rockne was anxious to go, but Father Walsh was not. As a former vice president and thoroughly familiar with all aspects of the highly successful Notre Dame football enterprise, Walsh was worried about publicly identifying the university with the issues of overemphasis and overcommercialization currently plaguing intercollegiate football. Besides, the university's past experiences with the Rose Bowl Committee and with some Pacific Coast Conference teams had been unpleasant.

At the end of 1921, after completing a highly successful football season of ten wins and one loss, Rockne had started negotiations with the Rose Bowl Committee about a possible postseason appearance in Pasadena against the Pacific Coast Conference champion, University of California, Berkeley, on New Year's Day 1922. As a matter of fact, the *Chicago Tribune* reported on November 29, 1921, that an invitation to Notre Dame to play in the Rose Bowl was all but certain. However, when the wire services reported that three Notre Dame players had participated in a professional football game for the Green Bay Packers a week after the collegiate season had ended, the prospect of a Rose Bowl invitation collapsed. A member of the Rose Bowl Committee advised Rockne on December 14, 1921, that because of the stories about the professionalism of some of the Notre Dame players, the University of California had refused to play against Notre Dame.[39]

Again in 1923, after finishing the season with nine wins and one loss, Rockne heard from the Rose Bowl Committee about a postseason appearance in Pasadena. Mindful of the humiliating rejection of Notre Dame as an opponent for the University of California in 1921 and aware of Walsh's concerns about what postseason play would do to the academic image of the university, the Faculty Board in Control of Athletics refused to consider a formal invitation to play in the Rose Bowl. At this time, Rockne was unable to take his team to the West Coast.

Two years later, so much had happened during 1924 and so much had changed that Walsh was willing to reconsider, and then after some very hard negotiating he approved a postseason game for Notre Dame in the Rose Bowl on January 1, 1925. Walsh changed his mind for several reasons. First, he recognized what the intense media interest in Notre Dame football had done for the university as a whole. When reporters wrote about Rockne's success or the exploits of the Four Horsemen, they could not do so without also writing about the special religious and academic environment that had made such success and exploits possible. That sort of reporting, Walsh had been persuaded, was good for Notre Dame, for Catholic higher education, and for American Catholics generally in the bigoted climate of 1924.

Second, the Rose Bowl invitation provided an opportunity to resolve a long-standing, highly embarrassing problem involving finances, religious sensitivities, and gross presidential miscalculation. A flat guarantee from the Rose Bowl of $35,000 would allow the university to begin and complete a much-needed and desired expansion and renovation of the existing campus gymnasium.[40] This totally inadequate facility could be expanded and improved to include a new basketball arena with a seating capacity of 5,000.

The justifications for such a project in the presence of so many other pressing facility needs could be easily stated. An extremely important reason for expanding the present gymnasium was the present very embarrassing "undesirable arrangement" with the YMCA in South Bend for playing home basketball games. No one in the Notre Dame administration was happy with that. It was not the same as playing basketball in a Protestant church but came very close. So sensitive to the Protestant religious influences of that institution was the Notre Dame administration that in 1922 off-campus students had been prohibited from residing in the South Bend YMCA.[41] Another important reason for proceeding with the gymnasium expansion project was the simple but powerful fact that Rockne wanted it. He wanted a modern basketball facility so he could schedule better and more prestigious opponents.[42]

Concerned about this problem for several years, Walsh naively believed in 1923 that he had found a solution for it. In that year a possible donor for the gymnasium expansion project was referred to him. Walsh approached a very wealthy New Jersey Catholic, reputedly much interested in basketball, whose son had almost enrolled at Notre Dame two years earlier. Simply stated, for a donation of $27,000 Walsh offered to rename the improved athletic facility the Shanley Gymnasium.[43] Apparently, Walsh did not know and did not take the trouble to find out why the young Mr. Shanley had never enrolled as a student after a campus visit.

In 1921, Joseph Byrne, a devoted New York alumnus and friend of the Shanley family, had interested them in Notre Dame as a fitting place to send their son. Shanley seriously considered enrolling his son and a friend of his son who was an outstanding basketball player in the fall of 1921.[44] Shanley and the two young men visited the campus in May and were generally impressed by what they found, except for campus housing.

Shanley had expected that his son and friend would be accommodated in a two-room suite in one of the better residence halls. However, because of overcrowded conditions and because deposits already had been collected for virtually all campus rooms for the forthcoming year, the best that Father James A. Burns, president of the university, could find for these two young men was a single room with a very dark bath.[45] Burns absolutely refused to oblige Shanley by taking away a two-room suite already assigned. It would be the small single room with the dark bath or something in the city.

Used to preferential treatment in things that mattered, and apparently a proper room assignment for his son and friend mattered very much, Shanley left the university very angry and did not enroll either of the young men.[46] Why Walsh was so ignorant of the recent history of the relations between the Shanley family and the university is inexplicable. The Shanley Gymnasium was not to be. Shanley ignored Walsh's offer and did not respond.[47]

At the end of 1924 Walsh did not have to be convinced about the need for an expanded gymnasium and certainly wanted to forget about the Shanley gaffe, but he also continued to worry about the potential public relations damage of a postseason game in distant Pasadena. Walsh was particularly concerned about what Big Ten critics of the Notre Dame football program would say and do.[48] This whole project had to be done right if it was to be done at all.

When negotiations with the Rose Bowl Committee began in October, it appeared that this project was not going to be done right. From the perspective of the Rose Bowl Committee, Notre Dame was the attraction, Notre Dame would fill their stadium. Because the Rose Bowl Committee wanted to avoid repetition of the embarrassing circumstances of 1921, they decided to ignore the Pacific Coast Conference altogether and contracted with the Haskell Indians to play in the Rose Bowl as the West Coast representative. The committee had persuaded itself that the present Pacific Coast Conference champion, Stanford, would refuse to play against Notre Dame for the same reasons that the University of California, Berkeley, had refused in 1921: the alleged professionalism of some of the Notre Dame players and the alleged low academic standards of this Catholic university.[49] That was too much for Walsh. What was good enough for Stanford was good enough for Notre Dame. The Faculty Board in Control of Athletics dutifully refused to accept a postseason game with a school as academically suspect as the Haskell Institute.

At this point, the University of Southern California, runner-up in final Pacific Coast Conference standings, offered its team as an alternative to Stanford. However, a better financial guarantee from the Rose Bowl Committee persuaded the academic and athletic leadership of Stanford to reconsider their position. In late November, the West Coast school agreed to play Notre Dame in Pasadena for an even split of 60 percent of the net gate receipts, which in the end amounted to payments by the Rose Bowl Committee of $52,000 each to Notre Dame and Stanford.[50]

Finally, there was irresistible pressure from Father O'Hara, prefect of religion and unofficial keeper of the institutional conscience, to take the football team to Pasadena. O'Hara had a special gift of being able to talk Walsh into almost anything, and the matter of a trip to the Rose Bowl was a case in point. O'Hara saw the Rose Bowl invitation as an almost providential opportunity to counter the extremely negative Klan-inspired image of Notre Dame as an institution populated by well-to-do Irish American Catholic thugs and hooligans who were not serious about academic pursuits. More than that, if properly organized and managed, O'Hara believed, the Rose Bowl trip might well turn out to be the most successful advertising campaign for the spiritual ideals and practices of American Catholicism yet undertaken in this century.

O'Hara explained his hopes for the Rose Bowl trip after the fact in his *Religious Survey* for 1924–25. "Successful in every contest," O'Hara wrote, "the team travelled from coast to coast, winning friends by the qualities of gentlemanliness and true sportsmanship. Daily communion was an essential part of the season. . . . the fruits of Catholic education were recognized in the gentlemanly conduct of the team while bigotry and prejudice received an abrupt set back."[51]

With respect to the place of Notre Dame football within God's divine plan for the world, which O'Hara sometimes broached in his more euphoric moments of reflection on the memorable events of 1924, he did not address the question directly in the *Religious Survey* for 1924–25. However, some years later, in the *Religious Survey* for 1930–31, he raised as a rhetorical question the "far-fetched" idea that by showing that frequent Holy Communion was acceptable practice for full-blooded athletic champions, "God has made use of the Notre Dame football team to spread devotion to the Blessed Sacrament."[52] O'Hara also questioned rhetorically whether or not through the prestige of Notre Dame football achievement God had called attention to the aims, ideals, practices, and successes of Catholic education. O'Hara gave no explicit answers to either of those rhetorical questions in the *Religious Survey* for 1924–25 or for 1930–31; he did not have to.

However theologically simplistic or insightful O'Hara's idea of the Notre Dame football team as a providential instrument might turn out to be, Walsh was of no mind even to think about arguing with his popular prefect of religion about it. He had neither the energy nor inclination to do so. If that was what O'Hara wanted to believe and propagate, so be it.

A man who could believe such things and say so publicly without fear of embarrassment was so supremely self-confident to be capable of almost anything. Indeed, such a man ought to have a major role in the Rose Bowl project and did. After signing the contract for a Notre Dame appearance in Pasadena on New Year's Day, Walsh turned over the management of the Rose Bowl enterprise to O'Hara. He was the only Holy Cross priest to travel to Pasadena with the team.

Once in charge, O'Hara with full cooperation from Rockne proceeded to plan and then organize a three-week American Catholic public relations spectacular. Influential individual alumni, alumni clubs, and local Knights of Columbus councils were all enlisted as local organizers, hosts, and sponsors of a series of demonstrations of Catholic pride and achievement.

As planned by O'Hara, defeating Stanford and claiming the national intercollegiate football championship was only one of several reasons for going to Pasadena. Much more was involved in this trip than winning an important football game. Here were extraordinary opportunities to redeem the university and Indiana Catholics from the widely disseminated bigoted aspersions of the Klan and to display the manliness and wholesome spirituality of Catholic religious practices to as many journalists and ordinary people as possible. In this enterprise O'Hara was to receive strong support from enthusiastic alumni and Knights of Columbus councils from all over the country.

Among the most important alumni participating in the Rose Bowl project was Angus D. McDonald, a member of the university's Lay Board of Trustees and an executive with the Southern Pacific Railroad Company.[53] McDonald made available for the team and traveling party several Southern Pacific railway cars, including one specially outfitted as a rolling chapel, wherein O'Hara could celebrate Mass for the team, hear their confessions, and distribute Holy Communion on a daily basis. McDonald also facilitated arrangements for an elaborate schedule of complicated routings and stopovers on the way out to Pasadena and then for the return to South Bend.

The Notre Dame traveling party was composed of forty people: Father O'Hara, Coach Rockne, Assistant Coach Tom Lieb, thirty-three players, a student manager, and an influential alumnus and his two young sons. This Notre Dame party boarded their private railway cars in South Bend and went first to Chicago. The arrival of the team in Chicago was a news event and local reporters covered just about everything that happened to them while they were in the city. Local alumni and Knights of Columbus councils turned out in large numbers to honor the team and to be photographed with them. That was to be the pattern in city after city as the trip progressed.

The Notre Dame party reboarded their private railroad cars in the evening of December 20 and then, cheered by a large crowd, departed for Pasadena by heading south to Memphis. Arriving in Memphis in the morning of December 21, the players and coaches received their first taste of southern hospitality. After attending a special mass in the city, they were guests of local alumni and the Knights of Columbus at a hurried breakfast. From Memphis, O'Hara, Rockne, and their charges traveled south to New Orleans, where they enjoyed two hectic days of interviews, luncheons, banquets, receptions, a yacht trip in the Gulf of Mexico, and a tea dance.

The team was a huge favorite of the large local Catholic population, who turned out in large crowds to cheer and follow the players as they enjoyed the city.[54] In between social events, Rockne even managed to hold several workouts for the players in the Tulane stadium, one of which was an utter disaster. The players were so stuffed with oysters and creole food that they could barely run.[55] Rockne was so angered by the physical condition of the team that when two first-team linemen, Edward Huntsinger and John Weibel, broke his ten o'clock curfew to buy postcards in their hotel lobby to send to their families, the coach ordered them to pack up and return to South Bend. Only an eloquent plea for mercy by the team captain, Adam Walsh, and perhaps a kind word from O'Hara caused Rockne to relent and allow the two curfew breakers to continue the trip.[56] However, Rockne's anger with the squad's inordinate consumption of New Orleans hospitality continued unabated.

After the New Orleans episode, the Notre Dame entourage headed west along the Southern Pacific route to Houston, arriving there on December 24. In that city, the team was greeted and hosted at several functions by Father Matthew Schumacher, president of St. Edward's College in Austin.[57] Rockne worked the team hard in practice sessions in the Rice Institute stadium where their performance showed a great improvement over what it had been in New Orleans. After mass and Holy Communion on Christmas Day, O'Hara played Santa Clause for the players at a private party. The holiday spirit continued at a magnificent Christmas dinner hosted by the Knights of Columbus.[58]

The next day, the Notre Dame party left Houston, decided to cancel a scheduled stop in El Paso, and went directly to Tucson, where they stayed for six days. In Tucson the players enjoyed the hospitality of the local Lawyer's Club at a luncheon, visited an old Spanish mission, attended a grand banquet hosted by the Knights of Columbus, and were honored guests at several other dinners. The team also endured four days of vigorous football practice at the University of Arizona stadium. In Tucson the Notre Dame coaches were joined by Edward "Slip" Madigan, a former Rockne player, who was then head football coach at St. Mary's College in the Bay Area. Madigan had scouted Stanford for Rockne and had noted a sideline screen pass that the Stanford coach used two or three times a game. Quickly Rockne devised a defense for this pass play. While in Tucson he drilled his defensive backs, especially Crowley and Layden, to recognize situations when the play might be used and to cope with it.[59]

All pregame festivities and celebrations ended in Tucson. When the team and traveling party arrived in Los Angeles at 7:00 A.M. on December 31, they were greeted by several thousand supporters at the railroad station. At that early hour and place, local alumni, Knights of Columbus councils, and chapters of the Ancient Order of Hibernians presented a large silver football to the team.[60] After this presentation, Rockne and O'Hara wasted little time there. They took their charges directly to the Hotel Maryland in Pasadena and prepared for an afternoon practice session in the Rose Bowl.

In Pasadena all social activities and public appearances by the team either had been scheduled or were rescheduled as postgame events. New Year's Eve celebrations of any sort were scrupulously avoided. To insure that nothing untoward would occur on the night before the game, Rockne ordered an 8:30 bed check for all players on New Year's Eve and instructed the hotel telephone switchboard to hold all incoming calls to players until the next day when the game was over.[61] Thus isolated and protected, the players awaited the greatest moment in Notre Dame football history. On January 1, 1925, that great moment was upon them. After Mass, Holy Communion, and a hearty breakfast, the team and coaches went out to the Rose Bowl physically and psychologically ready to play, firmly believing that they could not lose. That belief, so firmly held when the team began its pregame warm-up in the Rose Bowl at 1:45 P.M., was to be severely tested before the day was out.

— iv —

The enormous pregame promotion and publicity notwithstanding, both Notre Dame and Stanford lived up to their respective football reputations and gave the 53,000 fans crowded into the Rose Bowl the great individual and team performances that they had come to see. Notre Dame defeated Stanford 27 to 10, but the issue was in doubt until the closing minutes of the final period. Even though the Notre Dame defense could not contain the running and passing of Stanford's huge fullback and All-American candidate, Ernie Nevers, it was a few timely spectacular defensive plays that won the game for Notre Dame.

Indeed, in game statistics Stanford outplayed Notre Dame in every important category except points scored. Stanford outrushed Notre Dame from scrimmage, registering seventeen first downs to only seven for Rockne's men. Stanford also outpassed Notre Dame, completing eleven out of fourteen attempts for 128 yards. Notre Dame completed only three out of seven attempted passes for forty-eight yards. Moreover, Stanford's powerful line managed to stop the running attack of the Four Horsemen, and after the start of the second period kept the Notre Dame offense contained well within its own territory.[62] Yet, Notre Dame won the game, because Elmer Layden played the best football game of his life.

Once again, Rockne started his second team, and they quickly showed themselves unable to stop Stanford's bruising running attack. Stanford scored first, early in the game, by kicking a field goal. Offensively, Rockne's first team proved to be no better than the reserves. The Four Horsemen could not mount a sustained drive against the huge but agile Stanford line. A game break occurred late in the first period when a poor Stanford punt put the Notre Dame offense on the Stanford thirty-two yard line. Seven plays later, Layden scored the first Notre Dame touchdown on a three-yard run early in the second quarter.[63] Crowley's try for the extra point was blocked, but Notre Dame had taken the lead in this game, 6 to 3. That touchdown was to be the only one scored by the Notre Dame offense in the entire game.

Stanford fought back fiercely, driving to the Notre Dame six yard line. After failing to gain on an off-tackle rush, Nevers attempted the long-awaited sideline screen pass which Madigan had alerted Rockne to expect. Layden was perfectly positioned to intercept, which he did, and then ran seventy yards for Notre Dame's second touchdown. Crowley kicked the extra point, giving Notre Dame a halftime lead of 13 to 3.[64]

During early moments of the third quarter, Stanford moved the ball well but was unable to cross the Notre Dame goal line. They had two missed field goals. Notre Dame could do nothing offensively and were contained within their own thirty yard line throughout the period. About halfway into the third quarter, a Stanford halfback fumbled a punt reception on his own twenty yard line. An alert Notre Dame end—Edward Huntsinger, one of the players almost sent home from New Orleans—scooped up the ball and ran for a touchdown. Again, Crowley kicked the extra point, thereby increasing Notre Dame's lead, 20 to 3.[65]

Stanford's best scoring opportunity came toward the end of the third period when Nevers intercepted a Layden pass on the Notre Dame twenty-nine yard line. Seven plays later, Nevers threw a ten-yard touch-down pass. Cuddeback kicked the extra point, narrowing Notre Dame's lead to only ten points.[66]

The final quarter opened with Stanford intercepting a pass on the Notre Dame thirty-one yard line. In seven running plays Stanford moved the ball to a fourth down situation inside the Notre Dame one yard line. Never's rush for the touchdown failed by inches, and the ball passed over to Rockne's men on downs. Notre Dame was unable to move the ball and punted it away. Stanford drove down the field deep into Notre Dame territory, only to lose the ball on a pass interception.

After an exchange of punts and with about two minutes to play, Stanford had the ball on the Notre Dame thirty-five yard line. Once again, Nevers attempted a sideline screen pass. Once again, Layden was properly positioned, intercepted the pass, and ran seventy yards for his third touchdown of the day. Crowley kicked the extra point, giving Notre Dame a comfortable lead, 27 to 10. The game ended shortly thereafter with Notre Dame in possession of the ball on their own twenty-two yard line. The national intercollegiate football championship indisputably belonged to Rockne's team. Celebration of that fact followed the team wherever it went in Los Angeles and elsewhere and lasted for twelve days.

For the players, the Rose Bowl game had been so physically exhausting that no one thought seriously about celebrating their great victory that evening. Most of the players were too tired to attend a postgame dinner dance that had been scheduled for them. Instead, they elected to retire early in order to be rested and refreshed for the many events and activities that the Notre Dame Alumni Club of Los Angeles had organized for them on Friday, January 2.[67]

The day began with a grand tour of Hollywood and its studios. Movie stars and starlets were present and waiting for the team. Photograph opportunities were abundant. Movie stars posed with players, and photographers captured the moment. Agents handed out studio publicity pictures of their clients, and the stars were there to autograph them. This very busy day ended with an elegant dinner dance for the team and traveling party hosted by the Notre Dame Alumni Club in the Hotel Biltmore in Los Angeles. It was an affair to remember, described by one the participants as "one of the outstanding events of the trip."[68] If O'Hara can be believed, through all of this socializing in circumstances rife with the most dangerous sort of temptations, the players always deported themselves as good Catholic gentlemen. They were a credit to their university and to their religion and probably an utter astonishment to some of their Hollywood hosts.

In the early morning of Saturday, January 3, the Notre Dame traveling party boarded their railroad cars and headed north for San Francisco with O'Hara and assistant coach Tom Lieb in charge. Rockne and his wife remained behind in Los Angeles resting and attending to personal business. O'Hara, Lieb, and the team arrived at the Palace Hotel in time for still another magnificent dinner dance hosted by local alumni and several Knights of Columbus councils and attended by the Irish American mayor of the city and other local dignitaries. Once again, the players and coaches were charming, properly dressed, and well behaved.

On Sunday, the team rose early and traveled to the cathedral for a Mass celebrated by Archbishop Edward Hanna. The players greeted parishioners after Mass and then returned to the hotel for breakfast. Next followed an automobile tour of San Francisco, ending at the home of Senator James Phelan, Montalvo, about fifty miles south of the city. Phelan had arranged a formal reception for the team, and they spent most of the day at Montalvo, returning to San Francisco in time to be guests of the cast of *Mitzi*, then playing at the Columbia Theatre. After the performance and cast party, the Notre Dame group boarded their railroad cars and departed for Salt Lake City.[69]

After arriving in that Mormon-dominated community in the morning of January 5, the team was given a bus tour of the city and of points of historic interest. Apparently O'Hara made a quick decision that the famous Mormon Tabernacle was not really a non-Catholic church and allowed his charges to visit this historic building and attend an organ concert there. After the concert, there was dinner, a reception, and late evening departure for Cheyenne and a taste of the Wild West. When they came into the capitol of Wyoming on January 6, O'Hara, Lieb, and the rest quickly discovered that local Catholics intended to make the most of their visit. The team was supplied with six-gallon cowboy hats, serenaded by a local military band, given the key to the city, and feted at a western barbecue. On leaving Cheyenne in the evening of January 6, the Notre Dame party proceeded straight south to Denver, where the Notre Dame Alumni Club had organized what turned out to be the most spectacular reception of the entire trip. Every moment of their time in Denver was accounted for and nothing was left to chance.[70]

A huge crowd thronged the Denver railroad station to greet them. In the first rows of this crowd was a large group of mothers of Notre Dame students from the Denver area and elsewhere in Colorado. Behind the mothers were rows of attractive, well-dressed young ladies who surged forward to decorate the players with flowers and kisses. Liberated from the young ladies by Alumni Club leaders, the team and coaches were piled into Packard cars and driven up Seventeenth Street through the heart of the financial district. They received continuous ovations from crowds lining their route, which ended at the Denver Athletic Club. The Notre Dame party escaped into that facility, where they were able to rest and get some refreshment.[71]

That evening, the Notre Dame team and coaches were honored at a grand banquet held in the University Club of Denver. They formed a receiving line and stood in it for almost two hours. Everyone in Denver of any standing from the governor of the state on down passed through it. Over two hundred attended the banquet, including college presidents, football coaches, newspaper publishers, and sports writers. Notre Dame colors were everywhere, and Notre Dame songs were sung.

The Denver business and professional community heard more about the athletic and academic history of Notre Dame that night than they could ever possibly internalize and remember. Tom Lieb spoke for the team and for the Notre Dame administration at the banquet when he tried to tell the audience in a simple but convincing way what the university meant to them. First, he introduced the players one by one. Then, when speaking about the university Lieb made points that O'Hara and enthusiastic alumni had been making in every place visited on the trip.

The purposes and values of American Catholic higher education—instruction in a morally and philosophically secure environment—had been articulated so often by so many that neither Lieb, O'Hara, nor any of the the other Catholics there present needed to do more than allude to them. Indeed, Catholic assumptions that Thomistic philosophy born and developed in the thirteenth century could teach correct thinking processes to contemporary students and provide worthy answers to the great philosophical and ethical dilemmas of the modern era were not shared by many Americans of the other persuasions or by those of no persuasion at all.

However, the idea that morality could be taught and learned, that human behavior could be changed, that people could be improved—that is, made better persons for having taken a specific set of college courses—was something that Americans of all persuasions wanted to believe. That was the aspect of Catholic higher education, the morally secure environment of Notre Dame and the moral improvement going on there, that Lieb addressed in the Denver Athletic Club. He tried to explain to his audience that what made Notre Dame different and special was the religious and moral spirit of the place. Everyone at the university was touched by it.[72]

No one attending the Notre Dame banquet that evening, wrote one account of Lieb's speech, "could ever forget that Notre Dame builds character, manliness, and uprighteousness, along with wonderful football elevens."[73] The appearance and mien of the players reinforced everything that Lieb had said. The Denver press picked up on Lieb's explanation of the Notre Dame spirit and lavishly praised "the quiet unassuming young men who came through as the University's football heroes."[74] The message about Notre Dame and American Catholic education that O'Hara wanted to deliver had been delivered all across the country. If Denver was any example, this message was received and believed.

The next stop after Denver was Lincoln, Nebraska, and because of past anti-Catholic and anti–Irish American expressions by locals when the team had played there, no one in the Notre Dame party knew what to expect. The team arrived in Lincoln on Thursday morning, January 8, and the people of Lincoln were on their best behavior for the short time Rockne's men were there. The Notre Dame party was greeted and treated in a manner befitting the new national intercollegiate football champions. They were hosted at an informal dinner by the chancellor of the University of Nebraska, the head football coach, and other university officials. The highlight of the stay in Lincoln was a collective invitation to attend the inauguration of the new governor of the state.[75]

Exhausted by the required socializing of the last nine days, and by now sick to death of nonstop smiling in receiving lines, the Notre Dame party returned to their railroad cars in the late evening of January 8 for a night's sleep and an early morning departure to Chicago. When they arrived in the Windy City on January 9, the Notre Dame traveling party broke up. Some remained in the city to be entertained by alumni, others visited family and friends in the Chicago area, and others went directly to South Bend. One way or another, the entire Notre Dame group was back in South Bend and at the university by January 12. Rockne arrived shortly thereafter.

Indeed, the heroes were home at last. The great cross-country tour was over, and no one who made it would ever forget the experience. They would not forget because there simply had never been anything like this Notre Dame Rose Bowl tour in the entire history of American intercollegiate football up to this time. Even more important, because the circumstances surrounding the tour were so extraordinary there would never be another like it ever again.

The Rose Bowl victory and triumphant tour was too glorious an event to be remembered only as a football game. The sort of historical experiences encountered by the Notre Dame community during 1924 could not be repeated. In particular, for O'Hara the emotional experience of the trip to Pasadena and back, constant attention from the press, and recognition as national champions was too much for him to internalize in a totally rational way. He saw the hand of God clearly at work during the football season of 1924. In route to the Rose Bowl most of the Catholic players received Holy Communion every day, and in O'Hara's mind this extraordinary example of religious observance by renowned athletes had profound consequences for the team, the university, and perhaps even the whole country. This trip and the religious behavior of the players making it, O'Hara believed, turned out to be among other things a great "crusade for the spread of Holy Communion."[76]

Moreover, in the trip to and from the Rose Bowl, O'Hara saw and articulated an extraordinary relationship between a "properly guided sport" such as football and good religious practices.[77] Simply stated, O'Hara considered football as developed and played at Notre Dame as an aid to religion and as a character builder. Because of the physical risks attendant upon playing the game, good Catholic players acquired the desirable habit of frequent prayer, that is, by praying for protection from football injuries.[78]

Beyond the value of prayerful habits, there was, of course, a high probability that temptations of the flesh would be lessened. Players simply would not have enough time for such diversions. By occupying all idle time and by providing the disciplinary training of physical mortification, submission of the will, and by promoting such natural virtues as courage, initiative, generosity, equanimity, dependability, alertness, and frankness, football was in many of its effects spiritually uplifting.[79] This form of argument was original to O'Hara at the time and has generally remained such ever since. Not many other responsible academic and athletic administrators since those inspiring days of 1924 and 1925 have had the nerve to use it.

Actually, O'Hara pushed this argument about as far it could go by contending that the university varsity monogram had historic associations and special religious sensibilities attached to it. According to O'Hara, that monogram was regarded by the players as being another type of devotional aid, much like a rosary, scapulars, or holy pictures. The monogram was seen by most of the players "as a badge of Our Lady, the heavenly patroness of the school; and its wearers looked upon themselves as her knights, performing a lowly honorable service in her honor, just as the fabled Juggler of Notre Dame did his tricks before her shrine, and as David danced before the Ark of the Lord."[80] Given the utterly corrupt world of intercollegiate athletics, this sort of argument went very far indeed and was credible only to the most uncritical true believers of Notre Dame mythology.

Having said that, however, and even after discounting O'Hara's emotional excesses, one must recognize that the religious spirit informing the football team during the season of 1924 was so powerful and evident that even Coach Rockne, the great motivator, was touched by it. Although he was normally undemonstrative about religion, some time after the Rose Bowl victory and triumphant national tour Rockne asked for religious instruction, was baptized, and was received into the Catholic Church in November 1925.[81]

— v —

In the end, the Notre Dame team had played and convincingly defeated an academically respectable opponent and had visited the West Coast and many other places for the first time. With the Rose Bowl payment of $52,000 in hand, Walsh got an improved and expanded gymnasium, but improved and expanded far beyond what he had initially considered.

The relatively modest expansion originally envisaged in the earlier Shanley scheme, which would cost only $27,000, escalated significantly. As Walsh saw the present situation, the university needed a basketball facility that it could be proud of.[82] That meant not only a facility with a seating capacity of at least 5,000 but also dressing room accommodations worthy of the athletic reputation of the institution. Notre Dame athletics, Walsh argued, was on the "crest of a wave" and with the right kind of a basketball facility "high class teams could be brought to the University."[83]

When plans for the gymnasium expansion were completed, Walsh expected the cost to be $50,000. The first bids received from contractors priced the project at $180,000. Changes in the plans reduced the costs to $149,000, but even that amount was too much for Father Gilbert Français, the superior general, to approve for a gymnasium. Only after Father Charles L. O'Donnell, the provincial superior, assured Français that there would be no need to borrow money for the project because football profits would provide the cash to pay for it, did he approve the expenditure of $149,000 for the basketball arena.[84] Begun in the summer of 1925 and completed in the fall, the new facility opened formally on November 20,

1925, with a memorable concert performance by the celebrated Irish tenor John McCormack.

O'Hara's idea of turning a trip to the Rose Bowl into a spectacular cross-county Catholic public relations tour with many stops en route as well as his management of that tour had been brilliant. In this whole episode, O'Hara's unfailing optimism, good sense, and indefatigable energy marked him as one probably destined for future leadership roles in the university community and perhaps even in the American Catholic Church itself. Not only was O'Hara a highly successful pastoral innovator, but he was very much a practical man of affairs. He understood money and possessed excellent managerial skills. Most people liked him personally and would usually take his advice or do what he asked.

For the university, the tour was a public relations triumph. For American Catholics generally, Notre Dame's victory over Stanford was an achievement that no one could diminish, and the tour was a magnificent opportunity for them to express collective pride and group solidarity. Not only were these extraordinary athletes and coaches from a Catholic university a group of genuine American heroes, but they had behaved on and off the field as exemplary Catholic gentlemen. Rockne's ever-present smile and wry sense of humor made friends for the university at every stop. Layden's modest off-field demeanor combined with his superb performance in the game was inspiring. Lieb's simple but moving exposition of the Notre Dame spirit in Denver was unforgettable. All of this, O'Hara orchestrated brilliantly. These Catholic gentlemen athletes from Notre Dame were special men from a special place. Forgotten and now totally replaced was the recent Klan-inspired image of Notre Dame students as hooligans.

For the Four Horsemen, the Rose Bowl was a fitting climax to a splendidly played and expertly managed intercollegiate football career. The adulation heaped upon them was overpowering, and at least one of them was not able to handle it well. Crowley, never a strong student, had tried both the College of Arts and Letters and the Law Course of Studies and was unable to finish either one. He stopped going to classes during the spring semester of 1925. There are no existing university records indicating that Crowley ever graduated from Notre Dame. Stuhldreyer graduated from the College of Arts and Letters *cum laude* in June 1925. Miller and Layden managed to complete the Law Course of Studies and graduate with their class.

After leaving the university, each of the Four Horsemen tried to make the most of their celebrity status. Each of them played professional football for one team or another on weekends, and all became college coaches at one time or another and enjoyed modest to great success in that very uncertain trade.[85] Of course, Layden returned to Notre Dame and served as head coach, 1934–1940, moving on to become commissioner of the National Football League, and later an executive in the transportation industry. The others all enjoyed varying degrees of success in business after leaving coaching. Because the American public would not forget them, the Four Horsemen were always in great demand as speakers and presenters. Like it or not, these men would always have a public life of some sort and each in his own way had to adapt himself to the demanding role of an untarnishable American sports icon.

With regard to Stanford, beyond the financial guarantee it is not clear what that university got out of this entire Rose Bowl episode. The Stanford coaches and players made mistakes which lost them a game that they probably should have won. The great Ernie Nevers made this same point in a slightly different way. Responding to an interview about this game thirty-five years after the event, Nevers observed, "A total of 150 yards in two tries and two touchdowns makes the passing combination of Layden of Notre Dame and Nevers of Stanford the best in Rose Bowl history."[86] In any case, Stanford and Notre Dame did not play another intercollegiate football game until 1942.

11

Power Won,
Then Thrown Away

Precisely when the peak of Klan power and influence in American public life during the 1920s occurred is difficult to determine. By the time the great election successes of 1924 had been achieved, the earlier bastions of power in the South and West were already deteriorating. The Indiana organization was deeply divided. Growth and expansion of the Klan in Illinois and Ohio were over. Nonetheless, national Klan leaders were justifiably jubilant over their many successes in the elections of that year and proceeded to act as if their moment of greatest opportunity had arrived. The national Klan leaders believed that many state legislators, governors, congressmen, and senators were now much beholden to them. Even though the president was not one of them, clearly he was not publicly against them either. As a matter of policy, Coolidge had handled all requests and demands from Klansmen and anti-Klansmen in the same equally nonresponsive way.[1] In late November 1924, from the perspective of the national Klan leadership, the present and future had never looked better.

Evans had many good reasons to be pleased by the elections of 1924 and showed it. After the enactment of the immigration restriction law of 1924, Evans proclaimed the national and state elections of that year as the greatest and most recent of Klan triumphs. Immediately after the elections, Evans boarded his private railway car and headed west on a grand tour of those states where Klan-supported candidates had done so well.[2] He convinced himself and others that with such an enormous enlargement of Klan political influence in Congress as well as among state legislators, enactment of a Klan-inspired legislative agenda for the country was now possible.

At the center of Klan domestic legislative concerns was creation of a national department of education with cabinet-level status for its head. Klan leaders also pressed for enactment of the Towner-Sterling education bill, which would have increased significantly federal participation in and control of the entire elementary and secondary school system. Similarly at the state level, friendly legislators in Oregon, Washington, and Michigan introduced a variety of antiparochial-school measures.[3] What the Klan and other groups fearful of the alleged divisive effects of Catholic schools hoped to obtain by such ambitious national and local efforts was more money for what they perceived to be a much-needed Americanizing public education monopoly.

For such true believers, a correct form of public education would follow from better trained teachers, higher paid teachers, better physical education programs and facilities, and new campaigns to combat illiteracy and Americanize aliens. Only the federal government could provide the direction and financing as well as the enforcement/regulation procedures required to raise and Americanize educational standards for all children throughout the country.[4] For that sort of federal aid to education, the time was not to be now. President Coolidge and other states' rights advocates were not ready for anything like a national department of education, and enthusiastic Klan support of it turned out to be counterproductive.[5]

In any case, considering the source of inspiration for a national department of education, clerical and lay Catholic leaders, ever anxious to protect and preserve their schools, adamantly opposed all forms of federal aid to and federal control of education and stridently maintained that opposition for the next forty years. Opponents of a national education department and of Towner-Sterling proved indefatigable and managed to sidetrack or defeat such measures whenever advocates proposed them.[6]

Postelection euphoria notwithstanding, the greatest Klan success in Washington, D.C., occurring during 1925 was not that of influencing legislation. It was in public relations. Klan leaders obtained permission to hold a national meeting in the city and parade through the capitol area unmasked but otherwise in full regalia during the second week of August. Klansmen expected that Coolidge would be in Washington in August for the parade because at one time when Governor of Massachusetts, he had addressed a meeting of the Catholic Holy Name Society. Klan leaders reasoned that having spoken to an exclusively Catholic group, the president owed the Protestant Klan at least a presence at their grand national parade. As was his style, Coolidge said nothing one way or the other about the Klan parade in the nation's capitol and spent August at his summer home in Swampscott, Massachusetts. The only notice of the event taken by the president was to authorize deployment of a special detail of marines to guard the Treasury Department while the Klansmen were in the city.[7]

The Klansmen came to Washington in force for the weekend of August 7, 1925, and the city and country were much impressed. On Saturday, August 8, more than forty thousand Klansmen and Klanswomen in full regalia marched sixteen to twenty abreast down Pennsylvania Avenue to Fifteenth Street, where they wheeled left into the grounds of the Washington Monument. Attired in a flowing royal purple robe trimmed in gold, Evans was in the lead contingent. Bossert, Evans' man in Indiana, walked beside him dressed in a business suit. Sometimes they marched silently, but usually bands played patriotic anthems or hymns such as "Onward, Christian Soldiers" and "Oh, Come All Ye Faithful."[8]

Most of the eastern states had units in the parade. The largest contingents had come from Pittsburgh and Akron.[9] The most photographed marchers were Virginia's nubile platoon of Kluxettes, carrying two enormous American flags, who stretched across Pennsylvania Avenue to collect donations. By the end of that very busy day, Klan leaders had produced a most impressive display of numbers, enthusiasm, and organization. It was the largest Klan parade ever, not equaled before or since.

After the parade, there were wreaths to be placed on the tombs of the Unknown Soldier and the recently deceased champion of Protestant Fundamentalist America, William Jennings Bryan. There were speeches to be delivered and an enormous cross to be burned in the Arlington Horse Show Grounds. When all of this was over and the last of these predominantly northern Klansmen had departed for their homes, there was a Klan public policy agenda to be enacted and implemented. For Evans and those around him, that agenda was easily and simply stated. It was time, at long last, that Catholic power in America be significantly and permanently reduced.

Klan efforts to keep Catholics in their place had foreign policy dimensions as well as domestic ones. Perfervid Klan opposition to United States participation in the Permanent Court for International Justice derived as much from contemporary anti-Catholicism as from those enduring fears of possible American involvement in any sort of League of Nations activities. Klan leaders worried about the possibility of the World Court somehow overturning United States immigration restriction laws in order to flood the country with Catholic aliens.[10] Similarly, Klan leaders, especially Evans, were extremely outspoken about the American government maintaining a strict noninterventionist policy toward Mexico.

When American Catholic leaders protested against the anticlerical policies of the new government in Mexico, Klan leaders regarded President Calles campaign against clerical control of education in that country as part of a great struggle to obtain religious liberty and said so. Evans publicly praised the education policy of the Mexican government and rhetorically offered to extend Klan protection to Mexico against subversion and attack by worldwide Catholicism.[11]

With regard to the serious domestic problem of curbing Catholic power and influence in American life, Evans frequently denounced the extraordinarily arrogant official Catholic position of no salvation outside of their Church and often railed against Catholic discriminatory and restrictive marriage practices. Obtaining any sort of federal legislative relief on such matters, Evans believed, was hopeless. Catholic lobbyists were too affluent, too well organized and effective to expect that Congress would ever act on behalf of Protestant interests in anything. For those very practical reasons, in the spring of 1927 Evans and local Klan leaders looked to state legislatures to protect Protestant America.

With little regard for First Amendment rights, friendly state legislators introduced Klan-inspired bills that would punish public criticism of civil marriages, prohibit prenuptial agreements prescribing the religion of children born of interfaith marriages, and ban interracial marriages.[12] Some legislators went so far as to introduce bills banning the Catholic fraternal organization Knights of Columbus. None of these bills were ever enacted. By 1927 so many embarrassments had occurred, especially in Indiana, that Klan membership had declined precipitously. Indeed, times had changed and in this matter very quickly. Though anti-Catholicism remained alive and respectable in America for many years and would enjoy a powerful renaissance in the national election of 1928, the time for such anti-Catholic bills ever being enacted by state legislatures had passed.

— ii —

While most Hoosiers and certainly most Indiana newspapers had followed the fortunes and savored the triumphs of the Notre Dame football team in the Rose Bowl, there is no evidence that either D.C. Stephenson, leader of the break-away Indiana Ku Klux Klan organization, or Walter Bossert, leader of those Indiana Klansmen still affiliated with the national Klan organization, had paid much attention to what the team had accomplished in Pasadena or had done on its trip back to Indiana. Both these men were preoccupied with planning strategies and agendas for the next session of the Indiana legislature. Stephenson, as the governor-elect's principal political advisor, had the additional task of organizing Ed Jackson's gubernatorial inauguration ceremony on January 12 and post-inaugural gala later that evening.

Jackson was inaugurated in grand style. The ceremony began at noon on January 12, 1925, in the main corridor of the state house. A light snow failed to diminish the enthusiasm of the more than 5,000 Republican faithful who crowded into the statehouse, blocking stairways, and filling up halls and corridors to watch their new governor take the oath of office. The people present did not see much and heard hardly anything at all. Jackson's inaugural speech was marvelously unspecific and mercifully brief, lasting only three minutes. With the formalities over, the serious business of celebrating could begin.[13]

Ordinarily, Indiana Republicans held their inaugural parties in their own private place, the Columbia Club on Monument Circle, right in the heart of Indianapolis. However, in January 1925 the Columbia Club was closed for renovation and reconstruction. For that reason, the Republicans moved their party up Meridian Street to the newly completed rival Democrat facility, the Indianapolis Athletic Club. The center of social activities that evening was to be on the fourth floor in the magnificently ornate ballroom. Tables had been arranged around the dance floor to accommodate about 150 leading Indiana Republicans and their wives and guests.

Great attention had been given to seating arrangements to insure that known incompatibles would not be forced to endure one another and thereby dampen festivities. As a matter of fact, Bossert had not been given an invitation and did not attend. In the lottery of dispositions worked out, Stephenson found himself placed at a well-located table, seated across from Madge Oberholtzer, an attractive, well-informed, ambitious, twenty-eight-year-old enthusiastic Republican volunteer campaign worker who was employed as the manager of the Indiana Young People's Reading Circle, a special section of the Indiana Department of Public Instruction.

The Athletic Club orchestra performed well. Speeches from the governor, other state officials, and honored guests were tolerable, but the entertainment provided by the Republican State Committee was disappointing. William Herschell, a local poet known best for extremely sentimental verse, had agreed to recite one of his rustic favorites, "Ain't God Good to Indiana," and did. Then, an Indianapolis entertainer, Roltaire Eggleston, told some jokes and tried to amuse the audience with magic tricks.[14]

In the course of a long and otherwise very boring evening, Stephenson exhibited no interest in either Herschell's recitation or in Eggleston's sleight of hand. Though accompanied by a lady, Stephenson's attention became more and more centered on Miss Oberholtzer. Before the evening was over, Stephenson and Oberholtzer talked at length about a variety of subjects, and when the dance music began, he invited his new friend out on the floor.[15] Indeed, both Stephenson and Oberholtzer left the Athletic Club that evening with their earlier escorts. Nonetheless, the acquaintanceship between Stephenson and Oberholtzer begun that night would develop and in four months' time would lead to terrible tragedy for one and disaster for the other.

—   iii   —

As the January opening of the Indiana legislature approached, Klansmen and their many thousands of sympathizers throughout the state expected great things from their newly elected Republican governor and Republican-controlled state senate and house of representatives. At long last, morality, patriotism, and Protestantism had a fair prospect of being revived and restored as meaningful influences in Indiana public life. That was what Klan candidates and their supporters had promised, and that was what the Indiana legislature was expected to do.

Pressure for enactment of a 100 percent Americanist legislative program was supposed to come from Klansmen legislators and from local Klan organizations, but in Indiana the Klan was sharply and deeply divided into two and sometimes into three factions. In January 1925, as the leader of the national Klan organization in the state, Bossert was very serious about developing a new legislative program based on Klan principles. Indeed, Bossert was a bigot, honest about that and also honest about most other things as well. As leader of the Indiana Klan, Stephenson had his own very ambitious personal legislative agenda and cared little about Klan principles or about principles of any sort. Publicly, Stephenson was not very honest about that, and as events would soon show, he was not really very honest about much of anything.

Bossert and his supporters were extremely candid about their legislative intentions in the forthcoming session of the Indiana state legislature. As a matter of fact, Bossert held a widely publicized meeting of national Klan organization loyalists in the Indianapolis Athletic Club on January 6, 1925—six days before Jackson's inaugural party in the same facility—to plan and prepare a regular Klan program for the legislative session.

Out of this meeting came a national Klan organization consensus in the state to press for legislation that would prevent Catholics from teaching in Indiana public schools, abolish Catholic parochial schools in the state, and require the formal introduction of Protestant religious values into public school curricula. However, Bossert and his friends meeting in the Indianapolis Athletic Club were not content with simply trying to drive Catholics out of Indiana public and private education.[16] Also, ways had to be found to employ state power on behalf of righteousness, that is, enact laws that would encourage a greater sense of personal moral responsibility among Hoosiers and otherwise protect and improve the overall moral climate of the state.

In due course, Bossert's friends in the state legislature introduced two bills to ban Catholics from teaching in the public schools. First, a bill to prohibit the wearing of religious garb in the public schools was directed at a very small number of nuns who had been hired by a few school boards in some parts of the state.[17] Because only a handful of nuns were involved in such situations, the problem addressed by this bill was more symbolic than real. It was a fact of Hoosier political life, however, that paying Catholic nuns for any reason with public money was unpopular. In the end, the religious garb bill won approval in the Indiana House of Representatives, 67 to 22, but failed overwhelmingly in the state senate, 40 to 6. Most senators had been persuaded by their leaders that if the employment of a few nuns as teachers in one or two public school districts was a problem, it should be resolved locally, not by the state legislature.

Bossert's second bill was more serious. If enacted, his teacher qualification bill would have established a public school education as a requirement for a public school teaching license in the state of Indiana. Under the provisions of this bill, persons educated in Catholic schools or in other private schools would be denied Indiana teaching licenses and thereby disqualified from employment as public school teachers anywhere in the state.[18] This bill also commanded significant support throughout Indiana. It confronted legislators with a very difficult choice, a choice that turned out to be too difficult for most of them to make. Ultimately, the bill failed in the state senate but not by a direct vote for or against. The senate voted, 41 to 5, to postpone consideration of it until an impossible day.

Abolition of Catholic parochial schools in Indiana was attempted by a sweeping but constitutionally suspect measure that simply would prohibit all parochial schools and all private nonmilitary schools from operating in the state. This bill also provided fines and jail sentences for parents who sent their children to such schools.[19] While long established military schools such as Culver and Howe were not included in the ban, other Indiana private schools and academies were. The bill was much too broad based—attacking all private nonmilitary schools—and far too draconian in prescribed penalties to have much chance of enactment. Again, the bill passed in the House, but failed in the senate. Despite these notable and widely publicized failures, the Klan's legislative assault on Indiana Catholic schools went on. Several other Klan-inspired bills tried to cope with the perceived problems of foreign and disloyal influences permeating Indiana Catholic schools in other ways. One bill required all Catholic schools to adopt the same textbooks used in the public schools. This bill passed the House by a wide margin but died in the senate.

However, there were some successes. A bill requiring all public and private schools in the state to display the American flag publicly was enacted into law. A bill mandating that all children attending any school in the state must study the Constitution of the United States at an appropriate time in their curriculum also became law.[20]

At least two bills dealt with the issue of formally introducing Protestant religious values into the public schools. The strategy employed was that of simply universalizing common practices in many Indiana school districts. One bill required public school teachers to lead their students in prayers and read portions of the Bible—King James version—to their students on a daily basis. This bill passed the House by the very wide margin of 75 to 11, but lost in the senate by only six votes. Opponents of this bill in the senate insisted that it was patently unconstitutional. One very frustrated senator felt obliged to remind his colleagues that their body was, after all, a legislative assembly, not a religious synod. Measures of this sort had no business coming before them.[21]

Nonetheless, bills of a religious nature continued to appear on the legislative calendar. A bill introduced in the state senate went far beyond praying and Bible reading and directly challenged the First Amendment. The state senate bill extended the public school curricula by two hours a week and mandated that those additional two hours be devoted to religious instruction.[22] This bill passed the senate but failed in the House.

The problem of finding ways to use state power to promote personal moral responsibility and improve the general moral climate of Hoosier social life proved to be perplexing and difficult. To be sure, the experience of trying to enforce Prohibition laws on an unwilling and uncooperative population had been neither edifying, successful, nor a model for any other sort of moral improvement strategy. Nevertheless, supporters of this great social experiment were of no mind in 1925 even to think about abandoning it. Although the idea that morality could be and ought to be legislated commanded wide acceptance throughout the state, deciding what to do and how to do it did not. The best that Klan leaders were able to do for Hoosier morals in the legislative session of 1925 was to offer a bill that would establish a state commission to censor "immoral motion pictures."[23] That bill died in the state House of Representatives.

As has been seen many Klan-inspired educational and moral improvement measures were introduced, but only two of the most innocuous ever became laws. Certainly, the American flag display law and the provisions mandating study of the United States Constitution in all Indiana schools intimidated no one, nor did it force new policies or programs in the cases of most school districts. The flag was already publicly displayed at virtually every Indiana school and studying the United States Constitution was already part of every school curriculum.

These Klan-sponsored education bills failed in the Indiana legislature for two principal reasons. First, many Hoosier state senators, particularly those elected from sharply contested districts, were fearful of turning all Catholic voters against them by casting recorded votes against parochial schools. Second, Senator James J. Nedjl of Lake County, chairman of the state senate education committee was an inveterate opponent of the Klan and of all Klan-inspired measures. Nedjl either stopped such bills in his committee or let them come to the floor of the senate only when in search of headlines and when defeat was certain.[24]

Recorded floor votes on defeated Klan bills were newsworthy events that were widely reported in newspapers across the state. It would appear that in the minds of the many Hoosier true believers in the Klan principles of Protestantism and "100 percent Americanism," the utter failure of Klan leaders to carry any sort of anti-Catholic program through the Indiana legislature marked them as being no different and certainly no better than other Indiana politicians. Thus began a popular disenchantment with both Klan organizations in the state that other events would very soon intensify. Those other events were consequences of the extraordinary ambitions and bizarre behavior of D. C. Stephenson.

— iv —

As one of Governor Jackson's principal political advisors, Stephenson's ideas about what to do with his greatly increased influence and power in Indiana public affairs after the election of 1924 were vastly different from those of Bossert and other true believers in Klan principles. It would be incorrect to argue that Stephenson cared nothing about trying to incorporate Klan principles into legislation intended to reform and improve Hoosier educational programs and social life. Indeed, he cared about that, but he cared much more about increasing his personal wealth and political power. Stephenson saw the election results in Indiana in 1924 as providing himself with extraordinary opportunities to increase the one and expand the other.

Great political influence with the governor and power in the state leg-islature had a very high cash value in Indiana in 1925 because lobbying activities in the state legislature had gotten completely out of hand. Lob-byists seemed to be everywhere, operating out of offices, private clubs, the better restaurants, and even in the halls of the statehouse itself. The lobbying situation in 1925 had become so flagrantly open and uncontrol-lable that the lieutenant governor and Speaker of the House had to do something. Lieutenant Governor Harold Van Orman delivered a power-ful public denunciation of special-interest influences in the legislature on February 5, 1925, which was widely reported in the Indianapolis press. Van Orman complained that lobbyists had crossed the line between legitimate informational and educational activities and unabashed im-propriety. According to Van Orman, lobbyists brazenly summoned sena-tors and representatives out of their respective chambers to receive vot-ing instructions. Some lobbyists went so far as to enter the chambers themselves and actually occupy the seats and desks of senators and repre-sentatives.[25] For the lieutenant governor and Speaker of the House that sort of unconscionable effrontery was too much. They ordered General Assembly gatekeepers to banish all lobbyists from the floors of the senate and house.[26]

This highly competitive, totally corrupt world of avaricious legislators and affluent lobbyists was one in which Stephenson was very comfort-able. By all accounts, he navigated through it with ease and skill. Stephen-son always knew what he wanted and worked very hard to discover what others needed. His ingenuity lay in an extraordinary ability to bring those two sets of circumstances together for mutual benefit.

The two most important measures directly affecting Stephenson's per-sonal interests to come before the Indiana legislature in 1925 were bills to reform the state highway commission and to require nutrition education in the public schools of the state. In these matters as in others during the course of the session, Stephenson planned to do very well for himself by appearing to do good things for others.

When the legislature opened in January 1925, the honesty of the state highway commission was highly suspect. Rumors abounded about the disposal of an estimated $8 million of surplus war material given to the state by the federal government. This material consisted of trucks, wagons, and heavy machinery dating from 1917. All of this equipment had been turned over to the state highway commission for appraisal and disposition. By most accounts this material was mostly inoperable, rusted, in bad repair, and damaged from lack of maintenance. The com-missioners decided to sell most of it for scrap metal. Two Indianapolis scrap metal dealers—Victor and Moses Goldberg—purchased most of this surplus material. Conventional wisdom maintained that they had done so on extremely favorable terms.

Allegations of graft and corruption by the commissioners were made by individual state legislators so often and carried in the local press that the Marion County Grand Jury looked into the matter. Indictments were returned charging the commissioners with grand larceny and embezzlement. On March 4, arrest warrants were issued for John D. Williams, Director of the State Highway Commission, Earl Crawford, a commissioner, and the Goldberg brothers. This alleged scandal was front-page news for weeks in the Indianapolis press, and editorials calling for an immediate reform of the state highway commission were numerous.[27]

Despite the enormous negative publicity connected with this affair, highway and construction lobbyists rallied to the defense of the beleaguered commissioners and their manner of doing business by protesting that the charges against them had been exaggerated and that the whole investigation had been politically motivated. From the perspective of the lobbyists, something else seemed to be intended but no one could be sure what it was. As the case wound its way through the courts, the lobbyists turned out to be right insofar as Indiana judges and jurors were concerned. The value of the surplus war material had been vastly overstated, the terms of the sale were reasonable, and no larceny or fraud by anyone was provable. Nonetheless, the idea of reforming the state highway commission had been firmly planted in the public mind, and Stephenson was ready with a plan.[28]

First, Governor Jackson spoke out in favor of a new state highway commission that would be more responsive to the needs of the people. Next, William N. Kissinger, a Republican state representative from Columbia City, drafted and introduced a bill that would dismiss the present state highway commission and authorize the governor to appoint a new one in its place. Opposed vigorously by highway lobbyists who were content with the present system and suspected that more was at stake here than administrative reform, the Kissinger measure became known in the press as the "road ripper bill."[29] Revealed later in court proceedings was the fact that Stephenson had initiated and orchestrated press reporting of the alleged scandalous activity of the present highway commissioners and intended to influence Jackson's choice of a new director and of new commissioners.[30]

Stephenson's motives for publicizing allegations of scandalous activity by the state highway commissioners and for promoting reform of that commission were uncomplicated. With a new highway commission in part named by him, Stephenson assumed that he and some of his new friends highly placed in the Indiana Republican party would be advantageously positioned to obtain some of the most lucrative state contracts presently held by others.[31]

Soon after Jackson had been elected, Stephenson and his friends had formed a new company—the Hammond Construction Company—to handle the business which a new and properly reformed and staffed state highway commission could send their way. In addition to this new company there were some older established ones anxious to do business with a new commission. George V. "Cap" Coffin, head of the Marion County Republican organization expected a percentage of cement contracts, and Lawrence Cartwright, Republican chairman of the Eighth Congressional District, owned a company ready and able to supply the state highway commission with crushed stone.[32] As Stephenson had intended, once the "road ripper" bill became law, there should be something for everyone with demonstrated loyalty to the Jackson regime.

However, even the most thoroughly prepared plans could not anticipate and cope with every possible contingency. In this instance Stephenson had underestimated the amount of influence exercised by the highway lobby in the Indiana legislature. That very important special interest group wanted no change in the personnel or structure of the present state highway commission. Nonetheless, despite spirited and apparently well financed opposition to the "road ripper" bill, it passed all three readings in the House of Representatives. The lobbyists prevailed in the senate. They managed to stop it on the last day of the session. Stephenson's friends in the senate were unable to bring the bill to the floor for a final vote. The session ended before a final vote could be taken.[33]

Disappointed certainly at the end of the session over the fate of the highway commission reform bill, Stephenson managed that disappointment very well. After all, other measures touching Stephenson's personal interest introduced earlier had fared much better. Enactment of a nutrition education law by the state legislature in early March was entirely Stephenson's work and shrewdly calculated to make a great deal of money for him.[34]

This newly enacted nutrition education law directed and authorized the state superintendent of public instruction to provide proper rules and regulations for the teaching of a course in diet and nutrition in all elementary and secondary schools in the state. As enacted, this law detailed precisely what the content of such a course should be. While the law did not mention a specific textbook by name as fulfilling the content requirements of such a course, there was only one that did.[35]

Stephenson had hired Madge Oberholtzer, an employee of the Department of Public Instruction, to help write *One Hundred Years of Health,* a textbook precisely organized and written to meet all of the content objectives of the new nutrition education law. Stephenson also purchased a small Indianapolis publishing company, McClure Publishing, to prepare, print, and market this book throughout the state.[36]

Stephenson had met Miss Oberholtzer for the first time at Jackson's inaugural gala, and in time his interest in her would go far beyond whatever writing ability she might have had and her strategic placement in the Department of Public Instruction. For the moment, however, Stephenson saw Oberholtzer as an important part of a process to get his nutrition education book written, adopted by the Department of Public Instruction, and then purchased by all Indiana public schools.

To be sure, Stephenson's scheme was ingenious. Knowledge of the food needs of the human body and of how to combine and balance foods properly was important information for Hoosier parents and school-children to have. Yet, Stephenson's scheme for delivering that information was also an object lesson in how to translate political influence into real money without getting caught. Altogether, this scheme was Stephenson doing what he did best.

Also, during the legislative session Stephenson attended to and successfully pursued more traditional, tried and true, methods of influence peddling. Friends in the House of Representatives cooperated to introduce a bill that would prohibit public utility holding companies operating in the state from holding stock in other public utility holding companies. This bill was extremely complicated, understood by few, and never intended by its sponsors to have been enacted. The sole purpose of introducing the measure was to extort money from utility companies to insure defeat of it. In this totally nefarious enterprise Stephenson appears to have succeeded grandly. According to one account, Samuel Insull, the celebrated Chicago utility magnate, was supposed to have paid Stephenson $200,000 to stop the bill, which he did.[37]

Two other bills provided Stephenson with opportunities to sell his influence to lobbyists anxious to purchase it. First, a bill prohibiting manufacturers from dumping trash into streams was introduced early in the session and alarmed several companies engaging in that practice. This bill went nowhere. A Stephenson associate testified in later court proceedings that his boss had planned to ask the affected companies for $75,000 to defeat the bill. Whether anyone actually paid for Stephenson's influence on this matter is unknown.[38]

Second, Indiana fire insurance companies strongly opposed a bill that would have encouraged competition in their industry by repealing an existing law prohibiting out-of-state insurance companies from selling fire insurance in the state at rates lower than those set by the Indiana Insurance Rate-Making Bureau. Stephenson offered his services to the insurance lobby to kill this bill, which he managed to do. On February 12, the House voted to postpone consideration of the bill to an impossible day. How much Stephenson received for his services, if anything, in this instance is also unknown.[39]

Finally, a bill sponsored by the dairy industry requiring more descriptive labeling of packages of oleomargarine encountered unexpectedly strong opposition early in the session in the House of Representatives. One of Stephenson's associates testified later that he approached dairy lobbyists for donations to insure enactment of this special interest legislation. Whether any donations for this project were forthcoming is anyone's guess, but on February 26 the bill failed in the House by one vote.[40] Overall during the legislative session of 1925, Stephenson's influence in the Indiana state legislature proved to be sufficient to stop any measure he wanted defeated but insufficient to insure enactment of all bills he wanted passed.[41]

Stephenson's ability to deal successfully with lobbyists depended on their perceptions of his political influence with the governor and in the state legislature. He represented himself as a political mastermind who could get anything done for anyone for a price. During the winter of 1925, Stephenson worked very hard to embellish and expand perceptions of himself among lobbyists as an expert political fixer by arranging who would be the next Republican candidate for mayor of Indianapolis. If Stephenson could arrange candidate selection for that important office in the May primaries and then win the general election in the fall, he would be the most powerful political manager in the state, having very close ties to the governor, to many members of state legislature, and to the mayor and city government of Indianapolis. Stephenson's boast, much reported later in the press, that in Indiana he was the law would be very close to being true.

Stephenson decided to support John L. Duvall, present Marion County treasurer, for the Republican nomination for mayor of Indianapolis in the May primary elections. Duvall's only serious opponent for the mayoralty nomination, Ralph Lemcke, was the candidate of the reigning Indianapolis Republican party boss, William Armitage. A man used to exercising virtually unlimited power in the city and county and reputed to be closely connected with local gamblers, Armitage was of no mind to share ill-gotten gains or anything else with a political newcomer such as Stephenson. Armitage was an old-line Republican party war horse who was neither impressed nor intimidated by local Klan rhetoric or organizational power.[42]

As Stephenson saw the political situation in Indianapolis, the issue to be resolved in the May primary elections was control of the local Republican party. That could be achieved only by defeating Armitage's mayoralty candidate, Lemcke, in the May elections. Because Stephenson was prepared to mobilize Indianapolis Klansmen for any mayoralty candidate unconnected with the Armitage machine, Duvall was almost an irrelevant player in the fight between Stephenson and Armitage for control of the Indianapolis Republican organization. In pre-election meetings and strategy sessions, Stephenson treated Duvall as such.

According to Duvall's recollection of the circumstances surrounding his decision to run for mayor of Indianapolis, written thirty years later, he was visited by a committee of fourteen Indianapolis Klansmen a few weeks before Christmas in 1924. This committee of Klansmen assured Duvall that their organization was so powerful in the city that their support would be sufficient to nominate and later elect Duvall or anyone else mayor of Indianapolis. Duvall considered this extraordinary offer for about two weeks and then accepted it.[43]

Next, a few days before Christmas, Duvall was summoned to appear before Stephenson in his offices in the Kresge building, where the terms for obtaining Indianapolis Klan support were clearly set out. Duvall had to agree to make no appointments to any position as mayor without first consulting Stephenson. Duvall agreed to do so. Stephenson presented him with a written agreement specifying what Duvall had promised to do about future appointments. Duvall signed this agreement, which Stephenson described at the time as a contract, and filed it as an assurance of Duvall's good behavior after becoming mayor of Indianapolis.[44]

However, that one written agreement was only the beginning of Stephenson's demands upon Duvall. After the legislative session had closed and the opening of the primary election season approached, Stephenson met with Duvall and with about thirty Klan members of the Indianapolis Klan organization in the Washington Hotel in mid-March to plan election strategy. So certain of the primary and general election outcomes were the men at this March meeting that at the end of it Stephenson called Duvall aside and asked him to speak with Claude Worley for a few moments.[45]

A close friend of Stephenson and a former sheriff from Franklin, Indiana, Worley was Stephenson's candidate for the post of chief of police of Indianapolis after Duvall became mayor. It was reasonable that Worley should make the future mayor's acquaintance. Duvall spoke with Worley and then agreed with Stephenson that he was the man for the job. Duvall also agreed with Stephenson that a city highway commissioner ought to be added to the city's Board of Public Works and that his friend and mentor in the Kresge building ought to be the one to name him. Stephenson and his new Republican friends might have lost easy access to state highway and paving contracts, but Duvall's election as mayor of Indianapolis would give them a virtual monopoly of city road repair and paving business.[46] After all, something was better than nothing. This arrangement could turn out to be a reasonable compensation for the loss of the "road ripper bill."

Indeed, Stephenson's rapid rise to prominence in Indiana Republican politics was absolutely unprecedented. There simply never had been anything like D. C. Stephenson in Indiana politics. Although no one attending the meeting at the Washington Hotel in mid-March suspected that Stephenson's extraordinary career was about to change, his descent began in the late evening of March 15 and turned out to be even more spectacular than his rise.

— v —

On Sunday, March 15, 1925, Miss Madge Oberholtzer returned to her parents' home, where she lived, in the Irvington section of Indianapolis at 10:00 P.M. after an evening out with a gentleman friend. Upon arrival, she learned from her mother that earlier in the day Stephenson's secretary, Fred Butler, had called her with an important message from his boss about the nutrition education book that she was working on. Madge returned the call and spoke with Stephenson, who requested that she come over to his mansion, a short distance from the Oberholtzer home, at once to discuss some important matters before he left for Chicago that same evening. Stephenson offered to send one of his bodyguards, Earl Gentry, to the Oberholtzer home to escort Madge down the street to the Stephenson mansion.[47]

Madge agreed to go as summoned, informed her parents about what was happening, and, accompanied by Gentry, departed for the Stephenson mansion. At that moment, everything seemed quite proper. However, Madge never returned home that night, nor by March 16 had she directly communicated with friends or family. Her parents had become seriously alarmed. Given the nature of the situation in which they found themselves, the Oberholtzers called their family lawyer, Asa J. Smith, for advice about they ought to do.

Smith responded sympathetically and professionally to the distraught parents. He tried to calm them down by saying that everything would probably turn out to be alright. He told them not to worry, that he would investigate and call them back when he had something to report. Next, Smith called Bert C. Morgan, a Prohibition enforcement officer, who also did investigative work for local lawyers. Morgan was also a close friend of Harry G. Leslie, Speaker of the House in the General Assembly. Morgan knew something about Stephenson's power and influence in Indiana politics and cautioned Smith about rash and precipitate action. He warned against driving over to the Stephenson mansion and demanding to see the Oberholtzer girl. Morgan suggested a slower approach, that is, to try and find out as much as possible about what had happened before confronting Stephenson.[48]

Later in the day, Mrs. Oberholtzer received a telegram from her daughter saying that she was being driven to Chicago but would return to Indianapolis on an evening train. Smith, Ermina Moore, a close friend of Madge, and Morgan went to the Union Station in the early evening to meet all of the trains coming from Chicago. Madge was not on any of them. When the last train left at 10:00 P.M., Morgan went home, and Smith drove Moore to the Oberholtzer home. By now it was past 11:00 P.M., but Smith, Moore, and Mrs. Oberholtzer decided to drive to the Stephenson mansion. After knocking on the door for fifteen minutes, the two women roused Fred Butler and one other Stephenson employee. Both of these men denied any knowledge of Stephenson's whereabouts. With no information forthcoming and with nothing else to do, Smith drove the women to their homes and then went home himself.[49]

The first break in this mysterious disappearance occurred in the morning of March 17 when Madge was delivered to her home in Irvington by a man later identified as Earl Klinck, one of Stephenson's bodyguards. Mrs. Oberholtzer was out of the house when Madge was returned. A woman boarder with the Oberholtzers, Eunice Schultz, answered the door and watched Klinck carry Madge up to her bedroom. Klinck told Miss Schultz that Madge had been in an automobile accident. She was hurt but had suffered no broken bones. Klinck left the house as soon as possible, identifying himself as Mr. Johnson from Kokomo. Miss Schultz looked at Madge and observed that she was in a terrible condition. She was conscious, groaning, had bruises on her face, and lacerations on her chest. Schultz called the Oberholtzer family doctor, John K. Kingsbury, who lived nearby. Dr. Kingsbury went directly to the Oberholtzer home to examine Madge, and after asking several probing questions about how she got herself into such a desperate condition, she began to tell him an incredible story about the events of the past three days.[50]

According to what Madge Oberholtzer told Dr. Kingsbury on March 17 and repeated later for Smith, her lawyer, when she arrived at Stephenson's house he was very drunk and clearly indicated that she would not be allowed to leave. Two other men were drinking in the kitchen and together with Stephenson, they forced her to take several drinks. Stephenson told her that they were all going to Chicago on the late evening train. She was forced into a car and driven to Union Station, where Madge, Stephenson, and Earl Gentry, a Stephenson bodyguard, boarded a sleeping car bound for Chicago. She was forced into a private compartment and then into a lower berth with Stephenson, while Gentry climbed into the upper berth in the same compartment. At this point, Stephenson forced Madge to disrobe and for the next several hours proceeded to assault, rape, bite, chew, and pommel her. According to Madge, Stephenson bit and chewed all over her body. She had bite marks on her neck, face, tongue, breasts, back, legs, and ankles.[51]

Perhaps wary of the legal consequences of taking Madge in her present situation across a state line, Stephenson, Madge, and Gentry got off the train in Hammond, Indiana. With daybreak several hours away, the Stephenson party proceeded directly to the Indiana Hotel in that city. They registered for two rooms, one for Stephenson and Madge and the other for Gentry. Stephenson and Madge laid down on the bed in their room and very quickly Stephenson fell asleep. According to what Madge told Kingsbury and repeated for Smith later, she slipped Stephenson's revolver from his pocket and considered killing him as he slept. Thinking better of such a horrendous act and of the disgrace it would bring upon herself and her family, Madge decided to kill herself instead. She passed into the bathroom with Stephenson's revolver and actually placed the barrel of the gun to her temple, checking in the mirror to be sure the shot would go where intended. After looking at herself in that pose a while, she thought better of this course of action as well and decided to find some other means of ending her life.[52]

When Stephenson awoke she asked him for money to buy a hat, because she had left her home without one, and to purchase some cosmetics. Stephenson gave her fifteen dollars and ordered Gentry to accompany her to some nearby stores. He remained in the hotel awaiting the arrival of his car and driver from Indianapolis. Madge and Gentry went first to a milliner's shop where she bought a small silk hat and then to a drugstore to purchase a lipstick. Once in the drugstore, she went to the back of it away from and out of Gentry's hearing and asked a clerk there for a box of bichloride of mercury tablets, a popular disinfectant and in some circles an agent for inducing abortions. The clerk provided the tablets without question. She paid for them and immediately concealed the box in her purse.

Though out of Gentry's scrutiny and hearing for several minutes, she asked the clerk for nothing else, no help, no police assistance, and passed no notes of any sort. After completing her purchases, Madge and Gentry returned to the hotel. Once back in her room, Stephenson and Gentry left the room to confer with Stephenson's driver, who had arrived from Indianapolis with the car. Though left alone, apparently Madge gave no thought to attempting to escape from her captors. Instead, she arranged the bichloride of mercury tablets in groups of threes on her bedside table and swallowed six tablets. She had intended to take them all but could only manage six because the pain and distress in her stomach was immediate and extremely intense.[53]

Madge started vomiting and may have fainted. Sometime in the afternoon Stephenson's driver came into Madge's room and asked what had happened. She told him. Stephenson rushed into the room demanding to know why she had taken poison. Madge responded simply by saying that after what had been done to her, she wanted to kill herself. Stephenson called her a fool and then immediately took charge of the situation. He sent Gentry out to buy a bottle of milk which he forced Madge to drink and ordered his driver to get the car so they could return to Indianapolis.[54] Some consideration was given to the possibility of taking Madge to a hospital in Hammond to have her stomach pumped, but that option was abandoned as being too risky.[55] Instead, the group piled into Stephenson's car in midafternoon and headed for Indianapolis.

For Madge, the seven-hour drive to Indianapolis was an utter horror. The milk therapy prescribed by Stephenson did not work. Wedged between Gentry and Stephenson in the rear seat of the car, and kept in a sitting position, Madge became violently ill during the trip and vomited all over the inside of the car. She cried and screamed throughout most of the journey from Hammond to Indianapolis. The group reached Stephenson's mansion in the early hours of Tuesday, March 17. Madge claimed later that once in Indianapolis, she had begged Stephenson to get her medical help, but he refused. Instead, he raved and ranted that she would stay where she was until she agreed to marry him, thereby eliminating the possibility that she might testify against him in court. By morning, Madge had fallen asleep and Stephenson's temper had calmed. Klinck woke Madge and indicated that he was going to take her home, which he did.[56]

That was the story Madge told to Dr. Kingsbury and would later tell to Smith and others. For the moment, however, Kingsbury was most concerned about treating his patient. Apparently, he ruled out transporting her to a hospital. Instead, he contacted the Nurses' Exchange and engaged

a full-time nurse to stay with Madge. With the help of the nurse, Kingsbury inserted a tube down Madge's throat and flushed out her stomach.
Next, he tried to raise her low body temperature with blankets. By the
early afternoon, Kingsbury believed that everything he could do to treat
and comfort his patient had been done. He left Madge in the care of the
nurse and promised to check back on her progress later in the afternoon.[57]

After the doctor had departed, the Oberholtzers called Smith, who
came right over to the house to talk with Madge. He saw at once that she
had been brutalized, was told that Stephenson was responsible, and that
Madge had ingested a quantity of bichloride of mercury. At this point
Smith took charge of this incredible situation, and things began to
happen.[58]

To Smith, Madge Oberholtzer's situation appeared to be an open and
shut case of assault and battery, rape, and possibly kidnapping. All that
Smith needed to proceed in this matter was permission from the woman's
parents to file formal charges against Stephenson. However, there were
other considerations. If Madge recovered from the poison, would the
Oberholtzers be willing to endure the lurid publicity attendant upon the
trial of a celebrity such as Stephenson? As Smith evaluated the situation,
there was no need to move hastily until they had a better understanding of
Madge's physical condition and prognosis.[59]

Madge had no doubts at all about her physical condition. Many times
during conversations with Smith, Madge stated that she did not expect to
get well and was in such agony that she wanted to die. Kingsbury confirmed Madge's self-diagnosis. He told Smith that she would probably not
live longer than three or four weeks.[60] Though well aware of Kingsbury's
opinion that Madge would probably die, Smith made no move toward the
police or the county prosecutor's office. Instead, joined by another attorney, Smith decided to confront Stephenson with what he knew about
Madge's ordeal and then begin a discussion about some sort of out-of-
court financial settlement for Madge in the event that she recovered and
for the Oberholtzers if she did not.[61]

Smith and his partner had some difficulty getting an appointment
with Stephenson. A meeting was arranged, but nothing came of it. After a
brief but pointless conversation, Smith was referred to Stephenson's
lawyer, Robert Marsh, for further discussion of the Oberholtzer matter.
Smith met with Marsh later that day, and in the course of this meeting
Marsh denied that Stephenson had any connection with the assault and
rape of Madge Oberholtzer. Marsh stated to Smith that an incident of that
nature had occurred in Stephenson's mansion and that his client knew the
man responsible. Because the incident had occurred in Stephenson's

house he was prepared to admit some financial responsibility and pay a reasonable settlement to keep his friend out of court and off the front pages of the local press.[62]

Smith told Marsh that he did not believe a single word of Stephenson's story. Marsh responded by asking what the Oberholtzers intended to do about this business. Smith stated unequivocally that Madge Oberholtzer ought to be liberally compensated for what had been done to her. Marsh offered to recommend a compensatory payment of $5,000, but not a dollar more. Smith rejected that first offer out of hand, and the lawyers ended their meeting with nothing decided except that they would meet again during the next few days to discuss the matter further. In the course of the week, the lawyers met several times with Marsh standing firm on his initial offer of $5,000 and with Smith insisting upon at least $10,000.[63] On March 26, Smith learned that Madge's condition had deteriorated. Kingsbury told the family that Madge was dying, and her lawyers should try to get a formal statement about her ordeal as soon as possible before it was too late to do so.

Assisted by Ermina Moore, Smith spent the next two days working with Madge and stenographers preparing a formal account of her abduction, assault, and rape. Smith and Moore completed this account, a dying declaration by the victim, and obtained Madge's notarized signature on it.[64] Smith did not have to think very long about the next step, because at long last the Marion County prosecutor's office began to move into the case.

Will Remy, recently elected Marion County prosecutor, was one of the few Indianapolis Republican election winners without ties or obligations to Stephenson for election assistance. Remy had heard the same courthouse rumors about Stephenson's problems as everyone else, and on Saturday, March 28, he called Smith and asked whether there was anything they should talk about. Smith indicated that there was and arranged a meeting with the prosecutor for Sunday morning, March 29, in Remy's father's house.[65]

Remy was a very strong Republican but also intensely anti-Klan. He had no use for Klan principles and deeply resented the virtual takeover of the Indiana Republican party by Stephenson and his Klansmen friends. Because of Remy's anti-Klan stance and past associations with former governor McCray, now in a federal prison, Stephenson had tried unsuccessfully to exclude Remy from the Republican ticket in Marion County. Despite Stephenson's efforts, Remy won the primary and general elections handily, getting more votes in Marion County than even President Coolidge. Moreover, at a postelection victory party for Marion County

Republican election winners, Remy was the only one among them who refused to praise Stephenson publicly for the money and effort expended on behalf of Marion County Republican candidates. Remy did not like Stephenson personally or politically and was eager, almost enthusiastic, about proceeding against him.[66]

At his meeting with Remy, Smith read Madge's statement aloud to the prosecutor, who listened intently and asked questions about when and how the statement had been prepared. After hearing Smith's reading of Madge's statement, Remy knew that the entire case against Stephenson rested upon it. The next day, Monday, March 30, Remy began gathering information and other statements necessary to proceed with a prosecution. He collected a statement from Madge's father, George Oberholtzer, about the events of March 15 to 17 and received the signed originals of what was now being described as Madge Oberholtzer's dying declaration. By Thursday, April 2, Remy had a warrant for Stephenson's arrest prepared; and indeed, later on that day, Stephenson was arrested in his suite of rooms in the Hotel Washington on charges of assault and battery with intent to commit murder, kidnapping, and conspiracy to commit a felony.[67]

Stephenson was brought to the Indianapolis police headquarters, questioned briefly by the supervisor of detectives, and then brought into the lockup area for formal booking. One of Stephenson's attorneys contacted two bail bondsmen, who posted a $25,000 bond required for his release. Stephenson was back on the street only a few hours after being arrested. Remy announced immediately that a Marion County grand jury would begin investigating the case on the next day, April 3, which they did.[68] The grand jury returned an indictment against Stephenson on April 4. The *Indianapolis Star* carried a full account of Stephenson's arrest and release on April 2 while papers in other parts of the state reported the events on April 3.[69]

Arraignment had been scheduled for Friday, April 3, but had to be delayed until Monday, April 6 because Klinck and Gentry, also named in the arrest warrant, were out of town for the weekend. Finally, on April 6, Stephenson was arraigned alone before Judge James A. Collins, a local politician who had been identified in *Tolerance* two years earlier as a Klan member. Klinck and Gentry would be arraigned together later in the day.

Stephenson had secured the services of Euphraim Inman, the best known criminal lawyer in Indianapolis during those years. At Stephenson's arraignment, Inman pleaded his client not guilty and then requested that Judge Collins quash all further proceedings on the grounds of insufficient evidence. Collins responded by agreeing to hear Inman's argument for dismissal on Saturday, April 11.[70]

After leaving the court in very good spirits, Stephenson spoke briefly with reporters, stating that the charges against him were nothing but political chicanery, and the Oberholtzer case was just another effort by the Evans-Bossert Klan faction in Indiana to discredit and punish him. That faction was extremely fearful of his political influence with Hoosier voters and worried about what he might be able to do in the primary and general elections of 1926. He assured reporters that there was absolutely nothing to the charges lodged against him and then, exuding supreme self-confidence, went away to attend to normal business matters.[71]

For the moment Stephenson's business was anything but normal. He had to round up Klinck and Gentry and personally deliver them to the office of Omar N. Hawkins, sheriff of Marion County. Hawkins was an avowed Klansman and very sympathetic to Stephenson in his present circumstances as well as beholden to him for past political and financial support. Hawkins knew Klinck personally, because Klinck had been on the sheriff's payroll as a deputy since the November elections. After Klinck had been named in the arrest warrant, Hawkins took him off the county payroll but remained on friendly terms with him.

Hawkins brought Klinck and Gentry before Judge Collins forthwith, and both men pleaded not guilty. After posting a bond of $5,000 each, both men were released from custody. As scheduled by Judge Collins, Stephenson, Klinck, and Gentry, accompanied by Inman, appeared in court to argue for dismissal of all charges. Both Inman for the defendants and Remy for the people spoke at length about the charges and the evidence that underlay them.

Inman argued that the indictment returned by the grand jury on April 4 was improperly drawn, biased, and not an impartial investigation. According to Inman, the grand jury had been presented only with evidence of persons who claimed to have heard alleged statements made by Miss Oberholtzer. No direct testimony of any sort had been presented to the grand jury. He insisted that the indictment was founded on wholly unreliable hearsay and incompetent testimony.[72] Judge Collins said very little during or after the arguments, announcing only that he would study all aspects of the case and rule on Inman's request for dismissal on Thursday, April 16.[73]

Between April 11, when Judge Collins heard Inman's arguments for dismissal, and April 16, when he had promised to rule on them, Madge's physical condition deteriorated severely. On April 2, the day Stephenson had been arrested, she slipped into a coma from which she never revived.

Specialists were brought in to examine her, but by April 12 the medical consensus was that death could occur at any moment. The local press followed all releases of medical information very closely. On April 13, though Madge was still unconscious, her temperature was reported down a few degrees. On the basis of that new medical information, the *Indianapolis Star* carried a headline, "Miss Oberholtzer reported better."[74] That sort of journalistic wishful thinking may have helped sell a few more newspapers but was in fact medical nonsense. Madge Oberholtzer died the next day, April 14, 1925, at 10:30 A.M. in her home with her parents and a nurse at her bedside.[75]

An official autopsy was performed at once by a pathologist from the Indiana University School of Medicine. On April 15, after completion of the formal inquest, Indianapolis newspapers carried County Coroner Paul F. Robinson's verdict. Robinson was a public official who had been also identified as a Klansman by *Tolerance* two years earlier. The coroner's verdict was straightforward. Madge's death had been caused by the ingestion of bichloride of mercury tablets. By now, through detailed newspaper accounts, the public was aware of virtually everything that had happened to Madge, and public sentiment was building rapidly against Stephenson. Madge's funeral on April 16 was a major civic event.[76]

Hundreds of people gathered about the Oberholtzer home waiting for a glimpse of the casket. Florist vans arrived with floral arrangements that filled the dining room and living room, overflowed to the front porch, and lined the outside walkways. All three Indianapolis dailies sent reporters and photographers, including society and entertainment writers who described in great detail the dress and jewelry worn by the deceased. Whatever horrors may have been visited upon Madge, wrote Mary E. Boastwick of the *Indianapolis Star*, "had left no trace on her face. Her expression was serene and peaceful."[77] Madge was interred in the Memorial Park Cemetery amid mountains of flowers. From victim, Madge now had become a martyr whose tragic demise could not be allowed to remain unavenged.

Later, in the early hours of April 17, several cars pulled into the long driveway of Stephenson's mansion and men from those cars broke into the building. Since Stephenson's first arrest, he no longer lived in the mansion. He had removed most of his personal belongings from the house and had moved into the Hotel Washington as a permanent resident. At about 1:30 A.M., the neighborhood was roused by an explosion in the Stephenson mansion. Neighbors could see flames raging inside the house. All of the cars parked in the driveway were gone. The fire department managed to extinguish the flames in about an hour. Investigators discovered that all the gas jets in the house had been turned on and gasoline had been liberally sprinkled about the lower floor of the house to feed the fire. There was no doubt that this explosion and fire in the Stephenson mansion was a premeditated act of arson.[78] Though Klinck, Gentry, and Fred Butler, Stephenson's secretary, were later charged with conspiracy to commit arson with intent to defraud an insurance company, no one was ever convicted and punished for this crime.[79]

Earlier on April 16, the day of Madge Oberholtzer's funeral, Judge Collins announced that he had denied Inman's request to quash further proceedings against Stephenson. Public indignation, especially among women's organizations, had reached such extreme levels that whatever Collins' personal feelings might have been, he had no choice except to let the case go forward. Two days later, Remy went back to the grand jury to raise the principal charge against Stephenson to first degree murder and to obtain another warrant for his arrest.[80] Judge Collins received the warrant on Saturday morning, April 18, and immediately passed it on to Sheriff Hawkins for action.

Hawkins received the warrant while eating lunch and delayed acting upon it until 3:00 P.M. When the sheriff's men began their belated search for Stephenson, he was nowhere to be found. As a matter of fact, Stephenson remained at large all day Sunday, April 19. Local newspapers speculated that he had left Indianapolis permanently.[81] However, on Monday, April 20, Stephenson, Klinck, and Gentry were all arrested by Sheriff Hawkins in Inman's office. All three prisoners were taken to the Marion County Jail, booked, and lodged in cells. Judge Collins announced that prisoners arrested on murder indictments would be denied bail.[82] For the first time in his life, Stephenson was behind bars in Indiana. As events would soon show, Stephenson would remain behind bars in Indiana for a very long time.

Specifically, Stephenson, Klinck, and Gentry were indicted on four counts. The first count charged the men with kidnapping, assault, and denying Madge medical assistance while she was kept in forcible custody. The second count charged the three men with causing her to take poison by her own hand while under duress, fear, and compulsion. The third count charged Stephenson and the others with felonious assault and intent to commit forcible rape upon Madge, causing her to sicken, languish, and die. The fourth and final count charged the accused men with kidnapping, assault, biting, and denial of medical assistance, which caused her death.[83] All of these counts were based on Madge's dying declaration. The prosecutors correctly assumed that the judge would admit the dying declaration as evidence in this case and then persuaded themselves that a jury would believe every word in it.

It was clear that Stephenson was in very serious trouble with the Indianapolis criminal justice system and increasingly over the next few weeks found himself isolated and an object of contempt with both former supporters and long-standing enemies. Because of the Oberholtzer tragedy, Stephenson had become a pariah. All local politicians and the Republican party power brokers wanted to break all ties with him.

For Stephenson, there would be no extenuating circumstances for anything he had done or was accused of doing. He had betrayed and embarrassed far too many people. There would be no forgiveness and no mercy. His personal and political destruction had begun, and no one in public life was of a mind to try to stop it.

12

Indiana's Trial
of the Century

All three Indianapolis daily newspapers extensively reported events relating to the Oberholtzer case occurring between Stephenson's first arrest on April 2 and his second arrest for first-degree murder on April 20. Parts of the Oberholtzer story emerged in piecemeal fashion during those three weeks until scarcely a single literate newspaper reader could have been ignorant of Madge's abduction and abuse. Because the story was so prominent, a major shift in public opinion about the role and sincerity of the Klan organization was underway. After all, Stephenson had been the former head of the Indiana Klan, an organization ostensibly committed to moral improvement and to the protection of virtuous American womanhood. The utter hypocrisy of Stephenson's alleged behavior with Madge and others tarred the entire Klan organization. Thousands of Hoosiers were embarrassed by past involvements with Klansmen and Klan-sponsored events and wanted to forget about their misguided flirtation with that organization.[1] Although a great many Hoosiers clearly had become disenchanted with the Klan organization, there is little evidence to suggest that such disenchantment led to any massive rejection of Klan principles. So-called 100 percent Americanism and public commitments to Protestant religious and moral values remained as strong as ever throughout the state.

Moreover, Klan participation in the May primary elections was evident everywhere. Except for Indianapolis and a few other places, however, Klan-endorsed candidates fared poorly. For example in South Bend, Klan endorsements were publicly rejected by most of the candidates who had received them. Seven candidates made the point that they were neither Klansmen nor Catholics and wanted to be judged on their own merits.[2]

In this primary election in South Bend, Klan-endorsed candidates were soundly defeated. According to John B. Chester, a reporter for the *South Bend Tribune,* who had covered the primary elections in St. Joseph County, the Klan was a disintegrating organization whose claim to influence in city politics was totally unfounded.[3]

In Indianapolis, the situation was more complicated. The local Klan organization tried to salvage some credibility and influence in public affairs by joining the hue and cry against Stephenson. Walter Bossert, Stephenson's successor as Grand Dragon of the national Klan organization in Indiana, had no use for the man even before the Oberholtzer affair had surfaced. Walter Bossert had no difficulty whatsoever in denouncing the man who had brought so much shame and embarrassment upon the organization. Bossert stated publicly that justice required swift and condign punishment of Stephenson for all of his criminal misdeeds.[4]

The hue and cry against Stephenson was heard everywhere. Five hundred residents of Irvington turned out for a meeting in the local Methodist church to protest rumored efforts to allow Stephenson, Klinck, and Gentry to be released on bail. This meeting was addressed by Thomas Carr Howe, a former president of Butler College. Howe excoriated both Stephenson and the Klan, asserting that Stephenson was guilty of murdering Madge Oberholtzer. He could not be more guilty if he had used a gun and shot her dead in broad daylight. Howe also announced the establishment of a special fund, of all things, to assist the prosecution in pursuing the case against Stephenson.[5] In the following weeks other groups held similar meetings and demanded that justice be done, meaning conviction and punishment of Stephenson. Church organizations and women's groups issued statements urging not only that justice be done but that it be done quickly.

A week after Stephenson's second arrest, an otherwise lethargic and dull Indianapolis Republican mayoralty primary election campaign was energized when one of the candidates, Ralph A. Lemcke, tried to make Stephenson an issue. In speeches all over the city, Lemcke insisted that John Duvall, incumbent county treasurer and front-runner in the Republican mayoralty campaign, was backed by Stephenson and his organization. Lemcke claimed that a vote for Duvall was really a vote for Stephenson. Though Duvall had actually signed a contract with Stephenson promising him patronage approvals in exchange for financial and political support, Duvall issued a sworn statement repudiating Stephenson and his organization.[6]

The Stephenson political organization had a special fascination for Charles Maurice of the *South Bend Tribune.* According to Maurice, after

Stephenson's banishment from the national Klan organization in early 1924, he had turned himself into an aggressive political captain with loyal political followers in every section of the state.[7] The basic question in Maurice's mind was whether or not the Stephenson organization would function as efficiently without Stephenson in the May primary elections as it had with him in charge during the primary and general elections of the previous year. The machine had not functioned well in South Bend at all. Indianapolis would be different.

What those followers in the capitol city would do now that their leader had been disgraced, incarcerated, and had become such an object of public scorn and hatred was anyone's guess. That question was answered clearly enough by Indianapolis Republican voters in the primary election on May 5. Lemcke's effort to identify Duvall with Stephenson failed to move very many hard-core Klan supporters in the city away from Duvall. Stephenson's "military machine" without Stephenson delivered the necessary votes in the city. Duvall won the primary election by 7,000 votes.[8] He won again handily in the November general election and was inaugurated as mayor of Indianapolis.

The *Indianapolis Star* reported also that in the November election all five candidates running on the Klan-backed "United Protestant" school board slate had also been elected, placing control of the Indianapolis public schools in the hands of Klan-supported politicians.[9] Duvall enjoyed his November victory immensely. But in the following weeks and months, he proceeded to form and preside over one of the most corrupt administrations ever to govern the city.

Notwithstanding Duvall's victory in the May primary election, public opinion in Indianapolis had been thoroughly aroused against Stephenson. The attempted burning of Stephenson's mansion, Howe's impassioned public denunciation of Stephenson, the reactions of women's groups to the entire Oberholtzer affair, Bossert's attack on Stephenson, as well as the intensity of local press coverage combined to convince Euphraim Inman that Stephenson could not possibly get a fair trial in Indianapolis. Therefore, he filed a petition with Judge Collins requesting a change of venue for Stephenson's trial.

Judge Collins had denied virtually every motion and petition filed by Inman up to May 23, but not this one. Collins was much relieved with the opportunity of getting out of the case and getting the case out of Marion County. After some delays, Hamilton County, about twenty-five miles north of Indianapolis, was found agreeable to all parties as a suitable venue for the trial. The case was transferred to the circuit court of Judge Fred E. Hines. On May 25, Stephenson, Klinck, and Gentry were delivered into the custody of Charles Gooding, Hamilton County sheriff, in Noblesville. The prisoners were immediately placed in ordinary four by fifteen foot cells in the forty-year-old county jail.[10]

Noblesville was the county seat for Hamilton County. It was a typical Indiana small town with less than five thousand people living there. The town was strongly Republican in politics and was run by farmers and small business men. Noblesville was also typical of the towns in that part of the state wherein over the last few years a very active and highly visible Klan organization had developed. Torchlight parades had been frequent. Fiery crosses had been burned regularly in open-air evening Klan ceremonies only a few yards away from the county jail where Stephenson was now held. The principles of 100 percent Americanism and Protestant virtues for all had appeared in Noblesville long before the Klan had come to town and would remain popular there after Klansmen had put away their robes and the organization had disappeared.[11]

Once in Noblesville, Stephenson and Inman decided to expand the defense team. Stephenson engaged two additional lawyers to assist Inman. One of the new lawyers was the celebrated Ira Holmes, a distant cousin of U.S. Supreme Court Justice Oliver Wendell Holmes. Active in Republican politics, a lawyer of flamboyant reputation, and widely known for successful defenses of Indianapolis bootleggers, Holmes commanded the highest fees in the capitol city.[12] One newspaper reported that Stephenson had transferred ownership of the fire-damaged mansion in Irvington as a retainer for legal services.[13] The second new lawyer was Floyd Christian of Noblesville. Christian was a member of the oldest law firm in Hamilton County, a Mason, a pillar of the local Presbyterian church, and skilled in handling murder cases. He brought knowledge and respectability to the Stephenson side of the bench.

The principal task of this very impressive array of Hoosier legal talent was to persuade Judge Hines to dismiss the charges against Stephenson, Klinck, and Gentry or, failing that, to get a reasonable bail so that the prisoners could be released. Judge Hines proved to be as intransigent on these issues as Judge Collins.

Judge Hines did not appreciate at all what had been visited upon him and his court. He greatly resented having been pressured into receiving and adjudicating overflow cases from Indianapolis. Hines believed strongly that the city ought to take care of its own problems. Hines already had one celebrity juvenile murder case from the capitol city to deal with and did not need the Stephenson spectacular to complicate his life. Hines was also nervous about, perhaps even fearful of the publicity, regional and national, that high-priced, showcase criminal lawyers would bring to his court. He was thoroughly uncomfortable being center stage in what promised to be an extravagant courtroom drama and was absolutely determined not to be bullied by Stephenson's costly counsel. That Hines did not like either Inman or Holmes was clear from their first encounter in court, and very soon the extent of that dislike was apparent to all.[14]

Inman began his defensive moves by filing motions with Judge Hines to quash the indictments against his clients. Hines rejected them almost out of hand. Next, Inman requested a bail bond hearing. Hines agreed to hear arguments about bail on June 10. Having a date for a bail bond hearing, Inman proceeded with another motion requiring the prosecution to turn over copies of Madge's dying declaration and the register page of the Indiana Hotel in Hammond to the defense for examination. On June 12, Hines ruled that no dying declaration had been submitted to him as evidence for the prosecution, but if one was, the court would require that copies be provided to the defense before the bail bond hearing set for June 16.[15] Inman's opening strategy was clear. He intended to attack the substance and manner of preparing and obtaining the dying declaration at the bail bond hearing and try to persuade Judge Hines to exclude it from the trial.

The prosecution complied with the judge's ruling in the matter of the dying declaration in due course. However, copies of the dying declaration were released to the press before one was delivered to Inman. Inman's strategy failed utterly because the prosecution had made certain that Madge's dying declaration would become part of the public record of this case before Judge Hines had a chance to rule on the admissibility of it. The judge did not protest the behavior of the prosecution in this matter or in any other. In the end, on Thursday June 25, Judge Hines ruled that the dying declaration was admissible and that all defendants should be denied bail.[16]

Inman responded with a request that the trial begin as soon as possible, as early as Monday June 29. Judge Hines and the prosecutors were visibly shocked by Inman's totally unexpected move. Hines studied his calendar and declared that he could not possibly begin the trial before Monday July 6. Next, Inman moved that Stephenson be tried separately from Klinck and Gentry, Hines denied this motion on July 2 and ruled that all three defendants should be ready for trial as scheduled on Monday July 6.

On that trial date, the judge and prosecutors were present and ready to begin, but Inman and his team were not. They simply failed to appear and sent no notice explaining why. After waiting the entire morning for the defense to enter his courtroom and becoming totally exasperated, Hines declared the court adjourned and stated that the case would not be heard until sometime during the October session. Minutes after Hines had adjourned the court, Inman ambled into the courtroom and asked Hines to reopen the court. Hines refused and angrily asserted that any further motions with respect to this case could be submitted to him privately during the recess.[17]

Inman would not give up. He filed another motion on July 26 brazenly requesting another bail bond hearing, but Hines would have no more of that and peremptorily denied the motion. Aware that at this stage of the proceedings that Judge Hines had lost all patience and could barely stand the sight of Inman in his courtroom, the lawyer made his ultimate and final move against Judge Hines. On August 10, the defense filed a motion for a change of judges, claiming that Hines had been biased in his rulings and was prejudiced against the defendants.[18]

Judge Hines was appalled. He vigorously denied Inman's allegations and insisted that such statements were nothing but plain perjury. Clearly, Judge Hines could not continue and did not. He stated that this court was no longer interested in this case and wished that it could be taken out of the county. After two months of legal fencing with Inman, Hines was delighted to be out of the case and free of him. It is not clear whom Hines despised more, Stephenson or Inman. However, before Hines could be rid of the case and the lawyers, he would have to find some other judge in Hamilton County to take his place. Finding a judge that the prosecution and defense would accept was not easy, but the task was completed in two days' time on August 12. By process of elimination from a list of three judges, Will Sparks of Rushville turned out to be Hines' successor. He was no one's first choice. Availability and a willingness to take on the case at this late hour appeared to be the only reason for choosing him.[19] In time, the defense would deeply regret the choice of Sparks. He was a most determined and stubborn man.

Judge Sparks was no more eager for the publicity and showcase lawyer antics certain to be attendant upon the Stephenson trial than had been his predecessors, Collins and Hines. Having spent seventeen years on the Rush County Circuit Court, Sparks was an experienced judge. He was driven into the case, to be sure, by a sense of duty but also by a touch of personal ego that he, Will Sparks, would undertake and complete a controversial case that two of his colleagues had abandoned. For Sparks, there was much satisfaction in that thought.

Sparks was fifty-three years old, a Methodist, a strong Republican, and a Mason, but Klan principles and activities had no attraction for him whatsoever.[20] He had watched local Klansmen in Rushville transform that town from an open community into one where neighbors mistrusted one another and where the most absurd rumors about Catholic intention and possible future actions were believed by many good people who should have known better. Sparks' own secretary was a Catholic woman who in the face of increasing local anti-Catholic hostility had offered to resign her post prior to the last election to prevent any embarrassment or untoward electoral consequences being visited upon her employer.

Sparks would not hear of his secretary quitting her job in order to save his. He responded by saying that if he lost the election because of her religion, the election was not worth winning. The secretary's anxiety over this matter was unnecessary, because the issue of her religion never came up during the election. Nonetheless, this incident confirmed and intensified Sparks' latent hostility to the Klan and positively insured that he would approach the Stephenson case ready to believe the worst and excuse nothing.[21]

During the late summer of 1925 while the Stephenson case was being passed from judge to judge in Indiana, Evans and others in the national Klan organization decided that ignoring the Oberholtzer case and the events transpiring in Noblesville was bad policy. Evans was well informed about the progress of the Stephenson case and about the state of affairs in Indiana. A contingent of Hoosier Klansmen had traveled to Washington, D.C., to participate in the Klan march down Pennsylvania Avenue on August 8. Bossert, unrobed and wearing a business suit, marched side by side with Evans during this massive Klan demonstration and undoubtedly found time to discuss the details of the Stephenson case with him. In any case, once the Washington demonstration was over, Evans immediately boarded a train to Noblesville to attend a Klan-sponsored Chautauqua in that place on August 9. Local Klansmen had organized a series of lectures, plays, and concerts for the community. Crowds from all over Hamilton County came into Noblesville to attend the events and to hear Evans.[22]

Evans' intentions in coming to Noblesville at this time are clear enough. He wanted to remind people in Indiana and elsewhere that Stephenson had been expelled from the Klan months before the Oberholtzer incident had occurred. Evans was determined to banish all and any lingering impressions that the Klan was in any way responsible for or implicated in the death of Madge Oberholtzer. Precisely what Evans said in Noblesville on August 9 is unrecorded, but whatever he did say was put into a speech delivered in the courthouse square within earshot of Stephenson's second-floor cell. No one expected Evans to be fair or express any sort of sympathy for Stephenson, and he did not. For Stephenson and his lawyers, the presence of Evans denouncing the former Indiana Grand Dragon in Noblesville, where Klan principles had some standing, was a thoroughly depressing experience. But it was only the beginning.[23]

According to an account given by Stephenson to a reporter fourteen years later, the streets and sidewalks of Noblesville had been filled with hooded Klansmen throughout the day and evening of August 9. As Stephenson remembered the day, death threats were shouted at him from the Klansmen gathered near the jail. The sheriff actually had to intervene twice during the day to disperse the crowd from the environs of the jail. Thereafter, Stephenson claimed, local Klansmen met regularly during the rest of August and in September and October in Noblesville and elsewhere in Hamilton County plotting how to stir up public sentiments against him.[24]

In this increasingly hostile environment on October 12, Judge Sparks began the protracted process of jury selection. All but one of the first one hundred jurors interviewed were rejected. Jury selection continued until October 28, whereupon, after 260 interviews, a jury was finally impaneled. No one in the courthouse could recall a more lengthy jury selection process in the history of the state.[25]

During that process occurred what was probably the crowning irony and disappointment of Stephenson's relatively short-lived public career. On October 14, after more than a year of poor health, United States Senator Samuel M. Ralston finally died. Stephenson had hoped to obtain this seat for himself by gubernatorial appointment. However, incarcerated in the Hamilton County jail, Stephenson was clearly unavailable. Instead of appointing Stephenson, Governor Jackson chose Arthur M. Robinson, a friend of Stephenson and a frequent attorney for the Indiana Klan, to serve out the remaining two years of Ralston's term. Before leaving for Washington, Robinson was one of the very few of Stephenson's former political friends not to foreswear and desert him during this time of increasing desperation. As a matter of fact, before leaving for Washington, D.C., Robinson contributed $5,000 to a defense fund of $17,000 collected from a few Marion County Republican officials and secretly delivered to Stephenson in the Noblesville jail.[26]

Stephenson must have been deeply disappointed by the appointment of Robinson, but at the moment he had much more important matters to worry about. With the jury selection completed on October 28, Judge Sparks was of no mind to waste any more time. He ordered the trial of Stephenson and the others to begin on the next day, October 29, 1925, before a Hamilton County jury of ten farmers, a truck driver, and a gas plant manager.[27] The man who declared so often that in Indiana he was the law was about to discover just how Indiana law and justice functioned in an unpopular celebrity case such as this one during the 1920s.

— ii —

On the first day of the trial, October 29, the prosecution laid out its strategy for convicting Stephenson of murder in the first degree. Despite all of the pretrial publicity and the generally hostile state of public opinion against Stephenson, the case was far from being open and shut. The state was prepared to spare no efforts or expenses in obtaining a conviction. In order to be certain that territorial interests were represented, the state assigned a Hamilton County assistant prosecutor, Ralph K. Kane, to join Remy, Marion County prosecutor, in managaing the Stephenson prosecution.

Beyond that, the state also added Charles Cox, a highly experienced trial attorney and former judge to the prosecution team. Like Inman, Cox was an accomplished courtroom orator of the old school. He was a master of emotional pleading, skilled at simplifying complex issues, and temperamentally unable to avoid purple phrases and extreme overstatement. Cox had been engaged by the prosecution because he was the best available courtroom orator ready and willing to challenge Inman at his own game.

For the prosecutors, this case was a very special one, indeed. However, special or not, Indiana law was very clear about a central element in it. Suicide was not a crime in Indiana. There had to be an accessory before or after the fact to prove that a crime had been committed. There was absolutely no evidence even suggesting that Stephenson had been an accessory to Madge Oberholtzer's ingestion of the bichloride of mercury tablets, and the prosecution wasted no time arguing that he had.

Similarly, to prove a charge of first-degree murder, the prosecutors would have to prove that premeditation was a factor, and that was impossible to do. Again, there was absolutely no evidence indicating that Stephenson had forced Madge to swallow any of the poison tablets so the prosecutors simply ignored the issue of premeditation with regard to the ingestion of the tablets and had to try to work it into their case in some other way.

The tack taken was to argue that the bichloride of mercury tablets was not the cause of Madge's death. After all, the prosection insisted, Madge had lived twenty-nine days after swallowing the tablets. They argued that the cause of death was a massive infection in the deceased's lungs and respiratory system. This infection had been derived from bites and lacerations inflicted by Stephenson on several parts of Madge's body during the train ride from Indianapolis to Hammond.[28] According to the prosecution, germs from Stephenson's teeth had caused the infection that killed Madge Oberholtzer. That was what the jurors had to be persuaded to believe.

In the course of the trial, this unfortunate woman of twenty-seven years was represented by the prosecutors as being a horrible example of ravaged and murdered innocence. She had been entrapped, defiled, raped, and in the end fanged to death by a moral degenerate turned sadist, D. C. Stephenson. Such was the case presented by the prosecutors, abetted and supported by a parade of professors, medical experts, and toxicologists from the Indiana University School of Medicine and elsewhere who testified that such a theory was scientifically and medically credible. Before the trial was over, it was clear enough to all involved that many powerful persons of great influence in the state were determined that Stephenson had to be convicted, utterly discredited, and removed from society for a very long time.

Defense strategy was simple. Inman and his colleagues argued that Madge had taken her own life and that the cause of her death was self-administered ingestion of bichloride of mercury tablets. Like the prosecutors, Inman also produced a number of medical experts and toxicologists to support that theory of cause of death. Consistent with the theory that self-administered poison had killed Madge, Inman claimed that Stephenson was not and could not be guilty of first-degree murder under Indiana law because the conditions for such a crime had never existed. While there may have been some evidence of assault and possibly even abduction in this case, premeditation of murder was unprovable. Moreover, Inman argued, there was no evidence that Stephenson had in any way forced Madge to take the poison tablets which he insisted had caused her death.

Secondarily, Inman and other members of the defense team were prepared to argue and to present witnesses who would testify that Madge was not the paragon of ravaged innocence that the prosecution had made her out to be. Inman had collected witnesses willing to testify that Madge enjoyed more than an occasional drink of gin. Beyond that, there were witnesses ready to recount incidents involving public displays of affection for Stephenson and at least one other ready to accuse Madge of blatant promiscuity.

Inman had turned up an Indianapolis housewife, Cora Householder, a neighbor of the Oberholtzers, who claimed that her husband had been involved with Madge in an on-going affair shortly before her death. According to Mrs. Householder, her husband had left her and was living in the Oberholtzer home as a boarder when Madge had her tragic encounter with Stephenson.[29] However, the jury heard none of this. Judge Sparks allowed testimony about gin drinking, but excluded witnesses testifying about Madge's personal life and character.

In Sparks' court Inman was not to be allowed to paint a scarlet letter on this deceased woman's reputation.[30] The prosecutors had said that Madge was "clean of soul" and that was that. Nasty stories alleging otherwise would not be told in Judge Sparks' court by anyone even if there was a possibility that they might be true.[31] In that court, Sparks' extraordinary sense of chivalry had the effect of disarming Stephenson's defense and virtually insuring the conviction that public opinion was demanding.

The trial went on until November 14. Neither Stephenson, Klinck, nor Gentry testified. In later years, Stephenson insisted that he had been warned against speaking out on his own behalf while in the Noblesville jail by Klan representatives. He claimed to have been told that if he testified and revealed any Klan secrets, he would be killed whether in prison or not.[32] For the two weeks of the trial, the local press followed every development very closely. In virtually all defense motions, Judge Sparks ruled for the prosecution. Since most of the witnesses were medical experts, there were few opportunities either for lawyers or the press to sensationalize. That was to be saved for the closing arguments, which took almost three days with three lawyers on each side participating.

When delivered, the closing arguments of both the defense and prosecution were classic examples of Hoosier grandiloquent courtroom oratory. The defense dwelt upon inconsistencies, of which there were many, in Madge's dying declaration. They urged the jurors to bear in mind the definition of reasonable doubt, find the courage of heroes, eschew what public opinion wanted, and write their verdict on the basis of the evidence as presented. Inman was startlingly and perhaps even bravely specific about what this case had become. According to Inman, the special attorneys for the prosecution had been "hired for money to get blood in this case. The state had drawn pictures not with brush and paint but with brush and mud."[33]

There were mysterious powers operating the state of Indiana, Inman continued, that were behind the persecution of these men, trying to send them to the electric chair. Other "men are jingling the gold now of the enemies who seek their destruction."[34] Inman stated directly to the jury that whatever had happened on the train from Indianapolis to Hammond, Madge Oberholtzer had died by her own hand, from self-administered poison. At the same time, Inman implied that Klansmen and politicians beholden to the Klan were now using this terrible tragedy to revenge themselves on Stephenson for what he had done to their organization and to their legislative program in Indiana. This trial, Inman concluded, was really about political persecution, and Stephenson, Gentry, and Klinck were the unfortunate victims of it.[35]

The prosecution's closing arguments went in an entirely opposite direction. Remy began his three-hour presentation by assuring the jury that the defendants had had a fair trial, "no one in the history of jurisprudence has ever had a fairer one. These men had a fairer trial than they ever gave Madge Oberholtzer."[36] She would be alive today, Remy continued, if it were not for the unlawful acts of the defendants. They destroyed her body. They tried to destroy her soul, and in the last few days had tried to befoul her character.[37]

According to Remy, the defendants tried to make the jurors think that Madge Oberholtzer was a bad girl. That had been the most shameful part of the history of the case. They put their gang on the stand, Remy declared, men who worked for or under Stephenson. Some of these so-called witnesses were paid by him and were put on the stand because he could find no one else. Yet, Madge Oberholtzer's character still shined untarnished. The girl's life might have been saved, Remy continued, indeed there had been cases where the lives of persons suffering from bichloride of mercury poisoning had been saved even though many hours passed without treatment. In this instance, there was an abscess on her lung contributing to her death that had been brought on by the fangs of D. C. Stephenson.[38] Remy concluded by recalling that according to Madge Oberholtzer, Stephenson had said that he was the law in Indiana. "Thank God, he can't say that he is the law in Hamilton County."[39]

It was Charles Cox, however, who provided the most emotive and most condemnatory final presentation of the state's case and, he took the better part of two days to do it. He argued that the enormity of the crime demanded what the laws of Indiana allowed in a case such as this, the death penalty for all three defendants. According to Cox, Stephenson was a sadist. Klinck was a gorilla, and Gentry was a coward. All three should be killed by law.[40]

The defendants probably did not intend to kill Madge Oberholtzer, began Cox, but they are liable criminally. They are responsible to the law for everything that naturally and probably flowed from the things they did to her. These brutal men killed her, murdered her, Cox raged—these degenerates, these perverts, drunk with power must never be set free to go out into the world and commit other outrages against other innocent women. Despite the stellar performance of the man with the melodious voice—meaning Inman—Cox continued, good men will not allow these fiends to escape their just deserts.[41]

Kane also had his moments of media attention. In his closing argument, Kane attacked the defense team of lawyers almost as severely as he attacked the defendants. He excoriated the defense team for deceit, hypocrisy, and denied vehemently that special prosecutors had been hired by the state in this case or that political conspiracy was driving the prosecution of it.[42]

During his part of the prosecution's closing arguments, Kane was less descriptive but more confrontational than Cox. He argued with and shouted at witnesses during cross-examinations. During the cross-examination of one defense witness, Kane actually offered to meet the witness on the street and settle the matter of whether the man had perjured himself or not.[43] The next day Kane appeared in court with a large black eye. He explained the injury by claiming that he had bumped his head on a cellar door the previous evening.[44]

Black eye or not, throughout his closing argument Kane minced no words. The defendants, he declared "are as guilty of the murder of Madge Oberholtzer as though they had stabbed her with a knife."[45] We cannot bring Madge Oberholtzer back to life and restore her to her bereaved parents, Kane continued, but we can make an example of them for the protection of other daughters. The people of this nation, Kane concluded, wish to know whether an Indiana jury will permit vagabonds to commit fiendish crimes of this sort. Finally, Kane wanted "to know whether there is a man in this community who would sign a verdict to acquit this hideous monster who preys upon the virtuous young daughters of this state."[46]

So there it was. The defense had represented their clients as victims of political persecution, guilty of something perhaps, but not of the crimes for which they had been charged. The prosecution portrayed the defendants as fiends deserving the severest penalties the law would allow. By 11:00 A.M., November 14, both sides had said everything they could think of to say. It was time for this Hamilton County jury of ten farmers, a truck driver, and a businessman to determine whether the defendants were victims or fiends.

Judge Sparks spent twenty-five minutes instructing the jury about the distinctions between first- and second-degree murder and explained the grounds for finding the defendants guilty of one or the other. Following lunch, the jurors began their deliberations, and after only four hours were ready to deliver their verdict. The jurors decided that Stephenson was indeed a fiend, but that Klinck and Gentry were victims. Stephenson was found guilty of murder in the second degree, while the verdict on Klinck and Gentry was not guilty.

Conviction of murder in the second degree required a minimum of twenty years of penal servitude. Although good behavior and the possibility of parole could reduce the amount of time actually served, among Indiana lawyers and judges such a sentence was commonly called life imprisonment.[47] The sentence of twenty years to life was under the law the most severe that Judge Sparks could assign, and that was what he actually assigned.

Immediately after sentencing, Stephenson's lawyers requested from Judge Sparks a stay of sentence while they prepared a petition for a new trial. Sparks denied their request, and on November 21, Stephenson was transported from Noblesville to the Indiana State Prison at Michigan City to begin his sentence.[48] Among those persons witnessing Stephenson's predawn departure in a two-vehicle convoy was Judge Sparks. He had traveled the seventy miles from his home in Rushville to Noblesville and spent the night in a hotel there in order to be on site and present at the Noblesville jail at 4:00 A.M. when Stephenson departed for Michigan City. Indeed, this act was an example of supreme devotion to duty or perhaps of something a bit less noble.

Indiana's criminal trial of the century was ended, and justice had been done. The *South Bend Tribune* editorialized that many people throughout the state had expected an acquittal or a hung jury, believing that Stephenson was too powerful and had too many powerful friends to be convicted.[49] According to this editorial, the verdict in the Stephenson trial had been a vindication of the Indiana criminal justice system.

While applauding the verdict in this trial, the editorial writers also managed to harbor a few reservations about it. The state had decided that Stephenson had murdered Madge Oberholtzer by indirection and that he should go to prison for it. However, the editorial writers commented, if Stephenson was "guilty of the conduct recited in the evidence of the state he should be electrocuted forthwith."[50] That he was not sentenced to death must be attributed to the spirited defense conducted by his lawyers. Stephenson's criminal lawyers were among the best in Indiana and demonstrated that fact by presenting an array of witnesses and testimony sufficient to raise doubts in the minds of the jury about the fairness of the charge of murder in the first degree.

The editorial also expressed disappointment over the acquittal of Gentry and Klinck. If Stephenson was guilty of murder, then they should be tried again for conspiracy. Their guilt in the bad business of "transporting Madge Oberholtzer from Indianapolis to Hammond, Indiana, remains to be demonstrated to a jury."[51] The writers concluded that the trial had been scrupulously fair, thanks to Judge Sparks, and that "Indiana criminal justice has been given a desirable tonic by the sensible and efficient conduct in this celebrated murder case."[52]

At long last for the public at large and especially for the thousands of Klan sympathizers and devotees of Klan principles, this embarrassing ordeal was over. How much had been changed by it all remained to be seen. Anti-Catholicism continued to be an unpleasant fact of American political and social life, especially in Indiana, for many years. During the election campaign of 1928 anti-Catholicism intensified and exploded in ways that shocked Catholics and embarrassed many Protestants.

— iii —

Stephenson went to jail in November 1925 firmly believing that he would not be there very long.[53] Appeals had been filed, and, most important of all, Stephenson was confident that his good friend and political and financial beneficiary, Governor Ed Jackson, would find a way to deliver a pardon or a parole to him. As the months passed without a word from the governor's office, Stephenson became convinced that perhaps Jackson needed a little push. In early 1926 he began preparing one.

Stephenson's scheme was simple and direct. He intended to intimidate Jackson by threatening to release damaging information about him and about other Republican officials. In this scheme Stephenson intended to move slowly and incrementally, expecting that important Republican politicians, fearful of what Stephenson could reveal, would pressure Jackson into some sort of clemency action or commutation of sentence.

Stephenson implemented his scheme by leaking reports out of prison that he was about to divulge information linking high-ranking Republican state officials with corrupt practices and deals.[54] When rumors of that sort failed to achieve any result, Stephenson had friends retrieve damaging letters and cancelled checks from his so-called "black boxes" hidden in barns and other secure locations.

With such documents in safe hands—sometimes actually smuggled into his prison cell [55]—Stephenson began releasing them one by one over a period of time to the press. The first of the documents released related to John Duvall, the serving mayor of Indianapolis. Stephenson managed to deliver to Boyd Gurley, editor of the *Indianapolis Times,* a facsimile copy of Duvall's contract with Stephenson promising him control of the city's boards of public works, of parks, and of public safety.[56]

Soon Gurley and his reporters hotly pursued other details, all of which culminated in a series of long articles entitled "What Stephenson Could Tell" published in the *Indianapolis Times* in the fall of 1926. The articles were based on Stephenson's letters smuggled out of prison and dealt with a system of graft and corruption operating at all levels of Indiana state government. There were revelations about protection money paid by bootleggers and payments from the Insull public utility interests destined for the Republican State Committee but which allegedly wound up in the pockets of Governor Jackson. The articles were accompanied by facsimile illustrations of key incriminating letters in Stephenson's handwriting.[57]

These revelations were spectacular and attracted the attention of Thomas H. Adams, editor and publisher of the *Vincennes Commercial,* a life-long Republican and an active member of the Republican Editorial Association. Adams was much concerned about the future of the Indiana Republican party and was no admirer of Jackson. After receiving a letter from Stephenson wherein the prisoner insisted that he could prove that Jackson owed him $825,000 in campaign expenses and that the mayors of three major cities and forty small towns were indebted to him for campaign expenses, Adams pressed for a public investigation of Stephenson's allegations.[58]

The extent of political corruption in Indiana seemed so widespread and persuasive that even the United States Senate took notice of it. Senator James Reed (D-Mo.) sent investigators from the Department of Justice to interview Stephenson and others. Specific attention and publicity was given to the fact that Senator Arthur Robinson (R-Ind.) had received strong financial and political support from the Klan.[59]

Finally, in the fall of 1926, Remy, acting in his capacity as Marion County prosecutor, obtained a special grand jury and launched a full-scale investigation of political corruption in his jurisdiction. Among those persons brought before the grand jury was Stephenson. However, his appearance turned out to be a disappointment. He refused to answer questions, citing constitutional guarantees against self-incrimination. Why Stephenson, already serving a life prison term, should worry about self-incrimination is no mystery. In truth, he was not worried about self-incrimination at all. Hopeful that Jackson would change his mind and grant him a pardon in exchange for silence, Stephenson decided for the moment that he would not repeat to the grand jury what he had told Remy in private.[60]

Jackson simply refused to do anything for Stephenson. Consequently, by the spring of 1927 Stephenson decided to cooperate with another grand jury and tell what he knew about corruption and corrupt practices in the state. He arranged to deliver two of his "black boxes" to Remy. While the documents in the boxes were not quite the treasure trove that Remy had expected, they were rich enough in incriminating information to present to a grand jury. There were thirty-one cancelled checks with notations about their purposes. Some of the checks had been made out to Jackson. Others went to Jackson supporters. The boxes also contained pledges from Republican congressmen Ralph Updike of Indianapolis and Harry Rowbottom of Evansville promising Stephenson approval of patronage appointments in exchange for financial and political support in the election of 1924.[61]

Stephenson told the grand jury how he had raised $23,000 from public utility interests, including $15,000 from the Insull Utility group in Chicago, who had operations and facilities in Indiana. According to Stephenson, the money had been given to Jackson personally to deliver to the Republican State Committee. Again according to Stephenson, none of the money ever reached the State Committee. Stephenson claimed that Jackson used the money to buy a farm in Hancock County and pay off a promissory note.[62] All in all, Stephenson insisted that he had spent $227,000 on Jackson's primary and general election campaigns. In return for this campaign money, Stephenson claimed to have received a written contract from Jackson promising that Stephenson would be recompensed by receiving the coal contract for the state and by obtaining control of the State Highway and State Purchasing Commissions. Stephenson also admitted to bribing the publisher of an Indianapolis Black newspaper and a popular local Black minister to help out in the Jackson campaigns.[63]

The most damaging testimony against Jackson involved the attempted bribery of Governor Warren McCray in 1923, when Jackson had been Indiana Secretary of State. Stephenson told the grand jury how Jackson, at that time acting as an agent for the Klan, had offered McCray $10,000 on December 8, 1923, if he would appoint a Klan attorney as Marion County prosecutor. Though in desperate financial straits at the time, McCray refused and appointed the strongly anti-Klan Republican William Remy instead. As a result of this testimony Governor Jackson was indicted along with George A. Coffin, Marion County Republican chairman, and Robert Marsh, a Klan attorney, on September 9, 1927, for conspiracy and bribery.[64]

While pursuing Jackson, Remy and the grand jury also had been look-ing into the affairs of John Duvall, the Klan-dominated Indianapolis City Council, and other lesser public officials. Duvall's contract with Stephen-son was already in the public record, but Duvall had made deals with others as well. According to testimony presented to the grand jury, Duvall had received a campaign contribution of $14,000 in 1925 from William H. Armitage, reputed to be the Marion County slot machine boss, in return for promises much like those made to Stephenson. Moreover, by failing to report Armitage's campaign contribution, Duvall had violated the In-diana Corrupt Practices Act.[65]

Duvall had reached out to at least one of the local Protestant churches. He had promised the Reverend George Henniger, pastor of the East Tenth Street Methodist Church and head of the local Klan political action com-mittee, that as mayor he would make 85 percent of his patronage ap-pointment from a list of persons recommended by the Klan. He also promised Rev. Henniger that he would appoint no Catholics to any city employment whatsoever.[66]

In the end, Duvall was indicted for violating the Corrupt Practices Act. Six Republican Klansmen on the Indianapolis City Council were also indicted for soliciting and accepting bribes. Duvall's trial began on Sep-tember 12, 1927. He was convicted, fined $1,000, and sentenced to thirty days in jail. The court also ruled that he was barred from holding any public office retroactive to January 1, 1926. He duly resigned the mayoralty in February 1928. After a long series of appeals, Duvall finally went to jail and served out his sentence of thirty days in 1931. The six Klan members of the city council pleaded guilty to lesser charges of corruption, paid small fines, and resigned their posts.[67]

Jackson, Coffin, and Marsh went to trial for bribery and conspiracy before Judge Charles McCabe of the Marion County Circuit Court on February 9, 1928. In the course of the trial, the guilt of all three defendants was clearly established, but all three went free under a two-year statute of limitations. Even though the state successfully proved that a conspiracy to bribe Governor McCray had existed, the prosecution had failed to prove that the defendants had attempted to conceal their crime. Proof of con-cealment was essential in this case because under Indiana law, if a felony charge was not filed within two years of the act, homicide excepted, de-fendants could not be convicted unless they had been out of the state or had managed to conceal their crime.[68]

Since almost four years had passed between the time of the alleged bribe and when charges were filed, Judge McCabe directed the jury to return a verdict in this case of proved but not guilty as to all three defendants. The case was outside of the statute of limitations, and the defendants escaped conviction on a technicality. To be sure, Jackson was pressed to resign but would not and served out the remainder of his term. Upon leaving the governor's office, Republican party leaders wanted nothing more to do with him. He was a pariah that active and aspiring Republican politicians wanted to forget. Coffin managed to maintain control of the Republican party organization in Marion County, and Marsh returned to his law practice.[69]

— iv —

Certainly, all Indiana politicians had been severely shaken by the entire Stephenson affair. Many elected Republican state officials had some sort of past associations with Stephenson or had received favors from him. Those who did had something to hide and were scrupulous about doing so. They did everything possible over the next decade to distance themselves from Stephenson and from Klansmen of any stripe.

As for Stephenson himself, the assistance given to prosecutors investigating political corruption in the Jackson and Duvall administrations did him no good at all. He remained in prison with virtually no prospect of parole or early release. As a matter of fact, Stephenson served more time for the crime of murder in the second degree than any other person in the history of the state. Too many important people wanted him where he was and commutation or parole was not possible until several of them died.

Though Stephenson filed numerous appeals over the years and was picked clean of his ill-gotten gains by a succession of lawyers, he stayed in prison under better than tolerable conditions until March 1950, when the respected Democratic governor Henry F. Schricker commuted his sentence and allowed him parole to take a job as a printer in Carbondale, Illinois. Stephenson's freedom was short-lived indeed, only eight months. He was returned to prison after missing a meeting with his parole officer, leaving Carbondale without permission, and taking a job in Minnesota under an alias. Stephenson remained in prison for six more years.

Finally, in December 1956 a Republican governor, George N. Craig, initiated a Christmas clemency program wherein sixty prisoners were freed. Stephenson was among them and was given a complete discharge from prison. This discharge was a total surprise. Only a week before the release, Hugh O'Brien, chairman of the State Correction Board, a Catholic and former professor of sociology at the University of Notre Dame, had told a reporter that Stephenson was unsuitable for parole because he was unable to cope with the outside world.[70] However, Governor Craig thought otherwise. He told reporters that releasing Stephenson was the right thing to do. After all, he had served longer for a second-degree murder conviction than anyone else. Once the boss had gone public on this matter, O'Brien had a sudden change of heart. He responded to reporters' questions by saying that since Stephenson was all right mentally, there was no reason why he could not cope successfully with life on the outside. Stephenson was released on December 20, 1956, on the condition that he leave the state of Indiana.

After release, Stephenson ignored the condition about leaving the state. He moved to Seymour, Indiana, where he married his third wife, Martha Dickinson, and worked at his old trade as a newspaper printer. Five years after his release he found himself in trouble with the law once again. He was arrested on a charge of molesting a young girl in Independence, Missouri. Stephenson argued that the incident was no more than a misunderstanding, paid a $300 fine, and was ordered to leave the state.

He returned to Seymour and to his wife in 1961. Perhaps because of the Missouri incident, he and Martha separated that year. Sometime in 1962 Stephenson left Indiana, never to return. Stephenson made his way to Jonesboro, Tennessee, in 1963 to be treated at the Veterans' Hospital there. He settled in Jonesboro, met and married a local widow, Martha Murray Sutton, nineteen years younger than himself, without bothering to divorce Martha Dickinson Stephenson, who was alive and well in Seymour, Indiana. Later, Mrs. Sutton claimed no knowledge of Stephenson's lurid past or of his other wife in Indiana. Stephenson lived quietly in Jonesboro with Mrs. Sutton for two years. He died in June 1966 and was buried in the local Veterans' Administration cemetery.

Of those who had been close to Stephenson during his triumphant years most were dead by the time he was released from prison. Jackson and Gentry were among those who had died. Klinck had simply disappeared. Of his principal enemies, Evans continued until 1939 to head the national Klan, which was much diminished in size and influence everywhere, with active local branches largely confined to the South. In 1936 Evans tried to revive Klan fortunes by announcing his intentions to deemphasize racial and religious matters in order to concentrate on the growing threats and power of communism and the CIO.[71]

National Klan finances were in such a sorry state in 1936 that Evans was forced to sell the conspicuous Imperial Headquarters on Peach Tree Street in Atlanta. An insurance company purchased the property and, much to Evans' embarrassment, that company immediately sold it to the

Catholic Diocese of Atlanta as a site for the new Catholic Cathedral of Christ the King.

Construction of the cathedral and ancillary buildings on the site took about three years. When completed, Bishop O'Hara of Atlanta, in a moment of wry humor, invited Evans to attend the dedication ceremonies. Surprisingly, Evans accepted the invitation, attended the ceremonies, and allowed himself to be photographed flanked by Bishop O'Hara and Cardinal Dougherty of Philadelphia. This incident was too much for local hard-core Klansmen to digest, and Evans was forced to resign his office and retire from Klan affairs.

Evans was replaced by his chief of staff, James Colescott, a veterinarian from Terre Haute, Indiana. This change in leadership affected the fortunes of the organization not one whit. It was virtually moribund except in the southeast in 1939 and continued to be so throughout the country until after World War II.

Stephenson's old rival in Indiana Klan affairs and longtime Republican party activist, Walter Bossert, took over leadership of the national Klan organization in Indiana after Stephenson's expulsion in 1924. Bossert could not have been displeased by Stephenson's troubles in 1925, and during the trial he publicly urged swift and condign punishment for the now disgraced former Klan leader. Once installed as head of the national Klan organization in Indiana, Bossert very quickly found himself in sharp disagreement with Evans over Klan political activities in the state.

After Stephenson went to jail, Evans embraced Senator James E. Watson as the candidate most worthy of Klan support in the election of 1926. Evans backed Watson even though he had been a political friend and associate of Stephenson. For Bossert, Watson was the worst sort of self-serving politician that true believers in the Klan principles of 100 percent Americanism and Christian morality ought to abhor.

When Evans ordered Indiana Klansmen to vote for Watson in the forthcoming election, Bossert refused to do so and resigned his post as Grand Dragon of the Indiana Klan. Having crossed Evans once, Bossert's presence in Klan affairs was no longer to be tolerated. He withdrew from Klan activities but generally remained true to Klan principles. Bossert remained hostile to Catholics for the rest of his life, believing them to be a divisive and alien force in American life. He continued to be active in Indiana Republican party politics and actually ran as a candidate in the Republican senatorial primary election in 1938. He was defeated and then retired from public life.[72]

Concerning Senator Watson, he was reelected for a second term in 1926 with Klan support. Two years later, Watson actively opposed the nomination of Herbert Hoover for president, aspiring to that office himself. When Hoover actually became president in 1928, Watson was elected majority leader in the Senate. Hoover and Watson disliked one another intensely, and with Watson as majority leader cooperation between the president and the Senate leadership on some issues was difficult, so difficult in fact that Hoover tried unsuccessfully to have Watson replaced as majority leader by the more congenial Senator David A. Reed of Pennsylvania.

Throughout his political career, Watson was a staunch conservative and worked diligently on behalf of railroads, banks, and other corporations. As chairman of the Senate Finance Committee, Watson was indefatigable in his advocacy and support of high tariffs. He was a confirmed isolationist and an advocate of strict immigration restriction. Watson's long public career ended in the Democratic landslide of 1932, when he was defeated by Frederick Van Nuys. Retiring from politics, Watson did not return to Indiana. He remained in Washington, D.C., practicing law there and generally serving the same interests as a lobbyist that he had supported as a senator. Watson died in Washington at the age of eighty-three. There is nothing in his official biographical materials or in his *New York Times* obituary about any associations with Stephenson, Evans, or the Ku Klux Klan.

Senator Arthur R. Robinson, the Indianapolis Klan lawyer who received the appointment to the U.S. Senate in October 1925 that Stephenson believed should have been his, also established himself as a strident and rigid conservative. He was elected in 1926 for a term expiring in March 1929 and then reelected for a full term in 1928. After Roosevelt's great electoral victory in 1932, Robinson turned out to be one of the president's most vituperative critics and opposed virtually every New Deal measure. He insisted that the "blundering busy bodies" of the New Deal were destroying basic American values.[73]

Robinson's conservative rhetoric did him little good in the senatorial election of 1934, when Sherman Minton defeated him by 50,000 votes. Robinson retired from politics, returning to Indianapolis to practice law with offices in that city and in Washington, D.C. He died in 1961, at eighty years of age. Again as in the case of Watson, there was nothing in his official biographical materials or in his *New York Times* obituary about Robinson's Klan associations and activities in Indiana.

About the future of the very malleable Hugh O'Brien, chairman of the State Correction Board in 1956, after Governor Craig left office at the end of that year O'Brien returned to Notre Dame as a sociology professor and finished his career in that capacity. The brash, outspoken Pat Emmons, who was head of the South Bend Klan organization during the height of tensions in South Bend during the spring and fall of 1924, lost his job as a foreman at the Studebaker Corporation. Next, he was punished by Evans for his loyalty first to Stephenson and then later to Bossert. The South Bend Klan lost its charter from the national Klan organization in September 1926 for refusing to remit portions of locally collected dues to Atlanta as a protest over the appointment of W. Lee Smith as Bossert's successor. Emmons described Smith as not being a Christian man. The South Bend Klan organization gave up its headquarters and went out of existence in February 1928. Emmons emigrated to Canada and dropped out of sight.

Much like Senators Watson and Robinson, the hundreds of thousands of true believers in Klan principles in Indiana and in other northern states were embarrassed by their association with an organization so utterly disgraced by Stephenson. Most of the true believers in pure Americanism, conservative social and moral principles, Protestant religious values, and continuation of Prohibition who had flirted with the Klan in the 1920s had rejected the organization by 1930. In that year, Klan membership had dropped from an earlier high of about five million to less than three hundred thousand, most of them concentrated in the South.[74] How many former Klansmen and unreckoned numbers of Klan sympathizers rejected Klan principles as completely as they had rejected the Klan organization is problematic. There is no way of knowing.

Certainly, Klan principles were powerfully operative in the presidential election of 1928 and contributed to the overwhelming defeat of the country's first Catholic presidential candidate. Later, other great national and local causes would find support from those who had been anti-Catholic, anti-Semitic, anti-Black, and had applauded the hooded marching men and women who had burned fiery crosses during the 1920s. Ironically, the most important of those causes—isolationism and anti-communism— that appealed to so many former true believers in Klan principles during the 1930s also appealed to a majority of American Catholics. This was not the first or last time in American history that old enemies would put aside ancient hostilities and forget past indignities to form alliances in order to confront new social and moral threats perceived as being more immediately dangerous and destructive to the body politic than traditional religious and racial conflicts had ever been. Such formal and informal alliances happened in the 1930s and would happen again.

PART III

— 13 —

THE PRESIDENT
AND THE COACH

F or the entire university community, the encounter with the Klan, the elections of 1924, and the revelations of the sordid Stephenson affair had been a chastening experience. If the people at Notre Dame did not already know the realities of being Catholic in America during the early 1920s, they learned about them very quickly in 1924. Among the things learned were that hundreds of thousands of Americans had been persuaded that Catholics in this country owed allegiance to a foreign power, that American Catholics were secretly and sometimes openly contemptuous of Protestantism as a religion and of Protestant social values, and that because of priestly influence among them they could never behave as free, autonomous individuals. In short, people of this mind-set believed that American Catholics were an unassimilatable minority, who, as long as they remained Catholic, could never become loyal Americans and trustworthy citizens.

To be sure, none of these attitudes were entirely new, but the highly successful manner whereby Klansmen and their sympathizers had propagated them was. During the 1920s, the Klan movement helped establish anti-Catholicism as a socially tolerable prejudice in American private and public life. Being anti-Catholic was not exactly chic, but in many circles one could be so in speech and writing without apology or embarrassment.

Perhaps the most chastening part of the whole Klan encounter experience was the realization that the present state government was hostile to Catholics and to Notre Dame. The Republican legislative agenda during 1925 was proof positive of that. In addition, university leaders had learned that city government could not be trusted to act routinely in university interests. Local politicians had other constituents as well as the university and had to be mindful of them. Generally, local officials were more ambivalent than overtly hostile to university interests. In future encounters of the sort experienced in May 1924, university officials had persuaded themselves that they could look only to their own local constituencies and resources for support and protection.

Being on their own in such situations was not altogether bad or unreasonable. As good Irish nationalists, Walsh and his colleagues understood thoroughly the concept, virtues, and goals of Sinn Fein, meaning self-reliance, we ourselves, or in some interpretations, ourselves alone. If the university could rely only on themselves alone, better they should know it and develop some principles for living as independently as possible from state and local government.

Henceforth, except for athletic relations, all Notre Dame presidents and other officials for the next thirty years would have as little to do with state government and state educational institutions as possible. Communication and associations occurred only when absolutely necessary. The days of fraternal and cooperative relations with Indiana University and Purdue University that had existed during Father Burns' time were over. Distance made this arrangement workable and unembarrassing.

With city government, separation was more difficult. Both were contained within the same county, and communication and associations of some sort simply could not be avoided. Yet, a means of maintaining independence was already firmly in the hands of Notre Dame administrators. After all, the university was located in Notre Dame, Indiana, and not in South Bend, Indiana. For the foreseeable future, all university presidents would stridently and inexorably oppose all efforts by city officials to annex and incorporate Notre Dame into the city. That was the enduring lesson of the events of 1924 and annexation and incorporation was then and still remains a non-negotiable proposition.

Present and future relations with local and state governments was only one of several enduring problems responsible for the severe job stress suffered by the presidents of Notre Dame during the 1920s. Given the infrastructure of the university and the traditional internal organization of the Holy Cross order, delegation and decentralization were not viable options for Walsh and his successors. Decisions had to be made by those priests appointed to offices where the power to do so had been concentrated. The only way to minimize the enormous stresses of being the president of Notre Dame was to escape from the university and leave the country. Walsh visited Ireland and England as often as he could and set foreign travel precedents that his successors made the most of.

Student behavior problems were endemic, annoying, and largely irresolvable. Spectacular examples of misbehavior were reported almost immediately by students who enjoyed shocking their overanxious parents and interested alumni. Such parents and alumni were quick to admonish Walsh for allowing such things to happen. For example, according to student gossip reported to parents, the senior ball in May 1923 had gotten completely out of hand. One local alumnus complained that the ball had been well patronized "by cigarette smoking girls and booze toting boys."[1]

Holding Walsh responsible for everything that happened at Notre Dame, this alumnus, blessed with a gift of sarcasm, hoped that Klan newspapers would not hear of this event and publish an account of the racy social life of these brilliant Notre Dame boys—Catholic gentlemen all, properly outfitted with the refinement and culture of a great Catholic university.[2]

Indeed, the senior class of 1923 must have been a particularly wild bunch. The class officers had contracted with an Ohio company to supply seniors with graduation pins. Funds for purchasing the pins were collected, but the company was never paid in full for them. A balance of $673 remained after the class had graduated and the students had dispersed. The Ohio company engaged a local lawyer to handle collection proceedings, and the first thing that the lawyer did was to write to Walsh.[3] The lawyer did not know what to do because the seniors involved had left for their respective homes or for parts unknown. He trod a very delicate line. Mindful of angering Walsh by accusing Notre Dame students of dishonesty, he urged the president to do something. The lawyer insisted that the bill ought to be paid regardless of any dissensions that may have existed in the class and of "any controversy over the honesty of the men having charge of the monies."[4]

The lawyer concluded his appeal by making a point that Walsh could neither answer nor avoid. While not blaming the university for the malfeasance of a few students, he noted how humiliating it was "to think that a crowd of graduates from a Catholic university with the standing of Notre Dame would leave the account to innocent strangers unpaid."[5] All that Walsh could think of doing at the moment was to pass the problem on to his prefect of discipline, Father J. Hugh O'Donnell, for resolution.

O'Donnell wrote to the lawyer acknowledging the justice of the company's claim for payment and advised him that efforts were being made to call a conference of class officers within two weeks and to devise some method for collecting enough money for the class to pay its just debts.[6] Whether the conference was ever held or whether the bill was ever paid at all by the class of 1923 is unknown. This incident annoyed Walsh and

O'Donnell severely. Indeed they were embarrassed, if not humiliated, by it. It mocked the carefully crafted public relations language about the morally superior environment of Catholic universities which was so frequently and loudly professed to the world. Walsh and other university officials consoled themselves by attributing this incident as well as others to the baneful influences of off-campus students on the rest of the student body.

As has been noted, the status of lay faculty at the university during the Walsh years was not a happy one. Walsh would have preferred doing without them. As Shuster had said, lay faculty were treated as necessary evils and paid as little as possible. With the objective of doing without them in mind, Walsh carefully considered a recommendation from Burns that facilities in the Holy Cross House of Studies at the Catholic University of America in Washington, D.C., be expanded and improved. He expressed some concern over how this $100,000 expansion should be financed but agreed in principle that the facility ought to be improved so that the work of Holy Cross seminarians and priests could be "advanced in such a way as to provide necessary priests and teachers for the future."[7]

Being a realist, Walsh knew that the Holy Cross Congregation could never even hope to find enough trained priests to staff programs in the Colleges of Science, Engineering, Commerce, and Law. However, professors and instructors for the College of Arts and Letters were another matter. Walsh and others had convinced themselves that teaching humanities and social science courses could be done by almost anyone. Seminarians and priests could be trained in their House of Studies and then assigned to do that.

Apart from the very uncertain future for lay faculty teaching humanities and social science courses, Walsh had serious reservations about providing salary increases for potentially expendable lay employees. Why burden the institution by raising the salaries of men soon to be replaced by Holy Cross priests with advanced degrees?

The very high anxiety level of lay faculty in the College of Arts and Letters is understandable. It was derived in large part from the simple fact of not having the same kind of alternative employment opportunities as were available to their lay colleagues in the Colleges of Science, Engineering, Commerce, and Law. Catholic teachers of English, history, or languages at college and university levels were largely limited in employment opportunities to teaching those subjects at Notre Dame or at other Catholic colleges and universities. Opportunities for Catholic teachers at state colleges and universities continued to be very few indeed. Because Catholic critics of the kind of education offered at such institutions had been very public and so severe, Catholic teachers correctly perceived that they would not be welcome there. Few applied and shamefully fewer were ever hired.

More than that, at this time in the College of Arts and Letters, lay faculty did not have anyone in or close to the upper levels of the administration willing and able to speak for them and look out for their interests. To be sure, lay deans in the Colleges of Science, Engineering, Commerce, and Law were generally powerless in deciding matters of salary increases and contract renewals, but they could and did argue for deserving individual cases.

However, the priests serving as deans in the College of Arts and Letters were either disinterested in such matters or fearful of encroaching upon the prerogatives of the director of studies and the president. Lay faculty in the College of Arts and Letters simply did not talk to their reverend deans about such matters. They had to look elsewhere. Lay faculty in other colleges were better off. For example, because of a close friendship with O'Hara and of the mistaken expectation that sooner or later he would probably join the Congregation of Holy Cross, the lay faculty member with most influence with the administration was James E. McCarthy, dean of the College of Commerce.

McCarthy always looked out for himself, but he was also willing to act on behalf of others. With regard to himself, McCarthy was usually dissatisfied with his own salary increases, and when contracts with salary notifications were sent out in May, he usually was among the first to register his dissatisfaction with the president. Sometimes McCarthy's humble requests for salary reconsideration were successful, but most of the time during the Walsh years, they were not.

While always looking out for his own interests, McCarthy would frequently intervene with the president on behalf of other lay faculty members for salary reconsideration. As a matter of fact, in May 1925, McCarthy asked for salary increases for one of the four lay faculty members teaching in his college and also for two members of the English department who taught many undergraduate commerce students.[8] Though in this instance McCarthy's requests for salary reconsideration went unheeded, he certainly had distinguished himself by trying to get something more for his faculty and friends.

Actually, at this time McCarthy's salary reconsideration efforts went far beyond these three cases. He proposed and offered to prepare a university-wide salary scale for all Notre Dame lay faculty.[9] McCarthy argued that a possible remedy for the annual anxiety bouts over salary increases and contract renewals could be mitigated, if not ended, by the establishment of "a salary scale for deans, professors, associate professors, and instructors that provides a maximum and minimum salary limit based on length of service that each in his field may eventually attain." According to McCarthy, such a scheme would be equitable if based on "an understanding of living costs, a willingness to pay a saving wage rather than a living one, a full measure of understanding that by doing so our teaching staff may be made permanent, enthusiastic, and more willing to give full service."[10]

Although properly reinforced with a splash of Catholic sociology, the idea of a salary scale that lay faculty would know about was far too radical for Walsh to consider or for that matter for any of his successors to consider. Walsh was not about to tell anyone anything about university finances or salary policies that they did not need to know. The difficulties and faculty morale problems embedded in such an idea as a published university salary scale were too great to risk. The principle that the less lay faculty knew about university finances and salary policies the better has endured and has successfully resisted all efforts to modify it down to the time of this writing. Walsh disposed of the McCarthy scheme by not responding to it.

— ii —

Another extremely important constituency that caused continuing problems for Walsh and his successors but could not be managed by the tactic of nonresponse was the American Catholic hierarchy. The problems with the bishops generally and especially with Bishop John F. Noll of the Fort Wayne Diocese in which the University of Notre Dame was located had nothing to do with theology or with ecclesiastical discipline. The problems had to do with football. Their excellencies made requests for postseason games for charitable purposes and for football tickets to important games that sometimes drove Walsh and his immediate successor, Father Charles L. O'Donnell, to distraction. For a member of a Catholic religious order to say no to a bishop in the 1920s was not something easily or lightly done. Notre Dame football was perceived by many of the bishops as O'Hara had perceived it, as one of the great triumphs of twentieth-century American Catholicism, and they wanted to share in it.

To be sure, more than postseason football games for charitable purposes and football tickets for popular games was at issue here, especially with Bishop Noll. Frequently, he would write to the president of the university on behalf of some deserving young man for special treatment in the admissions process or in the allocation of student jobs. Charles O'Donnell did not appreciate outside interference in the affairs of the university for any reason at any time, and in a tone of tempered exasperation tried to explain to the bishop how complicated the allocation of student jobs was and that outside advice in such matters was not needed.

O'Donnell informed the bishop that about 2,200 students were eligible for student employment, and of that number only about 600 competed for about 400 jobs. What O'Donnell did not say was that about fifty of those jobs went to student athletes. What he did say was that seniors were given priority, leaving not very many jobs for freshmen. O'Donnell made the point that "for every poor but deserving boy who wants to enter college, there is a poor but deserving boy who will have to quit college if he cannot receive some help." The problem was not an easy one of solution, O'Donnell concluded, but "we try to do our best to all concerned."[11]

Noll was an avid Notre Dame football fan and missed few opportunities to attend games, especially if they were played in interesting places. On one occasion in 1930, Bishop Noll accompanied the great team of that year on a week-long trip to California by train to attend the game with the University of Southern California in Los Angeles. Notre Dame's undefeated team won that game handily 27 to 0 before 73,000 people in the Coliseum.

Noll was overwhelmed with pride in the performance of these Catholic young men, aided by two spectacular Jewish running backs, Marchmont Schwartz, who had been recruited away from Loyola of New Orleans, and Marty Brill, who had transferred to Notre Dame from Penn State.[12] Noll wrote Walsh about the overall experience of being in Los Angeles for this great game. The crowd of 5,000 Notre Dame fans cheering their arrival at the Los Angeles railroad station, the triumphal stops at railroad stations across the country on the return trip, ending in Chicago with an enormous ticker-tape parade through the city, and then a crowd of 25,000 awaiting their arrival and greeting them in South Bend[13] was almost too much for Noll to handle rationally.

"I knew that the men would not spare themselves," Noll wrote, "because it was their last game, that they were going to win another national championship for their alma mater, for Rockne, and for the glory of the Church."[14] There was not much glory around for anyone in 1930 and people grasped it wherever they could find it. Noll found it in the Coliseum, at railway stations across the country, in Chicago, and in South Bend. It was as a priest friend attending the game noted to Walsh later, the

Methodists of the country may have defeated Al Smith in 1928, but the Methodists of the University of Southern California could not beat Notre Dame.

On another occasion, Noll's passion for Notre Dame football almost got him into serious trouble. He traveled to New York for the Army game in November 1928, a game that Notre Dame barely managed to win. While in the city, he was wined and dined as befitted his station by Notre Dame alumni and other prominent local Catholics. Several of the gentlemen attending the bishop were investors, stockbrokers, and investment bankers. These men were all experienced players in the stock market and apparently regaled Noll with stories about the enormous sums individuals had made by trading on inside information, at that time a legal but morally suspect activity. Apparently, the bishop was deeply impressed by what he had heard about fortunes being easily won in the stock market. The stories heard in New York stayed with him when he returned to Fort Wayne. The bishop decided to write to one of his New York hosts, James J. Boylan, with an extraordinary proposition.

In a letter sent to Boylan on November 23, 1928, Noll stated that while he had never been interested in the stock market, "If the gentlemen of whom you spoke as having books with the proper tips could help me out in saving a very important institution which is going bankrupt in this diocese, I would be willing to advance some money and let him buy and sell as his own information would dictate."[15]

The bishop of Fort Wayne proposed using diocesan funds to buy and sell stocks on inside information in order to rescue a Catholic hospital from near bankruptcy. Apparently, the question of beneficent and noble ends never justifying employment of morally suspect means never entered Bishop Noll's head. This incredible moral oversight by the official moral teacher of the Catholic diocese of Fort Wayne was exceeded only by the bishop's naiveté about the nature and state of the stock market in 1928. All players were not winners. Noll was saved from himself by Boylan, whose prescience about the risks of playing in the current market turned out to be timely and wise.

Boylan responded to Noll in early December expressing sympathy for the bishop's situation and a willingness to offer whatever assistance he could. At the same time, Boylan warned the bishop about the uncertainties in the present market. Neither Boylan nor any of his friends would assume responsibility for putting diocesan funds in the market at this time. In Boylan's judgment, the market was out of the hands of professionals and most anything could transpire. The advice of his friends, Boylan concluded, was to get out of the present market and stay out. It was no time for anyone to debut.[16] Noll heeded Boylan's advice, and by next October when the stock market crashed, he was very glad that he had.

Other bishops did not try to intervene so directly in Notre Dame affairs as did Noll, but both Walsh and O'Donnell, especially after the great Rose Bowl and triumphal tour of 1925, were continually pressed by bishops for postseason charity football games in their regions. Bishop Noll had a Catholic hospital in Fort Wayne that needed to be rescued from near bankruptcy, Archbishop Hanna of San Francisco had institutions in his archdiocese that needed help, and even a Holy Cross College in Texas devastated by a tornado asked for a charity postseason game.[17] All of this pressure prompted Charles O'Donnell to observe to a friend in November 1928, "how many persons there are who are anxious to give us opportunities of doing good."[18]

Combined with this seemingly endless series of requests from bishops for postseason charity football games was pressure from other sources. In the early 1920s the Big Ten prohibited members of their conference from participating in postseason games, including the Rose Bowl, a prohibition that lasted more than twenty years.[19] Whatever the Big Ten chose to do about regulating intercollegiate football Walsh was always of a mind to follow. At the same time, a report from the Carnegie Foundation recommended a ban on all postseason contests. Grateful for the significant contribution of the Carnegie Foundation to Father Burns' first fund drive and hopeful of going back to that source for other grants in the future, Walsh took their recommendations very seriously.

The result of all of this pressure on Walsh in the spring of 1925 was a decision to decline all invitations to postseason games. The ban was unpopular initially in many quarters on campus and off, but it remained in place and effective, except for one year during the Great Depression, until 1969, when university administrators at that time had no knowledge of why it had been instituted in the first place and rescinded it. The ban was formally announced on June 12, 1925, in a letter from Walsh to Bishop William Lillis. In this letter Walsh made no mention of the annoyance of episcopal pressure and attributed the ban to the necessity for following the Big Ten and his fear of charges of commercialism and of bad publicity for the university.[20]

Even Rockne, with some reluctance, accepted the ban as a fact of life and work at Notre Dame. He advised one friend that the ban on postseason charity games made sense because there were so many requests for them. Playing even a single postseason charity game could create major public relations problems for the university. Notre Dame would not only incur the enmity of the eminent persons and good causes that were turned down in a given year, Rockne concluded, but we would be morally obligated to continue the practice and accept other such games in the future.[21] Once the ban on postseason games had been announced, most of the world accepted it, and the university received positive public relations credits for having done so.

The matter of dealing with escalating episcopal and other pressures for complimentary, well-placed seats at important Notre Dame football games consumed an enormous amount of presidential time and annoyed both Walsh and O'Donnell severely. As was his way, O'Donnell often indicated his annoyance by using sharp doses of sarcasm. Walsh was more resigned and taciturn about their excellencies' demands.

In the fall of 1928 O'Donnell complained acidly about the number of bishops seeking tickets for the game that year in New York. Bishop Noll was among the first in line. According to O'Donnell, Noll had written to him offering to be O'Donnell's guest in the presidential box in Yankee Stadium. Bishops Finnegan and Mitty intended to attend the game and insisted that O'Donnell accompany them, even though he had decided not to travel to New York for the game. "I don't know how much longer I can hold out against such pressure," he wrote to a friend. "What can a mere college president do against the successors of the Apostles?"[22] The reasons for complying with these requests was prudence, a form of insurance, and a way of earning goodwill.

In 1929 and 1930 the football team managed two undefeated and untied seasons while playing before 431,000 and 331,000 fans respectively in those two years. By 1930 the stock market had crashed and the country was in the grip of the Great Depression. Clearly, Notre Dame administrators had much more import matters to worry about than football tickets for bishops, yet pressure for them intensified.

O'Donnell became so exasperated with these demands that he wrote to a priest friend about them in language that he never expected anyone else would read. To Father Joseph Boyle, O'Donnell wrote, "I shall send another ticket, not necessarily in my box to Bishop Kelly of Winona, feeling of course that it is wasted. Why these fat heads of bishops should take up good seven dollar space at our games is more than I can understand. There is not a backside in the hierarchy worth that much insurance."[23]

O'Donnell's sarcasm got even stronger as he went along in his letter to Boyle. Bishop Dunn of New York was coming to Chicago for the Notre Dame-Army game in Soldier Field. Bishop Cassidy of Fall River was flying out to Chicago for the same game, and from there "twittering out to California." I rather "admire the Fall River fool for jeopardizing what is left of his life in this fashion," O'Donnell added. "It shows a commendable interest in the future of us younger men who are ready to pull on purple sox."[24]

On still another occasion, O'Donnell confided to a layman friend, "There has been so much trouble about tickets that I am able to agree with the Carnegie Foundation that college football ought to be done away with."[25] Needless to say this was another example of O'Donnell's sarcasm. Neither he nor anyone else at Notre Dame at this time thought seriously of abolishing intercollegiate football at Notre Dame or anywhere else. The university simply could not afford to do so. In quieter and less aggravated moments, O'Donnell became and remained throughout his presidency an avid defender of Notre Dame football against all criticism from whatever source.

In any case, the episcopal penchant for trying to find ways of exploiting Notre Dame football, perhaps the premier American Catholic achievement of the decade, for charitable purposes is understandable. The negative reactions of Notre Dame administrators is equally so. To appreciate the passion of some bishops to attend and be seen at Notre Dame football games in large cities, such as New York, Chicago, and Los Angeles, one must realize that these football games had become celebrity events with powerful religious, ethnic, and even political overtones. A great many different flags, both large and small, had to be shown at them.

Accommodating all of the bishops who wanted to attend these important football games was extremely difficult for Notre Dame administrators because prudence required that such requests be honored, no matter how inconvenient. Catholic priests at this time rarely ever said no to a bishop. That just was not a prudent thing to do. Consequently, there were times when Walsh and O'Donnell would beg tickets from local Holy Cross priests who had them in order to meet episcopal demands.

All of these difficulties about charity games and football tickets were troublesome and often embarrassing for Notre Dame presidents, but the major problems arising from Notre Dame football successes did not come from opportunistic football-minded bishops. The biggest problems came from Rockne himself, a superb coach, an extremely ambitious and almost insatiable business entrepreneur, a media darling, and an absolutely uncontrollable and conniving university employee. If Walsh and O'Donnell had crosses to bear in this life, the heaviest one was Rockne.

— iii —

Rockne's personal relationship with the university and its leaders was ambiguous. As a graduate, as a football monogram holder, and as a convert to Catholicism Rockne was as qualified to be a full member of the Notre Dame family as anyone. Indeed, in almost all respects he was a true son of Notre Dame, but hardly an absolutely loyal one. Rockne wanted whatever he could get from the university as well as whatever his position there and win-and-loss record could command from outside sources.

Rockne never stopped pressing the university for salary increases, longer contracts, more staff, and better facilities. He varied the manner of making demands according to circumstances, but there always were demands. For example, as has been seen, as early as 1921, Rockne apprised two influential alumni that he needed more money and was thinking about moving to Northwestern University to get it. These two alumni approached Father Burns and helped negotiate a 40 percent salary increase, raising it to $7,000 and a five-year contract, something entirely unprecedented in university history.

Rockne made no moves in 1922—the first year of Walsh's presidency—toward threatening to leave the university for more money elsewhere, more autonomy, or better facilities. However, in 1923, Rockne's team won nine games, including one over Princeton that class-conscious American Catholics savored for months. That year Notre Dame lost only one close contest against Nebraska in Lincoln, a game enlivened by anti-Irish and anti-Catholic crowd reactions. After such a successful season, Rockne convinced himself that he was worth more money and was unappreciated by Notre Dame administrators and faculty. He took advantage of outside offers to leverage the university into providing more money and better working conditions.

The first threat under Walsh's presidency came near the end of 1923 when a Pittsburgh newspaper carried the story that Carnegie Tech had made overtures to Rockne about coming to that institution beginning in 1925. Persons knowledgeable about the Carnegie Tech football program in Pittsburgh assured Walsh that no such overtures had been made. Indeed, that may have been true, but the fact of those newspaper reports were enough to raise anxieties among influential Notre Dame alumni about the prospect of Rockne leaving.[26]

More serious was the situation with Iowa. Iowa officials approached Rockne by asking him to recommend candidates for the now-vacant position of head football coach at their institution. Rockne was noncommittal, but after reaching an impasse with Walsh's vice president, Father Thomas Irving, and with the Faculty Board in Control of Athletics over getting permission for a postseason game in California that he had already agreed to play, Rockne told Iowa officials that he would consider an offer from them.[27]

Iowa officials were delighted, and according to one account offered Rockne a three-year contract at $8,000 a year. There is no clear evidence that Rockne ever signed such a contract. He appears to have sought it only as a ploy to improve his situation at Notre Dame. What is interesting about this episode is that the president of the University of Iowa who authorized this contract for Rockne was none other than Walter Albert Jessup, the same college president who had so severely criticized the Notre Dame football program in 1921.[28]

Rockne's old friend, Angus McDonald, orchestrated a formidable campaign to keep Rockne at Notre Dame. It was a role familiar to him because he had played it in 1921 with Burns. In the Iowa matter, McDonald knew how to manage Rockne and what to say to Walsh. After several letters and a personal visit to the campus from New York, McDonald persuaded Walsh to consider what he called reasonable requests from Rockne, including the hiring of a full-time business manager for the athletic department, a long-term contract for Rockne with a significant salary increase, and affording the coach a stronger influence in shaping the new constitution for the Faculty Board in Control of Athletics and in the general reorganization of athletic affairs then under way.

Walsh needed little persuasion to make Rockne an offer he could not refuse. The president knew that rising football revenues would pay for Rockne's salary rise as well as for the new business manager's stipend. Issues relating to the new constitution for the athletic board and Rockne's influence over it was another matter. Holy Cross priests simply would not tolerate lay interference in high-level administrative decisions. Walsh decided that Rockne would be shown the new document after it had been written and not before. Walsh also decided to appease Rockne on this issue by replacing Irving as board chairman with Father Joseph Burke, a long-serving academic administrator whom Walsh liked and trusted. On the issues of salary and contract length, Walsh went far beyond the Iowa offer. He presented and Rockne accepted a new ten-year contract with a salary of $10,000 a year for ten months' work. That was a staggering salary for any Notre Dame employee in 1924.[29]

Rockne was so delighted with the new contract and salary increase that he publicly professed in a Notre Dame publication an oath of loyalty to Notre Dame and stated that he was not interested in any other university or football program in the country and wanted to spend the rest of his professional career at the school that had done so much for him.[30] This was an oath probably seriously intended at that moment but easily forgotten over the next four years. Joseph Byrne, another influential New York alumnus deeply interested in Notre Dame's football fortunes, was also satisfied with Rockne's new contract. Byrne wrote to Walsh at the end of February 1924 advising the president that the best way to handle Rockne now and in the future was "absolutely to let by-gones be by-gones and start everything afresh as if nothing had happened."[31]

However well-intentioned, this advice turned out to be impossibly wrong. The truth of the matter was that no one could manage Rockne at any time for very long. Walsh did not take Byrne's advice, because he knew better and could not forget what had happened. He had capitulated on most points in this matter and resolved that he would not do so again. Next time, no matter how great alumni pressure might be, he would stand fast on the solid legal grounds of contractual obligations.

As has been already recounted, following the Klan riots in South Bend in May 1924, the football season of that year was a glorious triumph for the university and for American Catholics everywhere. Notre Dame went through the regular season as well as a postseason appearance in the Rose Bowl undefeated. The much-praised Four Horsemen captured the public imagination, and Rockne's celebrity status soared. With that increased celebrity status, the coach's value in many marketplaces increased greatly. Early 1925 was opportunity time for a coach who knew how to make the most of it.

In December 1924, an important alumnus of the University of Wisconsin approached Rockne about moving to that institution. Rockne did not pursue that offer. About the same time officials from the University of Southern California contacted Rockne about the head coaching job at that school. Apparently Rockne agreed to meet with them during the Rose Bowl visit. His intentions were disguised unknowingly by his old friend and protector, Angus McDonald, who wrote to Walsh in mid-December indicating that Rockne wanted to stay over in California "for the sake of his own and his wife's health." According to McDonald, "Rockne was in a highly nervous condition due to a long and difficult season, I fear that unless he takes a rest he will break down. . . . You should let Rockne know," McDonald concluded, "that his absence from the university will not seriously interfere with anything, and thereby relieve his mind."[32] Walsh agreed, and Rockne finalized arrangements to meet with Southern California officials after the Rose Bowl game had been played.

The meeting went well with the point being made that Mrs. Rockne liked the southern California climate and would rather live there than in South Bend. On January 15, 1925, the comptroller of the University of Southern California wired Rockne in South Bend that all of the conditions he had specified in the meeting would be met.[33] In Los Angeles, news of the offer was not a well-kept secret. A reporter published the details on

February 16, and the wire services picked up the story and distributed it throughout the country. All of this occurred before Rockne had a chance to speak with Walsh and try to talk his way out of his long-term contract with Notre Dame. Walsh heard about the offer from the press and responded by reminding Rockne that he had a contract with the university and that legal action was possible if he broke it.[34]

In a wire to Rockne, Southern California officials apologized for the news leak and the embarrassment that had followed from it. Included with this apology was a formal invitation from the trustees of the University of Southern California to come to their school.[35] Apparently, Walsh's threatening response had some considerable effect on the situation. Rockne had been frightened by the prospect of legal action and said so. He complained to Southern California officials about being constantly on the defensive since returning from California and was fearful that his standing with some influential alumni had been compromised.[36]

When Rockne finally advised Southern California officials that further negotiations were futile, one of those officials responded with the observation that it was almost criminal for Notre Dame to hold him to his contract if Mrs. Rockne would be happier in Los Angeles than in South Bend.[37] Apparently, as later events would suggest, at this time Mrs. Rockne entirely subscribed to this view and never really forgave Notre Dame for blocking the family's move to sunny southern California. While the University of Southern California did not get Rockne to head their football program in 1925, they did manage to get Rockne's team on their schedule for the season of 1926, initiating a series that has lasted to the present day.

With Rockne's employment situation stabilized for the moment, he faced the season of 1925 with some trepidation. The celebrated Four Horsemen had graduated, and only second-string players from the great team of the previous year along with young and inexperienced freshmen and sophomores were available to make up the squad in 1925. In many eyes, the season of 1925 was a failure. The team won seven games, lost two games (Army and Nebraska), and tied Penn State. No Notre Dame team had lost two games in a single season since 1914. Losing the final game to Nebraska in 1925 was painful in several respects and had serious consequences for Notre Dame-Nebraska athletic relations and for Rockne as well.

Previous Notre Dame football teams visiting Lincoln had encountered anti-Catholic and anti-Irish insults from local fans. However, Rockne and Notre Dame officials usually had been willing to ignore them as coming from the town rather than from the University of Nebraska for the sake of continuing the series and earning a substantial return from gate receipts.

Moreover, the warm and generous reception of the Rose Bowl team in Lincoln in January 1925 inclined Notre Dame officials to assume that anti-Catholic and anti-Irish verbal abuse and harassment in Lincoln was on the wane or over. That assumption turned out to be incorrect.

Remarks made about alleged rules violations and academic laxity at Notre Dame by members of the Nebraska traveling party after the Nebraska-Illinois game in mid-October 1925 were picked up by the press and repeated throughout the Midwest. Rockne responded to these press reports quickly and vituperatively.[38] The controversy over these widely reported but generally untrue allegations about rules violations formed the background for what happened before and during Notre Dame's final game against Nebraska on Thanksgiving Day, 1925.

When the Notre Dame team and fans arrived in Lincoln in late November, they were genuinely shocked by public displays of animosity against them. Placards appeared in store windows exhorting Nebraska to beat the Notre Dame roughnecks soundly. Notre Dame fans reported anti-Catholic and anti-Irish epithets intended to upset and rattle the Notre Dame team before and during the game from every corner of the stadium. Insofar as affecting the outcome of the game, Nebraska fan behavior probably did not matter very much. At Lincoln on Thanksgiving Day, 1925, Notre Dame was clearly outclassed, and Nebraska went on to win the game handily, 17 to 0.

Nebraska's obvious superiority on that day did nothing to diminish abusive crowd behavior. However, the most painful insults of all came not from the crowd but from a Nebraska student pep organization. In a tasteless halftime stunt a group of Nebraska students burlesqued the now celebrated Four Horsemen and Irish Americans generally in an unforgivable way.

Four Nebraska students appeared in midfield, each carrying a brickmason's hod and mounted on make-believe horses. They galloped around the field delighting the intensely partisan Nebraska crowd. Given the pregame controversy about rules violations and academic laxity at Notre Dame as well as the way the game was going, Notre Dame supporters were outraged. The messages of the stunt were clear enough, namely, that the Four Horsemen were the intellectual equivalents of hod carriers rather than bona fide college students and that Irish Americans were fit only for menial jobs.

The *South Bend News-Times* reported the incident, noting that this halftime stunt had ridiculed Irish Americans, Rockne, and the University of Notre Dame.[39] Notre Dame officials attending the game assumed that someone in the University of Nebraska student affairs office must have approved the stunt or it never would have happened. No matter what the outcome of the game turned out to be, this ethnic insult from an organization apparently sanctioned by some officials in the University of Nebraska could not be forgiven and was not.

When the Notre Dame traveling party returned to South Bend, Dean McCarthy advised Walsh that members of the athletic board believed that Nebraska should be dropped from next year's schedule and the series ended.[40] Walsh agreed. The game with Nebraska for the season of 1926 was canceled and all negotiations for future games were dropped as well. Thus was the Notre Dame-Nebraska series played regularly every year since 1916 ended. Though Rockne strongly opposed canceling the Nebraska series and indeed distanced himself personally from the athletic board's decision in public relations releases and in private correspondence, this was a decision with very long-lasting consequences. Notre Dame did not play Nebraska again until 1947, when most of the men involved in the original decision were either off the athletic board, retired, or deceased, and the reasons for making it had been forgotten.

In 1925, however, Klan anti-Catholic activities were at their peak, and for Holy Cross priests and the wider Notre Dame community the time for ignoring anti-Catholic and anti-Irish insults from anyone had passed. The practical realities of this decision were clear enough. Nebraska needed Notre Dame on its schedule more than Notre Dame needed Nebraska. Only Notre Dame had enabled Nebraska to sell out its new stadium. Moreover, Notre Dame could and did play before larger crowds and obtain high financial returns by scheduling other opponents in large urban stadiums.[41]

In 1925, the Notre Dame-Nebraska game had been played before 35,000 people in Lincoln. A year later, the first game with the University of Southern California, who replaced Nebraska as a regular annual opponent, was played before a crowd of 74,000 people in Los Angeles. The decision to drop Nebraska was certainly justifiable in view of the ethnic and religious sensitivities of that time and in the long run probably made financial sense, but Rockne did not see it that way.

Rockne was outraged over the fact that Walsh and the athletic board had overruled him in the Nebraska matter and had intervened in what he believed was his personally sacrosanct area of scheduling. Rockne did not know how often such interventions would be repeated in the future. Angry and frustrated over the ego-bruising Nebraska affair, Rockne persuaded himself that he had experienced enough interference from Notre Dame officials and that it was time to move elsewhere and to do so quickly.

— iv —

The month of November 1925 turned out to be a very busy and aggravating time for Rockne. After losing a game decisively to Army, 27 to 0, in Yankee Stadium in mid-October and then winning two close games against Minnesota and Georgia Tech, Notre Dame managed a tie against Penn State on November 7. That was certainly not a good beginning for the last month of a lackluster season. Notre Dame won an easy victory over Carnegie Tech and a harder one over Northwestern before facing Nebraska in the final game of the season and as things worked out the final game of this series.

Just prior to the Nebraska game and much to the delight of Mrs. Rockne and of Notre Dame officials, Rockne was received formally into the Catholic Church, being baptized, taking Holy Communion, and accepting Confirmation in mid-November.[42] Apparently Rockne exhibited none of the zeal for the Church and it ministers usually exhibited by recent converts. Acceptance of the Catholic faith had no impact whatsoever on his feelings for the university or for Notre Dame officials after the cancellation of the Nebraska series. He was so outraged and so personally humiliated by this action that he carried intensely bitter feelings with him when he departed for New York City in late November.

While in New York, Rockne met with James R. Knapp, an unpaid representative of the Columbia University athletic department. Whether Rockne or Knapp initiated this meeting is unclear.

What is certain is that Rockne signed a three-year contract to go to Columbia for $20,000 a year. Apparently, Rockne had signed the contract with the understanding that the whole business would remain secret until he returned to South Bend and arranged with Walsh to get released from his contract.[43] The way matters stood between Rockne, Walsh, and the athletic board at that time, a release from the contract was a distinct possibility.

However, Rockne never had a chance to pursue that strategy because he went to Philadelphia rather than to South Bend immediately after the signing on December 1, 1925, and Columbia officials leaked details of the signing to the press on December 4. Stories about Rockne's contract with Columbia appeared in evening editions on that day.

In the company of Joseph M. Byrne and John Neeson in the Benjamin Franklin Hotel in Philadelphia, Rockne first heard of the news leak from a local evening newspaper account. According to Byrne, Rockne turned white when he read the story. Byrne and Neeson questioned Rockne very closely for over a half an hour about what he had done and why. Next,

Byrne and Neeson compelled Rockne to call Father Walsh immediately, that is, shortly after midnight December 5, to explain what had happened. Exactly what Rockne told Walsh is unknown, but some sources suggest that he told the president what he said publicly later, namely, that he had sent Knapp a letter, probably on December 2 and presumably before leaving for Philadelphia, saying that his agreement with Columbia could not be carried out and that he wanted to remain at Notre Dame. Rockne claimed later that the letter had been sent from South Bend, but Rockne did not return to South Bend until after December 7.[44]

Next, in the early hours of December 5, Walsh spoke with Byrne and Neeson and tried to develop a strategy that would minimize public relations damage to the university and to Rockne. What they proposed to do was, first, to sequester Rockne, that is, never leave him alone for a minute and keep him away from the press. Second, for Byrne and Rockne to go to New York forthwith and confront Knapp and possibly other Columbia officials about the violation of Rockne's contract with Notre Dame and obtain a withdrawal of the Columbia offer.[45]

On Saturday morning, December 5, Byrne and Rockne left Philadelphia by train for New York. Upon arriving they went directly to the Astor Hotel, where they were joined by a Notre Dame alumnus, Rupert Mills, and a close friend of Byrne, Preston Walsh. Byrne and Mills went off to meet with Knapp in offices at Columbia University while Walsh remained with Rockne in the Astor Hotel, keeping a close watch over him and taking all telephone calls. At the Columbia meeting, Knapp indicated that Rockne would be released from his contract with Columbia if that was what he wanted and that he and Byrne should prepare a press release favorable to both universities. However, when Byrne brought Rockne to Knapp's office in the afternoon, Knapp and his wife both tried to persuade Rockne to forget about his Notre Dame contract and come to Columbia.[46]

Regarding this behavior as a breach of good faith, Byrne exploded and demanded an immediate meeting with Columbia's athletic board, which he did not get. After an acrimonious exchange, the parties agreed to meet later in the afternoon to finalize a mutually satisfactory press release. The truth of the matter was that a mutually satisfactory press release was impossible. Officials at Columbia were ready to withdraw their contract with Rockne on the patently spurious grounds of being unaware that the coach was still under contract to Notre Dame at the time of his signing with them. In their press release Columbia authorities insisted that their athletic board would not have offered a contract to Rockne if they had known he was still under contract to another university. Columbia regretted the entire situation and withdrew their contract.[47] However, this Columbia press release was issued while Byrne and Knapp were in the Astor Hotel trying to prepare a mutually satisfying press release of their own. Columbia authorities succeeded in getting their version of the incident out first.[48]

Back at Notre Dame, Walsh played a carefully controlled but partly disingenuous game. He admitted to no one that he had known about the Columbia contract since the early hours of December 5, when Byrne had compelled Rockne to call the president and tell him what had happened. Walsh did not release any statement about the affair until December 11 and did so only in response to calls from newspapers coming from every part of the country.

On this occasion, according to an Associated Press report originating in South Bend, initially Walsh stated that Rockne had told him by telephone that he had signed *no* contract and that he had no intention of leaving Notre Dame.[49] Walsh expressed surprise that Rockne had indeed signed a contract with Columbia. The president professed no knowledge of details and added that even Mrs. Rockne had expressed surprise at newspaper accounts of the signing.[50]

Walsh followed up this statement with another on December 12 that Notre Dame would not stand in Rockne's way if he wanted to go to Columbia. Rockne could stay or leave; it was up to him to decide. Moreover, Walsh added that he would be the first to congratulate him if he decided to leave.[51] This apparently magnanimous position was, of course, a pure public relations ploy, because Walsh had known for over a week from Byrne and Rockne that the coach would stay at Notre Dame.

If Walsh dissembled with skill and caution, Rockne's public accounting of the affair issued on December 18 was in effect a public Act of Contrition. Rockne declared himself heartily sorry for having embarrassed his beloved alma mater. He stated further that at no time had he intended to leave Notre Dame or had he at present anything but a strong desire to serve the school that had done so much for him. If and when the time came for him to leave Notre Dame, he would not do so without first obtaining a clear understanding with university authorities about when and why he was going.[52]

The persuasive impact of Walsh's and Rockne's public statements upon press commentators was minimal. Most commentators concluded that Rockne had not told the truth and that Walsh was cooperating with the coach in order to minimize public relations damage to all concerned.

Ed Hughes of the *New York Evening Telegram* put the public statements of Walsh and Rockne into perspective by observing that the "glistening coat of whitewash applied to Knute Rockne does not cover the football coach."[53] Indeed, it did not and Walsh knew that it did not.

As every priest knew, all too frequently penitents relapse. There was not much in Rockne's history to reassure anyone that the man would amend his life and do better. Consequently, Walsh prepared a "Memorandum for the Athletic Files" which Rockne must sign if this very troublesome matter was to be put behind all of them. Rockne agreed. He signed Walsh's memorandum without murmur or protest. Father George Finnegan, vice president of the university and soon to be appointed bishop of Helena, signed the same document as a witness.

Included in the memorandum were the points that Rockne had not asked for a release and that Notre Dame had been ignorant of the whole proceedings. Stated explicitly in the memorandum was a threat that if any future questions should be raised about these two points, the substance of this signed memorandum "should and would be given such publicity as might be necessary to fully acquaint the public with the attitude taken by the University of Notre Dame."[54] By signing this document Rockne attested to the truth of it and indicated his willingness to approve whatever publicity on these matters the perceived welfare of the university might require.[55] Simply stated, Rockne agreed that the reputation of the university must never be compromised or diminished in any way by the behavior and credibility of its football coach. Thus was the Columbia matter formally closed.

From New York, Walsh received a long, detailed account of what had happened from the ever-loyal Joseph M. Byrne. He admitted that Rockne was an irresponsible person and had embarrassed the university and himself on many occasions because of his thoughtless dealings and actions. We all have our faults, Byrne added, and probably Rockne had more than most. However, the real villain in this piece was Mr. Knapp. If Knapp had been a square shooter, Byrne concluded, the whole affair could have been settled quickly and quietly with little publicity "but Mr. Knapp was a dog of another color."[56]

Though Byrne was suffering from cash-flow problems since the failure of his brokerage business the previous August, he agreed to travel with Rockne to France on board the *DeGrasse,* leaving New York on January 6 and returning from Le Harve on February 10, 1926. The trip was, as Byrne put it, "the least I can do for my university to see Rock through his troubles . . . and will give Mrs. Byrne and myself a great deal of pleasure to return Rock to you as the same fine boy we knew as an undergraduate."[57] However, life was not that simple. The accumulated resentment and hostility between Walsh and Rockne was too great to forgive and forget.

Upon returning from Europe, Rockne was more subdued for a while. He complained bitterly to a friend that his life was now an open book, and "if they pick on me I presume I will have to stand it."[58] Clearly, Walsh had won this battle, but Rockne was not the kind of person who could accept defeat as a permanent condition. The conflict between Rockne and Walsh and other university administrators would go on but be waged by other means.

— v —

In early 1926, Walsh and his close advisors decided once again to apply for admission to the Big Ten. They had to be nervous about how all of the bad publicity surrounding the Columbia incident would affect their application. The timing of the application seemed propitious because rumors in athletic circles suggested that the conference was ready to expand. This appearance of opportunity apparently counted for more in Walsh's thinking than any possible consequences following from the *cause celebre* with Columbia. Whatever Walsh's reasons for approaching the Big Ten at that moment, the application was very serious on the part of the university, and strategies for winning approval were carefully planned.

First, Rockne made a goodwill tour of conference member schools to speak with coaches and athletic directors. Shortly thereafter, Dean McCarthy made the same sort of tour, giving his attention to faculty members on athletic boards. Rockne thought his tour had gone well except for Michigan, where it was clear that authorities at that state university were determined to oppose Notre Dame's application to join the Big Ten. The University of Chicago and the University of Illinois were doubtful as well. McCarthy's tour was even less encouraging. He returned to Notre Dame believing that Big Ten hostility and jealousy of Rockne was the principal obstacle to Notre Dame's entry into that conference.[59]

At this point, Walsh and his advisors changed their strategy. Instead of submitting a formal application in May, they asked the conference members to appoint a committee to visit Notre Dame to investigate all matters academic and athletic at the university. Depending upon the findings of this committee, Notre Dame would or would not submit an application for admission to the conference in December.[60]

A majority of Big Ten schools refused to consider the Notre Dame proposal. They dodged the issue and certain bad publicity attendant upon refusing Notre Dame's application by voting 6 to 4 not to enlarge the conference at this time. Walsh was deeply disappointed by the conference's action and decided to try resolving this matter by meeting with the presidents of the University of Chicago and of the University of Michigan, the principal opponents of the Notre Dame application. When he visited these two institutions, however, their presidents were reluctant to intervene concerning the positions taken by their respective athletic directors. Both presidents simply advised Walsh to submit an application for admission to the conference in December and hope for the best.[61] Their inaction on this matter was a measure of the status and power of coaches such as Yost and Stagg in their respective institutions. Walsh came away from the meetings with a clear understanding of how deep was the hostility of Yost and Stagg toward Rockne and the Catholic school that employed him. By words and actions those two coaches had made no secret of how much they loathed Rockne and envied his celebrity status and economic success. That special loathing was an insurmountable obstacle to Notre Dame obtaining admission to the Big Ten. If getting into that conference was perceived by Notre Dame officials as being so important, perhaps the time had come to think about ways of eliminating that obstacle.

With Walsh's silent approbation, Dean McCarthy visited a number of influential Notre Dame alumni and sounded them out about replacing Rockne. Speaking as the secretary of the Notre Dame athletic board, McCarthy insisted that Rockne was the principal obstacle to conference admission and that the coach's penchant for embarrassing the university by thoughtless statements and actions had become too much to bear. In effect, McCarthy argued that Rockne was preventing Notre Dame from achieving public recognition as a peer of their neighboring state and private universities. McCarthy's arguments were heard by the alumni groups but were not well received. Insofar as they were concerned, dismissing Rockne was unacceptable. Rockne had been too successful as a coach and was too much of a national celebrity even to think of replacing him with someone else. Rockne learned of McCarthy's visits to alumni groups a few months later and never forgave him for what he had tried to do as Walsh's proxy.[62]

During the spring and fall of 1926, Rockne tried almost heroically to be on his best behavior. He did not want to do anything that would jeopardize the university's application to the Big Ten. That decision would be made in December, but in the fourth game of the season, against North-western, Rockne was involved in an incident with an official that doomed the Notre Dame application.

Notre Dame had won their first three games handily against Beloit, Minnesota, and Penn State. Rockne and his team managed to defeat Northwestern, 6 to 0, before 41,000 people in Evanston on October 23, but it had not been easy. According to Rockne, one of the reasons for the difficult game with Northwestern was the officiating. A strong Michigan partisan, Meyer Morton, acting as referee, assessed ninety-five yards in penalties against Notre Dame and none against Northwestern. At game's end, Rockne encountered Morton and told him that his game officiating looked like "a Big Ten Suckhole."[63] The incident was exaggerated and reported in the Chicago press and elsewhere. For Yost in Ann Arbor, this incident was proof positive, if he needed any, that under no circumstances should Rockne and Notre Dame be allowed into the Big Ten.

In the weeks following the incident, Yost abetted by Stagg circulated stories about rules violations at Notre Dame and alleged that no matter how many courses a student athlete might fail, he would not be declared ineligible. All of these rumors and allegations, which were absolutely unfounded, were reported in the Chicago press.[64] Rockne stridently insisted publicly and privately that such stories were just stories and nothing more, the standard stock and trade of Yost and Stagg.[65]

The Big Ten conference meeting in December proceeded generally along the lines as scripted by Yost and Stagg, with others agreeing. The Notre Dame application was denied. Privately, Rockne attributed the rejection to Yost's undisguised anti-Catholicism, styling his enemy from Michigan as a Tennessee hillbilly who was very narrow in religion.[66]

The concerns, anxiety, and ultimate disappointment over the Big Ten conference application notwithstanding, Rockne was able to prepare the now matured players from last season into a winning team for 1926. Win they did until the next to the last game of the season. Rockne's team easily defeated Beloit, Minnesota, Georgia Tech, Indiana, and Drake. Only Northwestern and Army turned out to be genuine contests. After being severely tested, Notre Dame obtained one touchdown victories in each of them. By the last week in November, with only games against a reputedly weak Carnegie Tech squad and a strong Southern California remaining, midwestern reporters were proclaiming another Notre Dame national championship as a possibility.[67]

Clearly, Rockne underestimated the Carnegie Tech football team as a serious opponent for his present squad. He thought so little of Carnegie Tech's football ability that he turned game direction over to Hunk Anderson and did not himself travel with the team to Pittsburgh. Instead, Rockne went to Chicago to participate in promotional activities for himself and his growing outside business interests. Actually, this Chicago trip was the second time during this season that he relied on Anderson to direct team play while he was attending to personal interests elsewhere. The first such absence occurred in the game against Indiana in Bloomington on November 6 when Rockne went off to New York to tend to some promising entrepreneurial projects involving the use of his name.

Inspired play by the Carnegie Tech team, overconfidence by the Notre Dame squad, and poor coaching by Anderson resulted in a Carnegie Tech upset of Notre Dame, 19 to 0. Reporters were astonished. A writer in the *New York Herald Tribune* described the Carnegie Tech victory as "an upset of tremendous proportions . . . considered by many as the greatest upset in collegiate football annals."[68] Moreover, Rockne's absence from the game was widely known. The *Chicago Tribune* and other papers made a point of mentioning it in their game stories, and pictures of Rockne in Chicago on game day also appeared in the local press.[69] Once again Rockne had embarrassed the university, was himself humiliated, and for several days became the object of journalistic mockery.

Though all thoughts of a national championship disappeared with the Carnegie Tech loss, partial redemption was achieved quickly. The team returned from Pittsburgh early Sunday morning, November 28. On Monday, November 29, Rockne and the team departed on the four-day trip to Los Angeles. The players practiced and worked out at various stops along the route and were ready to play very hard against Southern California in the Coliseum before 72,000 people. In the game, Notre Dame scored first, but Southern California responded with two touchdowns and took the lead. In the final minutes of the game, Rockne worked another miracle. A reserve quarterback, Art Parisien, who happened to be ambidextrous, threw several left-handed and right-handed passes which thoroughly confused Southern California defenses, enabling Notre Dame to score a last-minute touchdown and win the game, 13 to 12.

— vi —

Rockne's absences from the Indiana and Carnegie Tech games were indicative of the extraordinary expansion of his outside business interests, especially after the Columbia fiasco in late 1925. If Rockne could not double his salary by going to Columbia, he would have to find other ways of augmenting it. This he did in a variety of new and ingenious ways. In fact, Rockne set standards of income augmentation that few collegiate coaches were able to meet at that time or later. Simply stated, Rockne rarely missed or forsook any opportunity to make money out of his celebrity status.

Rockne's private business dealings began early in his career. In late 1922, Rockne contracted with the Christy Walsh syndicate to do a series of newspaper articles and columns which the syndicate would place. Actually, the Christy Walsh group did more than place the stories, they supplied the ghostwriters who wrote most of them. As a matter of fact, during Rockne's later years, about all of Rockne that appeared in such articles was his name. In many instances, the first time that Rockne ever saw the articles was when they appeared in print. Christy Walsh placed ghostwritten football columns under a Rockne byline in about fifty Hearst and Pulitzer newspapers, netting Rockne in good years upwards of $6,000, or about half of his regular Notre Dame salary. His other early major publishing venture was an instructional book, *Coaching,* published in 1925, which brought him almost $7,000.[70]

In addition, there was a great deal of money to be made in coaching schools and conferences. Rockne developed what had been summer pastime activities into organized, highly profitable businesses. He got into the summer coaching business in the early 1920s through informal gatherings at the Culver Military Academy, about twenty-five miles from South Bend. In the summer of 1923, Rockne held one coaching school at Notre Dame and two others at out-of-state locations. Quickly Rockne realized that coaching schools were indeed an entrepreneurial idea whose time had come. Acting on his own and in partnership with others, Rockne expanded to five coaching schools in 1925 increasing thereafter to seven schools with over a thousand student coaches participating in his programs.[71]

Initially at Notre Dame, Rockne received one-half of the twenty-five dollars tuition paid for the coaching school programs. The other half went to the university, along with revenue from dormitory usage. Income from food services went to the local company managing and staffing the university cafeterias.[72] After winning the national championship, Rockne's bargaining position was much stronger, so he did not replicate the Notre Dame financial model at other institutions. He charged the student coaches a fee for tuition, thereby separating his profits from those of the host schools. Murray Sperber, who has studied Rockne's business dealings in detail, estimated that Rockne probably netted $22,000 a year for his summer coaching schools. Related to the summer coaching schools was Rockne's plan for summer coaching camps for young athletes. He established one, Camp Rockne in Wisconsin, in 1930 and planned to develop others on a large scale. However, fate intervened and he died before the scheme could be completed.

Coaching schools and summer camps preoccupied Rockne in June and July, but speaking engagements kept him busy throughout the year. Rockne signed a contract with the Leigh-Emmerich lecture bureau and spoke as often as that agency could book dates for him. His speaking fees rose from $125 per appearance in 1926 to over $400 in 1927.[73] Rockne was absent from the university in 1927 and 1928 so often that Father Walsh wrote a snappish letter reminding the coach that he was a very high salaried university employee and should spend more time tending to business there.[74] Indeed, Rockne did cut down his lecture program for Leigh-Emmerich but did not suffer much income loss for doing so. Other entrepreneurial opportunities were at hand, and Rockne took full advantage of them.

There was, of course, income from endorsements. He contracted with the Wilson Athletic Equipment Company to market and advertise his name, nickname, portrait, and facsimile signature on every piece of football equipment the company sold. From the Wilson contract, Rockne probably netted about $10,000 a year between 1928 and 1930.[75] Rockne also from time to time endorsed a number of personal care products, including Barbasol shaving cream under the slogan of "the right play at the right moment." This endorsement ran as an advertisement for several months in *Collier's* magazine during the fall of 1929.

Also, Rockne lent his name to a local travel agency and derived income from its bookings. In addition to steering business to his agency, he escorted a group of rich tourists to the Olympic games in Amsterdam in 1928, for which he was paid $10,000. Later in the same year, Rockne shepherded a group from the Football Coach's Association, after their meeting in New Orleans, on an unforgettable tour of the bars and flesh pots of Havana. As a matter of fact, there did not appear to be any events or products that Rockne would not endorse if the price was right.

Rockne was much beholden to Albert R. Erskine, president of the Studebaker Corporation and chairman of the Notre Dame Board of Lay Trustees. Rockne went willingly anywhere that Erskine wanted to send him, including opening the Chicago Auto Show in 1927, for which he received $500 for a twenty-minute talk.[76] This sort of activity, which Rockne made no effort to disguise, did not make him very popular with ordinary Notre Dame faculty, who were lucky to earn $2,500 a year on annual contracts.

Rockne's business life was so complicated and frenetic during 1928, 1929, and 1930 that he had to turn down some lucrative offers because of time constraints and because of objections from the Notre Dame administration based on propriety considerations. One such rejection was an offer to appear in an extensive one-man vaudeville tour, similar to those made by Will Rogers, providing inspirational monologues, witty sayings, and football chatter. However, one offer to which the university could not and did not object was an invitation made and accepted in 1928 for Rockne to become a vice president in the Studebaker Corporation and then give regularly scheduled lectures and motivational speeches to Studebaker employees and dealers as well as appearing as a Studebaker representative at special events.

The Studebaker appointment certainly regularized Rockne's outside business life insofar as Studebaker assignments necessarily reduced the number of his other appearances, but the Studebaker appointment in no way diminished his frequent and lengthy absences from the university. Sperber estimated that at the height of Rockne's earning power, 1928–30, the coach received from all sources about $75,000 a year, an enormous income for that time. Rockne's gross income exceeded even that of his patron, Albert R. Erskine of the Studebaker Corporation.[77]

If Rockne had lived, the Great Depression notwithstanding, there would have been even more to come. He opened a stocks and bonds brokerage office in South Bend in 1930. According to one account, Rockne had signed a radio contract just before he died that would have netted him $30,000 a year.[78] Finally, the ill-fated flight to California that took Rockne's life in March 1931 was for the purpose of signing a contract for $50,000 to appear in the role of the football coach in a Universal Pictures movie version of the popular Broadway play *Good News.*

In terms of making money out of celebrity status acquired through football coaching, Rockne was unmatched by anyone during his own time or later. Rockne was too much for either Father Walsh or his successor, Father Charles L. O'Donnell, to handle. The simple truth of the matter was that in public estimation and general newspaper interest, Rockne had a greater reputation and was more important and newsworthy than either Walsh or O'Donnell. To the general public, Rockne had become Notre Dame.

All of Rockne's business interests and ever-increasing celebrity status depended upon his ability to produce winning football teams. Recruitment of talented players and training them to perform well in his system was the foundation on which everything else rested. The Carnegie Tech fiasco in 1926 had dashed all hopes for a national championship and had ruined the season for that year. Rockne had hopes for the season of 1927 but was realistic about his prospects for defeating a formidable Minnesota team and the always dangerous overexperienced team from West Point.

Rockne knew, as did most sports writers in the country, that the Army team had two superb running backs, Red Cagle and "Light Horse" Harry Wilson, who were in their sixth and seventh years of major college football play. There was no doubt that these two players were superior to most of the professional backfield stars in the National Football League.[79]

The first five games of the season against tiny Coe College, the University of Detroit, the Naval Academy, Indiana University, and Georgia Tech were all easy victories. Reporters once again began to write about a possible national championship. Then, Minnesota came to South Bend on November 5 and played their hearts out. An exciting young sophomore, Bronko Nagurski, playing tackle, virtually shut down the Notre Dame offense after an easy first-quarter touchdown. Late in the game Nagurski forced a fumble that led to a tieing touchdown. The game ended in a 7 to 7 tie, ending a twenty-two-year home game winning streak. Nagurski went on to achieve All-American status as a lineman, and then the next year earned the same honor as a running back.

The Notre Dame team had stumbled badly against a great player in the Minnesota game but avoided a loss. The following week in Yankee Stadium before 65,000 people the Notre Dame team would face two great players. Despite the fact that Notre Dame donned green uniforms and changed the numbers of some Notre Dame players to confuse the opposition, Cagle and Wilson played up to and over their reputations. Army easily defeated Notre Dame, 18 to 0, and ended all talk of a national championship.

Two games remained in the season, but really only one mattered. The Notre Dame team easily overpowered Drake University in Des Moines, 32 to 0, on November 19 before only 8,400 people. The following week, Notre Dame encountered Southern California in Soldier Field before 120,000 fans. For most Chicago people, this match was the game of the year; and, indeed, it was the largest turnout for a football game in Chicago's history to that time. The game was as much a political and social event in Chicago as it was an athletic one. Celebrities, politicians, local notables, and even gangsters rubbed shoulders in the boxes at Soldier Field. Actually, people-watching and observing the antics of the crowd were much more interesting than the game.

Both teams scored early touchdowns, but Southern California failed in their extra point try. After three quarters of uninspired play and avoidable mistakes by both sides, the game ended with a narrow but controversial Notre Dame win, 7 to 6. Late in the game, officials ruled against a play that would have given Southern California a two-point safety and a probable victory.

Despite the disappointment over the tie with Minnesota, the loss to Army, and the dullness of the Southern California game, the season was a financial success, grossing over $331,000. However, this very good payout could have been even greater, if Notre Dame had a stadium of its own. Rockne claimed that both Minnesota and Notre Dame had lost at least $75,000 by playing at Cartier Field rather than in Chicago. Revenues from home games amounted to only one seventh of the gross for the entire season.[80] With the season of 1927 now history, Rockne turned his attention to the extremely difficult task of trying to persuade Walsh to approve a scheme for building a new stadium.

— vii —

Ever since Walsh had assumed the presidency of the university in the summer of 1922, Rockne had been pressing him and others in the Notre Dame community to replace the very limited Cartier Field facility with a new stadium. Walsh had resisted all such pressures, preferring to build dormitories, a new dining hall, a new field house and gymnasium, and also to improve some academic buildings. Walsh was also very sensitive to what other higher education authorities and foundation officials thought about the overemphasis and commercialization of intercollegiate athletics. During the 1920s the building of new large stadia was widespread and symbolized that sort of overemphasis and commercialization. Moreover, as Rockne's embarrassing behavior and entrepreneurial activities intensified in 1924 and thereafter, the fact that an idea about a major university policy decision came from Rockne was almost sufficient to damn it in Walsh's estimation.

However, because of lobbying by influential alumni, by the fall of 1927 Walsh's resistance to a stadium project had mellowed into hesitation about how and when to undertake it. At the November meeting of the Board of Lay Trustees just prior to the Minnesota game on November 5, Walsh agreed to establish a special committee of trustees with three subcommittees to inquire into the feasibility of the stadium project at this time.[81]

Of these three subcommittees, the one charged to investigate the general feasibility of the project, composed of Frank Herring and Fathers Walsh, Burns, and Charles L. O'Donnell, was the most important. The second subcommittee on finance included money men such as Albert R. Erskine and Edward N. Hurley. The third subcommittee directed to inquire into site selection and oversee construction included Rockne.[82]

All of these subcommittees were expected to present reports to a meeting of the special committee in December. Apparently, Rockne did not expect that the feasibility subcommittee dominated by Walsh, Burns, and O'Donnell would deliver a positive recommendation. In order to expedite or insure a positive recommendation from those men and to encourage others to pressure them, Rockne once again employed his ultimate weapon. First, Rockne started rumors among influential alumni indicating that if the stadium project was disapproved, he would accept the first outside offer extended to him in 1928.[83] Second, to add credibility to these rumors, Rockne submitted a very brief letter of resignation to Walsh on November 28, 1927, the day after the season-ending game against Southern California.[84]

Walsh neither accepted nor acknowledged Rockne's resignation at this time, because he had a fair understanding of what was behind it. Though Walsh publicly ignored the resignation for the time being, privately through Frank Herring he took some action. Acting on Walsh's behalf, Herring issued an addendum to the instructions given to the three subcommittees. Walsh's message was clear enough to those who received it. Notre Dame would not proceed with a stadium project if an undue financial burden was placed on the university and if any other adverse contingency, not at present foreseen, meaning Rockne's departure, should arise.[85] As a member of the site selection and construction subcommittee, Rockne certainly received a copy of this addendum to the subcommittee's instructions. Walsh was as good at the game of bluff as was Rockne, and the president wanted Rockne and everyone else involved in this project to know that he was still the boss.

Meanwhile the three subcommittees proceeded with their work and reported to the special committee in a meeting at Notre Dame on December 17, 1927. The feasibility subcommittee of Herring, Burns, Walsh and O'Donnell approved the idea that building a stadium for use in 1929 was desirable. At the same time, Walsh indicated his strong opposition to building a new stadium on credit, fearing criticism for not doing the same for urgently needed academic facilities. Hurley and other trustees on the special committee pointed out that the stadium project was very different from constructing a new classroom building. Self-financing programs were available for a stadium but not for academic facilities.

Hurley estimated that a new stadium suitable for seating 50,000 people could be built for $800,000. Since Rockne had managed to set aside $300,000 for the project in the athletic department account, only $500,000 would be required to complete the project.[86] Hurley believed that $500,000 could be easily raised by selling box seats to 100 men willing to pay $500 a year for ten years.[87] The idea was appealing even if some doubted that more than $150,000 could be raised by such means.[88] If the university was to proceed with the stadium project a self-financing scheme was the only way to go. There simply was no support for borrowing or for organizing a special fund drive.[89]

At this meeting on December 17, the feasibility subcommittee's report was approved. The finance and site selection subcommittees were charged to explore all possibilities and come up with recommendations at a later date. The idea of a stadium project had been approved, but the university was not yet committed to proceeding with it. That was as far as Walsh would go at this point. Required by canon law to leave the presidency of the university and the office of local superior that went with it in the summer of 1928, Walsh decided to leave the final decision about the stadium project to his successor.

Decision avoidance came easy to Walsh, and in his final year as president that disposition became increasingly evident. In addition to delaying action on the stadium project, Walsh found himself confronted with another much more delicate decision, especially within the context of Holy Cross politics, that he also managed to avoid. While serving on the feasibility subcommittee for the stadium project, Father Burns had learned of Rockne's $300,000 nestegg buried in the athletic department account. Believing that monies taken or borrowed from that account would be easily and quickly replenished and uncertain if and when the stadium project would proceed, Burns had in mind an alternative use for some of that now dormant money.[90]

Burns suggested to Walsh that he, as president, ought to divert $100,000 of the dormant money in the athletic department account to a project for renovating and generally improving the residential and academic facilities at the Holy Cross House of Studies in Washington, D.C., of which he was rector.[91] Walsh agreed that the facilities in Washington needed improvement and that anything to enhance the quality of life and educational opportunities for Holy Cross seminarians would be a very good thing indeed. However, if renovation of the Washington facilities was to proceed, Walsh insisted that the monies should come from the general funds of the university and not from the athletic department account. Walsh did not need another brawl with Rockne at this time. To Burns, Walsh simply stated that he did want to commit to such a project without the approval of his successor. Thus Walsh avoided another serious confrontation with Rockne that could not have remained private. In any case, Burns was willing to wait a bit longer and did not press Walsh to do anything that might cause controversy during the last few months of his presidency.

For his part, Rockne probably heard about Burns' designs. He reacted by complaining bitterly both publicly and privately about the torturously slow Holy Cross decision-making process. Nonetheless, Rockne signed a new ten-year contract with the university in April 1928. This new contract notwithstanding, Rockne was deeply frustrated. He wanted a new stadium for the season of 1929, but when no formal action had been taken in the spring of 1928, it was clear that the project could not be completed by the fall of 1929. All of these uncertainties and delays in 1928 made scheduling extremely difficult, because while the new stadium was under construction Cartier Field would be unusable and all games would have to be played away.

No wonder Rockne counted the days until Walsh would be out of office. Most likely Walsh also was counting the days. Like the good soldier he had been in 1917 and 1918, Walsh had served his religious community and the university since 1922 to the best of his considerable ability. Quite apart from the canon law requirement requiring Walsh to leave office, it was time for someone else to assume leadership and find ways of coping with the problems of Catholic education and of living and working in an environment of undiminishing anti-Catholic hostility.

The powers that be within the Holy Cross community put their faith and future into the hands of Father Charles L. O'Donnell, also a veteran of the Great War like Walsh but in personality traits and in energy a very different man indeed. That energy would be much appreciated and needed during the enormous crises facing the country, the university, and the American Catholic community in the next few years.

— 14 —

POLITICAL HUMILIATION
AND FOOTBALL TRIUMPH

C harles O'Donnell was a native Hoosier, born in Green-
field, Indiana, in 1884. He was the youngest of six children whose parents had been born in Donegal. Edu-
cated in the parochial schools of Kokomo, O'Donnell found a religious
vocation early and came to Notre Dame as a seminarian at the tender age
of sixteen. O'Donnell graduated from the university in 1906. In the fall of
the same year, he was sent to the House of Studies in Washington, D.C., to
do his theology and begin graduate studies in English literature at the
Catholic University of America. He completed his graduate work in 1910
with a dissertation on the prose works of the English Catholic Victorian
poet and writer Francis Thompson. Upon receiving his doctorate, he returned to Notre Dame, where he was ordained on June 24, 1910.

Like his presidential predecessor, O'Donnell was totally and absolutely
an Irish American. Deep affection for the Irish literary and cultural
heritage was an essential part of his intellectual persona. O'Donnell was
himself a poet of considerable talent. He was blessed, or perhaps cursed,
with extraordinary gifts of sharp wit and sarcasm, which he displayed
with an embarrassing regularity. O'Donnell was not a man to turn the
other cheek. He would not let pass criticisms, however well or ill founded,
of the university, the Catholic Church, Irish Americans, or the American
Catholic community. He was always ready to respond, publicly or privately, in ways that recipients would not soon forget. For this reason
O'Donnell's private and official letters are by far the most interesting of all
of the Notre Dame presidents of his generation.

O'Donnell had strong views about the role of religion in education
and about the importance of literary culture in American higher education. While he never argued that literary and cultural knowledge were the

only proper indicators of how well-educated a person might be, he came very close, for he strongly believed that religious values and literary culture were closely connected and ought to be integral parts of any authentic educational mission. Others in the Holy Cross community, particularly O'Hara and some of the university's Thomistic philosophers, would disagree. However, for as long as O'Donnell was president, after religion, literature would have as important a place in the Notre Dame curriculum as the classics or scientific and technological understanding.

Believing as strongly as O'Donnell did in the importance of literary culture, it should not be surprising that his own literature courses were regarded as memorable events by those students who took them.[1] Actually, O'Donnell's teaching career was relatively brief. He moved into university administration very early, serving as prefect of religion from 1912 until he went off to the Great War as a chaplain along with Walsh and four other Holy Cross priests in 1917.

After service in France and on the Italian front and saddened by what he had seen and heard while in Europe, O'Donnell returned to Notre Dame in 1919. He went back to the classroom momentarily, and then in the summer of 1920 was named provincial of the American Province of the Holy Cross community and as such was the superior of Presidents Burns and Walsh. This was an unusual appointment for a man of his age, being only thirty-six, but by all accounts he was successful in this office during a troubled time. When O'Donnell's six-year term expired, he was named first assistant to the superior general and then in 1928 was chosen to succeed Walsh as president of the university.

Given O'Donnell's wide range of experiences, he was extremely well prepared to assume the presidency in what quickly became a most difficult time for Notre Dame, the American Catholic community, and the country as a whole.

For vice president, O'Donnell chose a man who in personality traits was much *un*like himself, Father Michael A. Mulcaire. The new vice president had been born in Ireland in 1894 and had come to Notre Dame at the age of fifteen as a seminarian. Finding a religious vocation and leaving home at such an early age was by no means exceptional in his family. He was one of eight children, of whom four became priests and nuns. After graduating from Notre Dame in 1917, Mulcaire went off to the Catholic University of America to do his theology and begin graduate work in economics. He was ordained in 1922 and received his doctorate in economics in 1923.

Mulcaire returned to Notre Dame to teach economics from 1923 to 1928. As a teacher, Mulcaire was remembered as being very bright, aggressive, and one who did not suffer fools, or persons he believed were fools, gladly. Along with his intelligence and aggressiveness, unlike O'Donnell, Mulcaire was possessed with a very evident sociability and, alas, an affection for alcohol. In time this affection became an addiction and ruined the later years of his life.

The starkly opposite personalities of O'Donnell and Mulcaire combined in an administrative team inspired faculty wits irreverently to style their time in office as Notre Dame's poet and peasant era. Aggressive, direct, sometimes coarse, and knowing it, Mulcaire was not offended by the sobriquet of peasant. He was what he was. In 1928 what he was seemed to be precisely what the office of vice president and chairman of the athletic board required. O'Donnell and other influentials in the Holy Cross community believed Mulcaire to be the best available man to try to manage Rockne and bring the athletic department under closer supervision. As Mulcaire said to Hunk Anderson a few years later, the priests wanted to regain control over a situation that desperately needed correction.[2] That was Mulcaire's charge, and he undertook it with all the zeal, naiveté, and good intentions of inexperience. Rockne was not a man easily managed or intimidated by clerical authority.

However, in the fall of 1928 the principal preoccupation of the university community was not Rockne or football. It was the same as the rest of the country, the presidential election of 1928 with all of the anti-Catholic propaganda and hostility associated with it. Because of the Stephenson debacle in 1925, Klan organizations were a spent force in most American communities outside of the South in 1928. Generally, decent people everywhere no longer wanted to participate actively in Klan organizations or otherwise be associated with them.

Though Stephenson was in jail and Klan organizations in the North had been shattered, Klan principles, meaning anti-Catholicism, had not been widely discredited. In rural communities and in some urban ones throughout the South, Midwest, and West, there was little shame or embarrassment in publicly expressing or displaying anti-Catholic sentiments during those years.

To be sure, there were some quite carefully argued and reasoned public statements about the alleged divided political loyalties of American Catholics. Such pieces were answerable in civilized discourse. Although minds might not be changed one way or the other by them and disagreements remained, life could go on with some continuing suspicions but without rancor or public displays of bigotry.

However, other statements about alleged Vatican intentions and Catholic practices in America were based on the wildest sort of misinformation and rumor and for the most part were unanswerable in any form, civilized or otherwise. Some of the persons engaging in such strident anti-Catholic propaganda were people who had no way of knowing better. Others who should have known better chose to pander to this deeply held and long-standing American prejudice for a variety of religious, political, and social reasons.

During the presidential campaign of 1928, Methodists and Baptists were perhaps the most active in damning Alfred E. Smith's candidacy on religious grounds. Protestant fundamentalists tended to be the most extreme, but the whole range of Protestant opinion, from strict Lutherans to permissive Unitarians, contributed to the cacophony of anti-Catholic hostility against Smith. Anti-Catholicism was nothing new to Smith. He had encountered religious prejudice as early as 1918 in his first New York gubernatorial campaign, and it had plagued him ever since.

Anti-Catholicism and Klan principles had deadlocked the Democratic National Convention in 1924 and had led to the nomination of a decent but colorless candidate who had no chance of defeating Calvin Coolidge. Smith had tried to handle those several earlier anti-Catholic episodes by ignoring them, assuming that his widespread popularity and public record in the state of New York was more than sufficient to persuade voters to support him. In New York City and state politics, Smith was correct. Voters across the state supported him in increasing numbers after 1922. What was correct in New York and perhaps elsewhere in the northeast simply was not true for much of the rest of the country.

Religious bigotry aside, there were at least four important reasons why many Americans chose to vote against Al Smith in 1928. First, the issue of Prohibition deeply divided the country. Though most politicians tried to straddle the issue by shrouding their respective positions in clouds of ambiguity, Smith stood forthrightly for the restoration of legal beer and spirits and for repeal of the Eighteenth Amendment. For many true believers in the desirability of Prohibition, Smith was on the wrong side of the most important moral issue of the day.

Second, Republicans took full credit for the general prosperity of the country in 1927 and 1928. Their spokesmen insisted that prosperity would disappear if a Democrat were elected president. From the point of view of voters who were distrustful of Smith, more than the loss of prosperity was at risk if a Democrat won the election. Some of Smith's closest friends and associates were rich Catholics who were perceived as having been overly aggressive, unprincipled, and probably dishonest in their business practices. Such alleged predatory men would certainly turn up as members of Smith's cabinet or find themselves in other important government positions where their presumed wicked ways would be under no restraint in a

Smith administration. The principal villain in this scenario of predatory Catholic businessmen taking over the country was John J. Raskob, a successful financier, a former vice president of General Motors, and Smith's probable choice for the post of secretary of the treasury.

Third, notwithstanding Smith's affection for rich people, his Tammany Hall background and associations, in some eyes, branded him as a corrupt politician or at least overly friendly with some of the most notorious urban machine politicians in the country.

The fourth reason was a matter of snobbery. While Smith might have a large number of rich friends who enjoyed his company, he had only an eighth-grade education and was the only person of working-class origins in the entire twentieth century to win the presidential nomination in one of our major political parties. For many American voters, especially the newly enfranchised women voters, the very idea of the Smiths being installed in the White House was appalling. Smith's New York City accent simply affronted many midwestern, southern, and western Americans. His manner of pronouncing "raddio" for *radio,* "foist" for *first,* "woik" for *work,* and dropping "g's" from such words as *going, living, smiling,* and *praying* established Smith, in many minds, as an ill-bred, uncouth, ignorant political opportunist.[3]

At the same time, Katie Smith's dowdy appearance, unfashionable clothes, and penchant for saying nothing of interest to the press did not help the image of the Smiths as the country's first family. For many Americans of this sort of snobbish mind-set, it appeared that the cartoon characters of "Maggie and Jiggs" were about to move into the White House and defile that sacred space with generous helpings of corn beef and cabbage and lots of beer.

Certainly, each of these secondary issues were important in determining voter's choices, but none of them, either singly or in combination, would have been fatal to the Smith campaign without the extraordinary extent of religious bigotry displayed in the presidential election of 1928. The religious issue in presidential politics arose early in 1927. It began after the prospect had diminished that any other prominent Democrat would seriously challenge Smith for the nomination. To be sure, the nomination was not to be Smith's for the asking. However, as governor of New York and as a much-bruised veteran of the horrendous Democratic National Convention of 1924, it was clear that he had first refusal for the nomination in 1928, and in the spring of 1927, there were no signs that Smith was about to refuse it. The possibility of a Catholic becoming president of the United States was one that Protestants and other Americans had to confront.

Among the first to face the issue of a Catholic president was Charles C. Marshall, a New York City attorney and a leading Episcopalian layman. Marshall wrote an article, "An Open Letter to the Honorable Alfred E. Smith," which the *Atlantic Monthly* agreed to publish in March 1927. The magazine sent Smith galley proofs before publication and promised to publish a response from Smith in the May number of their magazine. In this article, Marshall absolutely eschewed the language of bigotry and tried to make his points about Catholics being unacceptable for the presidential office in constitutional terms.[4]

Marshall's principal point was that American Catholics found themselves in the impossible position of trying to serve two masters, the Roman Catholic Church and the American Constitution and state. In the manner of a legal brief, Marshall cited and quoted papal bulls, encyclicals, and other Church documents to make a case that neither Smith nor any other American Catholic could conscientiously serve as both president of the United States and as a loyal member of the Catholic Church. The issues for Marshall as well as for others who contributed opinions to this controversy were those of religious liberty and separation of church and state.

On the basis of a close reading of these Catholic Church documents, Marshall and others who agreed with him were convinced that Vatican authorities had not ever and did not now consider American conventions and practices in the areas of religious liberty and separation of church and state as correct. The American approach to religious liberty as well as to the constitutional doctrine of separation of church and state were tolerated by the Vatican because nothing could be done about them. According to Marshall and others, the great Protestant fear was that with a Catholic installed in the White House perhaps something would be done about them. For many Protestants including Marshall, the risks of having a Catholic in the White House were just too great to hazard.[5]

Though Smith was outraged by Marshall's article, his initial reaction was to ignore it. Two of Smith's aids who happened to be Jewish, Judge Joseph Proskauer and Belle Moskowitz, insisted that Smith had to answer it. According to one account, Smith admitted to Proskauer that he had never heard of the Vatican documents and books that Marshall had mentioned and that they had nothing to do with being a Catholic.[6] In the end, Smith gave the task of preparing his response to Marshall to Proskauer, who immediately sought help from Father Francis P. Duffy, former chaplain to the celebrated sixty-ninth Regiment of the Rainbow Division, and from Michael Williams, editor of *Commonweal*. What Proskauer, Duffy, and Williams prepared was edited by Smith and then presented to Archbishop Hayes for final approval. So it was that a Protestant challenge to the right of Smith or any other American Catholic to be elected president of the United States was answered in large part by a Jewish judge.[7]

When completed, the Proskauer response to Marshall, entitled "Catholic and Patriot: Governor Smith Replies," was logical, to a degree scholarly, but mainly rhetorical. It could hardly have been otherwise because the response-writing team could not deal with most of Marshall's points directly. The papal encyclicals and other documents said what Marshall had indicated. The main issues of religious liberty and separation of church and state had to be dealt with indirectly. For example, Proskauer and Duffy quoted from the *Catholic Encyclopedia,* a source that Marshall had used, about the virtue of tolerance. They also quoted statements from a series of Catholic prelates, especially Archbishop John Ireland of St. Paul, about their respective firm commitments to the constitutional doctrine of separation of church and state and to legal guarantees of religious freedom.[8]

Perhaps the most telling point in the response was when Proskauer and Duffy chided Marshall for thinking that all American Catholics were alike in mind and heart and therefore obligated in some way to accept and publicly defend every utterance and statement emanating from prelate or priest. That obligation was not demanded from Episcopalians or from other American Protestants. The authors of the response also affected to be mystified why the public perception of American Catholics was so different. They concluded by assuring Marshall that, as president, Smith would recognize no power in the institutions of his church that would conflict with the United States Constitution or interfere with the enforcement of the laws of the land.[9]

Smith's response was duly published in the May issue of the *Atlantic Monthly,* but it is uncertain how many people bothered to read the article and very doubtful that many minds were changed by it. The religious issue in the forthcoming campaign was in no way put to rest by Smith's reply. As a matter of fact, Dr. Albert C. Diffenback, editor of the *Christian Register* and a prominent Boston Unitarian minister, went over much of the ground already covered by Marshall in a speech delivered at the University of Virginia Institute of Public Affairs in Charlottesville on August 16, 1928.[10] In this speech, Diffenback declared that no Roman Catholic should ever be elected president of the United States. The reasons why were clear enough in Father John A. Ryan's book *The State and the Church,* published with an official Catholic Church imprimatur, meaning that nothing in the book was theologically objectionable. According to Diffenback, Ryan had demonstrated that no person could be a loyal Catholic while supporting the prevailing American constitutional doctrine of separation of church and state.[11]

Father John A. Ryan, a professor at the Catholic University of America who was a social liberal but a theological conservative, was not seriously misinterpreted on prevailing official Catholic doctrine on the American model of separation of church and state. Ryan argued that the American model was tolerable in the United States but not appropriate for export elsewhere. According to the Vatican point of view as explicated by Ryan, a model more approximating an ideal church-state relationship was the existing arrangement in Spain. In that predominately Catholic country at that time a close relationship between church and state was believed to be the best and most efficacious for all concerned.

Ryan speculated that if at some future time Catholics became a majority in the United States, perhaps something like the Spanish model would be the best and most efficacious for us as well. However, the likelihood that Catholics would ever achieve majority status in this country was so remote, Ryan added, that the present wall of separation between the Catholic Church and the state would remain forever intact, that is, firm and high. Ryan's explication of the official Catholic doctrine on separation of church and state and speculations about possible future church-state relations in the United States certainly dissatisfied and probably alarmed those Protestants and other Americans with informed interests in American Catholic affairs. In the minds of others who were generally untouched by arguments and speculations of this sort, this whole controversy was simply sound and fury that confirmed long-held suspicions. Not many of the latter were of a mind to care very much about what the pope, Vatican officials, John A. Ryan, or even Alfred E. Smith had said or not said about these issues.

It is undeniable that in 1928 Vatican officials and the conservative theologians at the Catholic University of America made the task for aspiring national politicians of being authentically Catholic and totally American very difficult. For a man like Smith, whose devotion to the Catholicism into which he had been born and raised was genuine, the controversy over whether his religion made him an unacceptable presidential candidate was at once unfair and tragic.

Smith could not and did not deny the official Church doctrines on religious freedom and separation of church and state that had been lately called to attention. What he tried to say in the response prepared by Proskauer and Duffy was that those positions were absolutely irrelevant to what he would do as president. The unstated implication in the assurances he gave in the *Atlantic Monthly* article and later in a speech delivered in Oklahoma City on September 20 were clear enough. In the special situation as president of the United States, he would behave as an American first and as a Catholic second. However, as events were soon to demonstrate, an overwhelming majority of Protestants and of unchurched people in the country did not believe him.

A substantial literature could be collected from the anti-Catholic propaganda issued in 1928 intended to frighten Americans into believing that if Smith were elected, the country would be utterly changed. Religious freedom as we know it would be lost forever. Actually, the propaganda against Smith proceeded on two levels. The lowest level of propaganda was predominately, but not exclusively, stock-in-trade, traditional anti-Catholic slanders. Most of these materials were unsigned booklets, broadsheets, pamphlets, and handbills run off on small-town printing presses and duplicating machines.[12]

Pulpit and platform speakers also contributed. To be sure, there were Protestant ministers and lay leaders who were appalled by what was being done to Smith and to American Catholics in the name of Protestant security and who protested publicly, but their voices went unheeded by the majority. Though a degree of anti-Catholicism was respectable in some circles, these literary and oratorical assaults in 1928 were unprecedented. Nothing like them had ever afflicted so much of America.[13]

These oratorical assaults included the famous evangelist Billy Sunday, who as a self-styled ambassador of God proclaimed a duty to defy the forces of hell, meaning Smith and the "damnable whiskey politicians, businessmen, crooks, bootleggers, pimps, and street-walking whores who were associated with him."[14] Other speakers and writers were less colorful but stridently poignant. The *Christian Index,* a Baptist publication in Atlanta, warned its readers that Smith and the men around him, particularly Raskob, were capable of anything. They intended to take over the country and had the money to do it. From now on, the *Christian Index* concluded, it will be "Rum, Romanism, and [General] Motors" running everything unless the country wakes up.[15]

Then there were those such as the editorial writer for the *Wesleyan Christian Advocate* in Atlanta who began an attack on Smith with defensive politeness but ended in the old way. The editorial insisted that Smith had a constitutional right to run for president even though he was a Catholic. At the same time, Protestants have a right to vote against him because he is a Catholic. We are strongly persuaded, the editorial concluded, that Catholicism is a degenerate religion which everywhere ought to be replaced by a purer type.[16]

Propagandists at a higher level were perhaps more implicitly anti-Catholic than explicitly so. Instead, they focused more on the candidate's anti-Prohibitionist stance and on his Tammany Hall background and associations. Bishop James Cannon of the southern branch of the Methodist Church, editor of the *Baltimore and Richmond Advocate,* a powerful member and influence in the Anti-Saloon League, and a leader in the campaign to win ratification of the Eighteenth Amendment, was a link between the lower and higher level anti-Smith propagandists.

As early as July 1928, Cannon and three other southern branch Methodist bishops issued a public statement out of Richmond affirming their intent to wage a militant campaign against Smith because of his anti-Prohibition policy.[17] More than Smith's anti-Prohibitionist stance was involved in Cannon's decision to oppose the Democratic candidate. While Cannon stated publicly that any means were justified in protecting and preserving Prohibition as the highest achievement of the American people in promoting general welfare,[18] beneath this very important issue was Smith's Tammany Hall background and his Catholicism.

As Cannon saw the world, the Democratic party had fallen under the control of New Yorkers who, by definition, were corrupt and immoral. According to Cannon, New York City was a satanic, foreign-populated place, a modern Sodom and Gomorrah from which no good could ever come. Cannon was convinced that Smith had not broken free of his old New York connections and that he would not do so in the future. The prospect of crooked Tammany politicians installed in the White House was too frightening even to consider.

However, beyond all of the important considerations relating to the presumed corrupt and immoral culture from whence Smith had come and which all of America ought to reject, there was that old principle bred in Cannon's bones that the bishop could neither ignore nor deny. Proclaiming himself free of all forms of bigotry, Cannon resolved that no subject of the pope could ever become president of the United States.[19] Cannon's commitment to this principle was absolute. His vigorous and unrelenting campaign against Smith helped persuade a majority of voters in five normally Democratic states, including his home state of Virginia, to vote for Hoover on election day.

One of the most celebrated, active, and distinctly high-level propagandists against Smith in the election campaign was Mabel Walker Willenbrandt, educator, champion of women's property rights, a strong Republican, and a serving assistant attorney general of the United States. President Harding had named Willenbrandt to the post of assistant attorney general at the age of thirty-one, making her the youngest woman ever to achieve that rank in the federal government.

Willenbrandt was a fiercely partisan Republican, an unquestioning passionate believer in Prohibition who also happened to be the chief enforcer of the Volstead Act. By 1925, Willenbrandt had been responsible for the prosecution of more than forty-five thousand Volstead Act violations in the federal courts. For her, Prohibition was more than a noble experiment. It was a "moral crusade under religious leadership frankly intended to save the people from a habit believed to be the chief cause of poverty and misery."[20] Willenbrandt had no tolerance whatsoever for anti-Prohibitionists and scarcely any for Democratic politicians, especially those who spoke in heavily accented New York City English. Not surprising, then, in 1928 that she became one of the most outspoken and most quoted critics of the Smith candidacy.

Willenbrandt insisted in later years that at no time during the campaign of 1928 had she ever faulted Smith for his Catholicism. Instead, she argued that her attacks upon Smith were directed toward his anti-Prohibitionist stance and for his association with predatory Tammany Hall politics. Having said this in a book published in 1929, *The Inside of Prohibition*, Willenbrandt, in a skillful lawyerlike manner, was probably technically correct.

While Willenbrandt may not have personally attacked Smith on religious grounds in 1928, in many speeches during the campaign she urged Prohibitionist Protestant ministers to try to convince the nation that Smith was a threat to Prohibition and to the Constitution of the United States, of which Prohibition was now a legal part.[21] Clearly, there was a special message in Willenbrandt's anti-Smith speeches during the campaign of 1928 that went beyond the issue of Prohibition. She managed to damn Smith and his friends as well as the social and political culture from whence they had come without specifying that he, they, or it were all Catholic and thereby menaces to Protestant notions of morality and right behavior. This message may have been unstated, but it was effectively delivered and widely understood.

Finally, there was, indeed, one high-level critic and strident opponent of Smith whom no one before the election campaign of 1928 could honestly accuse of bigotry. This critic and opponent was the celebrated William Allen White, editor and publisher of the *Emporia Gazette,* the reputed voice of small-town America and keeper of midwestern values, and an energetic author of magazine articles and books who had a national reputation for wisdom and objectivity. White was a Republican but not stridently so; he was a Prohibitionist and adamantly so. While White was no bigot, he did not understand and was at times utterly mystified by the realities and apparent contradictions of American Catholic culture that a man like Smith represented and articulated.

White had attacked and ridiculed the Klan often and vigorously in the pages of the *Emporia Gazette* during the 1920s and actually had run for governor of Kansas as an independent when neither of the candidates from the two major parties would publicly denounce the Klan. White lost that election, which he had no real chance of winning, but thoroughly enjoyed the opportunity of relentlessly attacking the Klan in towns and cities across the state when it was not politically prudent to do so.

White's attitude toward Smith initially wavered from deep suspicion of his Tammany Hall background to grudging support. As the campaign of 1928 heated up, White's small-town dislike of big city life and morals and his strong commitment to Prohibition captured his mind and soul, especially after receiving a slanderous pamphlet written by the Reverend O. R. Miller, superintendent of the New York Civic League. Actually, this pamphlet had been first published in 1918 by the Anti-Saloon League as an account of Smith's legislative record between 1904 and 1916. In this pamphlet, Reverend Miller falsely charged Smith with supporting laws favoring prostitution and gambling and keeping saloons open.[22] In this instance, White believed what he had read in Miller's pamphlet and persuaded himself that no matter how intelligent and progressive Smith might be, a man with his background, clear anti-Prohibitionist stance, alleged record supportive of vice, and Tammany associates should never be elected president of the United States.[23]

Once convinced of Smith's unsuitability as a presidential candidate, White said as much in speech after speech and in article after article throughout the campaign. On at least four separate occasions, White charged that Smith had voted against legislation in the New York State Legislature that would stop the illegal gambling and prostitution activities occurring in and around saloons.[24] White's rapid transition from ambiguity about Smith's candidacy to fanatical opposition was uncharacteristic of the man and embarrassing to members of his family.[25]

White insisted that it was neither Smith's religion nor his anti-Prohibitionist stance that made him unacceptable to middle America. It was his record, a record that indicated just what kind of president Smith would turn out to be, "a Tammany President . . . Tammany is Tammany, and Smith is his prophet."[26]

While it is hard to estimate precisely how much White damaged Smith's campaign, it must have been considerable. Those American Catholics aware of what White had been saying and writing would never forget or forgive him for what he had done to Smith and to them. No matter how much White protested that religion had no part in his strident opposition to the first Catholic candidate for the American presidency in history and no matter what stands he had taken for tolerance in the past, many, if not most, American Catholics did not believe him and regarded him as an enemy. No matter how important or noble White's future causes might be, almost instinctively because White supported them, many American Catholics, almost instinctively, were disposed to oppose them.

Election day, November 6, 1928, was also Katie Smith's birthday. Smith was determined that no matter how the election turned out, Katie's birthday would be properly celebrated. He ordered a huge birthday cake and oversaw other preparations at the Biltmore Hotel for the festivities.[27] However, before Katie Smith's birthday celebration had begun, the trend of the election was apparent. Smith and many of his Tammany Hall friends had gathered at the Seventy-first Regiment Armory in New York City to hear the election returns. By 9:30 P.M., Smith knew that the election was going to be lost.

Even in the state of New York, the tide ran heavily against Smith. He lost his home state while the Democratic gubernatorial candidate, Franklin D. Roosevelt, won his contest. Smith could not abide the commiserations and instant analyses of the event offered by his friends in the Armory. He retreated to the Biltmore Hotel and tried to make the best of a very bad day by hosting Katie's birthday party.[28]

Over the next few days the magnitude of Smith's defeat and the principal reason for it became clear. First of all, more votes were cast in this presidential election than in any previous one, a total of 36 million for both candidates with Hoover capturing 21 million and Smith receiving 15 million. Electoral votes cast for Hoover were 444 while Smith received only 87, which gave Hoover the largest electoral vote majority ever given to a winning presidential candidate up to that time. Moreover, in the election of 1928 women had registered and voted in much larger numbers than in 1924, and anecdotal evidence suggests that women were more aggressively anti-Smith than were men.[29] Pundits then and later insisted that no Democrat could have won in 1928. That may have been true, but no Protestant Democrat would have lost so decisively as did Smith, particularly in traditional Democratic southern and border state strongholds. That religion was the critical factor in assuring Smith's defeat in those areas and in the country at large cannot be doubted.

Smith only carried eight states, six in the South and heavily Catholic Massachusetts and Rhode Island. He lost five southern states—Virginia, North Carolina, Tennessee, Florida, and Texas—which traditionally had been solidly Democratic. Bishop Cannon's anti-Catholic campaigns in Virginia and in neighboring states had succeeded grandly. Hoover carried all of the border states—Maryland, Kentucky, West Virginia, Missouri, and Oklahoma—which in past elections had produced Democratic majorities. All of the southern and border states carried by Hoover, except Kentucky, elected Democratic senators and congressmen. Hoover even managed to carry the city of Chicago by 20,000 votes, and Wisconsin provided Hoover with the largest plurality ever given to a presidential candidate in the history of the state.[30]

All of these numbers suggest just how broad and deep were anti-Catholic sentiments during the campaign against Smith in 1928. Smith had been rejected in those five southern states and elsewhere in traditionally heavy Democratic constituencies, but generally the Democratic party and other Democratic candidates were not. The lesson derived from the campaign and from Smith's humiliating defeat was that in 1928 American Catholics were viewed by most of the larger society as a distrusted minority who were unfit for top leadership positions in what was still believed to be a Protestant country. This lesson was taken to heart by most American Catholic leaders and by many ordinary American Catholic citizens as well. Moreover, this lesson was acted upon. Never especially ecumenical-minded, American Catholics would be much less so in the years ahead. American Catholics would go their own way. Those other Americans not of the true faith who steadfastly refused to accept them as political and social equals could go wherever God in his infinite wisdom might choose to send them.

In a gesture of appreciation for how Smith had endured the slings and arrows of religious bigotry during the campaign, O'Donnell and the university recognized Smith as an outstanding American Catholic by awarding him the Laetare Medal at a special reception held in May 1929 at the Plaza Hotel in New York. O'Donnell made the presentation, with Cardinal Hayes attending. O'Donnell did not say explicitly but clearly implied that the governor had suffered political martyrdom for the sake of his religion, standing out "as a moving force and as a radiant inspiration." To be sure, the presentation speech was vintage O'Donnell, most certainly written by himself and delivered with such sincerity and conviction that most who heard it did not know whether to cry or cheer.[31] It was one of O'Donnell's finer oratorical moments.

As for Smith, he would have much preferred having been a winner than a martyr, but in view of what happened to the American and world economies a year hence he was probably lucky that the election of 1928 had been lost. He was young enough and sufficiently positioned within the party to think about trying again in 1932, a time when almost any Democratic presidential candidate ought to be able to defeat Hoover or any other Republican nominee.

— ii —

At Notre Dame, the course of the election of 1928 was closely watched. O'Donnell described himself later as a nonpartisan Democrat,[32] but his sympathies as well as those of an overwhelming majority of the university community were solidly with Smith. As a matter of fact, in a modest way O'Donnell was involved in the campaign. He had a lengthy correspondence with Michael Williams of the *Commonweal* about how to deal with the religious issue. However, by early September 1928, O'Donnell had convinced himself that Smith could not win. In O'Donnell's view, the Republicans were too skilled in running and winning presidential campaigns for the Democrats to have much hope for victory. Indeed, the Republicans had lost only four out of fifteen presidential elections between 1868 and 1924. O'Donnell believed that the Republicans understood organization and the Democrats did not. Superior organization and money was what won presidential elections, and Republicans were skilled in the one and had plenty of the other.[33]

However, there was one celebrated member of the university community, Coach Rockne, who at the urging of a Big Ten official and some rich Republican friends considered issuing a public endorsement of Hoover. Actually, Rockne had been approached by both national political parties seeking an endorsement of their respective candidates from the country's most successful and best-known college football coach.

The Democrats acted first. On September 13, 1928, Millard Tydings from the Democratic National Committee asked Rockne by telegram to deliver a national radio address on the subject of "Governor Smith—The Inspiration of America's Youth." Rockne turned down this invitation because he believed along with O'Donnell that Smith had no chance of winning. In early September, Rockne knew that an invitation to endorse Smith would be forthcoming from the Democratic National Committee, and on his own he decided to plead political neutrality in the campaign and politely refused the invitation. He advised O'Donnell of what he intended to do, and O'Donnell confirmed his judgment that it would not be well for Rockne to identify himself or Notre Dame with either presidential candidate.[34]

In effect, O'Donnell turned Rockne's judgment about maintaining a neutral stance in presidential politics into a university policy. Subsequently, this policy of neutrality in presidential politics was broadened to include controversial public policy issues of any sort. To insure that the university would not be directly or indirectly identified with controversial public personalities or public causes, henceforth, only the president of Notre Dame was authorized to speak for the university on such matters.

Other members of the university community were expected to maintain a discreet silence on presidential politics and on public policy issues. Though not understood to be political censorship at that time, that was precisely what that policy turned out to be. This policy, in effect, initiated by Coach Rockne and confirmed by O'Donnell might have been prudent and made sense in the special circumstances of 1928, but it was one that would cause serious internal difficulties and great public embarrassment to the university in the years ahead.

The Republican approach to Rockne came through Major John Griffith, commissioner of the Big Ten, and longtime business associate of Rockne. On September 20, 1928, Griffith wrote to Rockne and argued that the athletic prosperity which all in the college football business had enjoyed during the last eight years had been connected with the country's business prosperity. If Smith were elected and a business recession followed, Griffith feared an athletic recession might fall upon the country and all that had been built up in the last eight years would be in serious jeopardy. Griffith asked Rockne to make a brief statement explaining why he was for Hoover. With such a statement in hand the Republican National Committee could do much good in the campaign by sending copies of it to schools and colleges.[35]

Rockne responded quickly to Griffith's letter. In spite of Rockne's recent stance of neutrality in the presidential campaign professed to the Democrats and O'Donnell's establishment of neutrality in such matters as university policy, he thought seriously about obliging Griffith. Rockne had opted for neutrality in order to maintain a public image of being a national figure who was above politics and to further his business interests. He wanted to be able to sell himself and his endorsed products to as many consumers as possible, especially those millions of citizens voting against Smith. Self-interest would be most effectively satisfied by maintaining a public stance of neutrality in public affairs.[36]

However, to Griffith, Rockne passed the blame for not obliging his Republican friends on the Notre Dame administration. To be sure, Rockne had few personal political convictions of any sort. Yet, he advised Griffith that university officials had insisted that because his name was so closely connected to Notre Dame and regardless of his personal feelings in this matter, he had to maintain a public stance of neutrality. Having left Griffith with the opinion that in his heart he was a Republican and favored Hoover, Rockne concluded by observing that university officials believed that neutrality was best because at some future time favors might have to be asked from both sides. According to Rockne the true Machiavellians in this matter were university officials, certainly not himself.[37]

Though it is difficult to be certain about any of Rockne's motives in controversial situations, Rockne appears to have tried to make amends for deserting Smith during the campaign and for being indifferent to the assaults upon American Catholic dignity and patriotism issuing from Smith's opponents. On November 10, 1928, only four days after Smith's humiliating election defeat, Rockne managed one of the most celebrated Notre Dame football victories in history by beating Army 12 to 7 in Yankee Stadium before a crowd of 78,000. A headline from the *New York Herald Tribune* on November 11 summed up the anti-Catholic turmoil of the last several months by screaming, "After the election came Rockne's revenge."

The football season of 1928 had begun poorly and ended badly. Winning only five out of nine games for the season, this team had the worst record up to that time of any football squad in modern Notre Dame football history. It was the poorest team that Rockne ever fielded, and he knew it. Prior to the Army game, this team had lost two out of its first six games but had won only two against major opponents. Most important, the team had been unable to score more than a single touchdown in games against major opponents. Facing the possibility of a humiliating defeat by a superior Army team before an enormous crowd, only four days after Smith's disastrous election defeat, and with the sports writing elite of the country in attendance, Rockne was ready to try anything and did.

According to Grantland Rice's memoirs published a quarter of a century after the Notre Dame-Army game of 1928, Rockne's "Win one for the Gipper" speech delivered in the locker room on November 10, 1928, was a carefully planned performance. There was nothing spontaneous about it at all. Rice claimed that Rockne had spent much of the evening before the Army game on November 10 attending a party in his Fifth Avenue apartment. Rice recalled Rockne saying during the party that he intended to ask "the boys to pull one out for Gipp."[38] Indeed, at the time, Rice added, it appeared that the Notre Dame football team of 1928 needed all of the help it could get from whatever source.

The problem with this account of the origins of Rockne's "Win one for the Gipper" locker room speech was that Rice's memory was faulty or his imagination was overactive. The party at Rice's New York apartment in the evening of November 9 never occurred. Rice was out of town covering the Georgia Tech–Vanderbilt football game in Atlanta.[39] Apparently, Rice, ever a scoop-minded sportswriter, invented this imaginary party on the eve of the Army game to give himself an exclusive preview of the most famous locker room speech in sports history. It was not the same as his spectacular Four Horsemen coup, but it was something.

A more likely source of the idea of using the memory of Gipp to inspire the Notre Dame team to play beyond themselves against a very strong West Point squad was one of Rice's colleagues on the *New York Herald Tribune,* W. O. McGeehan. On Friday, November 9, 1928, McGeehan treated his readers to a full laudatory column on "Gipp of Notre Dame," recounting Gipp's performance against Army in 1920 and describing him as the greatest football player he had ever watched. After describing Gipp's tragic and untimely death, McGeehan implied that his hero for this column had been a decent person, good citizen, and an appropriate role model for the youth of the country.[40] This extraordinary rehabilitation of Gipp's unsavory reputation as a gambler, pool shark, drinker, and utterly indifferent to academics by a celebrity sports writer who should have known better was enough for Rockne. He proceeded to make use of Gipp's memory as he saw fit.

Rockne delivered his famous speech to the team in a locker room in Yankee Stadium on November 10, 1928. Exactly when he delivered it is uncertain. In the ghostwritten *Collier's* article published under Rockne's name two years later, the coach claimed to have done it at halftime. An assistant coach recalled on one occasion that indeed the speech was given at halftime. Yet, the same assistant coach on another occasion was sure that Rockne spoke to the team just before the kickoff.[41] Francis Wallace, who had reported the speech to the *New York Daily News,* November 12, 1928, two days after the game, insisted that Rockne gave it after the pregame warm-up.[42]

Wallace's account has Rockne explaining to the players that when on his deathbed, George Gipp had told him that someday, when the time came, Gipp wanted Rockne to ask a Notre Dame team to beat Army for him. Wallace had not been in the locker room when the speech was delivered. His source for what was said was Joseph Byrne, who was present. Neither Wallace nor Byrne made any mention of Rockne using the specific phrase "Win one for the Gipper." That came two years later and was probably invented by John B. Kennedy in his much more creative and emotional ghostwritten piece published by *Collier's* in 1930. Kennedy's *Collier's* article including the "Win one for the Gipper" story was reprinted in the posthumously published *Autobiography of Knute Rockne* in 1931, and finally sanctified as truth by the Warner Brothers film *Knute Rockne—All American* in 1940.

Whatever Rockne said to the team in Yankee Stadium, there is no doubt that Rockne believed absolutely in the power of inspired words to improve athletic performance. He used inspired words often with skill and success during the 1920s. Yet, football success during that decade and thereafter depended on such fundamentals as talent, size, speed, training, and a bit of good luck. Generally, ordinary athletes could not be talked into championship performances. Rockne knew that. However, once in a while inspired words persuasively delivered could make a difference when football fundamentals were absent or weak. That happened in the Army game in Yankee Stadium on November 10, 1928.

As to the game, whether Rockne urged his players to go out and "Win one for the Gipper" before the game, at the half, or not at all, the Notre Dame team played much better than expected during the first half. Neither team was able to score. Army broke the tie in the third quarter by scoring a touchdown but missed the conversion. Notre Dame countered with a long drive in the same quarter that ended also with a touchdown and a missed conversion.

The 6 to 6 tie held until late in the fourth quarter when substitute end John O'Brien, making his first and only appearance in a varsity game, caught a desperation pass from John Niemic and stumbled into the end zone for the tie-breaking score. Indeed, for this feat O'Brien earned a permanent place in Notre Dame football lore as the celebrated "Johnny One Play O'Brien." Notre Dame was ahead in this game, but it was not won until an eighty-three-yard Army drive stalled on the Notre Dame one inch line at game's end.[43] However, game's end turned out to be very controversial.

Before the Army team could make another play after reaching the one inch line, the referee blew the final whistle ending the game. According to the rules, if Army had made a first down, they were entitled to another play. Rockne insisted that Army had not made a first down, even though they had reached the one inch line. As Rockne saw the situation, possession of the ball reverted to Notre Dame, and the game was over. Upon reflection, the referee who had blown the final whistle, Walter Eckersall, a *Chicago Tribune* sportswriter and longtime friend and client of Rockne for game officiating assignments, was not so sure. He admitted that as time ran out, he had not paid attention to whether the ball should have reverted to Notre Dame or stayed in possession of Army.[44] This controversy went nowhere after a few days of press coverage and quickly faded from the public memory. The game had been won, and the inspiring circumstances associated with it would live and grow and become the most enduring legend in American sports history.

Rarely an underdog during the Rockne years, the Notre Dame team played that role brilliantly against an excellent Army team on that day in

Yankee Stadium. The team managed to win a game they should have lost. However, sports miracles do not occur in threes. Outplayed and out-coached against Carnegie Tech on November 17 at Cartier Field, Notre Dame suffered a humiliating loss, 27 to 7, the first defeat at home since 1905. The final game against Southern California before 72,000 people in Los Angeles was not much better. The issue was never in doubt with Notre Dame losing, 27 to 14.

At the end of the season, there was not much worth remembering except for the Army game. On that day against a superior Army team, in-spired words persuasively delivered had transformed journeymen players into champions for an afternoon. This fact resonated throughout the American sports world in 1928 and continues to do so today. Ironically, Rockne's greatest athletic moment, now an established American sports legend, occurred not during one of his best seasons but in his worst ever.

— iii —

While the won and lost record of the Notre Dame football team in 1928 had been Rockne's worst ever, net profits from football for that season approached $500,000.[45] Though a Chicago newspaper reported Notre Dame's share of the proceeds from the Southern California game as being $140,000, the record football profits for the year were not public knowledge and consequently did not much mitigate the team's overall poor performance or in any way blunt criticism from some sportswriters. Noting the newspaper report about Notre Dame's apparent windfall from Los Angeles, O'Donnell observed to a friend that he hoped the report was true because "In the absence of glory we can make good use of this tan-gible asset."[46]

On top of the disappointing win-loss record in 1928, Rockne evi-denced an increasing frustration over the very slow and cautious Holy Cross decision-making process regarding the stadium building project. With such an abundance of cash in hand, he could not understand why firm decisions about the size of the stadium, costs, and methods of fi-nancing had not been made. In addition, by the summer of 1929, Rockne had found other things to worry about.

Rockne did not like Father Mulcaire and resented all of the vice presi-dent's efforts to restrain and render him more accountable to university authorities for how he spent athletic department funds and how he man-aged his program. Then in February 1929, President O'Donnell delivered a speech in New York deploring the identification of Notre Dame as a football factory[47] and followed that up by asking Rockne to mention the university's academic achievements in his off-campus speeches.[48]

There were also the matters of hiring a basketball coach that Rockne did not want and installing Father Vincent Mooney as head of the athletic department without consultation or input from him. Also, listing Mooney's name above Rockne's name in the university catalogue infuriated the coach. That listing angered Rockne because of the inevitable embarrassment that would fall upon himself when outsiders, unfamiliar with the relationship between priests and lay faculty at Catholic colleges and universities, examined the catalogue.[49]

Rockne also asserted that a group of young Notre Dame faculty who resented his financial success and free-wheeling management of the football program had organized a cabal to drive him out of the university. According to Rockne, the members of this group were second-rate men who had failed at most things in life and were conspiring to replace him as athletic director with Father Mooney.[50]

Finally, on July 1, 1929, after an appeal to President O'Donnell for reinstatement of a promising halfback who had been dismissed from the university for academic failure was rejected, Rockne submitted his resignation to O'Donnell. At once, the coach began negotiating with Ohio State officials about moving there.

O'Donnell received the resignation letter but took no action on it. He knew Rockne well enough and was fully cognizant of the coach's past history of resignations during Walsh's time to accept this resignation as authentic. Rockne wanted something, and O'Donnell had to figure out just how much he ought to give. O'Donnell knew that nothing could ever completely satisfy Rockne, but a few careful compromises might be worked out for the time being for the mutual benefit of the coach and of the university.

O'Donnell was disposed toward compromise because of the status of the stadium building project. That project simply could not go on without Rockne. He was needed as a kind of collateral to insure and facilitate financing and to work out a financially appealing no-home-game schedule while construction was under way. Also, O'Donnell was moved toward compromise by Albert R. Erskine of the Studebaker Corporation and of the Notre Dame Board of Trustees, who was prepared to do whatever was necessary to keep Rockne at Notre Dame and in South Bend.[51]

After several meetings, O'Donnell assured Rockne that the stadium building project would go forward, that contracts with the Osborne Construction Company of Cleveland would be signed for a 54,000 capacity stadium, that excavations would begin in the summer of 1929, and that the entire project would be completed for the opening of the football season in October 1930. Total project costs approached $900,000 and would be financed out of cash-in-hand plus receipts from the sale of 240 six-person prime location box seats for ten years.[52] Over $150,000 was subscribed for box seats from South Bend alone.[53] After all of the financial details of the project had been sorted out, the university would get a new stadium that was virtually debt free.

With the question of the stadium building project resolved to everyone's satisfaction, O'Donnell negotiated the rest of Rockne's complaints. The president insisted upon keeping Mulcaire as vice president and as head of the athletic board, but was willing to give up Mooney. That very decent man, former friend but now enemy of Rockne, would be given a leave of absence from the university to pursue graduate studies at the Catholic University of America. While Rockne was glad to be rid of Mooney and the threat from the faculty that he represented and was pleased by the approval of the stadium building project, a most compelling reason for him to forgo Ohio State and stay at Notre Dame was Erskine's very attractive offer.

The president of the Studebaker Corporation provided Rockne with a personal services contract that would pay the coach $5,000 for addressing twenty-one meetings of Studebaker dealers between January and March 1929. This contract was to be only the beginning of a long and profitable association with the Studebaker Corporation. There would be additional personal service contracts with higher pay in the years ahead. There were promises of a full-time appointment as a manager of Studebaker sales promotion activities when Rockne retired from coaching and of a vice presidency in the future Rockne Motors subsidiary, the intended producer of the "Rockne," a new low-priced sedan to be built in Detroit.[54] These were offers and prospects that could not be refused. Nothing more was heard about resigning or moving to Ohio State. Both O'Donnell and Rockne had much to attend to.

While Rockne and the on-going never-ending public relations wars inspired by Notre Dame's football fortunes were continuing problems for O'Donnell, he had quite a bit more on his mind during his six-year presidency than athletics and stadium building. O'Donnell was a man who had to balance within himself an acute sense of practicality and acceptance of reality with deeply rooted intellectual and cultural interests. He wanted Notre Dame to become a great Catholic university and a significant contributor to the intellectual and cultural life of the Church and of the nation. While successful achievement of those noble aspirations required resources that were unavailable at the moment, O'Donnell resolved to do what he could with what he had.

What O'Donnell had, depended upon the current state of university finances. In 1928–29, total instructional and operational costs approached a million dollars. Income from tuition fees and the lay faculty endowment amounted to only $653,000, or about 65 percent of total instructional and operating costs.[55] This $350,000 shortfall was made up from profits generated by room rents, food services, other local auxiliary enterprises, and an amount from football revenues. For new buildings and one-time educational and cultural projects, O'Donnell could only pray for gifts and dip into remaining football profits after operating costs had been met. The importance of the football enterprise to the well-being and future educational progress and cultural improvement of Notre Dame was clear enough to those university officials privy to financial information and much suspected by those who were not.

The centrality of football revenues to the development of Notre Dame was such that O'Donnell had little patience with those persons in college and university leadership positions and in some of the major foundations who denounced intercollegiate football as a threat to the integrity of American higher education. This is not to say that O'Donnell saw nothing distressing in the way intercollegiate football was currently being managed and regulated or that he was willing to wink at rules violations for the sake of money and public relations glory. What aggravated O'Donnell most in these matters was the hypocrisy of many of the college and university officials who had spoken out forcefully against abuses in intercollegiate football generally, while saying nothing about athletic conventions and practices at their own institutions.

A case in point was the vigorous president of Columbia University, Nicholas Murray Butler. Notre Dame administrators remembered very well the behavior of Columbia University representatives and officials in 1925 when Rockne flirted with the idea of breaking his contract with Notre Dame and moving to Columbia. There was so much lying and dissimulation by all of the parties in that widely publicized embroglio that no one escaped from it with an intact reputation.

Consequently, when Butler attacked intercollegiate football as a menace to education and culture, O'Donnell reacted bitterly to what he perceived to be an example of Butler's supreme hypocrisy and unforgivable condescension. To Bishop Noll, an avid supporter of Notre Dame football and writing to him as Catholic to Catholic, O'Donnell scoffed at the notion that culture was imperiled by intercollegiate football. To be sure, O'Donnell believed that contemporary culture was in danger, but, as he saw the world, that danger came more from the materialistic and atheistic philosophies propagated in secular college classrooms than from athletics.

Those protesting savants of whom Butler was a leader, O'Donnell wrote, "should turn their attention to the doctrines taught by professors in their universities and not bother their heads about college football." What ironically passes for education in most secular colleges and universities today, O'Donnell continued, was far more menacing to American life than athletics could ever be. "If football destroys Columbia," O'Donnell concluded, "so much the credit to football."[56]

Neither O'Donnell nor Noll had much understanding of or sympathy for the kind of academic freedom found at Columbia or at other peer institutions. In truth, however, neither a misunderstanding of academic freedom nor untested assumptions about the impact of academic philosophies of any sort on student and faculty behavior were at issue in this outburst. O'Donnell admired strongly resonating, quotable statements, especially his own, and this one certainly must have resonated with Noll. While this outburst against Butler and secular colleges and universities was standard Catholic rhetoric for the time, these were the words of a very angry practical man who perceived athletic deemphasis movements at this time by well-endowed and long-established universities to be a threat to the prosperity and progress of his institution. To grow and develop, Notre Dame needed football profits. O'Donnell knew that but would not or could not say so publicly in ways that critics would accept. In conflicts between morality and money during the 1920s, morality usually had the best and most persuasive arguments, but in the end money usually, not always, decided the issue.

O'Donnell was genuinely interested in the state of culture and social values in the country at large and at Notre Dame. He could not do very much in a practical way about the state of things in the country at large, but he could certainly try to expand the cultural horizons of the Notre Dame community. O'Donnell and his successors were all true believers in the efficacy of celebrity guest lecturers for raising academic standards as well as for increasing general cultural understanding.

Though celebrity guest lecturers would come and go, O'Donnell had convinced himself that the experience of seeing and hearing them would have a lasting impact on students and faculty. In truth, the strategy of celebrity guest lecturers was the only practical option for improvement in cultural awareness open to Notre Dame officials. For a variety of religious, financial, and political reasons, they chose not to try to purchase, on a permanent basis, celebrity and near celebrity academics and intellectuals from other institutions. However, O'Donnell and those in his inner circle were willing, perhaps even anxious, to spend generous amounts of money for that time to bring celebrity intellectuals to Notre Dame for short periods.

Given the perceived low level of intellectual performance among American Catholic intellectuals, Notre Dame officials generally sought academic and cultural improvement from European Catholics. In humanities areas, as one might suspect, Catholic celebrity intellectuals coming for short-term stays and appearing before exclusively English-speaking audiences were most available in England and Ireland. Among the first of such celebrity intellectuals to be approached during the O'Donnell years was the English Catholic historian and essayist Hilaire Belloc.

O'Donnell wrote to Belloc in September 1928 and had to do so again in October before receiving a reply. Belloc expressed an interest in coming to Notre Dame for a short stay but indicated that his financial situation was so precarious that he could not consider coming for less than a thousand pounds.[57] Actually, Belloc, in effect, set the price for what the university was willing to pay for a visit by a European celebrity intellectual. O'Donnell responded to Belloc's asking price with an offer of $5,000 plus travel expenses for a spring visit. For this salary, Belloc was asked to deliver a series of six lectures and stay at Notre Dame long enough to deliver a commencement address and receive an honorary degree.

This offer to Belloc for much less than a semester's work was two and a half times what most Notre Dame professors would earn in a year. Indeed, for its time, O'Donnell's offer to Belloc was a princely one, and Belloc agreed to come in the spring of 1929.[58] However, Belloc never reached South Bend. He traveled as far as New York when failing health forced him to return to England.

Having failed with the Belloc project, O'Donnell did not give up. He approached the eminent English Catholic writer and literary essayist Gilbert K. Chesterton with a similar offer to come to Notre Dame in the spring of 1930. O'Donnell made this offer notwithstanding the fact that O'Hara had denounced Chesterton and other English and Irish Catholic writers and intellectuals as being hypercritical of traditional Catholic practices in the *Religious Bulletin*. In this instance, O'Donnell gave not a minute of thought to what O'Hara had written in the *Religious Bulletin*, and O'Hara was of absolutely no mind to remind him of it.

Indeed, Chesterton agreed to come but illness delayed his arrival at Notre Dame until October 1930. He had contracted to give two series of lectures over a six-week period on some phases of English literature or

English history and to receive an honorary degree at a special convocation to be held in early November. In most things, while at Notre Dame for six weeks, Chesterton exceeded expectations. The Notre Dame community had never before encountered anyone quite like him. His profound learning, brilliant wit, and soft-spoken voice were accompanied by an enormous physical presence. Chesterton weighed almost three hundred pounds and had to move slowly and deliberately. Students wondered how such a small voice could emanate from such a very large man.

Chesterton's lectures were always well attended and long remembered as exciting intellectual experiences. The man himself later was more modest about his performance at Notre Dame. Except for difficulty satisfying a very large appetite for alcohol in a formally prohibitionist country, Chesterton appeared to have enjoyed his entire stay at Notre Dame.

Chesterton had a genuine gift for saying with heartfelt sincerity the right things to most people at the right time. For example, at the special November convocation when he received an honorary degree, Chesterton left hardly a dry eye in Washington Hall after describing how coming to a university named and devoted to Our Lady had affected him. Where Our Lady had erected her pillars, Chesterton observed in a voice that most present had to strain to hear, "all men are at home, and I knew that I should not find strangers."[59] He did not.

At Notre Dame, Chesterton was liked and much appreciated. He responded in kind. While the substance of his lectures would soon pass from the memory of those who had heard him, recollections of his charm, wit, and presence would not. Simply stated, Chesterton did about everything during his brief stay at Notre Dame that a guest lecturer could do. He set standards of discourse and intellect and exemplified at that time how much joy and excitement could be experienced in pursuing the life of the mind.

In due course, other English and Irish celebrity intellectuals would come to the university. William Butler Yeats visited in 1932 and was incomprehensible. Of course, after 1934, a succession of European intellectuals, scholars, and scientists would find their way into permanent positions at Notre Dame. However, none who came later, no matter how valuable their contributions to the university, ever captured the imagination of the total Notre Dame community as had Chesterton in the fall of 1930.

Even before Chesterton's arrival on campus, O'Donnell was aware that more than inspiring guest lecturers would be required to transform Notre Dame into a great university. O'Donnell believed that for intellectual activity and cultural awareness to flourish and grow at Notre Dame, the university had to create a new facilitating infrastructure. At the center of this new infrastructure were graduate programs and new buildings. O'Donnell attempted to provide both.

In early 1930, O'Donnell renewed contacts with the General Education Board to explore with officials there the possibility of obtaining a grant to strengthen graduate studies at Notre Dame. O'Donnell was specially concerned about the 1,200 students enrolled in the summer session seeking higher degrees. He also hoped to receive funds for advanced work in education and chemistry. What O'Donnell wanted from the General Education Board was, in effect, a renewal of the previous lay faculty endowment grant, only this time directed toward graduate studies. Salary money was needed for the recruitment of young faculty with Ph.D. degrees and research experience.[60]

The representative of the General Education Board, D. H. Stevenson, who met with O'Donnell, was interested in the new Notre Dame graduate studies project but made no promises nor did he offer much encouragement. In February 1930 the General Education Board simply had no funds for additional activities of the sort that O'Donnell had proposed. Notwithstanding the refusal of the General Education Board to consider further O'Donnell's proposal, Stevenson advised the president that he would submit a summary of the graduate studies situation at the university, indicating that in his opinion Notre Dame had "the greatest opportunity of any Catholic institution in the country in this particular form of service."[61]

In the very grim economic environment of 1930, O'Donnell could not have been surprised by the outcome of his interview with Stevenson; it was clear that whatever was done about developing graduate studies at Notre Dame would have to be done by themselves alone. O'Donnell was no more anxious to initiate new costly instructional programs at this critical time than had been the General Education Board. Yet, he did not want to turn away completely from a step that seemed so essential for the intellectual and cultural development of the university. He proceeded slowly and very cautiously in what seemed to him to be the right direction.

In 1931, O'Donnell persuaded the Provincial Chapter of Holy Cross to appoint a committee to study all of the problems of providing the university with a thoroughly efficient graduate school and to manage graduate activities presently in place.[62] The type of graduate school envisioned would be open to men and also to nuns during both the summer session and the regular academic year. This committee of eight members included O'Donnell, four of the principal clerical academic administrators of the university, Walsh, and two future presidents, John F. O'Hara and John J. Cavanaugh. From this beginning, this committee remained in charge of graduate studies at Notre Dame until a dean was appointed in 1944.

The second aspect of O'Donnell's intellectual and cultural infrastructure improvement plans for Notre Dame, new facilities, fared better and progressed faster than did graduate studies. Despite the very harsh economic environment of those years, O'Donnell was able to find funds from football revenues and two fortuitous gifts to mount a major building program.

After the stadium building project was under way, O'Donnell responded to a long-standing need and pressed for a new law college building. In 1929 the university contracted with the Boston architectural firm of Magininis and Walsh for a design of a new Gothic-like structure costing about $400,000. The new building provided classrooms, a law library, moot court facilities, and a small auditorium. Funding for this project had to come from internal sources. Construction began in the fall of 1929 and was completed a year later. The most costly of O'Donnell's building projects also funded from internal sources were two new elegant revenue-producing dormitories designed to house 600 students.[63] At long last he was redeeming Father Burns' pledge to build a dormitory memorializing the generosity of the Old Student group who had allowed funds they had raised for a dormitory to be used instead to complete the fund drive of 1922.

Named Alumni Hall and Dillon Hall and costing $950,000, these two new student residences designed by Magininis and Walsh were also of Gothic-like character, complete with niches, statuettes, figurines, and plaques decorating the exterior walls. The design reflected O'Donnell's preference for buildings that would combine the beauty of the Middle Ages with the necessities of modern living. Given the university's authoritarian structure in matters such as this, the president's architectural preferences always prevailed. In any case, ground for these new dormitories was broken in March 1931 and construction was completed seven months later.[64]

The ravages of the Great Depression notwithstanding, the university was blessed with a gift of $200,000 from Edward Nash Hurley for the construction of a two-story building for the College of Commerce and a gift of $300,000 from John F. Cushing for a new three-story engineering building. Though neither of these gifts covered initial construction costs estimates, because of the severe economic conditions in the country and in the region, the university was able to bargain down initial estimates and make up the unfunded balances from internal sources.

Construction of the commerce building was completed in 1931, while the engineering building was opened in 1932. O'Donnell's building program was completed with construction of a new steam and water pumping plant costing $250,000 that went on service at the end of 1931. O'Donnell's very ambitious building program including the stadium approached $3,000,000 in total costs, a very large expenditure at that time for an institution of the size and resources of Notre Dame.

Given the economic condition of the country and region in 1930 to 1934 and the fact of declining enrollment after 1932, O'Donnell's building program was at once courageous, foolhardy, and a test of his faith that somehow Our Lord and Our Lady would provide for the survival and prosperity of her school. The football bonanza continued, albeit nowhere near the record levels of 1928 and 1929, but there was always enough from that source to keep the university solvent and complete the building program. O'Donnell had no way of knowing that such would be the case when the university contracted for the new buildings, but he believed that it would and proceeded with his plans. O'Donnell established himself as one of the great builders of new facilities in university history. Moreover, he did it in the riskiest of times.

— iv —

While O'Donnell worked to improve intellectual and cultural life at Notre Dame and provide new facilities, Rockne labored to improve the performance and win-and-loss record of the football team. There was an unusual urgency about team preparation during September 1929, although no one imagined at that time that O'Donnell's building program as well as the future financial solvency of the university might depend on how well Rockne's teams performed in 1929 and 1930.

The football season of 1929 was different. Because of on-going construction of the new stadium, all nine games on the schedule had to be played away. Of those nine games, three were played in Chicago before very large crowds in Soldier Field and one was played in Evanston. One game was played in Baltimore against Navy before 65,000 persons and another against Army in Yankee Stadium before 79,000 people. Though the other three games drew smaller crowds, a seasonal attendance record of 551,000 was attained in 1929 and remained unsurpassed until after World War II.

Of these games, Rockne was only able to attend four. A severe attack of phlebitis in his right leg prevented walking and much traveling. He ran practices from a wheelchair and dramatically appeared at three games similarly equipped. In truth, between October 5 and November 30 with game preparation, game-playing time, and getting in and out of Pullman sleeping cars, there was very little time for players to tend to, or even think about, academics. In 1929, few people at Notre Dame were of a mind to raise the issue of lost academics, and no one did. The circumstances of that year were so special that whatever was happening would never happen again. So better to get on with it than to complain about it.

Rockne's teams in 1929 and 1930 were the best ever. Several circumstances conspired to make them so. Many of the players returning from the squad of 1928 had matured and improved greatly. Also, Rockne had managed to recruit Marty Brill away from the University of Pennsylvania and Marchmont Schwartz away from Loyola of New Orleans. Brill, son of a Jewish millionaire, and Schwartz, who was half Jewish, had come to Notre Dame for no other reason than to play football on a Rockne-coached team, and play they did, especially in 1930. Rockne found a brilliant quarterback in Frank Carideo and a fast, bruising fullback in Joe Savoldi, who along with halfbacks Jack Elder, Brill, and Schwartz formed the best backfield that Rockne ever developed. These players were bigger, faster, and better than the more celebrated Four Horsemen of 1924.

Rockne's football team in 1929 appeared to be so good that, uncharacteristically, even he predicted a highly successful season for it.[65] That prediction turned out to be a bit premature. Before only 16,000 people against Indiana in the opening game of the season, Notre Dame managed only a lackluster defeat of a very weak team, 14 to 0. Because of Rockne's phlebitis attack, the coach did not travel with the team to Baltimore for the game against Navy on October 12. He left field direction to assistants and tried to inspire the team with pep talks delivered to each individual starter by telephone.

Though locker-room observers reported the players much moved by Rockne's telephone calls, the effect of them did not transfer into superior performance on the field. Before a crowd of 64,000, Notre Dame barely defeated a scrappy but ordinary Navy team, 14 to 7. The game against Wisconsin in Soldier Field before 90,000 spectators was different. Notre Dame won easily with the punishing fullback Joe Savoldi emerging as a star and as a potential All-American candidate.

Remembering two recent losses to Carnegie Tech, Rockne accompanied the team to Forbes Field in Pittsburgh, where on October 26 a crowd of 66,000 waited to see whether the Tartans could win again. Despite a rousing pep talk by Rockne delivered from a wheelchair before the game and during the half, the Carnegie Tech team almost did it again. Coach

Walter Steffen of the Tartans devised a clever defense that contained the Notre Dame running attack for almost three quarters. Finally, Savoldi broke loose for a touchdown run, and Notre Dame won the game, 7 to 0.

The next two games against Georgia Tech in Atlanta on November 2 and against Drake on the following weekend in Soldier Field were easy victories. Though Rockne did not attend either game, Notre Dame overwhelmed Georgia Tech, 26 to 6, and defeated Drake, 19 to 7. Even without Rockne's presence or inspirational pep talks, Elder, Carideo, and Savoldi were unstoppable. Actually, these two games were warm-up performances for a major clash between an undefeated Notre Dame and an undefeated Southern California team in Soldier Field on November 16.

Despite the stock market crash and deteriorating economic condition in the country and the region, the demand for tickets was unsatiable. Over 112,000 persons, the largest crowd in Chicago sports history, poured into Soldier Field to watch what was trumpeted as the game of the decade. Rockne addressed the team in the locker room and urged them to overwhelm the Trojans in the first few minutes of the game and seize an early lead. The players responded, scoring an early touchdown, but Southern California did the same. By halftime the two teams had played to a tie, 6 to 6. During the halftime interval, Paul Castner, a former player, spoke about the importance of Rockne to the team, and how he had risked his health by coming to the game. According to observers, the players were visibly moved, some almost to tears. Early in the third quarter, Savoldi scored a touchdown and Carideo kicked the extra point. Southern California responded with a spectacular ninety-six-yard touchdown run but failed to make the extra point. The game ended with Notre Dame winning, 13 to 12.[66]

Rockne was too exhausted after the Southern California game to return to Chicago for the Northwestern contest on November 23. He really was not needed. Over 50,000 people watched Notre Dame batter Northwestern, 26 to 6, with Savoldi scoring two touchdowns. With a national championship in sight, Rockne devoted himself to preparing the team for the final game against Army on November 30.

In 1929 Army did not appear to be as formidable as in the past. Army had lost to Yale and had been tied by Harvard. However, with Navy still off the Army schedule, the team trained very hard for what was for them the biggest game of the year. Sports enthusiasts in the New York area agreed. Tickets were in very short supply, and scalpers commanded outrageous prices. Over 79,000 people crowded into Yankee Stadium on a cold, blustery day to witness the finale of a great Notre Dame football season. Rockne was not among them. Because of the distance and cold weather, the coach remained in South Bend and once again communicated with the team by telephone and followed the course of the game by listening to the radio broadcast.[67]

The terrible weather hampered the offensive play of both teams. Notre Dame and Army struggled to a scoreless tie until late in the second quarter when Jack Elder intercepted an Army pass close to the Notre Dame goal line and sprinted the length of the field for what turned out to be the only touchdown of the game. Notre Dame played very conservative defensive football during the second half and managed to win an otherwise dull game, 7 to 0. Some controversy appeared in the press about Notre Dame's conservative play in the second half, but most supporters were immensely satisfied with an undefeated season. Indeed, the errors and mistakes of the previous season were easily and quickly forgotten. Football glory might be fleeting but was a most joyful experience when one's team had it. In 1929 Notre Dame had it.

Perhaps even more satisfying than the glory of the moment was the knowledge that all of the backfield stars, except Elder, would be back next year. The prospect for two consecutive national championships was very good. Most satisfying of all for the Notre Dame administration were the record football profits earned during the season. Net football profits for 1929 amounted to a spectacular $541,000. There would never be another seasonal payday like this one for fifty years.

In Notre Dame chronology, the historic stock market crash in 1929 occurred a few days after the Carnegie Tech game. The effects of this cataclysmic event were not immediately apparent to the Notre Dame community. Certainly, ticket scalper prices for the Southern California and Army games were not affected at all. Yet, the portents of economic disaster were clear to those prescient enough to look for them. For example, many of Al Smith's rich friends were heavy stock market players, and many were ruined in a matter of days. Business failures and unemployment mounted. No one could be sure which companies would survive and which would be forced to close. Jobs lost were lost forever. Virtually all past certainties about living, acquiring, and spending were shattered. Most Americans resigned themselves to living one day at a time, hoping for the best but not knowing from where the best would come.

Despite some anxiety over the large financial commitments to O'Donnell's building program, Notre Dame officials saw the immediate future as grim but not yet life-threatening. The new stadium would be ready in the fall of 1930 to accommodate crowds of 59,000 for home games. The football money machine was intact and preparing for another spectacular season. All would be well if some of the enormous ticket demand experienced in Chicago and New York would transfer to the South Bend area.

Even more important than the possibility of additional football revenues from the new stadium was the fact that the university entered this new and very difficult economic period with the record seasonal football profits of $541,000 for 1929 in hand. Thus situated and fortified, though fearful and cautious, Notre Dame officials wanted to believe that if the national and regional depression did not last too long, Our Lady's university ought to survive and would be ready for the better days that public officials assured the country would come.

—— 15 ——

THE END OF AN ERA

B etween 1930 and 1934, the Great Depression spread slowly but inevitably from the major urban centers into every region across the entire country. Twentieth-century Americans had no previous experience of an economic disaster of this magnitude. Most could not believe what was happening and were at a loss about how to cope. The country's financial system bent, cracked, and in some regions collapsed. During the first five years of the new decade approximately 21,000 American financial institutions failed including 10,000 banks.

Overwhelmed by pessimism and doubt and without adequate sources of credit, entrepreneurs and businessmen discovered that a free-market solution to the present crisis was not working. By 1934 the gross national product had declined 30 percent from the levels of 1929, while unemployment soared to an unprecedented 25 percent of the work force. Businesses failed everywhere, and those still employed found themselves working longer hours for less money than in the previous decade.

The Great Depression brought a massive general deflation to all parts of the country affecting both prices and wages, though wages declined farther and faster than prices. All sectors of the economy suffered and higher education was no exception. Public universities experienced significant reductions in funding. Private institutions watched their enrollments decline, charitable giving diminish, and profit margins from intercollegiate athletics disappear. For American colleges and universities, the years between 1930 and 1934 were the worst of times.

When the severity of the economic crisis became clear in 1930, Notre Dame found itself fortuitously situated in the short run to cope with the effects of depression and deflation. Overall enrollment remained steady and actually reached a record high of 3,227 in the fall of 1931. To be sure, football profits for 1930 were only a few thousand dollars under the record high attained in 1929 but that modest decline was a portent of things to come. By 1931 football profits had declined to $400,000 or 26 percent below the level of 1929. Lost income of that magnitude was a shock, and the university tried to cope with it by implementing tight cost controls and nonexpansion of instructional and student services.

Conventional wisdom would have us believe that Notre Dame neither terminated lay faculty nor cut lay faculty salaries during the years of the Great Depression. That may have been true after 1934 but was not the case for the years 1930 through 1933. All lay faculty contracts were for one year only, so any faculty member could be terminated by simply not renewing his contract. No special explanations for such an action were given or expected.

Even during a contract year, lay faculty could be dismissed on one month's notice for a number of specific causes. A lay faculty member's conduct toward associates and students was supposed to be marked by a gentlemanly courtesy and a sufficiently obliging disposition, a demeanor that young men would be inclined to emulate. Causes for reproach or scandal on campus or elsewhere, whether from overindulgence of intoxicating liquor or the commission of acts discreditable or reprehensible, were grounds for dismissal. So also was dishonorable behavior of lay faculty in the domain of Catholic education, as well as any conduct jeopardizing the confidence and goodwill of patrons and friends of the university.

Behavior threatening the university's good name or reputation for efficiency in education—for example, striking or having personal encounters with students—was unacceptable and cause for dismissal.[1] Finally, death or long-term disabling illness terminated a lay faculty member's contract and obligated the university only to pay a pro rata portion of the salary from the date of termination to the end of the month, not to the end of the contract year.[2]

The severity of Notre Dame lay faculty employment contracts as well as the engagement of a Chicago collection agency to recover delinquent student accounts were practical measures believed to be necessary and in the best interests of the university. Nonetheless, policies such as these gave a man as sensitive to the human condition as O'Donnell moments of pause. As O'Donnell explained to a nun who had solicited a student job for an incoming freshman in 1931, "No body seems to understand that our operating expenses are tremendous. Taking care of the very life of the school puts us in the ungracious position of seeming to be at times impervious to the appeals of charity."[3] This was something that every lay faculty member knew and understood to be an absolute condition of employment.

With preserving the life of the school very much in mind, the Notre Dame administration adopted a cautious strategy of watchful waiting and nonexpansion of lay faculty and other services during 1931. Father James McDonald's return to the university from Oxford, where he had been taking some graduate courses, is a case in point. McDonald's return prompted O'Donnell and his director of studies, Father Leonard Carrico, not to renew the contract of a young lay teacher in the English department.[4]

The young man was one of the bachelor dons living in Lyons Hall. He had taught Freshman English and French since 1925, and there were no complaints about the man's performance. He was terminated in order to make room for McDonald and to save a modest salary, that is, to replace a salaried layman with an unsalaried priest.[5] The young man appears to have accepted his fate without a murmur. As a matter of fact, O'Donnell persuaded the man to resign in exchange for positive letters of recommendation for possible positions elsewhere. A resignation was submitted, accepted with regret, and followed by a written testimonial from O'Donnell that was glowing.[6]

As economic conditions worsened in 1932, the treasurer of the university was authorized to harass lay faculty with overdue accounts in the dining hall,[7] football scholarships were cut back from thirty-six to twenty,[8] student jobs were limited generally to athletes and to seniors,[9] and more lay faculty experienced the shock of contract nonrenewal. The reason offered for such actions and terminations was a need to reduce personnel because of economic conditions.[10]

O'Donnell even politely but firmly refused a request from Bishop Noll to find employment at Notre Dame for a former Protestant minister lately converted to Catholicism. O'Donnell professed a fear of having the university acquire a reputation as a "refugium" for convert ministers but stated clearly to the bishop that "At this time we are cutting down rather than expanding our teaching personnel."[11]

Increasing administrative anxiety over what O'Donnell had called preserving the life of the school can be illustrated by an inquiry sent to O'Donnell from an Ohio building and loan society in May 1932. Given the precarious conditions of financial institutions throughout the country, many persons with money in banks to pay higher-education tuition bills could not access their own funds for that purpose.[12]

Written on stationery with the slogan "Where Your Money Grows," the Bellfontaine Building and Loan Society advised O'Donnell that in the fall of 1931, in order to protect depositors and borrowers, the society had to limit disbursement of withdrawal accounts to a percentage of receipts. Withdrawals had to be limited to meeting the necessities of life, such as, food, fuel, and extreme emergencies. Withdrawals for education were not allowed under these rules. A depositor who had requested funds from his account to pay tuition at Notre Dame had been denied.[13]

The building and loan society wanted to know if Notre Dame would accept, in lieu of cash, interest-bearing certificates of deposit redeemable when the present economic situation had improved. The society pointed out that some colleges in Ohio had agreed to accept such certificates. O'Donnell responded quickly that such an arrangement was unacceptable at Notre Dame.

As economic conditions worsened day by day in the spring of 1932, the leadership of the university made a major decision about lay faculty contracts for 1932–33. O'Donnell sent a letter along with contract renewals announcing that an unprecedented situation confronted the university at this time. Up to now, O'Donnell wrote, the financial situation of the university had not been seriously affected and normal salary scales and wages had been maintained. How long the university could continue this policy was uncertain.[14]

With regard to employment contracts issued for 1932–33, no salary increases, even in cases of promotion, would be given. Depending on conditions at midsemester, salaries could be adjusted up or down. Moreover, because a significant decrease in enrollment might leave the university overstaffed, a new clause was included in all contracts. This new clause allowed the university to cancel a contract after giving thirty days notice, whereupon the employment covered under it would cease.[15] Being serious about preserving the life of the school above all else, O'Donnell prepared for the worst. Providentially, the worst did not come.

In late July 1932, O'Donnell reported to a friend that university finances were no longer a special concern. The worst seemed to be over. We should rest easier, he wrote, if freshman registration for the fall "would begin to pick up. At present, it is fifty percent below normal."[16] O'Donnell was able to rest a bit easier, because when the fall semester opened, freshman registration had improved to about two-thirds of normal, enough to push overall enrollment up to 2,780. Though overall enrollment for 1932–33 was down 400 from the previous year, the number of students registered was sufficient to avoid implementation of the draconian clause lately included in lay faculty contracts for 1932–33.

While the fall enrollment for 1932–33 was 14 percent below the record high of 3,227 in 1930–31, that decrease was not much lamented. Virtually all of the 2,780 students registered in the fall of 1932 lived in the residence halls on campus, reducing significantly, at long last, the student overflow into South Bend. While remaining solidly Catholic, henceforth, Notre Dame would also be characterized as a residential institution, meaning that an essential part of a Catholic education as delivered at Notre Dame would be student residential life.

In the fall of 1932, O'Donnell was about as optimistic about the future as anyone could be at that time. "Unless a cataclysm occurs," he wrote, "we shall, with the help of God, weather the storm."[17] No economic cataclysm occurred to overwhelm the university, but there was unexpected calamity in late March 1931. Rockne died in an airplane crash. Yet, the university managed to cope with this tragic loss and with all of the public relations furor associated with it as well as with the continuing economic hardships of the Great Depression. Though enrollment would decline further in 1933–34 before turning upward again in 1934–35, during these years life at Notre Dame in the residence halls, in classrooms and laboratories, in faculty lounges, and on the playing fields generally went on much as before.

— ii —

While O'Donnell struggled to keep his building program on track and the university solvent during the early years of the Great Depression, Rockne attended to his many outside business ventures, laboring diligently to keep the money flowing. Actually, Rockne was at the height of his earning power during the months following the stock market crash. Sperber estimated Rockne's income from Notre Dame and from outside sources at that time to be about $75,000 a year, more than the president of the Studebaker Corporation and approaching that of the president of the United States.[18] No less significant than the money made were the money-making opportunities rejected. For example, Rockne turned down an offer of $50,000 to go on a vaudeville tour with Will Rogers. He passed on this offer because of personal health problems and because O'Donnell did not want him to take it.[19] For the moment, Rockne's income from outside enterprises continued to rise and seemed shielded from the powerful negative forces besetting other parts of the economy.

In the meantime, construction work on the new stadium had proceeded apace and the edifice was ready for use in the fall of 1930. A game against Southern Methodist had been scheduled for October 4, and an elaborate stadium dedication ceremony had been planned for the Navy game on October 11. Team preparation for the forthcoming season also proceeded apace with expectations for another national championship soaring with every practice day. The team Rockne fielded in 1930 was the most experienced and most talented squad up to that time in Notre Dame history.

The Notre Dame football team of 1930 was experienced and talented, but they got off to a slow start against Southern Methodist on October 4. This first game ever played in the new stadium almost turned out to be a disaster. Only one other team during the season played Notre Dame closer than did Southern Methodist. With less than 15,000 persons attending and looking very lonely in the new stadium, Savoldi returned the opening kickoff ninety-eight yards for a touchdown. After that spectacular opening, Southern Methodist played Notre Dame to a 14 to 14 tie until the closing minutes of the final quarter. Carideo returned a punt for twenty-nine yards deep into Southern Methodist territory, and Schwartz scored a touchdown, winning the game, 20 to 14.

Perhaps the players and the coach had been looking a week ahead to the much-bruited stadium dedication ceremony and the game against Navy. Certainly, all of the public relations resources of the university and of their friends in the media employed every trick of their respective trades to deliver as large an audience as possible for the events of October 11. Notre Dame officials hoped to celebrate the new stadium by filling it. That goal was much easier stated than achieved. After all, attendance for the Southern Methodist game had been no better than what a similar contest in Cartier Field would have drawn. No one could guess whether the Southern Methodist experience would be an exception or the norm for future home games against ordinary teams.

Promoters advertised special excursion trains from Chicago, but no amount of public relations trumpeting and train chartering could possibly deliver 58,000 people to the new Notre Dame stadium in 1930 for an early season game against an ordinary Navy team. The presence of naval dignitaries, local worthies, the prospects of a blessing by Bishop Noll, and an oration by O'Donnell were not enough. The fundamentals for a big attraction were just not there. In the end, only 40,000 people appeared for the ceremony and the game. Since this was much less than expected and officials were fearful of what a partially filled stadium would imply about the spectator appeal of Notre Dame football, the photographer hired to take publicity pictures touched up the foregrounds of his shots to make the stadium appear full.[20]

In preparation for the stadium dedication ceremony, Notre Dame publications glorified the university's football past in the most extravagant terms. Football heroes were secular saints, and the unforgettable George Gipp was perhaps the saintliest of all. Even O'Donnell's healthy cynicism about such matters did not immunize him from the emotions of the moment. In his dedication address, the president transformed Gipp into a Chaucerian perfect Christian knight of the gridiron enlisted in the service of Our Lady.[21] Surely, O'Donnell knew better. Yet, he did it anyway, believing that a little or even a lot of truth-stretching for the good cause of projecting a positive image of Notre Dame football and perhaps filling up the new stadium thereby was forgivable.

After the hyperbole of the dedication ceremony, the game against Navy was anticlimactic. It was a runaway for Notre Dame. The Navy team had virtually no offense and could not contain the Notre Dame running attack. Notre Dame won handily, 27 to 2, with Savoldi scoring three touchdowns.

Savoldi's performance against Navy completed a public relations process that had begun earlier. Known now as Jumping Joe after leaping over a goal line defense to score a touchdown, the big fullback with a strong Italian accent became a sportswriter's darling. Savoldi had come virtually from out of nowhere, Three Oaks, Michigan, to achieve star status in a sport that he had only recently learned to play in one of the largest and most competitive football programs in the country. Writers represented Savoldi as big, fast, and dumb, interpreting his Italian-accented English as an indicator of ignorance and severe cultural deprivation. He was recognized by the press as a great natural football player but as not really capable of handling authentic college-level academics.

This image was, of course, totally false for both him and the university. To be sure, in enrolling as a physical education major Savoldi had not elected a demanding program, and he received academic credit for courses in Italian, a language in which he was fluent. Yet, required courses in English, mathematics, science, and especially the courses required for teacher certification that he took and passed were academically challenging. Moreover, during his time at Notre Dame, Savoldi avoided academic probation and maintained a grade point average sufficient to maintain athletic eligibility. While he was not an honor roll student, few varsity football players at Notre Dame or elsewhere were. Though false, the image of Savoldi created by the sports writing fraternity persisted because it made interesting copy.

With Savoldi running brilliantly, the Notre Dame team had clearly lived up to expectations against Navy and did so again the following week against Carnegie Tech. The Tartans had played hard in a close but losing effort against Notre Dame the previous year in Pittsburgh. Rockne's gloomy press comments about his team's prospects were calculated to attract as large a crowd as possible into the new stadium. He wanted Notre Dame supporters in Chicago, Detroit, and Cleveland to believe that the game would be very close with the outcome much in doubt.

Rockne's purposeful exaggeration of the football ability of the current Carnegie Tech squad had some effect. Upwards of 30,000 people came to the stadium and found relatively uncrowded comfortable seating wherein they watched Notre Dame easily defeat the Tartans, 21 to 6, with Schwartz passing for two touchdowns and scoring one himself. For the next game, Rockne's team traveled to Pittsburgh to play the Panthers in their new stadium on October 25. Notre Dame had not played the University of Pittsburgh since 1912, and a large crowd of 66,000 came to see Rockne's team perform. What they saw was unforgettable. Notre Dame scored five touchdowns in twenty-five minutes and defeated an outmatched Pittsburgh team, 35 to 19. Schwartz ran sixty yards for one touchdown, while Savoldi scored twice, one on a one-yard plunge and the other on a thirty-yard run after intercepting a Panther pass.

The Notre Dame team returned to South Bend and prepared for the first visit of a Big Ten team, Indiana, to the new stadium. On game day, November 1, Notre Dame was ready to play, but few supporters were willing to give money and time to watch them. Before only 11,000 persons, Notre Dame ran the Indiana team into the ground. Savoldi, Schwartz, and Brill each scored two touchdowns in the one-sided win, 27 to 0.

A week later, the Notre Dame team made its first and only trip to the East Coast in 1930 to play the University of Pennsylvania in Philadelphia. On November 8, more than 75,000 people, many down from New York for the game, crowded into Franklin Field to watch Notre Dame overwhelm the Pennsylvania team, 60 to 20. All members of the starting Notre Dame backfield scored, and the greatest accolade for the day's performance went to Marty Brill, who scored three touchdowns on long runs. Born and raised in Philadelphia, Brill savored his day of glory enormously. He had left the University of Pennsylvania for Notre Dame because the coaches at Pennsylvania had refused to start him. Brill had clearly demonstrated how flawed the judgments of those coaches had been.

After the Pennsylvania game, the team returned to South Bend to prepare for their final home appearance against an unheralded squad from Drake University on November 15. There was not much that public relations chicanery could do to make this game an attraction, so none was attempted. The game was scheduled, would be played, but the issue was never in doubt.

However, while the interests of Notre Dame supporters in the South Bend area and elsewhere were not much piqued by dispatches from the practice field, public attention in a massive way immediately focused on a revelation that appeared in the *South Bend Tribune*. The hero of the present football season, Joe Savoldi, the country's leading scorer and a strong candidate for All-American honors had filed for a divorce in a South Bend court. The shock from this revelation resonated throughout the Notre Dame community and among football enthusiasts in South Bend and across the country. What would have been hardly newsworthy at other intercollegiate football centers provoked a major crisis at Notre Dame.

No one at Notre Dame, including the coaches, even knew that Savoldi had been married to a local South Bend girl since 1928. Yet, everyone associated with or familiar with the university knew that this was too serious a matter to be ignored and that action of a draconian sort would be sure to follow. Resolution of this case was, of course, a presidential decision, but the decision taken by the president would be decisively influenced by the recommendations of Father O'Hara, prefect of religion.

O'Hara was a strong supporter of Rockne and of Notre Dame's role as a major participant in intercollegiate football, but in moral theology he was very much a strict constructionist. Indeed, O'Hara was inclined to see the hand of God actively manipulating the fortunes of Notre Dame football. As the only noncoaching Notre Dame official traveling with the team to the Rose Bowl in 1925, he had spoken and also written many times on that theme in the *Religious Bulletin*. After discussing the Savoldi case with several Notre Dame priests, O'Hara concluded that it had been visited upon the university as a test of the institution's commitment to religious principles, "as if Almighty God had laid his cards on the table to test our willingness to place principle above everything else."[22]

In this case, finding meaning in the historical precedents of King Heny VIII's celebrated divorce of Catherine of Aragon in the sixteenth century, O'Hara believed strongly that once again important religious principles were involved. First of all, the university did not knowingly admit married men as undergraduate students. Savoldi had violated this convention. More important was the circumstance of filing for a divorce. While there were canonical ambiguities about this case that a skilled canon lawyer might have exploited to find a less painful resolution of it, neither O'Hara nor O'Donnell sought such counsel. The fact that Savoldi had been married before a justice of the peace in a civil service regarded as invalid in the eyes of the Church changed nothing for O'Hara. Even if Savoldi had withdrawn the divorce petition as some claim he did,[23] the university process against him would still have gone forward.

Arguments derived from the canonical invalidity of civil marriages had no appeal for O'Hara or for many other Catholic spokesmen at this time. Such arguments had been used by anti-Catholic speakers and writers during the presidential campaign of 1928 with devastating effect. Catholics had been falsely represented as believing that only marriages performed under Church auspices were valid. All others however, wherever, and by whomever performed were not authentic; the participants in such unions were adulterers and adulteresses and all offspring of them were bastards. Echoes of those diatribes could still be heard in 1930, and no one wanted to revive them by issuing public statements trying to explain how a canonically invalid civil marriage exempted a star athlete from university rules violations and kept him eligible to play intercollegiate football.

According to O'Hara's interpretation of Church teachings on marriage at the time, marriage was a sacred institution, so sacred that even if canonically invalid, once entered into could not be dissolved for the convenience, no matter how compelling, of one or both of the marital partners. The issue in such cases was divorce, that is, dissolution of a marriage, not remarriage after divorce as became the norm in many dioceses over the next fifty years.

Moreover, in O'Hara's view, when divorce was undertaken, the offense was so grave that there were no innocent parties. Regardless of the type of specific behaviors that had led to a divorce, both parties were responsible for the dissolution of the marriage. If the traditional three conditions for mortal sin were present—grave matter, full knowledge, and full consent—both partners had sinned mortally and would be denied sacramental participation until their lives had been appropriately amended, the sin forgiven, and a proper penance performed. To O'Hara and other priests in the Notre Dame community, the traditional conditions for mortal sin were patently self-evident in the Savoldi case, and only one form of resolution was possible. As O'Donnell admitted to a friend, there was simply nothing else to do except dismiss the young man.[24] The Savoldi matter was resolved quickly. O'Hara wrote a piece about the case in the *Religious Bulletin* under the title of "Idols with Feet of Clay," and Savoldi was allowed to withdraw from the university. In the end, university officials believed they had taken a stand on the very high moral ground of the sanctity of marriage, even the sanctity of a canonically invalid one.

The gravity of divorce to people living and working in the Notre Dame community at this time cannot be exaggerated. Separation from the university because of divorce had happened before. John P. Tiernan, the law professor who had managed the highly questionable reinstatement of George Gipp to academic good standing and football eligibility in the fall of 1920, later briefly became dean of the Notre Dame Law School and the highest paid lay faculty member after Rockne. This important local status did not save him. Involved in a divorce proceedings that told all, Tiernan was persuaded to resign and left the university in 1923 without benefit of testimonials for good service or references for a position elsewhere. So offensive to the Notre Dame concept of Catholic character was divorce that being involved in a dissolved marriage remained a cause for dismissal or, at best, nonpromotion and nonretention of lay faculty members until the 1960s.

Savoldi's departure from Notre Dame was sad but by no means ruinous to the young man's life. Though Savoldi only played in six games during the season of 1930, he was selected as a second team All-American fullback. Rockne facilitated a modest contract with the Chicago Bears, where he briefly played in the same backfield with Red Grange and Bronco Nagurski. From Chicago, Savoldi went to Green Bay for a short time before abandoning professonal football for the imperfect athletic/entertainment world of professional wrestling.[25]

Though Savoldi's marital problems continued over the next few years (he married again in 1931 and divorced a second time in 1932, then married still again in 1933 and stayed with this wife for the rest of his life), his wrestling career prospered. He became a headline performer on the wrestling circuit for several years and later worked as a wrestling match promoter. When the country entered the war in 1941, Savoldi went into the army, and because of his fluency in Italian, especially the northern Italian dialects, he was selected for duty in the Office of Strategic Services (OSS) and served with distinction behind enemy lines in Italy.

After the war, Savoldi returned to the South Bend area, where he worked as an insurance agent for several years. Then, at the age of fifty-four, Savoldi decided to change careers. He entered Evansville University and by 1962 had completed his undergraduate degree requirements, accumulated credits for high school teacher certification in science, and earned a master's degree in education. He taught high school science in Henderson County, Kentucky, near his wife's home town, from 1962 until 1972 and was highly respected as a gifted teacher. Savoldi died in 1972 at the age of sixty-five. Some human stories with sad beginnings have happy endings. This was certainly one.

Back at Notre Dame, the decision of officials to force Savoldi out of the university turned out to be noncontroversial. Even Rockne kept quiet about it. In the world outside of Notre Dame, most sports writers could not or would not understand the nature of Savoldi's offense and believed that the university had acted unrealistically, if not foolishly, in jeopardizing the football team's prospects for winning another national championship. Catholic circles responded favorably to Notre Dame's stand on religious principle. O'Donnell summarized the local and public reactions to Savoldi's departure by observing to a correspondent, "There has been no squawk from the coaches or from the boys themselves, nor from anybody except from a few illiterates who write anonymous letters in lead pencil."[26]

Alas, for the distant future the precedent of 1930 was forgotten. There would be a later time when, after local rules had been broken and criminal laws possibly violated, offenses under those local rules would be redefined downward to allow suspensions rather than dismissals for star athletes. Affidavits alleging criminal behavior were filed and then withdrawn. Thus were promising athletic careers allowed to continue at Notre Dame.[27] Even allowing for drastically different circumstances and utterly changed times, imagining how Charles O'Donnell and John O'Hara would have handled a similar situation hardly taxes one's mind.

For Rockne in mid-November 1930, with the Savoldi matter behind him, there was preparation for the Drake game on November 15 and selection of a replacement fullback. He settled on Larry Mullins, perhaps a bit faster than Savoldi but twenty pounds lighter. On game day Rockne hardly needed a fullback at all. The game with Drake, as expected, turned out to be no contest. Barely 10,000 people came out to the stadium to see Schwartz run forty-three yards for a touchdown and watch Notre Dame overwhelm Drake, 28 to 7.

The rout of Drake was the last home game of the year. Preparations began at once for a match with a much more serious opponent in Evanston on November 22. Northwestern was undefeated after seven games and anxious to avenge the humiliating loss of 1929. Despite the Depression and ever-increasing unemployment in the Chicago area, ticket demand was very high. So high was that demand that some thought was given to moving the game to the cavernous Soldier Field and then donate part of the much-enhanced gate receipts to the city of Chicago for poor relief. However, in one of its most dismal moments, the Big Ten leadership refused to oblige Notre Dame or Chicago's destitute. They denied Northwestern permission to transfer the game to Soldier Field.

The game was played in Evanston before only 44,000 people, whereas three times that number had been expected to appear at Soldier Field.[28] Even though the city of Chicago did not receive a much-needed donation for poor relief from the game, it was a well-played contest and well worth the price of admission even in those increasingly grim times. Marchy Schwartz led the Notre Dame running attack and, as quarterback, Frank Carideo probably played the best game of his career. Notre Dame defeated Northwestern, 14 to 0, scoring all of their points in the last ten minutes and knowing at game's end that they had been severely tested.

The following week Notre Dame returned to Chicago, only this time to Soldier Field, where the annual confrontation with Army would be played before 110,000 people. Both teams were well prepared for what had become for each the biggest game of the year. Chicago's rich, famous and infamous, along with tens of thousands of ordinary folk, traveled to the massive stadium by Lake Michigan to watch a slow and brutal game, made so by terrible weather.

A cold drizzle, sometimes changing to pouring rain, turned the playing field into a bog. Mud and slush soiled uniforms and obscured numbers to such an extent that the players were virtually indistinguishable. The two teams battered each other without much respite and were locked into a scoreless tie until the middle of the fourth quarter. Then, Marchy Schwartz, following blockers well initially, slipped and slid his way through the mud for a fifty-four-yard touchdown run. Carideo kicked the extra point giving Notre Dame a seven-point lead. However, that lead seemed short-lived indeed when, in the closing minutes of the game, Army blocked a punt in the Notre Dame end zone and recovered it for a touchdown. Despite the terrible weather, crowd reactions intensified, erupting into an enormous roar when the Army kicker missed the extra point. When time expired, Notre Dame had won an extremely physical game played in impossible weather conditions by the narrowest of margins, 7 to 6.

The team returned to South Bend with barely enough time to dry out before preparing to leave for the final game of the season against the University of Southern California in Los Angeles on December 6. After the victory over Army, at the university there was not much interest or time for academics. The Army game had been played on November 29, and the team departed for the West Coast on December 2. This final game had all of the makings of a clash of Titans. The Trojans had enjoyed an excellent year, winning all eight previous games, some by forty and fifty points. This apparently formidable Southern California squad was all that stood between Notre Dame and an undisputed national championship. In the Notre Dame community, all eyes and minds were focused on Los Angeles.

At a time in the country when optimism of any sort was in very short supply, the prospect of a national football championship for Notre Dame, and by extension, for Catholic America was intoxicating. With the humiliating presidential election of 1928 only two years distant and still very much in mind, Rockne's team in 1930 seemed to many to be a providential instrument for the restoration of American Catholic self-esteem. There was a sense in the university community, among alumni, and in the hearts of Notre Dame football supporters across the country that a great moment had arrived, that history of some sort was about to be made. The Great Depression and deteriorating economy notwithstanding, those who could afford the trip west wanted to be there when it all happened.

Packaged tours for the game were heavily marketed and successfully sold. Alumni groups chartered railway cars in order to travel with the team. All was set and ready for a transcontinental spectacular when the team and entourage departed for Los Angeles in early December. One witness described the trip west as the movement of an entire city on wheels.[29]

The train stopped in Tucson long enough for Rockne to hold a full-scale practice session and to entertain and confuse Los Angeles sportswriters about who would be his starting fullback. Traveling from Tucson, the Notre Dame entourage reached Los Angeles on December 5, where a crowd of 5,000 alumni and well-wishers greeted the team and followed them to their hotel.[30] On Saturday over 73,000 people filled the Coliseum to watch Notre Dame easily defeat Southern California, 27 to 0.

Everything attempted that day by Notre Dame worked well, while their opponents could neither mount an offense nor contain the Notre Dame running attack. Bucky O'Connor, a seldom-used halfback converted to fullback for this game, broke loose for a run of eighty yards and a touchdown. All of the regular Notre Dame backs ran up impressive yardage totals, leaving the Trojan team as stunned as had been those of the University of Pennsylvania and Drake. After the opening kickoff the outcome of this game had never been in doubt.

After the final score of this game was reported by the news services, never in doubt either was Notre Dame's claim to the national intercollegiate football championship. Seven different agencies selected the Notre Dame football team in 1930 as the best in the land. Rockne certainly enjoyed universal public recognition as being the best, but he generally managed adulation well. To be sure, he would with affected modesty admit that those Notre Dame enthusiasts who proclaimed his team to be the greatest in American football history were probably correct. At this most euphoric of sports moments, this level of self-praise was acceptable.

American Catholics, ever-conscious of their minority status in the country, savored these wonderful weeks of sports glory as much or perhaps even more than did the coach, players, and university leaders. Almost in the spirit of a holy day of obligation, priests, nuns, parochial school students dismissed for the day, Catholics of all degrees of religious attachment showed their appreciation for what the team had done for their pride and self-esteem by turning out en masse at railroad stations along the route from Los Angeles to Chicago to cheer their heroes homeward.

When the Notre Dame team arrived in Chicago on December 10, the city fathers, responding to the enthusiasm of that city's large Catholic population, organized a ticker tape parade through the loop area which had been decorated with blue and gold Notre Dame banners. Thousands of people, both in and out of work, forgot their many personal troubles for a day and lined Michigan Avenue and State Street to applaud the Catholic football champions of America and their two outstanding Jewish halfbacks. Nothing like this extraordinary public demonstration of ethnic and religious pride in sports achievement would occur ever again in Notre Dame history.

After the magnificent welcome in Chicago, Rockne and the team received more of the same when they arrived in South Bend on December 10. University officials and the city fathers cooperated to make the arrival of the team in South Bend a memorable event. Upwards of 25,000 people greeted them at the railroad station. Classes were suspended for the day at the university, and the entire community there turned out to welcome the coach and players home. Municipal offices and businesses in South Bend closed for the afternoon. Notre Dame students stayed in town and, joined by local supporters, organized and executed in the business district what was reported as the largest snake dance in the history of the city. The snake dancers and others celebrated well into the evening hours with a minimum of rowdy behavior. By December 12, at long last, the great and unforgettable football season of 1930 was over. Now it was time for Notre Dame officials to assess the football program's financial impact on the university during the past year and to determine what changes, if any, ought to be considered for future years.

That Rockne would continue to field national championship teams year after year was statistically unlikely. That football revenues would increase or even remain stable given the continuing deteriorating national and regional economies, no matter how well Rockne's teams performed, was also unlikely. That Rockne might leave the university and go elsewhere, given his history, was always a possibility. Whether a Notre Dame football team without Rockne could attract crowds sufficient to meet athletic department costs and still be able to support other university activities was at best doubtful in the present economic climate. The experience of major football programs at other institutions suggested that, in this time of Depression, the great crowds of the past would not appear and that football profits would certainly diminish or perhaps even vanish.

O'Donnell and his advisors had much to speculate about, but two matters seemed very clear. First, the balance sheet for the past season disclosed a disturbing trend and what could become an alarming situation. As has been noted, football profits for 1930 had declined only slightly from the record high of 1929. However, there was not much joy in that statistic. While revenues for 1930 had increased, costs had escalated significantly. Stadium and practice field costs were new items, travel expenses moved higher, and the outlay of $14,500 for new uniforms, more than the total library purchasing budget for the same year, embarrassed those who knew about it. The trend of modest revenue increases accompanied by rapidly rising costs was disturbing and provided an additional rationale for tighter cost controls throughout the university.[31]

More alarming was the inability of Rockne's greatest team to fill the new stadium. In 1930, home game attendance was only 42 percent of capacity, with over 140,000 seats remaining unsold. Without the revenues from away games played in Soldier Field, the Los Angeles Coliseum, Yankee Stadium, and other large-capacity sites, the Notre Dame football program would have been in serious financial difficulty.

O'Donnell was quite worried about this situation but was fearful of doing anything to aggravate it. He feared, and correctly so, that for the foreseeable future the new stadium rarely, if ever, would be filled to capacity. Even under the best of circumstances, as in 1930 with a national championship team playing in the stadium, operating costs would be covered but not much more. Without a Rockne-coached team playing there, the prospect of actually losing money on the stadium was real.

The second matter about which there was little disagreement among Notre Dame officials was recognition of Rockne as an invaluable university asset. Rockne's public relations value was incalculable. His much-demonstrated ability to bring money into the university through football revenues could not be found in any other football coach of his generation. No matter how difficult the coach was or might become, his continuing presence at Notre Dame during these very difficulty economic times was essential for the prosperity of the institution.

To be sure, Rockne's ego tantrums and whims were annoying and all too frequent. Yet, for the immediate good of Our Lady's university, they had to be endured by those priests charged with running the place.

Henceforth, O'Donnell and especially Mulcaire would do their best to oblige Rockne, keep him contented, and at Notre Dame. They would try to do so with forbearance and with as much forgiveness as could be mustered. Neither of these two priest/administrators were accustomed to treating lay faculty in such a delicate manner, but, after all, Rockne was different.

— iii —

Indeed, Rockne was different. In 1931, when most Americans worried about keeping businesses solvent and finding jobs, Rockne was at the peak of his earning power. In mid-March 1931, with sales declining precipitously, Albert R. Erskine, president of the Studebaker Corporation and chairman of the Board of Lay Trustees of the university, appointed Rockne manager of sales promotion for the corporation.[32] It is not clear when this appointment was to begin, whether O'Donnell knew about the appointment, or what O'Donnell could do when he found out about it. How Rockne intended to combine his football coaching and other business activities with what amounted to a full-time job with a major corporation confronting the most serious financial crisis in its history is unknown, but Rockne must have believed that somehow he would find a way to do so.

In addition to this new Studebaker appointment, Hollywood had beckoned, offering Rockne an opportunity to become a movie star. During the previous year, Rockne's agent, Christy Walsh, had started negotiations with Universal Pictures for Rockne to appear in a film version of a popular Broadway play, *Good News*, as a football coach.[33] By mid-March 1931, Rockne's film deal with Universal Pictures was set, and he made arrangements to travel to Hollywood and sign a contract to appear in the film.

The months of February and March 1931 were hectic ones for Rockne. First, the coach had a confrontation with Mulcaire and the athletic board over renewing the football contract with the University of Southern California. Mulcaire and others objected to renewal because of the travel time involved.[34] How Rockne responded to the board is unknown, but some mention must have been made of the great financial advantages of playing in a large capacity stadium like the Coliseum. Certainly, Mulcaire was aware of how dependent the football program was on revenues from games played in large-capacity sites. What is known about this confrontation is that tempers on both sides appear to have been controlled, no easy task for Mulcaire, and the football series with Southern California continued.

Next, Rockne traveled to Florida to visit his wife and youngest son, who were vacationing there, and discuss future plans. From Florida, the coach returned to South Bend briefly and tried to arrange a meeting with O'Donnell to explain the details and time commitments of the film contract. O'Donnell was unavailable during the short time that Rockne was in South Bend, so the coach left the president a letter in which he affected a personal indifference to the project but would consider it only because of what it might do for the university.[35]

According to Rockne, Universal Pictures had offered the coach $50,000 to appear in the film version of *Good News*. He stated explicitly in his letter to O'Donnell that this project "doesn't interest me at all." However, he added, "there might be a chance to put out a picture that might be instructive and educational as regards Notre Dame in every sense of the word."[36]

In this letter to O'Donnell, Rockne's inelegant and tortured prose notwithstanding, the coach stretched credibility beyond the limits of reasonable discourse. If Rockne was uninterested in receiving a personal payout of $50,000 for any sort of project in the spring of 1931, he must have been the only person in the country so inclined.

Having done his best to avert presidential disapproval of the film project, Rockne left South Bend for Chicago, took a train to Kansas City to visit two of his sons who attended a boarding school there. On March 31, 1931, Rockne boarded an airplane that was to take him from Kansas City to Los Angeles, with intermediate stops in between. There were no intermediate stops. Ice formed on the wings of the aircraft over western Kansas. The pilot lost control, and the plane crashed, killing the crew and all eight passengers.

Back at Notre Dame, Mulcaire received the telephone call from the news services reporting that the famous Notre Dame coach had been a passenger on the downed plane and had been killed along with the others. Upon Mulcaire fell the doleful task of informing the Notre Dame community that Rockne was dead.

— iv —

Rockne's remains were returned to South Bend on April 2, and the funeral service, which became a national event, was held on Saturday,

April 3. The Columbia Broadcasting Company requested and was granted permission to broadcast the funeral services to the nation. Tributes were received from the president of the United States and from the king of Norway. The mayors of New York and Philadelphia—James J. Walker and Harry Mackay—traveled to South Bend to attend the funeral services in person. Condolence messages flooded into the university from celebrities and ordinary people all over the country. Businesses in South Bend and elsewhere in the country closed for the day. All of the streetcars and buses in the cities of South Bend, Mishawaka, Elkhart, and Michigan City stopped at three o'clock, when funeral services began, and remained motionless for two minutes. Neither the university community nor the South Bend area had ever experienced or would ever again experience an event as moving, as grand, and as national as the Rockne funeral. Everything that could be done by the diocese, university, and city to make it so was done.

Because April 3 was Holy Saturday of Easter week, Church rules prohibited a Mass of Requiem on that day so the services could not begin until the afternoon. The timing of the funeral services did not matter. Only 1,400 of Rockne's closest friends and relatives were allowed into Sacred Heart Church. Crowds outside the church overflowed all over the campus. Those unable to get into the church followed the services over loudspeakers. The entrance to the new stadium was draped in black. Bishop Noll was present at the church door to receive the casket, borne by six of Rockne's current players. The Moreau Seminary choir performed brilliantly, and Charles O'Donnell's highly emotional funeral oration initiated what became, in effect, a popular canonization of a new secular saint.

With Sacred Heart Church packed and three former university presidents who had all known Rockne very well—Fathers Cavanaugh, Burns, and Walsh—present at the altar, O'Donnell began his long funeral oration. He began in the manner of the great seventeenth-century French philosopher/orator, Bishop Bossuet. First, O'Donnell read a long scriptural passage emphasizing the ever-present tenderness of God. Then, he asked rhetorically, who was this man Knute Rockne? Without trying to answer this question himself, O'Donnell simply stated that the president of the United States and the king of Norway knew who Rockne was and what he had accomplished. So did ordinary people across the country. O'Donnell implied that in some mysterious way great men are known to us and that Rockne was that sort of great man.

Next, O'Donnell asked another rhetorical question, why did Rockne enjoy such incredible popularity? Confessing no answer to this question either and declaring against the irreverence of trying to guess, he proceeded to do exactly what he had declared against doing. The picture that O'Donnell painted of Rockne was absolutely extraordinary. Rockne was a great man because "he loved his neighbor and fellow man with genuine deep love."

In an age, O'Donnell continued, "that has stamped itself as the era of the 'go-getter'—a horrible word for what is all too often a ruthless thing—he was a 'go-giver'—a not much better word but it means a divine thing." Rockne was, more than most of us, "quite elementarily human and Christian, giving himself, spending himself, like water, not for himself, but for others." Rockne was "an inspirer of young men in the direction of high ideals that were conspicuously exemplified in his own life."

It was fitting, O'Donnell concluded, that he should be brought here to his beloved Notre Dame, Our Lady's school, and "that his body should rest awhile in this church where the light of Faith broke upon his happy soul." In life and work, Rockne honored Our Lady in the "principles he inculcated and the ideals he set up in the lives of the young men under his care. He was her true son."[37] O'Donnell's portrait of St. Knute was complete for the moment, but there would be later embellishments.

After the Mass of Requiem had ended and the final blessings were administered, the Rockne cortege proceeded solemnly from the church down Notre Dame Avenue and out to Highland Cemetery, where final prayers and interment rites were performed. Rockne, the man, was gone, but the myth of Rockne as saint, which O'Donnell had proclaimed in his funeral oration, lived on and developed. Why O'Donnell chose to create this image of secular sainthood for his deceased football coach and to do so in the most public way possible with the clear compliance and support of three past university presidents requires some sort of explanation.

The obvious motives of concern for the Rockne family, grief over the loss of a longtime friend and colleague, responding to the thousands of expressions of sympathy from celebrities and ordinary people, and the timeless motive of not wishing to speak ill of the dead were all present and operative in this situation. However, those powerful motives by themselves do not explain why O'Donnell went as far as he did or why Cavanaugh, Burns, and especially Walsh went with him.

Praise was entirely appropriate at this time of tragedy and sorrow. Hypocrisy was not. Clearly, O'Donnell crossed the line between praise and hypocrisy in his oration by attributing attitudes and behaviors to Rockne that he and the three former presidents as well as most of the faculty and alumni close to the athletic department knew were utterly preposterous. The easy answer to the question of why O'Donnell crossed that line is that, given the liturgical and psychological contexts in Sacred Heart Church on that sad day, the president's emotions got the better of him and he said what he wanted to believe and wanted the world to believe. Indeed, that may be the answer, but circumstances suggest that there may be another.

Many different perceptions of studying and living at Notre Dame drew students to the university. First of all, Notre Dame was the largest and best-known Catholic residential university in the country. Perceptions of the strong religious character of the place and of opportunities for Catholic living and liturgical participation motivated middle-class Catholics to send their sons there. At the same time, most of those sons, attracted by perceptions of the school's celebrated athletic culture, were anxious to attend.

It would be incorrect to contend that in 1931 the quality of education delivered at the university was the principal reason why students came. Perceptions of that quality were positive among the parents electing to send their sons to Notre Dame. However, parents did not send their children to Notre Dame or to other Catholic colleges and universities because they believed them to be academically better. The relative scientific and scholarly excellence of an institution was not an issue in such decisions.

To most Catholic parents of this generation, it did not matter that prohibited books were not read and that certain subject areas were not studied in Catholic schools. Modern notions of academic freedom simply were unknown or, if known, not highly valued by parents or by Catholic colleges and universities, including Notre Dame. Parents chose to send their sons to Catholic schools, and especially to Notre Dame, because they believed them to be safe, well-supervised places where education was delivered in a philosophically and morally secure environment. Students could be educated for life and work in the contemporary world and in the process become stronger Catholics and better persons. That was the point of it all.

In 1931, Notre Dame could not and did not boast of scientific and scholarly distinction. Though O'Donnell had begun a modest institutional thrust toward encouraging research and scholarly activity, advancing the frontiers of knowledge was only a very small part of academic life at Notre Dame. The educational outcome desired there was graduation of educated, patriotic Catholic gentlemen who would be credits to their families, their Church, and their communities. Anecdotal evidence suggests that those desired outcomes were largely achieved.

If graduation of good men, not necessarily great scholars, was the point of it all, then O'Donnell's canonization of Rockne as a good man carried its own logic. Whether thought through or not, the mythologizing of Rockne's life and accomplishments turned out to be extraordinarily utilitarian and opportunistic. As the best-known Notre Dame man in the country, a mythologized life of Rockne was advanced and accepted as proof that Our Lady's university was succeeding. After O'Donnell's initiating funeral oration, other Notre Dame officials who had known Rockne well carried the mythologizing process several steps further.

James Armstrong, director of the Alumni Association, put together a special commemorative issue of the *Notre Dame Alumnus* in May 1931 that became a primary source for Rockne mythology. The full text of O'Donnell's funeral oration appeared in it as did pieces by Bishop Francis C. Kelly of the Diocese of Oklahoma City-Tulsa, Armstrong, Christy Walsh, and others. O'Donnell's oration represented the official Notre Dame position on the late coach. For Armstrong, Rockne was a believer in God, a humble man, an advocate of clean living and right thinking, an inspirer of youth, a maker of men, and an apostle of sportsmanship. Armstrong added three new elements that would be developed further nine years later in the Warner Brothers film *Knute Rockne—All American,* at a time when research and scholarship had become much more important in academic life at Notre Dame. According to Armstrong, Rockne had been one of the school's greatest teachers, best scholars, and had died trying to help a friend in California by fulfilling a speaking engagement there.

Christy Walsh, sports agent and a highly successful professional mythmaker, contributed a few paragraphs entitled "Happy Landings," wherein he reinforced Armstrong's point about the trip to Los Angeles. Walsh asserted that Rockne had died thinking of others waiting for him in California, not mentioning that those waiting were executives at Universal Pictures. Walsh knew the truth about the California trip but did not choose to tell it.

Bishop Kelly knew virtually nothing about Rockne or his many entrepreneurial activities but believed him to be a highly successful, very popular Catholic celebrity. Ministering in a region where Catholics were no more than 3 percent of the population and anti-Catholic attitudes were widespread, Bishop Kelly knew the importance of attractive Catholic public relations assets. Rockne had been in life and could continue in death to be such an asset. His Excellency chose to speak out and associate his name and moral authority with Rockne mythology. The bishop's contribution to the commemorative issue of the *Notre Dame Alumnus* probably amused as many as it inspired. He described Rockne as a Sorin without cassock and breviary. A description perhaps befitting the mythological St. Knute but certainly not even close to the Rockne known to administrators, faculty, coaches, and close observers of the Notre Dame scene.

There were, of course, a spate of books hastily published in 1931 to profit from the national interest in the late coach. Among the first in print was Harry Stuhldreyer, one of the coach's Four Horsemen, with an effort entitled *Knute Rockne: Man Builder,* ghostwritten by his wife and Pete Martin of the *Saturday Evening Post.*[38] Perhaps even more worshipful was Warren Brown's *Rockne,* also published in 1931. O'Donnell was so pleased and supportive of Brown's work that he wrote a foreword for it, testifying to the author's accuracy and authentic depiction of his subject.

Similarly, when Bobbs-Merrill brought out the *Autobiography of Knute Rockne,* derived principally from John B. Kennedy's ghostwritten Rockne articles previously published in *Colliers,* Cavanaugh provided a preface, a postscript, and helped Mrs. Rockne prepare an introduction for it. In so doing, Cavanaugh and Mrs. Rockne, in effect, legitimized the "win one for the Gipper" story.

Significantly absent from this list of Rockne mythologizers was Matthew Walsh, who had known and seen the best and worst of the man. Perhaps endowed with a clearer sense of history than O'Donnell and Cavanaugh, Walsh remembered what he had written in a confidential memorandum for the university archives about Rockne's behavior and duplicity during his Columbia escapade. Walsh, being the kind of man he was, would neither speak ill of the dead nor pay homage to false images. This former president opted for silence in this cause, content to observe, perhaps wince at what was being said and written, but not participate in it.

Of course there were other persons close to the Notre Dame administration who remembered Rockne as he was and ignored the entire mythologizing effort. Cap Anson, close friend of O'Donnell and member of the Board of Trustees, had known Rockne and was thoroughly familiar with the Notre Dame scene. Much moved by the coach's death, Anson wrote to O'Donnell six weeks after the funeral observing that because Rockne was such a complicated man his true value could not be closely gauged. Certainly, in a public relations way the coach had been a great asset to Notre Dame, and results showed the full service rendered. "I think," Anson continued, "Knute Rockne loved Notre Dame with a deeper attachment than he may have outwardly shown; some people are just like that. . . ."[39] Indeed, as all of the presidents who had to deal with the coach were well aware, Rockne was like that.

After the funeral, O'Donnell and Mulcaire had to address the question of a replacement for Rockne. They decided to separate the posts held by Rockne into an athletic director and a head football coach, that is, replace

Rockne not with one man but with two. For athletic director, O'Donnell first approached Major John Griffith, commissioner of the Big Ten. When Griffith declined, O'Donnell turned to Jess Harper. This former Notre Dame football coach and mentor of Rockne accepted. Charged by the Notre Dame administration to impose strict cost controls and financial accountability, Harper took control of athletic programs and operations in May and immediately began closely scrutinizing every expenditure, no matter how trivial.[40]

With recommendations for the post of head football coach pouring into the university from every quarter, O'Donnell ended speculation by announcing that no new coach would be hired. Rockne would be replaced by his assistant, Heartley "Hunk" Anderson as senior coach and by Jack Chevigny, a former player, as junior coach, an arrangement that neither lasted long nor worked very well at all. When Chevigny resigned at the end of 1931 to go to Texas, Anderson was named as head coach.

Despite Harper's scrutiny of expenditures and the threats to cut back athletic scholarships and on-campus jobs for athletes, Anderson still had about a hundred players who subsidized one way or another from which to select a varsity squad. However, in several important respects, there was to be a new order of things in the athletic department and football program. Both Harper and Anderson were told explicitly by Mulcaire that the old free-wheeling days of Rockne's time were over. The priests were determined to reclaim control over athletic operations and virtually nothing was to be done or undertaken without prior approval of Mulcaire and/or the athletic board.[41] The only place and time when Anderson would be boss was on the practice field or on game day. Rockne was gone, and despite what Rockne mythologists were writing, O'Donnell and Mulcaire never wanted to have another athletic director/coach as autonomous and uncontrollable as he had been at Notre Dame. That was to be the new order of things.

The strictures and standards imposed upon Harper and Anderson notwithstanding, O'Donnell accelerated the Rockne mythologizing process by committing the university to a Rockne film and to a fund-raising project for a suitable Rockne memorial. Shortly after Rockne's death, the ever-resourceful Christy Walsh persuaded Universal Pictures to recognize the profit potential in the massive display of national grief attendant upon the coach's death and rework the script of their intended Rockne film to exploit the new circumstances. Studio executives agreed. The title of the film was changed from *Good News* to *The Spirit of Notre Dame*, the story line was changed, and Lew Ayres was cast in the leading role.

For his part, Walsh promised to deliver former Rockne players Stuhl-dreyer and Layden for walk-on appearances in the picture and obtain the approval and cooperation of the president of Notre Dame for the project. Walsh managed to do what he promised. While the players were paid a pittance for their appearances and the university's compensation was to be in the coin of public relations, Walsh took very good care of himself in the negotiations with the studio and was paid handsomely for facilitating the project.[42]

O'Donnell cooperated with Universal Pictures to the extent of dis-patching a Holy Cross priest out to Hollywood to act as a liaison between the studio and Notre Dame. O'Donnell and his man on the spot were naive enough to think that these master filmmakers would be willing and sufficiently skilled to employ some cinematic technique capable of pro-jecting the spirituality of Notre Dame by adjusting light and shooting through filtered lenses down the nave of Sacred Heart Church. The presi-dent's man in Hollywood tried dutifully to do so. He gave advice which the producer and director ignored. They did it their way.

In the end, this hastily shot, low-budget production disappointed everyone. Audiences did not come. O'Donnell viewed the film in a cam-pus premiere in September and probably regretted that he had ever let Christy Walsh talk him into lending the name and reputation of the uni-versity to such a project. The president communicated his disappoint-ment to the head of Universal Pictures in September 1931 by observing that campus viewers saw little of the real Notre Dame in it.[43] Apparently, no one else did either.

This experience with a Hollywood film studio was not entirely nega-tive. Lessons were learned, and the next time the university got involved in a Hollywood film endeavor, things would be done differently. Notre Dame officials resolved that in any future film project, they would deal with the studio directly and not through an unscrupulous intermediary such as Christy Walsh. Indeed, nine years later in altogether altered cir-cumstances, Notre Dame did deal directly with a Hollywood studio. This approach was not without serious problems for the university and for the studio, but in the end the final product enjoyed much greater success.

Finally, there was the matter of a suitable memorial for Rockne. Through the ages, the most beloved saints of a region enjoyed their own special holy days, and the most beloved of all had shrines erected by devo-tees able to organize mass support. Sometimes this process took cen-turies. In the case of St. Knute, local devotees believed that a proper shrine could be constructed in a few years. Early on, a special annual memorial

Mass and Communion breakfast for Rockne was established. It was held shortly after graduation exercises were over, and members of the Rockne family usually attended. Rockne certainly qualified as a most beloved secular saint. Popular support for a suitable memorial building was perceived as being easily organized. Planning began a few months after the coach's death, and O'Donnell announced the project on June 6, 1931.

The project was an extremely ambitious one. O'Donnell envisaged a nationwide campaign to raise a fund of $650,000 for the construction of a Rockne Memorial Field House and $350,000 for a maintenance endowment. The ever-reliable Albert R. Erskine was chosen to head the campaign, with celebrities such as Al Smith, Admiral Richard E. Byrd, and Will Rogers serving on the project's board of directors. The task of trying to raise a million dollars in the midst of the greatest economic depression in American history proved to be formidable. The strategy adopted was to solicit the very rich and then get whatever was possible from everybody else. The board of directors went so far as to authorize the passing of collection plates at college football games across the country.

Nothing worked, the early 1930s was not a propitious time for a fund drive of this magnitude. The celebrities who had been so forward in expressing grief and the enormous sense of national loss at Rockne's untimely passing were not in a giving mode. As a matter of fact, few people were. The tried and true sources of money for past drives were exhausted. Only 10 percent of the alumni contributed anything, and student contributions amounted to less than $500. By the end of 1931, with only $126,000 collected and an additional $34,000 pledged, O'Donnell accepted reality and suspended the drive.

Nonetheless, the university commitment to build a Rockne memorial remained firm. The drive was revived under a new president in 1937 and raised an additional $200,000. At that time, university officials decided to proceed with the project on their own. The original plans for the memorial were modified to fit available resources, and maintenance costs for the new facility were integrated into the overall university maintenance budget. The new facility, completed in 1938, was situated at the west end of the campus mall and included a swimming pool, basketball courts, handball and squash facilities, and a display area for football memorabilia. The Rockne Memorial was formally dedicated during commencement week in June 1939.

The failure of the fund drive combined with a 25 percent decline in football profits during Anderson's first coaching year in 1931 surprised O'Donnell and Mulcaire. Along with virtually every other business in the country at this time, the great Notre Dame football enterprise was slowing down. With further declines in football profits expected in 1932 because ticket prices had been reduced to spur sales, and with enrollment certain to drop as it was doing at other universities, the immediate future of the university seemed likely to mirror that of the rest of the country and promised to be grim.

Times were changing, but to what extent no one knew. What most thinking men and women around the country in 1932 knew was that an era had ended. New leaders would have to emerge with new policies to get America moving again. So it was to be during the presidential election of 1932. So it was also to be in the American Catholic community and at Notre Dame.

— 16 —

EPILOGUE

T he impact of the Great Depression was worldwide. The major industrial powers of Europe and North America were particularly hard hit. Political leaderships in those regions were seriously challenged and generally replaced. Shattered economies in central Europe generated malevolent political forces producing a generation of political leaders who in their pursuit of nationalist goals and power would destroy millions of people and change that region forever. The social costs of a failing free-market economic system in western Europe intensified class divisions and so utterly perplexed and confounded incumbent political leaders there that consensus about national purpose was lost, and confidence in democratic institutions eroded. Confused about what to do or which way to go, the people of the western European democracies were uncertain about which leaders or which parties to follow. Democratic governments drifted, and events took charge.

In America, as the Depression deepened in 1931 it became clear that those in charge of the federal government could not cope with it. Unendowed with personal charisma of any sort, all that the incumbent Republican could offer the disenchanted and frightened American voters of those years was a firm Protestant religious background and professions of faith that in time free-market capitalism would correct itself and the economy would improve. Indeed, prosperity was just around the corner, and voters should trust Hoover to lead them to it.

However, in 1932 for most Americans that sort of trust was not forthcoming. Given the mysterious nature of business cycle analysis and the uncertainties about the practicalities of fiscal policy management and monetary theories, new leadership in the White House might not do much better than the present incumbent, but a new administration could not do worse. As the presidential campaign season approached, it was clear that almost any Democrat would defeat Hoover. It was also increasingly clear that Al Smith, Catholic America's most successful national politician, would not be the Democrat to do it.

Smith's message about how to deal with the economic catastrophe visited upon the country was not much different from that of Hoover. Yet, Smith believed that for what he had suffered and endured in the past for the Democratic party, he deserved a second chance at the greatest political prize of all. Virtually put aside in New York politics by the new governor, Franklin D. Roosevelt, and not liking it at all, Smith's aspirations for a second chance at the presidency proved to be a fantasy that faded fast.

After Roosevelt won reelection as governor of New York in 1930 with a plurality of 725,000 votes, he became a front-runner for the Democratic presidential nomination. State and local Democratic leaders generally were of no mind to risk reviving the religious issue at this most opportune of times. Though Smith managed to defeat Roosevelt by three to one in the Massachusetts primary election, the results in that heavily Catholic state were an exception. Smith had neither the energy, money, nor organization required to enlist enough delegates in all of the states to become a successful contender. Roosevelt had all three and won the Democratic presidential nomination in Chicago on the fourth ballot.

With the support of Smith and of all other prominent Democrats, Roosevelt went on to win the presidential election in November handily, capturing 57 percent of the popular vote and carrying forty-two states. Only Delaware, Pennsylvania, Connecticut, Maine, New Hampshire, and Vermont went for Hoover. Indeed, the Hoover landslide of 1928 had been reversed.

Though Roosevelt had vanquished Hoover more completely than Hoover had defeated Smith in 1928, the old happy warrior found little comfort in the result. He watched other prominent Catholic politicians, many from New York, receive important positions in the Roosevelt administration and hopefully expected a call for a job in Washington, but no such call was ever placed. State appointments as a trustee of the New York State College of Forestry, as a Commissioner of the Palisades Interstate Park, and as an honorary curator of the Bronx Zoo were all that came Smith's way. In the very pragmatic world of American Depression politics, like Hoover, Smith was a has-been. A major political force behind the rise of the American Catholic minority was now spent.

Deeply disappointed and perhaps feeling more betrayed than forgotten, Smith turned away from his progressive political past, seeking and finding solace and companionship from rich Catholic friends who continued to admire him. In addition to the Laetare Medal awarded to Smith by the University of Notre Dame in 1929, other Catholic honors came to him, including an honorary degree from the Catholic University of America and investment with the uniform and dignity of a Privy Chamberlain in the Papal Household. Though recognized and praised for his public service by both Harvard University and New York University with honorary degrees, Smith's interests and activities narrowed to those of his inner circle of friends and business associates.

One of those interests was, of course, the Empire State Building. Despite all of Smith's extraordinary salesmanship, the building remained largely unoccupied during the mid-1930s, and only extreme efforts prevented bankruptcy. So precarious was the financial position of the Empire State Building that Smith traveled to Washington to ask Roosevelt to rent federal office space in it. The effort proved futile for a number of very good reasons, the most important being that Smith's time for expecting favors of any sort from Roosevelt had passed.

Perhaps alarmed by the direction of New Deal legislation and programs, by the mid-1930s Smith had moved sharply to the right in politics and as a member of the American Liberty League adopted a public anti-Roosevelt stance. As a matter of fact, in early 1936 Smith delivered a speech to the American Liberty League that was broadcast by radio to the nation. In this speech he denounced the Roosevelt administration as a socialistic enterprise concentrating too much power in the federal bureaucracy. Smith puzzled and saddened former supporters by turning away from the Democratic party and declaring for Republican presidential candidates Landon in 1936 and Wilkie in 1940.

Cut off from his own past and demonstrably ineffective in national politics, Smith gave more of his time to Catholic charities and to organizations concerned with public morality, such as the Legion of Decency. Apparently, the severe psychological wounds of 1928 had never completely healed. For Smith and millions of American Catholics the annoying sense of inferiority remained.

When Smith died in October 1944, his recent embarrassing political behavior was forgotten. He was given the equivalent of a state funeral at St. Patrick's Cathedral with virtually the entire city of New York closing down for most of the day. Thousands attended the services and lined the streets to honor the man and remember the humiliating experience that so many American Catholics had shared with him. The very long-standing, informal, but formidable religious test for presidential candidates of not being Catholic, affirmed by the election results in 1928, would remain operative and unchallenged for another thirty years.

— ii —

While major leadership changes were occurring in American national politics during the early 1930s, similar changes characterized state politics as well. Under the impact of the Depression, Republican incumbents generally did not fare well. In Indiana, of course, special conditions prevailed following from the disgrace, trial, and conviction of D. C. Stephenson and the collapse of the organized Klan movement in the state. As already noted, Governor Jackson, a close friend and associate of Stephenson, had been forced into retirement by Republican leaders in 1928. That move was strategically sound, because another Republican, Harry G. Leslie, was elected governor in the Hoover sweep of the state in that year.

In 1932, impacted severely by the Depression, Hoosiers voted for Roosevelt and other Democratic candidates with a vengeance. In Indiana, Democrats won everywhere. Roosevelt carried the state by 135,000 votes. Sixteen consecutive years of Republican control of the governor's mansion ended when Paul V. McNutt easily defeated Raymond S. Springer. By a substantial margin Frederick Van Nuys bested Klan favorite James Watson, ending a senatorial career of twenty-eight years in Washington, D.C. Moreover, Democrats carried every congressional district in the state.

However, these Democratic election victories in early 1932 were not long lasting. They certainly did not reflect a significant change in the basic political and social conservatism of Hoosier voters. Distrust of Catholics and fear of their alleged loyalty to a foreign potentate remained endemic, although less openly acknowledged. Ironically, the great public causes of anti-Communism and isolationism so popular in the region in the years ahead attracted thousands of former Klan supporters as well as a majority of Catholics. While there is little evidence of formal cooperation between former Klan supporters and Catholics in any sort of common public-advocacy enterprise, both of those causes found stalwart champions among Hoosier politicians and voters of all religious and political persuasions. In the face of new political and social menaces, some of the older, traditional ones no longer seemed so threatening.

In South Bend the progress of the Depression profoundly impacted the Studebaker Corporation, forcing a change in leadership there that seriously affected both the city and Notre Dame. Erskine's belief in the virtues and efficiencies of free-market capitalism had been undiminished by the stock market crash and by the collapse of demand for goods and services that followed it. His prescription for the return of prosperity was more enterprise, not less. To further that end, Rockne had been appointed manager of sales promotion for the corporation in March 1931. If anyone could promote more enterprise, Rockne was the man to try.

In addition to the Rockne appointment, throughout 1931 and 1932 Erskine continued to develop new models and pay regular dividends to Studebaker shareholders. As a matter of fact, Erskine actually increased the dividend payout in 1931 over what it had been in previous years.[1] In the end, however, Erskine's more enterprise strategy did not work. The corporation suffered significant losses in 1931 and went into receivership in March 1933. A new court-appointed management team of two long-serving Studebaker officials, Paul Hoffman and Harold Vance, were given control of the corporation and forced Erskine into retirement.

Though Erskine's loss of salary ($100,000) did not leave him cash poor for the moment, decreasing income and values from his real estate holdings did not bode well for the future. More important, Erskine was under an order from the Federal Board of Tax Appeals to pay $730,000 in income taxes unpaid on Studebaker stock options executed by his wife since 1926.[2] Erskine simply could not cope with being pushed aside by a judge and by two of his vice presidents. To relieve his increasing personal stress, Erskine began reducing public service commitments. Among others, in June Erskine asked to resign from his place on the Notre Dame Board of Lay Trustees.[3] Apparently, neither this resignation nor any of the others diminished personal stress or growing anxiety about the future. Leaving a note to his family declaring that he could not go on, Erskine shot himself on July 1, 1933.

Hoffman and Vance managed to save the corporation from bankruptcy by liquidating unsold inventories through steep dealer discounts, by eliminating models, laying off workers, cutting wages, wiping out pension and vacation benefits, and reducing the work week to two or three days.[4] Indeed, the corporation survived when many of its smaller competitors in Indiana and elsewhere did not. However, as the largest business and employer in the South Bend area, the effect of these painful but necessary corporation survival measures on local firms doing business with Studebaker, on workers, and on the city was devastating. Until Studebaker could come back, the people and the city would have to bide their time and hope for the best.

Erskine's suicide shocked and saddened the South Bend community and everyone at Notre Dame who had known or worked with him. The *South Bend Tribune* carried a headline proclaiming the loss to the community of a very great benefactor. As for Notre Dame, although Erskine was a Protestant, his contributions to the modernizing and development of the university over the previous fifteen years had been immeasurable.

More than any other layman, Erskine had been responsible for the success of Father Burns' fund drive. No person did more to keep Rockne contented and at Notre Dame than Erskine. His work raising funds for the new stadium was critical. Erskine's advice about accounting procedures and business methods was well received and usually acted upon.

Possibly, the incident most revealing of Erskine's character and deep attachment to Notre Dame was occasioned by investment advice for endowment funds given in his capacities as chairman of the Board of Lay Trustees and a member of the Investment Committee. Erskine recommended an investment of funds from the lay faculty endowment in some automobile company bonds. When those bonds dropped in price and were sold, Erskine made up the losses incurred by the endowment from his personal resources. He was an extraordinary man for any place or time.

Though three presidents of Notre Dame and other university officials attended his funeral, perhaps the manner of his death or a lack of funds or both precluded the university from memorializing this very important man in Notre Dame history with a building, prize, or plaque. The city of South Bend was under no such theological constraint. Erskine's memory was preserved in South Bend by giving his name to a public golf course.

— iii —

Though unrelated to the Depression, leadership changes occurred within the Catholic Church during the late 1930s that profoundly affected the role and influence of the Church in American public life. Pope Pius XI died in early 1939. He was succeeded on March 2, 1939, by Archbishop Eugenio Pacelli, a long-serving papal diplomat and the papal secretary of state since early 1930.

Taking the name Pius XII, the new pope began his pontificate at one of the most critical times in modern European history. Upon the outbreak of the Second World War in September 1939, Pius XII was necessarily preoccupied with the challenges and horrors which that terrible conflict visited upon the people of Europe and elsewhere. Consequently, the direct papal management of Catholic Church affairs in different parts of the world through individual bishops as practiced by the pope's predecessors became impractical in a world at war.

Pius XII elected to delegate more decision making in local affairs to a trusted bishop or archbishop who, in effect, would act as an informal papal liaison with other prelates in a region. Those bishops or archbishops most trusted in such roles were either men the pope knew personally or had himself elevated to their present ecclesiastical dignities. The implementation and fruits of this policy were most readily apparent in the United States. With the very important Archdiocese of New York vacant, Pius XII surprised most Vatican watchers by elevating a slightly known auxiliary bishop of Boston, Francis J. Spellman, who was on bad terms with the archbishop there, to the most prestigious archdiocese in the country. Combined with Spellman's appointment as archbishop of New York was another one designating him as military vicar to the United States military forces.

The pope chose an obscure auxiliary bishop of Boston for these two highly important posts because he knew Spellman better than any other American prelate. As a matter of fact, Spellman was a close personal friend of the pontiff and had been so for many years. That friendship began and developed during Spellman's several assignments in Rome, especially between 1925 and 1932, when he was the first American priest ever to be attached to the Vatican secretariat of state. Pius XII knew that Spellman was the man he wanted in New York and wasted little time settling the appointment. Only six weeks after his formal installation as pontiff, the pope simply put aside other higher-ranking candidates considered by his predecessor and appointed Spellman.

Because of Spellman's continuing friendship with the pope and because his status as vicar to the American armed forces provided access to the White House and opportunities for meeting and establishing a personal relationship with President Roosevelt, Spellman quickly became the most powerful Catholic churchman in our nation's history. To be sure, Spellman was not the pope of America, as some of his American clerical opponents were wont to describe him. He did not dominate everything and everyone in the Church, but given his influence in the White House as well as what he had in Rome, Spellman came closer to doing so than any prelate before or since. It was no great exaggeration when clerical insiders and journalists described the New York chancery offices and the archbishop's residence as the power house.

Power was what Spellman sought, was what he obtained, and was what he knew how to use. Power derived from close relationships with great men made Spellman the most reported and most authoritative Catholic spokesman in America on public policy issues and a most important voice in the selection of American bishops. Midwestern bishops managed to resist his influence over bishop selection in their respective areas, but for dioceses in the eastern United States and in some parts of the Far West, Spellman's protégés were usually installed.

Spellman's emergence as the most powerful and visible leader of American Catholics was a major event in the history of the Church in America. It was also an event that impacted directly on the University of Notre Dame. One of Spellman's most successful protégés, who was eventually installed as archbishop of Philadelphia, was Father John F. O'Hara of Notre Dame.

— iv —

Leadership changes came also to Notre Dame in the early 1930s, driven not by the Depression but by natural causes and internal Holy Cross politics. Charles O'Donnell's second term as president of the university expired in the summer of 1934. Under existing rules and conventions, a new president would have to be chosen at that time. However, O'Donnell's failing health forced Father Burns, now provincial of the Congregation of Holy Cross, and other influentials in the religious community to consider a successor as early as the summer of 1933.

O'Donnell's serious health problems began in 1931 when a streptococcus infection settled in his throat, then traveled to his ear, producing a partial deafness. Treatment provided some relief, but the man was to be severely affected by throat problems for the rest of his life. During the winter of 1932–33, O'Donnell was very ill, spending much time in the university infirmary and in St. Joseph's Hospital. His condition failed to improve during the spring of 1933, and he was barely able to appear at graduation exercises that year.

Finally, in late June 1933, O'Donnell visited the Mayo Clinic and was diagnosed as suffering from an inoperable throat cancer. Relieved from all duties at this time but retaining the title of president, O'Donnell, knowing that he would not recover, accepted medical retirement with equanimity and prepared himself spiritually for the inevitable. O'Donnell died on June 4, 1934.

As a man and a priest, O'Donnell was a unique person. He was always interesting. O'Donnell did not know how to be dull or even ordinary and never was. Not particularly gregarious and not having many very close friends, even within the religious community, O'Donnell gave all of his devotion and emotional energy to the university. Blessed with charm and wit and perhaps cursed a bit with an enormous talent for sarcasm and irony, he found many more occasions for exhibiting the latter than the former. More than any other Notre Dame president, O'Donnell regularly entered the very rough and sometimes nasty arena of image making and breaking to defend the good name and interests of the university. Any perceived criticism of Notre Dame was quickly redressed.

In such situations and when in top form, O'Donnell's answers were always sharp, unforgettable to those receiving them, and in calmer moments sometimes regretted. President of the university at a most critical and challenging time, O'Donnell, as has been noted, was an active and highly successful builder. Having said that, his contributions to university development went far beyond erecting new buildings and expanding facilities. The enormous improvement in faculty quality and academic activities experienced by Notre Dame between 1930 and 1940 had been initiated by O'Donnell. He charted a course toward academic distinction which his gifted successor diligently followed.

The matter of O'Donnell's successor had to be faced directly in the late spring of 1933 when the president's deteriorating health and increasing debility became obvious. During O'Donnell's periods of incapacitation during 1931 and 1932 and especially between April and September 1933, Mulcaire served as acting president. In these instances the peasant proved himself an inadequate replacement for the poet. Mulcaire's aggressive manner, sharp tongue, and drinking persuaded Father Burns, as provincial, after discussions with Matthew Walsh to take Mulcaire out of the succession to the presidency.[5]

Initially, Burns had intended to replace Mulcaire as vice president with someone else but keep him at the university as an executive assistant to O'Donnell. However, Burns changed his mind and decided to remove him from Notre Dame altogether.[6] Mulcaire was given leave to visit his mother in Ireland during the summer of 1933 and was then transferred to a Holy Cross college in Portland, Oregon, where he served as vice president from 1933 to 1945. He returned to Notre Dame after World War II, and though afflicted with poor health and occasional bouts with alcoholism, outlived most of his contemporaries. He died in 1964.

Once the decision to remove Mulcaire had been made, selecting a successor for O'Donnell was easy. Burns turned to a longtime protégé, Father John F. O'Hara, and appointed him vice president in place of Mulcaire in July 1933. At first reluctant to give up his post of prefect of religion and job as editor of the *Religious Bulletin*, O'Hara, understanding fully the nature of religious obedience and the meaning of duty, accepted the appointment as vice president and chairman of the athletic board. Immediately, O'Hara took over the day-to-day operations of the university, first as vice president and then as acting president.

Mulcaire's banishment and O'Hara's appointment completely surprised the university community. There had been no inkling that Mulcaire was going out or that O'Hara was coming in. Though O'Hara had no advanced degrees of any kind and was untrained in any academic specialty, most faculty and staff approved the change. Some faculty in the College of Arts and Letters worried about O'Hara's known anti-intellectual proclivities, casual attitudes about academic freedom issues, and affection for book censoring, but nobody wanted Mulcaire back. Certainly, O'Hara had many admirable qualities. Virtually everyone praised his energy and lack of pretensions and vainglory. He was expected to be decisive, fair in most things, perhaps a bit idiosyncratic in other things, and demanding of everyone. After all, O'Hara was the best available man, perhaps not one for all seasons and times, but the fittest at this time to lead the university community out of the despair of the Depression and the pessimism of the Mulcaire interregnum.

O'Hara'a first major challenge as vice president was a familiar one: all was not well with the football program. Anderson's performance as head coach had been extremely disappointing. Though his teams win and loss records of six wins, two losses, and one tie for 1931 and seven wins and two losses for 1932 were far from being shameful, the performance of his teams was close to being so. Wins over demonstratively weak teams had become close contests, Anderson's offenses were predictable, playing errors multiplied, and the number of penalties increased. Anderson's teams in those two years simply had not played as well or as hard as had those in Rockne's time.

If the seasons of 1931 and 1932 were disappointing, the one of 1933 was disastrous. Notre Dame won only three games, lost five, and tied one. Only the 13 to 12 win over Army in the final game of the season was a worthy Notre Dame performance. The rest of the games, wins, losses, or the tie were all poorly coached and poorly played. What drove O'Hara to ask for Anderson's resignation at the end of the season in 1933 was not so much his win and loss record, the quality of play, or the torrents of complaints about Anderson from patrons, alumni, and supporters; it was the precipitous decline of football profits between 1930 and 1933.

With football profits reduced to only $177,000 in 1933, that is, one third of the net amount earned in 1930, a crisis was at hand. That amount of revenue loss was unsustainable. Even the most conservative fiscal management could not possibly make up that loss and enable the university to balance its overall budget. All branches of the university would have to pay some part of the price of Anderson's failure to win and attract ticket buyers. Something had to be done and was. After conducting polls of alumni and friends close to the football enterprise and compiling list after list of potential candidates, O'Hara believed that he had found his man, Elmer Layden.

Layden had not been a consensus first choice, but he was almost everyone's second choice. More important, Layden was a man whom O'Hara had known and liked as a student and who still possessed qualities that appealed to him. Layden had been an exemplary Catholic student athlete at Notre Dame and was an exemplary Catholic layman as an adult. He was, of course, the hero of the Rose Bowl victory in 1925 and a consistently winning coach at Duquesne.

O'Hara met with Layden in New York before the Army game in late November 1933, agreed to combine the jobs of head football coach and athletic director, and offered Layden the new position. Layden accepted on the spot and signed a contract, but any public announcement had to be delayed until O'Hara could collect resignations from Anderson and Harper. That took about a week's time. The announcements of the resignations and of Layden's hiring were released in early December. Anderson and Harper dutifully did the right thing. They departed gracefully, both pledging everlasting heartfelt affection for Notre Dame. The former went first to North Carolina State and eventually to the Chicago Bears as a line coach, while the latter retired to his ranch in Kansas.

O'Hara was proud, and rightly so, of his management of the Anderson/Harper departures and of the signing of Layden. The Layden appointment was widely approved in the Notre Dame community and acclaimed elsewhere. Indeed, the public perception of the event was that the right thing had been done. If the dangerous decline in football profits could be reversed, O'Hara believed that together he and Layden could do it.

O'Hara's successful handling of the football situation at the end of 1933 convinced Burns and the Holy Cross community generally that he should be the next president of the university. About a month after O'Donnell died, to no one's surprise the Provincial Council chose O'Hara to be the new president and local superior.

As president, this man with virtually no academic credentials worth mentioning and with a widely known history of anti-intellectual public statements and an apparent passion for book censoring turned his attention and energy to improving the quality of academic life and faculty hiring at the university in ways scarcely imagined before.

Following a course charted by Burns and begun by O'Donnell, O'Hara recruited distinguished European refugee scientists and scholars. In six years' time he authorized the hiring of more faculty with doctorates than had been hired by all of his predecessors together. O'Hara provided resources and firm presidential support for the establishment of a graduate school and for the expansion of graduate education in the strongest departments of the university. He found money for the improvement of research and teaching activities in mathematics, the sciences, Thomistic philosophy, and political science.

O'Hara provided funds for holding major scientific and political science symposiums at the university and for scholarly publications as well. Perhaps most important of all for the growing academic reputation of the university, he approved the establishment and permanent financing of a new scholarly journal, the *Review of Politics*, whose contributors regularly included many of the most eminent European and American intellectuals of the decade. All of this, moving so much so far so fast, would be an amazing achievement for any university president anywhere.

Why and how a man with O'Hara's educational and intellectual background and experiences would undertake such an exciting but totally out-of-character academic venture, and what were the consequences for the university, American Catholics, and the country is, indeed, another story that will have to be told in another book.

Notes

1. Catholic, French, and Irish American

1. Marvin R. O'Connell, "Ultramontanism and Dupanloup: The Compromise of 1865," *Church History*, June 1984, 201; Patrick Corish, *The Irish Catholic Experience: A Historical Survey* (Wilmington, Del.: M. Glazier, 1985), 194. What follows about changes and developments in European Catholic affairs comes largely from O'Connell and Corish.

2. Corish, 194.
3. O'Connell, 206.
4. Ibid.
5. Ibid., 212.
6. Ibid., 232.
7. Ibid., 212.
8. Ibid., 194.
9. David Joseph Arthur, *The University of Notre Dame, 1919–1933: An Administrative History* (Ann Arbor, Mich.: University Microfilms, 1973), 86.
10. Ibid., 340.
11. Canon Etienne Catta and Tony Catta, *Basil Anthony Mary Moreau*, English translation by Edward L. Heston, C.S.C. (Milwaukee: Bruce Publishing Co., 1955), 1:4.
12. Ibid., 27.
13. Ibid., 76.
14. Ibid., 82.
15. Ibid., 818–19.
16. Bouvier once referred to Moreau as one of those "individuals who are extremely hard to handle and who think they can find a protection in Rome." Ibid., 786.
17. Ibid., 790.
18. Ibid., 324.
19. Ibid., 448–49.

20. Ibid., 328, n. 10.
21. Ibid., 446–47.
22. Ibid., 434.
23. Ibid., 436–37.
24. Ibid., 441.
25. Arthur, 86.
26. Catta, 346–48.
27. Ibid., 387–88.
28. Ibid., 392.
29. Ibid., 393–95.
30. Ibid.
31. Ibid., 405.
32. Ibid., 474.
33. Ibid.
34. Ibid., 501.
35. Arthur J. Hope, C.S.C., *Notre Dame One Hundred Years,* revised edition, Introduction by Thomas J. Schlereth, (South Bend, Ind.: Icarus Press, 1978), 11.
36. Catta, 502.
37. Ibid., 503, n. 38.
38. Ibid., 502–3.
39. Ibid., 503.
40. Ibid., 446–47.
41. Rev. Edward F. Sorin, C.S.C., "Chronicles," 76, AUND.
42. Ibid., 25.
43. Gerald Philip Fogarty, S.J., *Denis J. O'Connell: Americanist Agent to the Vatican, 1885–1903* (Ann Arbor, Mich.: University Microfilms, 1970), 88.
44. Hope, 170.
45. Ibid., 67.
46. Cullen to Mathew, October 10, 1841, in Rev. Peadar MacSuibhne, *Paul Cullen and His Contemporaries* 5 vols. (Naas: Leinster Leader, 1961–1977), 2:9–10.
47. Hope, 116–17.
48. Ibid.
49. Ibid., 117–18.
50. William Corby, *Memories of Chaplain Life* (Notre Dame, Ind., 1893), 112.
51. Ibid., 137.
52. Hope, 138.
53. Ibid., 186.
54. Brother Francis de Sales to Sorin, September 3, 1877, Sorin General Administrative Correspondence, 1874–1877, Microfilm, AUND.
55. Colovin to Hudson, 1880, CAMM, X, 2, F, AUND.
56. See Brother Francis de Sales to Sorin, September 3, 1877, Sorin General Administrative Correspondence, 1874–1877, Microfilm, AUND and Colovin to Hudson, 1880, CAMM, X, 2, F, AUND.

57. Ralph E. Weber, *Notre Dame's John Zahm* (Notre Dame, Ind.: University of Notre Dame Press, 1961), 36–37.

58. Maurice Francis Egan, *Notre Dame Scholastic,* XXII (1888–89), 322; Weber, 36–37.

59. Weber, 36–37.

60. Egan, 322.

61. Hope, 344.

62. Weber, 119, 121.

63. Ibid., 121.

64. Ibid., 130.

65. Quoted from Sorin's circular letter in Arthur, 211.

66. Fitte to Edwards, July 13, 1905, CEDW, XII, 2, h, AUND.

67. Ibid.

68. Morrissey to Edwards, March 1, 1906, CAMM, XI, 2, 1, AUND.

69. Cavanaugh to the General Education Board, January 8, 1906, General Education Board File, folder 1, AUND.

70. Ibid.

2.   The President and the Professor

1. Charles Veneziani, *A Plea For The Higher Education Of Young Catholic Men Of America With An Exposure Of The Frauds Of The University Of Notre Dame, IND, Preceded By A Circular Letter To The Archbishops, Bishops, And Prominent Clergy Of The United States* (Chicago: no publisher listed, 1900), 11–13, AUND.

2. See Morrissey's letter to Zahm, March 22, 1900, printed by Veneziani in his *A.M.D.G.,* no date but estimated by AUND to be probably 1912, sheet 3, Treasurer's Office, Legal Papers, Microfilm M505, reel 2, odometer 70, AUND.

3. Ibid.

4. Ibid.

5. Ibid.

6. Ibid.

7. Veneziani, *A Plea,* 15.

8. Ibid.

9. Ibid., 14.

10. Ibid., 13–14.

11. Ibid., 14.

12. Ibid., 16.

13. Ibid.

14. Ibid.

15. Ibid., 9.

16. Ibid., 17.

17. Ibid., 18.

18. Ibid., 10.

19. Veneziani, *A.M.D.G.*, sheet 3.

20. Ibid.

21. Ibid., sheet 2.

22. Veneziani, *A Plea*, 7.

23. Veneziani, *A.M.D.G.*, sheet 3.

24. Ibid.

25. Ibid., sheet 2.

26. Ibid.

27. Ibid.

28. Ibid.

29. Ibid.

30. Ibid.

31. Charles Veneziani, *Frauds Of The University Of Notre Dame, Notre Dame, Indiana, Or How The Catholic University Of Notre Dame With Her Fraudulent Doctor's Degrees, Courses, Etc., Prostitutes The Prestige Which A Religious Order Enjoys In The Eyes Of Catholics To Obtain Their Money Under False Pretenses* (n.p., 1901), 19–28, AUND.

32. Ibid., 11.

33. Charles Veneziani File from the Treasurer's Office, Legal Papers, Microfilm M509, odometer 70, AUND.

34. Veneziani, *A.M.D.G.*, sheet 4.

35. Ibid.

36. For Veneziani's recollection of his conversation with Archbishop Falconio in October 1904, see Veneziani to Français, January 2, 1918, Charles Veneziani File from the Treasurer's Office, Legal Papers, Microfilm M509, reel 2, odometer 70, AUND.

37. Veneziani, *A.M.D.G.*, sheet 4.

38. Ibid., sheet 3.

39. Ibid.

40. Ibid.

41. Ibid., sheet 2.

42. Ibid.

43. Ibid.

44. Ibid., sheet 3.

45. Ibid.

46. Ibid.

47. Ibid.

48. Ibid.

49. James M. O'Toole, *Militant and Triumphant: William Henry O'Connell and the Catholic Church in Boston, 1859–1944* (Notre Dame, Ind.: University of Notre Dame Press, 1992), 197.

50. Charles Veneziani File from the Treasurer's Office, Legal Papers, Microfilm M509, reel 2, odometer 70, AUND.

51. Ibid.

52. Ibid.
53. Ibid.
54. Ibid.
55. Veneziani, *A Plea,* 23.
56. Ibid., 24.
57. Veneziani, *Frauds Of The University Of Notre Dame,* 13.
58. Veneziani, *A Plea,* 28.
59. Veneziani, *Frauds Of The University Of Notre Dame,* 13.
60. Ibid., 14–15.
61. Arthur, 230.

3.   Making a Place in the World as It Is

1. Hope, 281.
2. Cavanaugh to Lt. E. G. Lenihan, May 11, 1918, UPBU, 46, L, AUND.
3. Ibid.
4. Ibid.
5. Ibid.
6. For a general discussion of the problem of error and of the freedom to teach from an early-twentieth-century American Catholic perspective, see John A. Ryan and Francis J. Boland, C.S.C., *Catholic Principles of Politics,* revised edition of "The State and the Church" (New York: Macmillan, 1958), 174–76.
7. Foik to Mrs. John Donaldson, February 12, 1919, Library Correspondence Miscellaneous, AUND.
8. Ibid.
9. Cavanaugh to Burns, March 30, 1920, UPBU, January–June 1920, Box 43, AUND.
10. Hope, 281.
11. Cavanaugh to Morrissey, October 13, 1917, "Memo on the Summer School," UPBU, Box 43, AUND.
12. Ibid.
13. Arthur, 219.
14. Ibid.
15. Ibid.
16. Ibid., 297–99.
17. Hope, 244.
18. Ibid., 240.
19. Ibid., 241.
20. Arthur, 299.
21. Francis Wallace, *Knute Rockne* (New York: Doubleday, 1960), 37–38.
22. Hope, 299–300.
23. Michael R. Steele, *Knute Rockne: A Bio-Bibliography,* Popular Culture Bio-Bibliographies (Westport Conn.: Greenwood Press, 1983), 12.

24. Wallace, 81.

25. Ibid., 144.

26. Ibid., 102.

27. Cavanaugh to Burns, Memorandum on Athletic Salaries, 1919, UPBU, Box 4, A, #1, AUND.

28. Ibid.

29. Anne Kearney, "Rev. Paul J. Foik, C.S.C.: Librarian and Historian," prepared for the Seventh Annual Conference on the History of the Holy Cross Congregation, June 25, 1988, St. Mary's College, Notre Dame, Ind. Bound typescript catalogued in the Hesburgh Library, University of Notre Dame.

30. Foik to Cavanaugh, no date, Report of Present Library Condition, Library Correspondence, 1911–1916, Box 2, AUND.

31. Foik to Earl Dickens, November 18, 1915, Library Correspondence, 1915–1916, Box 2, AUND.

32. Ibid.

33. Foik to Twining, January 13, 1916, Library Correspondence, 1913–1917, Box 2, AUND.

34. Foik to Burns, November 17, 1915, Library Correspondence, 1913–1917, Box 2, AUND.

35. Ibid.

36. Foik to Byrne, November 23, 1915, Library Correspondence, 1913–1917, Box 2, AUND.

37. Foik to Miss M. E. Aherne, November 19, 1915, Library Correspondence, 1913–1917, Box 2, AUND.

38. Ibid.

39. Kelley to Foik, July 21, 1915, Library Correspondence, Box 2, 1913–1917, AUND.

40. Foik to Aherne, November 19, 1915, Library Correspondence, Box 2, 1913–1917, AUND.

41. Ibid.

42. Ibid.

43. Ibid.

44. Foik to Dickens, November 18, 1915, Library Correspondence, Box 2, 1913–1917, AUND.

45. Foik to Tilton, September 25, 1918, Library Correspondence, Box 2, 1913–18, AUND.

46. Foik to Tilton, December 7, 1918, Library Correspondence, Box 2, AUND.

47. Foik to Tilton, September 25, 1918, Library Correspondence, 1913–1918, Box 2, AUND.

48. Ibid.

49. Foik to Tilton, December 7, 1918, Library Correspondence, 1913–1918, Box 2, AUND.

50. Tilton to Cavanaugh, November 27, 1918, UPWC, 35/30, AUND.

51. Ibid.

52. Tilton to Foik, August 1, 1918, Library Correspondence, Miscellaneous, AUND.

53. Ibid.

54. Ibid.

55. Cavanaugh to Tilton, April 29, 1918, UPWC, 38/30, AUND.

56. Tilton to Foik, September 10, 1918, Library Correspondence, 1913–1918, Box 2, AUND.

57. Ibid.

58. Foik to Tilton, November 9, 1917, Library Correspondence, 1913–1918, Box 2, AUND.

59. Foik to Tilton, December 7, 1918, Library Correspondence, 1913–1918, Box 2, AUND.

60. Cavanaugh to Miss Anna Frances Levens, June 5, 1918, UPBU, Box 45, L, AUND.

61. Arthur, 86–87.

62. Ibid.

63. Ibid., 87.

64. Ibid.; Kearney, 111.

65. Quoted from Français' Circular Letter, December 16, 1918, in Arthur, 87–88.

66. Ibid., 88, 91.

67. Ibid., 91.

68. Ibid.

69. Cavanaugh to Miss Anna Frances Levens, October 13, 1917, UPBU, Box 45, L, AUND.

70. Cavanaugh to Lt. Emmit Lenihan, May 11, 1918, UPBU, Box 46, L, AUND.

71. *Scholastic,* May 4, 1917.

72. Ibid.

73. Cavanaugh to Sister Mary Irene, January 30, 1919, UPBU, Box 44, I, AUND.

74. Cavanaugh to Royce, March 26, 1919, UPBU, Box 44, I, AUND.

75. Ibid.

76. Cavanaugh to Sister Mary Irene, January 30, 1919, UPBU, Box 44, I, AUND.

77. Moloney to Cavanaugh, April 17, 1919, UPBU, Box 43, AUND.

78. *South Bend Tribune,* October 15, 1918, and *passim.*

79. Quoted in Hope, 333.

80. *South Bend Tribune,* October 15, 1918.

81. Ibid., October 23, 1918.

82. Arthur, 84.

83. Ibid., 92.

84. Ibid., 88.

85. Ibid., 92, n. 43.

86. Ibid.

87. Hope, 346.

4. The Burns and O'Hara Revolutions

1. The source of this recollection was Father Charles E. Doremus, C.S.C.

2. Burns to Edward Elliott, Chancellor of the University of Montana, October 10, 1921, UPBU, Box 44, AUND.

3. Ibid.

4. Burns to F. Wile, September 7, 1920, UPBU, Box 46, W, 7, AUND.

5. Hope, 34.

6. James A. Burns, C.S.C., "The Catholic High School Movement," *Proceedings of the Association of Catholic Colleges in the United States*, III (April 1901), 33.

7. Arthur, 208–9.

8. Ibid., 244.

9. Ibid., 246.

10. Ibid., 247.

11. Ibid.

12. Ibid.

13. Morrissey to Joseph C. Kenny, April 1, 1921, UPBU, Box 44, K, 5, AUND.

14. Ibid.

15. Burns to Unknown, June 21, 1921, UPBU, Box 46, S, 3, AUND.

16. Ibid.

17. Burns to Vernon Kellogg, November 2, 1920, UPWL, Box 51, AUND.

18. Burns to Father Louis Kelley, November 30, 1919, UPBU, Box 44, I [4], AUND.

19. The absence of organized programs of collateral reading in the library to supplement classroom work was a complaint frequently made by the librarian about all of the colleges, but this problem was most severe in the College of Commerce because so many students were enrolled in its programs. See Foik's Special Report on the Library, August 4, 1923, UPWL, Box 47, AUND.

Not much money was spent for library materials at that time. Total library expenditures for the College of Commerce for the first semester, 1922–23, was less than $100.

This level of expenditure continued. The dean of the College of Commerce complained to the director of studies in 1926 that there was "not enough money for technical commerce books,[and] not much in the library for students to read." McCarthy to Hubbel, June 21, 1926, UPWL, Box 49, Miscellaneous, McA-McD, #2, AUND.

20. Burns to Very Rev. Edward A. Pace, February 13, 1920, UPBU, Box 43, AUND.

21. See James A. Burns, C.S.C., "A Constructive Policy for Catholic Higher Education," *Catholic Education Association Bulletin*, XVII (1920), 48–56; also reprinted in the *Notre Dame Scholastic*, LIV (1920). See also Kearney, 159–63.

22. Burns, C.S.C., "A Constructive Policy . . ."

23. Burns to Sauvage, November 29, 1919, UPBU, Box 47, AUND.

24. Ibid.

25. Ibid.

26. Burns to Sauvage, February 19, 1920, UPBU, Box 47, folder Sa, AUND.

27. Burns to Cavanaugh, January 31, 1922, UPBU, Box 43, January–July 1922, AUND.

28. Burns to Sauvage, February 19, 1920, UPBU, Box 47, folder Sa, AUND.

29. James A. Burns, C.S.C., "A Constructive Policy for Catholic Higher Education," reprinted in *Notre Dame Scholastic,* LIV (1920), 8–9.

30. The prose works of Francis Thompson was the subject of O'Donnell's doctoral dissertation at the Catholic University. O'Donnell received his Ph.D. from that institution in 1910. Hope, 399.

31. Shuster, Autobiography, 286, AUND.

32. Shuster Memoir, AUND.

33. Shuster, Autobiography, 286, AUND.

34. Rockefeller Foundation Archives Endowment Fund, 2421, Xerox copies, AUND. Hereafter cited as Rockefeller file.

35. Rockefeller file, AUND.

36. Contract and Lease between the University of Notre Dame and Olen A. Clarke, July 31, 1920, UPWL, Box 52, AUND.

There was more to the denial of contract renewal to Tsiolis and the Balbanes brothers than a need for higher rent. It would appear that these restauranteurs could not handle the flood of new customers following from the enrollment increase of 1919. In any case, a serious food poisoning incident in the winter of 1919–20, allegedly attributed to an unhygienic kitchen, turned Burns against these Greek restauranteurs. He insisted that they vacate Badin Hall and be off Notre Dame property on the day of contract expiration, September 15, 1920.

Burns to Mrs. F. H. Smith, February 2, 1920, UPBU, Box 46, S [4]; Burns to Tsiolis and Balbanes Brothers, June 2, 1920, UPBU, Box 43, C, 3, AUND.

37. Burns to James Hines, March 23, 1920, UPBU, Box 44, H, 9, AUND.

38. Hope, 348.

39. Ibid., 232.

40. Ibid., 255.

41. Arthur, 254.

42. *Notre Dame Scholastic,* November 2, 1920, 27.

43. Arthur, 256.

44. Ibid., 258.

45. Ibid., 257–58.

46. Ibid., 259.

47. Shuster Memoir, AUND.

48. Philip Gleason, *Keeping the Faith: American Catholicism Past and Present* (Notre Dame, Ind.: University of Notre Dame Press, 1987), 167–68. Most of what follows about the role of neoscholasticism in the intellectual life of the Church and in American Catholic higher education is either taken directly from or suggested by this excellent study by my friend and colleague.

49. Ibid., 26–27.

50. John T. McNicholas, O.P., Archbishop of Cincinnati.

51. Gleason, 169.

52. Ibid.

53. Ibid., 170

54. Ibid., 168, n. 47.

55. William M. Halsey, *The Survival of American Innocence* (Notre Dame, Ind.: University of Notre Dame Press, 1980), 55.

56. Philip Gleason, "American Catholic Higher Education: A Historical Perspective," in Robert Hassenger, ed., *The Shape of Catholic Higher Education* (Chicago: University of Chicago Press, 1967), 49.

57. Ibid., 48.

58. Miltner to Burns, 1920–21, Reports of the Colleges, UPBU, Box 47, AUND.

59. Ibid.

60. Gleason, *Keeping the Faith,* 143.

61. Very Rev. Thomas E. Cullen, "Teaching Religion?" *Catholic Education Association Bulletin,* November 1924, 178.

62. Ibid.

63. Ibid.

64. Rev. Joseph V. McClancy, "Aims and Purposes in Teaching Religion," *Catholic Education Association Bulletin,* November 1922, 161–62.

65. Ibid.

66. Ibid., 162.

67. Ibid., 158.

68. Ibid., 163.

69. "Frequency of Communion," *New Catholic Encyclopedia,* vol. 4 (Washington, D.C.: The Catholic University of America Press, 1967), 39.

70. McClancy, 158.

71. Ibid., 164.

72. The following character sketch of John F. O'Hara, C.S.C., during his Notre Dame years is drawn largely from material in Thomas T. McAvoy, C.S.C., *Father John O'Hara of Notre Dame, the Cardinal Archbishop of Philadelphia* (Notre Dame, Ind.: University of Notre Dame Press, 1967), and from conversations with retired Notre Dame lay faculty and Holy Cross priests who knew and remembered him.

73. McAvoy, 93.

74. Ibid., 100.

75. Ibid.

76. Ibid., 112.

77. *Religious Bulletin,* March 3, 1931.

78. Religious Survey, 1924–25 in the Official Bulletin of the University of Notre Dame, XXXIX, no. 1, 128.

79. See J. F. O'Hara folder, May 1928, UPWL, Box 49, AUND.

80. Ibid.

81. Hope, 449.

82. Ibid.

83. Ibid.

84. John F. O'Hara, C.S.C., Report on the State of Religion, June 19, 1921, UPBU, Box 45, AUND.

85. McAvoy, 103.

86. Ibid.

87. Ibid.

88. John F. O'Hara, C.S.C., Miscellaneous Remarks on Discipline from the Religious Survey, 1921, UPBU, Box 45, AUND.

89. McAvoy, 115.

90. O'Hara to Burns, no date, folder Off-Campus Students, UPBU, 1921, AUND.

91. Report of the prefect of religion, 1922–23, UPBU, Box 45, AUND.

92. Ibid.

93. McAvoy, 108.

94. O'Hara to Walsh, July 16, 1922, UPWL, Box 49, AUND.

95. Ibid.

5.   Ideologies and Money

1. Burns to DeValera, September 16, 1919, UPBU, Box 43, D, 4, AUND.

2. *South Bend Tribune,* October 16, 1919.

3. Hope, 354; *Scholastic,* LIII, 58.

4. *South Bend Tribune,* October 14, 15, 16, 1919.

5. Hope, 354; *Scholastic,* LIII, 71.

6. Burns to Jolly, October 1, 1920, UPBU, Box 43, AUND.

7. Announcement of Celtic Subjects, 1919, UPBU, Box 43, AUND.

8. Ibid.

9. Foik to Cavanaugh, November 12, 1919, UPBU, Box 43, AUND.

10. Burns to Deery, August 16, 1920, UPBU, Box 43, D, 14, AUND.

11. Foik to Thompson, February 11, 1920, Library Miscellaneous, T, Box 2, 1917–1922, AUND.

12. Kearney, 12.

13. Ibid., 13–14, 27–29.

14. W. E. Allen to George W. Green, May 21, 1919, and enclosure dated March 22, 1919, Library Miscellaneous, T, Box 2, 1917–1922, AUND.

15. Ibid.

16. Arthur, 118–19.

17. Ibid., 124.

18. Hayden to Cavanaugh, March 3, 1916, UPOH, Box "General Education Board," AUND.

19. Arthur, 122.

20. Ibid., 123.

21. Ibid., 124.

22. Ibid., 160.

23. Ibid.

24. By-Laws of the Lay Board of Trustees, 1922, UPWL, Box 13, AUND.

25. Walsh to Edward C. Elliott, President of Purdue University, July 29, 1927, UPWL, Box 51, Miscellaneous, Ei-Er, AUND.

26. Ibid.

27. Ibid.

28. Arthur, 164.

29. Ibid.

30. Ibid.

31. Ibid., 125.

32. Ibid.

33. Bryan to Buttrick, January 21, 1920, UPOH, General Education Board, AUND.

34. Buttrick to Bryan, January 27, 1920, UPOH, General Education Board, AUND.

35. Arthur, 126.

36. Burns to the General Education Board, March 20, 1920, UPOH, General Education Board, AUND.

37. Arthur, 126.

38. Burns to Buttrick, May 28, 1920, UPOH, General Education Board, AUND.

39. Arnett Memorandum on Site Visit to Notre Dame, February 11, 1921, UPOH, General Education Board, AUND.

40. Arthur, 127–28.

41. Arnett to Burns, March 2, 1921, UPOH, General Education Board, AUND.

42. Burns to the General Education Board, March 6, 1921, UPOH, General Education Board, AUND.

43. Arthur, 129.

44. Walsh to Neuman, August 27, 1923, UPWL, Box 18, AUND.

45. Burns to Wallace Buttrick, March 7, 1921, UPWL, General Education Board, AUND.

46. Ibid.

47. Ibid.

48. Ibid.

49. *Scholastic,* March 5, 1921, 322.

50. Ibid.

51. Arthur, 131.

52. Ibid.

53. Ibid.

54. Ibid., 132.

55. *Scholastic,* June 4, 1921, 506.

56. Ibid.
57. Arthur, 133.
58. Burns to McPhee, July 3, 1922, UPBU, Box 43, AUND.
59. Arthur, 132.
60. Burns to unknown, March 5, 1922; Burns to Dowling, March 6, 1922, UPBU, Box 43, AUND.
61. Burns to O'Brien, February 14, 1922, UPBU, Box 43, AUND.
62. Walsh to Burns, March 30, 1922, UPBU, Box 48, folder Walsh, AUND.
63. Burns to O'Brien, no date, UPBU, Box 43, AUND.
64. Erskine to Cavanaugh, November 6, 1919, UPWC, AUND.
65. Ibid.
66. Report September 20, 1921, UPBU, Box 44, E, 3, AUND.
67. Burns to Kelsey, September 19, 1921, UPBU, Box 44, K, 3, AUND.
68. Burns to Byrne, October 3, 2921, UPBU, Box 43, B, AUND.
69. Contracts, 1921–22, UPBU, Box 44, AUND.
70. Burns to the Armour Company, April 2, 1922, UPBU, Box 43, A, 1, AUND.
71. *Scholastic,* June 11, 1921, 1.
72. Burns to the Armour Company, April 2, 1922, UPBU, Box 43, A, 1, AUND.
73. Burns to the Honorable Elbert H. Gary, no date, UPBU, Box 43, AUND.
74. Ibid.
75. Burns to Judge Gary, August 3, 1921, UPBU, Box 43, AUND.
76. Ibid.
77. McGinn to Burns, August 27, 1920, UPBU, Box 43, AUND.
78. Ibid.
79. Ibid.
80. Ibid.
81. Ibid.
82. Burns to McGinn, August 31, 1920, UPBU, Box 43, AUND.
83. Burns to Thomas P. Hardy, September 26, 1920, UPBU, Box 43, AUND.
84. McGinn to Burns, August 27, 1920, UPBU, Box 43, AUND.
85. Ibid.
86. Ibid.
87. McGinn to Benson, September 20, 1920, UPBU, Box 43, AUND.
88. Ibid.
89. Ibid.
90. Schwab to Erskine, November 21, 1921, UPBU, Box 44, E, 3, AUND.
91. Kern Organization Contract, January 28, 1922, UPBU, Box 44, K, 5, AUND.
92. Burns to the Armour Company, April 2, 1922, UPBU, Box 43, A, 1, AUND.
93. Marshall Field to Burns, April 20, 1921, and Burns to Marshall Field, May 2, 1922, UPBU, Box 44, AUND.
94. Walsh to Burns, October 27, 1921, UPBU, Box 48, folder Walsh, AUND.
95. Ibid.

96. McGinn to Burns, March 15, 1922, UPBU, Box 43, AUND.

97. Marshall Field to Burns, May 21, 1922, UPBU, Box 44, AUND.

98. James T. Foley to Walsh, July 3, 1922, UPWL, Box 51, Miscellaneous, Fo, AUND.

99. Ibid.

100. Ibid.

101. Arthur, 137.

102. Burns to Ainsberry, May 30, 1922, UPBU, Box 43; Burns to Stephen B. Fleming, May 31 1922, UPBU, Box 44, F, 4, AUND.

103. Arthur, 137–38; see also note 65.

104. Ibid., 138; see also Arnett's memorandum on Burns' visit, June 26, 1922, UPOH, General Education Board, AUND and Burns to McPhee, July 3, 1922, UPBU, Box 43, AUND.

105. Arthur, 138.

106. Burns to McPhee, July 3, 1922, UPBU, Box 43, AUND.

107. Arthur, 139.

108. Ibid.

109. Shuster Memoir.

110. Arthur, 141.

111. Dickens to Walsh, May 28, 1923, UPWL, Box 53, Miscellaneous, Di, AUND.

112. Burns to the General Education Board, January 15, 1923, UPOH, General Education Board, AUND.

113. Arnett to Burns, February 15, 1923, UPOH, General Education Board, AUND.

114. Arthur, 144.

115. Walsh to McLaughlin, May 7, 1923, UPWL, Box 49, McL to McZ, AUND.

116. Speech of Albert R. Erskine, April 18, 1924, UPWL, Box 51, Universal Notre Dame Night, AUND.

117. Ibid.

118. Arthur, 143.

119. Hope, 354.

120. Arthur, 143.

6.   The Development of the Notre Dame Football Enterprise

1. Arthur, 143.

2. See "The Constitution, By-Laws and Regulations of the Faculty Board in Control of Athletics at the University of Notre Dame," in M. A. Quinlan, C.S.C. and M. William Dempsey, *The Notre Dame Athletic Record* (Notre Dame, Ind.: University of Notre Dame Press, 1929), 239–44.

3. See President Daniel Russell Hogdon's letter to Burns, December 28, 1920, apologizing for and explaining what had happened. Included in Hogdon's

letter were copies of two letters from Rockne to the Valparaiso coach about Burns' reaction to the incident. UPBU, 1920, AUND.

4. UPBU, 1920, AUND.

5. Ibid.

6. Minutes of the Faculty Board in Control of Athletics, November 4, 1920, AUND.

7. Ibid.

8. Hogdon to Burns, December 28, 1920, UPBU, AUND.

9. Ibid.

10. Minutes of the Faculty Board in Control of Athletics, January 30, 1921, AUND.

11. Ibid.

12. Minutes of the Faculty Board in Control of Athletics, 1920, AUND.

13. Ibid., January 16, 1921.

14. Ibid.

15. Ibid.

16. Ibid.

17. Ibid., January 20, 1921, AUND.

18. Ibid.

19. Athletics Report, 1919–1920, UPBU, Box 43, AUND.

20. Kanaley to Burns, December 7, 1921, UPBU, Box 44, K, AUND.

21. Ibid.

22. Ibid.

23. Kanaley to Rockne, December 7, 1921, UPBU, Box 44, K, AUND.

24. Ibid.

25. Burns to McDonald, December 27, 1921, UPBU, Box 44, M, 6, AUND.

26. Notre Dame Athletic Association Reports for 1919–20 and 1920–21, UPBU, Box 43, Athletics, AUND.

27. Michael R. Steele, *Knute Rockne: A Bio-Bibliography* (Westport, Conn.: Greenwood Press, 1983), 37; Arthur, 329–30.

28. Arthur, 329–30.

29. Ibid., 327.

30. Ibid., 362.

31. Heartley W. "Hunk" Anderson with Emil Klosinski, *Notre Dame, Chicago Bears and "Hunk,"* A Sports Immortals Book (Oviedo, Fla.: Florida-Sun Gator Publishing Company, 1974), 24.

32. Paquet to Burns, December 1920, UPBU, Box 45, P, AUND.

33. Steele, 19.

34. Knute K. Rockne, *Autobiography of Knute Rockne* (Indianapolis: Bobbs-Merrill, 1931), 222.

35. *South Bend Tribune,* September 22, 1920.

36. Anderson, 35.

37. Ibid.

38. Mrs. Raymond Wright to Burns, October 12, 1921, UPBU, V-Z, AUND.

39. Ibid.

40. Burns to Mrs. Wright, October 18, 1921, UPBU, V-Z, AUND.

41. Ibid.

42. Arthur, 332.

43. Report on Failures, January 22, 1922, UPBU, Box 44, F; March 3, 1923, Box 46, F, AUND.

44. "Constitution, By-Laws and Regulations of the Faculty Board in Control of Athletics at the University of Notre Dame, April 1924," in Quinlan and Dempsey, 243.

45. Arthur, 333.

46. Ibid., 332.

47. George Gekas, *Gipper: The Life and Times of George Gipp, A Biography* (South Bend, Ind.: And Books, 1987), 16.

48. Ibid., 12.

49. Ibid., 36.

50. Ibid., 45–46.

51. Ibid., 46–47.

52. Ibid., 49–50.

53. Ibid., 63–64; Steele, 20.

54. George Gipp Academic Transcript with grades and disciplinary action deleted, AUND.

55. Gekas, 73.

56. *South Bend Tribune*, September 25, 1919.

57. Ibid., November 2, 1919.

58. Gekas, 100.

59. Foik to Cavanaugh, November 14, 1919, Library Correspondence, Miscellaneous, AUND.

60. Anderson, 41–42.

61. Gekas, 104.

62. Ibid., 109.

63. Ibid., 114.

64. *South Bend Tribune*, January 10, 1920.

65. Gekas, 115.

66. Vurpillat to Burns, March 29, 1920, Burns Correspondence, Box 46, V, AUND.

67. Gekas, 118; Anderson, 40.

68. Gekas, 118.

69. Ibid., 120.

70. Ibid.

71. Ibid.

72. Notre Dame Athletic Association Reports for 1919–1920 and 1920–1921, UPBU, Box 43, AUND.

73. Petition to the Very Reverend James Burns, president of the University of Notre Dame, nd, UPBU, Box 43/2, folder marked Miscellaneous, AUND.

74. Ibid.

75. Ibid.

76. Patrick Chelland, *One for the Gipper* (Chicago: Henry Regnery, 1973), 30. Chelland has the right day but the wrong year. The *South Bend Tribune* reported that Gipp had been reinstated on May 7, 1920, because of the petition presented to Father Burns by South Bend businessmen.

77. Gekas, 125.

78. Ibid.

79. Ibid., 128

80. Ibid.

81. Ibid., 126–27.

82. Ibid.

83. Ibid., 129.

84. Ibid.

85. Minute Book of the Faculty Board in Control of Athletics, 1920, AUND.

86. *South Bend Tribune*, September 22, 1920. See also entry dated September 27, 1920, in Minutes of the Faculty Board in Control of Athletics, 1920–1921, AUND.

87. See entry for September 27, 1920, in the Minutes of the Faculty Board in Control of Athletics, 1920–1921, AUND.

88. Ibid.

89. Ibid.

90. Ibid.

91. Ibid.

92. Gekas, 134.

93. Knute Rockne, "Gipp the Great," *Collier's*, November 22, 1930, 14–15.

94. Chelland, 135–38; Coles Phinizy, "Win One for the Gipper," *Sports Illustrated*, September 17, 1979, 99–112; Steele, 20–21.

95. Minutes of the Faculty Board in Control of Athletics, September 28, 1920, AUND.

96. *South Bend Tribune*, September 29, 1920.

97. Gekas, 145–46.

98. *South Bend Tribune*, November 16, 1920.

99. Johnson to Burns, March 21, 1921, UPBU, Box 46, AUND.

100. Gekas, 185.

101. Ibid.

102. Steele, 21–22.

103. Ibid., 23.

104. Francis Wallace, *Knute Rockne* (New York: Doubleday, 1960), 85.

105. Chelland, 182–84.

106. *South Bend Tribune*, November 23, 1920.

107. Gekas, 192.

108. *South Bend Tribune*, November 30, 1920.

109. McMeel to Burns, March 16, 1921, folder Dr. C. H. Johnson and the George Gipp Case, 1921–1923, Burns Presidential Correspondence, Box 46, AUND.

110. Burns to Cavanaugh, December 6, 1920, Burns Presidential Correspondence, Box 43, AUND.

111. Johnson to Burns, March 3, 1921, Dr. C. H. Johnson and the George Gipp Case, 1921–1923, Burns Presidential Correspondence, Box 46, AUND.

112. Gekas, 202.

113. Walsh to Armstrong, January 8, 1925, Walsh UPWL, Box 51, Miscellaneous, Ao-Az, AUND.

114. Burns to Paquet, December 14, 1920, UPBU, Box 45, Folder P, 4, AUND.

115. Walsh to Professor Frank W. Cavanaugh, May 1, 1923, UPWL, Box 52, Miscellaneous, Ca-Cp, 2, AUND.

116. Ibid.

117. Burns to Cavanaugh, December 6, 1920, UPBU, Box 43, AUND.

118. Walsh to Professor Frank W. Cavanaugh, May 1, 1923, UPWL, Box 52, Miscellaneous, Ca-Cp, 2, AUND.

119. *South Bend Tribune*, December 17, 1920.

120. Gekas, 202–3.

121. Clippings from local newspapers were sent to Burns. Hugh O'Donnell to Burns, December 20, 1920, UPBU, Box 45, O, 3, AUND.

122. Burns to Paquet, December 14, 1920, UPBU, Box 45, P, 4, AUND.

123. Gekas, 203.

124. Johnson to Burns, April 29, 1921, UPBU, Box 46, Dr. C. H. Johnson and the George Gipp Case, 1921–23, AUND.

125. Johnson to Burns, March 3, 1921, UPBU, Box 46, Dr. C. H. Johnson and the George Gipp Case, 1921–1923, AUND.

126. Walsh to Armstrong, January 8, 1925, UPWL, Box 51, Miscellaneous, Ao-Az, AUND.

127. Johnson to Burns, April 29, 1921, UPBU, Box 46, Dr. C. H. Johnson and the George Gipp Case, 1921–1923, AUND.

128. Johnson to Burns, June 2, 1921, UPBU, Box 46, Dr. C. H. Johnson and the George Gipp Case, 1921–1923, AUND.

129. Lowenthal and Mums to Burns, March 31, 1922, UPBU, Box 46, Dr. C. H. Johnson and the George Gipp Case, 1921–1923, AUND.

130. Ibid.

131. Burns to Lowenthal, April 1, 1922, UPBU, Box 46, Dr. C. H. Johnson and the George Gipp Case, 1921–1923, AUND.

132. Johnson to Walsh, November 3, 1920, UPBU, Box 46, Dr. C. H. Johnson and the George Gipp Case, 1921–1923, AUND.

133. Ibid.

134. Walsh to Johnson, January 10, 1923, UPBU, Box 46, Dr. C. H. Johnson and the George Gipp Case, 1921–1923, AUND.

135. Johnson to Walsh, January 11, 1923, UPBU, Dr. C. H. Johnson and the George Gipp Case, 1921–1923, AUND.

136. Murray Sperber, *Shake Down the Thunder* (New York: Henry Holt, 1993), 95, 284–85.

137. Rockne, "Gipp the Great."

138. Gekas, 197.

139. Steele, 23.

140. Ibid., 250.

141. Ibid.

7. The Prefect and the Professor

1. Hope, 259.

2. Rev. Robert Austgen, C.S.C.

3. Hope, 359.

4. Arthur, 265.

5. Ibid.

6. Patrick Haggerty, C.S.C., "The Halls of Notre Dame," *The Dome*, 19 (1925), 155.

7. Report from Off-Campus Student Office for 1921–1922, UPWL, Box 51, Academic Matters, AUND.

8. Ibid.

9. Arthur, 271.

10. Ibid., 276.

11. Perceval Brooks Coffin to Walsh, October 30, 1926, UPWL, Box 52, Miscellaneous, Coa-Cok, AUND.

12. Arthur, 264.

13. Walsh to James D. Fogarty, July 14, 1924, UPWL, Box 51, Miscellaneous, Fo, AUND.

14. Ibid.

15. Ibid.

16. Arthur, 278.

17. Walsh to John F. Shea, May 6, 1925, UPWL, Box 47, folder Sh, AUND.

18. Hope, 361.

19. Ibid., 362.

20. Arthur, 279.

21. Hope, 362.

22. Walsh to Charles L. O'Donnell, C.S.C., November 19, 1926, UPWL, Box 49, Miscellaneous, Oa-Od, 3, AUND.

23. Arthur, 280.

24. Hope , 362.

25. Arthur, 280.

26. Ibid., 265.

27. Walsh to John F. Shea, May 6, 1925, UPWL, Box 47, folder Sh, AUND.

28. Report to the Lay Board of Trustees, November 15, 1925, UPWL, Box 48, Lay Board of Trustees, 1, AUND.

29. Ibid.

30. Arthur, 276–77.

31. Contract Files, 1923–1924, AUND.

32. McCarthy to Walsh, September 28, 1926, UPWL, Box 49, McA to McD, AUND.

33. Arthur, 328.

34. McCarthy to Walsh, January 21, 1926, UPWL, Box 49, McA-McD, 2, AUND.

35. McNamara to Walsh, December 17, 1923, UPWL, Box 49, Miscellaneous, McL-McZ, AUND.

36. Ibid.

37. Walsh to McNamara, December 17, 1923, UPWL, Box 49, Miscellaneous, McL-McZ, AUND.

38. Foik to O'Hara, October 28, 1922, Library Correspondence, AUND.

39. Ibid.

40. Ibid.

41. Ibid.

42. Coyle to Walsh, August 8, 1923, UPWL, Box 52, Miscellaneous, Co-Coz, AUND.

43. Walsh to Coyle, August 9, 1923, telegram; UPWL, Box 52, Miscellaneous, Co-Coz, AUND.

44. Foik to O'Hara, October 28, 1922, Library Correspondence, AUND.

45. Ibid.

46. Ibid.

47. *Religious Bulletin*, March 7–March 31, 1924.

48. Ibid., March 5, 1924.

49. Ibid.

50. Ibid.

51. Ibid., March 17, 1924.

52. Ibid., March 7, 1924.

53. Ibid.

54. Ibid., March 17, 1924.

55. Thomas E. Blantz, C.S.C., *George N. Shuster: On the Side of Truth* (Notre Dame, Ind.: University of Notre Dame Press, 1993), 375, notes 16 and 17. The Macmillan contract was dated November 8, 1921, and is in Shuster Papers, Box 6, AUND.

56. Graduate Committee Minutes, 1923–1930, Eighth Meeting, May 1, 1923, AUND.

57. Ibid.

58. Graduate Committee Minutes, 1923–1930, Ninth Meeting, May 15, 1931, AUND.

59. Graduate Committee Minutes, 1923–1930. Tenth Meeting, July 31, 1923, AUND.

60. Quoted in Blantz, 51.

61. Halsey, 93.

62. Ibid.

63. Shuster Memoir, AUND.

64. For a sampling of such views see Frank L. Christ and Gerard E. Sherry, *American Catholicism and the Intellectual Ideal* (New York: Appleton-Century Crofts, 1961), 135–252. The three major studies of this problem appearing in the late 1950s were John Tracy Ellis, *American Catholics and the Intellectual Life* (Chicago: Heritage Foundation, 1956); Gustave Weigel, S.J., "American Catholic Intellectualism—A Theologian's Reflection" in *Review of Politics* 19, July 1957, 275–307; Thomas F. O'Dea, *American Catholic Dilemma: An Inquiry into the Intellectual Life* (New York: Sheed and Ward, 1958).

65. Christ and Sherry, 72.

66. Ibid.

67. *Commonweal*, September 2, 1925, 372–78.

68. Quoted in Ellis, 45–47.

69. O'Dea, 42–48; Michael V. Gannon, "Before and After Modernism" in *The Catholic Priest in the United States*, ed. John Tracy Ellis (Collegeville, Minn.: St. John's University Press, 1971), 350 *passim*.

70. O'Dea, 83.

71. Ibid., 83–84.

72. Shuster Memoir, AUND.

73. George N. Shuster, "Have We Any Scholars?" *America*, August 15, 1925, 418–19.

74. Ibid.

75. Ibid.

76. Ibid.

77. Ibid.

78. Ibid.

79. Ibid.

80. Ibid.

81. "Insulated Catholics," *Commonweal*, August 19, 1925, 337–38.

82. Ibid.

83. Ibid.

84. Ibid.

85. Ibid.

86. Ibid.

87. Ibid.

88. Ibid.

89. Ibid.

90. Ibid.

91. Ibid.

92. Burns to Shuster, May 15, 1926, UPWL, Box 1, folder 2, AUND.

93. Ibid.

94. Ibid.

95. Shuster Memoir, AUND.

96. See Wooten to Williams, October 16, 1925, and a draft of Wooten's proposed article, "Infiltrated Catholics," Shuster Papers, AUND.
97. Ibid.
98. Ibid.
99. Ibid.
100. McAvoy, 431.
101. *New York Times,* November 7, 1925, 13:1.
102. *Commonweal,* November 4, 1925, 635.
103. Ibid.
104. *New York Times,* November 7, 1925, 13:1.
105. Hugh O'Donnell to Walsh, November 12, 1925, UPWL, Box 49, folder Hugh O'Donnell, AUND.
106. Shuster Autobiography, 287, AUND.
107. Ibid.
108. Blantz, 128–30.
109. Christ and Sherry, 228.

8.   The Ku Klux Klan Comes to Indiana

1. David M. Chalmers, *Hooded Americanism: The First Century of the Ku Klux Klan, 1865–1965* (Garden City, N.Y.: Doubleday, 1965), 30.
2. Wyn Craig Wade, *The Fiery Cross: The Ku Klux Klan in America* (New York: Simon and Schuster, 1987), 165.
3. Ibid.
4. *South Bend Tribune,* October 24, 1923.
5. Ibid.
6. Richard K. Tucker, *The Dragon and the Cross: The Rise and Fall of the Ku Klux Klan in Middle America* (Hampden, Conn.: Shoe String Press, 1991), 5.
7. Ibid.
8. Ibid.
9. Ibid., 10–11.
10. Ibid., 11.
11. Ibid., 126.
12. Wade, 226.
13. Ibid.
14. Ibid., 125.
15. *Fiery Cross* (Indiana Klan newspaper), July 13, 1923.
16. M. William Lutholtz, *Grand Dragon: D. C. Stephenson and the Ku Klux Klan in Indiana* (West Lafayette, Ind.: Purdue University Press, 1991), 55.
17. Wade, 213.
18. Tucker, 34.
19. Ibid.
20. Lutholtz, 56.

21. Ibid.
22. Ibid.
23. Ibid., 37.
24. Subtitle carried by each number of the *Fiery Cross.*
25. Wade, 223.
26. Ibid.
27. Ibid.
28. Tucker, 38.
29. Ibid., 39.
30. *D. C. Stephenson, Irvington 0492: The Demise of the Grand Dragon of the Indiana Ku Klux Klan,* compiled from the Papers of Harold C. Feightner by H. R. Greenapple (Plainfield, Ind.: SGS Publications, 1989), 20.
31. Tucker, 41.
32. *New York Times,* February 3, 1924.
33. Lutholtz, 131.
34. Ibid., 85.
35. Tucker, 43.
36. Ibid., 44.
37. Ibid., 44–45.
38. Lutholtz, 87.
39. Ibid., 45–46.
40. Tucker, 77–78.
41. Wade, 234.
42. Tucker, 93.
43. Ibid., 82.
44. Ibid.
45. Wade, 225.
46. Tucker, 82.
47. Ibid., 83.
48. Wade, 231.
49. Tucker, 94.
50. Wade, 231.
51. Lutholtz, 114–16.
52. Ibid.
53. Ibid., 147.
54. Anti-Catholic Complaints by the Indiana Klan, October 4, 1923, UPWL, Box 47, AUND.
55. Ibid.
56. Kenneth T. Jackson, *The Ku Klux Klan in the City, 1915–1930* (New York: Oxford University Press, 1967), 103.
57. Ibid.
58. Ibid.
59. Ibid.
60. Ibid., 106.

61. Ibid., 271, n. 44.

62. Ibid., 271, n. 45.

63. Ibid., 115.

64. *South Bend Tribune,* February 25, 1923.

65. Jackson, 116.

66. Ibid., 112.

67. Ibid., 113.

68. Ibid.

69. *South Bend Tribune,* April 6, 1923.

70. Ibid., March 14, 1923.

71. See a copy of a letter sent from Mayor Eli Seebirt to Erskine, July 20, 1923, and Erskine to Walsh, July 23, 1923, Ku Klux Klan Materials, 1/3, AUND.

72. *South Bend Tribune,* March 6, 1923.

73. Ibid., March 18, 1923.

74. Ibid., March 14, 1923.

75. Ibid.

76. Ibid.

77. Ibid., April 20, 1923.

78. Ibid.

79. "Meeting the Klan," *Scholastic,* February 17, 1923, 513.

80. Ibid.

81. *South Bend Tribune,* March 30, 1923.

82. Ibid., October 15, 1923.

83. Ibid., April 6, 1923.

84. Ibid.

85. Ibid., May 25, 1923.

86. Ibid., May 19, 1923.

87. Hope, 372.

88. Ibid.

89. P. O'Donnell to Erskine, July 12, 1923, Ku Klux Klan Materials, 1/3, AUND.

90. Froning to Walsh, July 17, 1923, UPWL, Box 51, Henry B. Froning, AUND.

91. Froning to Walsh, July 24, 1923, UPWL, Box 51, Henry B. Froning, AUND.

92. Ibid.

93. Walsh to Froning, July 27, 1923, UPWL, Box 51, Henry B. Froning, AUND.

94. P. O'Donnell to Walsh, May 26, 1923, Ku Klux Klan Materials, 1/2, AUND.

95. Hope, 372–73.

96. P. O'Donnell to Walsh, May 26, 1923, Ku Klux Klan Materials, 1922–1980, 1/2, AUND.

97. Jackson, 116.

98. *South Bend Tribune,* April 28, 1923.

99. Ibid., May 18, 21, 1923.

100. Ibid., May 28, 1923.

101. Ibid., June 30, 1923.

102. Ibid., June 12, 1923.

103. Ibid.

104. Ibid.

105. Ibid., June 14, 1923.

106. Ibid., June 22, 1923.

107. Ibid., June 24, 1923.

108. Ibid., June 26, 1923.

109. Copy of Mayor Eli Seebirt to Erskine, July 20, 1923, sent to Walsh by Erskine, July 23, 1923, Ku Klux Klan Materials, 1922–1980, 1/3, AUND.

110. O'Donnell to Walsh, December 20, 1923, with enclosure dated November 30, 1923, Ku Klux Klan Materials, 1/3, AUND.

111. Ibid.

112. *South Bend Tribune,* November 12, 1923.

113. Ibid., November 23, 1923.

114. Ibid., January 12, 1924.

115. Ibid.

116. Ibid.

117. Proctor named former Judge James S. Harman as the Klansman elected as president of the Elkhart Chamber of Commerce. In this instance Proctor was mistaken. Harman ran in the Democratic primary election for Congress on May 6, 1924, and won. In this election, Harman was not endorsed by the Klan. John T. McCutcheon of South Bend received Klan endorsement as the Democratic nominee for Congress in the Thirteenth District.

118. *South Bend Tribune,* January 12, 1924.

119. Ibid.

120. Ibid., January 9, 1924.

121. Lutholtz, 127–28.

122. Ibid., 128–29.

123. *South Bend Tribune,* February 2, 1924.

124. Ibid.

125. Ibid.

126. Ibid., April 2, 1924.

127. Ibid.

128. *Indianapolis News,* May 13, 1924.

129. *South Bend Tribune,* May 4, 1924.

130. Ibid.

131. Ibid., May 2, 1924.

132. Ibid., May 4, 1924. The candidates endorsed by the Klan in the St. Joseph County Republican primary elections were Ed Jackson, governor; Rev. A. L. Vermillion, Congress; Cyrus E. Pattee, judge; Jesse Hess, senator; Harry Taylor, prosecutor; A. N. DuComb, representative; Tom Dugdale, coroner; Thomas Goodrick, sheriff; Noah C. Lehman, treasurer.

According to the *South Bend Tribune,* May 6, 1924, a few days before the primary election local Klan leaders decided that Lehman had no chance whatsoever to win the Republican nomination for county treasurer. At that time, the local Klan withdrew its endorsement of Lehman and gave it to the front runner, George A. Swintz, hoping to be able to claim some credit for his near certain victory. Friends of Swintz were amused by the suggestion that he had any sympathy for the Klan. The race for county treasurer was hotly contested because this office carried with it the highest salary ($17,000) paid to any elected St. Joseph County official.

133. *South Bend Tribune,* April 6, 1924.

134. Ibid.

135. Ibid.

136. Lutholtz, 141. Lutholtz quotes from and cites a study by Jill Nevel, a Princeton undergraduate, completed as part of a senior honors essay requirement. The Nevel study is on deposit in the Indiana Historical Society in Indianapolis and the South Bend Public Library.

137. *South Bend Tribune,* February 2, 1924, 2.

138. Lutholtz, 141.

9.   Confrontation in South Bend and After

1. *South Bend Tribune,* May 6, 1924.

2. Tucker, *The Dragon and the Cross,* 102; *Indianapolis News,* May 12, 1924.

3. *South Bend Tribune,* May 7, 1924.

4. Ibid.

5. Ibid., May 10, 1924.

6. Ibid.

7. Ibid., May 13, 1924.

8. Ibid.

9. Ibid.

10. *Indianapolis News,* May 13, 1924.

11. *South Bend Tribune,* May 13, 1924.

12. Ibid.

13. Ibid.

14. Ibid.

15. Ibid.

16. Hope, 374.

17. Ibid. See also *South Bend Tribune,* May 18, 1924.

18. Grant's recollections of the events of May 16, 1924, appeared in Mary Ellen McAndrews, "The Day the KKK Came to Town," *The Observer,* April 30, 1974.

19. *South Bend Tribune,* May 18, 1924.

20. Ibid.

21. Ibid.

22. Ibid., May 17, 1924.

23. Ibid.

24. Ibid.

25. Ibid.
26. Hope, 376.
27. *South Bend Tribune,* May 18, 1924.
28. Hope, 376; *South Bend Tribune,* May 18, 1924.
29. *South Bend Tribune,* May 18, 1924.
30. Ibid.
31. Ibid.
32. Ibid.
33. Ibid.
34. Ibid.
35. Ibid.
36. Ibid.
37. Ibid.
38. Ibid.
39. Ibid.
40. Ibid.
41. Ibid.
42. Hope, 375.
43. This KKK banner was kept for many years in a package stored in the old library. From there, it passed to the university art gallery and finally found permanent storage into the Notre Dame Archives. An unsigned and undated note describing the flag-raising incident was included in the storage box with the banner. Also O'Hara alluded to student misbehavior on this occasion in the *Religious Bulletin,* May 26, 1924.
44. Hope, 376.
45. *South Bend Tribune,* May 20, 1924.
46. Hope, 375–76.
47. *South Bend Tribune,* May 20, 1924.
48. Ibid.
49. Ibid.
50. Ibid.
51. Ibid.
52. Ibid.
53. Ibid.
54. Hope's version of the events of May 19, 1924, provide one example of how myths about Notre Dame have been created and perpetuated. No text for Walsh's speech from the Civil War Monument exists because he spoke extemporaneously. Hope cited the *South Bend Tribune,* May 20, 1924, as the source of the version printed in his *Notre Dame One Hundred Years.* However, Hope's version, written twenty years after the event, differed significantly from what appeared in the *South Bend Tribune.* Hope puts words in Walsh's mouth unreported in the newspaper that make Walsh appear much more in charge of the situation than he could have been and presented the students as being more orderly and disciplined than they were.

In addition, Hope attributed actions and statements to Walsh on that occasion that simply could not have happened in the manner described. Hope has Walsh speaking from the ledge of the monument, pointing a finger directly at Klan headquarters and threatening it with destruction, "leaving no stone upon stone" (p. 377) if the spirit moved him. Then, according to Hope, the students surged toward the building only to be restrained by a word from Walsh. Next, after Walsh finished his speech, Hope has the students forming ranks in columns of fours and marching back to the campus. The absurdity of the students marching back to campus after enduring a severe police battering is surpassed only by the impossibility of Walsh pointing his finger directly at Klan headquarters during his speech from the monument. Hope was mistaken about the location of Klan headquarters. The Klan had rented space in the Knights of Pythias Building on the northeast corner of the intersection of Michigan and Wayne streets, two blocks south and one block east of the Civil War Monument from which Walsh spoke. Walsh could not have seen or pointed directly at Klan headquarters in the manner described.

55. *South Bend Tribune,* May 20, 1924.

56. Ibid.

57. Ibid.

58. Walsh to O'Donnell, October 11, 1924, UPWL, Box 49, folder Rev. Charles L. O'Donnell, AUND.

59. Ibid.

60. Hope, 278; *South Bend Tribune,* February 20, 1928.

61. Ku Klux Klan Materials, 1/3, AUND.

62. *Religious Bulletin,* May 24, 1924.

63. Ibid.

64. *Religious Bulletin,* May 26, 1924.

65. *South Bend Tribune,* May 20, 1924.

66. Lutholtz, 138–39.

67. Ibid., 139.

68. Ibid., 145.

69. Ibid., 140.

70. Ibid., 135.

71. *South Bend Tribune,* May 23, 1924.

72. Tucker, 102.

73. *South Bend Tribune,* May 26, 1924.

74. Ibid.

75. *South Bend Tribune,* May 21, 1924, 2.

76. See column "Watson Unconcerned," *South Bend Tribune,* May 24, 1924.

77. Ibid.

78. Ibid.

79. *South Bend Tribune,* May 25, 1924.

80. *Indianapolis Star,* May 26, 1924.

81. Tucker, 102.

82. *South Bend Tribune,* May 24, 1924.

83. See column "Watson Unconcerned," *South Bend Tribune,* May 24, 1924.

84. *South Bend Tribune,* May 21, 1924.

85. Wade, 197, 200.

86. Lutholtz, 147.

87. *New York Times,* June 10, 1924, 3.

88. Ibid.

89. Edgar Allen Booth, *The Mad Mullah of America* (Columbus, Ohio: Boyd Ellison, 1927), 89.

90. *New York Times,* June 10, 1924.

91. Arnold S. Rice, *The Ku Klux Klan in American Politics* (Washington, D.C.: Public Affairs Press, 1962), 136, n. 1.

92. *New York Times,* June 10, 1924.

93. Ibid.

94. Rice, 75.

95. *New York Times,* June 10, 1924.

96. Ibid., June 12, 1924.

97. Ibid.

98. Ibid.

99. Rice, 74–75.

100. *New York Times,* June 11, 1924.

101. Ibid., June 12, 1924.

102. Lutholtz, 146.

103. Ibid.

104. Ibid., 148–49.

105. Ibid., 149.

106. Chalmers, 208.

107. Ibid., 210.

108. Ibid., 212.

109. Card postmarked May 20, 1924, Ku Klux Klan Materials, 1/3, AUND.

110. A Klansman Now and Always to Walsh, May 19, 1924, Ku Klux Klan Materials, 1/3, AUND.

111. Unsigned and undated card addressed to Walsh, Ku Klux Klan Materials, 1/3, AUND.

112. Copy of *Fiery Cross,* May 30, 1924, with handwritten warning, Ku Klux Klan Materials, AUND.

113. Edgar Allen Booth claimed that the Lansing Klan organization was strongly pro-Stephenson during the internecine struggle between Stephenson and Evans. Booth, 98–99.

114. *Lansing State-Journal,* June 5, 1924. Clipping sent to Walsh with a letter dated June 6, 1924, Ku Klux Klan Materials, 1/3, AUND.

115. H. M. Trausch, *The Truth about the Notre Dame Riot on Saturday, May 17, 1924* (Indianapolis: Fiery Cross Publishing Company, no date), 7–8, 20, AUND.

116. *Fiery Cross,* October 24, 1924, Ku Klux Klan Materials, 1/6, AUND.

117. Chalmers, 302; Edgar Allen Booth asserts in *The Mad Mullah of America,* 167, that the *Fellowship Forum* was controlled by Evans and lavishly supported by Klan funds. Booth was a true believer in Klan principles but disgusted by the venality and incompetence of national Klan leadership. Though his book is written from the perspective of a Klan insider, it is a badly organized, sometimes incoherent collection of gossip, anecdotes, and hearsay and should be used cautiously.

118. Clipping from the *Fellowship Forum* sent to Walsh, no date, Ku Klux Klan Materials, 1/3, AUND.

119. *Youngstown Citizen,* May 24, 1924, 4. Clipping sent to Walsh, Ku Klux Klan Materials, 1/4, AUND.

120. Ibid.

121. Ibid.

122. Chalmers, 159, 179.

123. Emmons to Walsh, September 16, 1924, Ku Klux Klan Materials, 1/3, AUND.

124. Walsh to Rev. Charles O'Donnell, C.S.C., October 11, 1924, UPWL, Box 49, folder Rev. Charles O'Donnell, AUND.

125. Ibid.

126. Ibid.

127. Ibid.

128. Ibid.

129. Ibid.

130. Ibid.

131. Ibid.

132. Ibid.

133. *South Bend Tribune,* October 15, 1924.

134. Ibid.

135. Ibid., October 5, 1924.

136. Ibid., October 18, 1924.

137. Ibid.

138. Ibid.

139. Under the heading, "Thirteenth District," *South Bend Tribune,* October 5, 1924; *New York Times,* October 19, 1924, Section 2, 1.

140. *New York Times,* October 19, 1924, section 2, 1.

141. Ibid., 1–2.

142. *South Bend Tribune,* October 18, 1924.

143. Ibid.

144. Ibid.

145. *Fiery Cross,* October 24, 1924, explains what had been planned for the October 18 meeting in South Bend.

146. Ibid.

147. Walsh to Rev. Charles L. O'Donnell, C.S.C., October 11, 1924, UPWL, Box 49, folder Rev. Charles L. O'Donnell, C.S.C., AUND.

148. Ibid.
149. Ibid.
150. Ibid.
151. Ibid.
152. O'Donnell to Walsh, September 29, 1924, UPWL, AUND.
153. Walsh to O'Donnell, October 11, 1924, UPWL, Box 49, folder Rev. Charles L. O'Donnell, C.S.C., AUND.
154. *New York Times,* October 19, 1924, section 2, 2.
155. *Fiery Cross,* October 24, 1924, Ku Klux Klan Materials, 1/6, AUND.

10. Against a Blue-Gray Sky

1. This quotation from the *New York Times* and reprinted in the *Notre Dame Alumnus* appears in Murray Sperber, *Shake Down the Thunder: The Creation of Notre Dame Football* (New York: Henry Holt, 1993), 174.
2. Ibid., 121–23.
3. Ibid., 149.
4. Ibid., 142.
5. *Religious Survey,* 1923–24, 13, AUND.
6. *South Bend Tribune,* October 12, 1924.
7. Sperber, 38.
8. Ibid., 147.
9. Ibid., 265.
10. Ibid., 457.
11. Ibid., 184.
12. *New York Times,* October 19, 1924, section 10.
13. Ibid.
14. *South Bend Tribune,* October 19, 1924.
15. Ibid.
16. *New York Times,* October 19, 1924, section 10.
17. Rice's famous sports piece about the Four Horsemen appeared as a front page story in the *South Bend Tribune,* October 19, 1924.
18. Strickler had been born in South Bend and was well connected at Notre Dame. His father was manager of the university farms. In 1924, Strickler was a transfer student with sophomore standing. He had attended Indiana University for about a year and had played football until an injury ended his career there. He returned to Notre Dame and enrolled in the College of Commerce. Strickler's football prospects at Notre Dame were hopeless. However, because of parental influence, Rockne gave him a part-time job as a student press assistant. That part-time job became a full-time preoccupation for Strickler. He lived at home and not on campus. There is no evidence that he took or passed any courses while enrolled at Notre Dame. Strickler left the university at the end of the football season in early 1925.
19. Sperber, 178.

20. Ibid.

21. *South Bend Tribune,* October 19, 1924.

22. Ibid.

23. Sperber, 179–80.

24. Ibid., 180.

25. This estimate of Strickler's profits from the sale of Four Horsemen photographs comes from Dave Condon's extended obituary notice of Strickler in Condon's "In the Wake of the News" column in the *Chicago Tribune,* December 7, 1976.

26. Sperber, 180.

27. *New York Herald-Tribune,* October 26, 1924.

28. *South Bend Tribune,* November 2, 1925.

29. Sperber, 166.

30. Ibid., 149–50.

31. *South Bend Tribune,* November 16, 1924, Sports Section, 1, under headline "Pass Acid Test."

32. *South Bend Tribune,* November 16, 1924, front page.

33. Ibid., Sports Section, 1.

34. Quoted in Sperber, 167.

35. Ibid., 181.

36. *South Bend Tribune,* November 23, 1924, front page.

37. Ibid., November 30, 1924.

38. Ibid.

39. Sperber, 121.

40. Walsh to Schumacher, October 7, 1924, UPWL, Box 25, folder Schumacher, AUND.

41. Walsh to John H. Neeson, September 27, 1924, UPWL, Box 49, Miscellaneous, Na-Ne, AUND.

42. Walsh to Angus McDonald, May 15, 1925, UPWL, Box 49, Angus McDonald, Trustee, AUND.

43. Arthur, 286.

44. Ibid., 271.

45. Ibid.

46. Ibid., 272.

47. Ibid., 286.

48. Sperber, 168–69.

49. Ibid., 169.

50. Ibid.

51. Ibid.

52. *Religious Survey,* 1930–31, Introduction, AUND.

53. Sperber, 170.

54. *Notre Dame Alumnus,* January 1925, 116–18.

55. Elmer Layden with Ed Snyder, *It Was a Different Game: The Elmer Layden Story* (Englewood Cliffs, N.J.: Prentice Hall, 1969), 30.

56. Ibid.
57. Sperber, 170.
58. *Notre Dame Alumnus,* January 1925, 33.
59. Layden, 31.
60. *Notre Dame Alumnus,* January 1925, 117.
61. Ibid., 171.
62. *South Bend Tribune,* January 2, 1925, section 2, p. 3.
63. Ibid.
64. Ibid.
65. Ibid.
66. Ibid.
67. *Notre Dame Alumnus,* January 1925, 117.
68. Ibid.
69. Ibid.
70. Ibid.
71. Ibid., 115.
72. Ibid.
73. Ibid.
74. Ibid.
75. Ibid., 118.
76. McAvoy, 107.
77. Ibid., 107–8; *Religious Survey,* 1923–24, 11, AUND.
78. *Religious Survey,* 1923–1924, 11, AUND.
79. Ibid., 12.
80. Ibid., 12–13.
81. Hope, 425.
82. Walsh to John H. Neeson, September 27, 1924, UPWL, Box 49, Miscellaneous, Na-Ne, AUND.
83. Walsh to Angus McDonald, May 15, 1925, UPWL, Box 49, Angus McDonald, Trustee, AUND.
84. Arthur, 287.
85. Sperber, 181.
86. Layden, 34.

11. Power Won, Then Thrown Away

1. Chalmers, 286.
2. Ibid., 283.
3. Ibid., 284.
4. Ibid., 285.
5. Ibid.
6. Ibid.
7. Ibid., 286.

8. Ibid., 287. In some Catholic circles, particularly in the large northeastern cities, the popular Protestant hymn "Onward Christian Soldiers," frequently taught to public school students in the elementary grades and sung by them during school assembly programs, became so identified with anti-Catholic attitudes and positions that humorous parodies of it circulated among Catholic working-class youth in the public schools. The opening lines, "Onward, Christian soldiers, marching as to war, with the cross of Jesus going on before" became "Onward, Christian soldiers, marching as to war, with the cross of Jesus hid behind the door." The author of this work recalls that parodies such as this one were sung lustily and defiantly by Catholic boys during assembly periods in the public schools of East Orange, New Jersey, during the mid and late 1930s.

9. Ibid., 277–78.

10. Ibid., 285.

11. Ibid., 284.

12. Ibid., 290.

13. Lutholtz, 156–57.

14. Ibid., 158.

15. Ibid.

16. Ibid., 152–53.

17. Ibid., 153.

18. Ibid.

19. Ibid.

20. Ibid.

21. *South Bend Tribune,* January 23, 1923.

22. Ibid.

23. Lutholtz, 152.

24. Ibid., 154.

25. *Indianapolis News,* February 5, 1925.

26. Ibid.

27. Lutholtz, 173.

28. Ibid.

29. Ibid.

30. Ibid., 174.

31. See a series of stories on the state highway commission corruption investigation and on the progress of the so-called "road ripper" bill in the *Indianapolis Star,* March 5, 1925, March 7, 1925, March 9, 1925, and March 10, 1925.

32. Lutholtz, 174.

33. Ibid.

34. Ibid., 171.

35. Ibid.

36. Ibid.

37. Ibid., 155.

38. Ibid.

39. Ibid., 170–71.

40. *South Bend Tribune,* February 27, 1925.
41. Ibid., April 26, 1925.
42. Lutholtz, 175.
43. Letter From Duvall to the *Indianapolis Star,* April 25, 1955.
44. Lutholtz, 175.
45. Ibid., 175–76.
46. Ibid., 176.
47. Ibid., 176–77.
48. Ibid., 179.
49. Ibid., 180–81.
50. Ibid., 183.
51. Ibid., 184.
52. Ibid., 185.
53. Ibid.
54. Ibid.
55. Ibid., 186.
56. Ibid.
57. Ibid., 187.
58. Ibid.
59. Ibid., 189.
60. Ibid., 190.
61. Ibid.
62. Ibid., 191.
63. Ibid.
64. Ibid., 195.
65. Ibid.
66. Ibid., 195–96.
67. Ibid., 197.
68. *South Bend Tribune,* April 20, 1925.
69. Ibid., April 3, 1925.
70. Lutholtz, 201.
71. Ibid.
72. *South Bend Tribune,* April 6, 1925.
73. Lutholtz, 201–2.
74. *Indianapolis Star,* April 13, 1925.
75. Lutholtz, 202.
76. Ibid., 203–4.
77. *Indianapolis Star,* April 16, 1925.
78. Lutholtz, 204–5.
79. *South Bend Tribune,* November 16, 1925.
80. Ibid., April 20, 1925.
81. Lutholtz, 205.
82. *South Bend Tribune,* April 20, 1925.
83. Tucker, 141–42.

12.   Indiana's Trial of the Century

1. Lutholtz, 212.
2. *South Bend Tribune*, May 6, 1925.
3. Ibid.
4. Ibid.
5. Ibid.
6. Ibid., April 26, 1925.
7. Ibid.
8. Ibid., May 6, 1925.
9. Lutholtz, 257.
10. Ibid., 218.
11. Ibid.
12. Ibid., 216.
13. *Indianapolis Star*, May 14, 1925, 13.
14. Lutholtz, 214–15.
15. Ibid., 223.
16. Ibid.
17. Ibid.
18. Ibid.
19. Ibid., 225.
20. Ibid., 226.
21. Ibid., 226–27.
22. Ibid., 227–28.
23. Ibid., 228.
24. Ibid.
25. Ibid., 228–29.
26. Ibid., 250.
27. *South Bend Tribune*, November 14, 1925.
28. Lutholtz, 253.
29. Ibid., 271–72.
30. In the course of making a very long closing argument for the prosecution on November 12, Charles Cox actually used the phrase "write the scarlet Letter on her tomb." Ibid., 293.
31. Ibid., 273.
32. Ibid., 260.
33. Ibid., November 14, 1925, 3.
34. Ibid.
35. Ibid.
36. Ibid., November 12, 1925, 1–3.
37. Ibid.
38. Ibid.
39. Ibid.
40. *Indianapolis News*, November 13, 1925, 25.

41. Ibid.

42. *South Bend Tribune,* November 14, 1925.

43. Lutholtz, 271.

44. Ibid., 281.

45. *Indianapolis News,* November 15, 1925.

46. Ibid.

47. *South Bend Tribune,* November 15, 1925.

48. Ibid., November 21, 1925.

49. Ibid., November 16, 1925.

50. Ibid.

51. Ibid.

52. Ibid.

53. Tucker, 160.

54. Ibid., 161–62.

55. Ibid., 162.

56. Ibid.

57. Ibid., 162–63.

58. Lutholtz, 303.

59. Ibid., 305.

60. Tucker, 163–64.

61. Ibid., 164–65.

62. Ibid., 166.

63. Ibid.

64. Ibid., 166–67.

65. Ibid., 167.

66. Ibid.

67. Ibid., 168.

68. Ibid., 169–70.

69. Lutholtz, 309.

70. Ibid., 313.

71. Michael and Judy Ann Newton, *The Ku Klux Klan: An Encyclopedia* (New York and London: Garland, 1991), 189.

72. Newton, 66.

73. Obituary Notice, *New York Times,* March 18, 1961, 23:3.

74. Tucker, 184.

13.   The President and the Coach

1. Vitus Jones to Walsh, May 31, 1924, UPWL, Box 50, Miscellaneous, Jo-Jz, AUND.

2. Vitus Jones to Walsh, October 13, 1924, UPWL, Box 50, Miscellaneous, Jo-Jz, AUND.

3. Ibid.

4. Ibid.

5. Ibid.

6. J. Hugh O'Donnell to Walsh, nd, UPWL, Box 50, Miscellaneous, Jo-Jz, AUND.

7. Walsh to Burns, May 4, 1928, UPWL, Box 52, folder Buo-Buz, AUND.

8. McCarthy to Walsh, May 5, 1925, UPWL, Box 49, folder McA to McD, 3, AUND.

9. Ibid.

10. McCarthy to Walsh, May 15, 1925, UPWL, Box 49, McA-McD, 3, AUND.

11. Charles L. O'Donnell to Noll, September 15, 1928, UPCO, Box 53, folder Bishop of Fort Wayne, AUND.

12. Sperber, 299.

13. Ibid., 344–45.

14. Noll to Charles O'Donnell, December 13, 1930, UPCO, Box 53, folder Bishop of Fort Wayne, AUND.

15. Noll to James J. Boylan, November 23, 1928, UPCO, Box 53, folder Bishop of Fort Wayne, AUND. Copy of Noll's letter sent to O'Donnell from Boylan.

16. Boylan to Noll, December 7, 1928, UPCO, Box 53, folder Bishop of Fort Wayne, AUND. Copy sent to O'Donnell from Boylan.

17. Arthur, 450.

18. O'Donnell to James Metz, November 21, 1928, UPCO, Box 8/136, AUND.

19. Sperber, 189.

20. Walsh to Lillis, June 12, 1925, UVMU, Box 2, folder 48, AUND.

21. Rockne to John Bisset, November 8, 1927, Athletic Director Records, Box 7, folder 183, AUND.

22. O'Donnell to William Brady, October 8, 1928, UPCO, Box 53, Bra-Bre, AUND.

23. O'Donnell to Boyle, UPCO, October 30, 1930, Box 53, folder Rev. Joseph Boyle, AUND.

24. Ibid.

25. Charles O'Donnell to Boylan, November 22, 1929, UPCO, Box 53, Bo, AUND.

26. Clarence Overend to Walsh, December 28, 1923, UPWL, Box 49, Miscellaneous, DO-OZ, AUND.

27. Sperber, 154–55.

28. Ibid., 154.

29. UPWL, Box 53, folder Rockne and the Columbia Incident, AUND.

30. Sperber, 156.

31. Byrne to Walsh, February 29, 1924, UPWL, Box 52, Miscellaneous, BY, AUND.

32. McDonald to Walsh, December 16, 1924, UPWL, Box 49, folder Angus McDonald, AUND.

33. Sperber, 187.

34. Ibid.

35. Ibid.

36. Ibid.

37. R. Bovard to Rockne, January 27, 1925, Athletic Directors Records, 8/179, AUND.

38. Sperber, 200–201.

39. *South Bend News-Times,* November 27, 1925.

40. McCarthy to Walsh, November 29, 1925, UPWL, Box 43, folder McA-McD, AUND.

41. Sperber, 202–3.

42. Walsh to Thomas Clair, December 16, 1925, UPWL, Box 52, folder Ci-Cl, AUND.

43. Sperber, 203.

44. Byrne to Walsh, December 16, 1925; Rockne and the Columbia Incident, Associated Press story December 12, 1925, UPWL, Box 53, AUND.

45. Ibid.

46. Ibid.

47. *Cincinnati Enquirer,* December 13, 1925, UPWL, Box 53, Rockne-Columbia Incident, AUND.

48. Ibid.

49. Ibid.

50. *South Bend Tribune,* December 11, 1925.

51. Rockne-Columbia Incident, 1925, UPWL, Box 53, AUND.

52. Ibid.

53. Ibid.

54. Memorandum for the Athletic Files dictated by Father Walsh, December 18, 1925, UPWL, Box 53, AUND.

55. Ibid.

56. Byrne to Walsh, December 16, 1925, Rockne-Columbia Incident, UPWL, Box 53, AUND.

57. Ibid.

58. Quoted in Sperber, 206.

59. Sperber, 209.

60. Ibid.

61. Ibid., 208–9.

62. Ibid., 209.

63. Rockne to John Griffith, November 5, 1926, UADR, 12/83.

64. *Chicago Evening Post,* November 16, 1926.

65. Sperber, 211.

66. Rockne to Molloy, April 29, 1929, UADR, 15/120, AUND.

67. Sperber, 218.

68. *New York Herald Tribune,* November 28, 1926.

69. Sperber, 219.

70. Ibid., 224.

71. Ibid., 225.

72. Walsh to M. M. Pearce, March 26, 1925, UPWL, Box 50, Miscellaneous, Pe, AUND.
73. Sperber, 236.
74. Rockne to Leigh, March 22, 1928, UADR, 14/41, AUND.
75. Sperber, 234.
76. Ibid., 562.
77. Ibid., 239.
78. Delos Lovelace, *Rockne of Notre Dame* (New York, 1931).
79. Sperber, 265.
80. Ibid., 268.
81. Minutes of the Special Committee, December 7, 1927, UPWL, Box 47, AUND.
82. Ibid.
83. Sperber, 269.
84. Rockne-Columbia Incident, 1925–1927, UPWL, Box 53, folder 10, AUND.
85. Sperber, 270.
86. O'Donnell to Aborgast, March 31, 1929, UPCO, Box 53, AO-AZ, AUND.
87. Minutes of the Special Committee of the Lay Board of Trustees, December 17, 1927, UPWL, Box 47, folder Minutes, 1922–1928, AUND.
88. O'Donnell to Aborgast, March 31, 1929, UPCO, Box 53, AO-AZ, AUND.
89. Ibid.
90. Walsh to Burns, May 4, 1928, UPWL, Box 52, Miscellaneous, Buv-Buz, AUND.
91. Ibid.

14. Political Humiliation and Football Triumph

1. Hope, 400.
2. Anderson, 100–101.
3. *Commonweal,* November 7, 1928, 10.
4. Richard O'Connor, *The First Hurrah* (New York: Putnam, 1970), 177.
5. Charles C. Marshall, "An Open Letter to the Honorable Alfred E. Smith," *Atlantic Monthly,* April 1927.
6. O'Connor, 178–79.
7. Ibid.
8. Alfred E. Smith, "Catholic and Patriot: Governor Smith Replies," *Atlantic Monthly,* May 1928.
9. O'Connor, 180–81.
10. *Commonweal,* November 7, 1928, 12.
11. Ibid.
12. O'Connor, 206–7.
13. Ibid.
14. Ibid., 206.

15. Victor Short, "The Documents of Intolerance," *Commonweal*, November 7, 1928, 11–12.

16. Ibid., 11.

17. Ibid.

18. Oscar Handlin, *Al Smith and His America* (Boston: Little, Brown, 1958), 133.

19. Ibid., 132–33.

20. Norman H. Clark, "Mabel Walker Willenbrandt," in *Dictionary of American Biography*, supplement 7, ed. John A. Garraty (New York: Scribner's, 1981), 785–86.

21. Ibid.

22. Handlin, 186–87.

23. Ibid.

24. Ibid.

25. Irving Dilliard, "William Allen White," in *Dictionary of American Biography*, supplement 3, ed. Edward T. James (New York: Scribner's, 1973), 815–17.

26. Quoted in Handlin, 187.

27. O'Connor, 220.

28. Ibid., 221.

29. *Commonweal*, November 21, 1928, 65.

30. *America*, November 17, 1928, 126.

31. *Notre Dame Alumnus*, 1928–1929, 320–21.

32. O'Donnell to Cap Anson, November 7, 1932, UPCO, Box 53, AUND.

33. O'Donnell to Noll, September 29, 1928, UPCO, Box 53, folder Bishop Noll, AUND.

34. O'Donnell to Rockne, September 7, 1928, UPCO, Box 7, 63, AUND.

35. Griffith is quoted in Sperber, 273.

36. Ibid., 275.

37. Rockne to Griffith, September 22, 1928, UADR, 10/14, AUND.

38. Grantland Rice, *The Tumult and the Shouting: My Life in Sport* (New York: A. S. Barnes, 1954), 182.

39. Sperber, 283.

40. Ibid., 282.

41. Steele, 40.

42. Ibid.

43. Ibid.

44. Sperber, 287.

45. Ibid., 293.

46. O'Donnell to Brady, December 4, 1928, UPCO, Box 53, AUND.

47. *New York Times*, February 23, 1929.

48. O'Donnell to Rockne, April 26, 1929, UADR, 17/49, AUND.

49. Rockne to O'Donnell, July 4, 1929, UPCO, Box 7, 49, AUND.

50. Ibid.

51. Sperber, 294.

52. Hope, 403.

53. O'Donnell to Anson, April 25, 1929, UPCO, Box 53, AUND.

54. Michael Beatty, Patrick Furlong, and Loren Pennington, *Studebaker, Less Than They Promised* (South Bend, Ind.: AND Books, 1984), 16.

55. Hope, 408–9.

56. O'Donnell to Noll, January 3, 1931, UPCO, Box 53, folder Bishop Noll, AUND.

57. Hope, 416.

58. O'Donnell to Belloc, November 23, 1928, UPCO, Box 53, Belloc, AUND.

59. *Notre Dame Alumnus*, 1930–1931, 108.

60. Interview of Rev. Charles L. O'Donnell, President of the University of Notre Dame with D. H. Stevenson, February 18, 1930, General Education Board file, folder 3, AUND.

61. Ibid.

62. O'Donnell to Burke, November 13, 1931, UPCO, Box 53, Buo-Buz, AUND.

63. Hope, 404.

64. Ibid., 405.

65. Sperber, 312.

66. Ibid., 317.

67. Ibid., 320.

15.   The End of an Era

1. Contracts of Employment, UPCO, Box 53, AUND.

2. Ibid.

3. O'Donnell to Sister M. Aloysius, July 10, 1931, UPCO, Box 53, AO-AZ, AUND.

4. O'Donnell to Boyle, May 5, 1930, UPCO, Box 53, BO-BZ, AUND.

5. Ibid.

6. Ibid.

7. O'Donnell to Richard Bourland, November 25, 1930, UPCO, Box 53, BO-BZ, AUND.

8. Sperber, 374–75.

9. Mulcaire to Sister M. Annetta, August 8, 1932, UPCO, Box 53, AO-AZ, AUND.

10. O'Donnell to John Bohan, April 28, 1932, UPCO, Box 53, BO-BZ, AUND.

11. O'Donnell to Noll, June 9, 1932, UPCO, Box 53, Noll, AUND.

12. Bellfontaine Building and Loan Society to O'Donnell, May 11, 1932, UPCO, Box 53, AUND.

13. Ibid.

14. Contracts, 1932–1933, UPCO, Box 53, AUND.

15. Ibid.

16. O'Donnell to Anson, July 23, 1932, UPCO, Box 53, Anson, AUND.

17. O'Donnell to Brady, September 26, 1932, UPCO, Box 53, Brae-Bri, AUND.

18. Sperber, 238.

19. Robert Harron, *Rockne: Idol of American Football* (New York: A. L. Bunt, 1931), 122–23.

20. Sperber, 334.

21. *Notre Dame Alumnus,* October 30, 1930, 39–42.

22. Quoted in Sperber, 335.

23. Savoldi Case, UPCO, 7/123–124, AUND.

24. Sperber, 336.

25. Ibid.

26. Quoted in Ibid.

27. See the *South Bend Tribune,* July 26, 1974, 17 and *New York Times,* July 26, 1974, 18:1.

28. Sperber, 339–40.

29. *New York Post,* December 2 and 3, 1930.

30. *Chicago Tribune,* December 6, 1930.

31. VPMU, 1930, 2/52, AUND.

32. Beatty, Furlong, and Pennington, 16.

33. *Notre Dame Alumnus,* October 1931, 14.

34. Sperber, 350.

35. Rockne to O'Donnell, March 30, 1931, UPCO, Box 3, 59, AUND.

36. Ibid.

37. *Notre Dame Alumnus* 9 (1930–1931), 299–300.

38. Sperber, 537.

39. Anson to O'Donnell, May 18, 1931, UPCO, Box 53, Anson, AUND.

40. Sperber, 373.

41. Anderson, 100–101.

42. Stuhldreyer to Cavanaugh, April 11, 1940, UVOC, Box 8, 57, AUND.

43. O'Donnell to G. Laemmle, September 28, 1931, UPCO, Box 8, 79, AUND.

16.   Epilogue

1. Beatty, Furlong, Pennington, 18.

2. *New York Times,* July 1, 1933, 12:1.

3. Burns to O'Donnell, June 29, 1933, UPCO, 1/67, AUND.

4. Ibid.

5. Ibid.

6. Ibid.

Bibliography

Manuscript Material in the Archives of the University of
Notre Dame (AUND)

Athletic Business Manager's Records
Athletic Director's Records
Faculty Board in Control of Athletics, Minutes of Meetings
Correspondence of James F. Edwards
Correspondence of Andrew J. Morrissey, C.S.C.
General Administrative Correspondence: Sorin, Microfilm
General Education Board Papers
Library Correspondence
Ku Klux Klan Materials
Shuster Personal Papers
Shuster Memoir
Sorin's Chronicles

Presidential Correspondence

John William Cavanaugh, C.S.C., 1905–1919 (UPWC)
James A. Burns, C.S.C., 1919–1922 (UPBU)
Matthew J. Walsh, C.S.C., 1922–1928 (UPWL)
Charles L. O'Donnell, C.S.C., 1928–1933 (UPCO)
John F. O'Hara, C.S.C., 1934–1940 (UPOH)

Vice Presidential Correspondence

John F. O'Hara, C.S.C., 1933–1934 (UVOH)
Michael J. Mulcaire, C.S.C., 1928–1933 (UVMU)
F. Hugh O'Donnell, C.S.C., 1934–1940 (UVOC)
John J. Cavanaugh, C.S.C., 1940–1946 (UVOC)

Printed Sources located in the University of Notre Dame Archives

Notre Dame Alumnus
The Dome
The Observer
The Scholastic
Religious Bulletin
Religious Survey

Charles Veneziani. *A.M.D.G.* Estimated date, 1912.

Charles Veneziani. *A Plea For The Higher Education Of Young Catholic Men Of America With An Exposure Of The Frauds Of The University Of Notre Dame, IND, Preceded By A Circular Letter To The Archbishops, Bishops, And Prominent Clergy Of The United States.* Chicago, no publisher listed, 1900.

Charles Veneziani. *Frauds Of The University Of Notre Dame, Notre Dame, Indiana, Or How The Catholic University Of Notre Dame With Her Fraudulent Doctor's Degrees, Courses, Etc., Prostitutes The Prestige Which A Religious Order Enjoys In The Eyes Of Catholics To Obtain Their Money Under False Pretenses.* 1901–1902.

Books

Anderson, Heartley W., with Klosinski, Emil. *Notre Dame, Chicago Bears and "Hunk."* A Sports Immortals Book. Oviedo, Fla.: Florida-Sun Gator Publishing Company, 1974.
Arthur, David Joseph. *The University of Notre Dame, 1913–1933: An Administrative History.* Ann Arbor, Mich.: University Microfilms, 1973.
Beatty, Michael; Furlong, Patrick; Pennington, Loren. *Studebaker, Less Than They Promised.* South Bend, Ind.: AND Books, 1984.
Blantz, Thomas E., C.S.C. *George N. Shuster: On the Side of Truth.* Notre Dame, Ind.: University of Notre Dame Press, 1993.
Booth, Edgar Allen. *The Mad Mullah of America.* Columbus, Ohio: Boyd Ellison, 1927.
Catta, Canon Etienne, and Catta, Tony. *Basil Anthony Mary Moreau.* 2 vols. English translation by Edward L. Heston, C.S.C. Milwaukee: Bruce Publishing Company, 1955.
Chalmers, David M. *Hooded Americanism: The First Century of the Ku Klux Klan, 1865–1965.* Garden City, N.Y.: Doubleday, 1965.
Chelland, Patrick. *One for the Gipper.* Chicago: Henry Regnery, 1973.
Christ, Frank L., and Sherry, Gerard E. *American Catholicism and the Intellectual Ideal.* New York: Appleton-Century Crofts, 1961.

Corby, William. *Memories of Chaplain Life.* Notre Dame, Ind., 1893.

Corish, Patrick. *The Irish Catholic Experience: A Historical Survey.* Wilmington, Del.: M. Glazier, 1985.

Ellis, John Tracy. *American Catholics and the Intellectual Life.* Chicago: Heritage Foundation, 1956 (reprinted from *Thought,* XXX, 351–88, Autumn, 1995).

Fogarty, Gerald Philip, S.J. *Denis J. O'Connell: Americanist Agent to the Vatican, 1885–1903.* Ann Arbor, Mich.: University of Michigan Microfilms, 1970.

Gekas, George. *Gipper: The Life and Times of George Gipp, A Biography.* South Bend, Ind.: AND Books, 1987.

Gleason, Philip. *Keeping the Faith: American Catholicism Past and Present.* Notre Dame, Ind.: University of Notre Dame Press, 1987.

Greenapple, H. R., ed. *D. C. Stephenson Irvington 0492: The Demise of the Grand Dragon of the Indiana Ku Klux Klan.* Compiled from the Papers of Harold C. Feightner. Plainfield, Ind.: SGS Publications, 1989.

Halsey, William M. *The Survival of American Innocence.* Notre Dame, Ind.: University of Notre Dame Press, 1980.

Handlin, Oscar. *Al Smith and His America.* An Atlantic Monthly Press Book. Boston: Little, Brown, and Company, 1958

Harron, Robert. *Rockne: Idol of American Football.* New York: A.L. Burt, 1931.

Hope, Arthur J., C.S.C. *Notre Dame One Hundred Years.* Revised edition, Introduction by Thomas J. Schlereth. South Bend, Ind.: Icarus Press, 1978.

Jackson, Kenneth T. *The Ku Klux Klan in the City, 1915–1930.* New York: Oxford University Press, 1967.

Layden, Elmer. *It Was a Different Game: The Elmer Layden Story.* Englewood Cliffs, N.J.: Prentice Hall, 1969.

Lovelace, Delos. *Rockne of Notre Dame.* New York, 1931.

Lutholtz, M. William. *Grand Dragon: D.C. Stephenson and the Ku Klux Klan in Indiana.* West Lafayette, Ind.: Purdue University Press, 1991.

MacSuibhne, Rev. Peadar. *Paul Cullen and His Contemporaries.* 5 vols. Naas: Leinster Leader, 1961–1977.

McAvoy, Thomas T., C.S.C. *Father John O'Hara of Notre Dame, the Cardinal Archbishop of Philadelphia.* Notre Dame, Ind.: University of Notre Dame Press, 1967.

O'Connor, Richard. *The First Hurrah.* New York: G. P. Putnam and Sons, 1970.

O'Dea, Thomas F. *American Catholic Dilemma: An Inquiry into the Intellectual Life.* New York: Sheed and Ward, 1958.

O'Toole, James M. *Militant and Triumphant: William Henry O'Connell and the Catholic Church in Boston, 1859–1944.* Notre Dame, Ind.: University of Notre Dame Press, 1992.

Quinlan, M. A., C.S.C., and Dempsey, William. *The Notre Dame Athletic Record.* Notre Dame, Ind.: University of Notre Dame Press, 1929.

Rice, Arnold S. *The Ku Klux Klan in American Politics.* Washington, D.C.: Public Affairs Press, 1962.

Rice, Grantland. *The Tumult and the Shouting: My Life in Sport.* New York: A. S. Barnes, 1954.

Rockne, Knute K. *Autobiography of Knute Rockne.* Indianapolis: Bobbs-Merrill, 1931.

Ryan, John A., and Boland, Francis T., C.S.C. *Catholic Principles of Politics.* Revised edition of "The State and the Church." New York: Macmillan, 1958.

Sperber, Murray. *Shake Down the Thunder: The Creation of Notre Dame Football.* New York: Henry Holt, 1993.

Steele, Michael R. *Knute Rockne: A Bio-Bibliography.* Popular Culture Bio-Bibliographies. Westport, Conn.: Greenwood Press, 1983.

Trausch, H. M. *The Truth about the Notre Dame Riot on Saturday, May 17, 1924.* Indianapolis: Fiery Cross Publishing Company, nd.

Tucker, Richard K. *The Dragon and the Cross: The Rise and Fall of the Ku Klux Klan in Middle America.* Hampton, Conn.: Shoe String Press, 1951.

Wade, Wyn Craig. *The Fiery Cross: The Ku Klux Klan in America.* New York: Simon and Shuster, 1987.

Wallace, Francis. *Knute Rockne.* New York: Doubleday, 1960.

Weber, Ralph. *Notre Dame's John Zahm.* Notre Dame, Ind.: University of Notre Dame Press, 1961.

Articles

Burns, James A., C.S.C. "A Constructive Policy in Catholic Higher Education." *Catholic Higher Education Association Bulletin*, XVII, 1920.

———. "The Catholic High School Movement." *Proceedings of the Association of Catholic Colleges in the United States*, III, April 1901.

Cullen, Very Rev. Thomas E. "Teaching Religion?" *Catholic Education Association Bulletin*, November 1924.

Egan, Maurice F. *Scholastic*, XXII, 1888–1889.

Gannon, Michael V. "Before and After Modernism." In *The Catholic Priest in the United States*, ed. John Tracy Ellis. Collegeville, Minn.: St. John's University Press, 1971.

Gleason, Philip. "American Catholic Higher Education: A Historical Perspective." In Robert Hassenger, ed., *The Shape of Catholic Higher Education*, The University of Chicago Press, 1967.

Haggerty, Patrick, C.S.C. "The Halls of Notre Dame." *The Dome*, 19 (1925).

Kearney, Anne. "Rev. Paul J. Foik, C.S.C.: Librarian and Historian." Paper prepared for Seventh Annual Conference on the History of the Holy Cross Congregation, June 25, 1988. St. Mary's College, Notre Dame, Ind.

Marshall, Charles C. "An Open Letter to the Honorable Alfred E. Smith." *Atlantic Monthly*, April 1927.

McAndrews, Mary Ellen. "The Day the KKK Came to Town." *The Observer*, April 30, 1974.

McClancy, Rev. Joseph V. "Aims and Purposes in Teaching Religion." *Catholic Education Bulletin*, November 1922.

"Meeting the Klan," *Scholastic*, February 17, 1923.

O'Connell, Marvin R. "Ultramontanism and Dupanloup: The Compromise of 1865." *Church History*, June 1984.

Phinizy, Coles. "Win One for the Gipper." *Sports Illustrated*, September 17, 1979.

Rockne, Knute. "Gipp the Great." *Collier's*, November 22, 1930.

Short, Victor. "The Documents of Intolerance." *Commonweal*, November 7, 1928.

Shuster, George N. "Have We Any Scholars?" *America*, August 15, 1925.

Smith, Alfred E. "Catholic and Patriot: Governor Smith Replies." *Atlantic Monthly*, May 1928.

Weigel, Gustave, S.J. "American Catholic Intellectualism—A Theologian's Reflection." In *Review of Politics*, 19, July 1957.

Reference Works

Dictionary of American Biography. 10 vols., nine supplements. New York: Scribner's, 1957–1994.

New Catholic Encyclopedia. 15 vols. Washington, D.C.: Catholic University Press, 1967.

Newton, Michael and Judy Ann. *The Ku Klux Klan Encyclopedia.* New York: Garland, 1991.

Index